Russian and Soviet Policy in Manchuria and Outer Mongolia

By the same author

Communist China Today: Domestic and Foreign Policies

PETER S. H. TANG

RUSSIAN AND SOVIET POLICY IN MANCHURIA AND OUTER MONGOLIA
1911-1931

Introduction by
Philip E. Mosely

DUKE UNIVERSITY PRESS
Durham, North Carolina, 1959

DUKE UNIVERSITY PRESS, DURHAM, N. C.
CAMBRIDGE UNIVERSITY PRESS, LONDON N.W.1, ENGLAND

PRINTED IN THE UNITED STATES OF AMERICA
BY THE SEEMAN PRINTERY, INC., DURHAM, N. C.

DEDICATED
TO THE MEMORY OF
MY MOTHER AND FATHER
AND TO
THE OTHER MARTYRS
AND FIGHTERS FOR FREEDOM
OF OUR TIME

The publication of this book was assisted by a grant to the Duke University Press by the Ford Foundation.

INTRODUCTION

Manchuria and Outer Mongolia have held a special place in Sino-Russian relations of the last one hundred years, as testing grounds of imperial and revolutionary power and policies. To China, striving to find a new place of strength and unity in a drastically changed political world, Manchuria, by 1911, meant the opening up of new opportunities for settlement, for agricultural and industrial development, and for modernization. To Japan and Russia, control of Manchuria's strategic routes and resources spelled potential domination of East Asia. Outer Mongolia, once the center of a conquering empire, was still, for China, a neglected border region; for Russia, an alternative route of expansion toward the major centers of Chinese power.

In his authoritative study, Dr. Peter S. H. Tang has traced the evolution of imperial Russian and Soviet policy toward these two "fault-areas" of world politics between 1911 and 1931. The choice of these initial and terminal years is, for the student of politics, a felicitous one, for it enables him to examine in detail and compare the aims, tactics and methods of the pre-1917 and post-1917 Russian regimes.

Before as after 1917, the status of Outer Mongolia lent itself to a complicated pattern of maneuver. While outwardly upholding China's suzerainty as a device for avoiding the "internationalizing" of the problem of Outer Mongolia, both imperial and Soviet empire-builders zealously built up political, economic, and military strongholds of influence. The proclamation, on Soviet soil, of the Mongolian People's Republic was only the most dramatic act of interference in the evolution of modern Mongolia. By 1931, Mongolia was far more closely bound to the Soviet Union, and far more completely cut off from China, than ever before in its history. From a

wide variety of sources—Chinese, Russian, and Western—Dr. Tang
has drawn a clear picture of the methods by which Russia advanced
its ambitions there, and the role and fate of the first "people's democracy," as the reader will discover for himself, are strikingly similar
to those of later exemplars.

In Manchuria, imperial Russia had to be content, by 1911, with
a sphere of influence, retained by it in growing co-operation with
Japan. The development, until 1917, of its military, economic, and
administrative control over its extensive sphere has been traced here
with skill. The collapse of Russian control after the October Revolution, the complicated struggle between different Russian factions
and among China, Japan, and the Western powers, and the re-establishment of Russian predominance in a Soviet form, are described
with care. The conflicts between Soviet, Chinese, and Manchurian
regional interests are brought out clearly, down to the point, in 1931,
when Japan's expansionist ambitions overwhelmed its potential rivals.

From a careful study of the available documentary and secondary
materials, in Chinese, Russian, and other languages, and from insights
gleaned from his own experience in diplomacy, Dr. Tang has made
a valuable contribution to our understanding of the role of Manchuria and Outer Mongolia in Russian and Soviet diplomacy, 1911-
1931.

PHILIP E. MOSELY

PREFACE

The face that the Soviet Union presents to the world today is both threatening and enigmatic. A frightening number of nations have already yielded to Soviet pressure, and many more are now engaged in a conflict with Communist infiltration, subversion, and outright attack. In an age when nations are seeking to understand one another and to work out their problems in the interest of world harmony and mutual assistance, international attention is drawn to the expansionist policies of the U.S.S.R.

The fact is that modern Russian history is a more or less consistent record of territorial expansion. The Janus-face of the Soviet Union is not new to students of history. And the countries which border Russia—the giant which sprouted from the seed planted by the minuscule state of Muscovy—have confronted it since the time of Ivan the Terrible.

Now that the whole world has this face to confront, the time seems particularly appropriate to examine the record of Russia's past activities in relation to certain bordering states, and to analyze her ambitions, her goals, and her tactics. The task is undertaken in the hope of casting light on the present and future objectives of the Soviet Union, and perhaps on her methods of dealing with her problems.

A single study, however, can treat of only a small portion of this history in the detail that such a work demands. The purpose of the present book, therefore, is to bring under close scrutiny that part of Russian diplomacy, pre-Revolutionary and Soviet, involved in the dealings with Manchuria and Outer Mongolia during the two decades between the Chinese Revolution of 1911 and the Japanese attack on Manchuria in 1931.

In the period under consideration, Russian-Soviet policy in Man-

churia and Outer Mongolia presents a record of diplomatic intrigue
through which China was partially dismembered, and the severed
peripheral regions were attached, either officially or unofficially, to
Russia.   As far back as 1858, Russia had begun her acquisition of
Chinese territory with the annexation of the Amur region, followed
in 1860 by that of the Maritime Province.   The quiescent period
which followed was not one of true peace, for it was not long before
a bold drive on Manchuria was launched.   When that effort was
checked by the impact of a strong Japan and her demands, Northern
Manchuria began to receive Russia's attention, and Outer Mongolia
became the focal point of her ambitions.

That Russia was able to achieve such a record in the brief span
of twenty years was due to several factors; foremost among them
was the construction and operation of the Chinese Eastern Railway.
It was through the manipulation of this railroad that Russia secured
economic dominance, strategic control, and political influence over
Manchuria, which, after 1924 became fertile ground for the sowing
of Communist propaganda.   The Chinese Eastern Railway became
an instrument of critical strategic importance by virtue of its crossing
one of the world's danger spots—Manchuria—where the vital interests of the nations competing for influence directly clashed.   For
Russia, the existence of the railway justified an endless series of demands which violated the sovereign rights of China.

In Outer Mongolia, Russian influence stimulated a movement
toward independence which ultimately resulted in the establishment
of a Mongol government quite distinct from that of China.   Misunderstandings and antagonisms helped weaken the ties between
Chinese and Mongol, while Russia began to enjoy special economic
and political privileges.   As for the Chinese government, malad-
ministration by its officials and general organizational weakness left
it unable to cope with the activities of its Russian neighbor.   Although
impartial observers agree that Outer Mongolia was entitled to self-
determination, association with her ever-spreading northern neighbor
has brought not a solution but merely Russian domination in lieu of
Chinese.

Most of the important materials having bearing on this subject,
although widely scattered and difficult of access, including Russian

and Chinese documents, have been examined by the author in preparation for this work.

The author is very much indebted to Professor Philip E. Mosely, director of studies at the Council on Foreign Relations and formerly director of the Russian Institute, Columbia University, under whose guidance this study was first undertaken. President Grayson L. Kirk and Professors John N. Hazard, Oliver J. Lissitzyn, Thomas P. Peardon, Nathaniel Peffer, Geroid T. Robinson, and C. Martin Wilbur were kind enough to read the manuscript either in full or at various stages in its preparation, and all made valuable suggestions. He wishes also to express his gratitude to Dr. Margaret Starbuck, Dr. Harold Engle, Mr. Liu Ching-chang, Mrs. Carrie Kim, and particularly to Mrs. Edna C. Law, who generously contributed their time and efforts to help produce this work. Special mention must be made of the assistance of Miss Joan Maloney and Mrs. Sandra W. Thornton, staff assistants of the Research Institute on the Sino-Soviet Bloc, of which the author is Executive Director. The invaluable encouragement and co-operation of Mr. Ashbel G. Brice, director of Duke University Press, has helped over the past five years to bring this work to fruition. The author's heartfelt appreciation and thanks must also be expressed for the assistance and inspiration of his wife during the final phase of preparation of this study for publication. The author is grateful to the American Council of Learned Societies and the American Philosophical Society for grants received while the book was being completed, and which will primarily be used for further study. The cost of typing the manuscript was covered in part by a grant from the Tsing Hua University Teaching and Research Funds, administered by President Y. C. Mei. There are, of course, many others, too many to permit separate mention here, who gave of their time and advice, and the author hopes that all of them are aware of his sincere appreciation for their assistance. He alone, of course, is responsible for the views and judgments, and for any errors which this work may contain.

PETER S. H. TANG

Washington, D. C.
September, 1959

TABLE OF CONTENTS

LIST OF MAPS

ABBREVIATIONS USED IN FOOTNOTES

B.S.E. *Bol'shaia Sovetskaia Entsiklopediia (Great Soviet Encyclopedia)*. 1st and 2nd editions. Moscow, various dates.

C.C.W.C.S.L. *Ch'ing Chi Wai-Chiao Shih-Liao (Chinese Diplomatic Documents for the Late Ch'ing Period)*. Peiping, 1932.

C.L.S.L. *Ch'ien-Lung Shih-lu (The Factual Records under the Reign of Emperor Ch'ien-Lung)*.

C.L.T.C. *Chi-Lin T'ung-chih (Gazetteer of Kirin)*. 1891.

C.O.H.T.W. *Chung-O Hui-i Ts'an-kao Wen-chien (Sino-Russian Conference: Reference Documents)*. Peking, 1923.

C.T.M.C.Y.L.K. *Ch'ing-Ting Man-Chou Yuan-liu Kao (A Study of the Origin of the Manchus by Imperial Orders)*. 1778.

C.T.S.L.C.P. *Chiao-Tung-Shih Lu-chen-pien (History of Communications: Part of Road Administration)*. Nanking, 1931.

C.Y.B. *The China Year Book*. London & N. Y., 1912-19; Peking & Tientsin, 1921-.

D.I.B.Z.D.I. *Die Internationalen Beziehungen im Zeitalter des Imperialismus*.

E.L. *Entsiklopedicheskii Leksikon (Encyclopedic Lexicon)*. St. Petersburg, 1835.

E.S. *Entsiklopedicheskii Slovar' (Encyclopedical Dictionary)*. St. Petersburg, 1896.

F.R.U.S. *Foreign Relations of the United States*. Washington, D. C.

I.M.I.D. *Izvestiia Ministerstva Inostrannykh Del (Bulletin of the Ministry of Foreign Affairs)*. Petrograd, 1912-17.

I.W.S.M. *Ch'ou-pan I-wu Shih-mo (Records on Foreign Relations)*. 1929-30.

K.A.	*Krasnyi Arkhiv* (*The Red Archives*).
K.H.T.Y.	*Kuang-Hsu Tiao-yo* (*Treaties under the Reign of Kuang-Hsu*).
K.V.Zh.D.	*Kitaiskaia Vostochnaia Zheleznaia Doroga* (*The Chinese Eastern Railway*).
L.C.C.L.	*Lung Chiang Chih-lueh* (*A Concise Study of Heilungkiang*). 1891.
L.F.Y.T.L.	*Li-Fan-Yüan Tse-li* (*Code of the Board of the Administration of Dependencies*). 1908.
M.O. v E.I.	*Mezhdunarodnye Otnosheniia v Epokhu Imperializma* (*International Relations during the Period of Imperialism*). Moscow, 1931-39.
M.S.E.	*Malaia Sovetskaia Entsiklopediia* (*Small Soviet Encyclopedia*). 1st and 2nd editions. Moscow, various dates.
R.A.	*Russkii Arkhiv* (*The Russian Archives*). St. Petersburg, 1878.
S.C.T.C.	*Sheng-Ching T'ung-chih* (*Gazetteer of Shengking*). 1736.
S.D.D. po M.V.	*Sbornik Diplomaticheskikh Dokumentov po Mongol'skomu Voprosu* (*A Collection of Diplomatic Documents Relative to the Mongolian Question*). St. Petersburg, 1914.
S.F.P.C.	*Shuo-fang Pei-ch'eng* (*Studies of the Northern Regions*). 1860.
S.S.	*Skhidnii Svit* (*The World of the Orient*). Kharkov.
S.S.E.	*Sibirskaia Sovetskaia Entsiklopediia* (*Siberian Soviet Encyclopedia*). Moscow, 1932.
S.U.R.	*Soviet Union Review*, published by the Soviet Union Information Bureau, Washington, D. C.
T.C.H.T.S.L.	*Ta-Ch'ing Hui-tien Shih-li* (*The Institutes of the Great Ch'ing Dynasty*). 1908.

Part One. THE CHINESE EASTERN
RAILWAY: INSTRUMENTALITY
OF RUSSIAN AND SOVIET
POLICY IN MANCHURIA

I: HISTORICAL BACKGROUND

MANCHURIA AND RUSSIAN EXPANSION

It was in the middle of the seventeenth century that Manchuria first became known as a geographical area of some significance in the international arena.[1] Since then both Russian and Chinese cartographers and historians have concurred in treating Manchuria as the Northeast region or Tung-San-Sheng (Three Eastern Provinces) of China.[2]

Manchuria's first international boundary with Russia, fixed by the Nerchinsk Treaty of 1689, started from the Argun River and proceeded along the Yablonoi (Yablonovoi) Mountains and the Stanovoi (Dzhugdzhur) Range to the Ud Bay of the Sea of Okhotsk.[3]

[1] Emperor Ch'ien-Lung to the Cabinet, Imperial Edict, Oct. 9/Aug. 19 (Chinese lunar calendar), 1777, in A-Kuei & others, *Ch'ing-Ting Man-Chou Yuan-liu Kao* (*A Study of the Origin of the Manchus by Imperial Orders*, referred to hereinafter as *C.T.M.C.Y.L.K.*) (1778), Book of Introduction, sh. 1; Hsieh Shou-ch'ang & others, *Chung-Kuo Ku-ching Ti-ming Ta-tz'u-tien* (*A Gazetteer Containing Ancient and Contemporary Names of Places in China*) (Shanghai, 1931), p. 1098.

[2] "Manchzhuriia" ("Manchuria"), I. E. Andreevskii, K. K. Arsenev, & others, *Entsiklopedicheskii Slovar'* (*Encyclopaedical Dictionary*, referred to hereinafter as *E.S.*) (St. Petersburg, 1896), XXXVI, 574; Yang Wen-hsun & others (ed.), *Chung-Kuo Ti-li Hsin-chih* (*A New Chinese Gazetteer*) (Shanghai, 1935), bk. 7, p. 1; Wang Hua-lung, *Tung-Pai Ti-li Tsung-lun* (*A Geographical Survey of the Northeast*) (Peiping, 1933), pp. 5-6; Hsü Hsi, *Tung-San-Sheng Chi-lueh* (*The Annals of the Three Eastern Provinces*) (Shanghai, 1915), p. 1; Chow Chih-hua, *Tung-San-Sheng Kai-lun* (*A Sketch of the Three Eastern Provinces*) (Shanghai, 1931), p. 1.

[3] Russia, Imperial Academy of Sciences, *Atlas Rvssicvs Mappa vna Generali et Vndeviginti Specialibvs Vastissimvm Imperivm Rvssicvm cvm Adiacentibvs Regionibvs* (referred to hereinafter as Russia, Imperial Academy of Sciences, *Atlas Rvssicvs*) (St. Petersburg, 1745), Mappa Generalis Totius Imperii Russici and nos. 17, 19; Ch'ou Tai-chün, *Chung-O Chieh-chi* (*A Record of the Sino-Russian Boundary*) (Wuchang, 1911), sh. ii, bk. I, sh. 14-22; Lou T'ung-mao & Yang Tseng-wei, "Geography," in Northeastern University (ed.), *Tung-Pei Yao-lan* (*Survey of the Northeast*) (Santai, 1944), p. 49; "Eastern, Central and Southern Asia" (map), Albert Herrmann, *Historical and Commercial Atlas of China* (Harvard-Yenching Institute Monograph Series, Vol. I) (Cambridge, Mass., 1935), pp. 58-59.

As a result, Manchuria included the present-day Amur and Primor-
skaia (Maritime) Provinces, modern Manchuria, and a large portion,
or presumably the whole, of Sakhalin Island.[4] Historical atlases for
this period as well as Russian, Chinese, and Western atlases of the
day clearly show this boundary as provided for in the Nerchinsk
Treaty.[5] For 170 years it held unchanged. In the treaties of Aigun
(1858) and Peking (1860) Manchuria was pared down, so that, with
the exception of the small Chinese *irredenta* near Blagoveschensk—
Chiang-Tung-Lu-Shih-Szu-T'un (Sixty-Four Settlements or villages
to the East of the Amur),[6] it was reduced to its present dimensions,

[4] Russia, Imperial Academy of Sciences, *Atlas Rvssicvs*, nos. 17, 19; E. G.
Ravenstein, *The Russians on the Amur* (London, 1861), pp. 73, 76, and map "The
Regions of the Amur to illustrate Events of the 17th Century," facing p. 1; Herrmann, *op. cit.*, pp. 58-59; H. S. Tanner, *New Universal Atlas of the World* (Phila-
delphia, 1836), nos. 55, 56; T'ung Shih-heng, *Li-tai Chiang-yü Hsing-shih I-lan-t'u*
(*An Atlas of the Territorial Domains of the Successive Dynasties*) (7th ed.; Shanghai, 1926), map 17. Sakhalin was said to have been occupied by Russia later, by
force and without treaty arrangement (Lou & Yang, *op. cit.*, pp. 49-50).

[5] "Sibir'" ("Siberia"), A. Voshchinin, *Geografícheskii Atlas Rossüskoi Imperii*
(*The Geographical Atlas of the Russian Empire*) (St. Petersburg, 1851), no. 15;
"Karta Sibiri, 1581-1886 gg." ("Map of Siberia, 1581-1886"), E. Zamyslovskii,
Uchebnyi Atlas po Russkoi Istorrii (*School Atlas according to Russian History*)
(St. Petersburg, 1887), no. 9; Russia, Imperial Academy of Sciences, *Atlas Rvssicvs*,
Mappa Generalis Totius Imperii Russici and nos. 17, 19; *Huang-Yü Ch'üan-t'u* (*A
Complete Atlas of Royal Territory*) (K'ang-Hsi ed., 1719); "Sheng-Ching Yü-ti
Ch'üan-t'u" ("A Complete Map of Shengking"), Wang Ho & others, *Sheng-Ching
T'ung-chih* (*Gazetteer of Shengking*, referred to hereinafter as *S.C.T.C.*) (1736),
Book of Introduction, sh. 4-6; "Chi-Lin Choi-chieh Ch'üan-t'u," ("A Complete Map
of the old Boundary of Kirin") *Chi-Lin T'ung-chih* (*Gazetteer of Kirin*, referred to
hereinafter as *C.L.T.C.*), Vol. I (1891), preface 1; Yeh Kwei-shou, *Ta-ti Ch'üan-
ch'iu K'ao-lüeh chih T'u* (*A General Map of the Globe*) (Chinan, 1846); T'ung,
op. cit., map 17; T'ung Shih-heng, *Ch'ing-ch'u Chiang-yü T'u* (*A Map of the
Territorial Domain of the Early Part of the Ch'ing Dynasty*) (Shanghai, 1916);
Su Chia-jung, *Chung-Kuo Ti-li Yen-ko T'u* (*Atlas of Successive Geographical
Changes of China*) (3rd ed.; Shanghai, 1930), map 81, sh. 24; Herman Moll,
Atlas Minor (London, 1732 [?]), nos. 30, 37; J. Gibson, *Atlas Minimus* (Phila-
delphia, 1798), no. 3; "The World," "Moral and Political Chart of the Inhabited
World," and "Comparative, Geographical and Statistical Map of Asia," William C.
Woodbridge, *Modern Atlas* (Hartford, 1831); Tanner, *op. cit.*, nos. 55, 56; "Map
of the World," and "Political Map of Asia," W. C. Woodbridge, *School Atlas*
(Hartford, 1845); Herrmann, *op. cit.*, pp. 58-59; "Russian Advance into Siberia to
the death of Peter the Great 1725," George Goodall (ed.), *Soviet Union in Maps:
Its Origin and Development* (London, 1949), p. 4; Karl von Spruner, *Historisch-
Geographischer Hand-Atlas Zur Geschichte Asiens, Africas, Americas und Austra-
liens* (Gotha, 1855), map no. XIX; "Waereld," "Asiae," and "Tartaria Sive Magni
Chami Imperium," Nicolaes Visscher, *Atlas Minor sive Geographia Compendiosa*
(Amsterdam, n.d.).

[6] Chiang-Tung-Lu-Shih-Szu-T'un is located across the Zeiia (Chinch'ili) River
to the south of Blagoveshchensk and across the Amur to the east of Aigun. In 1858,
by the Treaty of Aigun, China ceded territory north of the Amur to Russia with

the somewhat ambiguous proviso that the Manchu inhabitants in the Chiang-Tung-Lu-Shih-Szu-T'un area be permitted to reside there in perpetuity under the protection and control of the Manchu authorities. Thereafter the Manchu Court exercised its jurisdiction over this area and regarded it as a part of the empire. In 1883 border mounts were erected for demarcation purposes. In the summer of 1900, however, as a result of the Boxer uprising and Sino-Russian hostilities across the Amur near this area, the Russians drove all these Manchus and the Chinese merchants in Blagoveshchensk, more than 7,000 in all, into the Amur River. Only about one hundred of these people survived to take refuge on the west bank of the Amur (Aigun). Since then this area has been occupied by the Russians and not by China. So far no change has been contemplated for treaty consideration. For the foregoing, see "Hailanp'ao," Hsieh & others, *op. cit.*, p. 727; Yang & others, *op. cit.*, bk. 7, p. 126; Hsü, *op. cit.*, pp. 15-16; Fang Lo-t'ien, *Tung-Pei Kuo-chi Wai-chiao (International Diplomacy Concerning the Northeast)* (Shanghai, 1933), p. 15; Ho Han-wen, *Chung-O Wai-chiao-Shih (Sino-Russian Diplomatic History)* (Shanghai, 1935), pp. 199-200; Ch'en Po-wen, *Chung-O Wai-chiao-shih (Sino-Russian Diplomatic History)* (1st ed.; Shanghai, 1928), pp. 53-54; Lou & Yang, *op. cit.*, p. 49. It is noteworthy that all maps produced under the Manchus and the Chinese Nationalists continued to include the Chiang-Tung-Lu-Shih-Szu-T'un area within Chinese territory or, with a few exceptions, it was marked Chinese *irredenta*. See Tsou Po-Chi, *Huang Yü Chüan-t'u (A Complete Atlas of Royal Territory)* (1874), "Map of the Three Eastern Provinces"; T'ung Shih-heng, *Chung-Hua-Min-Kuo Hsin-ch'ü-yü T'u (Atlas of the New Territorial Divisions of the Chinese Republic)* (4th rev. ed.; Shanghai, 1917); Ch'en Hao-chi, *Chung-Kuo Hsin yü-t'u (New Atlas of China)* (4th rev. ed.; Shanghai, 1925), no. 6; Ko Suicheng, *Tsui-hsin Pen-kuo Ti-t'u (The Newest Domestic Atlas)* (Shanghai, 1930), no. 8; Ting Wen-chiang, Weng Wen-hao & Tseng Shih-ying, *Chung-Hua-Min-Kuo Hsin Ti-t'u (New Atlas of the Chinese Republic)* (Shanghai, 1934), nos. 8, 12; Liu Chi-ch'en & Lee Ch'ing-ch'ang, *Chung-Kuo Fen-sheng T'u (Atlas of China in Provinces)* (Shanghai, 1938), no. 23; "Heilungkiang," Lee Ch'eng-san, *Chung-Kuo Fen-Sheng Ti-t'u (Atlas of the Provinces of China)* (Chungking, 1945); Yang Ching-hsiung & Li Ch'ing-cheng, *Chung-Hua-Min-Kuo Tsui-hsin Fen-sheng Ti-t'u (The Newest Atlas of the Provinces of the Chinese Republic)* (Shanghai, 1946), no. 31; Ching Ching-yü, *Hsiu-cheng Chung-Kuo Fen-sheng Chin-t'u (A Detailed Pocket Atlas of China in Provinces)* (9th rev. ed.; Shanghai, 1946), no. 25.

On the other hand, Russian maps subsequent to the Aigun Treaty of 1858 have never made any distinction of the Chiang-Tung-Lu-Shih-Szu-T'un area as a unit but have included it with Russian and Soviet territory. See Russia, Headquarters of the Chief of Staff, *Karta Aziatskoi Rossii (Map of Asiatic Russia)* (St. Petersburg, 1865); U.S.S.R., TsIK (the CEC), *Atlas Soiuza Sovetskikh Sotsialisticheskikh Respublik (Atlas of the Union of Soviet Socialist Republics)* (Moscow, 1928), maps facing pp. 10, 24; U.S.S.R., TsIK (the CEC), *Bol'shoi Sovetskoi Atlas Mira (Great Soviet Atlas of the World)* (Moscow, 1937), pp. 84-85; *Malaia Sovetskaia Entsiklopediia (Small Soviet Encyclopedia*, referred to hereinafter as M.S.E.) (1st ed.), Vol. IV (Moscow, 1929), cols. 535-536; *Bol'shaia Sovetskaia Entsiklopediia (Great Soviet Encyclopedia*, referred to hereinafter as B.S.E.) (1st ed.), Vol. XXXVIII (Moscow, 1938), cols. 73-74; B.S.E. (2nd ed.), XXI (Moscow, 1953), map between pp. 168 & 169. Likewise maps published under the Chinese Communists, which specifically acknowledge Soviet maps as their prototype, follow the Soviet map-drawing policy of ignoring the Chinese *irredenta*. See Kuang-Hua Geographical Society (ed.), *Hsin Chung-Kuo Feng-sheng Ti-t'u (Atlas of the Provinces of New China)* (Peking, 1950), no. 13; Chin Chu-an, Ch'en Chih-fang, & Yang Po-ju, *Chung-Hua-Jen-Min-Kung-Ho-Kuo Ta-ti-t'u (Great Map of the Chinese People's Republic)* (Shanghai, 1950); *Chung-Hua-Jen-Min-Kung-Ho-Kuo Feng-sheng Ti-t'u (Atlas of the Chinese People's Republic in Provinces)* (Shanghai, 1953), no. 26.

less than one-half its original size.[7]

When alluding to older Manchuria, Russian literature put English geographical knowledge of Asia at that time next in importance only to Chinese historical records on Eastern Asia.[8] The eighth edition of the *Encyclopaedia Britannica* described the pre-1858 Manchuria as "a large district in the Northeast of Asia constituting a government of the Chinese Empire";[9] and the seventh edition gave the following information.

The frontier of China on the side of Russia . . . is as follows: Commencing at the north-eastern extremity where the Uda [Ud] falls into the Sea of Olchotsk [Okhotsk], in the 55th parallel of northern latitude, it stretches west and west-southwest along the limits of the Tungousi Tartars, the Duourian Mountains, and along the Kerlon, which divides it from the Russian province of Nertchinsk, till it meets the 50th parallel.[10]

The survival of traces of the greater Manchuria of older times is of some interest to historians. Foremost among these is the Genghis Khan Wall, an archeological treasure, known in Russian literature and believed to have been erected at the time of the Mongolian domination in Manchuria. This wall runs from the Amur basin to Hailar, "crosses the Argun River," and stretches into "the present Russian possessions."[11]

Another is the ruins of the Buddhist temple or the Monastery of Eternal Repose (Yung-Ning-Szu) constructed early in the Ming dynasty on the summit of a bold cliff about half a mile below the village Tyr, near the mouth of Amgun River and about ninety-five versts (one verst is equal to 0.66 miles), or sixty-three miles, from the Liman of the Amur.[12] In the Museum of Vladivostok are

---

[7] "Chung-O Chieh-chi Piao" ("Chart of the Sino-Russian Boundary Record"), Ch'ou, *op. cit.*, sh. 2; Lou & Yang, *op. cit.*, p. 49; Wang, *op. cit.*, p. 52; Wu Hsiang-hsiang, *O-Ti Ching-lüeh Chung-Kuo Shih* (*A History of Aggression of Russian Imperialism on China*) (Tapei, 1954), pp. 12-13; Russian literature sometimes refers to the older Manchuria as "the then Manchuria," e.g., *Opisanie Man'chzhurii* (*Description of Manchuria*) (St. Petersburg, 1897), p. 15.

[8] "Aziia" ("Asia"), *Entsiklopedicheskii Leksikon* (*Encyclopaedic Lexicon*, referred to hereinafter as *E.L.*) (St. Petersburg, 1835), I, 253.

[9] "Manchooria," *Encyclopaedia Britannica* (8th ed.; Boston, 1857), XIV, 260.

[10] "China," *Encyclopaedia Britannica* (7th ed.; Edinburgh, 1842), VI, 548.

[11] *Opisanie Man'chzhurii*, p. 11.

[12] V. Vasil'ev, "Zapiska o Nadpisiakh Otkrytykh na Pamiatnikakh Stoiashchikh na Skale Tyr, bliz Ust'ia Amura" (Dolozheno v Zasedanii Istoriko-Filologicheskogo Otgeleniia 14-go fev. 1896 g.) ("Note on the Inscriptions Discovered on the Monuments Standing on the Tyr Cliff, near the Mouth of the Amur" [Reported at the

exhibited two stone tablets inscribed in Chinese bearing testimony to this Buddhist temple not far from the mouth of the Amur in older Manchuria.[13] The Russian historian Vasil'ev recorded in detail the story on these historical tablets:

The Temple of Iun Nin Sy [Yung-Ning-Szu], as it appears, was constructed in the eleventh year of the reign of Emperor Iun-Lo [Yung-Lo] of the Ming dynasty (1413) in the land of Nurgan inhabited by the Tszi-Me-Li people. According to the inscriptions on the monuments, the first attempts to infiltrate this land may have been made under the first Ming Emperor Khyn-Vu [Hung-Wu] (1368-98) but without success. Only in the spring of 1411, Ishikha, a court official . . . , was sent there with more than one thousand government . . . soldiers on fifty-five big ships. He introduced there a local administration: Nurgan was reorganized into the province of Du-Sy, in which officials receiving seals and ranks of all kinds were installed . . . apparently all from among the natives, because they were said to administer themselves. This incorporation, however, as seen from the story on the tablets, was accomplished not by the force of arms, but through lavish gifts. Ishikha, besides providing costly entertainment, distributed clothes, food and household articles to the inhabitants of Nurgan, as well as to the barbarians Ku (-i) [Ku-I] living beyond the sea, i.e., on the island of Sakhalin. Evidently, the Chinese Government, desirous of establishing a civil state, constructed this temple for the propagation of knowledge, as it was said.[14]

According to European topographical and geographical scientists of the nineteenth and previous centuries, "the natives look upon this spot [the ruins of Yung-Ning-Szu] with veneration and . . . carry on here their religious rites," and "the Russians knew of the existence of these monuments in the seventeenth century."[15] In about the year 1690, N. C. Witsen (1641-1717) wrote:

It is said that some thirty or forty years ago, Russian warriors found a bell weighing six hundred and sixty pounds, . . . and several stones bearing Chinese inscriptions. The natives living there said, that long ago a Chinese

Conference of the Historical-Philological Division on Feb. 14, 1896]), *Izvestiia Imperatorskoi Akademii Nauk* (*News of the Imperial Academy of Science*), Vol. IV, no. 4 (St. Petersburg, April, 1896), pp. 365-367; Ravenstein, *op. cit.*, pp. 193-194; Li Chi, "Manchuria in History," *The Chinese Social and Political Science Review* (Peiping, July, 1932), Vol. XVI, no. 2, pp. 251-252, & plate III.

[13] Li, *op. cit.*, pp. 251-252.
[14] Vasil'ev, *op. cit.*, pp. 365-366.
[15] Ravenstein, *op. cit.*, p. 195.

emperor had come to the Amur by sea, and erected the monuments and left the bell in commemoration, whence it was concluded that China and Japan might be reached this way.[16]

A manuscript of 1678 was said to have mentioned "the same facts."[17] Russian literature of the first half of the nineteenth century sometimes referred to the lower Amur basin as Dauriia, describing it as "the northernmost district of China, connected with the Manchurian region."[18] The long island facing the mouth of the Amur was "first called Sakhalin—the Manchurian name of the Amur."[19]

Today the Russian specialists still believe that "according to their natural, ethnographical and historical condition . . . the closely linked Russian and Chinese parts of the Amur territory" are "not different countries, but only parts of the one and the same geographical unit . . . , undivided by natural boundaries."[20]

Historically, Manchuria became "known only through ancient Chinese accounts."[21] Russian works on early Manchurian history, with few exceptions, rely solely on Chinese annals, which they regard as the only sources.[22]

At various times, the people living in Manchuria, though principally of the same stock,[23] had "repeatedly changed their names,"[24] and were said occasionally to have "adopted the names of a prominent leader."[25] They were first mentioned as Sushen in recorded Chinese history beginning about the latter part of the Shang dynasty

[16] Nicolaas Corneliszoon Witsen, *Noord en Oost Tartarijen* (*North and East Tartary*) (Amsterdam, 1692), I, 67, cited in Ravenstein, *op. cit.*, pp. 195-196.

[17] The manuscript was referred to by Ravenstein as in the possession of the library of the Siberian Department (possibly of the British War Office, since Ravenstein's book was dedicated to Colonel Sir Henry James, R.E., Director of the Topographical and Statistical Department of the War Office), *ibid.*, p. 196.

[18] "Amur," *E.L.*, II, 161.

[19] *Ibid.*, II, 162.

[20] V. E. Gluzdovskii (ed.), *Primorsko-Amurskaia Okraina i Severnaia Man'chzhuriia* (*The Maritime-Amur Borderland and Northern Manchuria*) (2nd rev. ed.; Vladivostok, 1917), p. 169.

[21] "Puteshestvie po Man'chzhurii Missionera de-la-Briunera" ("Missionary de la Bruner's Journey in Manchuria"), *Sovremennik* (*The Contemporary*) (St. Petersburg), Vol. XVIII, no. 12, sec. V (Dec., 1849), p. 179.

[22] "Aziia III: Aziia Izvestnaia v Srednie Veki" ("Asia III: Asia as Known in the Middle Ages"), *E.L.*, I, 257.

[23] "T'i-yao" ("Outline"), *C.T.M.C.Y.L.K.*, Book of Introduction, sh. 1; Vol. VI, sh. 4; Vol. VII, sh. 1, 3; *passim.*

[24] *Opisanie Man'chzhurii*, pp. 6-7; Gluzdovskii, *op. cit.*, p. 51.

[25] Gluzdovskii, *op. cit.*, p. 51.

(*circa* 1400-1102 B.C.).[26]   This name remained through the Chou
(1122-250 B.C.) and the Ch'in (Ts'in) (255-207 B.C.) dynasties.
Through the Han (206 B.C.—220 A.D.) and the Tsin (265—419
A.D.) dynasties, they were called Ilou; Wuchi during the epoch of
the Northern and Southern dynasties (420-588 A.D.), Moho in the
Sui dynasty (589-618), Pohai in the Tang dynasty (618-907),
Nuchen in the Liao (907-1125), Western Liao (1125-68), Chin
(1115-1260), Sung (960-1127), Southern Sung (1127-1280), and
Yüan (1280-1368) dynasties, Chienchou in the Ming dynasty (1368-
1644), and Manchu in the Ch'ing dynasty (1644-1911).[27]

In their day, the Sushens and the Ilous lived in Eastern Manchuria, including the Ussuri territory.[28]   In the later Han dynasty
(25-221), when the Fuyüs dominated Western Manchuria, the Ilous
were said to have controlled an extensive area as far as the lower
Amur.[29]   Russian geographical studies record these facts about the
Ilous:

Vestiges of the Ilou domicile are preserved in the Ussuri region in the
form of a number of pits, former mud-huts . . . and enormous piles of
kitchen refuse with a large quantity of polished stone tools and fragments
of household utensils . . . . These dwellings of "stone-men" were often
found on the shores of the Amur firth.[30]

The early inhabitants of Manchuria were divided in a large num-
ber of tribes and clans, which were quite hostile to one another.[31]   In
the fifth century the land of the Mohos again "extended to the
Amur."[32]   However, it was not until the seventh century that Ta
Tso-yung, the leader of the Sumos (one of the seven original Ilou,
Wuchi, and, later, Moho tribes), united them into a great, powerful

---

[26] "Wu-Ti-Chi" ("The Age of the Five Rulers"), Lei Hsioh-ch'i, *Chu-Shu Chi-
nien (The Bamboo Annals)*, Vol. I, sh. 7; "Chou-Chi" ("The Chou Dynasty"),
ibid., Vol. IV, sh. 2; Li, *op. cit.*, p. 234.
[27] Cf. n. 23; also "Pu-tsu" ("Tribes"), *C.T.M.C.Y.L.K.*, Vol. I, sh. 4; Vol. II,
sh. 6; Vol. V, sh. 3-4; Vol. VI, sh. 5-7; Vol. VII, sh. 1-5; "Chiang-yü" ("Territorial Domain"), *ibid.*, Vol. VIII, sh. 8-9; Vol. IX, sh. 3, 6-8; "Liao-Tung K'ao"
("On Liaotung"), Wei Huan, *Huang-Ming Chiu-pien K'ao (A Study of the Frontiers of the Ming Dynasty)* (1541), Vol. II, sh. 1-15; Hsi Ch'ing, *Hei-Lung-Chiang
Wai-chi (Notes on Heilungkiang)* (Canton ed., 1900), Vol. I, sh. 1.
[28] Gluzdovskii, *op. cit.*, p. 51.
[29] "Chiang-yü" ("Territorial Domain"), *C.T.M.C.Y.L.K.*, Vol. VIII, sh. 8-9.
[30] Gluzdovskii, *op. cit.*, p. 51.
[31] *Ibid.*
[32] Ravenstein, *op. cit.*, p. 5.

country under the name of Pohai (668-925).[33] At the height of its power, the state of Pohai stretched from the middle of Korea to the area beyond the Amur, and from the Eastern Ocean to the Great Khingan Mountains,[34] and boasted five capitals and seventy-seven cities connected by good highways.[35] According to Gluzdovskii, "traces of these [roads and] ruins of fortresses of this epoch have been preserved in many parts of the Southern Ussuri region." "One of these huge fortresses," he said, "may be found at three versts from Nikol'sk and can be seen from the windows of trains approaching that city from Vladivostok."[36]

At the end of the ninth century, a powerful Ch'itan tribe rose in an area to the west of Manchuria, moved eastward and attacked the Pohai state. In 916, when the Ch'itans were organizing their Liao (Iron) dynasty in Manchuria, Pohai already had yielded a considerable portion of its domain. By the middle of the tenth century Pohai had been reduced to but "a narrow strip of the littoral from Lake Khanka to the coast of the Sea of Japan."[37]

At the beginning of the twelfth century, however, the Nüchens, a Manchurian tribe related to the Pohais and descendants of the Sushens, the Ilous, and the Mohos,[38] conquered the Liao empire, quelled the remnant of Pohai,[39] and founded the Chin (Golden) dynasty, "with boundaries up to the mouth of the Amur."[40] A Russian source indicates that "many of the relics of monuments left by the ancient inhabitants of the Ussuri region were related to this [Chin] dynasty."[41]

In the thirteenth century the Chin dynasty fell into the hands of Genghis Khan, under whose Mongol rule Manchuria was reported to have been devastated. Not until the beginning of the seventeenth century were the inhabitants of the Ussuri region able to show signs of recovery.[42] Soon thereafter the Manchus, who were indirectly related to the Nüchens and also descended from the

[33] "Pu-tsu" ("Tribes"), *C.T.M.C.Y.L.K.*, Vol. II, sh. 4-5; Vol. V, sh. 4; Vol. VI, sh. 1, 4.

[34] *Opisanie Man'chzhurii*, p. 7; Ravenstein, *op. cit.*, p. 5.

[35] "Pu-tsu" ("Tribes"), *C.T.M.C.Y.L.K.*, Vol. VI, sh. 2, 6-7; Gluzdovskii, *op. cit.*, p. 52.

[36] *Ibid.*   [37] *Ibid.*

[38] "Pu-tsu" ("Tribes"), *C.T.M.C.Y.L.K.*, Vol. VII, sh. 1.

[39] *Ibid.*, Vol. VII, sh. 6-7.

[40] Gluzdovskii, *op. cit.*, p. 52.

[41] *Ibid.*   [42] *Ibid.*

ancient Sushens, Ilous, and Mohos, began to subdue their sister tribes and to seize the power of the declining Ming dynasty.[43] They brought along related tribes from Manchuria into China proper for further conquest and garrison.[44]

Concerning Manchuria's relation to China, a consensus seems to have been established. Ravenstein wrote: "We find the destinies of Manchuria almost uninterruptedly connected with those of China."[45] His explanation for this state of affairs was that the Manchurian tribes "prefer conquest in the south, rather than to rely upon their own strength, and to found an independent empire in Manchuria."[46] Russian sources recognize the interplay in history between periodic nomadic invasions from Manchuria into China and the Chinese assimilation and subjugation of the Manchurian tribes.[47]

Pursuing the same line of thought Li Chi, of the Academia Sinica, on the basis of findings by Chinese historians, concludes: "Manchuria's history is . . . only a part of Chinese history,"[48] because "it is impossible to relate the history of Manchuria by itself. Events in Manchuria are but reflections of the happenings in China proper: the Chinese domination in the Northeast, the nomadic invasions, the uprisings and downfall of the various tribes are all phases of Chinese history in general."[49]

According to historians, "as early as the neolithic time, both racially and culturally, South Manchuria belonged to the same area as North China."[50] As a matter of fact, it was reported that the Sushens of North Manchuria were first at the court of Emperor Shun with tributes of bows and arrows as early as 2225 B.C.[51] In all Chinese classic literature, such as *Tso-chuan, Kuo-yu, Chou-shu, Shu-hsü, Shih-chi,* and *Han-shu,* "frequent mention was made . . . of

[43] Emperor Ch'ien-Lung to the Cabinet, Imperial Edict, Oct. 9/Aug. 19 (Chinese lunar calendar), 1777, *C.T.M.C.Y.L.K.,* Book of Introduction, sh. 1; "Pu-tsu" ("Tribes"), *ibid.,* Vol. I, sh. 1.
[44] Gluzdovskii, *op. cit.,* p. 52.
[45] Ravenstein, *op. cit.,* p. 3.
[46] *Ibid.*
[47] *Opisanie Man'chzhurii,* pp. 2-3, 7.
[48] Li, *op. cit.,* p. 226. His article "Manchuria in History" is an abstract on a larger work in Chinese, compiled by Messrs. Fu Ssu-nien, Hsü Chung-shu, Members of the Institute of History and Philosophy of the Academia Sinica, and Fang Chuang-yu, Fellow of the Normal College of Peiping.
[49] *Ibid.,* p. 258.
[50] *Ibid.,* p. 226.
[51] "Wu-Ti-Chi," Lei, *op. cit.,* Vol. I, sh. 7; *Opisanie Man'chzhurii,* pp. 6-7.

big stone arrow-heads as the typical products manufactured by [the] Sushen[s] and sent to the court of the Chou dynasty as their main tribute."[52] Later the Ilous "borrowed the technique of agriculture from the Chinese."[53]

From the time of the Kingdom of Yen of the "Warring States" (403-221 B.C.) when it had annexed South Manchuria in the fourth century B.C.,[54] the tribes of Manchuria played one of three roles in their relation to China: they either served as tributaries to the imperial courts of China,[55] asserted "native rule," or launched invasions into China proper. During the Han dynasty, Emperor Wu made South Manchuria into the Provinces of Chenfan and Hsüant'u, which included the present-day Russian territory around Vladivostok.[56] He also controlled the Fuyüs and the Ilous as tributaries.[57] Similarly the Moho tribe paid tribute to the Sui dynasty.[58] Even the powerful Pohai state was, for a time, considered a "tributary" of the Tang and its succeeding dynasties.[59] On the other hand, the "self-rule" of the Pohais and the uprisings and the subsequent invasion of first the Ch'itans (based in Manchuria), then the Nüchens, and, later, the Manchus, had been achieved largely through the Chinese, particularly those Chinese who were serving in their armies.[60]

---

[52] *Ibid.*, p. 7; Li, *op. cit.*, p. 231.   [53] Gluzdovskii, *op. cit.*, p. 51.
[54] Li, *op. cit.*, p. 235.

[55] These tributary tribes were required to patrol the empire frontiers in order to maintain commercial intercourse with the provinces, to pay homage to the emperor, and to obey orders from the commissioner (*ibid.*, p. 239). For regulations of the tributary system and royal grants in the Ming Dynasty, see "Liao-Tung K'ao" ("On Liaotung"), Wei Huan, *op. cit.*, Vol. II, sh. 16-17. For a description of the collection of tributes from the Jü-P'i-Ta-Tzu (Fish-Skin Tartars) and others in the lower Amur basin in the Ch'ing dynasty, see "Puteshestvie po Man'chzhurii Missionera de-la-Briunera," *Sovremennik* (*The Contemporary*), Vol. XVIII, no. 12, sec. V (Dec., 1849), p. 181.

[56] Li, *op. cit.*, p. 238; cf. *Opisanie Man'chzhurii*, p. 3.

[57] Li, *op. cit.*, pp. 239-240.

[58] The Sui Emperor actually told the Moho tribal envoy: "As I consider you my children, so should you consider me your father" (*Sui Shih* [*History of the Sui Dynasty*], chap. lxxxiv, cited in Li, *op. cit.*, p. 245).

[59] Ta Tso-yung, the founder of the Pohai state, was originally "a sub-officer of the Chinese army," and subsequently appointed "Prince of Pohai and Governor of Hukhan Province." Pohai "continued to pay tribute to the imperial court all through the Tang and succeeding dynasties without any interruption" (*Tang Shih* [*History of the Tang Dynasty*], chap. ccxix, cited in Li, *op. cit.*, p. 245). Russian source notes that during the period between 766 and 779 the envoys of Pohai went to the Tang Court twenty-five times (*Opisanie Man'chzhurii*, p. 9).

[60] Li Chi points out that "the Mohos, the Ch'itans and the Nüchens had been all

During the Yüan and the Ming dynasties, Manchuria in the eyes of the world appeared under the auspices of the imperial houses of China.[61] In 1215 the Mongols led by Genghis Khan began their conquest of the Chin empire. By 1234 they had annexed Manchuria, and soon after their subjugation of the Southern Sung dynasty in 1279 the Yüan dynasty of the Mongols governed Manchuria as one province, Liao-Yang-Hsing-Sheng.[62]

Under the Ming dynasty, Manchuria, forming the northern territory of Shantung, was divided into twenty-five *wei* (garrisons) and a number of *suo* (posts), all under one military commander with the title of the *Tu-ssu* of *Liaotung*.[63] Later another *Tu-ssu* was established for Nurgan "at the far-away mouth of the Amur."[64] In addition, a large number of native *wei* were created. A total of 384 *wei* and 24 *suo* were reported.[65] According to one Chinese historian, "the majority of these places, scattered all over North and East Manchuria, including the Maritime and Amur provinces of Siberia, have been identified."[66] A Russian source regards the *wei-suo* system of the Ming dynasty in Manchuria as a significant effort on the part of the Chinese at agricultural colonization.[67]

Under the Ch'ing dynasty, Manchuria achieved a new status, for it was the home of the imperial house. As for the Manchus, they were now ruling an extensive empire; they were realizing the cen-

depending on Chinese support and utilizing expert Chinese service" (Li, *op. cit.*, p. 242). On another occasion, he said: "These Chinese [immigrants and their descendants] served in their [the Ch'itans' and the Nüchens'] army and were encouraged to intermarry with the native tribes" (*ibid.*, p. 250). For Chinese serving in the Manchu military system before the conquest of China proper, see Owen Lattimore, *Manchuria: Cradle of Conflict* (New York, 1935), pp. 45-46.

[61] *Opisanie Man'chzhurii*, p. 12.

[62] *Ibid.*, p. 11; the full name of the province was Liao-Yang-Teng-Ch'u-Chung-Shu-Hsing-Sheng, with jurisdiction over seven *lu* (*S.C.T.C.*, Vol. X, sh. 2; Ch'en Fang-chi, *Li-Tai Ti-li Yen-ko Piao* [*Charts of Successive Geographical Changes of the Various Dynasties*], 1895, Vol. III, sh. 38).

[63] *Opisanie Man'chzhurii*, p. 11; Ch'en Fang-chi, *op. cit.*, Vol. III, sh. 38.

[64] Japan, Tao-Keizai Chosakyoku (East Asiatic Economic Investigation Bureau), *The Manchuria Year Book 1932-33* (Tokyo, 1932), p. 32; Vasil'ev, *op. cit.*, p. 365; Li, *op. cit.*, pp. 251-252.

[65] *Ta-Ming Hui-tien* (*Imperial Gazetteer of Great Ming*) gives a complete list of the names of such *wei* and *suo*; Li, *op. cit.*, p. 252.

[66] Li, *op. cit.*, p. 252.

[67] It was reported that Chinese forces stationed in Liaotung were quartered in fortresses, yet constituted military-farming colonies. They were said to have a clearly designated staff of settlers responsible for paying into the treasury a stipulated amount of grain products (*Opisanie Man'chzhurii*, p. 12).

turies-old ambition of their nomadic ancestors to conquer China. But more important, another phase of Chinese history had begun.

As early as in the eighteenth century, the British had made the following observation on the historical process of the multi-national Chinese world or society:

The most interesting particulars of the Chinese history relate only to the incursions of the Tartars, who at last conquered the whole empire, and who still continue to hold the sovereignty, though by transferring the seat of the empire to Peking, and adopting the language, manners, etc. Tartary would seem rather to have been conquered by China, than China by Tartary. These incursions are said to have begun very early; even in the time of emperor Shun. . . .[68]

Further illustrating this historical process of the Chinese political pattern, Lattimore explains:

Wherever the old populations and old social conditions of Manchuria can still be detected, it is easy to discern the effects of a well-defined historical process; the periodic assault on China of barbarian tribes from the north, alternating with Chinese reactions which threw back the invaders and extended Chinese authority and influence into barbarian territories. Manchuria, sometimes as an appendage of Mongolia, occasionally through the independent action of Manchurian tribes, has for more than a score of centuries been concerned in this cyclical process.

The process itself can be concisely described, for it has followed a curiously regular, almost stereotyped course. At different periods barbarian tribes north of the Great Wall have descended on China, establishing kingdoms and sometimes empires of greater or less territorial extent. Thus . . . in the tenth and eleventh centuries the Liao (Khitan) dynasty, originating in Manchuria, conquered China as far as the Yellow River, with a capital first at Liaoyang in Manchuria and then at Peking. In the twelfth century the Liao were overthrown, not by the Chinese but by another Manchurian horde, that of the Chin (Nüchen), who extended the conquest of China as far as the Yangtze. The Chin, in turn, were overthrown by other barbarians—the Mongols, who established the Yüan dynasty and completed the conquest of China . . . .

Owing, however, to the fact that each alien dynasty, as it matured, became more and more Chinese, the reflex action of Chinese culture north of the Great Wall was never lacking. Invariably the conquerors took

[68] "China," *Encyclopaedia Britannica* (3rd ed.; Edinburgh, 1797), p. 653. For an illustration of this historical process, see *ibid.*, IV, 653-660.

over the Chinese dynastic model for their ruling families and Chinese forms of government for their new territories; and, gradually losing the characteristics of conquering aliens, became essentially a Chinese ruling class. Just as invariably, when the power of the dynasty waned, a Chinese reaction, tinged with racial animosity, took place. The dynasty was overthrown, the Chinese power moved north once more . . . . Whoever seized the power after the overthrow of the alien dynasty established a new dynasty; and when this in turn decayed the next invasion from the north swept over the Great Wall.[69]

Apparently as a result of this historical "destiny," "the Manchus, from a very early period, not only looked on China as a country to conquer, but on Chinese civilization as something to aspire to."[70] Furthermore, Lattimore observes, "long before the [Manchu] Conquest, the largest numerical element in the Manchu armies must have been Chinese."[71] Agreeing with the view that the Manchu rule over China "represented only a dynastic change,"[72] he describes the Manchu conquest of China as one of the Chinese civil wars in history:

The Manchus, for their part, had taken on a thoroughly Chinese color. Their two emperors who ruled from Mukden before the entry into China were emperors in the Chinese manner. It it not too much to say that the final Manchu conquest of China was less an alien invasion than the triumph of the strongest regional faction in a colossal Chinese civil war.[73]

On the other hand, for one reason or another, the Manchu Court had for a prolonged period instituted a perplexing policy of closing up Manchuria to Chinese immigration.[74] But after the Manchus migrated en masse to China proper as officials and "bannermen,"[75] Manchuria, with the exception of the old Chinese settlement in Liaotung,[76] became largely depopulated. To remedy the serious situation thus created, in 1665 the Manchu Court actually issued a

[69] Lattimore, *op. cit.*, pp. 36-38.
[70] *Ibid.*, p. 44; cf. *Opisanie Man'chzhurii*, pp. 13-14.
[71] Lattimore, *op. cit.*, p. 46.
[72] Li, *op. cit.*, p. 227.
[73] Lattimore, *op. cit.*, p. 46
[74] "Man'chzhuriia," *E.S.*, XXXVI, 358; Gluzdovskii, *op. cit.*, p. 174; Li, *op. cit.*, pp. 255-256.
[75] Li, *op. cit.*, p. 255; *Opisanie Man'chzhurii*, p. 12.
[76] Li Chi observes: "In the *History of Liao* and the *History of China*, we find frequent mention of mass migration of inland Chinese to Liaotung. In the Mongol dynasty such migration continued, so that the Liaotung area became almost entirely settled by the Chinese" (*op. cit.*, p. 250).

mandate to encourage settlement in Manchuria.[77] In 1673, however, the Court reversed its policy by forbidding the Chinese (Han-Jen) to settle beyond Mukden and by stopping the Mongols at the Outer Fengtien Wall.[78] In 1776, Emperor Ch'ien-Lung reiterated this policy and issued the following edict, which actually was intended for most of Manchuria:

Shengking and Kirin are the home of the dynasty. To permit immigrants to settle down there would greatly affect the Manchu mode of life. . . . Let . . . orders be given out that immigrants are forever prohibited from entrance.[79]

This policy of exclusion was reportedly due to several causes: (1) The imperial house desired a monopoly of Manchurian trade in fur, ginseng, and pearl. (2) The Manchus placed considerable faith in Chinese "Feng-shui," or geomancy, and did not want the surface features of their native land changed by Chinese tillers. (3) The early Manchu emperors wanted to keep the ruling race pure, even if only nominally so.[80] Thus, Manchuria was looked upon by the Manchu emperors as their "patrimony,"[81] and in the early days of the Ch'ing dynasty Heilungkiang and part of Kirin, which constituted the historically significant part of older Manchuria, were "kept as royal parks, where the common people were forbidden to go."[82]

As history shows, Chinese migration into Manchuria was not and could not be checked by the Manchu policy of "closed territory" ("Feng-chin"), especially when the ruling house after the time of Emperor Ch'ien-Lung began to show signs of increasing weakness and gradual decline.[83] By 1790, when the Court had its hands full

[77] *Ibid.*, p. 255.
[78] The country south of Mukden remained predominantly Chinese in population, and the Chinese had free access to Mukden itself (*ibid.*, p. 256; "Man'chzhuriia," *E.S.*, XXXVI, 358).
[79] Emperor Ch'ien-Lung to Grand Councilor of State, Imperial Edict, *C.L.T.C.*, Vol. I, sh. 34. Cf. also Edict of Emperor Chia-Ch'ing, *ibid.*, Vol. II, sh. 8-9.
[80] Li, *op. cit.*, pp. 225-256. Emperor Yung-Cheng attempted to prevent assimilation of the Manchus by the Chinese, while Emperor Ch'ien-Lung created a Manchu entity immune to Chinese influence; see "Feng-T'ien-Fu Chih-chang" ("Official Duties of the Fengt'ien Prefecture"), Li Hung-chang & others, *Ta-Ch'ing Hui-tien Shih-li* (*The Institutes of the Great Ch'ing Dynasty*, referred to hereinafter as *T.C.H.T.S.L.*) (1886), Vol. MXCIII, sh. 1. Cf. also Gluzdovskii, *op. cit.*, p. 174; "Man'chzhuriia," *E.S.*, XXXVI, 358.
[81] Gluzdovskii, *op. cit.*, p. 177.   [82] Li, *op. cit., p.* 257.
[83] *Ibid.*; *The Manchuria Year Book 1932-33* (Tokyo, 1932), p. 34; Gluzdovskii, *op. cit.*, p. 174.

with the Pai-Lien (White-Lotus Sect) rebellion, it was forced to accept the accomplished fact of fresh Chinese immigration and limited its efforts in that direction to the mere prevention of further inflow.[84] Yet, when the Chinese immigrants continued to move into the forbidden land, the Court, with no desire to incur added public resentment, did not try to enforce the exclusion. At the same time it was unwilling to repeal the law of the "sacred ancestors."[85] Therefore, as a kind of last stand, the Court attempted to colonize the Sungari Valley with the Manchus then congesting Peking.[86] This, however, proved as unsuccessful as its policy of excluding Chinese from Manchuria.[87]

During the second half of the nineteenth century, Chinese immigration into Manchuria became considerably intensified, despite administrative measures. Finally, faced by the T'ai-P'ing rebellion (1850-64) and its aftermath, the Manchu Government had to acknowledge the *fait accompli* of Chinese colonization and in 1878 officially opened Manchuria for Chinese immigrants.[88] For this reason, as in Mukden, Chinese civil administrative machinery was set up for Kirin in 1882, and later for Heilungkiang as well.[89] Unfortunately, these decisions, which could have fortified the border and perhaps discouraged Russian advance into Manchuria, came almost half a century too late.[90]

As early as in the middle of the seventeenth century, four decades before the era of Peter the Great, Russia had demonstrated its interest in the Far East. Following Vasilei Poyarkov's (1643-46) and Erofei Khabarov's (1649-52) Cossack "expeditions,"[91] it had ex-

---

[84] Edict of Emperor Chia-Ch'ing, 1810, *C.L.T.C.*, Vol. II, sh. 8.

[85] *T.C.H.T.S.L.*, Vol. MXCIII, sh. 2-3; Hsü, *op. cit.*, p. 38.

[86] Edicts of Emperor Chia-Ch'ing, 1814, 1821, 1823, 1824, 1825, 1829, 1831, 1842, *C.L.T.C.*, Vol. II, sh. 15-16; Vol. III, sh. 1, 8-9, 11, 17-18, 31, 41.

[87] Hsu Tsung-liang, *Lung Chiang Chih-lueh* (*A Concise Study on Heilungkiang*, referred to hereinafter as *L.C.C.L.*) (1891), Vol. IV, sh. 6.

[88] Gluzdovskii, *op. cit.*, p. 174.

[89] Shen T'ung-sheng (ed.), *Kwang-Hsu Cheng-yao* (*A Collection of the More Important Documents of the Reign of Kwang-Hsu, 1875-1908*) (1909), Vol. IV, sh. 22; *L.C.C.L.*, Vol. IV, sh. 8.

[90] Cf. Gluzdovskii, *op. cit.*, p. 174.

[91] The Russians first settled at the foot of the Ural Mountains toward the end of the fifteenth century. In 1581, three years before the death of Ivan the Terrible, Yermak crossed the Ural and commenced the conquest of Siberia. Subsequently, the Russians founded Tobolsk in 1587; Tomsk, in 1604; Yeniseisk, in 1619; Yakutsk, in 1632; and Okhotsk, in 1638. From the accounts of an exploring party of Cos-

panded its power eastward to the Amur basin. A British source states: "An invasion was made into Manchuria by the Russians in the seventeenth century, but although they established themselves for forty years on the Amur, they were at last driven out by the Manchus."[92]

Some Russian authors, even during the time of the Tsars, regretted the "outrageous" Cossack raids on the Amur region of the Manchu Empire and their "treacherous and cruel behavior towards the natives."[93] For example, Davidov wrote in 1911:

It is regrettable that from the beginning of our early acquaintance with

sacks in 1636, they first learned of the Amur, and exploration of the region was first considered and planned by Peter Petrovich Golovin, the first *voivod* of Yakutsk. For the details of Poyarkov's and Khabarov's adventures, see Ravenstein, *op. cit.*, pp. 9-13, 14-25; Vladimir, pseud. (Zenone Volpicelli), *Russia on the Pacific and the Siberian Railway* (London, 1899), pp. 102-108, 110-126. Khabarov's first report of 1650, "asking for 6,000 men to accomplish the conquest of the Amur" (*ibid.*, p. 158) must have reached Moscow some time before Russia decided in 1654 to interfere in favor of Little Russia and wage war with Poland. At this juncture, "the conquest of the Amur had already been under consideration for some time" by Muscovy (Ravenstein, *op. cit.*, p. 24). It was "resolved in Moscow to despatch 3,000 *strielitz* to the Amur" (Vladimir, *op. cit.*, p. 125). Khabarov himself "wished to conquer Manchuria" (*ibid.*, p. 115) and was actively engaged in "his work of conquest" (*ibid.*, p. 116). In all, 532 Russians had left Siberia for the Amur at one time or another under Khabarov's command (Ravenstein, *op. cit.*, p. 25). The adventurers declared themselves in the service of the Emperor Alexis Mikhailovich, "Grand Duke of all Russia" (Vladimir, *op. cit.*, p. 121). After Khabarov came Onuphrius Stepanov, less colorful but no less adventuresome, who in 1654 "penetrated into the heart of Manchuria as far as the town of Ningut" (*ibid.*, p. 131). In 1658 he perished with about 270 of his men in one of his annual raids up the Sungari, where they were caught in a trap by the Chinese fleet. The annihilation of Stepanov and his forces ended "the first Russian occupation of the Amur" at a time when Muscovy, under Alexis Romanov, had just concluded a truce with Sweden and was waging a second war with Poland (*ibid.*, pp. 132, 158-159). Nikiphor Romanov Tchernigofskii then took up the challenge and built a new fort on the site of one burnt by the Chinese in 1658. By 1681, Tchernigofskii had surpassed his predecessors, "having extended the Russian power over the river Ussuri and part of the Sungari up to the mountains" (Lt. Col. Rogosa, *Short Account of the Occupation of the Amur Region*, cited in *ibid.*, p. 134). His successor, *voivod* Alexis Tolbuzin, was the defender of Albazin during the Chinese siege in 1685 and again in 1686. Killed by a cannonball in 1686, Tolbuzin was succeeded by Athanasius Beiton (*ibid.*, pp. 134-136).

[92] "Manchooria," *Encyclopaedia Britannica* (8th ed.; Boston, 1857), XIV, 260. Chinese literature recorded that the Lo-Ch'a or Russians had disturbed the frontier of the Manchu Empire for more than thirty years. See Ho Ch'iu-t'ao, *Shuo-fang Pei-ch'eng* (*Studies of the Northern Regions*, with special reference to Sino-Russian relations, referred to hereinafter as *S.F.P.C.*) (1860), Book of Introduction, sec. I, sh. 5-14.

[93] Ravenstein, *op. cit.*, p. 13. The peaceful natives, mostly peasants, who had first received the Russians "with open arms" and "provided them with food," were

[our] great peace-loving neighbor, our attitude had not always been just nor based on mutual understanding of one another. . . . [As to] Russian activities in the east and south . . . all information available to us concerning the given period sketches a horrible picture of the inhumanity of the first Russian emigrants toward the various tribes living by the Amur [River] and paying tributes to their princes. Such harsh violence against the peaceful natives forced them first to move southward to the Amur, and then further from the Amur to the upper Nonni River. The sites left behind by the dislodged tribes were then settled by the Russians.[94]

The author goes on to say that the Russians then advanced "in the absence of a fixed border line" and under the urge to reach a "natural boundary," at which time "the Chinese Government, primarily motivated by the feeling of self-preservation and self-defense, . . . stopped the further invasion of the Lo-Ch'a, i.e., the Russians, by armed force."[95]

Davidov compares Russian invasion of Manchuria with Chinese forbearance:

So long as the Russians came in contact only with the various tribes living to the north of the present Manchurian territory, plundered and violated

---

"exposed to all sorts of extortion." They were subjected to "unlimited levies of tribute," "barbarous tortures" as hostages, and massacres. As "all [along] the way the Cossacks lived by plunder," the natives subsequently "took to flight at the approach of the Russians" (*ibid.*, pp. 11-13, 16-20, 25; Vladimir, *op. cit.*, pp. 104, 107, 111-112, 114, 116-117, 119, 124, 131). "Khabarov himself admits to having tortured and burnt his hostages. The memory of this treatment by the early Russians still lives among the natives of the Amur, and Middendorv was told in 1845 by a Nigidal (Natki), that the early Russians were devils, who made gridirons of the parents to roast the children" (Middendorv, *Siberische Ruise*, IV, 174, cited in Ravenstein, *op. cit.*, p. 19, n. c.). Khabarov also wrote: "The fear of God fell upon the heathen dogs [natives] and they could not stand the terror of the Tsar and our weapons, and they fled, and we ran at their backs, killing many and seizing [many] prisoners . . ." (cited in Vladimir, *op. cit.*, p. 119). At the hands of Khabarov and his band alone, "the loss of the natives and Manchu[s], in [number of dead] amounted, as far as can be ascertained, to about 1,600 men" (Ravenstein, *op. cit.*, p. 25). Besides, the Cossacks' "capricious violence and wasteful plunder exhausted the resources of the natives" (Vladimir, *op. cit.*, p. 131).

[94] D. A. Davidov, *Kolonizatsiia Man'chzhurii i S.-V. Mongolii* (*Colonization of Manchuria and Northeastern Mongolia*) (Vladivostok, 1911), pp. 11-12. In 1671 the Russian settlement at Albazin was organized by several farming families, with an Orthodox church constructed in the same year (*ibid.*, p. 12). For the Chinese record of Russian encroachment and behavior, see *S.F.P.C.*, Book of Introduction, sec. I, sh. 7-8, 10, 12-13; "Chiao-She Chih" ("Records of Negotiations"), *Hei-Lung-Chiang Chih-kao* (*Draft Gazetteer of Heilung-kiang*) (1930), Vol. XXXIV, sh. 1-2, *et al.*

[95] Davidov, *op. cit.*, p. 12.

only these people, the Manchus were quiet and did not take any step against us. But as the robbery began to extend to their own territory and to affect the whole large region along the lower reaches of the Amur and in the Sungari basin, the Manchu Government was driven to the defense of the fatherland of its people. It despatched first not an army, but an enquiry to the Russian authorities, in which it pointed out the disturbance caused by the marauding of the Russians, and requested the regulation of frontier relations. When that and subsequent enquiries did not produce any result, the Manchus in growing exasperation took up arms to repay in kind the injuries they had suffered.[96]

After observing the cautious and nonbelligerent edict issued by Emperor K'ang-Hsi in 1683 relative to the Russian incursions, Davidov could not help noting "how contrary were the attitudes of the two peoples: sincerity and love of peace on the one side, robbery accompanied by slaughter on the other."[97]

In the spring of 1685, following an initial reconnaissance, "the Manchu army advanced to the town [fort] of Albazin, destroyed it, and took as voluntary prisoners forty-five Russians."[98] However, the Russians disregarded "such a lesson . . . and once again went back to the ruins of Albazin and fortified it."[99]

The renewed Russian transgression precipitated a warning from Emperor K'ang-Hsi, who sent "the Manchu army to Albazin again to begin its siege." Only then did the Russian proposal to negotiate a peaceful settlement of all boundary questions reach Peking, where-upon the Manchu Court immediately called off the siege pending diplomatic arrangements.[100]

Negotiations followed shortly afterwards. Russia and China concluded the Nerchinsk Treaty on August 27, 1689, in which the long-needed frontier line was drawn and the Russian encroachment was halted for a century and a half. The failure of Russia to make further advances at this stage was attributed to the power of China.[101] Although the Nerchinsk Treaty has been considered at times "a

[96] *Ibid.* The first measure against the Russian invasion was the construction of the city of Aigun on the bank of the Amur, about 500 versts or 330 miles down the stream from Albazin (*ibid.*, pp. 12-30).

[97] *Ibid.*, pp. 13-14.

[98] *Ibid.*, p. 14; cf. *Opisanie Man'chzhurii*, p. 15.

[99] Davidov, *op. cit.*, p. 14.

[100] *Ibid.*

[101] D. Romanov, "Prisoedinenie Amura k Rossii; Period I: Otkrytie i Zavoevanie Reki Amura 1636-1689" ("The Annexation of the Amur to Russia; Period I: The

complete failure for Moscow diplomacy,"[102] it was viewed by a Russian specialist as having "advantageous aspects for [Russia] . . . [e.g.] the right of tariff-free trade with China.[103]

After the signing of the Nerchinsk Treaty in 1689, the prolonged period of tranquillity between Russia and China which ensued was not broken until the Russian Amur expeditions and occupations of the 1850's. This is not to say that Russia desisted from all activity where Manchuria was concerned. Under the surface there was a kind of watchful waiting between the two neighbors and there were some Russian infringements of local character which did not entirely escape the eye of the Manchu Court. Nor had the Russian sovereigns given up altogether their designs on the Amur.

In the century following the signing of the agreement outlining the Nerchinsk boundary, the Manchu dynasty attained the height of its power, yet its authorities paid little attention to the defense of its frontiers. As a matter of fact, the center of border defense was moved inward first from Aigun to the left bank, then to Mergen, then to Tsitsihar. Boundary inspections took place only once a year for some places, once every three years for some others, and not at all for the more remote areas and so the Russian peasants and Cossacks following in the footsteps of the Chinese frontier inspectors were able to hunt game in these areas and collect tribute from the people.[104] In 1737-38, at the suggestion of Academician Müller, Russian surveyors Shobelzin and Shetilov extended their labor to Chinese territory. Early in the nineteenth century Major Stavitskii, botanist Turczaninov, and Colonel Landyshinskii each explored the Amur as far as Albazin.

As for Russia's ruler at this time, there was no lack of interest. While most of his reign was devoted to the Turkish and the Swedish Wars, Peter the Great (1689-1725) did in his later years cherish ambitions of conquering the region at the mouth of the Amur and proceeding "to the Great Wall of China."[105] One of his agents,

Opening and Conquest of the Amur River 1636-1689"), *Russkoe Slovo* (*The Russian Word*) (St. Petersburg), April, 1859, Part I, p. 200.

[102] George Vernadsky, *Political and Diplomatic History of Russia* (Boston, 1936), p. 222; Vladimir, *op. cit.*, p. 165. Golovin was described as "a man of weak will and understanding" in addition to his "ignorance of China" (Vladimir, *op. cit.*, p. 164).

[103] Davidov, *op. cit.*, p. 15.   [104] Ravenstein, *op. cit.*, p. 71.

[105] Vladimir, *op. cit.*, pp. 167-168.

A. P. Volynskii, stated a few years after Peter had ordered Captain Bering to explore the North Pacific in 1724: "If Peter had lived longer, he would have tried to reach India. At the same time he secretly dreamed of opening a way to China as well."[106]

Catherine II (1763-95), though busy with Polish affairs (1763-95), the Turkish Wars (1768-74, 1787-92), as well as domestic troubles, including the Pugachev uprising (1773-75), did not neglect to carry on Peter's plans both in Europe and in the Far East. She sagaciously remarked: "If the Amur were useful only as a convenient way to supply our possessions in Kamchatka and on the Sea of Okhotsk, its possession would be important."[107] These plans, however, were not carried out. The Russian Government was confined to the conclusion of a series of conventions, namely, the Treaty of Kiakhta, supplementary articles in 1768, and the International Act of 1792, regulating frontier questions and the overland trade through Kiakhta.

Alexander I (1801-25) did little to further these plans, for he was preoccupied with the Napoleonic (1805-7, 1812-14), the Swedish (1808-9), the Turkish (1806-12), and the Persian (1804-13) Wars, as well as with international congresses and domestic reforms.[108]

But his successor, Nicholas I (1825-55), saw the gradually increasing importance of the Russian settlements in Kamchatka and the fur trade of the Russian-America Company in Alaska, and, like Peter the Great and Catherine II, gave serious thought to the idea of "recovering" the Amur. Russia's renewed interest in and drive on the Amur during the reign of Nicholas I is usually attributed to the challenge from Great Britain in the Pacific following the latter's victory in the Opium War (1840-42). In the first place, when Great Britain seized Hong Kong, Russia felt its appetite for territory whetted. When China lost the Opium War and had to open five ports to British trade, Russia knew that its favored position in overland trade was indeed threatened. And, in the final analysis, "the Russians had always coveted the Amur, and were now in constant dread of being forestalled by England, whose occupation of the mouth of the Amur would destroy forever the prospects of annexing Siberia and permanently arrest expansion eastward to the Pacific."[109]

---

[106] Cited in Vernadsky, *op. cit.*, p. 240.
[107] Cited in Vladimir, *op. cit.*, p. 168.
[108] *Ibid.*, p. 169.   [109] *Ibid.*, p. 172.

In 1846 Nicholas I sent an expedition under Lieutenant Gavrilov to explore the mouth of the Amur in spite of the cautious advice to the contrary by Count Nesselrode, who feared that it would provoke the formidable Manchu enemy to belligerence. Though information derived from this expedition was fragmentary and erroneous, the Tsar took care to find immediately the right man for the task ahead. On September 7, 1847, Nicholas I personally selected thirty-eight-year-old General Muraviev, then Governor of Tula, and appointed him the Governor-General of Eastern Siberia with special emphasis on the Amur.[110] Subsequently, with the zealous assistance of Captain Nevelskoi, Muraviev was able to secure the use of the waterway of the Amur.[111]

On January 20, 1849, the Tsar appointed a special committee to study the Amur question, and on February 8 he approved its proposal to send a maritime expedition to explore the mouth of the Amur. Nevelskoi was appointed commander of the expedition.[112] Nevelskoi, who had left the Black Sea port of Cronstadt in August, 1848, on commission to Petropavlovsk in Kamchatka, reached the mouth of the Amur in the summer of 1849.[113] In mid-1850, on his own responsibility, Nevelskoi proceeded up the forbidden Amur itself and at twenty-five versts from the mouth established a post, which, in honor of the Tsar, he called Nikolaevsk. Here on August 6, 1850, the Russian military flag was hoisted. To mark the occupation of the Amur, an open violation of the still existing Nerchinsk Treaty, Nevelskoi left five armed men to guard the first Russian post on the long-coveted river.[114]

In November, 1850, when Muraviev in person reported this event to St. Petersburg, Nesselrode and his party urged an immediate withdrawal, "without awaiting the complaints of the Chinese, thus avoiding 'extreme danger.'" On January 19, 1851, however, Nicholas I ordered that "the post of Nikolaevsk be maintained, and even guarded by a vessel during summer months." On this occasion the Tsar had these memorable words to offer: "Where the Russian flag has once been hoisted, it must not be lowered." Nominally the

[110] Ivan P. Barsukov, *Graf Nikolai Nikolaevich Murav'ev Amurskii po Ego Pis'mam, Dokumentam, Rasskazam Sovremenikov i Pechatannym Ictochnikam* (*Count Muraviev Amurskii According to His Letters, Documents, Tales of Contemporaries and Printed Sources*) (Moscow, 1891), I, 170-171.
[111] *Ibid.*, I, 172 ff.   [112] *Ibid.*, I, 195.
[113] *Ibid.*   [114] *Ibid.*, I, 278-279.

post was accredited to the Russian-American Company. It was thought by St. Petersburg that this distinction between a private company and the Russian Government would veil the real objectives behind the appearance of the Russians at the mouth of the Amur and the establishment of Nikolaevsk and lull any suspicion on the part of either the Chinese or the natives.[115]

Muraviev's next task was to build up a large armed force in Eastern Siberia in the hopes that Russia might eventually "act as the protector of China." His plan was to convert the peasants registered at Nerchinsk into Cossacks. From a population of twenty-nine thousand males he wanted to form twelve battalions (each one thousand strong) of Cossack infantry. On April 27, 1851, Nicholas I approved this conversion program and later, on June 27, orders to that effect were issued, thus creating the infantry battalions of the Transbaikalian army.

Meanwhile, in the course of 1851-53, Nevelskoi and his men were busy exploring and occupying the lower reaches of the Amur, the coast to the south of the river mouth, and Sakhalin for the defense of the latter. In March, 1853, the post of Alexandrovsk was established at the bay of De Castries, that of Mariinsk near Lake Kizi, and later, that of Constantinovsk at Imperatorskii Bay. On June 12, 1853, instructions from Muraviev came to Nevelskoi that the Tsar had sanctioned the occupation of De Castries, Kizi, and the Island of Sakhalin. Circling the coast of Sakhalin and sailing northwards into the Gulf of Tartary, Nevelskoi hoisted the Russian military flags at Constantinovsk on August 1, at Alexandrovsk on August 5, and at Mariinsk on August 7, 1853. By the end of the same year the most important harbors in the Gulf of Tartary had been occupied, posts had been established in Sakhalin, and the Amur navigated for 300 versts. In the spring of 1854, a body of 250 men was sent down the Amur to guard the posts on the coast.

In 1854 Russia was at war with Turkey and thus became involved also in a destructive war with England, France, and Sardinia. The Crimean War (1854-56), however, only served to provide Muraviev with a better reason for accomplishing the Russian aim of acquiring

[115] *Ibid.*, pp. 282-283. Later, April 11, Nicholas I ordered the occupation of Sakhalin by the same Russian-American Company. While the company received for this purpose an adequate sum from the government, it was Nevelskoi who was expected to carry out the order.

the Amur territory. In a confidential report to Grand Duke Constantine, then Admiral-in-Chief, he stressed the necessity of strengthening the Far East and navigating the Amur.[116] He pointed out the weakened state of the Chinese Empire and requested full power to deal with the latter:

While the Western Powers could not inflict any serious loss on Russia in Europe, they might easily deprive her of Kamchatka and of the mouth of the Amur in the Far East. The Empire of China, now insignificant on account of its military weakness, might become dangerous under the influence and guidance of England and France—Siberia might even cease to be Russian. The loss of this vast region . . . could not be compensated by any victories or conquests in the West. It was therefore necessary to guard Kamchatka, Sakhalin, and the mouth of the Amur, thus also *acquiring enduring influence on China.* This was possible with the means now disposable in Eastern Siberia, prepared during the last five years, provided full powers were given to the Governor-General to settle all questions without the loss of time entailed by reference to St. Petersburg.

. . . At the same time troops, provisions, and artillery must be sent down the Amur. . . . The navigation on the Amur would not meet with much opposition from the Chinese, as three years' experience at the mouth of the river had shown they cared little about the question. (Moreover, it was easy to explain that the measure was necessary for the defense not only of the sea-coast but of Manchuria itself, which would be exposed to great danger by the neighboring conquests of the Western Powers.) It was also necessary to bear in mind that the Chinese Government was fully occupied by its domestic troubles, half the empire being in the hands of the rebels.[117]

In the same report, Muraviev assured his statesman correspondent that "it would not be necessary to send a large force down the Amur, as the English in their war with China had never been able to land more than 3,000 men." On the other hand, he enumerated the forces at his disposal in Eastern Siberia as a result of five years' preparation—"16,000 infantry and 5,000 cavalry, out of which a total of 13,000, with 20 guns, could be sent across the borders."[118]

Muraviev's suggestion was duly referred to a special committee

[116] Barsukov, *op. cit.*, I, 306-307, 313-314.
[117] Muraviev to Grand Duke Constantine, Confidential Report, Nov. 29, 1853; cited in Vladimir, *op. cit.*, pp. 202-204. Italics added.
[118] *Ibid.*, pp. 202, 203.

under the Heir-Apparent. On January 11, 1854, the Tsar directed Muraviev to settle directly with the Peking Foreign Office all questions concerning the frontier in the Far East. A decision was also reached "to start navigation on the Amur, even if the consent of the Chinese were not obtained, and to send reinforcements to Kamchatka by that river."[119]

On May 14, 1854, Muraviev personally led his first expedition down the Amur.[120] A dispatch had been sent to Peking stating that, on account of war with other powers, officials and troops had been ordered down the Amur for the defense of the Russian possessions on the littoral. At the same time the Chinese Government was requested to appoint a time and place for a conference of plenipotentiaries to settle frontier questions. On May 18 the flotilla, consisting of one steamer and seventy-five barges and rafts transporting a line battalion about eight hundred strong, a *sotnia* (one hundred) of Cossacks, and a division of mountain artillery, solemnly entered the Amur, which had been closed to Russia since the Treaty of Nerchinsk.[121]

On May 28, when the expedition approached the Chinese fortified town of Aigun, Muraviev sent officers to inquire whether its governor had received instructions from Peking. Since no answer to Muraviev's dispatch about the navigation of the Amur had reached him, the Chinese governor was greatly embarrassed. He attempted to assert Chinese sovereignty and the inviolability of the Amur, but the formidable sight of the flotilla and especially the unfamiliar steamer so intimidated him that his only wish was to remove them from his town.[122] Consequently, Muraviev met little opposition as he reached the Sungari on June 2, the Ussuri on June 5, and Mariinsk on June 12. On his arrival at Nikolaevsk, after a tour of inspection, he found the answer of the Chinese Foreign Office, which had been forwarded after him down the river, stating that the Chinese were ready to appoint officials to inspect the places on the frontier.[123]

[119] Barsukov, *op. cit.*, I, 345.

[120] *Ibid.*, I, 368.

[121] *Ibid.*, I, 371.

[122] *Ibid.*, I, 372; Ching Shun, Military Governor of Kirin, to Emperor Hsien-Feng, Memorial, June 24/May 29 (Chinese lunar calendar), Wen Ch'ing, Chia Cheng, Pao Yün, & others (comp.), *Ch'ou-pan I-wu Shih-mo* (*Records on Foreign Relations*, referred to hereinafter as *I.W.S.M.*), Hsien-Feng Ch'ao (under the reign of Emperor Hsien-Feng) (Peking, 1867), Vol. VIII, sh. 5-6.

[123] Barsukov, *op. cit.*, I, 373, 375.

On the completion of his successful navigation of the Amur, Muraviev sent Major Korsakov to St. Petersburg with a report of the events. At the capital, Korsakov was immediately taken to the War Office and thence to the Heir-Apparent and to Grand Duke Constantine. When Korsakov was presented to Nicholas I the following day, the Tsar "embraced him, and announced the promotion of all the officers of the expedition."[124]

Soon Muraviev prepared his second expedition. On October 30, 1854, and February 18, 1855, he forwarded dispatches to Peking, declaring that under the instructions of the Tsar, he was leading a second expedition down the Amur to its mouth with artillery and provision to repulse the probable attacks of the allied fleet.[125] When he reached Aigun in May, 1855, Muraviev notified the Manchu governor that "104 large boats, including a steamer, were to follow, transporting 300 horses, 300 cattle, and over 8,000 persons of both sexes, besides cannon, rifles, and war materials," and requested that "the vessels not be detained."[126] Greatly surprised by the size of the expedition and the presence of women and cattle, the Chinese were left with no doubts as to the intent of the Russians to establish permanent settlements on the Amur.[127]

In the meantime Peking proposed that the meeting of Russian and Chinese plenipotentiaries be held at Urga, the capital city of Outer Mongolia. Muraviev replied that he was presently engaged in leading reinforcements to the mouth of the Amur and would remain there until September to treat the question of the frontier with the Chinese plenipotentiaries that would be sent for the purpose.[128] On September 8, 1855, the Chinese plenipotentiaries sent down the Amur reached Muraviev's headquarters at Marinsk. Negotiations commenced on the following day. During the conference Muraviev and his deputy, Admiral Zavoiko, proposed that all the places on the Amur which had been occupied by Russia against allied attack as well as all the coast should definitely belong to Russia. In order to secure uninterrupted communications between the troops and the fortresses at the mouth of the Amur and the inland provinces, they needed a chain of settlements on the left bank of the Amur, which would thus constitute the best natural frontier between the

[124] *Ibid.*, I, 384.
[126] *Ibid.*, I, 424.
[128] Barsukov, *op. cit.*, I, 422-423.

[125] *Ibid.*, I, 410, 417-418.
[127] Vladimir, *op. cit.*, p. 209.

two empires. For reply, the Chinese plenipotentiaries read the Russian senate note of June 16, 1853, embodying Foreign Minister Nesselrode's conservative view on the question. Muraviev paid little attention to the note. Instead he requested the plenipotentiaries to communicate to Peking his intention of sending another expedition down the Amur, where he would now establish permanent communications between the troops and fortresses at the mouth of the Amur and the inland provinces.[129]   Thus, according to a Russian source, "by the end of 1855, the Amur [region] had been definitively occupied by the Russians."[130]

When Muraviev's third military expedition started down the Amur in the middle of May, 1856, the Crimean War had come to an end with the signing of the Treaty of Paris. His expedition was composed of 110 boats and rafts conveying 1,636 men and 24 officers of the 13th and 14th line battalions. On May 21 it had reached Aigun, and General Korsakov, military governor in the absence of Muraviev, went ashore to confer with the Chinese mandarins. He outlined his plan of sending a large number of vessels up and down the river during the summer and setting up provisions and garrisons on the left bank of the Amur. The Chinese had not received any instructions about the navigation of the river, but they would not restrict the free movement of the Russian vessels. What they objected to was the establishment of garrisons and storehouses on the left bank. Korsakov was carrying out the instructions of Governor-General Muraviev and requested the mandarins of Aigun to report the matter to Peking. When the Chinese asked about the number of Russian troops at the mouth of the Amur, Korsakov said there were about ten thousand, and five thousand more were expected. More surprising still was the announcement that five hundred men were to be stationed at the mouth of the Zeia opposite Aigun.[131]

After the conference the third Russian expedition proceeded down the Amur and founded four posts, each with a garrison, on the left bank: Kumarski, opposite the mouth of the Kumara; Ust-Zeiski, at the mouth of the Zeia; Khinganski, at the commencement of the Little Khingan Range; and Sungariiski, opposite the mouth of the

[129] *Ibid.*, I, 427-429.
[130] *Opisanie Man'chzhurii*, p. 17.
[131] Barsukov, *op. cit.*, I, 449-452.

Thereupon, Li Hung-chang telegraphed his Government, recommending the concession:

Russia possesses enormous stretches of land, which are settled very sparsely. She will not, therefore, encroach upon one foot of soil owned by others. And, as for China, bonds of intimacy link her with that country. She has no motive for wishing to connect the railway in Manchuria, except the prompt conveyance of troops. And that again was wanted in order to come to China's aid effectually if at any time she should be in straits, so that the line would not be solely for Russia's benefit. The building of the railway is beyond China's financial capacity. But if she granted the concession to the Russo-Chinese Bank at Shanghai, she could, by means of fitting stipulations, secure for herself the right of control and no difficulties would arise. Transactions of this kind are in vogue in every country. On those grounds the Tsar solicited me to turn over the offer in my mind, to close with it definitely. He urged that China did not know how soon trouble would be stirred up for her, . . . but she could at least make it possible for Russia to come to her rescue. In the discharge of my duty, I note these words for the guidance of the Crown.[221]

In China the proposed concession was initially opposed by Prince Ch'ing, who was in charge of the Tsungliyamen or Foreign Office, and Chang Chih-tung, the Viceroy of Hupeh. They had reacted similarly in the previous year, when the Russian railway project was first reported by the foreign press.[222] However, the concession as recommended by Li was later approved, in principle, by the Empress Dowager Tzu-hsi.[223]

The Sino-Russian Alliance was then signed by Lobanov-Rostovskii, Witte, and Li Hung-chang on June 3/May 22, 1896, in Moscow, where the coronation took place.[224] It is important to note that the alliance thus concluded was a limited and conditional one, providing

[221] Li Hung-chang to the Tsungliyamen (Chinese Foreign Office), Tel., Apr. 29, 1896 (Chinese lunar calendar), *C.C.W.C.S.L.*, Vol. CXXI, sh. 5-6.

[222] Memorial of the Tsungliyamen to the Throne, Oct. 19/Sept. 2 (Chinese lunar calendar), 1895, citing Chang Chih-tung's memorial, dated between Sept. 19 and Oct. 17, 1895 (identical to Aug., 1895, according to Chinese lunar calendar), in "Memorials Relating to the Russian Agreements," *Kuang-Hsu Tiao-Yo* (*Treaties under the Reign of Kuang-Hsu,* referred to hereinafter as *K.H.T.Y.*), Vol. XLV, sh. 3; Sun Chi-i, *Chung-O Chiao-she Lun* (*Sino-Russian Negotiations*) (Shanghai, 1931), p. 72.

[223] Sun, *op. cit.*, p. 72.

[224] Khvostov, "Nachalo," in Potemkin, *op. cit.*, II, 117. The text of the 15-year secret treaty was first published in the London *Daily Telegraph*, April 15, 1910, on its expiration by Li Ching-mai, and was reproduced in MacMurray, *op. cit.*, I, 81. Cf. Witte, *Memoirs*, pp. 92, 93.

for Russian assistance to China only in the event of attack from Japan. There is reason to doubt whether this limitation of the *casus foederis* had been made explicit in the arguments initially advanced by Witte to persuade Li to accept the alliance.[225] Certainly Li did not convey the idea of any such restriction in his memorial to the Chinese throne.[226] Exactly how the limitation was first introduced, and at what stage of the negotiations, thus remains a mystery.

In his memoirs, Witte indicates that he introduced the change at the last minute, just before the signing of the agreement, but that he did so to correct an ill-advised alteration of his original version which had crept into the text due to the negligence or ignorance of Prince Lobanov-Rostovskii and Tsar Nicholas II.[227] Prior to his check, re-check, and last-minute appeal for revision, the text of the agreement would have provided "for the mutual defense of the two countries in the event of an attack upon either of them not by Japan alone, but by any other Power."[228]

Whatever the explanation for the earlier looseness of the text, and whatever Witte's original proposals regarding the *casus foederis,* his political wisdom was apparent in the reasoning by which he supported the last-minute change: "Several European Powers, including France, our ally, and England, have interests in China, and to obligate ourselves to defend China from all those countries meant to arouse them all against us and to invite no end of trouble."[229] Lobanov-Rostovskii died on August 30/18, 1896, without leaving a firsthand explanation of his negligence.

In the face of these considerations, it would perhaps have been unrealistic for the Chinese to expect to obtain a blanket commitment for Russian assistance. It is also possible that Li Hung-chang had no choice other than to accept as it was the final and limited version of the alliance, for the position of his government at home was extremely weak, and his attention abroad was almost entirely absorbed by the nightmare of troubles with Japan.

The terms of the alliance contained China's pledge of a strategic railway concession for Russia. Article VI of the Moscow treaty provided that the Treaty of Alliance would not take effect until the railway contract stipulated in Article IV was confirmed by China.

[225] Cf. p. 43, *supra.*   [226] Cf. p. 45, *supra.*
[227] Witte, *Memoirs*, pp. 90-93.   [228] *Ibid.*, p. 91.
[229] *Ibid.*

The basic agreement concerning the projected Manchurian railway was the Contract for Construction and Operation of the Chinese Eastern Railway, negotiated by P. M. Romanov, Russian Assistant Minister of Finance, and Shu King-ch'eng, China's envoy to Russia and Germany, in Berlin,[230] and signed there on September 8/August 27, 1896, by Shu and the representatives of the Russo-Chinese Bank, Rothstein and Prince Ukhtomskii.[231] According to the contract, the Russo-Chinese Bank was to form an organization to be known as "The Chinese Eastern Railway Company"[232] under a Chinese president named by and with the seal of the Chinese Government for the purpose of constructing and operating a railway of the same name (Article I). The period of the concession was to be eighty years "from the day on which the line is finished and traffic is in operation." Thereafter, "the line, with all its appurtenances, will pass free of charge to the Chinese Government." China, however, reserved the right to buy back the railway "at the expiration of thirty-six years" from the date of the completion of the railway (Article XII).

Witte was pleased that "the terms of the railroad concession granted by China were very favorable for Russia." He even thought that Russia could probably perpetuate this concession, because "the terms of the redemption were so burdensome that it was highly improbable that the Chinese Government would ever attempt to effect the redemption."[233] Thus, Romanov stated that the entire concern of Witte was in perpetuating the exploitation of the railway "for the interests of Russia."[234] Li, on the other hand, was probably mistaken in his reliance upon Russia's non-expansionist policy.

Incidentally, it has often been reported in Russian sources that Li was bribed by Witte in the railway dealing.[235] Witte, however, denied this completely. "I must say that there is not a particle of

[230] *Ibid.*, p. 95.

[231] For Russian text of the Contract, see IU. V. Kliuchnikov and Andrei Sabanin (eds.), *Mezhdunarodnaia Politika Noveishego Vremeni v Dogovorakh, Notakh i Deklaratsiiakh* (*International Politics of Most Recent Times in Treaties, Notes, and Declarations*), Part I (Moscow, 1925), pp. 278-280; for Chinese text, see *K.H.T.Y.*, Vol. XLV, sh. 6-10; for English text, see MacMurray, *op. cit.*, I, 74-77.

[232] Referred to by Witte in his *Memoirs*, p. 92, as the "Eastern Chinese Railroad Corporation." Cf. p. 44, *supra*.

[233] Witte, *Memoirs*, p. 95.

[234] B. A. Romanov, *op. cit.*, p. 128.

[235] Khvostov, "Nachalo," in Potemkin, *op. cit.*, II, 117, 118; B. A. Romanov, *op. cit.*, p. 117.

truth in this rumor."[236]   Neither is there support for this charge in the published Russian documents, although there is some alleged evidence of Li's having accepted bribes in two other cases: the lease of Port Arthur and Dairen and the loan arrangement of 1898.[237] Even these reports, however, are not entirely credible, as they imply that Li would have shared these bribes with his bitter rival, Finance Minister Weng T'ung-ho.[238]   As for Professor V. M. Khvostov's remarks on a bribe of three million rubles promised to Li for the extension of the southern branch of the Chinese Eastern Railway,[239] these are not in conformity with the documents published in *The Red Archives*.

Contrary to the expectation of Li Hung-chang, the Chinese Eastern Railway Company formed by the Russo-Chinese Bank under the 1896 contract did not bear a truly private character.   But the Chinese had little to say about the matter.   In disregard and even in contravention of some of the important provisions of the contract, the statute of the C.E.R. Company was issued unilaterally and without Chinese consent, appearing as a Russian ordinance signed by Nicholas II "in his own hand," on December 16/4, 1896.[240]

The Russian-proclaimed statute bound the railway very closely to the Russian Government and made it an all-out Russian colonial enterprise in Manchuria.   The railway bonds, which constituted a significant portion of the capital of the C.E.R. Company, were to be issued "each time with the special sanction of the [Russian] Minister of Finance" (Article XI).   The reserve capital of the company "must be kept in Russian state interest-bearing securities, or in railway bonds guaranteed by the Russian Government" (Article XIV). The Russian Government, through its Finance Minister, made up the insufficient working funds of the company and met the annual payments due on the railway bonds (Article XVI).   In regard to

---

[236] Witte, *Memoirs*, p. 95.

[237] "Perepiska O Podkupe Kitaiskikh Sanovnikov Li-Khun-Chzhana i Chzhan-In-Khuana" ("Correspondence Regarding the Bribery of the Chinese Officials, Li Hung-chang and Chang Yin-huan"), A. I. Pavlov, Russian minister at Peking, to Muraviev, Russian Foreign Minister, tel., Jan. 24/12, 1898, *K.A.*, II, 288; Pavlov to Muraviev, tel., Jan. 27/15, 1898, *ibid.*, II, 289; P. M. Pokotilov, representative of the Russian Ministry of Finance at Peking, to Witte, tel., March 21/9, 1898, *ibid.*, II, 290.

[238] Pavlov to Muraviev, tel., Jan. 27/15, 1898, *ibid.*, II, 289.

[239] Khvostov, "Nachalo," in Potemkin, *op. cit.*, II, 118.

[240] Text in MacMurray, *op. cit.*, I, 84-90.

the personnel of the C.E.R. Company, the election of its vice-president and of the members of the audit committee, the appointment of the engineer-in-chief, engineers, and the departmental chiefs were all subject to the "approval of Russian Minister of Finance" (Article XXVII). Equally, the procedure of railway management and technical requirements were "to be submitted for confirmation by Russian Minister of Finance" (Article XXVII). Thus, Romanov correctly concluded that "the Russian Government found itself, in fact, the complete proprietor of the railway."[241]

Furthermore, in the absence of an announcement in the *Official Gazette,* the subscription of the shares of the C.E.R. Company began at 9 A.M. on December 29/17, 1896, and closed a few minutes later.[242] "In this manner," said Romanov, "the five-million-ruble share capital of the company fell into the item or 'the expenditures of the Russian Treasury on the Far East.' "[243] This was undoubtedly a flat violation of Article I of the railway contract, which stipulated that "the shares of the company can be acquired only by Chinese or Russian *subjects* [not *Governments*],"[244] in order to assure the private character of the projected Chinese Eastern Railway.

Soon after the surveying for the construction of the railway had started in the autumn of 1897, the Tsarist Government made a move which went beyond anything Witte had intended, and which he later characterized as "aggression involving the violation of treaties, the breaking of freely given promises and the disregard of the elementary interests of other nationalities."[245] This was the cabinet decision of November 26/14, 1897, over his strong protest, to seize Port Arthur and Dairen, and to construct a branch line linking them with the Trans-Siberian Railway.[246]

Following the German occupation of Kiaochow on November 17, 1897, a squadron of Russian warships in turn occupied the two Liaotung ports early in December.[247] At this unsavory Russian move, Witte was outraged over his own government's duplicity.

[241] B. A. Romanov, *op. cit.,* p. 125.

[242] Rothstein to Witte, letter, Dec. 29/17, 1896, cited in B. A. Romanov, *op. cit.,* p. 121.

[243] *Ibid.,* pp. 44, 121.

[244] Italics added.

[245] Witte, *Memoirs,* p. 102.

[246] Popov, "Pervye Shagi," Journal of the Conference of the Council of Ministers, Nov. 26/14, 1897; referred to in *K.A.,* LII, 108 n. 1.

[247] Witte, *Memoirs,* p. 101.

He emphatically reminded the Tsar and the ministers that "we had declared the principle of China's territorial integrity and . . . on the strength of that principle we forced Japan to withdraw from the Liaotung peninsula."[248]   He further pointed out that Russia had concluded a secret defensive alliance with China, ". . . thus obligating ourselves to defend her from Japan's encroachments upon her territory."[249]   Vigorously protesting the occupation, Witte warned that "the seizure of a Chinese port would be the height of treachery and faithlessness."[250]   What is more, such a measure would be not only "extremely dangerous" but also against Russia's own self-interest, because it would arouse China "against us, thus endangering the railroad construction."[251]

However, Nicholas II had always thought that Russia's future "open port should be on the Liaotung Peninsula or at the northern corner of the Korean Gulf."[252]   And so, ignoring Witte's strong arguments, Nicholas II chose to follow the advice of his Foreign and War Ministers, Muraviev and Vanovskii, and adopted forceful measures for "his own thirst for military glory and conquest."[253]   Therewith, a cabinet conference drafted a set of demands for the lease of the Liaotung Peninsula and a southern extension of the C.E.R., which the new War Minister, Kuropatkin, considered "a strategic necessity."[254]   On March 27/15, 1898, three weeks after Germany had secured the lease of Kiaochow, Russia succeeded in imposing upon China a convention for a lease in the Liaotung Peninsula,[255] the very place recovered from Japan through Russian-led intervention.   The formal agreement for the extension of the Chinese Eastern Railway to the southern seaports was signed on July 6/ June 25, 1898, between the Chinese Eastern Railway Company and China.[256]   The new line was to bear the name of the South Manchurian Branch of the Chinese Eastern Railway (Article I).

[248] *Ibid.*, p. 99.   [249] *Ibid.*, pp. 99-100.
[250] *Ibid.*, p. 100.   [251] *Ibid.*

[252] Popov, "Pervye Shagi," Nicholas II to Muraviev, note, Nov. 23/11, 1897, *K.A.*, LII, 102.

[253] Popov, "Pervye Shagi," Muraviev to Nicholas II, report, Nov. 23/11, 1897, *ibid.*, LII, 105; Witte, *Memoirs*, p. 101.

[254] Witte, *Memoirs*, p. 102; Popov, "Pervye Shagi," Journal of the Conference of the Council of Ministers, Nov. 26/14, 1897, referred to in *K.A.*, LII, 108 n. 1.

[255] Text in MacMurray, *op. cit.*, I, 119-121.

[256] Text in *ibid.*, I, 154-156.

Witte later characterized the Russian policy of seizing Port Arthur and Dairen as "child's play which would end disastrously."[257] As it turned out, this was indeed one of the fatal steps which led to the Russo-Japanese War of 1904-5. Since, as a result of Russia's defeat, the South Manchurian Branch of the C.E.R. between Kwanchengtze and Port Arthur was ceded to Japan, this study will deal only with the northern section of the C.E.R., which remained under Russian control after 1905.

[257] Witte, *Memoirs*, p. 103.

II: THE CHINESE EASTERN RAILWAY UNDER SOLE RUSSIAN MANAGEMENT UP TO 1917

RUSSIAN COLONIAL POLICY AND PRACTICE THROUGH THE RAILWAY

Russia's role in Manchuria was described by the Russian historian Rykachev in 1910 in the following words: "If a colony implies a land remote from the metropolis, a land which represents a particle of the fatherland transplanted to a foreign country, then Harbin, with the [coming of the] Chinese Eastern Railway, is now the first and unique Russian colony."[1] Gluzdovskii further described the Russian influence in Manchuria in 1917:

The northern part of Manchuria lies in the sphere of economic and political influence of Russia; the Russian Government has the right to establish its own administration, to keep troops of a definite number for the guarding of the railway and the whole zone of the leased land, and to exploit natural resources; the Russian subjects are granted the right of trade and industrial activities as well as the right of lease in the zone put aside by the Chinese Government for the use of the [Chinese] Eastern Railway.[2]

The importance of the Chinese Eastern Railway for Russian interests in Manchuria was also noted later by Soviet jurist Lashevich: "The building of the Russian colony in Manchuria was closely connected with the organization and development of the C.E.R. Company."[3]

[1] A. Rykachev. "Russkoe Delo v Man'chzhurii," *Russkaia Mysl'* ("The Russian Business in Manchuria," *The Russian Idea*), Vol. XXXI, no. 8, 1910, p. 122.

[2] V. E. Gluzdovskii, *Primorsko-Amurskaia Okraina i Severnaia Man'chzhuriia (The Maritime-Amur Borderland and North Manchuria)* (Vladivostok, 1917), pp. 175-176.

[3] G. Lashevich, "Sudebno-Administrativnaia Reforma v. Osobom Raione Man'chzhurii 1920-1921 gg." ("Legal-Administrative Reform in the Special District of Manchuria"), *Mezhdunarodnaia Zhizn' (International Life)* (Moscow), no. 1, 1924, p. 68.

It will be recalled that the Chinese Eastern Railway Company was originally intended by its founding fathers, Witte and Li Hung-chang, at the insistence of the latter, to be an agency for a private concessionaire, the Russo-Chinese Bank, which was to undertake the construction and operation of the C.E.R. under Chinese protection and territorial jurisdiction.[4] However, no sooner had the operation of the railway begun, than the function of the C.E.R. underwent a sweeping transformation. As Lieutenant General Martynov, Commander of the Trans-Amur Frontier District, 1911-13, said, "It is a well known fact that the private C.E.R. Company represents a plain fiction, inasmuch as it exists exclusively at the state's expense."[5] He further stated:

The Chinese Eastern Railway Administration represents, in the full sense of the word, a *colonial government* with all functions inherent to it. The manager of the railway administers at the same time the territory of the zone together with its population through all branches and in all respects; he is even endowed with the power of diplomatic relations, for which there is a special department in the structure of the administration.[6]

In investigating the development of this situation, under which, in the words of Lashevich, "this part of Chinese territory [North Manchuria] was gradually brought to a position near to the status of a Russian colony,"[7] one must turn to the Russian colonial policy in Manchuria, centering on the Chinese Eastern Railway, as advocated and conducted by Count V. N. Kokovtsov, the Russian Prime Minister, 1911-14, and S. D. Sazonov, 1910-16. It is essential to bear in mind that Kokovtsov and Sazonov fully agreed that "the annexation of North Manchuria was for us [the Russian Government] an imperative necessity," and that Russia was only awaiting a favorable time.[8] Events were to show that in striving incessantly for this goal of eventual annexation of North Manchuria through

---

[4] Witte, *Vospominaniia (Memoirs)*, I, 48. Cf. Article IV of the Russo-Chinese Treaty of Alliance, May, 1896, and Articles I, II, IV, & V of the Railway Contract, Sept. 8, 1896, in MacMurray, *Treaties and Agreements with and Concerning China, 1894-1919*, I, 81, 75-76.

[5] E. I. Martynov, *Rabota Nashikh Zheleznodorozhnykh Del'tsov v Manchzhurii (Work of Our Railway Businessmen in Manchuria)* (Moscow, 1914), p. 13.

[6] *Ibid.*, p. 17, italics added.

[7] Lashevich, *op. cit.*, p. 72.

[8] Protocol of an Extraordinary Meeting of the Ministerial Council at St. Petersburg, Dec. 2/Nov. 19, 1910, in B. De Siebert & G. A. Schreiner, *Entente Diplomacy and the World* (New York & London, 1921), pp. 25-27.

securing political, economic, and military advantages based on the C.E.R., Russia resorted to contractual confusion and diplomatic pressure in its relations with China to get an initial foothold, and then sought through bargaining and understandings with other Great Powers to strengthen its position and push forward its advantage.

CONTRACTUAL CONFUSION AND DIPLOMATIC PRESSURE

Often contractual confusion and diplomatic pressure have proved to be the most convenient and effective tactics by which the strong powers may prevail over the weak. It is quite clear that China lost important sovereign rights as the result of unjustifiable interpretation and unilateral implementation of ambiguous treaty and other contractual provisions by the strong foreign powers.[9]

It is regrettable that the history of Sino-Russian relations could not be free from, rather than punctuated with, instances of contractual confusion.[10] These have been detrimental to China, because contractual confusion first furnishes the weak with a false sense of security and later lends the strong a false justification for encroachment.

The very treaty which had provided the basis for the Chinese Eastern Railway—the Sino-Russian Alliance of 1896—clearly offered an example of diplomatic pressure, through the threat of withholding Russian assistance against future Japanese aggression unless a railway concession were granted. But contractual confusion may also have been used as a technique to bring China to yield the railway concession, with fateful consequences. This point cannot be established with certainty; but as was indicated above, there is some reason to believe that more was promised during the course of the negotiations, in the way of assistance to China against outside aggression, than was provided in the final version of the agreement.[11]

[9] Westel W. Willoughby, *Foreign Rights and Interests in China* (Baltimore, 1920), I, 297, 298; Chou Keng-sen, *Pu-Ping-Teng-Tiao-Yueh Shih-chiang* (*Ten Lectures on the Unequal Treaties*) (Shanghai, 1928), pp. 16-17, 26, 47-48, 59-60, 87-88, 94-95, 102-108, 123-125; Chang Ting-hao, *Pu-Ping-Teng-Tiao-Yueh ti Yen-chiu* (*A Study on the Unequal Treaties*) (Shanghai, 1927), pp. 45, 108, 109, 133-134; Chiu Tsu-ming, *Chung-Wai Ting-yueh Shih-chuan Lun* (*The Loss of Chinese Sovereign Rights through Agreement with the Foreign Powers*) (Shanghai, 1926), pp. 31-32, 43-45.
[10] To which the Agreements of 1945 and of 1950 may be added.
[11] Cf. p. 43, *supra*.

In the case of the railway itself, Russian use of contractual confusion was shown in the divergence in the interpretations of a single phrase of the railway contract of 1896—a divergence from which emerged what the able and frank Russian authors cited above have regarded as a Russian colonial empire in North Manchuria.

The single phrase in question is contained in Article VI of the Contract for the Construction and Operation of the Chinese Eastern Railway signed in Berlin on September 8/August 27, 1896, by Shu King-ch'eng, Chinese minister to Russia, and the representatives of the Russo-Chinese Bank, Rothstein and Prince Ukhtomsky. This article reads in Chinese: "yu kai-kung-shih i-shou ching-li," meaning "to be managed by the said [C.E.R.] Company single-handedly."[12] Special attention is directed to the fact that in the Chinese text, the moot phrase is contained within the clause which reads: "all the land utilized by the said [C.E.R.] Company is to be exempted from land taxation and to be managed by the said company single-handedly."

Unfortunately, the Russian version of the above phrase and the French and English versions derived from it diverge from the Chinese text to a surprising degree, so that the phrase is separated from its related clause and is made to stand alone, not merely as an independent sentence but as an independent paragraph, with its related clause belonging to the preceding paragraph. The arrangement and the divergent wording may be noted as follows:

. . . The lands belonging to the company will be exempt from all land taxes. (Russian version: ". . . *Zemli, prinadlezhashchie obshchestvu, budut svobodny ot vsiakikh pozemel'nykh nalogov.*")

The company will have the *absolute* and exclusive right of *administra-*

---

[12] For Chinese and French texts of the contract, see China, Ministries of Communications and Railways, *Chiao-tung-shih Lu-cheng Pien* (*History of Communications: Part of Road Administration,* referred to hereinafter as *C.T.S.L.C.P.*) (Nanking, 1931), Vol. XVII, chap. vii, pp. 3-14. For Russian text, see E. D. Grimm, *Sbornik Dogovorov i Drugikh Dokumentov po Istorii Mezhdunarodnykh Otnoshenii na Dal'nem Vostoke* (*Collection of Treaties and Other Documents on International Relations in the Far East*) (Moscow, 1927), pp. 110-113. The Russian text does not appear in F. F. Martens' and I. A. Ovchinnikov's collections, nor in the Russian Foreign Office Collection of 1891-1906, but it is found in Kliuchnikov and Sabanin (eds.), *Mezhdunarodnaia Politika Noveishego Vremeni v Dogovorakh, Notakh i Deklaratsiiakh* (*International Politics of Most Recent Times in Treaties, Notes, and Declarations*), Part I, pp. 278-280, with the moot section and a few other points surprisingly omitted.

tion of *its land*. (Russian version: "*Obshchestvu predostavliaetsia pravo bezuslovnogo i iskliuchitelnogo upravleniia svoimi zemliami.*")[13]

It was under the pretext made possible by the transformed version of the controversial section of Article VI of the railway contract and the railway statute[14] based on it, the latter unilaterally issued by Russia without Chinese consent, that Russia assumed her "absolute and exclusive right" to establish throughout the railway zone a system of municipal, judicial, and police administration which the Soviet writer Skalov called "a state within a state."[15]

The railway contract was not a formal treaty between states, but merely a concession contract entered into by the Chinese Government and a foreign private concern, the Russo-Chinese Bank, for a commercial undertaking within Chinese territory and under Chinese jurisdiction. This jurisdiction included issuing the seal and appointing the President for, and giving protection to, the C.E.R. Company. Consequently, in the absence of any provision in the contract or the clear intention of the contracting parties to the contrary, and following the ordinary meaning of the words of the contract (whether or not the other principles for the interpretation of treaties under international law be considered applicable), the Chinese text should have been considered the standard for interpretation in case of inconsistency, divergence, and controversy. It would therefore appear necessary to construe the moot point from the construction and wording of the Chinese text.

The Russian text and its derived French and English versions in circulation containing "the absolute and exclusive right of administration of its land" by the railway company, are at obvious variance with the Chinese text in sentence construction, in exact meaning of the context, and in the choice of words.

First, the sentence construction of the moot point in various texts[16] indicates reorganization and rearrangement which deviates from the Chinese original.

[13] Cf. p. 55, *supra;* the added italics show the divergent wording as compared with the Chinese original.

[14] For Russian text of the railway statute, see *C.T.S.L.C.P.*, Vol. XVII, chap. vii, pp. 32-55; for Chinese text, see Chih Jen-hsi, *Tung-T'ieh Wen-ti (The C.E.R. Question)* (Shanghai, 1929), Appendix II, pp. 1-22; for English text, see MacMurray, *op. cit.*, I, 84-88.

[15] G. B. Skalov, *Sobytiia na Kitaiskoi Vostochnoi Zheleznoi Doroge (Events on the C.E.R.)* (Moscow, 1929), p. 23.

[16] Cf. pp. 55-56, *supra.*

Secondly, since in the Chinese text, Article VI contains only one paragraph and is entitled "Land Utilized by the Railway and Its Tax Exemption" (*"Tieh-Lu Yung-Ti pin Mien-Shree"*), the lands referred to under this article are naturally "the lands *utilized by* the company," not "the lands *belonging to* the company"; if the lands actually belonged to the company, and if it had full governmental power over them, there would be no need for tax exemption. Similarly, since the controversial phrase "to be managed by the company single-handedly," appears within the paragraph, and is preceded by its immediately related clause, "all the land utilized by the company is to be exempted from land taxes," the "single-handed" management by the company in regard to lands, as authorized under this Article (VI), is understood to be further confined to business administration, with a specific provision for tax exemption; it is not a grant of absolute power, touching upon political, judicial, and police matters. It is clearly not a surrender of territorial jurisdiction, because otherwise the provision of tax exemption would be superfluous. This arrangement is not too much different from that for the estates of educational, religious, and public welfare institutions in the United States. Thus, no sense of "the absolute right of administration of its land" by the company could have been contemplated.

Thirdly, the most simple, common, and proper English translation of the Chinese words *"ching-li"* per se is not "to administer," but "to manage," as the same Chinese words, when used as a noun referring to a person, do not mean "administrator" but "manager." It would be absurd to equate the word "administration" with the Chinese context of the organic sentence and paragraph concerned. This is especially true as the same Chinese word *"ching-li"* reappears in the next clause, which concerns telegraph facilities—and which also should not have been rearranged into an independent sentence and placed as an individual paragraph in the translations—where it is translated as "to operate." The translation would probably be improved if "to operate" were replaced by "to manage," but it would certainly sound strange if "to administer" were used instead.

The point of view developed in part in the foregoing analysis was in fact the one expressed by the Chinese Foreign Office in February, 1908, immediately after the Russians had established a municipal council in Harbin, in a note of protest to the Russian

Government refuting the latter's claims of rights under the moot phrase of Article VI of the railway contract.[17] The note reads in part:

In accordance with Article VI of the original contract, the company does have the right to manage [here the Chinese words *"ching-li,"* meaning business administration, are used] its land singlehandedly; it means to manage such land solely, but will not attempt to administer [here the Chinese words "chih-li," meaning political administration, are used] the inhabitants within the railway areas.

Moreover, Your Excellency asserted that the company under Article VI has unlimited authority [over its land], etc., but this Department cannot find such phraseology in Article VI of the contract.   Article V, furthermore, explicitly grants the Chinese Government the authority to protect the land from both internal and external disturbances.   In short, that company has only the authority to manage [*ching-li*] its land but not to administer [*chih-li*] the inhabitants of the railway areas.[18]

The Chinese interpretation of the moot phrase is completely in accord with the later attitude of the United States when the State Department, in a note of November 6, 1909, replying to the Russian *aide-mémoire*[19] asserting "the absolute administrative right" of the C.E.R. Company "in Harbin and the other localities on its lands,"[20] said:

The claim of the Chinese Eastern Railway Co. that China has granted to it the municipal power necessary to the government of all cities and towns built upon the railway's leased land is not considered by the Government of the United States to be justified by the language of the original contract of 1896 between the Chinese Government and the Russo-Chinese Bank, which is the concession under which the Chinese Eastern Railway was built and exists today.   The administration by the railway company of its leased lands provided for in Article VI of the contract can refer only to such business administration as may be necessary to the 'construction, exploitation, and protection' of the railway, these being the objects expressly mentioned in the article for which these lands were granted by China.

[17] C. Walter Young, *The International Relations of Manchuria* (Chicago, 1929), pp. 94-95.

[18] Hsu Shih-chang, *Tung-San-Sheng Cheng-lueh* (*The Record of the Administration of the Three Eastern Provinces*), Vol. XI, sh. 37.

[19] Chargé Schuyler to the Secretary of State, no. 560, Oct. 9, 1909, Inclosure 2, *Foreign Relations of the United States* (hereinafter referred to as *F.R.U.S.*), *1910*, pp. 217-218.

[20] *Ibid.*, p. 217.

This was, without doubt, the understanding of China as evidenced by the Chinese translation of Article VI and by the protest of the Chinese Government against the attempts by the railway company to administer the municipal government of Harbin.[21]

After explaining that even the word "administration" in English is "quite commonly used of all sorts of business administration, while the same word in French and the equivalent word in the Chinese version of the contract are still more commonly used of business and nongovernmental administration," the note continues:

It is thus clear that this contract was for the establishment of a business enterprise, and it is impossible to read into it any context from which the use of the word in a political sense could be inferred.

The position of the United States, therefore, briefly stated, is that the claims of the Russian Government on behalf of the Chinese Eastern Railway are out of harmony with the natural interpretation of the text of the agreement referred to. . . .[22]

From the foregoing reasoning, it must be concluded that Russia's claim to "the absolute administrative right" of political, judicial and police character in the railway zone through the C.E.R. was in fact a manifestation of its colonial policy and practice in Manchuria as advanced by contractual confusion—a conclusion with which many authorities on this subject seem to be in full concurrence.[23]

With regard to diplomatic pressure applied by Russia upon China in her colonial policy and practice in Manchuria as shown by the C.E.R. incident, a few examples will prove to be adequate. The first case was the Russian demand for further railway concessions in North Manchuria. The demand was met with the reasonable reply from the Chinese Foreign Minister in April, 1914, that China would study the proposed railway lines carefully in order to decide which one should be built. If China did not have sufficient funds for the task, she would confer with the Russian merchants regarding a loan.[24]

[21] Note verbale of the Department of State to the Russian Embassy, file no. 4002/249a, Nov. 6, 1909 (*ibid.*, p. 219).

[22] *Ibid.*, p. 220.

[23] Willoughby, *op. cit.*, I, 298; Lancelot Lawton, *The Empires of the Far East* (London, 1912), II, 1304; Tao-shing Chang, *International Controversies over the Chinese Eastern Railway* (Shanghai, 1936), p. 70.

[24] Krupenskii to Sazonov, tel. no. 174, April 10/March 28, 1914, *Mezhdunarodnye Otnosheniia v Epokhu Imperializma* (*International Relations during the Period of Imperialism*, referred to hereinafter as *M.O. v E.I.*), Ser. III, Vol. II, doc. no. 201, p. 280.

But this answer was unacceptable to V. N. Krupenskii, Russian minister at Peking, as he reported to S. D. Sazonov, the Russian Foreign Minister, 1910-16, saying: "I replied by word of mouth to the [Chinese] Minister of Foreign Affairs that I consider the answer unsatisfactory and contrary to all the friendly assurances given to me in recent times . . . by the President himself and other Chinese dignitaries."[25]

In order to put more pressure on the Chinese Government for these additional concessions, the strong language of colonial practice was employed. A. A. Neratov, Assistant Minister of Foreign Affairs, thus instructed Grave, the Russian chargé at Peking:

We expect from the Chinese Government a demonstration of sincerity for these assurances and shall judge, first of all, on its attitude towards our desires concerning the question of railways in North Manchuria, to which we attach paramount importance . . . . Refusal to the Russians of these concessions we shall be compelled to consider as an act unfriendly to Russia.[26]

Another case was the Russian demand that China make enormous compensations to the Russian owners of gold mines in North Manchuria for the losses they suffered after the Russo-Japanese War. The case was, in fact, admitted by the Russian authorities to be a weak and "unjust" one because of the Chinese denial of the validity of the unratified concession agreements, "the abuse of the concessionaires," "the excessive statement of losses," and the supposed responsibility of the Russian Government as a result of its intermediary role in obtaining concessions from local authorities, and "the general position of extraterritoriality of the foreigners."[27]   Nevertheless, the Chinese Foreign Minister, Lou Tseng-tsiang, was obliged to give his consent to enter into negotiations on this matter because China was anxious to settle the Hulunbuir (Barga) problem.[28]

This effort was reminiscent of Russian pressure in 1910-11 for the renewal of the Russo-Chinese Commercial Treaty of 1881 through

[25] *Ibid.*
[26] Neratov to Grave, tel. no. 874, May 13/April 30, 1914, *M.O. v E.I.*, Ser. III, Vol. II, doc. no. 416, p. 538.
[27] Sazonov to Finance Minister P. L. Bark, letter, March 22/9, 1915, *M.O.v E.I.*, Ser. III, Vol. VII, Part II, pp. 504-507.
[28] Note of the Chinese Foreign Minister to Krupenskii, Nov. 6/Oct. 24, 1915, *M.O. v E.I.*, Ser. III, Vol. IX, doc. no. 210, enc. 1, p. 213.

resort to an ultimatum and a projected military demonstration,[29] and also of the Russian demand, backed by prepared enforcible measures, for Chinese renunciation of all financial operations of the international syndicate.[30] Finally, Russian diplomatic pressure was contemplated in an effort to widen the role of the C.E.R. and strengthen the Russian position in Manchuria. In the case of the C.E.R., the terms sought through diplomatic action were summarized by Sazonov in his memorandum to Tsar Nicholas II:

We for our part must try to obtain an assurance from China to enter into an agreement with us on the following points: (1) The construction of railways in Manchuria and in the adjoining parts of Inner Mongolia. (2) The strength and distribution of the Chinese fighting forces in Manchuria. (3) An acknowledgement on the part of the Chinese Government that the Chinese Eastern Railway possesses not only freedom of action in purely technical railway questions, but can also assume the entire administration in the expropriated zone. These three points, precisely formulated, must be placed before China.[31]

GREAT POWER UNDERSTANDING AND BARGAINING

Where the Chinese Eastern Railway is concerned, the most vivid illustration of Russia's use of understandings with the Great Powers and imperialistic bargaining to advance her colonial policy and practice is found in the series of Russo-Japanese secret agreements of 1907, 1910, 1912, and 1916.

The Russo-Japanese Secret Convention of July 30/17, 1907,[32] drew a specific line of demarcation between North Manchuria and South Manchuria for the respective Russian and Japanese spheres of exclusive interests and political and economic activities. Their "rights and privileges" on the Chinese Eastern and the South Man-

---

[29] Sazonov to Russian Minister at Peking, tel., Feb. 6/Jan. 24, 1911, De Siebert & Schreiner, *op. cit.*, pp. 29-30.

[30] Sazonov to Izvolskii and Benckendorf, tel. no. 475, March 18/5, 1912, *M.O. v E.I.*, Ser. II, Vol. XIX, doc. no. 652, pp. 294-295.

[31] Sazonov to Nicholas II, report, Jan. 23/10, 1912, *M.O. v E.I.*, Ser. II, Vol. XIX, doc. no. 379, p. 34.

[32] For the Russian text of the Secret Convention, see Grimm, *op. cit.*, pp. 168-170; it does not appear in Kliuchnikov and Sabanin, *op. cit.*; for the English text see E. B. Price, *The Russo-Japanese Treaties of 1907-1916 Concerning Manchuria and Mongolia* (Baltimore, 1933), Appendix B, pp. 107-108; it does not appear in MacMurray, *op. cit.*, I, 84-88. By this convention Japan also recognized the Russian sphere in Outer Mongolia.

churian railways were fully protected for future use as convenient fulcra for colonial empire-building. As the Soviet author Savvin points out, with the conclusion of the Russo-Japanese Secret Convention of 1907 it was "already as if there were a single front of Russia and Japan against China, which was unable to react by any measures whatever to the accomplished situation in Manchuria."[33] He concludes that this 1907 "Secret Agreement between Russia and Japan concerning their spheres of influence in Manchuria meant its actual division."[34]

It was this state of affairs created on her territory that made China "very much upset by the news of the conclusion of the Russo-Japanese covenant" of 1910, as the Russian minister at Peking reported to Izvolskii.[35] But this news gave the Russian Foreign Minister only cause for rejoicing over the three years' experience which had proved the "expediency" of the Russo-Japanese Treaty of July 30/17.[36] Thereafter a Supplementary Agreement was concluded with Baron Motono, the Japanese ambassador at St. Petersburg, on July 4/June 21, 1910,[37] "in order precisely to establish, and bring into conformity, their joint interests in Manchuria."[38] In describing the function of the 1910 agreement, Izvolskii says:

The first [Public Agreement] promotes closer joint action between Russia and Japan in Manchurian railways and confirms anew the firm resolution of both Governments to maintain the status quo in these districts. The Secret Treaty defines more precisely the two spheres of interest, as well as the limitations to which they subject themselves in order to reinforce their mutual relations and to preserve the position proper to them in Manchuria from all interference on the part of other Powers.[39]

The Chinese Revolution of 1911 gave further impetus to Russian colonial policy and practice through understandings with Japan

---

[33] V. P. Savvin, *Vziamootnosheniia Tsarskoi Rossii i SSSR c Kitaem* (*Relations of the Tsarist Russia and the U.S.S.R. with China*) (Moscow, 1930), pp. 64-65.

[34] *Ibid.*, p. 65.

[35] The Russian minister at Peking to Izvolskii, tel., May 12/April 29, 1910 (De Siebert & Schreiner, *op. cit.*, p. 16).

[36] Izvolskii to the Russian ambassador in London, Strictly Confidential Letter, June 24/11, 1910, De Siebert & Schreiner, *op. cit.*, p. 16.

[37] For the Russian text, see Grimm, *op. cit.*, pp. 176-177; for the English text of the Public Agreement, see MacMurray, *op. cit.*, I, 803-804; for that of Secret Convention, see Price, *op. cit.*, Appendix C, pp. 113-114.

[38] Price, *op. cit.*, Appendix C, pp. 113-114.

[39] Izvolskii to the Russian ambassador in London, Strictly Confidential Letter, June 24/11, 1910, De Siebert and Schreiner, *op. cit.*, p. 16.

in Manchuria. In a memorandum submitted to the Tsar in January, 1912, when the abdication of the Manchus was imminent, Sazonov declared: "Russia and Japan must use the present favorable moment to fortify their position in China . . . . The Manchurian question occupies the first place . . . . As our interests in Manchuria coincide with those of Japan, our task will be greatly facilitated by co-operation with Japan."[40]

Although Japan was not easily won to the idea of co-operation with Russia, especially to the recognition of Russian interests in Sinkiang,[41] the Russo-Japanese Secret Convention of July 8/June 25, 1912,[42] was signed by Sazonov and Motono in St. Petersburg. While this Secret Convention completed the previous secret agreements of 1907 and 1910, and extended the line of demarcation fixed by the 1907 agreement, the expansion of the Russian sphere continued to radiate, of course, from its power center of the Chinese Eastern Railway in North Manchuria.

After the outbreak of the World War in 1914, Russia was even more anxious to arrange further co-ordination with Japan through their mutual ally, England, principally to enable Russia to concentrate her attention on Europe. As Sazonov remarked: "We need a possible security in the Far East, which will, best of all, be guaranteed by friendly and even allied relations with Japan."[43] Sazonov also told Sir George Buchanan, the British ambassador at St. Petersburg, that he "had always been in favor of including Japan in our alliance," and hoped that Sir Edward Grey, the British Foreign Secretary, would clear up the situation.[44]

Grey did what he could. Although the Japanese ambassador in London told him that "so long as the War is in progress, it is difficult to draw up conditions of a permanent alliance between Russia and Japan," and although Japan considered herself bound to the

[40] *Ibid.*
[41] Verbal note of Japanese ambassador in St. Petersburg to Sazonov, May 27/14, 1912, *M.O. v E.I.*, Ser. II, Vol. XX, Part I, doc. no. 86, p. 81.
[42] For the Russian text, see Grimm, *op. cit.*, p. 180; for the English text, see Price, *op. cit.*, Appendix D, p. 117. For additional reference to the Secret Agreement, see *M.O. v E.I.*, Ser. II, Vol. XX, Part I, doc. nos. 220, 241, 248, 284, pp. 213, 234-235, 240-241, 278.
[43] Sazonov to Benckendorf, Russian ambassador in London, tel. no. 4713, Sept. 23/10, 1915, *M.O. v E.I.*, Ser. III, Vol. VIII, Part II, doc. no. 754, p. 243.
[44] Buchanan to Grey, tel. no. 696 (deciphered at the Russian Foreign Office), May 31/18, 1915, *M.O. v E.I.*, Ser. III, Vol. VIII, Part I, pp. 60, 62.

Agreement of September 5, 1914, through her alliance with England, Grey still endeavored to bring the two countries into a closer direct alliance. "Russia might prefer," he noted, "to be more directly connected with the government of Japan than she was at present through their mutual alliance with Great Britain."[45]

Then, during a visit of Baron Ishii, Japanese ambassador in Paris, to London in September, 1915, Sir Edward again took the opportunity of explaining to him what he "understood to be the desire of Russia for an alliance with Japan."[46] Grey even addressed Sazonov and the French Government, asking whether they wished that the three allies should invite Japan to adhere to the agreement of September 5, 1914.[47]

While Japan's response to the Russian desire for alliance was not enthusiastic,[48] the Russian Government was so eager for an agreement with Japan that it even considered turning over to Japan the remaining southern section of the Chinese Eastern Railway.[49] When Japanese Foreign Minister Ishii proposed that "if Russia could yield to Japan the railway between Changchun and Harbin at the highest price," then Japan "might comply with the Russian wishes."[50] Russia was ready to meet Japan half way. In replying to a Japanese note referring to this arrangement as a "demonstration of Russian appreciation towards Japanese friendship and assistance,"[51] the Russian Foreign Office declared: "The Russian Government could render a corresponding service to the Japanese Government by yielding to Japan, for instance, subject to a price to be agreed on, a part of the southern section of the C.E.R. which lies in the Japanese sphere of

[45] Memorandum of British Embassy at Petrograd to Russian Foreign Office, no. 145, Aug. 6/July 24, 1915, *M.O. v E.I.*, Ser. III, Vol. VIII, Part II, doc. no. 440, pp. 7-8.
[46] Memorandum of British Embassy at Petrograd to Russian Foreign Office, no. 181, Sept. 3/Aug. 21, 1915, *M.O. v E.I.*, Ser. III, Vol. VIII, Part II, doc. no. 628, pp. 202-203.
[47] *Ibid.*
[48] Russian ambassador in Tokyo, Malevskii, to Sazonov, dispatch no. 71, Sept. 20/7, 1915, *M.O. v E.I.*, Ser. III, Vol. VIII, Part II, doc. no. 736, pp. 326-327.
[49] Memorandum of the Russian Foreign Office to the Japanese ambassador in Petrograd, Motono, no. 453, Feb. 25/12, 1916, *M.O. v E.I.*, Ser. III, Vol. X, doc. no. 254, p. 273; also *M.O. v E.I.*, Ser. III, Vol. X, doc. nos. 245, 264, 275, pp. 259-261, 231-232, 290-291.
[50] Ishii to Motono, tel. (deciphered at the Russian Foreign Office), Feb. 14/1, 1916, *M.O. v E.I.*, Ser. III, Vol. X, p. 206.
[51] Memorandum of the Japanese Embassy at Petrograd to Sazonov, Feb. 18/5, 1916, *M.O. v E.I.*, Ser. III, Vol. X, doc. no. 217, p. 224.

influence in Manchuria, namely, between the city of Kwanchengtze [near Changchun] and the Sungari."[52]

It was in this spirit of understanding between the Great Powers that Russia reaffirmed her position in another note to Japan: "The Secret Conventions of 1907, 1910 and 1912, having served the fundamental and most friendly relations between Russia and Japan, should, evidently, remain in force."[53] It was in the same spirit that Russia concluded her desired alliance with Japan on July 3/June 20, 1916.[54] Through this Secret Treaty of Alliance attached to the Convention regarding co-operation in the Far East, the respective Russian and the Japanese "special interests" evolved into their combined "vital interests" which could be realized only at the expense of China as a whole and which led them to unite in order to oppose the possible hostile intervention of any third Power.[55] In addition, as the Chinese historian Ho Han-wen comments, "it gave the Japanese 21 Demands of 1915 a new stimulus, violated Chinese independence and destroyed the balance in the Far East."[56] It goes without saying that owing to this ironclad alliance of 1916, Russia's colonial policy in Manchuria based on the C.E.R. was not only safeguarded, but further strengthened through concerted action and "armed co-operation" with her like-minded Japanese ally.

In Russia's effort for understanding and bargaining with Japan, an example of commercial compromise may be noted. In order not to antagonize Japanese commercial interests in South Manchuria and to stimulate Japanese competition in North Manchuria, the Russian Foreign Office had carefully instructed its consul at Kwanchengtze to decline support to a Russian streetcar concessionaire in that city in his application to the Chinese Government, despite the absence of a definite prohibition in the Russo-Japanese Secret Conventions. The Russian Assistant Minister of Foreign Affairs thereupon instructed

[52] Cf. n. 49.
[53] Memorandum of the Russian Ministry of Foreign Affairs to Motono, Japanese ambassador in Petrograd, March 18/5, 1916, confidential, *M.O. v E.I.*, Ser. III, Vol. X, doc. no. 380, pp. 419-420.
[54] For the Russian text, see Grimm, *op. cit.*, pp. 191-192; for the English text, see MacMurray, *op. cit.*, II, 1327-1328 and Price, *op. cit.*, Appendix E, pp. 121-122. It is surprising that Ho in his *Chung-O Wai-chiao Shih (History of Sino-Russian Diplomacy)* gives the impression that Japan took the sole initiative to conclude the alliance, while Russia was quite indifferent. Cf. Ho, *op. cit.*, pp. 17-18 and footnotes.
[55] E. B. Price, *op. cit.*, p. 86.
[56] Ho, *op. cit.*, pp. 358-359.

the Russian representatives in Peking and Tokyo to convey this decision to Japan's Foreign Minister and to the Japanese representative
in Peking as an expression of Russian goodwill.[57]

In order to uphold and develop her interests in Manchuria based
on the Chinese Eastern Railway, Russia, though directing special
attention to her colonial understanding and bargaining with Japan,
had by no means neglected the other Great Powers. Least of all did
she overlook the fact that Great Britain and France were her allies
during this period. It was Sir Edward Grey who had received with
appreciation the transmission of the texts of the Secret Russo-Japanese
Conventions and had endeavored to promote the Russo-Japanese
Alliance of 1916. And it was France who took the part of "intermediary and natural interpreter" of the Russo-Japanese negotiations,
provided a "formula" for the Russo-Japanese Entente of 1907, and
hailed their conventions enthusiastically.[58]

In 1912, in the words of the Russian minister in Peking, even
"the American representative [in China] categorically declared that
his instructions contained nothing which would cause him to thwart
our [Russian] actions in Mongolia and Manchuria."[59] Krupenskii
was convinced after discussions with his foreign colleagues in Peking
that "we [the Russian Government] need at present fear no opposition on the part of the foreign Powers, should we deem it necessary
to take . . . military measures in North Manchuria, Mongolia, and
West China."[60]

Furthermore, Sazonov did try in 1914-15, during his conversa-
tions with Sir George Buchanan, Maurice Paléalogue, and Baron
Motono, the British, the French, and the Japanese ambassadors in
Petrograd, to effect a general political agreement between Russia,
France, Great Britain, and Japan, for which he thought "the favor-
able moment has come."[61] Thus, in winning Great-Power under-

[57] Artsimovich, Russian assistant foreign minister to Malevskii, Russian ambassador in Tokyo, and Grave, Russian chargé in Peking, letters nos. 434 & 435, *M.O.
v E.I.*, Ser. III, Vol. IV, doc. no. 213, pp. 254-255.

[58] A. Gerard, *Ma mission au Japon, 1907-1914* (Paris, 1919), pp. 6, 7, 28-29;
Price., *op. cit.*, pp. 30-31, 38.

[59] Krupenskii to Sazonov, dispatch no. 32, May 14/1, 1912 *M.O. v E.I.*, Ser. II,
Vol. XX, Part I, doc. no. 5, p. 4.

[60] *Ibid.*

[61] Sazonov to Benckendorf, Russian ambassador in London, tel. no. 4456, Dec.
28/15, 1914, *M.O. v E.I.*, Ser. III, Vol. VI, Part II, doc. no. 777, p. 281; Daily
Record of the Ministry of Foreign Affairs, Jan. 2, 1915/Dec. 20, 1914, *M.O. v
E.I.*, Ser. III, Vol. VI, Part II, doc. no. 745, pp. 339-340.

standing and in bargaining with other Powers for the advancement of her colonial policy in Manchuria, itself hinging on the Chinese Eastern Railway, Russia had displayed masterly skill and uncommon effectiveness in practice.

RUSSIAN POLITICAL ADVANTAGES THROUGH THE RAILWAY

Speaking of Russian political advantages in Manchuria through the Chinese Eastern Railway, A. Izvolskii, Russian Foreign Minister (1906-10) and ambassador to France (1910-17), had this to say, with some bitterness, about the situation created there by Count Witte:

Taking Cecil Rhodes as a model and copying his role as an 'Empire Builder,' Count Witte made of this [C.E.R.] zone . . . a domain over which he ruled with quasi-sovereign powers . . . . A multitude of functionaries . . . administered the leased territory, which constituted, in fact, an important colonial possession on the remote confines of Russia in Asia. . . .[62]

In similar tenor, Soviet writer Skalov described Russian political advantages in Manchuria based on the C.E.R.:

In the railway zone, only the Russian laws and the Russian courts functioned . . . . Harbin, the most important junction of the C.E.R., . . . was in fact, a Russian city . . . . The Tsarist servants had already looked upon North Manchuria as a Russian borderland. Their attitude towards the Chinese was arrogant and contemptuous. They treated the Chinese like an inferior race. It was possible to insult and even beat the Chinese in the railway zone with impunity, as the judges were Russian, while the guilty person always turned out to be a Chinese.[63]

Thus the Russian Government, using the device of contractual confusion analyzed in the previous section, was able to carry through a number of unjustifiable policies and practices. It was able, without Chinese approval and in direct contravention of the provision in Article V of the railway contract,[64] to assert for the Chinese Eastern Railway Company the jurisdictional authority in the railway zone, by estab-

---

[62] Alexander Iswolsky (A. Izvolskii), *Recollections of a Foreign Minister* (New York & Toronto, 1921), p. 121.

[63] Skalov, *op. cit.*, pp. 23-24.

[64] Article V provides: "Criminal cases, lawsuits, etc., upon the territory of the railway, must be settled by the local authorities in accordance with the stipulations of the treaties."

lishing criminal and civil court systems affecting not only the Russian but also Chinese subjects. It created municipalities on appropriated lands through abuses of local arrangements. And it was able to interfere with the internal affairs of the Chinese border region of Hulunbuir.

RUSSIAN JUDICIAL ADMINISTRATION IN THE RAILWAY "ZONE"

By an Imperial ukase of August 2/July 20, 1901[65]—originally secret,[66] but later made public in the course of a judicial proceeding— the jurisdiction of Russian courts generally typical of the Empire was extended to the territory of the Chinese Eastern Railway. A detailed system of lower and higher courts with appeal from the justices of peace to the district courts was thereby ordained. The appointment of the justices of peace established on the line of the C.E.R., as well as the determination of their number, their place of residence, and their dependence upon the district courts of the Russian Empire, was entrusted to the Russian Minister of Justice after a preliminary understanding with the Russian Minister of Finance. The expenditures of these courts were to be determined by the Russian Minister of Justice, likewise in accord with the Russian Minister of Finance. Though the amount was to be inserted annually in the budget of the Russian Ministry of Justice, it was to be reimbursed by the treasury of the Chinese Eastern Railway.

By 1901, trials of civil and criminal cases involving Russian subjects in the zones marked out by the Russian Government along the C.E.R. were under the jurisdiction of three Russian district courts—at Chita, Vladivostok, and Port Arthur. After the outbreak of the Russo-Japanese War on February 4, 1904, the district court at Port Arthur was removed to Harbin "without," as Soviet jurist Lashevich commented, "any agreement, consent or acquiescence whatsoever by China."[67] By an Imperial Order of April 23/10, 1904, the entire railway zone was placed under the jurisdiction of the Russian district court at Harbin,[68] and the new status of this tribunal

---

[65] For English translation of the text, see MacMurray, *op. cit.*, I, 88-90.
[66] *Ibid.*, I, 88; Lashevich, *op. cit.*, p. 71.
[67] *Ibid.*
[68] C.E.R. Company, *North Manchuria and the Chinese Eastern Railway* (Harbin, 1924), p. 42.

was formalized in 1906, when its name was changed to the frontier court.

In 1913 Russia completed the legal system in the railway zone by establishing separate civil and criminal district courts, a public prosecutor's office and an appeal court at Harbin, with the final appeal going to the Privy Council in St. Petersburg. In addition, there were altogether eleven courts of the first instance along the Chinese Eastern Railway line and five prisons—at Harbin (capacity: five hundred persons), Manchuli, Hailar, Pok'ot'u, and Huantaohotze. It may also be noted that the circuit system was adopted and that the function of the judicial police was performed by the railway police.[69] The Russian courts thus "perpetually established on the Chinese territory" and "applying Alexander II's codes of law," says Lashevich, "functioned down to their liquidation in 1920."[70]

According to the aforementioned decree of 1901 signed by Nicholas II, the jurisdiction of the Russian courts "includes matters arising on the line of exploitation of the Chinese Eastern Railway between Russian subjects exclusively, and particularly in criminal matters, where the accused and the injured parties are Russians; and in civil matters, where both sides, plaintiff and defendant, are Russian subjects."[71] This provision *per se* was an infringement upon China's sovereign right, because Harbin at that time was not a treaty port. As Miller, the American consul at Newchwang, pointed out in a communication of March 17, 1903, to Minister Conger in Peking, such a court system in the railway zone was without legal justification.[72]

Moreover, the Russian Imperial Decree of 1901 implied the extension of the jurisdiction of the Russian courts "to employees of the Chinese Eastern Railway . . . at a time to be determined by the Ministers of Justice and Finance."[73] By a series of local arrangements of 1899, 1901, and 1902, the extension of Russian judicial authority over Chinese subjects in the railway zone became increasingly facilitated, advancing actually in the form of "mixed attendance."[74]

Thus on May 31/18, 1899, a local arrangement concerning the handling of cases involving Chinese subjects was signed by the

[69] *C.T.S.L.C.P.*, Vol. XVII, chap. vii, p. 142.
[70] Lashevich, *op. cit.*, p. 71.   [71] MacMurray, *op. cit.*, I, 89.
[72] *F.R.U.S.*, *1903*, pp. 50, 51.   [73] MacMurray, *op. cit.*, I, 89-90.
[74] Lashevich, *op. cit.*, p. 71.

Tartar General (Chiang-Chun) of Kirin Province, Yang, and the Engineer-in-Chief of the railway, Yugovich. Under this arrangement, a Principal Department of Foreign and Railway Affairs (Tieh-Lu Chiao-Sheh Tsung-Chu)[75] was to be created as a liaison office between the Chinese provincial government and the Railway Administration. This department and the Russian Engineer-in-Chief were to have joint jurisdiction over all Chinese subjects employed by the railway; and, by implication, also over other Chinese as well in

. . . all cases arising in Kirin Province if these cases directly or indirectly touch the interests of the Chinese Eastern Railway Company, and also directly or indirectly touch the interests of persons working on the Chinese Eastern Railway, and also the interests of contractors of every sort for the supply of labor and work, and of artisans.[76]

This agreement was supplemented by another on July 18/5, 1901, which extended the jurisdiction of the Principal Department to include "other Chinese, temporarily or permanently residing in the leased zone of the railway, even if the nature of their occupation does not have any direct relation to the railway" in all cases "directly or indirectly" affecting the interests of the railway.[77] On January 14/1, 1902, a similar agreement was signed by Sah Pao, acting Chiang-Chun of Heilungkiang, and Yugovich to be applied in that province through the creation of the principal Heilungkiang bureau, also at Harbin.[78] In addition, however, this agreement (Article 2) extended the jurisdiction of the bureau to all cases "directly or indirectly" affecting the interests of the railway outside the railway zone but within the province.

It is to be noted that these local agreements entered into principally during the period of the Boxer uprising and Russian occupation of Manchuria, were not immediately reported to, nor fully approved by, Peking. The Chinese Imperial Court especially objected to the granting of consultation rights to the Russian Engineer-in-Chief in the appointment of members of the Heilungkiang bureau "as an

[75] *C.T.S.L.C.P.*, Vol. XVII, chap. vii, p. 138.

[76] *Ibid.*; English text in MacMurray, *op. cit.*, I, 277-278.

[77] For Chinese text, see *C.T.S.L.C.P.*, Vol. XVII, chap. vii, pp. 139-140; for English text, see MacMurray, *op. cit.*, I, 274-277.

[78] For English text, see MacMurray, *op. cit.*, I, 321-324.

infringement of Chinese sovereignty" and ordered its revision.[79] Moreover, the annual expenses of the Kirin department and of the Heilungkiang bureau were to be met by the railway through the the Russian Engineer-in-Chief. By these arrangements the institutions became convenient tools for the extension of Russian judicial authority.[80]

The examples of Kirin and Heilungkiang were followed by the province of Fengtien (Mukden) when on April 20/7, 1907, it entered into a similar arrangement with Yugovich and established a principal bureau in Liaoyang and a branch bureau in Harbin.[81] This local agreement was again concluded when all of Manchuria was under Russian occupation following the Boxer rebellion in 1900. It may be recalled that the Russo-Chinese Convention regarding the Russian evacuation of Manchuria was not signed until April 8/March 25, 1902, and that the actual partial evacuation did not occur until six months later, creating further complications in the process. Thus, in view of the prevailing circumstances, the validity of these local arrangements per se was questionable.

Even supposing that these local arrangements were concluded in due order, still they could not stand against the basic provisions of the original railway contract signed by the Peking Government. While objecting to the Russian action in establishing municipalities in 1908-9, China also rejected the assumption of jurisdiction by the railway authorities over Chinese subjects involved in civil and criminal cases.[82] Her basis for protest was Article V of the railway contract of 1896, which provided that "criminal cases, lawsuits, etc. upon the territory of the railway, must be settled by the local authorities in accordance with the stipulations of the treaties." It was quite evident that in the absence of specifications, "the local authorities" referred to Chinese local authorities because there were no Russian authorities at the time of the signing of the railway contract in 1896. Likewise, "the stipulation of the treaties" undoubtedly referred alike to all treaties signed between China and Russia prior

[79] *C.T.S.L.C.P.*, Vol. XVII, chap. vii, p. 140.

[80] Provisions in MacMurray, *op. cit.*, I, 276, 323.

[81] *C.T.S.L.C.P.*, Vol. XVII, chap. vii, p. 141. C. Walter Young seemed to be unaware of the Fengtien Agreement of 1902 when he wrote in 1929 before the publication of the preceding series in 1931; cf. Young, *op. cit.*, p. 21. The said agreement does not appear in MacMurray's collection.

[82] Young, *op. cit.*, p. 21.

to the 1896 contract, none of which provided for Russian supervision of the judicial organ.

Russia, however, answered the Chinese protest by citing as the source of the assumption of judicial authority the statutes of the C.E.R. Company, which she promulgated unilaterally on December 4/November 21, 1896, about three months after the signing of the railway contract. Though Section 7 of the Russian-promulgated railway statutes provided that "offences, litigation, etc., on the territory of the Chinese Eastern Railway shall be dealt with by local authorities, Chinese and Russian, on the basis of existing treaties,"[83] it could hardly be considered binding in its effect or of any real value in international law, because it was not of bilateral nature.

As a rule, Russia also claimed that the railway authorities had judicial rights on the basis of the moot phrase in the transformed non-Chinese version of the railway contract relative to "absolute and exclusive right" of administration.[84] As analyzed in the previous section, this Russian justification was merely a resort to contractual confusion. Since Russia was persistent in her attitude, China's protest was naturally of no avail. Thus, the Sino-Russian conflict over judicial authority in the railway zone was not settled until November, 1920, when the Chinese took over the Russian courts there.

RUSSIAN CIVIL ADMINISTRATION IN THE RAILWAY "ZONE"

As Lashevich points out, "in the field of civil administration in the settlements of the railway zone there functioned city self-government in a form reminiscent of that in Russia."[85] As early as 1898, the year of the founding of Harbin,[86] the then Colonel Dmitrii L. Horvath, General Manager of the Chinese Eastern Railway and concurrently Russian consul-general at Harbin, published a series of municipal rules and regulations, probably in rudimentary form, governing Harbin and the lands adjacent to, and appropriated by, the railway. This Russian action was immediately and strongly protested by the Chinese in North Manchuria,[87] and the Imperial Man-

---

[83] Cf. n. 14; MacMurray, *op. cit.*, I, 86.

[84] Cf. pp. 55-56, *supra*.   [85] Lashevich, *op. cit.*, p. 71.

[86] K.V.Zh.D., *Spravochnik po Severnoi Manchzhurii i K.V.Zh.D.* (The C.E.R. Company, *A Reference Book on North Manchuria and the C.E.R.*) (Harbin, 1927), p. 560.

[87] It is apparently due to its Russian authorship and supervision that *North Manchuria and the Chinese Eastern Railway*, published by the C.E.R. Company, states:

chu Court dispatched Governor Hsu Shih-ch'ang, later the President
of the Chinese Republic, to Harbin to organize a "Self-Administra-
tive Government." Thus, the Russo-Chinese disputes over civil
administration along the railway began as early as 1898.[88]

Russia's systematic attempt to exercise political-administrative
power through the C.E.R. Company was shown in her large-scale
endeavor to establish municipalities along the railway line. The
first step was to appropriate lands adjacent to the railway to furnish
the territorial basis on which to organize such units.[89] Russia's
tactics in this maneuver were to resort once again to contractual confusion. Since Article VI of the Railway Contract of 1896 merely
referred to "the lands actually necessary for the construction, operation and protection of the line, as the lands in the vicinity of the line
necessary for procuring sand, stone, lime, etc." without specifying
the exact amount, "the Russian authorities of the C.E.R. Company
used this provision as a pretext for occupying enormous lands along
the line in Kirin and Heilungkiang without limit or account since
August 1897."[90]

In 1902, when Manchuria was still under Russian occupation,
Chou Mien, Director of the newly founded Heilungkiang bureau, was
persuaded by the Russians to sign, without the authorization of the
Tartar General, Chen Te-chuan, an agreement to extend the area of
the land used by the railway company.[91] Though the fulfilment of
this invalid agreement was later frustrated because of the constant
and vigorous protests of China,[92] yet "further encroachment on lands
by the railway company continued unscrupulously."[93] In November,
1904, the C.E.R. Company even established within its system of
administration "land offices, which took control of land taxes, the
issue of title deeds, the transfer of titles, the construction of houses

---

"Historically, from the very beginning of its activity, the C.E.R. Co. was forced
to organize administrative police functions . . . . This phase of administrative activities of the Company, being unavoidable, met during the time of its existence with no
protest either on the part of the population of the railway's territory . . . or on the
part of the Chinese authorities" (p. 42); Tsao Lien-en, *The Chinese Eastern Railway: An Analytical Study* (Shanghai, 1930), p. 32.

    [88] Tsao, *op. cit.*, p. 32.
    [89] *C.T.S.L.C.P.*, Vol. XVII, chap. vii, p. 240.
    [90] *Ibid.*
    [91] Hsu Shih-chang, *op. cit.*, Vol. XI, sh. 13.
    [92] Cf. n. 88.
    [93] *C.T.S.L.C.P.*, Vol. XVII, chap. vii, p. 240.

and public highways and the general disposition of lands of civilians as well as of the railway."[94]

In order to put an end to further Russian encroachment on lands through the pretext of the railway, two similar contracts were authorized and concluded by the Chinese Imperial Foreign Office and the Russian minister at Peking on August 30/17, 1907, one signed by Sung Hsiao-lien and the agent of the General Manager of the C.E.R., Daniel, for Heilungkiang, and the other by Tu Hsueh-yin and Daniel for Kirin.[95] A definite limit upon the lands was set up by Article I of the two contracts, which provided that "the whole quantity of land required for the railway has been included in this agreement" and that "the Chinese Eastern Railway will never make any further expropriations." These contracts greatly reduced the quantity of the lands (about five hundred square miles) as compared with the invalid Chou agreement; but now Russia had obtained official Manchu sanction for lands thus acquired through the C.E.R.

As soon as these land-expropriation contracts were concluded, the Russian authorities of the railway launched a comprehensive program to create municipalities around various population centers and stations of the railway line. Even a year earlier, in 1906, foundations had been carefully laid for a system of municipal self-governing administration for the principal cities along the railway line, to supplement the general administration in the railway zone by the C.E.R. Company.[96] The system was promulgated by the "General Regulations of Civil Administration" (*"Min-Cheng Tsu-chih Ta-kang"*) of the C.E.R. zone, which had been drafted by General Ivanov, Commander-in-Chief of the Far Eastern Army; enacted in October, 1906, after deliberation by the Ministers of Finance, Foreign Affairs, the Army, and the Navy of Russia; and approved and published by the Board of Directors of the C.E.R. Company on December 29/16, 1906.[97]

[94] *Ibid.;* Tsao, *op. cit.,* p. 32.

[95] For Russian texts, see R.S.F.S.R., People's Commissariat for Foreign Affairs, *Soglasheniia Mezhdu Rossiei i Kitaem po Voprosam Zhelezno-dorozhnym, Pochtovo-telegrafnym i Tamozhennym (Agreements between Russia and China in regard to Railways, Posts, and Telegraphs, and Customs,* referred to hereinafter as *Soglasheniia*) (Petrograd, 1918), pp. 33, 38; for Chinese texts, see Hsu Shih-chang, *op. cit.,* Vol. XI, sh. 4-7; for English translations, see MacMurray, *op. cit.,* I, 663-674.

[96] *C.T.S.L.C.P.,* Vol. XVII, chap. vii, pp. 142-143.

[97] For Chinese text of the Regulations, see *ibid.;* Toa-Keizai Chosakyoku (East-Asiatic Investigation Bureau), *The Manchuria Year Book 1931* (Tokyo, 1931), p. 34.

Thus, "from 1906 on," says Gluzdovskii, "in Harbin and in settlements within North Manchuria such as Hailar, Tsitsihar, Pok'ot'u, and Huantaohotze, public administration was introduced and its work was placed under the superintendence of the C.E.R. Company's Department of Civil Administration."[98] In accordance with the above-mentioned "General Regulations of Civil Administration" this department was set up in July, 1907, and was placed "in charge of all municipal administration in the railway zone"; it, in turn, issued "Regulations for the Municipal Council" based on the "General Regulations."[99]

In that same year, 1907, Governor Hsu Shih-ch'ang secured a copy of these regulations, which were being put into effect in Harbin through the creation of a Russian municipal council there, and immediately outlined to the Waiwupu (the Chinese Ministry of Foreign Affairs preceding the Waichiaopu) a strong protest of four counts against such Russian action: (1) The municipal bodies were entirely under the control of the railway company and the presidents of the municipal executive committees (*chang tung*) were required to be Russians (Regulation 43). (2) Under the guise of electing executive officers, the political administrative authority passed entirely to the Russians, as the result of the removal of the existing Chinese officers. (3) Such over-all Russian control would interfere with Chinese administration and political rights and would certainly infringe on Chinese sovereignty and violate the territorial integrity of China. (4) The railway company assumed the authority of issuing regulations and of imposing taxes on all merchants.[100]

On January 27, 1908, the Waiwupu sent its first note of protest to Pokotilov, the Russian minister at Peking, contending that the railway contract of 1896 did not confer on the railway authorities the right of creating municipalities on the land of exploitation; and the Russian minister was asked "to give the necessary instructions that this new order of things must cease and the municipal regulations be canceled."[101] In his reply Pokotilov, in justifying the railway com-

---

[98] Gluzdovskii, *op. cit.*, p. 176.

[99] *C.T.S.L.C.P.*, Vol. XVII, chap. vii, p. 143; for Chinese text of the "Regulations for the Municipal Councils," see *ibid.*, pp. 144-152; its English version may be found in Lawton, *op. cit.*, II, 1302 ff.

[100] Hsu Shih-chang, *op. cit.*, Vol. XI, sh. 13.

[101] The Prince of Ch'ing to Chargé Fletcher (an inclosure), Feb. 25, 1908, in *F.R.U.S., 1910*, p. 203.

pany's action, resorted to the practice of contractual confusion regarding Article VI of the railway contract in the non-Chinese version, saying that the railway company had an absolute and exclusive right of administering its lands.   In her counterreply made in February, 1908, China denied the existence of such phraseology in the Chinese text of the railway contract and emphatically protested: "the action of the railway company in instituting municipal administrations at any of the various places on the line is evidently a usurpation of China's sovereignty," and "it is absolutely impossible for the Board of Foreign Affairs to recognize their rights in so doing."[102]

In spite of these Chinese representations, General Horvath proceeded vigorously with the program of Russian civil administration through the railway.   In March, 1908, the election of municipal councilors was held, and the Harbin municipal council was formed. In the meantime an ordinance was issued imposing fines or imprisonment upon those who should fail to comply with the Russian regulations, particularly those relating to the police, building, sanitary, and trade regulations and all taxes and dues imposed at the will of the administration of the municipalities, notably Harbin, Hailar, etc. Both Chinese and other nationalities, however, refused to pay these taxes imposed upon them "on the ground that any attempt at collection by the Russian authorities was illegal."[103]   As a result, "a large number of Chinese shops at various places along the line were forcibly closed, and for a time the business of the natives was reduced to a state of stagnation."[104]

When China lodged a strong protest with Russia on legal grounds respecting the administration of the railway zone, she was joined by the consuls of Great Britain, Germany, and particularly the United States stationed at Harbin, in protest against the collection of taxes at the discretion of Russia; only the Japanese, who apparently harbored similar designs toward South Manchuria, abstained.[105]

The American opposition to the Russian assumption of civil administration in the railway zone originated in 1907 when her consul, Mr. Fred D. Fisher, challenged the Russian demand that foreign consuls should receive permission from the Russian Government to establish consulates at Harbin. Fisher insisted that "he was accredited

---

[102] *Ibid.;* cf. pp. 55-56, *supra.*
[103] Lawton, *op. cit.,* II, 1305-1306.   [104] *Ibid.,* II, 1306.
[105] Hsi Shih-ch'ang, *op. cit.,* Vol. XI, sh. 13.

solely to the Chinese Government" and that Harbin was Chinese territory under Chinese jurisdiction.[106]   In reply to a Russian memorandum of February 4, 1908, Secretary Elihu Root upheld Consul Fisher and questioned the Russian right of establishing the municipal government at Harbin.   The note reads in part:

> The grant by the instrument of September 8, 1896, to the railroad company of a right of railroad administration over its own lands could not, even if standing alone, be deemed to carry a right of political administration which would amount to a transfer of sovereign rights; but the same instrument, by the French as well as the Chinese text, contains also an express provision reserving the political jurisdiction over these lands to the Government of China.   This view appears to agree entirely with that expressed by the Government of Russia in the declaration of the treaty of Portsmouth—that Russia has no territorial advantages or preferential or exclusive concessions in Manchuria of such a nature as to impair the sovereignty of China or which are incompatible with the principle of equal opportunity.[107]

In conclusion, Secretary Root emphasized that "political authority cannot be derived from the grant to the railroad company."[108]

As the critical situation developed in Harbin and other cities along the railway, China, after further protests, ordered Sao-ke Alfred Sze, chief magistrate of Harbin, accompanied by Horvath, to Peking to make explanations and to see whether a settlement would be possible.[109]   After considerable negotiation, a preliminary agreement was signed by J. Korostovetz, Russian minister in Peking, and D. Horvath for Russia, and Liang Tun-yen, Alfred Sze, and Yu Szu-hsiang for China, on May 10/April 27, 1909.[110]

Although this preliminary agreement was concluded on a so-called compromise basis, it proved, under the prevailing circumstances, to be detrimental to China.   In the first place, in return for the nominal and superfluous recognition of China's sovereignty over the railway zone (Article I), which had never been the legal ques-

---

[106] Lawton, *op. cit.*, II, 1301.

[107] The Secretary of State to the Russian Ambassador, April 9, 1908, File no. 4002, *F.R.U.S.*, *1910*, p. 204.

[108] *Ibid.*, p. 205.

[109] Hsu Shih-ch'ang, *op. cit.*, Vol. XI, sh. 13; for the related notes, see *ibid.*, Vol. XI, sh. 31-39.

[110] For Russian text, see Soglasheniia, p. 13; for Chinese text, see Hsu Shih-ch'ang, *op. cit.*, Vol. XI, sh. 13, and Ho, *op. cit.*, pp. 264-266; for English text, see MacMurray, *op. cit.*, II, 1185-1186.

tion, China consented to the establishment of the new Russian-organized municipal governments.

Secondly, the arrangements for municipal administration provided Russia with a camouflage for actual political control in the railway zone through the C.E.R. Company because "the power of control and personal revision" was reserved to the president of the Chiaoshechu (Bureau of Foreign and Railway Affairs) and the director (i.e., general manager) of the railway, who occupied "a position superior to that of the presidents of the assemblies of delegates and of the committees" (Article XIII).   Moreover, "important questions . . . should be referred to the president of the company conjointly with the principal administration [board of directors]" of the C.E.R. Company.   These provisions seem neither reasonable nor logical since a mere private concessionaire should respect the jurisdiction of the local authorities of a sovereign nation, and not vice versa.   Thirdly, the preliminary agreement left all detailed arrangements to a later conference to be convened within a month (Article XVI).   Since there was no guarantee that the conference would materialize, it enabled Russia not only to keep the existing situation going, but to issue and enforce unilaterally soon afterwards a fifty-five article regulation which brought the municipalities under the strict surveillance of the C.E.R. Company.[111]

The Russo-Chinese Preliminary Agreement of 1909 was not accepted by any of the "Treaty Powers" except Japan.   The position of the United States was particularly noteworthy, as Secretary P. C. Knox pertinently commented:

The preliminary arrangement, while eliminating some of the objectionable features of the former regulations and providing for a share in the supervision of the municipal organization by an official representative of China, still vests in the manager of the Chinese Eastern Railway Co. at Harbin and the board of directors at St. Petersburg virtual control over all important acts of the municipality, and it is further provided that pending the elaboration of a detailed scheme of administration the former intolerable regulations shall remain in force.[112]

Russia's determination to grasp and consolidate civil administra-

[111] C. L. Chu (ed.), *Chin-shih-lien lai chi Chung-O Kuan-hsi* (*Russo-Chinese Relations of the Last Ten Years*) (Harbin, 1926), pp. 150 ff.

[112] The Secretary of State to J. W. Riddle, U. S. ambassador in St. Petersburg, Aug. 6, 1909, *F.R.U.S., 1910*, p. 213.

tion in the railway zone through the C.E.R. Company was shown in her continuous and strenuous efforts at winning the acquiescence of the other Powers. As Russian Assistant Foreign Minister Neratov said, "we are most interested in settling—at least with France— the problem of the rights of the C.E.R. Company regarding its lands in Manchuria."[113] He was gratified not only that "the [French] Republican Government was ready to render Russia support in all matters relating to the safeguard of our political interests in the three Manchurian provinces,"[114] but also that "the views of the Powers on this problem [of Harbin's self-governing administration] begin to approach ours," that "the United States Government has already agreed to permit American nationals in Harbin to pay public levies,"[115] and that the British Government was willing to discuss the matter with Russia.[116]

It was France, Russia's intimate ally since 1894, who first gave her consent to the Russian scheme of civil administration in the railway zone through the C.E.R. Company, thus setting a precedent for the later Anglo-Russian Agreement. On February 11/January 29, 1914 the French Ministry of Foreign Affairs, in an *aide-mémoire*, gave Izvolskii the assurance of Prime Minister Gaston Doumergue that the French Government "fully recognizes" the obligation on the part of French nationals "to observe the Russian municipal regulations and to pay municipal taxes in the towns situated on the territories of the Chinese Eastern Railway."[117]

On December 3/November 20, 1914, the Anglo-Russian Agreement respecting the inclusion of British subjects within the scheme of municipal administration and taxation established in the area of the Chinese Eastern Railway was concluded by the exchange of notes between J. N. Jordan and B. Krupenskii, British and Russian ministers in Peking, to confirm the draft Agreement signed on April 30/ 17, 1914, in Harbin by H. E. Sly, British consul, V. Trautshold,

[113] Neratov to Izvolskii, letter no. 5, Oct. 5/Sept. 22, 1911, Confidential, *M.O. v E.I.*, Ser. II, Vol. XVIII, Part II, doc. no. 533, p. 77.

[114] *Ibid.*

[115] *Ibid.;* on June 1, 1910, Secretary Knox instructed Consul Greene at Harbin to permit American nationals to pay their just portion of municipal taxes "as a matter of equity"; cf. *F.R.U.S., 1910*, pp. 230-231.

[116] Neratov to Izvolskii, letter no. 5, Oct. 5/Sept. 22, 1911, confidential, *M.O. v E.I.*, Ser. II, Vol. XVIII, Part II, doc. no. 533, p. 77.

[117] *Izvestiia Ministerstva Inostrannykh Del* (*Bulletin of the Ministry of Foreign Affairs*) (Petrograd, 1914), II, 39.

Russian consul general, and E. Daniel, delegate of the C.E.R. Administration.[118]

By this agreement the British Government conceded that British subjects residing in Harbin and other settlements in the area of the C.E.R. should pay "the same dues and taxes paid by Russian subjects," and observe from January 1, 1915, "the local Regulations and By-laws." On the other hand, Russia assured the British that "all taxes and dues collected in the railway settlement at Harbin and in other settlements situated in the area of the Chinese Eastern Railway shall be devoted to municipal and public purposes," that a representative of the non-Russian community be admitted to the Harbin city council, and that the same right and privileges, particularly in matters of trade, industry, and leases of land, enjoyed by Russian subjects be granted to British subjects in the railway zone.

Subsequently, during a period of years, the Anglo-Russian Agreement of 1914 concerning the status of British subjects in the area of the C.E.R. was adhered to by other Powers: The Netherlands, on September 25/12, 1915; Belgium, on November 19/6, 1915; Spain, on December 2/November 19, 1915; France, on December 23/10, 1915; Denmark, on March 20/7, 1916; Italy, on May 23/10, 1916; and Japan, on March 10/February 25, 1917.[119] The United States was a notable exception to these adherences, though Krupenskii once hopefully reported to Sazonov that a similar arrangement might be made.[120]

As a result of these developments, the anomalous Russian civil administration in the railway zone based on the instrumentality of the C.E.R. Company persisted until 1920, when China recovered her administrative rights in that area. During the period under review, in spite of the fact that no formal agreement other than the preliminary arrangement of 1909 was signed between Russia and China, "Russia actually adopted the municipal system according to her own free will."[121]

[118] For Russian and English texts, see *Izvestiia Ministerstva Inostrannykh Del* (*Bulletin of the Ministry of Foreign Affairs*) (Petrograd, 1915), II, 1-10; the English text also appears in MacMurray, *op. cit.*, II, 1181-1184; for Chinese translation, see *C.T.S.L.C.P.*, Vol. XVII, chap. vii, pp. 152-154.

[119] *M.O. v E.I.*, Ser. III, Vol. VIII, Part I, p. 228 n.; cf. MacMurray, *op. cit.*, II, 1184-1185.

[120] Krupenskii to Sazonov, tel. no. 632, Dec. 3/Nov. 20, 1914, *M.O. v E.I.*, Ser. III, Vol. VI, Part II, doc. no. 597, p. 163.

[121] *The Manchuria Year Book 1931*, p. 34.

RUSSIAN INTERVENTION IN HULUNBUIR (BARGA)

Hulunbuir, also known by the popular local name, Barga, originating from the old tribal name, Bargo,[122] "comprises practically all of Heilungkiang Province to the west of the Manchurian Hinghan range."[123] It is flanked by Russian Siberia to the north and Outer Mongolia to the west. In area Hulunbuir is approximately 76,000 square miles[124] or 155,600 square kilometers,[125] about one quarter of Heilungkiang or "one third larger than the State of Illinois of the American Union."[126] In addition to vast virgin forests, fertile agricultural and grazing lands, and fisheries, Hulunbuir is rich in gold mines, which "may rival the Klondike in treasure,"[127] and in coal, iron ore, lead-silver ore, and rock-crystal.[128] The Chinese Eastern Railway intersects the territory of Hulunbuir from east to west, having 372 kilometers of its 944-kilometer-long western section within the region from Station Hingan to Station Manchuli.[129] Among five other stations in the area, there are Chalainor and Hailar, one kilometer from the political center of Hulunbuir.[130]

Hulunbuir was under the jurisdiction of the Liaotung *Chun* (prefecture) during the Han dynasty (206 B.C.-A.D. 280), of the Heishui *Tu-T'u-Fu* (prefecture) in the Tang dynasty (618-907), of the Holin *Lu* (prefecture) in the Yuan dynasty (1280-1368), and of the Hulunbuir *Fu-Tu-Tung* (lieutenant governor) in the Ch'ing dynasty (1644-1911).[131] Hulunbuir became known to Russia in the

---

[122] Owen Lattimore, *The Mongols of Manchuria* (New York, 1934), p. 156. For tribes of Hulunbuir, see also E. J. Lindgren, "North-Western Manchuria and the Reindeer-Tungus," *Geographical Journal* (London), LXXV (May, 1930), 518-519; Chang Chia-fan, *Hu-Lun-Pei-Erh Chih-lieh* (*Annals of Hulumbuir*) (Shanghai, 1923); Tsou Shan-yu & Chu Cheng-hsin, *Hu-Lun-Pei-Erh Kai-yao* (*An Outline of Hulumbuir*), 1939.

[123] "The Soviet Attempt to Steal 76,000 Square Miles of Chinese Territory," *China Weekly Review* (Shanghai), LI (Dec. 28, 1929), 129. Maps in *B.S.E.* (1st ed.) (1934), Vol. LX, col. 298 (2nd ed.) (1950), IV, 236; Chang Chia-fan, *op. cit.*; Tsou & Chu, *op. cit.*

[124] *China Weekly Review*, LI (Dec. 28, 1929), 129; Tsou & Chu, *op. cit.*, p. 5; Lattimore gives the figure as 75,000 sq. mi. (*op. cit.*, p. 156).

[125] *B.S.E.* (2nd ed.), IV, 236.

[126] *China Weekly Review*, LI (Dec. 28, 1929), 129.

[127] *Ibid.*

[128] *B.S.E.* (2nd ed.), IV, 237.

[129] *B.S.E.* (1st ed.), Vol. LX, col. 298.

[130] Hsieh Shou-chang and others (eds.), *Chung-Kuo Ku-ching Ti-ming Ta-tz'u-tien* (*A Comprehensive Chinese Gazetteer*), p. 435; Liu Chun-jen, *Chung-Kuo Ti-ming Ta-tsu-tien* (*Chinese Gazetteer*) (Peiping, 1933), p. 150.

[131] Liu Chun-jen, *op. cit.*, p. 150; Tsou & Chu, *op. cit.*, pp. 47-52.

seventeenth century, when (in 1675), according to a Russian source, "Prince Gantimur of Barga was unwilling to be under Manchu rule and adopted Russian citizenship. [Thus,] Barga entered into the Russian domain."[132]

In sharp contrast, Chinese sources assert that Russian Cossacks invaded Hulunbuir at this time and that they had, in fact, been disturbing the area for some forty years. China and Russia fought there twice, in 1685 and 1686, and finally concluded the Treaty of Nerchinsk in 1689,[133] which definitely excluded Russia from Hulunbuir, and fixed the boundary line at the Argun River. Yet in slightly over two hundred years, due to the presence of the Chinese Eastern Railway, Hulunbuir had attracted large numbers of Russian immigrants, including railway workers, guards, and troops, so that the Russians were outnumbered only by the Mongols there.[134] This was the situation in Hulunbuir on the eve of the Chinese Revolution of 1911.

According to an authoritative Soviet interpretation, the Barguts revolted after the Chinese Revolution and "joined forces with Outer Mongolia, which had declared its independence with the assistance of Russian imperialism."[135] The important part played by Russia in the secession of Hulunbuir from China has already been disclosed by a well-informed neutral source, *The China Year Book*, edited by H. G. W. Woodhead.[136] Chinese sources give many detailed accounts of the way Russia stirred the Barguts into rebellion and lent them assistance in their "independence" activities, thus hampering the Chinese in their necessary handling of the Hulunbuir disturbances. These accounts are worth noting.

On November 27, 1911, the Civil Governor of Heilungkiang reported that the Barguts had declared independence in accordance

---

[132] *B.S.E.* (2nd ed.), IV, 157.

[133] Tsou & Chu, *op. cit.*, p. 52; Chang Chia-fan, *op. cit.*, p. 79.

[134] Chang Chia-fan, *op. cit.*, pp. 22–24; in the absence of earlier census, the total population of Hulunbuir in 1927 numbered 72,022, including 22,658 Russians and 17,177 Chinese; the population in the railway zone was estimated at 40,000, of which 54 per cent were Russians, 45 per cent were Chinese, with the Mongols comprising 1 per cent. *B.S.E.* estimates the population of Hulunbuir in 1930 at 70,000, of which Mongols comprised 45 per cent, Chinese 25 per cent, Soviet citizens 20 per cent, and White Russians 10 per cent; see *B.S.E.* (1st ed.), Vol. LX, col. 278.

[135] *M.S.E.* (2nd ed.), Vol. I (Moscow, 1937), col. 715.

[136] *The China Year Book* (referred to hereinafter as *C.Y.B.*) *1914* (London & New York), p. 622.

with instructions from Urga, the capital of Outer Mongolia. He was immediately ordered by the Manchu Government, still functioning in Peking, to send troops for its suppression and dissolution. On November 29 the military governor of Manchuria telegraphed the report that Hulunbuir had received arms and ammunition from Russia for its fight for independence. Meanwhile, the governor of Heilungkiang reported a note from the Russian consul stating that according to the instruction of his Government, Russia would remain neutral in the event of Chinese-Bargut warfare. No conflicts between the Chinese and the Bargut forces should be permitted in the railway zone, and no Chinese troops should be transported by the Chinese Eastern Railway. But shortly thereafter on December 6 the governor of Heilungkiang again reported the Russians had openly intervened in favor of the Barguts, and that while the Barguts were besieging Manchuli, the railway authorities refused to transport Chinese troops. On December 28 he further telegraphed that the Russian troops of the 15th Column of the Siberian Frontier Army in disguised uniforms had helped the Bargut forces in a joint attack on Manchuli. On February 24, 1912, both governors jointly reported that there were definite evidences of the assistance rendered the Bargut forces by the Russians in the attack on Manchuli, and that the foreign residents of that city had given signed testimony as documentary proof. On March 7 scores of Russian military maps used in the campaign were transferred to Peking by the Heilungkiang governor. On March 14 both governors again reported that in addition to their exploitation of fisheries, gold mines, and coal fields through secret contracts with the Barguts in Hulunbuir, the Russians had undertaken the training of the Bargut forces.[137] In short, with strong Russian assistance, the Barguts seized Hailar on January 2, 1912, occupied Manchuli on February 22, and during the course of the following month seceded completely from China.[138]

It was not until after the Sino-Russian Declaration in regard to Outer Mongolian autonomy under Chinese suzerainty on November 5/October 23, 1913, that Sazonov made a parallel move to settle the status of Hulunbuir on terms favorable to Russian interests, by

---

[137] The account related in the foregoing paragraph is from Hsü Hsi, *Tung-San-Sheng Chi-lüeh* (*The Annals of the Three Eastern Provinces*), pp. 205-206 and Tsou & Chu, *op. cit.*, pp. 58-59.
[138] Tsou & Chu, *op. cit.*, pp. 57-58.

initiating Russian "mediation" between China and Hulunbuir.[139]   His motives for this effort may have been threefold: First, from a telegraphic report from S. V. Afanasev, Russian consul at Tsitsihar, he knew that there were Chinese military preparations in that area apparently directed against Hulunbuir.[140]   Second, delay in the negotiations with China on Hulunbuir might involve the danger of "the Chinese coming to an understanding with the Barguts without us [Russians]," as Krupenskii had suggested.[141]   Third, since Hulunbuir's two major cities, Manchuli and Hailar, were treaty ports, their inclusion in autonomous Outer Mongolia would have led to unnecessary friction with other Powers.[142]   Consequently, Sazonov set Russian policy regarding Hulunbuir in the following words:

We did not include Barga in Autonomous Mongolia, and in principle we agree with the restoration of sovereignty of China in this province.   But this must be done through peace negotiations in which we might take upon ourselves the role of intermediaries.   However, submission of Barga to China by armed force would affect Russian interests so much that we cannot regard it with indifference.[143]

This step of Russian policy was interpreted by Pi Kwei-fang, then Governor of Heilungkiang, as meaning the restoration of Hulunbuir nominally to China in exchange for maintaining *de facto* Russian advantages in that region.[144]

In order to secure the role of "arbiter," Sazonov further agreed with Finance Minister Kokovtsov, (who was soon to become Prime Minister), that "the instructions given to the General Manager of the Chinese Eastern Railway and the Commander of the Trans-Amur District of the Frontier Guards concerning the necessity of prevention of the Chinese forces going into Hailar [Hulunbuir] should remain in force."[145]   This, however, proved to be unnecessary.   When

---

[139] For an account of similar Russian "mediation" between China and Outer Mongolia, cf. chap. x, *infra*.

[140] Sazonov to Krupenskii, secret tel. no. 3143, Nov. 18/5, 1913, *K.A.*, XXXVII (1929), 23.

[141] Krupenskii to Sazonov, tel. no. 32, Feb. 6/Jan. 24, 1914, *M.O. v E.I.*, Ser. III, Vol. I, doc. no. 191, p. 233.

[142] *Die Internationalen Beziehungen im Zeitalter des Imperialismus*, referred to hereinafter as *D.I.B.Z.D.I.*), I, 7, note of the German editor, p. 459.

[143] Sazonov to Krupenskii, cf. n. 140.

[144] Pi Kwei-fang, *Hu-Lun Pei-Erh Wen-t'i* (*The Problem of Hulunbuir*) (Peking, 1914), sh. 2.

[145] Sazonov to Kokovtsov, letter no. 91, Feb. 10/Jan. 28, 1914, confidential, *M.O. v E.I.*, Ser. III, Vol. I, doc. no. 216, pp. 267-268.

Krupenskii was charged with declaring to the Waichiaopu that "Russia would not tolerate any decision on the destiny of Barga without her collaboration and would not recognize an agreement made directly between the Chinese Government and the Barga authorities,"[146] China "was compelled to accept Russian mediation."[147]

The reasons for Chinese consent were given by Governor Pi as follows: "The Republic [of China] was recently recognized by the Powers and did not intend to employ force in Hulunbuir. And the use of force there must depend on the Chinese Eastern Railway, which was within the Russian sphere of influence."[148]

At this point Sazonov's four "conditions for the re-establishment of China's sovereignty in Hulunbuir" were formally proposed to the Waichiaopu by Krupenskii on February 23, 1914.[149] They might be enumerated as follows: (1) The Barga tribes should be permitted to keep their local authorities. (2) "The Peking Government must confirm those contracts made by the Russian subjects with the Bargut authorities in the time of their *de facto* independence." (3) Russian subjects must have preferential rights to build such roads of approach to the Chinese Eastern Railway as should prove necessary. (4) Russian gold mine proprietors who had lost their concessions obtained before the Russo-Japanese War must be recompensed by the Chinese Government.[150]

In the meantime, Krupenskii replied to Sazonov's instruction by suggesting the advisability of making inquiries of the Barga authorities themselves as to the form of administration they desired.[151] Sazonov adopted this proposal; and the Russian vice consul at Hailar, Usatyi, telegraphed back the answer of the Barga authorities. They would prefer to remain under the power of the Mongolian Bogdo Khan (Living Buddha in Urga); but if this were not possible they would remain subordinate to China under eight conditions, including granting of the same autonomous status enjoyed by Outer Mon-

---

[146] Pi, *op. cit.*, sh. 1.

[147] *Ibid.*

[148] *Ibid.*

[149] *Ibid.*; Krupenskii to Sazonov, tel. no. 65, Feb. 23/10, 1914, *M.O. v E.I.*, Ser. III, Vol. I, doc. no. 307, p. 402.

[150] Sazonov to Krupenskii, tel. no. 290, Feb. 19/6, 1914, *M.O. v E.I.*, Ser. III, Vol. I, doc. no. 280, pp. 351-352; for Chinese text of the Russian conditions, see Pi, *op. cit.*, Appendix 1.

[151] Krupenskii to Sazonov, tel. no. 79, Feb. 28/15, 1914, *M.O. v E.I.*, Ser. III, Vol. I, p. 403 n. 1.

golia and a Russian guarantee of no Chinese interference with it.[152] Krupenskii thought that these conditions were "in the main unrealizable, as they would place Barga in the same position is Khalka [Outer Mongolia],"[153] and that direct subordination of Barga to the Chinese central government would make Russian "intervention" there "more inconvenient than supervision by Tsitsihar authorities."[154] Yet Sazonov indicated approval of the proposals of Barga:

The transformation of Barga into an autonomous country on the conditions proposed by the Barguts would correspond with our interests. On the other hand, we should not like to take it upon ourselves to refuse the Barguts support of their demands before the Chinese Government. If these demands appear unacceptable to the Chinese, then on the basis of their counterproposals we can play the role of *mediator* between the opposing camps of the Chinese and the Barguts.[155]

On March 17, 1914, all the Bargut conditions except the last one regarding Russia's guarantee were officially transmitted by Krupenskii to the Waichiaopu.[156] Any specific mention of Russian guarantee for the inviolability of Hulunbuir's autonomy was decided by Sazonov to be unnecessary, since this guarantee would "follow from the fact of our [Russian] participation in its formation."[157]

Of these four Russian and seven Bargut conditions, the initial reply of the Chinese Government, according to Krupenskii, dealt only with the original four and was "completely silent on our [Russian] demands" regarding prohibition of colonization by the Chinese and of stationing of Chinese troops and officials in Barga.[158]

At the very outset, Sazonov saw no object in hurrying the negotiations on this question. He did not want to complicate the important talks then going on about Outer Mongolia and railway construction in North Manchuria. Moreover, he considered that "the mainte-

[152] Sazonov to Krupenskii, tel. no. 372, March 2/Feb. 17, 1914, *M.O. v E.I.*, Ser. III, Vol. I, doc. no. 357, pp. 471-472; tel. of consul at Hailar, March 7/Feb. 22, 1914, *M.O. v E.I.*, Ser. III, Vol. II, p. 13 n. 2. Chinese text of the first 7 conditions in Pi, *op. cit.*, Appendix 1.

[153] Krupenskii to Sazonov, tel. no. 115, March 14/1, 1914, *M.O. v E.I.*, Ser. III, Vol. II, doc. no. 10, p. 13.

[154] *Ibid.* Tsitsihar was the capitol of Heilungkiang Province.

[155] Sazonov to Krupenskii, tel. no. 493, March 16/3, 1914, *M.O. v E.I.*, Ser. III, Vol. II, doc. no. 16, p. 18.

[156] Pi, *op. cit.*, sh. 1; Krupenskii to Sazonov, dispatch no. 29, April 3/March 21, 1914, *M.O. v E.I.*, Ser. III, Vol. II, doc. no. 147, p. 193.

[157] Cf. n. 155.

[158] Krupenskii to Sazonov, dispatch no. 29, April 3/March 21, 1914, *M.O. v E.I.*, Ser. III, Vol. II, doc. no. 147, p. 194.

nance of *status quo* there [in Barga] for the time being by no means contradicts our [Russian] interests."[159] Chinese attempts to speed up the negotiations were rebuffed on the ground that the Barga problem would necessitate lengthy discussion.[160] As a result, the scores of conferences on Hulunbuir held over a period of one year between the Waichiaopu and the Russian minister bore no fruit.[161]

This Russian attitude of keeping the Hulunbuir question on ice persisted not only until after the Tripartite Agreement regarding Outer Mongolia was signed on June 7/May 25, 1915, but even up to the time of Krupenskii's report on the so-called "intrigue" of Prince Wuteh (Udai).[162]

On October 25/12, 1915, the Russian minister informed Sazonov that "Mongolian Prince Wuteh proposed to Shen Fu, the ruler of Hulunbuir, on behalf of the Heilungkiang governor, an agreement with the Chinese Government without Russian knowledge."[163] Thereupon Krupenskii requested Sazonov "to appoint a definite date to the [Chinese] Foreign Minister for the signing of the agreement on Barga."[164] He further mentioned that he had approached the Chinese President "through a trusted person with a solicitation that he order Lou Tseng-tsiang [the Chinese Foreign Minister] to conclude the agreement . . . without delay."[165] Then, with the permission of Sazonov, Krupenskii positively declared to Lou Tseng-tsiang that "the text of the agreement and the notes is already finally determined," and that he could "not support any change whatsoever."[166]

Finally, the Russo-Chinese Agreement on Hulunbuir was reported to have been concluded on November 6/October 24, 1915, "without any further difficulties."[167] China's complete submission to Russia's will in regard to Hulunbuir was explained as due to her "fear of diplomatic isolation following the conclusion of the Sino-

---

[159] Sazonov to Russian chargé d'affaires in Peking, Grave, tel. no. 1336, July 6/June 23, 1914, *M.O. v E.I.*, Ser. III, Vol. IV, doc. no. 96, p. 136.

[160] The Provisional Director of the 4th Political Division of the Russian Ministry of Foreign Affairs, Abrikosov, to Grave, tel. no. 1447, July 19/6, 1914, *M.O. v E.I.*, Ser. III, Vol. IV, doc. no. 281, p. 336.

[161] Pi, *op. cit.*, sh. 2.

[162] Krupenskii to Sazonov, dispatch, Nov. 10/Oct. 28, 1915, *M.O. v E.I.*, Ser. III, Vol. IX, doc. no. 210, pp. 210-213.

[163] *Ibid.*, p. 211 n. 1.   [164] *Ibid.*, p. 210.

[165] *Ibid.*   [166] *Ibid.*, pp. 210-211.

[167] *Ibid.*, p. 212.

Japanese Agreements of May 25, 1915, concerning the Twenty-one Demands."[168]

The terms of the Russo-Chinese Agreement concerning the situation of Hulunbuir reveal that nearly all of Russia's original proposals, which Sazonov and Krupenskii initially doubted the Chinese would accept,[169] were in fact adopted: Hulunbuir was to form a special district directly subject to the Chinese Central Government (Article I). In normal times only a local militia was to be maintained. In case the local authorities should be unable to keep order, troops of the Chinese Central Government might be sent, but only "after having given notice to the Russian Government; after the restoration of order, these detachments were to be withdrawn" (Article IV). Should a railway be constructed in Hulunbuir and foreign capital be required, the Chinese Government would in the first instance look to Russia to find such capital (Article VII). The contracts made between Russian contractors and the Hulunbuir authorities were to be confirmed by the Government of the Chinese Republic after examination by a Sino-Russian mixed commission (Article VIII).[170] In view of these provisions, Governor Pi had reason to criticize this Agreement as a grave diplomatic defeat for China.[171]

Soon after its conclusion, the agreement was used by Russia as the basis for a diplomatic intervention in Hulunbuir, occasioned by the incursion of a small detachment of Chinese troops into the region. The Chinese were concerned at this time over the military activities of one Babojab, an Inner Mongolian prince who, with the support of Outer Mongolia, had assembled a sizable force and was seeking the independence of Barga.[172] As early as November, 1915, the Chinese Government, through the regular diplomatic channels, had sought the opinion of the Russian Government as to what steps should be taken "to stop Babojab's further activities."[173]

[168] Pi, *op. cit.*, sh. 2.   [169] Cf. pp. 84-86, *supra*.

[170] For Russian text of the agreement and the notes exchanged, see Russia, *Sobranie Uzakonenii i Rasporiashenii Pravitelstva* (*Bulletin of Laws and Ordinances of the Government*), no. 42, sec. I, Feb. 26/13, 1917; for Chinese text, see Tsou & Chu, *op. cit.*, 59-62 and Pi, *op. cit.*, Appendix II; for English text, see MacMurray, *op. cit.*, II, 1247-1249 and *C.Y.B.*, *1921-22* (Peking & Tientsin), pp. 600-602.

[171] Pi, *op. cit.*, sh. 2.

[172] Sazonov to Krupenskii, tel. no. 6295, Dec. 20/7, 1915, *M.O. v E.I.*, Ser. III, Vol. IX, doc. no. 586, p. 611.

[173] Krupenskii to Sazonov, tel. no. 667, Nov. 15/2, 1915, *M.O. v E.I.*, Ser. III, Vol. IX, doc. no. 260, p. 267.

As it happened, however, Babojab was in confidential and "official" communication with the Russian vice-consul at Hailar.[174] With Russian knowledge and assistance, he received continuous subsidies from Outer Mongolia with which to procure Japanese arms for his "considerable force."[175] Babojab was known to Sazonov not only as "one of the Mongolian princes declaring their defection from China and recognizing the authority of the Urga Hutukhtu [of Outer Mongolia]," but also as the head of "those forces sent by the [Outer] Mongolian Government into Inner Mongolia."[176] When Tsar Nicholas II read about Babojab from a Hailar report, he marked "Bravo" on the margin.[177]

Under these circumstances, Russia did not hesitate to intervene when, in December, 1915, the Russian vice-consul at Hailar, Usatyi, reported the appearance in Hulunbuir of a Chinese detachment of 150 men engaged in battle with the 7,000-man army of Babojab. Sazonov instructed Krupenskii forthwith "to call the serious attention of the Chinese Government [to] its consistent violation of the agreements on Mongolia and Barga."[178] When Krupenskii conveyed this warning to the Chinese Foreign Minister,[179] the Chinese had no recourse but to give assurances that the "information about the withdrawal of the Chinese troops which had occupied the monastery of Iugutszur Hutukhtu was correct," and to explain that "the Chinese forces penetrated into Barga through a misunderstanding."[180]

Russian intervention made itself felt, too, in cases which should have concerned directly only the Hulunbuir region and the province of Heilungkiang, and indirectly China as the sovereign power in the territory. Thus on July 6/June 23, 1916, the Russian minister in Peking again lodged a strong protest, based on a report from the Russian vice-consul at Hailar, against both the Chinese border guards

---

[174] Russian vice-consul at Hailar, Usatyi, to Sazonov, tel. no. 60, April 13/March 31, 1915, *M.O. v E.I.*, Ser. III, Vol. VII, Part II, doc. no. 525, p. 134.

[175] Russian vice-consul in Hailar to Krupenskii, report no. 159, Sept. 18/5, 1915, *M.O. v E.I.*, Ser. III, Vol. VIII, Part II, doc. no. 729, p. 321.

[176] Sazonov to Nicholas II, report, April 16/3, 1915, *M.O. v E.I.*, Ser. III, Vol. VII, Part II, p. 134 n. 1.

[177] *Ibid.*

[178] Sazonov to Krupenskii, tel. no. 6295, Dec. 20/7, 1915, *M.O. v E.I.*, Ser. III, Vol. IX, doc. no. 586, p. 611.

[179] Krupenskii to Sazonov, tel. no. 782, Dec. 22/9, 1915, *M.O. v E.I.*, Ser. III, Vol. IX, p. 611 n. 4.

[180] *Ibid.*

on the watchtowers and the Chinese gold-mining industry in the disputed border land between Hulunbuir and the rest of Heilungkiang.[181] This land had not been considered a part of Hulunbuir at the time when that region had declared its independence and sought to join Outer Mongolia. Furthermore, the Chinese gold mines were said to have been in operation there for years.[182] The Waichiaopu accordingly replied to Krupenskii that since the provincial boundary line was a matter of domestic concern, it had already referred the matter to the Governor of Heilungkiang, who was to seek a settlement with the Fu-T'u-Tung of Hulunbuir.[183] Krupenskii, in turn, denied that the matter was a domestic affair and cited Articles IV and VI for support and insisted on the withdrawal of the Chinese guards and the closing of the Chinese gold mines in the area.[184]

In the mean time, the delegates of Hulunbuir arrived in Tsitsihar, capital of Heilungkiang, to negotiate a settlement. Though both sides were "full of cordial feelings," the delegates from Barga were hesitant "for fear of foreigners."[185] After their return from Hailar with fresh instructions, both sides could feel the increased pressure of intervention in Hulunbuir on the part of Russian Vice-Consul Usatyi.[186]

These misgivings over Russian intervention in Hulunbuir continued well beyond the Russian Revolution of 1917, until the cancellation of Hulunbuir autonomy by Chinese presidential mandate on June 28, 1920.[187] During the period under review, the persistence of Russian intervention and the political advantages gained through both the Chinese Eastern Railway and the Agreement of 1915 had made Hulunbuir in fact, as a Soviet source suggests a condominium "under the [joint] control of China and Russia."[188]

[181] Note of Krupenskii to the Waichiaopu, July 6/June 23, 1916 (in Chinese), Pi, *op. cit.*, Appendix III.
[182] Governor of Heilungkiang to the Waichiaopu, tel., July 14, 1916, Pi, *op. cit.*, Appendix III.
[183] Note of the Waichiaopu to Krupenskii, Sept. 8, 1916, *ibid.*
[184] Note of Krupenskii to the Waichiaopu, Sept. 13, 1916, *ibid.*
[185] Governor Pi Kwei-fang of Heilungkiang to the Waichiaopu, tel., Dec. 12, 1916, *ibid.*
[186] Governor Pi Kwei-fang of Heilungkiang to the Waichiaopu, dispatch, Jan. 11, 1917, *ibid.*
[187] The Waichiaopu to Governor of Heilungkiang, dispatch, Jan. 16, 1919, *ibid.*
[188] *M.S.E.* (2nd ed.), Vol. I, col. 715.

RUSSIAN MILITARY ADVANTAGES THROUGH THE RAILWAY

Skalov points out that "the railway zone maintained the Tsarist army and even the Tsarist police."[189]   Lieutenant General E. I. Martynov, Commander of the Trans-Amur District of the Frontier Guards, 1911-13, emphatically states: "Manchuria has still greater significance in its military respect . . . . North Manchuria is the strategic key for the whole of our [Russian] Far East."[190]   He further advocates that "the interests of the Russian state demand the annexation of Manchuria as soon as possible."[191]

China, however, has never given to Russia, by any "single provision" of any relevant agreement, authority to maintain military forces or guards along the Chinese Eastern Railway in Manchuria.[192] Russian sources to be cited in this section reveal that the Tsarist Government, through the C.E.R., had not only used the illegally installed railway police and the Trans-Amur army as the "vanguards" and "tentacles"[193] of its far-flung empire, but was actually engaged in strategic maneuver, military fortification, and the projection of territorial acquisition.

"RAILWAY GUARDS" AND THE TRANS-AMUR ARMY

The term "railway guards" or "railway police," like "railway zone," is without legal foundation.   It is not used in the Treaty of Alliance, nor in the railway contract of 1896, nor in the 1898 Agreement concerning the southern branch of the C.E.R.   The army of the Trans-Amur District of the Frontier Guards of Russia had its origin in those regular Russian armed forces that poured into Manchuria following the Boxer uprising in 1900 and subsequently remained and regrouped after the 1902 Convention for the withdrawal of Russian forces from Manchuria.   In January, 1901, the Russian railway guards, brought to Manchuria in 1897 by General A.A. Gerngross and at least five thousand strong since 1899,[194] were in-

[189] Skalov, *op. cit.*, p. 23.   [190] Martynov, *op. cit.*, pp. 6-7.
[191] *Ibid.*, p. 12.
[192] Willoughby, *op. cit.*, I, 297; Young, *op. cit.*, p. 22.
[193] Martynov, *op. cit.*, p. 94.
[194] The Board of Directors of the C.E.R., *Kitaiskaia Vostochnaia Zheleznaia Doroga: Istoricheskii Ocherk* (*The Chinese Eastern Railway: A Historical Sketch*, referred to hereinafter as *K.V.Zh.D.: I.O.*) (1896-1905) (St. Petersburg, 1914), I, 26-27.

corporated into the forces of the Trans-Amur District, already seventy thousand strong, under the command of General Gidilikhs.[195] The establishment of both the railway guards and the army of the Trans-Amur District as a whole was the product of a series of flagrant violations by Russia of her treaty and contractual obligations to China under Articles IV and V of the Treaty of Alliance, Articles V and VIII of the railway contract, and Article II of the 1902 Convention.

In regard to the policing of the railway, Article V of the railway contract explicitly entrusted the task to China. It stipulated: "The Chinese Government will take measures to assure the safety of the railway and of persons in its service against any attack."

With regard to armed forces, Article V of the 1896 Treaty of Alliance emphatically provided: "In time of peace, Russia shall have the same right for the transit of her troops and stores, with stoppages, which shall not be justified by any other motive than the needs of the transport service." Similarly, Article VIII of the railway contract did not permit Russian uniformed men to land and be stationed in Chinese territory. It reads as follows:

The [C.E.R.] Company is responsible [for seeing] that the Russian troops and war material, despatched in transit over the line, will be carried through directly from one Russian station to another, without for any pretext stopping on the way longer than is strictly necessary.

For the general safeguarding of property and lives, the 1902 Pact empowered and obligated China "to protect the railway and all Russian subjects and their undertakings."

As to the over-all problem of the respect for Chinese sovereignty and territorial integrity, Article IV of the Treaty of Alliance solemnly declared: "The junction of this [Chinese Eastern] railway with the Russian railway shall not serve as a pretext for any encroachment on Chinese territory nor for any infringement of the rights of sovereignty of His Majesty the Emperor of China."

Russia, however, tried to justify her action of instituting "railway guards" by relying solely upon section eight of the so-called railway statute[196] which she issued unilaterally on December 4, 1896, without Chinese consent. This section, which sharply contradicts Article V of the railway contract, reads:

[195] *C.T.S.L.C.P.*, Vol. XVII, chap. vii, p. 141.
[196] *K.V.Zh.D.: I.O.*, I, 25.

The Chinese Government has undertaken to adopt measures for securing the safety of the railway and of all employed on it against any *extraneous attacks*.

The preservation of law and order on the lands assigned to the railway and its appurtenances shall be confided to police agents appointed by the Company.

The Company shall draw up and establish police regulations for this purpose.

Basing their action on this unilaterally issued document, the Russians were able to assert their responsibility for safety measures *within* the "lands assigned to the railway," leaving to the Chinese the task of providing safety against "extraneous attacks" coming from *outside* railway property. This awkward division, into internal and external aspects, of the safety measures called for in Article V of the railway contract remained, however, without legal foundation, since no unilateral action can nullify bilateral treaty or contractual obligations.

To defend her actions in using the railway to reap her military advantage, Russia also frequently used the moot phrase "absolute and exclusive right of administration of its [the railway's] lands,"[197] transformed by Russia from the Chinese wording in Article VI of the railway contract.[198] Even supposing that this phrase were valid, the railway company would still have no right to institute "railway guards," for Article V had definitely granted to the Chinese Government the power of policing the railway and maintaining law and order in the railway zone. It was a power "which would naturally have appertained to the Chinese Government unless there were a specific waiver of specific sovereign rights in the railway area in favor of the Railway Company."[199]

In order to offer an excuse for stationing the Trans-Amur army in the railway zone, Russia tried to blame the Chinese Government for the alleged "inability to fulfil its obligation, under the railway contract of 1896, to protect the railway and its employees."[200] Since there had never been an official Russian protest against any lack of protection provided by the Chinese Government, this unfounded allegation could not give Russia grounds for violating her treaty

[197] Cf. pp. 55-56, *supra*.
[198] Lashevich, *op. cit.*, p. 72.
[199] Young, *op. cit.*, p. 23.
[200] *K.V.Zh.D.: I.O.*, I, 25.

obligations, or for assuming on her own the task of correcting the negligence charged to the Chinese.

In addition, Russian sources contain some dramatic, but fictionalized, descriptions of the *Hunhutze* (bandits) in Manchuria and their occasional encounters with the Russian armed units.[201] Chinese sources, on the other hand, charged that the *Hunhutze* frequently had illicit connections with the Russian guards and soldiery and made the railway zone their refuge, and that in so doing, they menaced the security of the area.[202]

Against these flagrant Russian violations of treaty obligations, through introducing "railway guards" and stationing the Trans-Amur army in the railway zone, China had constantly raised strong protests. As early as 1901-2, Prince Chun had repeatedly lodged protests and refused to sanction the Russian railway guards.[203] In February, 1901, Count Vladimir Nikolaievich Lamzdorf, Russian Foreign Minister (1901-6), presented to Yang Wu, Chinese minister in St. Petersburg, a draft agreement of twelve articles demanding Chinese sanction for the maintenance of Russian railway guards along with regular Russian troops in the railway zone (Article II).[204] China flatly refused to sign this proposed agreement and requested the mediation of the British, German, Japanese, and United States Governments.[205] As a result, the 1902 Convention empowered and obligated China to "protect the railway."[206]

Although Russia continued to retain her railway guards and the Trans-Amur armed units after the 1902 Convention, the Russian action was viewed by China and the Great Powers alike as a *de facto* usurpation of Chinese rights in violation of treaty obligations.[207]

[201] *Ibid.*, I, 28-30.

[202] Hsü Hsi, *op. cit.*, pp. 401-402.

[203] Great Britain, *Parliamentary Papers*, China, no. 1904: "Correspondence respecting the Russian Occupation of Manchuria and Newchwang," p. 5.

[204] Sir E. Satow, British minister in Peking, to Lansdowne, British Foreign Secretary, tels. Feb. 27 & March 6, 1901, text of the draft agreement attached, *ibid.*, pp. 7, 12-13; for Chinese text, see *O-Shih-Kuan T'ang-an* (*Archives of the Chinese Legation in St. Petersburg*), cited in Ho, *op. cit.*, pp. 205-206.

[205] Chinese Imperial Edict, Feb. 28, 1901, translation in Great Britain, *Parliamentary Papers*, China, no. 2, 1904, doc. no. 16, p. 8; Lansdowne to Satow, tel., March 1, 1901, doc. no. 17, *ibid.*

[206] For Russian text of the 1902 Convention, see Grimm, *op. cit.*, pp. 154-156; for Chinese text, see *K.H.T.Y.*, vol. LXVII, sh. 6; for English translation, see MacMurray, *op. cit.*, I, 326-329.

[207] Hsü Hsi, *op. cit.*, p. 402; Sun, *Chung-O Chiao-she Lun* (*Sino-Russian Negotiations*), pp. 106-107; Lansdowne to Satow, cited in n. 205, *supra*.

Together with repeated Russian demands advanced as a price for the evacuation of Manchuria in 1902-4, the continued presence of Russian railway guards of the Trans-Amur army was one of the factors which enhanced rivalry and suspicion between Japan and Russia and thus prepared the ground for war.

In spite of the fact that Russia and Japan, by the Treaty of Portsmouth, had reserved "to themselves the right to maintain guards to protect their respective railway lines in Manchuria," and fixed the maximum number not to "exceed fifteen per kilometer" (Additional Article I to Article III of the Peace Treaty of September 5/August 23, 1905),[208] China never recognized this "right" agreed upon by others at her expense and without her knowledge. Moreover, the subsequent Sino-Japanese Treaty and Additional Agreement of December 22, 1905, had absolutely no bearing on the Russo-Japanese self-assumed police right in question.[209] The Sino-Japanese Treaty not only limited its connection with the Portsmouth Treaty merely to Articles V and VI of the latter (Article I), but further stressed the validity of "the *original* agreements concluded between China and Russia" regarding "the matter of railway construction and exploitation" (Article II). The Additional Agreement, especially, noted "the earnest desire expressed by the Imperial Chinese Government to have the Japanese and Russian troops and railway guards in Manchuria withdrawn as soon as possible," and promised that "Japan will withdraw her railway guards simultaneously with Russia" (Article II).

Thus, the Chinese Government had never recognized or sanctioned the creation of the Russian "railway guards" and the stationing of the Trans-Amur army in the railway zone. In fact, it had "protested on many occasions the unlawful measures adopted by Russia."[210] Yet, Russia seemed to have paid little attention to these long-standing Chinese protests. Russia's empire-building efforts in

[208] For Russian text, see Russia, Ministry of Foreign Affairs, *Protokoly Portsmutskoi Mirnoi Konferentsii i Tekst Dogovora mezhdu Rossiei i Iaponiei* (*Protocol of the Portsmouth Peace Conference and the Text of the Treaty between Russia and Japan*) (St. Petersburg, 1906), pp. 97-107; for English text, see MacMurray, *op. cit.*, I, 522-526.

[209] For English text, see MacMurray, *op. cit.*, I, 549-553; for Chinese text, see *K.H.T.Y.*, Vol. XCV, sh. 3-6.

[210] China, Ministry of Foreign Affairs, *Memoranda Submitted by the Chinese Assessor to the Commission of Enquiry*, comp. by Wellington V. K. Koo, April-Aug., 1932, p. 138.

Manchuria were consequently assisted by a powerful military arm of railway guards and the Trans-Amur army.

Turning to the *de facto* situation, as early as in 1897 one may find the special guards established on the railway line following an arrangement between the Russian Finance and War Ministers with the approval of Tsar Nicholas II.[211] The original number of the guards was set at 700, but soon it was raised to 2,000. In 1898, in contemplation of guarding the construction work of railway and steamship communication along the Ussuri and the Sungari rivers, the Tsar authorized the increase of the railway guards to 5,000 men.[212] In the spring of 1899, the staff of the guards included 669 officers, nine instructors, three chaplains, and 4,658 enlisted men, which constituted 19 mounted centuries and eight infantry companies.[213] The annual expenditure for this was then about two and one-half million rubles.[214]

In 1899-1900, when the news of the Boxer movement was first in the air, State Secretary Witte agreed with the chief engineer of the C.E.R. Company, the commander of the guards, and General Sakharov, then inspecting the guards, to increase the latter's strength to 11,000 men. In June, 1900, a few days before the foreign seizure of the Taku forts and the siege of the legations, Witte secured the approval of the Tsar to send additional forces for the railway guards.[215] With the arrival of the reinforcements by both land and sea routes, the Russian railway guards in the C.E.R. area were organized into 33 centuries, 24 companies, and six batteries.[216] It was these railway guards "together with the regular Russian armies" that suppressed the Chinese Boxers and won "the sincere thanks of the Tsar."[217]

On December 24/11, 1900, after the suppression of the Boxers in Manchuria, the Russian Minister of Finance, in agreement with the Russian War Minister, solicited the Tsar's sanction for increasing the railway guard force to 16,000.[218] As a measure of reducing expenses, the cadres were to be recruited from those enlisted men who were about to be placed on reserve in the Pri-Amur military district.[219]

[211] *K.V.Zh.D.: I.O.*, I, 25.

[212] *Ibid.*, I. 26-27.

[213] *Ibid.*, I, 27; I, 100 n. 1.

[214] *Ibid.*, I, 27 n. 1.

[215] *Ibid.*, I, 99-100.

[216] *Ibid.*, I, 101.

[217] *Ibid.*

[218] *Ibid.*

[219] *Ibid.*

In order to conform to the general system of manning the armed forces of Russia, the railway guards were to be included in the composition of the Separate Corps of the Frontier Guards under the Minister of Finance.[220]

On January 22/9, 1901, the plan submitted by the Finance Minister was approved by Tsar Nicholas II. From that time on, the railway guards on the C.E.R. were organized into a special district under the name of "Trans-Amur" and attached to the Separate Corps of the Frontier Guards.[221] Consequently, the higher leadership in the upper ranks and the administration of the Trans-Amur District, like that of the other districts of the Separate Corps, was left with the Minister of Finance, who was Chief of the Frontier Guards.[222] This district, however, operating beyond the frontiers of Russia itself, was supported by the funds of the C.E.R.[223]

The military organization of the Trans-Amur District was divided into four brigades. Each brigade was formed by detachments which contained infantry companies, mounted centuries, and artillery batteries. The detachments in turn were divided into two categories: troops of the line and reserve troops. The former were assigned to the direct service of guarding the road, while the latter served as a mobile reserve in case of need and also as the training cadre for the new recruits of the district.[224] The strength of the Trans-Amur District army was fixed at 25,000 men constituting 55 companies, 55 centuries, 12 infantry and 12 mounted training commands, six batteries, and a police command.[225]

During the Russo-Japanese War of 1904-5, Russia, like Japan, employed more than 250,000 combatants in Manchuria, a fact which was brought out later in the protocol concerning the withdrawal of Russian and Japanese armies from Manchuria and the transfer of railways, signed on October 30/17, 1905.[226] After this war the Russian forces in Manchuria under the Trans-Amur District included three divisions of infantry, six regiments of cavalry and one division of artillery, totaling 70,000 men in the railway zone, with 30,000 in

[220] *Ibid.*, I, 102.

[221] *Ibid.*, I, 103.

[222] The function of the Russian Frontier Guards was primarily to combat smugglers (*ibid.*).

[223] *Ibid.*

[225] *Ibid.*, I, 104.

[224] *Ibid.*, I, 103-104.

[226] MacMurray, *op. cit.*, I, 527.

the Harbin area alone.[227]   During the period of 1911-13, when Lieutenant General E. I. Martynov was the commander of the district, he confirmed that the Trans-Amur army had 12 regiments totaling 21,000 men and recommended that the number be doubled.[228]

After the outbreak of the European war, a considerable part of the Trans-Amur army was gradually transferred back to Russia. Yet, when the Russian Revolution took place in 1917, the Trans-Amur District still had under its command some 8,000 men.[229]   It was not disbanded until the expulsion of General Horvath in March, 1920.

The task of the Trans-Amur army had been succinctly defined by General Martynov as follows:

> In case of war in the Far East, the army of the so-called Trans-Amur District of the Frontier Guards must, first, defend the Chinese Eastern Railway, our unique communication line, and second, select from its own staff the principal kernel for the organization of the vanguards of the active army.
>
> Moreover, by penetrating, while peace still prevails, into what will be the enemy's rear in the theaters of war of the future, the Trans-Amur men are like tentacles [reaching out] to contact the enemy and to gather the most trustworthy information about him.[230]

Slogans such as these were deliberately used "to enhance military preparedness" and to strengthen the Russian military position in Manchuria.[231]   Thus, the railway guards and the Trans-Amur army as a whole served to implement the Russian policy of securing the railway zone as an advanced base with enormous military advantages.

STRATEGIC FORTIFICATION AND TERRITORIAL PROJECTION

Russia not only maintained guards and armed forces under the Trans-Amur District in the name of protecting the C.E.R., but was also actively engaged in planning and constructing the strategic fortifications along the railway base on the same pretext in 1913-14.

---

[227] *C.T.S.L.C.P.*, Vol. XVII, chap. vii, p. 141; Tsao, *op. cit.*, p. 34; T. V. Butov, a former official of the C.E.R., in an interview, gave the numbers as 90,000 and 60,000 respectively.

[228] Martynov, *op. cit.*, p. 102.

[229] Weigh Ken Shen, *Russo-Chinese Diplomacy* (Shanghai, 1928), p. 250; Tsao, *op. cit.*, p. 34.

[230] Martynov, *op. cit.*, p. 94.

[231] *Ibid.*, pp. 95, 105-106.

These fortifications were considered by Krupenskii, when asked by Sazonov for his opinion, as "a new step towards the strengthening of our authority in North Manchuria, so that it will be evident to the Chinese Government that it cannot treat us with indifference."[232] He thought that "the Chinese protests" could be "disregarded," since there would be no special complications with China on the matter.[233] In addition, by interfering with Chinese military strength and formation in North Manchuria, Russia actually earmarked Kirin and Heilungkiang as a Russian protectorate for eventual annexation.[234]

Reviewing the Russian scheme of fortification, in March, 1913, the Russian War Minister deemed it necessary, on the basis of a report from General Evert, commander of the Irtusk Military District, concerning Chinese military preparedness in Manchuria, to construct defense works for the protection of "the important mechanical equipment of the C.E.R." Adjutant General Sukhomlinov thereupon decided it was essential to build temporary defense works immediately with a view to replacing them later by more permanent fortifications. In April, 1913, the Russian Finance Minister accordingly proposed to the Council of Ministers an extraordinary appropriation of 500,000 rubles for these fortifications along the Chinese Eastern Railway.[235]

At its session of May 8/April 25, 1913, the Russian Council of Ministers, after examining these presentations and in agreement with the Chief of the General Staff, recognized the wisdom of securing the C.E.R. by permanent fortifications instead of the projected temporary defense works.[236] The War Minister thereby explained the detailed aspects of the defense construction for the C.E.R. and estimated its total cost at 1,200,000 rubles. This sum, however, did not include the cost of guns, machine guns, and searchlights, nor the amount of 30,000 rubles due the C.E.R. Company for the demo-

[232] Sazonov to Krupenskii, tel. no. 107, Jan. 26/13, 1914, *M.O. v E.I.*, Ser. III, Vol. I, p. 157 n. 4; Krupenskii to Sazonov, tel. no. 19, Jan. 29/16, 1914, *M.O. v E.I.*, Ser. III, Vol. I, doc. no. 136, pp. 156-157.

[233] *Ibid.*, p. 157.

[234] Cf. Protocol of an Extraordinary Meeting of the Ministerial Council at St. Petersburg, Dec. 2/Nov. 19, 1910, De Siebert & Schreiner, *op. cit.*, pp. 24-27; Martynov, *op. cit.*, pp. 12, 109.

[235] Special Journal of the Ministerial Council, Dec. 25/12, 1913, and Feb. 26/13, 1914, *M.O. v E.I.*, Ser. III, Vol. I, doc. no. 330, pp. 438-439. This journal was read and so marked by Tsar Nicholas II on April 5/March 23, 1914.

[236] *Ibid.*, p. 439.

lition of certain constructions. The fortifications were to be constructed exclusively by Russian workers. Finally, the War Minister, recognizing the security problem of the C.E.R., requested the council to approve the appropriation in full.[237]

During the meeting of the Council of Ministers, the Assistant War Minister declared that "the Ministry of War always considered the proper guarantee of the security of the Chinese Eastern Railway a problem of essential significance for the [Russian] state."[238] The Assistant War Minister further stressed that "we felt urgently compelled to equip and dispatch considerable armed forces with all types of weapons to North Manchuria and Mongolia."[239] He concluded that "the defense of the Chinese Eastern Railway has for us a strategic importance of the first order."[240]

The Russian Council of Ministers appreciated the significance referred to in the testimony of the Assistant War Minister regarding "the extraordinary significance of the Chinese Eastern Railway as a strategic line," and the necessity of "defending it by all means from any possible injury."[241] The Foreign Minister, after being assured by the Russian envoys in Japan and China that no great complications would result from this step,[242] agreed with the scheme of fortification. The Council of Ministers thereby adopted the project, voicing the hope that the fortifications would be constructed as promptly as possible.[243]

Besides fortifying the C.E.R., Russia also had projects for the construction of other strategic railways, especially the line from Aigun to Harbin and Tsitsihar as proposed by the Minister of War.[244] The Provisional Director of the War Ministry then explained that this line was to equalize Russia's position in North Manchuria with Japan's in the south. He remarked that the Planning Commission for Railway Construction in North Manchuria had also reached the

---

[237] *Ibid.*, pp. 439-440. [238] *Ibid.*, p. 440.
[239] *Ibid.*, p. 441. [240] *Ibid.*, p. 442.
[241] *Ibid.*

[242] Krupenskii to Sazonov, tel. no. 19, Jan. 29/16, 1914, *M.O. v E.I.*, Ser. III, Vol. I, doc. no. 136, pp. 156-157; Malevskii to Sazonov, Jan. 29/16, 1914, tel. no. 6, *ibid.*, doc. no. 138, p. 158.

[243] Special Journal of the Ministerial Council, Dec. 25/12, 1913, and Feb. 26/13, 1914, *M.O. v E.I.*, Ser. III, Vol. I, doc. no. 330, pp. 442-443.

[244] The line was from Aigun to Harbin with a branch to Tsitsihar (Provisional Director of the Ministry of War to Sazonov, letter no. 4375, April 14/1, 1914, Confidential, *M.O. v E.I.*, Ser. III, Vol. II, doc. no. 222, p. 303).

same conclusion and that on November 24/11, 1913, the War Minister had already informed the Foreign Minister of the significance of this line.[245]

On April 4/March 22, 1914, this railway project was reported by the War Minister to Tsar Nicholas II, who had fully agreed with the strategic necessity of this line for Russia on the basis of the following considerations:

The Chinese Eastern Railway is exposed to attack from the south by the Japanese and the Chinese forces and, consequently, the connection between Manchuria and Transbaikal by this route is unreliable. With the presence of the [railway] lines from Harbin and Tsitsihar to Blagoveshchensk [opposite Aigun, across the Amur River], our forces gathered in North Manchuria would have a tenable tie with the empire through Blagoveshchensk by the Amur Railway.

Moreover, the presence of these lines would widen our base, allowing our forces active in North Manchuria to be based in the future not only on Transbaikal, but also on the Amur Region. . . .

In the end, the construction of these lines . . . will give us an outlet to Manchuria from the Amur [Railway] line and a completely secure bond between the Maritime and the Manchurian theaters of military operations, so that the transfer of the forces and materials from one theater to another will be fully guaranteed.[246]

This railway project, together with four others, was officially brought to the attention of the Chinese Government by Krupenskii.[247] But while seeking railway concessions for itself, Russia tried at the same time to prevent the construction by China of the Suihuasian-Hailunfu line, despite the fact that the funds were to be provided by the Russo-Asiatic Bank.[248] The Russian War Office advised the Russian Foreign Ministry of the absolute necessity of preventing China from constructing "any railway line to the north of Harbin," because the building of a line "of this orientation without our gauge and not for our exploitation and not leading to Blagoveshchensk

[245] *Ibid.*

[246] *Ibid.*, pp. 303-304.

[247] The other four projected lines were: (1) Harbin—Boduhe, (2) Imianpo—Hantienmen, on the lower stream of the Sungari, (3) Tsitsihar—Boduhe, and (4) branches of the C.E.R. in Barga (Sazonov to Krupenskii, tel. no. 471, March 14/1, 1914, *M.O. v E.I.*, Ser. III, Vol. II, doc. no. 3, p. 5).

[248] Tel. of Russian consul at Tsitsihar, March 16/3, 1914, *M.O. v E.I.*, Ser. III, Vol. II, p. 304.

would only harm us."[249]   It might facilitate the operations of an
enemy of Russia towards Blagoveshchensk.   The War Office, therefore, suggested the frustration of the Chinese plan by the construction of a line with an opposite direction, i.e., from Blagoveshchensk,
under Russia's control.[250]

Moreover, Russia had demanded information from China regarding the number of her forces in North Manchuria.   In reply
to Krupenskii, the Chinese Government gave the figure as 32,000
men.[251]   The Russian War Minister even attempted to secure an
agreement with China limiting the number of all types of Chinese
forces in Kirin and Heilungkiang to a special quota, and a pledge
by China not to exceed the Quota without Russian approval.[252]   The
Chinese Government was compelled to notify Russia of the time and
the size of the increase of its forces, but did not submit to the demand
that it give a month's notice before making such an increase.[253]

The Russian Government further interfered with the Chinese
program of strengthening military forces in Manchuria, on the
grounds that the Chinese units, lacking adequate cadre, would exhibit
a lack of discipline detrimental to the interests of Russians living in
the Eastern Provinces and to the Russian enterprise of the Chinese
Eastern Railway.   Krupenskii was at this time instructed to advise
the Chinese Government for the sake of its own interests to maintain
only a police force in Manchuria.[254]

These Russian demands and interferences of a military nature
might well have given a warning signal regarding Russian territorial
designs in Manchuria.   Late in 1910 the Russian War Minister had
indeed recommended to the Ministerial Council "as necessary on
strategic grounds the annexation of North Manchuria by Russia."[255]

[249] Provisional Director of the Ministry of War to Sazonov, letter no. 4375,
April 14/1, 1914, Confidential, *M.O. v E.I.*, Ser. III, Vol. II, p. 304.
   [250] *Ibid.*, pp. 304-305.
   [251] Tel. no. 712 of Krupenskii, Nov. 7/Oct. 25, 1913, *M.O. v E.I.*, Ser. III, Vol.
I, p. 350 n. 1; Sazonov to Krupenskii, tel. no. 288, Feb. 19/6, 1914, *M.O. v E.I.*,
Ser. III, Vol. I, doc. no. 278, pp. 349-350.
   [252] Sazonov to Krupenskii, tel. no. 288, Feb. 19/6, 1914, *M.O. v E.I.*, Ser. III,
Vol. I, doc. no. 278, p. 350.
   [253] Krupenhskii to Sazonov, tel. no. 96, March 9/Feb. 24, 1914, *M.O. v E.I.*,
Ser. III, Vol. I, doc. no. 405, p. 526.
   [254] Assistant Foreign Minister Neratov, to Grave, tel. no. 759, April 25/12,
1914, *M.O. v E.I.*, Ser. III, Vol. II, doc. no. 290, pp. 378-379.
   [255] Protocol of an Extraordinary Meeting of the Ministerial Council at St.
Petersburg, Dec. 2/Nov. 19, 1910, De Siebert & Schreiner, *op. cit.*, p. 24.

The War Minister was of the opinion that the moment was "all the more favorable for us to take possession of Manchuria in agreement with Japan," as the Japanese were "very evidently preparing the annexation of South Manchuria." The Russian Foreign Minister declared that "he was perfectly convinced that the annexation of North Manchuria was for us an imperative necessity," but he regarded the given moment as unfavorable.[256] Prime Minister Kokovtsov agreed with Sazonov by saying:

Naturally, it would be impossible to declare that Northern Manchuria will never be annexed by Russia; political events in future might make it necessary for us to do so, should the political situation be favorable at the time. By safeguarding at present all our treaty privileges in Manchuria we can best prepare for the possibility just referred to.[257]

The Ministerial Council thereupon adopted the following resolution:

So far as Northern Manchuria is concerned, the Ministerial Council regards an annexation as dangerous at the present moment, but is of the opinion that the trend of events may force Russia to this step. All ministers must therefore be guided by the consideration that our stipulated privileges in Northern Manchuria must be maintained in full to permit eventually an annexation at some future date.

The Ministerial Council sanctions the measures proposed by the Minister of Foreign Affairs to exert pressure upon China. In case of necessity, however, there must be no shrinking from forceful measures.[258]

This idea of eventual annexation of North Manchuria permeated Russian thinking for years. As General Martynov said, "the great importance of Manchuria in economic and military respects compelled us to hope for its incorporation into the Empire."[259] In order to annex Manchuria, he urged quick action for the reason that "the present weakness of China evidently will not last forever."[260] Not unlike the War Minister, he looked toward the simultaneous annexation of North Manchuria by Russia and of South Manchuria by Japan. He thought that China was then still impotent; yet the other Powers, he felt, far from coming to the aid of China, would in all probability not hesitate to press their own demands for compensation upon that same weak China.[261] Therefore, Martynov

[256] *Ibid.*, p. 25.
[258] *Ibid.*, p. 27.
[260] *Ibid.*, p. 10.
[257] *Ibid.*, p. 26.
[259] Martynov. *op. cit.*, p. 7.
[261] *Ibid.*, p. 11.

pointed out, an earlier incorporation of Manchuria would be to "Russia's national interest."[262]

Martynov's impatience for a showdown was manifested in a report he submitted to the Russian Government in 1912, in his capacity as commander of the Trans-Amur District. It contained a warning to the effect that "the Chinese proposed to organize in Manchuria an uprising of the Boxer type directed against the railway and the Russian settlers"[263]—a piece of intelligence that was certainly unfounded, and perhaps deliberately fabricated. Evidently his intention was to urge the Russian Government to take forceful measures in Manchuria under the pretext of protecting the C.E.R.

In short, had the Russian Government followed the drastic policy of the War Minister in 1910-11, or listened to General Martynov's provocative suggestions in 1912-13, North Manchuria would have been incorporated into Russia or pressed under Russian occupation in the same pattern of force that was demonstrated in the years following 1900. Although these extreme projects were not adopted, actual practices showed how Russia used the Chinese Eastern Railway to secure Russian military advantages in Manchuria.

RUSSIAN ECONOMIC AND OTHER ADVANTAGES THROUGH THE RAILWAY

A Soviet source points out that "Tsarist Russia endeavored to turn Manchuria into her colony."[264] Whether or not this was her immediate goal, Tsarist Russia lost no time in exploiting the country in every possible way, through economic means and the diplomatic, political, and military measures described above, these being mutually complementary. Russian economic penetration into Manchuria through the medium of the Chinese Eastern Railway often took the form of *de facto* assumption of rights at the outset, largely adjusted later by local arrangements. The economic advantages that

---

[262] *Ibid.*, p. 12.

[263] Provisional Director of the Ministry of Foreign Affairs Neratov, to Krupenskii and Malevskii, tel. no. 1992, Oct. 1/Sept. 18, 1912, *M.O. v E.I.*, Ser. II, Vol. XX, Part II, 1940, doc. no. 841, pp. 324-325; Krupenskii to Neratov, tel. no. 813, Oct. 3/Sept. 20, 1912, *M.O. v E.I*, Ser. II, Vol. XX, Part II, doc. no. 880, p. 350; Neratov to Kokovtsov, letter no. 1028, Oct. 9/Sept. 26, 1912, Confidential, *M.O. v E.I.*, Ser. II, Vol. XX, Part II, doc. no. 957, p. 403.

[264] *M.S.E.* (2nd ed.), Vol. VI (1937), col. 537.

Russia had thus secured included, notably, inland navigation and mining and timber concessions, as well as reduced customs rates. Through the C.E.R. Russia had controlled educational and cultural institutions in North Manchuria. Last but not least, using the C.E.R. as a prototype, Russia had solicited China to grant further concessions for additional railway construction in that region.

The Chinese Eastern Railway Company acquired special rights of inland navigation in Manchuria first by a bold interpretation of Article IV of the railway contract of 1896.[265] The article provided that "the Chinese Government will give orders to the local authorities to assist the company to the extent of their ability in obtaining, at current prices, . . . the means of transport by water and by land," and that "the Chinese Government should, as needed, take measures to facilitate such transportation." It evidently did not grant by this provision any right of inland navigation to the C.E.R. Company. Yet, in its very founding year of 1896, the company established a Navigation Department within its structure, with the steamers flying the C.E.R. flags found on all navigable waters in Kirin and Heilungkiang.[266] Later, to adjust the contractual stipulation to the situation created by Russia through the C.E.R. Company, Article II of the 1898 Agreement between China and the C.E.R. Company concerning the southern branch of the C.E.R. made the following provision:

In accordance with Article IV of the Contract of . . . 1896, which provides that the Chinese Government shall take steps as occasion may require to facilitate the bringing in of the materials needed for the construction of the line, whether transported by water or by land, *it is now agreed* that the Company may employ steamers or other vessels, and such vessels flying the Company's flag shall be permitted to proceed up the Liao River or any of its branches, and to enter Ying-k'ou [the port of Newchwang] or any port in the Neutral Territory which may prove advantageous to the work of constructing this line, and may there discharge cargo.[267]

On the strength of this provision, Russian vessels flying the flag of the C.E.R. Company consolidated their previously self-assumed

---

[265] *C.T.S.L.C.P.*, Vol. XVII, chap. vii, pp. 379-380.

[266] *Ibid.* Vol. XVII, chap. vii, pp. 380-381; Hsü Hsi, *op. cit.*, p. 399.

[267] Text in MacMurray, *op. cit.*, I, 154-156. The neutral territory referred to was a specified zone north of the frontier of the leased Liaotung territory; Chinese troops were to be admitted within this neutral zone only with the consent of the Russian authorities (Article V).

rights and navigated all the rivers and their tributaries throughout Manchuria. South of Mukden, Russian steamers navigated along the Liao River and into all the ports along the Pechili Gulf until after the Russo-Japanese War, and north of Mukden they were not only found in the Amur, Ussuri, and Tumen river systems, but also in inland waters such as the Sungari and Nonni rivers, of which the Sungari was of paramount importance.[268]

The right of Russian vessels to navigate in the inland waters of the Sungari River was another result of contractual confusion, this time derived from the Treaty of Aigun of 1858. The Aigun Treaty defined the boundary line between the two countries by providing that the territory on the left bank of the Amur River and part of the Sungari River (now the so-called Hun-T'ung Kiang or the "Mixed" River) from Habarovsk to Lahasusu (T'ungkiang) was to be recognized as Russian, while that on the right bank was to be Chinese. The inhabitants on both sides of the river and of both countries were entitled to the right of free trade. But Russia arbitrarily interpreted the right of navigation and of free trade thus provided as also applicable to the greater part of the Sungari River from Lahasusu inland to Harbin and Fuyu.[269] Russia had assumed the *de facto* right of navigation on the Sungari in 1895 on the basis of similar interpretation of Article 18 of the Sino-Russian St. Petersburg Treaty of 1881.[270] Owing to the restrictions placed by the local Manchu authorities and the lack of Russian vessels, no important development was recorded until the establishment in 1896 of the C.E.R. Company, which greatly facilitated Russian navigation on the Sungari.[271]

In 1898, the first five Russian steamers flying the C.E.R. flag reached Harbin.[272] Then Russia attempted to monopolize both the Amur and the Sungari shipping.[273] No official Chinese recognition was given to the Russian right of navigation on the Sungari until Article XI of the Sino-Russian Memorandum of Agreement concerning the provisional Sungari River Trade Regulations of August 8/ July 26, 1910, gave tacit acknowledgment of the presence of Russian

---

[268] Hsü Hsi, *op. cit.*, pp. 399-401; Gluzdovskii, *op. cit.*, p. 176.
[269] *C.T.S.L.C.P.*, Vol. XVII, chap. vii, p. 380.
[270] *K.V.Zh.D.: I.O.*, I, 57.
[271] *Ibid.*, I, 57-58.
[272] *Ibid.*, I, 58.
[273] *C.T.S.L.C.P.*, Vol. XVII, chap. vii, p. 380.

vessels on the Sungari by stipulating that the statements of tonnage and goods of Russian vessels would be received by the Harbin River Customs.[274] Thereafter, up to 1917 more than one hundred Russian vessels of the C.E.R. Company and other private companies "steered to the heart of the Sungari and made Sungari River traffic virtually an affiliated part of the C.E.R. Company."[275]

The pattern of *de facto* assumption followed in the case of inland navigation was once again utilized as Russia helped itself to the mining rights in Manchuria. Article VI of the railway contract of 1896 merely mentioned that there would be a special arrangement for mines. However, there were no officially sanctioned contracts for mining concessions until 1907.

Yet, on July 18/5, 1901, and January 14/1, 1902, when Manchuria was still under Russian occupation, two local arrangements for coal mining were made by the Russian engineer-in-chief, A. J. Yugovich, with the Tartar generals of Kirin and Heilungkiang respectively.[276] These arrangements were neither approved by the Chinese Central Government nor recorded in the collections of official documents as in the case of the 1907 contracts.[277] Nor were they referred to in the latter contracts. Moreover, Chinese sources emphatically point out that in 1902 "the Waiwupu definitely rejected the petition of the C.E.R. Company for the exploitation of coal mines in the vicinity of the railway and for signing the contracts thereof."[278] Therefore, the so-called 1901 and 1902 arrangements for coal mining should have no legal standing.

Nevertheless, despite the disapproval of the Imperial Manchu Government, the Russian management of the Chinese Eastern Railway opened coal mines at Fushun, Yentai in Fengtien Province, at Tsaishunkai, T'outaokou in Kirin Province, and at Chalainor in Heilungkiang Province, etc. Facing this *fait accompli* and perceiving that the indiscriminate exploitation of Chinese mines by an alien enterprise would be detrimental to the country, the Manchu Court

[274] Text in MacMurray, *op. cit.*, I, 807-809.
[275] *C.T.S.L.C.P.*, Vol. XVII, chap. vii, p. 381.
[276] *Ibid.*, p. 154; text of the 1902 arrangement in MacMurray, *op. cit.*, I, 661-662.
[277] Chinese text of the identical contracts of Aug. 30/17, 1907, in Hsu Shih-ch'ang, *op. cit.*, Vol. XI, "Records of Mining Negotiations," sh. 21-22, and in *C.T.S.L.C.P.*, Vol. XVII, chap. vii, pp. 154-156; Russian text in *Soglasheniia*, p. 42; English text in MacMurray, *op. cit.*, I, 658-661.
[278] Hsu Shih-ch'ang, *op. cit.*, Vol. XI, sh. 20; Hsü, *op. cit.*, pp. 393-394.

was compelled to send two special delegates, Tu Hsiao-ying and Sung Hsiao-lien, to Harbin in 1907 for the conclusion of two similar mining contracts with the Chinese Eastern Railway Company on behalf of Kirin and Heilungkiang respectively.[279]

Article II of the twin contracts of 1907 did provide the free exploitation of coal mines in territories 30 Chinese li (10 miles) from each side of the railway along the entire line. The same article, on the other hand, definitely eliminated the notion of the 1901 and the 1902 unauthorized local arrangements that the Chinese Eastern Railway Company had "the exclusive right" of coal mining within the 60-li-wide railway mining zone and "the prior consultation right" regarding mining projects outside of the zone.[280] This meant that Chinese and foreigners might be given concessions for mining within the zone with the consent of the railway and with permission from the Chinese authorities. As regards lands located outside the zone, "the permission for Chinese or foreigners to explore or operate the coal deposits therein shall depend entirely on the Chinese authorities" (Article II). Coal-mining taxation was regulated at 12/100 of a local tael per 1,000 kin (eq. 1.33 lb.), plus 17.64 taels in silver for each active shaft annually (Article VII). Up to 1917, China hoped to use these provisions to resist further Russian encroachment in coal mining through the railway.[281]

The Russian right of lumbering through the C.E.R. Company originated from Article IV of the 1898 Contract concerning the southern branch of the Chinease Eastern Railway, which read in part: "to allow the company to fell timber at its pleasure in the forests on government lands," at a fixed price. Minister Shu King-ch'eng, negotiator and signer of this contract, was definitely responsible for the vague wording of this article which made subsequent Russian abuse possible.

In 1903 there was another blunder on the part of Chou Mien, Director of the Heilungkiang Bureau, who negotiated with the C.E.R. Company and, without authorization, granted it the right of lumbering in several designated areas; namely, in the railway right-of-way areas from the Genghis Khan Station to the Yakeshan Station

[279]Hsü Hsi, *op. cit.*, pp. 393-394.

[280] B. A. Romanov, *Rossiia v Man'chzhurii* (*Russia in Manchuria*), p. 371; Young, *op. cit.*, pp. 98-99.

[281] Hsu Shih-ch'ang, *op. cit.*, Vol. XI, "Records of Mining Negotiations," sh. 20.

(measuring 600 li in length and 60 li in breadth), the Hulan-Lamin Rivers area (300 by 100 li), and the Mulin-Lunlun Rivers area (170 by 70 li). Despite the repeated rejection by the Heilungkiang governor of the validity of these arrangements, the Russian management of the railway considered these Chou grants as acquired rights.[282]

Because of the continuous disapproval by Governor Chen Te-chuan and the Waiwupu, the Russian minister in Peking finally agreed to the negotiation of new arrangements by the C.E.R. Company following the ending of the Russo-Japanese War.[283] After protracted debates and discussions lasting more than a year, regulations or contracts for the felling of timber in Kirin and Heilungkiang were signed on August 30/17, 1907, and April 5/March 23, 1908, respectively.[284] By these contracts, any previous unauthorized arrangements were thereby unequivocally rescinded and timber concessions were reduced to about one tenth of the *de facto* area in the previous period.[285] In the meantime, license and tax provisions were imposed.

During the period of 1911-17, the C.E.R. Company had three timber concessions along with others held by private Russian and Polish concessionaires. These concessions often had light rail tracks connecting them to the main line of the C.E.R.; from them was derived a total annual income of not less than one hundred million rubles.[286] Russian interest in this respect might be further noted from the remarks of Sazonov. In 1915 the Foreign Minister said that "the forests in Kirin Province had been exploited by Russians to a considerable degree."[287] He was anxious to prevent the employment of an American, W. F. Sherfesee, by the Chinese Government as a forestry adviser so as not to "interfere with the Russo-Chinese relationship in the wood cutting business." For this purpose, he had instructed Krupenskii to make representations to the Chinese Government that if a foreign expert on forestry was needed, the Chinese Government should employ not an American, Sherfesee,

[282] Hsü Hsi, *op. cit.*, pp. 397-398; B. A. Romanov, *op. cit.*, p. 372; Hsu Shih-ch'ang, *op. cit.*, Vol. XII, "Records of Lumbering Negotiations," sh. 27.

[283] Hsu Shih-ch'ang, *op. cit.*, Vol. XII, sh. 27.

[284] For Russian texts, see *Soglasheniia*, pp. 51, 46; for Chinese texts, see Hsu Shih-ch'ang, *op. cit.*, Vol. XII, "Records of Lumbering Negotiations," sh. 28-30, 31; for English texts, see MacMurray, *op. cit.*, I, 671-674, 721-724.

[285] Hsu Shih-ch'ang, *op. cit.*, Vol. XII, sh. 27.

[286] Hsü Hsi, *op. cit.*, pp. 398-399.

[287] Sazonov to Krupenskii, tel. no. 6136, Dec. 11/Nov. 28, 1915, *M.O. v E.I.*, Ser. III, Vol. IX, doc. no. 495, p. 507.

"but a Russian subject, whom we [the Russian Government] are ready to recommend."[288]

The Russian advantage of reduced customs rates was provided in Article X of the 1896 Railway Contract, which read in part:

> Merchandise imported from Russia into China by the railway, and likewise merchandise imported from China into Russia by the same route, will respectively pay the import and export duty of the Chinese Maritime Customs, less one-third.
>
> If merchandise is transported into the interior it will pay in addition the transit duty—equivalent to a half of the import duty collected—which frees it from any further charge.

With regard to the latter provision, Russia, however, soon contended that "goods subject to this reduced import duty [two-thirds] can be transported to any point along the railway lines in Manchuria without being liable to further duty.[289]   The Chinese replied that "the payment of two-thirds duty entitles such goods to pass the Chinese frontier only, and that they must pay transit dues [50 per cent additional] to clear them to points further in the country."[290] As a compromise, after several months' controversy, the Experimental Regulations for the establishment of customs houses in Northern Manchuria were agreed upon by Russia and China on July 8/ June 25, 1907.[291]   By these regulations, the areas in and near the railway zone which would be entitled to import goods with a one-third reduction from the Chinese customs rates were delimited. Within a radius of ten Chinese li from Harbin station, and within an area extending five li in all directions from the stations at Manchuli, Hailar, Tsitsihar, Kuanchengtzu, and a dozen other places, goods were to be allowed entry with a one-third reduction of duties; goods destined for or sent to the interior outside these areas were to be subject to the usual duties and charges under inland trade regulations.[292]

Article VII of the railway contract of 1896 also provided: "All goods and materials for the construction, operation and repairs of

---

[288] *Ibid.*

[289] Hsu Shih-ch'ang, *op. cit.*, Vol. XIII, "Records of Customs Negotiations," sh. 1.

[290] *Ibid.*

[291] Text in MacMurray, *op. cit.*, I, 648-650.

[292] Hsu Shih-ch'ang, *op. cit.*, Vol. XIII, "Records of Customs Negotiations," sh. 26.

the line, will be exempt from any tax or customs duty and from any internal tax or duty." However, from 1897 goods other than materials needed by the railway for various purposes were imported through Manchuli and Aigun almost without exception under the camouflage of railway materials in order to avoid the already reduced customs duties.[293]

In 1908, in accordance with the Provisional Regulations for Chinese Customs Houses at Manchuli and Pogranichnaia agreed upon by Russia and China on May 30/17 of that year,[294] a Chinese customs office operated in the frontier city of Manchuli. Yet, in August of the same year, the Russian management of the Chinese Eastern Railway suddenly sent Russian troops under the command of Parshevskii to surround the Manchuli customs office, disarmed the customs police agents, lowered the Chinese flag, and arrested the Chinese customs officials.[295] The explanation of Manager Horvath for this insult to the Chinese was the encroachment by the Chinese customs office on the railway's "absolute and exclusive right of administration of its lands," which, as analyzed above, was unjustifiable of itself. The ensuing dispute between the Waiwupu and the Russan minister was not settled until six months later when the pre-incident order was restored.[296]

Meanwhile, Russia liberally applied the provision of the 50-verst (100-li or 33-mile) duty-free zone originally established under the Treaty of 1881.[297] It was due only to China's persistent reluctance to renew the treaty in 1911-12[298] that Russia abolished the duty-free zone on her side of the frontier effective January 14/1, 1913, and authorized China to do the same on the Chinese side.[299] China did follow this step in June, 1914.[300] Russian advantages of preferential

---

[293] *Ibid.*, sh. 1.

[294] Chinese text in *ibid.*, sh. 27-36; English text in MacMurray, *op. cit.*, I, 651-657.

[295] Hsu Shih-ch'ang, *op. cit.*, Vol. XIII, "Records of Customs Negotiations," sh. 2, 23.

[296] *Ibid.*, sh. 23-24.

[297] *Ibid.*, sh. 2, 24.

[298] Report of Sazonov to Nicholas II, Jan. 23/10, 1912, *M.O. v E.I.*, Ser. II, Vol. XIX, Part II, doc. no. 379, p. 34; Krupenskii to Sazonov, tel. no. 532, June 19/6, 1912, *M.O. v E.I.*, Ser. II, Vol. XX, Part I, doc. no. 205, p. 197.

[299] Krupenskii to the Waichiaopu, Sept. 6/Aug. 24, 1912, in MacMurray, *op. cit.*, I, 650-651.

[300] Ho, *op. cit.*, p. 269.

customs rates in connection with the Chinese Eastern Railway continued throughout the period under review.

The Russian management of the C.E.R. also administered educational institutions in the railway zone through a separate department of education within its structure. It controlled all the elementary schools, high schools, and two universities, totaling more than a hundred schools with more than 20,000 students, predominantly (more than 90 per cent) Russian. In 1915 the total expenses borne by the railway for the maintenance of these schools amounted to 1,143,000 gold rubles, of which 200,000 were used for the Law Faculty and the Polytechnical Institute in Harbin.[301]

The C.E.R. Company also controlled a number of cultural institutions, such as a chain of libraries, railway clubs, the Manchurian Research Society, the meteorological station, etc. The Russian Orientalist Society published a scientific journal, *Vestnik Azii* (the *Asiatic Herald*), from 1909 to 1922.[302] The annual expenses of the libraries alone amounted to 70,000 gold rubles.[303] In addition, the Tsarist Government was said to have "strenuously disseminated Christianity in all North Manchuria."[304] As Skalov pointed out, "Harbin became one of the most important missionary centers, where the Orthodox priests taught the Chinese boys belief in 'the Russian God,' and also, which was perhaps more to the point, the belief in the Russian Tsar."[305]

In view of the excessive advantages in political, military, economic, and cultural influences derived from the Chinese Eastern Railway, Russia had the incentive to monopolize railway construction in North Manchuria. In March, 1914, Krupenskii, under instruction, presented to Sun Pao-ch'i, the Chinese Foreign Minister, "demands" for constructing additional railways there by Russia together with the right to exploit natural resources in the area of the projected lines.[306] Thereafter, V. Grave, the Russian chargé, visited Sun further to advance the Russian "demands" and to indicate

---

[301] Tsao, *op. cit.*, pp. 35-36; *C.T.S.L.C.P.*, Vol. XVII, chap. vii, pp. 382-383.

[302] *C.T.S.L.C.P.*, Vol. XVII, chap. vii, pp. 383-384; V. A. Anuchin, *Geograficheskie Ocherki Manchzhurii* (*Geographical Outlines of Manchuria*) (Moscow, 1948), p. 35.

[303] Tsao, *op. cit.*, p. 36.

[304] Skalov, *op. cit.*, p. 24.

[305] *Ibid.*

[306] Krupenskii to Sazonov, tel. no. 116, March 16/3, 1914, *M.O. v E.I.*, Ser. III, Vol. II, doc. no. 28, p. 28.

the form of arrangement to be followed.[307]   The Russian Foreign Ministry also instructed him to insist on obtaining the concessions.[308] The Chinese Government promised not to appeal to any source other than Russia for financing the construction of railways in North Manchuria,[309] but declined to grant the right of exploiting natural resources along the line because no such privileges had been provided in the other, analogous contracts.[310]   Finally, on March 28/15, 1915, a contract regarding the loan for the construction of the Harbin-Haihe railway was signed by the representative of the Russo-Asiatic Bank, Goierom, and the Chinese Ministers of Communications and Finance.[311]

In view of this record of exploitation in Manchuria, it is difficult to imagine to what lengths the Russian advantages secured through the Chinese Eastern Railway might have been carried, had the European war and internal disturbances not intervened to absorb and exhaust Russian resources and energy.

[307] Grave to Sazonov, letter, May 27/14, 1914, *M.O. v E.I.*, Ser. III, Vol. III, doc. no. 104, p. 120.

[308] Assistant Foreign Minister Artsimovich to Grave, tel. no. 1481, July 24/11, 1914, *M.O. v E.I.*, Ser. III, Vol. V, doc. no. 20, pp. 40-41; Artsimovich to P. A. Bark, Finance Minister, letter no. 472, July 24/11, 1914, *M.O. v E.I.*, Ser. III, Vol. V, doc. no. 24, pp. 43-44.

[309] Grave to Sazonov, tel. no. 374, July 28/15, 1914, *M.O. v E.I.*, Ser. III, Vol. V, doc. no. 207, p. 200.

[310] Krupenskii to Sazonov, tel. no. 490, Aug. 29/16, 1914, *M.O. v E.I.*, Ser. III, Vol. VI, doc. no. 187, pp. 180-181.

[311] Grave to Sazonov, dispatch no. 13, March 30/17, 1915, *M.O. v E.I.*, Ser. III, Vol. X, doc. no. 500 pp. 617-618; *ibid.*, p. 617 n.

III: THE CHINESE EASTERN RAILWAY IN TRANSITION, 1917-24

GENERAL HORVATH'S "RAILWAY STATE" 1917-20

The Russian Revolution of 1917 marked the passing of the role of the Tsarist regime in the control of the Chinese Eastern Railway; it also injected Russian domestic struggles for political power into the question of the future of the railway. According to G. Voitinskii, "the Chinese Eastern Railway played a most colossal part in the counterrevolutionary offensive against the U.S.S.R." He further indicated that "all the blood-stained records of the Civil War" involving the "Kolchaks, Horvaths, and Semenovs" were "directly connected with the Chinese Eastern Railway whence a deadly danger had more than once threatened the Soviet Far East and Siberia."[1]

The basis for this powerful counterrevolutionary center was Horvath's so-called "railway state" within a state.[2] With his headquarters in Harbin, General Dmitrii Leonidovich Horvath, general manager of the C.E.R. since 1902, attempted "to assume full governmental power as regards the Russian population in the Chinese Eastern Railway territory."[3] For fully three years, from March, 1917, to March, 1920, General Horvath held the Chinese Eastern Railway against all claimants. He succeeded in preventing the Bolsheviks from gaining ground in his then exclusive domain, and the Chinese authorities from recovering the railway. And, by currying favor, he fared quite well with the consular corps at Harbin, who,

[1] G. N. Voitinskii, *K.V.Zh.D. i Politika Imperialistov v Kitae* (*The C.E.R. and the Policy of the Imperialists in China*) (Moscow, 1930), p. 40.

[2] Mikhailov, *Chto Proiskhodit na Kitaiskoi Vostochnoi Zheleznoi Doroge?* (*Events Pertaining to the Chinese Eastern Railway*), p. 7.

[3] Georgii V. Chicherin, *Vneshniaia Politika Sovetskoi Rossii za Dva Goda* (*Foreign Policy of Soviet Russia in Two Years*) (Moscow, 1919), p. 11.

instead of protesting his *ultra vires* administration, pledged their co-operation.[4]

General Horvath was a Russian noble and a distant relative of the abdicated Tsar. A graduate of the Nikolas Engineering School, he first served in the Life-Guards of the Pioneer Battalion in 1878 and then, from 1885, worked on the railways. He became the head of the South-Ussuri Railway in 1895 and of the Trans-Caspian Military Railway in 1899. Horvath ruled the Chinese Eastern Railway in the capacity of general manager from 1902 to 1920. In 1912 he was promoted to the rank of lieutenant general, following previous promotions for meritorious transport service rendered during the Russo-Japanese War. His position during this period was thus of equal importance to that of the Governor-General of the Far East stationed at Vladivostok. After the 1917 Revolution, Horvath entrenched himself in the railway area and became "one of the White Guards' leaders in the Far East." Soviet sources specifically indicate that in 1918 Horvath received a subsidy from Japan through Colonel Araki and, in turn, subsidized the White Guards detachments of Ataman Semenov in Trans-Baikal, and of Kalmykov in the Maritime Province. In 1919 he was the High Commissioner of the Kolchak regime in Manchuria.[5]

Horvath was most unscrupulous in the conduct of political activities in the C.E.R. area during the three years following the Russian Revolution. In March, 1917, he established in the railway zone, despite protests from the Chinese Government, a "Provisional Russian Republic," wherein he assumed governmental functions and proclaimed independence from Petrograd.[6] In the meantime, he convoked a national assembly, conducted a general election, and appointed himself "Director General of the All-Russian Provisional Government."[7] Horvath's power, however, was soon greatly reduced by the so-called Republican Executive Committee, organized at Harbin by self-appointed representatives and claiming authority from the Petrograd Provisional Government. But Horvath was allowed to retain his position under the title of "Commissioner,"

[4] Chu (ed.), *Chin-shih-lien-lai chi Chung-O Kuan-hsi (Russo-Chinese Relations of the Last Ten Years)*, p. 27; Far Eastern Review, XV (March, 1919), 298.
[5] *B.S.E.* (1st ed.), Vol. LX, cols. 73-74.
[6] Tsao [Resident-Investigator in Manchuria], *The Chinese Eastern Railway: An Analytical Study*, p. 43.
[7] *C.T.S.L.C.P.*, Vol. XVII, chap. vii, p. 62.

since he enjoyed in this capacity the approval of the Russian population in the railway area.[8]

Meanwhile, the authority of the Republican Executive Committee and of Horvath had been challenged by the Council of the Soldiers and Workmen's Delegates at Harbin, a replica of the Petrograd Soviet, under the leadership of M. Rutin, a junior officer of the former Trans-Amur army, and his comrades, Salvin and Lutskii. On December 12, 1917, following the Bolshevik coup d'état, Lenin sent a personal telegram instructing the council to take action. Thereupon the council issued a proclamation declaring itself "the official representative" of the Petrograd Government; it would bring all public offices under its control and supervision. Six days later, the council ordered the dismissal of Horvath and others. It also replaced the Russian consul in Harbin, Popov, with one of its delegates, Purianov. The former consul was forced to take refuge at the Chinese Bureau for Foreign Affairs.[9]

Because of the disorder resulting from the "mutiny" of the Russian troops in the railway zone, China sent a regiment into that area to intervene if and when necessary.[10] When it appeared that the soldiers and workers of the railway were gaining the upper hand in the affairs of the railway, Horvath lost no time in enlisting the support of the Chinese authorities. China readily responded and asked him to see if he could not solve the problem. He declared that he had admonished the delegates to act tactfully, since the railway was in Chinese territory and political activities of Russians would not be permitted by China. Also he had discussed the matter with Commander Shamoilov of the railway guards, and the unreliable troops were to be sent back to Russia gradually.[11] While he claimed that his authority could not be rescinded by the delegates, Horvath admitted that it was beyond his personal capacity to maintain order in the railway zone.[12] Thus, when Rutin planned to arrest Horvath in order to take over the railway administration and obtain ammunition from the Russian depot, Horvath secretly requested the protection of the Chinese army.[13]

[8] Weigh, *Russo-Chinese Diplomacy*, p. 218.
[9] *C.T.S.L.C.P.*, Vol. XVII, chap. vii, pp. 62-63.
[10] *C.Y.B., 1921-22*, p. 651.
[11] *C.T.S.L.C.P.*, Vol. XVII, chap. vii, p. 63.
[12] Chu, *op. cit.*, p. 28.
[13] *C.T.S.L.C.P.*, Vol. XVII, chap. vii, p. 63.

Anxious to solve this anomalous situation by peaceful means, General T'ao Ch'iang-k'uei, Commander-in-Chief of the Chinese Eastern Railway Protective Army, approached Rutin and other delegates to persuade them to leave Chinese territory. This request was refused, and as the consular corps in Harbin demanded action, Rutin, Salvin, and their followers were disarmed and ejected from China on December 26, 1917.[14] Following this, the Chinese military authority after consultation with Horvath issued an order to the effect that peace and order was to be maintained by Chinese troops and Russian railway officials, and that Chinese soldiers were to be quartered at various stations along the railway line.[15]

Horvath's "dictatorial" control over the Chinese Eastern Railway during the years 1917-20 was derived from a decision of the extraordinary meeting of the shareholders of the Chinese Eastern Railway Company held in Peking on April 27, 1918. This meeting was convoked by the Russo-Asiatic Bank, which was reorganized in Paris under the protection and with the assistance of the French Government. Earlier, after the Bolshevik Revolution, the bank had been nationalized in Russia. Availing themselves of the provision in the statute of the company which allowed its Board of Directors (*Pravlenie*) to reside either in Petrograd or in Peking, the officers of the bank now called the meeting so as to revive and reorganize the board which had been shattered by the Bolsheviks. At the meeting, Horvath was elected a member of the board and was deputized by it to act as managing director.[16]

Politically, Horvath was rather closely connected with Admiral Aleksandr Vasilievich Kolchak both before and after the formation of the latter's regime in Omsk. Earlier in 1918 before he went to Omsk in October and accepted the post of War and Naval Minister in the Socialist Revolutionary Government on November 4 Kolchak had spent some time in Harbin. His mission there, as Soviet sources saw it, was "to organize the Far Eastern front against the Soviet Republic under the instructions of Great Britain."[17] In the winter of 1918 when Kolchak overthrew the All-Russian Anti-Bolshevik

[14] *Ibid.*, pp. 63-64; Chu, *op. cit.*, p. 35; *North China Herald* (Shanghai), Jan. 12, 1918, p. 70.
[15] *Millard's Review* (Shanghai), III (Jan. 5, 1918), 161.
[16] J. Yavdynsky, *The Chinese Eastern Railway Problem in Contemplation of the Law* (Shanghai, 1934), p. 34; *F.R.U.S.*, *1918, Russia*, II, 156.
[17] *B.S.E.* (1st ed.), Vol. XXXIII (1938), col. 518.

(but liberal) Government at Omsk and established his own regime, Horvath abandoned his self-styled "All-Russian Provisional Government" and gave his support to the Kolchak regime. The administration of the Chinese Eastern Railway was entrusted by Horvath to his supporter and representative, Vasilii D. Lachinov. In July, 1919, Horvath was given the title of President of the Council of Elders, and returned to the C.E.R. post.[18] After the fall of Omsk to the Red Army, Kolchak headed east apparently with the hope of joining forces with Horvath and Semenov in order to revive the "counterrevolutionary" movement.[19]

As regards military activities, Horvath recruited more than three thousand White Russian and Mongolian troops in January, 1918, under the pretext of protecting the railway, but in actuality for military service against the Bolsheviks. He was warned by the Chinese authorities against disturbing local peace and order. As Horvath persisted in arguing the usefulness of these forces, the Chinese military authorities dispersed Horvath's recruits and paid them off. When the "counterrevolutionary" forces gathered strength and established a government in Siberia, Horvath again recruited more than three thousand Chinese troops. These, in turn, were dispersed by the Chinese authorities.[20]

In May, 1918, Horvath, jointly with Preshkov, sponsored a National Salvation Association, otherwise known as the Far Eastern Volunteer Corps, with headquarters consisting of four departments: military, diplomatic, civil, and financial. Horvath was to have overall supervision, with Preshkov acting as Commander-in-Chief. Horvath also proclaimed martial law in the railway zone and established five district headquarters at strategic points along the line. The Chinese authorities thereupon protested and ordered the Chinese armed units stationed along the railway to prevent the carrying out of these projects.[21]

After returning from a confidential consultation with the Russian minister in Peking, Horvath secretly recruited more than a thousand Russian troops and dispatched them to Russian Siberia.[22]

[18] *C.T.S.L.C.P.*, Vol. XVII, chap. vii, p. 65.
[19] *B.S.E.*, Vol. XXXIII, col. 518.
[20] *C.T.S.L.C.P.*, Vol. XVII, chap. vii, p. 64.
[21] *Ibid.*
[22] *Ibid.*

On July 9, 1918, Horvath announced the reorganization of his All-Russian Provisional Government and appointed Ataman Grigorii Semenov as his field commander to combat the Bolsheviks in Siberia.[23] Semenov had organized the so-called Special Manchurian Detachment with the alleged "support of France, Great Britain and Japan," and was active in Trans-Baikal from March, 1918, to November, 1920.[24] At this time Semenov had a heterogeneous army of twelve thousand, which included some Chinese and Koreans in the ranks. These forces were defeated in the Chita area and retreated to Heilungkiang. In August and September, 1918, the Heilungkiang Provincial Government was, therefore, busy in establishing examining stations, in disarming the disorganized forces, and in issuing regulations for the scattered Russian troops. The weapons thus collected from these troops had been secretly given to them by Horvath.[25]

To maintain his position in Manchuria, Horvath also sought the support of the Japanese. The full details are not known, but there is some evidence tending to substantiate the reports of their collaboration. Soviet information suggests the payment of a so-called "subsidy" to Horvath.[26] In addition, the Japanese were planning to make a loan to the Chinese Eastern Railway, which would give them, under the usages of imperialism, a basis for intervention and control. This project was defeated before it could materialize, because it was discovered and assailed by the press in China.[27] After Japan had compelled China to sign the Agreement of Military Co-operation on May 16, 1918 (later utilizing and distorting it by stationing sixty thousand troops in the C.E.R. zone), Horvath turned over to the Japanese all the barracks at his disposal.[28] During the prolonged Japanese occupation of North Manchurian points and Siberia it was generally recognized that the Japanese were support-

---

[23] *Ibid.*

[24] *M.S.E.* (1st ed.), Vol. VII (1930), col. 775.

[25] *C.T.S.L.C.P.*, Vol. XVII, chap. vii, p. 65.

[26] Cf. p. 115, *supra*; *B.S.E.* (1st ed.), Vol. LX, col. 73-74.

[27] Horvath concluded the loan for recruiting troops. Cf. Minister in China (Reinsch) to the Secretary of State, telegrams of May 14 & 18, 1918, *F.R.U.S., 1918, Russia*, II, 161-162; T. F. Millard, *Democracy and the Eastern Question* (New York, 1919), p. 309.

[28] Tao-shing Chang, *International Controversies over the Chinese Eastern Railway*, p. 95.

ing Semenov and Horvath and that they wanted Horvath to support Semenov as well.[29]

One episode involving Horvath's collaboration with the Japanese is particularly worth mentioning. In July, 1918, the Japanese General Staff urged upon the Cabinet in Tokyo the immediate occupation of the whole of Manchuria by Japanese troops and "taking over the control of the Chinese Eastern Railway."[30] Had Japan carried out this plan, she naturally would have utilized Horvath's all-out assistance. This deduction seems to be correct, especially in view of the fact that the Japanese Foreign Minister confirmed the aid given to Horvath by his government.[31] Horvath also "frankly admitted [the] guarantee of Japan's assistance" even for the possible establishment of a constitutional monarchy under Grand Duke Michael Alexandrovich in Vladivostok.[32]

The activities of Horvath at last precipitated his downfall. On January 24, 1920, Horvath proclaimed that he was forced "to assume full governmental power as regards the Russian population in the Chinese Eastern Railway territory," pending "the renewal of contact with the Supreme Ruler [Kolchak]." He was duly admonished by General Pao Kuei-ching, Governor of Kirin and concurrently president of the C.E.R., who had succeeded Mr. Kuo Tsung-hsi in August, 1919. However, Pao's protests that Horvath had exceeded his power and violated international law and treaty obligations by carrying out political functions within Chinese territory were ignored for the time being.[33]

In March, 1920, all Russian employees of the C.E.R., acting on instructions from Moscow, declared a general strike. They demanded that Horvath be dismissed before they would return to work. The immediate cause of the strike was the angry protest against the two months' arrearage of wage and salary payments resulting from Horvath's use of railway funds for political purposes.

[29] The minister in China (Reinsch) to the Secretary of State, tel., June 5, 1918, *F.R.U.S.*, *1918, Russia*, II, 189; the consul at Harbin (Moser) to the Secretary of State, tel., June 6, 1918, *ibid.*, pp. 190-191.

[30] The ambassador in Japan (Morris) to the Secretary of State, tel., July 13, 1918, *ibid.*, p. 281.

[31] Same to the same, tel., July 23, 1918, *ibid.*, p. 300.

[32] The chargé in China (MacMurray) to the Secretary of State, tel., July 12, 1918, *ibid.*, p. 279; MacMurray reported that Horvath was "deeply mixed with Japan." See the same to the same, tel., July 13, 1918, *ibid.*, p. 280.

[33] *C.T.S.L.C.P.*, Vol. XVII, chap. vii, p. 65.

The strike paralyzed the whole railway system and endangered the lives of White Russians in the railway zone. The grave situation necessitated the intervention of China as the sovereign Power. Thereupon, on March 15, 1920, Pao notified Horvath:

I have frequently pointed out that the Chinese Eastern Railway is situated in Chinese territory in which the existence of another sovereignty is inadmissible, as strife between Russian political parties creates disorders and interferes with the work of the railroad. Owing to the fact that General Horvath, Assistant President of the Board [of Directors of the C.E.R.], has assumed the functions of government and proceeded to adopt a policy of military force for political ends, the Russian railway employees have declared a strike and begun a revolutionary movement. In order to defend China's sovereign rights and to maintain normal conditions on the railway, I have suggested that General Horvath shall renounce all political power in the railroad territory so as to enable China to fulfil her treaty obligations.[34]

Horvath most reluctantly resigned through the persuasion of Yen Shih-ching, special commissioner of the Chinese Ministry of Communications. The Board of Directors of the C.E.R. appointed Piminov in his place. Meanwhile, both Russian parties were disarmed and the railway was restored to operation. On April 16, 1920, the Chinese Ministry of Communications officially appointed Horvath as its railway adviser. In November, 1920, at the suggestion of the Ministry, the Board of Directors of the C.E.R. elected Horvath as its senior adviser with an office in Peking. On December 1 of the same year Horvath was given, in addition, the honorary vice-chairmanship of the newly created Commission on the Chinese Eastern Railway.[35] These appointments put an end to the colorful episode of Horvath's "railway state" in Manchuria.

INTER-ALLIED SUPERVISION OF THE RAILWAY 1919-22

For a short period during the Tsarist-Soviet transition, the technical aspect of the Chinese Eastern Railway was under the active supervision of the Inter-Allied Technical Board, which made its first appearance on March 10, 1919. The authority of this board was derived from the multilateral "Agreement regarding Inter-Allied

[34] *Ibid.*, p. 66.   [35] *Ibid.*

Supervision of the Siberian Railway System" of January 9, 1919.[36] This agreement was signed by the Powers participating in the Siberian intervention.   It is, therefore, natural for Soviet authors to assail this arrangement as a device of imperialistic intervention to make the Chinese Eastern Railway territory "one of the principal counterrevolutionary centers."[37]

Inter-Allied supervision, in retrospect, followed the Brest-Litovsk Treaty of March 3, 1918, which put the Soviet regime at the mercy of the Germans.   Previously, Japan had solicited China to sign agreements of military and naval co-operation. She proposed to land, in conjunction with China, a force in Siberia "to check the gradual extension of enemy influence towards the East."[38]

From December, 1917, to June, 1918, the United States Government had persistently opposed the repeated French-British proposals and Japanese agitation for Japanese or Allied intervention in Siberia.[39] Considering this move as inopportune, the American attitude was that "military intervention there would add to the present sad confusion in Russia rather than cure it," and that it would be "of no advantage in the prosecution of our [Allied] main design, to win the war against Germany."   The United States, therefore, refused to "take part in such intervention or sanction it in principle.[40]

Only after the Supreme War Council's appeal to President Wilson to support the Allied intervention as "an urgent and imperative

---

[36] Text in MacMurray (ed.), *Treaties and Agreements with and Concerning China 1894-1919*, I, 82-83.

[37] Voitinskii, *op. cit.*, pp. 37-40; Lashevich, "Sudebno-Administrativnaia Reforma v Osobom Raione Manchzhurii, 1920-1921 gg." ("Legal-Administrative Reform in the Special District of Manchuria, 1920-1921") *Mezhdunarodnaia Zhizn'* (*International Life*), I (1924), 72.

[38] *C.T.S.L.C.P.*, Vol. XVII, chap. vii, p. 67.

[39] Memorandum of Secretary of State Lansing of an interview with the Japanese ambassador (Sato), Dec. 27, 1917, *F.R.U.S., 1918, Russia*, II, 13; Secretary Lansing to French Ambassador Jusserand, letter, no. 2043, Jan. 16, 1918, *ibid.*, pp. 28-29; Acting Secretary of State Polk to Ambassador Morris in Japan, tel., Jan. 20, 1918, *ibid.*, p. 31; The Department of State to the British Embassy, Memorandum, Feb. 8, 1918, *ibid.*, pp. 41-42; Secretary Lansing to Ambassador Page in Great Britain, tel., Feb. 13, 1918, *ibid.*, pp. 45-46; Acting Secretary Polk to Morris, tel., March 5, 1918, *ibid.*, pp. 67-68; Lansing to Jusserand, letter, March 16, 1918, *ibid.*, p. 80; the same to the same, letter, no. 2131, May 7, 1918, *ibid.*, p. 154; Lansing to Ambassador Sharp in France, tel., May 31, 1918, *ibid.*, p. 182; Lansing to Minister Reinsch in China, tel., June 22, 1918, *ibid.*, p. 220.

[40] Secretary Lansing to the Allied ambassadors, *aide-mémoire*, July 17, 1918, *ibid.*, p. 288.

necessity,"[41] did the United States Government reluctantly agree in mid-July to a conditional participation by contributing a small force for saving the Czechoslovaks in Siberia.[42] The American policy was explained as follows: "Military action is admissible in Russia . . . only to help the Czech-Slovaks consolidate their forces and get into successful cooperation with their Slavic kinsmen and to steady any efforts at self-government or self-defense in which the Russians themselves may be willing to accept assistance."[43]

The United States further declared that she did not expect to "take part in organized intervention in adequate force" and would withdraw "if the plans . . . should develop into others" inconsistent with her policy. Moreover she proposed that all associated in this undertaking unite in assuring the people of Russia that "none of the governments uniting in action . . . contemplates any interference of any kind with the political sovereignty of Russia, any intervention in her internal affairs, or any impairment of her territorial integrity either now or hereafter."[44] These policies of the United States, with their delimitations in regard to the joint Allied intervention in Siberia, were reiterated later,[45] and were reflected in the letter of instruction from the American Government to Major General William S. Graves, who headed the United States expeditionary forces there.[46]

The routes for the Allied expedition into Siberia were the Chinese Eastern Railway and the Ussuri Railway via Vladivostok. In August, 1918, about eighteen thousand Japanese troops disembarked at Vladivostok. Six thousand additional troops moved by way of Changchun to the Manchuli front. The Japanese were "dominating everything possible," and "making [every] effort [to] control [the] operation [of the] railways." This situation was described as "critical" by Mr. John F. Stevens, sent to Russia by President Wilson in

---

[41] The diplomatic liaison officer, Supreme War Council (Frazier), to Secretary Lansing, tel., July 2, 1918, *ibid.*, p. 231; cf. also *ibid.*, pp. 242-246.
[42] Lansing to the Allied ambassadors, *aide-mémoire*, July 17, 1918, *ibid.*, pp. 287-290.
[43] *Ibid.*, p. 288.
[44] *Ibid.*, p. 289.
[45] Lansing to Ambassador Morris in Japan, tel., Sept. 9, 1918, *ibid.*, pp. 372-373; Lansing to Ambassador Page in Great Britain, tel., Sept. 26, 1918, *ibid.*, pp. 394-395.
[46] Cited in Lansing to Ambassador Morris in Japan, temporarily at Vladivostok, tel., Sept. 26, 1918, *ibid.*, pp. 392-394.

April, 1917, to head an American Railroad Commission to investigate and advise regarding operation of the Trans-Siberian Railway and to control the forwarding of American supplies through Vladivostok. In October of the same year he was made advisor to the Minister of Communications of the Provisional Government for the entire Russian railway system.[47] Foreseeing the Japanese influence, Stevens strongly urged the American Government to take a firm stand promptly in meeting the situation. He recommended that the "railways should be at once taken under military control and [their] operation be placed in [the] hands [of] my Commission and [the] Russian Railway Service Corps."[48] The corps had been formed in October, 1917, to assist him and comprised approximately three hundred skilled American railroad men.[49]

Thereupon, on August 30, 1918, Secretary Lansing instructed Ambassador Morris to propose to the Japanese Government that Mr. Stevens be placed in charge of the Trans-Siberian and the Chinese Eastern railways.[50] In the meantime, instructions were given Chargé MacMurray to urge the consent of China to the United States proposal for handling the Trans-Siberian Railway system, including the Chinese Eastern.[51]

The Japanese Government was not enthusiastic toward the American plan.[52] In order to meet the objection of General Otani of the Japanese Army, senior officer of the Allied forces in Siberia, Secretary Lansing made the following explanation:

Mr. Stevens, as the adviser of the Russian railway administration, and the Russian Railway Service Corps of American engineers who will assist him, represent Russia and not the United States or any possible interest of the United States. I consider this point essential for, as you [Ishii] are already

[47] *F.R.U.S.*, *1918*, *Russia*, III, 183-191, ambassador in Russia (Francis) to Secretary Lansing, tel., Oct. 27, 1917, *ibid.*, pp. 203-204; consul at Vladivostok (Caldwell) to Secretary Lansing (from Stevens), tel., Aug. 26, 1918, *ibid.*, p. 239.

[48] *Ibid.*

[49] Secretary Lansing to Ambassador Francis in Russia, tel., Oct. 5, 1917, *ibid.*, p. 201.

[50] Secretary Lansing to Ambassador Morris in Japan, tel., Aug. 30, 1918, *ibid.*, pp. 239-241.

[51] Secretary Lansing to Chargé MacMurray in China, tel., Aug. 31, 1918, *ibid.*, p. 241.

[52] Ambassador Morris in Japan to Secretary Lansing, tel., Sept. 3, 1918, *ibid.*, pp. 241-242.

aware, the United States has no desire or purpose to secure an interest in the railways of Russia or to control them for itself.[53]

Viscount Uchida, the Japanese Foreign Minister, did not object to control of the Trans-Siberian Railway by the Inter-Allied Commission, but he hesitated to agree to Stevens' operation of the Chinese Eastern Railway. To overcome his objections, United States Ambassador Morris, suggested a possible compromise: Stevens should name a Japanese railway expert "and assign him to duty exclusively on the Chinese Eastern, subject to Stevens' instructions in the operations of that road."[54] This was to prevent continuous Japanese pressure "for entire control of the Chinese Eastern."[55] Finally, the supervision plan as amended and revised by Japan was agreed upon.[56]

The Chinese Government at first refused to give its assent to the Allied-supervision proposal on the ground that the status of the Chinese Eastern Railway was not the same as that of the Siberian system, as the former was within the territory of China and under her sovereignty. Governor Kuo Tsung-hsi of Kirin, concurrently president of the C.E.R., and Governor Pao Kuei-ching of Heilungkiang petitioned the Central Government for a protest against the plan and suggested that the matter be brought before the Paris Peace Conference, with, at least, a limitation of the scope of supervision in mind.[57] On the other hand, Chargé MacMurray assured the Chinese Foreign Minister that the commission would show "due regard for the rights of all parties in interest, including China."[58] Secretary Lansing also stated the purpose of the United States on the subject "without any reservation whatsoever," and expected Chinese co-operation.[59] Subsequently, a compromise was reached whereby the protection of the Chinese Eastern Railway was to be undertaken by the Chinese military authorities.[60]

[53] Secretary Lansing to Japanese Ambassador Ishii, Oct. 25, 1918, *ibid.*, pp. 277-278; Lansing to Morris, tel., Oct. 23, 1918, *ibid.*, p. 276; Morris to Lansing, tel., Oct. 24, 1918, *ibid.*, p. 277.

[54] Morris to Lansing, tel., Oct. 26, 1918, *ibid.*, p. 280.

[55] *Ibid.*

[56] Ambassador Morris in Japan to Secretary Lansing, tel., Dec. 3, 1918, *ibid.*, pp. 288-290; same to the same, tel., Dec. 27, 1918, *ibid.*, pp. 301-303.

[57] Texts of Kuo and Pao telegrams in *C.T.S.L.C.P.*, Vol. XVII, chap. vii, pp. 68-71.

[58] MacMurray to Lansing, tel., Sept. 7, 1918, *F.R.U.S.*, *1918, Russia*, III, 243-245.

[59] Lansing to Chinese Minister Koo, Sept. 13, 1918, *ibid.*, pp. 252-253.

[60] *C.T.S.L.C.P.*, Vol. XVII, chap. vii, p. 78.

The Russian minister in Peking, N. A. Kudashev, also initially protested the American plan, objecting that "the proposal to associate Chinese commissioners with Stevens infringed the concession contract and Article 19 [constitution of the Board] of the statutes" of the C.E.R. Again, Chargé MacMurray assured him that "Stevens would act in the name of Russia and safeguard her interests" and that "management of railways by him does not pursue the creation of a precedent or of any rights whatsoever in favor of America or any infraction to the existing treaty rights of Russia with regard in particular to the Chinese Eastern Railway."[61] Kudashev desired a written guarantee that "after the work of the American engineer's mission has been finished, the *status quo ante* would integrally be restored on the Chinese Eastern Railway."[62] He also hoped for an American promise "to support before the Chinese, in case of any infringement by the latter of the 1896 contract, our [Russian] protest against such an infringement."[63]

Boris A. Bakhmetev, Russian ambassador in Washington, on the other hand, was entirely cognizant of, and sympathetic with, the plan.[64] He merely advised that Stevens "should co-operate with the existing board of directors" as well as "with the administration and the personnel" of the C.E.R.[65]

General Horvath's attitude toward the American proposal was based upon his desire "to avoid personal humiliation."[66] Since the Allies would support him in this effort, he assented in principle to the American plan after several long talks with Roland S. Morris, the United States ambassador to Japan, who was temporarily at Vladivostok.[67] Later, Horvath also formally agreed to the details of the plan for operating the railways.[68]

The Agreement regarding Inter-Allied Supervision of the Siberian Railway System was finally signed on January 9, 1919, by the

[61] MacMurray to Lansing, tel., Sept. 19, 1918, *F.R.U.S., 1918, Russia*, III, 259-260.

[62] *Ibid.*, p. 261.

[63] *Ibid.*

[64] Lansing to MacMurray, tel., Sept. 24, 1918, *ibid.*, p. 266; Lansing to Bakhmetev, Sept. 14, 1918, *ibid.*, p. 255; Bakhmetev to Lansing, Sept. 24, 1918, *ibid.*, pp. 264-266.

[65] *Ibid.*, p. 266.

[66] Morris to Lansing, tel., Sept. 26, 1918, *ibid.*, p. 268.

[67] Morris to Lansing, tel., Sept. 30, 1918, *ibid.*, pp. 270-271.

[68] Morris to Lansing, tel., Oct. 13, 1918, *ibid.*, pp. 274-276.

Powers participating in the Siberian intervention.[69] It created a special Inter-Allied Committee, consisting of representatives from each Allied Power having military forces in Siberia, including Russia, and headed by a Russian, to exercise "the general supervision of the railways in the zone in which the Allied forces are now operating." The Inter-Allied Committee was to be advised by a Technical Board under its control. The Technical Board was composed of "railway experts of the nations having military forces in Siberia, for the purpose of administering technical and economic management" of both the Siberian and the Chinese Eastern railways. Allied military forces were empowered to continue in charge of protecting the railway system. The Russian manager or director should continue the general management of each railway, but the board was competent to deal with the technical operation of the railways. The agreement was to remain in force until the "withdrawal of foreign military forces from Siberia," when "all the foreign railway experts appointed under this arrangement shall be recalled forthwith."

The Inter-Allied Technical Board was instituted on March 9, 1919, and Mr. John F. Stevens was appointed as its president. The board secured a loan of five million gold dollars to improve the technical operation of the Chinese Eastern Railway and to meet the heavy demands of the Allied expedition and repatriation of the Czechoslovak forces. Aside from the financial and technical assistance,[70] the Technical Board actually served as a "watchdog of the Chinese Eastern Railway" to help preserve the integrity of its system from being undermined by the Japanese.[71] For example, on April 14, 1920, the board strongly protested against the interference and high-handed actions of Japanese troops in regard to the affairs of the C.E.R. and on May 6 secured an assurance from the Japanese Government that it intended to live up to the Inter-Allied Agreement.[72]

By January, 1920, the forces of the United States and other Powers had begun to withdraw from Siberia. Japanese troops, how-

[69] Text in MacMurray, *op. cit.*, I, 82-83.
[70] Cf. U. S. Department of State, *American Assistance in the Operation of the Trans-Siberian Railway* (Russian Series 4), Confidential (later declassified), Washington, 1919.
[71] Hollington K. Tong, "Inter-Allied Watchdog of the Chinese Eastern Railway," *Millard's Review*, XIII (June 26, 1920), 210.
[72] *Ibid.*

ever, refused to do so. For this reason, the Technical Board continued its function at Harbin and notified the Japanese that it would not cease to function until Japanese troops had left Siberian soil, since they were "foreign" in accordance with the Supervision Agreement.[73]

For the period prior to the withdrawal of the Japanese forces from Siberia, two plans were put forward: a British plan for the inter-Allied control and financing of the Chinese Eastern Railway, proposed in May, 1920,[74] and a United States project for "international conservancy" for the railway as suggested by Secretary Hughes in December, 1921.[75] Owing to China's rejection of the proposals for its continuation, the inter-Allied supervision over the Chinese Eastern Railway was terminated on October 31, 1922, by official notification to China after Japanese troops had finally been evacuated from Siberia.[76] The Inter-Allied Committee had been dissolved on October 24 and the Technical Board was abolished at its last meeting of November 1, 1922.[77]

Soviet Russian circles were indignant about the inter-Allied supervision of the Chinese Eastern Railway. The views of several noted Soviet commentators are worth citing. M. Mikhailov, for instance, asserted: "The imperialistic Powers attempted to seize the Chinese Eastern Railway after the October Revolution." He indicated that "France tried to achieve this with the aid of the Russo-Asiatic Bank [formerly Russo-Chinese Bank], the United States through the Inter-Allied Committee and Japan, by way of the 1922 agreement [on tariff reduction]."[78]

Among the Allies, the United States was charged with the greater portion of the blame. Mikhailov pointed out that "the first venture of utilizing the C.E.R. proceeded from the United States in March, 1918," and that "the Inter-Allied Committee was actually under the

[73] Secretary Colby to Chargé Bell in Japan, tel., May 17, 1920, *F.R.U.S., 1920,* I, 690-691.
[74] Ambassador Davis in Great Britain to Secretary Colby, tel., May 22, 1920, *ibid.,* pp. 691-692.
[75] Secretary Hughes to Minister Schurman in China, tel., Dec. 24, 1921, *F.R.U.S., 1922,* I, 874-875.
[76] Hughes to Schurman, tel., Oct. 27, 1922, *ibid.,* pp. 925-926; Schurman to Hughes, Oct. 31, 1922, *ibid.,* p. 928.
[77] The president of the Technical Board (Stevens) to Secretary Hughes, tel., Nov. 1, 1922, *ibid.,* p. 928.
[78] Mikhailov, *op. cit.,* p. 7.

lirection of its president, an American engineer, Stevens."[79] Voitinskii also remarked that "the imperialists, principally the United
States, await impatiently the convenient time for active intervention
at the first moment, even through diplomatic channels."[80]

Meanwhile, *Izvestiia* poked fun at Japan because she did not get
her expected "freedom of action" during the period of European
turmoil. Its editorial stated that the Allied diplomacy of "joint
action in the Far East" had destroyed the Japanese plan for the
annexation of the Russian Far Eastern Provinces.[81] While Khodorov
had pointed out that the United States had "striven for the internationalization of the [Chinese Eastern]railway" for twenty years,[82]
Liubimov concluded that "undoubtedly America prepared a project
of internationalization of the Chinese Eastern and the Ussuri railways as a counterpoise to the intention of Japan to occupy them
outright.[83]

Khodorov also indicated that "the grievous legacy" of the period
of inter-Allied supervision was "the attempt of world capitalists" to
look down upon the Chinese Eastern Railway as "needing their
guardianship, if not administrative, then, at least, financial." He
feared that all the bother over international control of the Chinese
Eastern and the Ussuri railways would be used as "a basis for the
future internationalization of these railways, i.e., for their exclusion
from the possession and ownership of the Russian people."[84] Both
Khodorov and Liubimov praised the victory of the Russian sword
that had "laid a limit to the ventures of the imperialistic Powers
in the Far East,"[85] and "liberated the Ussuri and the Chinese Eastern railways from the Inter-Allied Committee" and from "all the
blessings through internationalization by the capitalists of the property of the Russian masses."[86]

[79] *Ibid.*

[80] Voitinskii, *op. cit.*, p. 37.

[81] *Izvestiia* (Moscow), Oct. 26, 1922, p. 1.

[82] E. A. Khodorov, "Kitaiskaia Vostochnaia Zheleznaia Doroga" ("The Chinese
Eastern Railway"), *Mezhdunarodnaia Zhizn'* (*International Life*) (Moscow), no. 1
1924), p. 24.

[83] N. N. Liubimov, *Ekonomicheskie Problemy Dal'nego Vostoka* (*Economic Problems of the Far East*) (Moscow, 1926), p. 9.

[84] Khodorov, *op. cit.*, p. 22.

[85] Liubimov, *op. cit.*, p. 9.

[86] Khodorov, *op. cit.*, p. 22.

CHINESE CONTROL AND THE RUSSO-ASIATIC BANK

Not until September 23, 1920, did the Chinese Governmen[1] through a presidential mandate[87] discontinue its recognition of the Tsarist minister, Kudashev, and of the Russian consuls in China in their official capacities. Then China, in the exercise of her sovereign rights, asserted her jurisdiction over the so-called Chinese Eastern Railway zone. China's assumption of the "supreme control" over the railway itself as a trust for Russia was authorized in the Agreement Supplementary to the Contract for the Construction and Operation of the Chinese Eastern Railway signed on October 2, 1920 between the Chinese Government and the Russo-Asiatic Bank, the parent body of the Chinese Eastern Railway Company.[88]

In the preamble to the Agreement, the Chinese Government declared that, in view of its share of five million taels in the construction and operation of the Chinese Eastern Railway, of the sum owed by the railway company to China, of the ensuing political disorganization in Russia, and of its sovereign rights over the railway areas, it was obliged to take measures for the maintenance of communications and for the effective protection of the regions as well as of the property of the railway. The Chinese Government, therefore, pending such arrangement concerning the railway as the government may reach with a Russian government that "may be recognized by China," decided to exercise provisionally supreme control over the railway.

The other salient points of the Agreement are: (1) the commercial nature of the railway and the injunction against all political activities at all times; (2) the right of China to appoint, in addition to the president, four members of Chinese nationality to serve on the Board of Directors and, similarly, two Chinese members to the Committee of Auditors; (3) the equitable distribution of the railway posts between Chinese and Russians; and (4) the return of five million Kuping taels and the interest due thereon to the Chinese Government.

[87] Text of the mandate in *C.Y.B.*, *1921-22*, p. 626; cf. note of Kudashev to the Waichiaopu, Sept. 24, 1920, *ibid.*, pp. 626-627.

[88] For the Chinese and Russian texts, see *C.T.S.L.C.P.*, Vol. XVII, chap. vi, pp. 94-101; for English text, see Minister Crane to Secretary Colby, Oct. 7, 1920 (Enclosure—Translations), *F.R.U.S.*, *1920*, I, 713-715.

While the Soviet author Khodorov accused the "reactionary clique of Peking" of "securing for itself a share of right on the Chinese Eastern Railway,"[89] a White-Russian jurist, Yavdynsky, applauded the Chinese move as based on a "well justified apprehension." He added that "in the circumstances, it was not only the right, but the direct obligation, of the Chinese Government to replace the deficient [Russian] authority by its own power."[90] He concludes: "Such being the right, nothing could be said against the ways or the manner in which it had to be exercised."[91]

It may be specially noted that there was a marked absence of a timely and official Soviet protest to the Chinese Government in connection with the 1920 agreement, despite the presence of *ad hom* missions and the exchange of communications on other matters. The explanation may be found in the then prevailing situation. At that time Soviet Russia was busy in concluding peace treaties with Latvia and Lithuania, in conducting a peace talk with Poland, and in coping with General Wrangel's forces in the Crimea. Moreover, a special Chinese Military-Diplomatic Mission headed by Lieutenant General Chang Shih-lin was in Moscow between September and December, 1920, negotiating with the People's Commissariat of Foreign Affairs, or the Narkomindel, of the R.S.F.S.R.[92] Soviet Russia was then hopeful for "good-neighbor relations" with China, in order to break through the "blockade" in the east and thwart the wishes of Japan and "other rapacious Entente Powers."[93] As proof, on October 27 of that year, the Narkomindel presented to the Chinese Government, through its mission in Moscow, certain proposals concerning "the fundamental principles of a desirable agreement with China."[94]

Not until September 19, 1922, did Adolf A. Joffe, Soviet repre-

[89] Khodorov, *op. cit.*, pp. 24-25.

[90] Yavdynsky, *op. cit.*, p. 38.

[91] *Ibid.*, p. 39.

[92] I. I. Mints, "Vashingtonskaia Konferenysiia i Dogover Deviati Derzhav" ("The Washington Conference and the 'Nine-Power Treaty'"), in V. P. Potemkin (ed.), *Istoriia Diplomatii* (*A History of Diplomacy*) (Moscow, 1945), III, 113.

[93] V. Vilenskii (Sibiriakov) "Kitai i Sovetskaia Rossiia" (China and Soviet Russia"), *Izvestiia*, Oct. 9, 1920, p. 1.

[94] Mints, "Vashingtonskaia," in Potemkin, *op. cit.*, III, 3; Chinese text of the letter of the Narkomindel to Gen. Chang dated Oct. 2, 1922, in China, Chinese Delegation to the Sino-Russian Conference, *Chung-O Hui-i Tsan-kao Wen-chien* (*Sino-Russian Conference: Reference Documents, referred to hereinafter as C.O.H. T.W.*) (Peking, 1923), Vol. II, sh. 6.

sentative plenipotentiary in China, send a note to the Chinese government, protesting the calling of the "so-called meeting of shareholders" of the Chinese Eastern Railway to be held at Harbin on or about September 25.[95] This note, which was rejected by a Chinese memorandum of September 26,[96] referred to "the existing situation" as "clearly illegal and not sanctioned by any treaty undertakings"; it seems to have stated for the first time, if only by implication, the official Soviet attitude toward the Supplementary Agreement of 1920.

On a subsequent occasion Soviet Acting Representative Davtian stated more directly the Soviet position on the 1920 Agreement. In an interview with a ROSTA[97] correspondent in August, 1923, in which he explained his protest of August 2 against an order of the local Chinese authorities transferring the Land Department of the Railway to a Chinese administration,[98] Davtian further remarked: "The Soviet Government . . . considered the so-called Supplementary Agreement of 1920 between the Russo-Asiatic Bank and the Chinese Ministry of Communications illegal," because the railway "is Russian property." "The bank had no right" and "the railway could not sign an agreement without the sanction of Russia." Thus he concluded: "Any alteration in the pre-revolutionary status of the railway is to be made only with the consent of Russia."[99]

The Soviet polemic in connection with the 1920 Agreement was directed mainly against the Russo-Asiatic Bank. It denounced the bank for utilizing the opportunity to betray Soviet interests as the

[95] Russian text in *Pravda*, Sept. 24, 1922, p. 2; Chinese text in *C.O.H.T.W.*, Vol. II, sh. 59.

[96] *Ibid.*, sh. 65.

[97] ROSTA is an official abbreviation for the Russian Telegraphic Agency (Rossiiskoe Telegrafnoe Agentstvo) which served the press of the R.S.F.S.R. with political and economic information. Founded after the October Revolution of 1917, ROSTA was a section of the Central Board of Political Education (Glavpolitprosvet) up to 1923 and under the All-Russian Central Executive Committee (VTsIK) between 1923 and 1925. Before the creation of TASS in 1925, ROSTA supplied telegraphic information to the entire territory of the U.S.S.R., with the exception of the Ukraine. From 1926 on, ROSTA existed as a telegraphic agency under the Council of People's Commissars (SNK or Sovnarkom) of the R.S.F.S.R. In January, 1935, ROSTA was liquidated and its functions transferred to TASS. Cf. "ROSTA," *M.S.E.*, 1st ed., Vol. VII, col. 429; also 2nd ed., Vol. IX (1941), col. 187.

[98] Russian Delegation to the Waichiaopu, memorandum, Aug. 2, 1923, *C.O.H. T.W.*, Vol. II, sh. 142.

[99] "An Explanation of the Protest of the Representative of the U.S.S.R. in China," a Peking dispatch, Aug. 8, 1923, in *Izvestiia*, Aug. 10, 1923, p. 1.

proprietor of the railway by entering into an agreement with the Chinese Government at a time when Soviet Russia was occupied with the liquidation of foreign intervention.[100] It raised the outcry that "all the activities of the Russo-Asiatic Bank on the railway proceeded in complete contradiction of the interests of Soviet Russia and China."[101]

Joffe personally commented on the status of the Russo-Asiatic Bank and its claim to the Chinese Eastern Railway. On October 23, 1922, in an interview, he declared: If the bank pretended to be a Russian institution, then it had already been nationalized in 1918 by the decree of the Russian Government. If the bank were a French establishment, then "it did not have the right to lay claim to the possession of the railway," because the 1896 Contract provided that the shares of the railway could "only be in the hands of Russians and Chinese." He therefore concluded: "In both cases, the Russo-Asiatic Bank did not have the slightest basis to perform the role of the owner of the railway."[102]

Von Goier, a former member of the board of the Russo-Asiatic Bank, claimed that the bank was the real proprietor of the railway and demanded that the Soviet treasury show the shares of the C.E.R. Company it held, if it denied the right of the bank and made a counterclaim. For this he was, of course, denounced by Soviet commentators. In Liubimov's words, "In not a single Russian national problem had our emigrant circles, especially those near the Russo-Asiatic Bank, played a more traitorous role than in the question of the Chinese Eastern Railway."[103]

Yet, in their arguments against the Russo-Asiatic Bank (which was known as the Russo-Chinese Bank before the latter merged with the French Banque du Nord in 1910) the Soviet exponent had to admit the "two simplest formulas" or legal bases of the bank's claim. These formulas were: (1) The Russo-Asiatic Bank had figured as a party to the 1896 contract; (2) being entrusted to organize the C.E.R. Company, the bank was the shareholder of the railway Company.[104]

On precisely these legal grounds, Yavdynsky contended that the Supplementary Agreement was "an act of capital importance," as

[100] Mikhailov, *op. cit.*, pp. 7-8.
[101] *Ibid.*, p. 8.
[102] *Izvestiia*, Oct. 26, 1922, p. 1.
[103] Liubimov, *op. cit.*, p. 9.
[104] Khodorov, *op. cit.*, p. 24.

"it plainly confirms the original attitude of the Chinese Government in regard to the bank as its direct counterpart in the railway enterprise." Hence, he concluded that the 1920 Agreement should be regarded as "a formal admission that the bank remains the owner of the totality of the shares of the Chinese Eastern Railway and, in this capacity, is entitled to transact on behalf of the [railway] company."[105] This interpretation emphasizing the private character of the bank and of its agency, the C.E.R. Company, seemed to be in full conformity with the persistent attitude expressed by Li Hung-chang a quarter of a century earlier at the very outset of the railway enterprise; he also had insisted the railroad be built and operated by a private company, and had made it a fundamental condition of the initial agreement.

By signing the 1920 Agreement with the bank, China's position towards the relationship between the bank and the C.E.R. Company was clear. In an address to the Committee on Pacific and Far Eastern Questions of the Washington Conference of 1921-22, Dr. V. K. Wellington Koo, the Chinese delegate, pointed out that "the said contract [Supplementary Agreement] with the bank was entered into by the Chinese Government after it had satisfied itself that the Bank represented all the stockholders and all the shares, which fact had been certified through the French Government."[106]

In fact, the bank had exercised the functions of the shareholders of the C.E.R. Company ever since its establishment, so far as the election of the directors and auditors as well as the audit of the accounts were concerned.[107] Moreover, the private character of the C.E.R. Company and of the bank should be stressed, especially since the Russian plenipotentiary had explicitly stated at the Portsmouth Peace Conference in 1905 that the Japanese Government should sign a contract with the Chinese Eastern Railway Company for the cession of the southern branch of the C.E.R., because the railway company was a private organization.[108] Therefore, the legal standing of the bank and its relationship with the C.E.R. Company, in theory at least, should not be denied, in view of the fact that even the Soviet

[105] Yavdynsky, *op. cit.*, p. 39.

[106] *Conference on the Limitation of Armament* (U. S. Senate Documents, 67th Congress, 2nd Session, Vol. X, doc. no. 126) (Washington, 1922), p. 753.

[107] Chih, *Tung-T'ieh Wen-ti* (*The Problem of the C.E.R.*), p. 32.

[108] *Ibid.*

nationalization decree could not have effect beyond Soviet borders before the recognition of the Soviet Government by China in 1924.[109]

The Chinese Government, however, was severely criticized by some of its patriotic citizens as having taken "the wrong track by signing the agreement with the Russo-Asiatic Bank," instead of accepting the Soviet offer to negotiate for the return of the railway without compensation.[110] At this juncture, blame had also been heaped on China and the Chinese authorities of the C.E.R. "for not recovering the railway *in toto* and immediately."[111] This Chinese opinion might seem to be justified by a statement of Mr. Elihu Root, chairman of the Subcommittee of Delegates on the Chinese Eastern Railway (former Secretary of State and former Senator of the United States), at the Washington Conference:

The Chinese Eastern Railway . . . had been built and was owned by a corporation which had received its seal from the Chinese Government and was, therefore, a Chinese corporation . . . . On October 2, 1920— while the Interallied Agreement was still in force and operative—the Chinese Government entered into an alleged contract . . . with the Russo-Asiatic Bank . . . . It was manifest . . . that China, in the exercise of her sovereign rights, was entitled to take possession of a railway which had been constructed in her territory and which was owned and operated by a Chinese corporation. China had both the right and power to take such a step.[112]

The Chinese Government, during its control over the Chinese Eastern Railway, undertook a gradual and piecemeal recovery of her lost sovereign rights by liquidating certain Russian interests acquired in contravention of the terms of the original railway contract of 1896.

In the field of judicial administration, "Regulations for the Organization of the Judiciary of the Special Manchurian Region" were at first promulgated by a presidential mandate of October 31, 1920.[113] Accordingly, a high court and a district court in Harbin and six subdistrict courts at other cities along the railway were set up to handle lawsuits in this special area. Appeals might be taken to a court of appeal at Harbin and ultimately to the Supreme Court at Peking. In the meantime, however, both the "diplomatic corps" at

[109] Yavdynsky, *op. cit.*, p. 29.   [110] Tao-shing Chang, *op. cit.*, p. 102.
[111] Tsao, *op. cit.*, p. 55.
[112] "Minutes of the Subcommittee of the Delegates on the Chinese Eastern Railway," *Conference on the Limitation of Armament*, pp. 676-680.
[113] Text in *C.Y.B., 1921-22*, pp. 638-639.

Peking and the British and French consuls in the C.E.R. area vehemently protested, apparently for fear that such regulations would weaken the general status of foreigners in China.[114]   Yet the Soviet jurist Lashevich considered the Chinese measure as natural, because the former Tsarist courts, which were established not by treaty provisions but by the "pressure of force," had now "lost the previous, actual threat, diplomatic, and perhaps, military as well."[115]

With regard to the civil administration in the railway zone, China established a "Bureau for Municipal Affairs in the Special Area of the Eastern Provinces" in February, 1920.   Regulations for this bureau were promulgated by the Chinese Ministry of the Interior in September of the same year.   Thereafter the municipalities in the area were no longer illogically subordinated to the railway company but were made subject to the direct control of the Chinese Government.[116]

Similarly, during the general strike of the C.E.R. in March, 1920, all Russian railway guards and military units of the former Trans-Amur army were disarmed and replaced by Chinese troops of the Railway Protective Army, which had been entrusted to guard the C.E.R. lines by a conference of Inter-Allied Powers in 1919.[117] The monopoly over navigation, the land bureau, and other railway assets illegally acquired were also gradually taken back by the Chinese authorities in the process of piecemeal recovery.[118]

During the period of Chinese control, the Chinese Eastern Railway was under the joint management of the Chinese Government and the Russo-Asiatic Bank in accordance with the 1920 Agreement. With the selection of B. W. Ostroumov as manager, the railway began to assume a commercial character, and for the first time in its history started to show a profit—7,949,660 gold rubles for 1922, and 8,314,306 gold rubles for 1923.[119]   Nevertheless, according to

[114] Paul S. Reinsch, *An American Diplomat in China* (Garden City, New York., 1922), pp. 114, 115.

[115] Lashevich, *op. cit.*, I (1924), 72.

[116] *C.T.S.L.C.P.*, Vol. XVII, chap. vii, pp. 122-125.

[117] *Ibid.*, pp. 109, 111-115.

[118] *Ibid.*, p. 168.

[119] Yavdynsky, *op. cit.*, p. 41; he described Ostroumov as an engineer of administrative capacity.   T. V. Butov, a former assistant chief of the Economic Bureau of the C.E.R. under Ostroumov, in his interviews with the writer, confirmed this judgment, saying that Ostroumov had reduced the expenditure of the railway company in a remarkable way, and that Soviet attacks on him were entirely for political reasons.

Soviet Acting Representative Davtian, Joffe and his delegation had "repeatedly called the attention of the Chinese Government to the criminal activities of the present administration of the C.E.R., demanding the dismissal and even the arrest of the Railway Manager Ostroumov."[120] It would appear, then, that the Ostroumov condemnation served merely as a prelude to the Soviet bid for the Chinese Eastern Railway.

SOVIET OVERTURES REGARDING THE CHINESE EASTERN RAILWAY

During the period of civil war and foreign intervention within her domain, Soviet Russia could not gain direct access to the Chinese Eastern Railway in Manchuria. Siberia was for the time being under the sway of Czechoslovak troops, Kolchak's White Army, and the Allied forces; and the Japanese had become all the more aggressive.[121] At this juncture, Soviet policy in regard to the Chinese Eastern Railway took the form of anxious overtures coupled with the generous offer to return the railway to China without asking for compensation. This expressed willingness to abolish all remnants of Tsarist imperialism in China was acclaimed as a typical example of Soviet policy towards the oppressed "peoples of the East."[122] The attractive initial offer regarding the C.E.R. put forward in the Karakhan Declaration of 1919 was, however, later denied by the Soviet authorities, including Karakhan himself,[123] when actual talks between the respective missions got under way. This record of Soviet diplomacy left the impression that the original Soviet offer, purely nominal in character since the railway was not in fact under Russian control, was probably a bait rather than a genuine gesture of good will.

As early as July, 1918, before the first Karakhan Declaration was made, George Chicherin, then Soviet Commissar for Foreign Affairs, had explicitly declared: "We notified China that we renounce the conquest of the Tsarist Government in Manchuria and we restore

[120] *Izvestiia,* Aug. 10, 1923, p. 1.

[121] Chicherin, *op. cit.,* pp. 10-11.

[122] Cf. Karakhan Declaration of July 25, 1919, in V. Vilenskii (Sibiriakov), *Kitai i Sovetskaia Rossiia (China and Soviet Russia)* (Moscow, 1919), p. 14.

[123] Karakhan to C. T. Wang, Chinese Plenipotentiary, letter, Nov. 30, 1923, *C.Y.B., 1924* (Peking and Tientsin, 1925), p. 875.

the sovereign rights of China in this territory, in which lies the principal trade-artery—the Chinese Eastern Railway, property of the Chinese and Russian people."[124]

Knowing that Chinese public opinion was aroused against the decision of the Treaty of Versailles regarding Shantung, Leo M. Karakhan, Soviet Vice-Commissar of Foreign Affairs, on July 25, 1919, issued a declaration with the purpose of winning the friendship of the Chinese people and recognition by the Chinese Government.[125]   This first Karakhan manifesto, which sounded to Chinese ears as a new "diplomatic Magna Carta,"[126] referred to a previous offer to China "to start negotiations for the annulment of the Treaty of 1896, the Peking Protocol of 1901, and all the agreements with Japan from 1909 to 1916."[127]   Thus, it reaffirmed that Soviet Russia was ready to give back to the Chinese people "all the power and authority which were obtained by the government of the Tsar by tricks or by entering into understandings with Japan and the Allies." Concerning the Chinese Eastern Railway, it unequivocally announced:

> The Soviet Government returns to the Chinese people, without demanding any kind of compensation, the Chinese Eastern Railway, as well as all the mining, lumber, gold, and other concessions which were seized from them by the government of the Tsars, that of Kerensky, and the brigands, Horvath, Semenov, Kolchak, the Russian ex-generals, merchants, and capitalists.

This Karakhan Declaration, although issued on July 25, 1919, did not reach Peking until March 26, 1920, in the form of a French text of the manifesto received by wire in Peking from M. Yanson, representative of the People's Commissariat for Foreign Affairs of Siberia and the Far East, and duly "signed by Karakhan as a true

[124] Chicherin to the Fifth Congress of Soviets in July, 1918, *Izvestiia*, July 5, 1918, p. 7.
[125] Savvin, *Vzaimootnosheniia Tsarskoi Rossii i SSSR s Kitaem (Relations of the Tsarist Russia and the U.S.S.R. with China)*, p. 97.
[126] Alfred L. P. Dennis, *The Foreign Policy of Soviet Russia* (New York, 1924), p. 316.
[127] For a complete or original Russian text of the 1919 Declaration, see Vilenskii (Sibiriakov), *Kitai i Sovetskaia Rossiia (China and Soviet Russia)*, pp. 14 ff.; the emasculated Russian text appears in Savvin, *op. cit.*, pp. 96-97 and in D. Bukhartzev, *Desiat' Let Sovetskoi Diplomatii (Ten Years of Soviet Diplomacy)* (Moscow, 1927), pp. 69 ff.; official Chinese translation based on the French text in *C.O.H. T.W.*, Vol. II, sh. 1-3; English translation by the Waichiaopu was reproduced in *C.Y.B., 1924*, pp. 868-870.

copy certified."[128]   It was generally hailed among Chinese liberal circles.   It created a "particular sensation" because of "the reported offer to return the Chinese Eastern Railway to China without any compensation whatsoever."[129]

The Chinese official reaction to the Karakhan Declaration was one of skepticism at the outset, coupled with some doubt as to the authenticity of the manifesto.[130]   Thus, like the position of the Persian Government toward the Trotsky note of January, 1918, and the Karakhan memorandum of June, 1919, but unlike that of the bold Persian Cabinets of 1920 and 1921,[131] the Peking Government did not avail itself of foresight, confidence or courage to meet the Soviet "offer of good will," mainly because of the unfavorable international repercussions which would follow the opening of direct Sino-Soviet negotiations.

With the improvement of the Soviet position in Siberia, the Soviet attitude towards the Chinese Eastern Railway question began to undergo a marked change.   In fact, the offer to restore the C.E.R. to China without compensation did not appear in the *Izvestiia* news release of August 26, 1919, which contained the remainder of the text of the Karakhan Declaration.   This offer was also omitted from the subsequent Russian texts of the declaration.[132]

Shortly after China suspended official intercourse with the Tsarist minister, Kudashev, on September 23, 1920, a restatement of Soviet policy was made.   Karakhan signed his second declaration on September 27, 1920, addressing it to the Chinese Minister of Foreign Affairs.   The Soviet Government thereby declared "null and void all the treaties concluded by the former government of Russia with China . . . and returns to China free of charge, and for ever, all that was ravenously taken from her by the Tsar's Government and by the Russian bourgeoisie."[133]

[128] *Ibid.*, p. 870; *C.O.H.T.W.*, Vol. II, sh. 3.
[129] Allen S. Whiting, "The Soviet Offer to China of 1919," *Far Eastern Quarterly*, X (Aug., 1951), 356.
[130] Hollington K. Tong, "Russian Soviet Would Befriend China," *Millard's Review*, XIII (June 5, 1920), 24.
[131] Louis Fischer, *The Soviets in World Affairs, 1917-1929* (2nd ed.), I (Princeton, 1951), 287, 289-290.
[132] Whiting, *op. cit.*, pp. 356-357, 362-364.
[133] For Russian text of the 1920 Declaration, see Savvin, *op. cit.*, Appendix, p. 128; official Chinese translation in *C.O.H.T.W.*, Vol. II, sh. 4-5; English translation in *C.Y.B.*, *1924*, pp. 870-872.

As to the Chinese Eastern Railway, however, the Declaration proposed only the conclusion of a "special treaty" by China, Russia, and the Far Eastern Republic "for the rules and regulations of exploitation of the Chinese Eastern Railway for the needs of the R.S.F.S.R." Unlike the contents and the spirit of the 1919 manifesto, therefore, the 1920 proposal prescribed reciprocal conditions for China to fulfil in order to meet Russian needs. It may be that China's actions concerning the C.E.R. during this period helped bring about the change in the Soviet attitude; in the interval between the two Declarations, Russia had realized that China was not going to take over the C.E.R. for herself as a sovereign right, but would merely control it in trust for whatever Russian Government would finally be established in Moscow.[134]

The second Karakhan Declaration of 1920 was delivered to General Chang Shih-lin, during his mission in Moscow, for transmission to Peking.[135] It thus reached the Waichiaopu on Chang's return in December the same year.[136] The 1920 Declaration was received by the Chinese Government with an equal lack of enthusiasm; the Chinese leaders still preferred to recall the previous Soviet offer to return the Chinese Eastern Railway unconditionally. Because of this attitude of indifference, the railway issue was not brought up when I. Yurin, representative of the Far Eastern Republic, arrived in Peking in December, 1920, to negotiate a commercial treaty. The Chinese lack of interest was reinforced subsequently, in part because of the restraining influence of certain "Treaty Powers," notably France and Japan, and even more because of the Soviet occupation of, and Bolshevik activities in, Outer Mongolia following the White Russian disturbances there.[137] Following Yurin came Alexander K. Paikes, head of the first fully accredited mission from Moscow, in 1921. In an interview given on his arrival, Paikes declared that the more important part of his mission was the return of the Chinese Eastern Railway to China without financial obligation or any other condition beyond a promise that she would not dispose

---

[134] *Ibid.*, p. 872.

[135] Karakhan to Chang Shih-lin, letter of transmittal, Oct. 2, 1920, *C.O.H.T.W.*, Vol. II, sh. 6.

[136] Waichiaopu to Yurin, note, Feb. 5, 1921, *ibid.*, sh. 11.

[137] Savvin, *op. cit.*, pp. 98-99.

of it to any other power.[138] Paikes failed in his mission, as had Yurin, to open official negotiations with the Chinese Government, because of "the inadequacy of his personal prestige and the circumstances of international politics."[139] Yet, Paikes's words were accepted in China as further proof of the authenticity of Yanson's version of the first Karakhan Declaration.

The Chinese Government meanwhile had sent Shen Chun-shung to Moscow in May, 1922, but negotiations on the railway question did not get under way until the Russians dispatched Adolf Joffe at the head of a delegation to Peking, where he arrived in August, 1922.[140] On September 2 Joffe formally proposed the opening of negotiations on the basis of the Karakhan declarations of 1919 and 1920.[141] V. K. Wellington Koo, then Chinese Foreign Minister, demanded the withdrawal of the Red Army from Outer Mongolia as a condition precedent to negotiations. In response Joffe argued that it was against the interests of Russia, China, and Outer Mongolia to order the immediate withdrawal of Russian troops,[142] and charged that the Chinese authorities failed to prevent the "Whites" from using Chinese soil to attack Soviet territory. While issuing an order of October 27, 1922, directing local authorities to disarm White Russian bands who might seek shelter in Chinese territory, the Chinese Government wanted the Red Army to evacuate Outer Mongolia before the commencement of the conference.[143]

At this juncture the Chinese Eastern Railway question became the center of interest, because Joffe was exerting pressure on the Peking Government through strong notes emphasizing Soviet interests in the railway zone. He protested against the convocation of the meeting of the shareholders of the C.E.R. Company in September, 1932, and demanded the arrest and trial of Manager Ostroumov in November.[144] But his most revealing statement of the change

---

[138] *North China Herald,* Dec. 31, 1921, p. 887; *Millard's Review,* XIX (Dec. 31, 1921), 190.

[139] Ho, *Chung-O Wai-chiao Shih (Sino-Russian Diplomatic History)* pp. 321-322.

[140] Savvin, *op. cit.,* p. 104.

[141] Joffe to the Waichiaopu, note, Sept. 2, 1922, *ibid.,* pp. 104-105; text also in *Pravda,* Sept. 16, 1922, p. 1.

[142] Joffe to the Waichiaopu, memorandum, Oct. 14, 1922, referred to in *C.Y.B., 1924,* p. 860.

[143] *C.Y.B., 1924,* p. 860.

[144] Joffe to the Waichiaopu, note, Nov. 3, 1922, *ibid.*

in the Soviet position came in a speech prepared for the fifth anniversary of the October Revolution and read in his absence to an audience of Chinese intellectuals and sympathizers; in it he not only stressed the significance of the Chinese Eastern Railway for Russia but also indicated that his government was now ready to make its own the historic Tsarist claims upon the railway:

As the Russian people, exhausted as they are by their sacrifice in the world war and the struggle against the imperialist intervention, lack the means to build just now a new railroad branch in Russia's own territory, they must inevitably accept their own heritage of the Tsar's regime . . . . But in this issue also, all that Russia hopes for is that her interest in the question of the Chinese Eastern Railway will be understood and satisfied by China, and that necessary guarantees will be given.[145]

This address aroused the open suspicion of the Chinese public toward Soviet statements. It was coupled with Joffe's note of November 6 repudiating any inference that Russian interests in China had been renounced by the declarations of 1919 and 1920:

Russia has denounced the predatory and violent policy of the Tsar's Government and promised to renounce those rights which had accrued to Russia from this policy. But first, until all these questions shall have been settled by a free accord between Russia and China, Russia's rights in China will not have lost their strength; and secondly, these declarations do not annul Russia's legal and just rights in China. In particular, for instance, even if Russia vests in the Chinese people her title to the Chinese Eastern Railway, this will not annul Russia's interests in this line, which is a portion of the Great Siberian Railway and unites one part of the Russian territory with another.[146]

In reply to the Russian notes, on November 11, 1922, Koo, while promising to look into Joffe's allegations of corruption on the part of Ostroumov, expressed his belief that "the best solution of this problem would be the complete restoration of the [Chinese Eastern] railway to China," and requested the Soviet Government "to declare once more its intention of returning all its rights and interests in the said railway to China without compensation."[147]

[145] A.A. Joffe, "Russia's Policy in China," *Living Age*, Jan. 13, 1923, pp. 73–76.

[146] Joffe to the Waichiaopu, note, no. 419, Nov. 6, 1922, *C.O.H.T.W.*, Vol. II, sh. 83; cf. *North China Herald*, Nov. 18, 1922.

[147] The Waichiaopu to Joffe, Nov. 11, 1922, *C.O.H.T.W.*, Vol. II, sh. 89; cf. *C.Y.B., 1924*, p. 861.

In Joffe's answering note on November 14 came the first open dispute on the text of the Karakhan Declaration of 1919. He categorically denied that the first declaration had proposed the restoration of the C.E.R. to China without compensation, asserting that the passage was not found in either declaration. As for the proposal of treaty annulment contained in the 1920 Declaration, that was conditional upon China's acceptance of certain reciprocal obligations. Joffe specifically denied that any concrete propositions were made in the 1919 Declaration.[148]

Adding to the mystery of the Soviet offer, Karakhan, the signatory of the 1919 manifesto, also denied the authenticity of the Yanson text as received in Peking: "Never and nowhere could I have said that all the rights of the Chinese Eastern Railway belong to China."[149] In February, 1924, Antonov-Ovseenko of the Narkomindel again denied the offer and referred to it as a mere "misunderstanding."[150] In 1930 Savvin commented on this disputed proposal of the Karakhan Declaration of 1919:

In spite of the steps taken so that the Chinese Governments might receive the text of this note, it was *intercepted* and *distorted* by some one from among the imperialist representatives, or by the former Tsarist minister in Peking. The text of the note which was received by the Peking Government and acknowledged as a copy of it, as later ascertained, was entirely different from the original.[151]

This change of Soviet attitude regarding the C.E.R. also found expression in Chicherin's own words, more than three years after his first important statement touching upon the subject.[152] In a note dated December 8, 1921, to the Foreign Ministers of Great Britain, France, Belgium, Japan, Italy, and the United States, in which he protested the "examination by the Washington Conference of the question of the Chinese Eastern Railway" and declared himself "against any decision" violating Russian rights thereon, Chicherin stated:

---

[148] Joffe to the Waichiaopu, note, Nov. 14, 1922, *C.O.H.T.W.*, Vol. II, sh. 93-95; cf. *C.Y.B.*, *1924*, p. 861.

[149] Karakhan to C. T. Wang, letter, Nov. 30, 1923, *C.Y.B.*, *1924*, p. 875.

[150] A. Antonov-Ovseenko, "Soglashenie o KVZhD," ("The Agreement on the C.E.R."), *Izvestiia*, June 12, 1924, p. 2.

[151] Savvin, *op. cit.*, p. 97; italics added.

[152] Cf. *Izvestiia*, July 5, 1918, p. 7.

Although the Russian Government declared its readiness to hand over this railway to the Chinese authorities, on condition that China furnished certain guarantees essential to its transfer, such transfer has not taken place, and Russian rights in this railway remain in full force. Only when agreement on this question is reached between the Russian delegation entrusted with this task and the Chinese Government will those changes in Russian rights to this railway enter into force which will be laid down in the agreement, but until then these rights remain, and will remain the same as heretofore.[153]

Yet, in view of the earlier Chicherin statement of 1918 and the Vilenskii version of the text of the 1919 Declaration, as cited,[154] the marked absence in the late Soviet version of any reference to so crucial an issue as the C.E.R. appears very strange. Since Vilenskii was probably the author of the declaration,[155] and since the disputed passage appears word for word in the identical position in the declaration, both as printed in a Vilenskii pamphlet published at the time when the manifesto was first released and as received by wire in Peking, there seems little doubt that the Yanson text which reached the Waichiaopu was the authentic one, and that the offer to return the C.E.R. to China without compensation was almost certainly included in the 1919 Declaration. In his findings on this question, Mr. Whiting reached this conclusion:

The Vilenskii pamphlet has answered at least one question plaguing students of Sino-Soviet relations for over thirty years: did responsible Soviet officials offer to return the Chinese Eastern Railway to China without compensation? The answer is in the affirmative, despite the repeated denials by Soviet representatives. The responsibility of any alleged "insertion" or "distortion" rests not with Peking, not with Yanson, . . . it rests solely with Soviet officials who, between July 25 and August 26, 1919, reversed their position concerning the renunciation of the C.E.R., and then exerted every effort to conceal the fact of that reversal.[156]

While the Sino-Soviet diplomatic struggle concerning the C.E.R.

[153] Note of Chicherin, Dec. 8, 1921, text in the U.S.S.R., N.K.I.D., *Sovetsko-Amerikanskie Otnosheneia, 1919-1933* (*Soviet-American Relations 1919-1933*) (Moscow, 1934), p. 52.

[154] Cf. n. 119.

[155] Cf. *Deiateli Revoliutsionnogo Dvizheniia v Rossii* (*Promoters of the Revolutionary Movement in Russia*) (Moscow, 1930), pp. 816-817; Whiting, op. cit., pp. 363-364.

[156] Whiting, *op. cit.*, p. 364.

became more intense, a series of frontier incidents occurred along the Siberian-Manchurian border. The Soviet authorities seized the wharves, terminals, and other properties of the C.E.R., including eleven steamers, at Egersheld, a section of the port of Vladivostok. These events gave rise to protests by the Waichiaopu. Joffe, nevertheless, retorted that China had arbitrarily interfered in the administration of the C.E.R. for five years.[157]

These fruitless exchanges of angry notes, added to the Soviet refusal to honor its initial offer concerning the C.E.R. and its continuing occupation of Outer Mongolia,[158] contributed to a mounting revulsion of feeling among the Chinese. The press in China even denounced "the Soviet Government's aggressive policy as an echo of the Tsar's."[159]

While it was still believed in Peking that the Sino-Soviet Conference would be opened early in 1923, Joffe quietly departed for Shanghai en route to Japan.[160] Soviet official quarters explained that his journey was for reasons of health and announced that his duty was to be performed by Counsellor Davtian as acting representative.[161] Later, Soviet sources often referred to Joffe's illness as one of the factors in "procrastinating the negotiations."[162] On the other hand, the Chinese view of the unexpected departure of Joffe was that it constituted an admission of failure to make headway with the Chinese Government in forwarding his schemes—a failure which led him to try to reach an understanding with Japan on the Chinese question in general and the C.E.R. problem in particular.[163]

Before sailing to Japan, Joffe had several conversations with Dr. Sun Yat-sen in Shanghai, following which they issued a joint statement. Concerning the Chinese Eastern Railway, the statement read in part:

In order to clarify the situation, Dr. Sun Yat-sen has requested Mr. Joffe for a reaffirmation of the principles defined in the Russian Note to the Chinese Government, dated September 27, 1920. Mr. Joffe has accordingly reaffirmed these principles and categorically declared to Dr.

[157] *China Review*, IV (Jan., 1923), 21.
[158] Cf. chap. xiii, *infra*.
[159] Tao-shing Chang, *op. cit.*, p. 117.
[160] *C.Y.B.*, *1924*, p. 862.
[161] Joffe to the Waichiaopu, note, Jan. 15, 1923, *C.O.H.T.W.*, Vol. II, sh. 123.
[162] Savvin, *op. cit.*, p. 106.
[163] *C.Y.B.*, *1924*, p. 862; Weigh, *op. cit.*, p. 81.

Sun Yat-sen that the Russian Government is ready and willing to enter into negotiations with China on the basis of the renunciation by Russia of all the treaties and exactions which the Tsardom imposed on China, including the treaty or treaties and agreements relating to the Chinese Eastern Railway . . . . And he [Dr. Sun] agrees with Mr. Joffe that the existing railway management should be temporarily recognized by agreement between the Chinese and the Russian Governments without prejudice, however, to the true right and special interests of either party. At the same time Dr. Sun Yat-sen considers that General Chang Tso-lin should be consulted on the point.[164]

Judging from this statement, Louis Fischer's assertion, without any reference to the actual situation or to any evidence, that "in 1924, Dr. Sun Yat-sen advised the Russians not to return the Chinese Eastern Railway to China lest the anti-Sun, anti-Kuomintang Mukden Government of Chang Tso-lin be thereby so strengthened as to be in a position to defeat the Southern Nationalists,"[165] may be considered quite unfounded.

After Joffe's departure the Russian mission in Peking continued to maintain contact with the Chinese Government. On January 30, 1923, the Soviet Government proposed that in vew of Joffe's protracted illness the negotiations be transferred to Moscow.[166] The Waichiaopu replied that Peking was the negotiation place originally agreed upon between Joffe and itself, and that a transfer to Moscow would mean the interruption of the preliminary talk and further delay of the conference.[167] Davtian did not press this point and notified the Waichiaopu that the conference would be held in Peking upon Joffe's return.[168] On March 26, 1923, C. T. Wang, a former Chinese Foreign Minister, was appointed head of the Russo-Chinese Negotiations Commission. Joffe was immediately notified of the appointment.[169] In reply, Joffe with some irony stated that he "appreciated the changing of the previous Chinese policy of procrastinating the conference," and promised that as soon as he was

[164] Text in *C.Y.B.*, *1924*, p. 863; a Russian summary in *Izvestiia*, Feb. 1, 1923.
[165] Fischer, *op. cit.*, II, 795.
[166] Davtian to the Waichiaopu, note, Jan. 30, 1923, *C.O.H.T.W.*, Vol. II, sh. 131.
[167] The Waichiaopu to Davtian, note, Feb. 13, 1923, *ibid.*, Vol. II, sh. 132.
[168] Davtian to the Waichiaopu, note, Feb. 23, 1923, *ibid.*, sh. 135.
[169] The Waichiaopu to Davtian, note, March 28, 1923, *ibid.*, sh. 137.

able to get out of bed he would be happy, even if still ill, to open the conference.[170]

It became evident, however, that the impasse of the Sino-Russian parley during the last phase of the Soviet overtures, as a result of Joffe's character and illness, could be broken through only by the skilful diplomatic hand of Leo Karakhan. Because of his intimate association with the 1919 and 1920 declarations, Karakhan was particularly well suited to serve as head of an Extraordinary Mission to China. Beginning his mission in July, 1923, Karakhan succeeded in less than a year in gaining an unusual victory for the policy of the young Soviet Republic.

[170] Davtian transmitting Joffe's cable to the Waichiaopu, note, April 2, 1923, *ibid.*, sh. 138.

IV: THE CHINESE EASTERN RAILWAY UNDER JOINT SINO-SOVIET MANAGEMENT 1924-29

THE CONCLUSION OF THE 1924 AGREEMENTS

Soviet interest in Manchuria through the Chinese Eastern Railway has been basically similar to that of Tsarist Russia. As Vilenskii pointed out, "in Manchuria, on Chinese soil, there is a huge Soviet property in the form of the Chinese Eastern Railway which employs tens of thousands of Russian workers."[1] In spite of its denunciation of "predatory" Tsarist policy, the Soviet Government considered the C.E.R. as its own inherited asset and demanded that China respect Soviet rights thereto.[2] The task of the Karakhan Mission to China in 1923-24 was not only to win diplomatic recognition from China, but also to change the existing status of the C.E.R. to Soviet Russia's advantage.

The dispatch of Karakhan after the Joffe episode, in which the C.E.R. problem had been so deeply involved,[3] indicated the determination of the Soviet Government to gain, in its turn, control of the Chinese Eastern Railway. In analyzing this line of Soviet policy in Manchuria, Vilenskii declared that "Soviet Russia sweeps away all claims to the Chinese Eastern Railway, including those of the Russo-Asiatic Bank with its French protector." "Soviet Russia," he continued, "cannot tolerate a situation under which counterrevolutionary groups hostile to her possess property belonging to the U.S.S.R. on Chinese territory, and receive the acknowledgment of the Chinese

[1] V. Vilenskii (Sibiriakov), "Kitaiskaia Agressivnost'" ("Chinese Aggressiveness"), *Izvestiia*, March 1, 1924, p. 1.

[2] V. Vilenskii (Sibiriakov), "K Russko-Kitaiskim Otnosheniiam v Manchzhurii" ("Russo-Chinese Relations in Manchuria"), *Izvestiia*, Nov. 14, 1923, p. 2.

[3] Cf. chap. iii, sec. 4, *supra*.

administration." He therefore concluded that in return for a Soviet China policy based on respect for China's sovereign rights, "we demand from China respect for the legal rights of the U.S.S.R."[4]

Having made a stopover at Harbin in August, 1923, Karakhan arrived in Peking and paid his first official visit to the Waichiaopu on September 7. He notified the Chinese Foreign Minister that "his Government required formal recognition before negotiations could be opened."[5] The Chinese Government, fearing that by granting *de jure* recognition they would automatically bring into force again all the old treaties with Tsarist Russia, suggested that negotiations be opened first. Karakhan, however, insisted upon the establishment of normal relations prior to the beginning of negotiations as "a preliminary evidence of sincerity and friendliness on the part of the Chinese Government." He explained that "the Russian people has the right to demand [such] a proof."[6] In reply, C. T. Wang, the Chinese negotiator, again asked Karakhan to set a date for the formal opening of a conference so that the question of the Chinese Eastern Railway, as well as other outstanding questions, might be discussed and settled.[7]

The negotiations following this exchange of views produced no compromises until February, 1924. During this period, Karakhan "bombarded" the Chinese Government "with notes of protests" on various subjects.[8] In one of his notes addressed to the Waichiaopu in February, Karakhan warned China that "no independent action should be taken regarding the affairs of the Chinese Eastern Railway without the consent of the Government of the U.S.S.R.," and that "the existing state of things should remain without alteration." He told the Chinese Government that "even the insignificant changes would have the most severe consequences for China."[9]

By March 14, 1924, a draft agreement providing for an immediate establishment of normal relations was signed. Simultaneously, an agreement for the provisional management of the Chinese East-

[4] V. Vilenskii (Sibiriakov) "Sovetskoe Imushchestvo na Kitaiskom Zemle" ("The Soviet Property on the Chinese Soil"), *Izvestiia*, Sept. 13, 1923, p. 1.

[5] *C.Y.B., 1924*, p. 866.

[6] Karakhan to Wang, note, Nov. 30, 1923; *C.Y.B., 1924*, p. 874.

[7] Wang to Karakhan, note, Jan. 9, 1924, *ibid.*, pp. 877-878.

[8] *Ibid.*, p. 867.

[9] Karakhan to the Waichiaopu, note, Feb., 1924, summary in *Izvestiia*, Feb. 29, 1924, p. 1.

ern Railway was drawn and signed by Wang and Karakhan.[10]   It very much resembled the Supplementary Agreement of 1920, with the Soviet Government taking the place of the Russo-Asiatic Bank as a party to the agreement.

The signing of the draft agreement was followed by an impasse stemming, on the one hand, from the refusal of the Chinese Government to approve the work of its negotiator without further modifications of the draft, and on the other hand, from the objections of third countries to a direct Sino-Soviet settlement.   The Chinese Cabinet found that in the draft agreement submitted by Wang three points were omitted: the cancellation of the Soviet-Mongolian treaties, the immediate evacuation of the Russian troops from Outer Mongolia, and the consideration of the transfer of churches and immovable property of Tsarist Russia in China in accordance with the request of the U.S.S.R.   Consequently, the Chinese Cabinet refused to ratify the draft agreement and ordered that these necessary modifications be made.[11]

Upon being notified of the decision of the Chinese Government, Karakhan addressed a three-day ultimatum to Wang, holding China responsible "for the breaking off of the negotiations and the breaking up of the agreement" and "for all the ensuing consequences."[12]   In his note to the Chinese Foreign Minister, Koo, the Soviet representative warned that "after the expiration of the same time limit, the Chinese Government will not be able to resume negotiations until it will have without any agreement and unconditionally established normal official relations with the Government of the U.S.S.R."[13]

About this time, the reactions of the other Powers entered the picture.   On March 12, 1924, France, which was particularly interested in the Wang-Karakhan negotiations, cautioned China that the interests of the Russo-Asiatic Bank must be protected by any agreement between China and Russia, and demanded that the French Government be consulted in any settlement concerning the Chinese

[10] M. Tanin, *Mezhdunarodnaia Politika SSSR 1917-1924 gg.*   (*International Politics of the U.S.S.R. 1917-1924*) (Moscow, 1925), p. 84; text in *C.Y.B.*, *1924*, pp. 880-883.

[11] Statement of the Chinese Cabinet, March 23, 1924, *ibid.*, pp. 883-884; Tanin, *op. cit.*, p. 94.

[12] Karakhan to Wang, letter, March 16, 1924, *C.Y.B.*, *1924*, p. 879; summary in *Izvestiia*, March 18, 1924, p. 1.

[13] Karakhan to Koo, note, March 19, 1924, *C.Y.B.*, *1924*, p. 880.

Eastern Railway.[14] On May 3 even the American Government reminded Peking of China's responsibility toward the foreign stockholders, bondholders, and creditors of the C.E.R. as regulated by a resolution of the Washington Conference,[15] although China was not a party to this resolution and Russia was not even a participant in the conference. The Wang-Karakhan negotiations thus entered a deadlock.

Dissatisfied with this situation, the Soviet press immediately reported that "the French, Japanese and American ambassadors, using threats, demand that the Chinese Government refuse to ratify the agreement between the U.S.S.R. and China concerning the reestablishment of diplomatic relations and other questions."[16] *Izvestiia* commented that the Soviets were well aware of the fact that "the governments of France, the United States, and Japan, until now following a policy of boycott and sabotage towards the Soviet Republics, put the strongest pressure on the Chinese Government for the purpose of preventing its agreement with the government of the Soviet Union."[17]

Despite the Soviet "ultimatum" regarding the draft agreement, the Chinese Government notified Karakhan that future negotiations would be conducted directly by the Waichiaopu, then under Koo. The Soviet envoy, however, refused to give his consent to this. On April 1, 1924, Koo, in another communication to Karakhan, while rejecting the latter's "right to impose a time limit on the Chinese Government," expressed his willingness to incorporate the three points in question in a supplementary exchange of notes, "should M. Karakhan see insurmountable difficulties in modifying the preliminary text of the proposed agreement."[18]

From then until May 31, the day of signing the 1924 agreements, the public was continually informed that the impasse remained unresolved. Just a few days before the consummation of the negotiations, Karakhan himself denied through a press interview that

[14] *China Weekly Review*, XXVIII (March 22, 1924), 126.

[15] *U.S. State Department Leaflets*, "China," June 18, 1924; C. A. Macartly and others, *Survey of International Affairs*, *1925*, II (London, 1928), 343-344.

[16] "Intrigi Derzhav" ("The Intrigue of the Powers"), March 16, 1924, *Izvestiia*, March 18, 1924, p. 1.

[17] IU. Steklov, "Doloi Boikotistov i Sabotazhnikov" ("Down with the Boycotters and Saboteurs!"), *ibid.*

[18] The Waichiaopu to Karakhan, note, April 1, 1924, *C.Y.B., 1924*, pp. 885-887.

the deadlock could be broken. Even prior to this deadlock, *Izvestiia* had made the Soviet attitude clear. Vilenskii described "the Chinese policy in Manchuria and especially its application to the Chinese Eastern Railway," as one which "cannot be called other than Chinese aggressiveness against the interests of Soviet Russia." He accused the Chinese Government of procrastinating the Russo-Chinese negotiations and warned that "we have already in China the fourth diplomatic mission . . . , even patience has its limit." "One way or another," Vilenskii declared, "either the present ruler of China really works for friendship with Soviet Russia, in which case he should refrain from an anti-Soviet policy in Manchuria, or official China, if it persists in this aggressive policy, should come out with it openly."[19] The Russian press also called upon the Chinese to emulate the examples of Afghanistan, Turkey, and Persia—all of which had recently concluded agreements with the Soviet Union—in pursuing a role of friendly co-operation in relations with their Communist neighbor.[20]

After these recriminations, pressures, and announcements of impasse from the Russian side, the Koo-Karakhan agreements were suddenly signed without advance notice on May 31, 1924, at Peking. In view of the earlier Soviet strictures against secret diplomacy in any form, the divergence between the public pronouncements of deadlock and the actual conduct of negotiations behind the scenes—in which Karakhan's proposals had the support of Chicherin[21]—seems rather ironic.

The Peking agreements of 1924, which were to provide in part the legal basis for the Sino-Soviet joint management of the C.E.R. for the next five years, consisted of an Agreement on General Principles, an Agreement for the Provisional Management of the Chinese Eastern Railway, seven declarations, and an exchange of notes.[22] Despite slight modifications in some of the declarations, these agree-

[19] Vilenskii (Sibiriakov), "Kitaiskaia Agressivnost'" ("Chinese Aggressiveness"), *Izvestiia*, March 1, 1924, p. 1.

[20] "Sovetsko-Kitaiskaia Druzhba" ("Soviet-Chinese Friendship"), *Izvestiia*, March 16, 1924, p. 1.

[21] George Chicherin, "The Agreement between the Soviet Union and China," *Soviet Russia Pictorial*, IX (Aug., 1924), 210.

[22] For the Russian texts, see Savvin, *Vzaimootniia Tsarskoi Rossii i SSSR s Kitaem* (*Relations of the Tsarist Russia and the U.S.S.R. with China*), Appendix pp. 133-135; Chinese texts in *C.T.S.L.C.P.*, Vol. XVII, chap. vii, pp. 126-133; English texts in Leonard Shapiro (ed.), *Soviet Treaty Series*, Vol. I, 1917-28 (Washington, D. C., 1950), pp. 242-244.

ments were basically similar to the Wang-Karakhan draft Agreement which the Chinese Government had refused to ratify. Thus they marked a step forward in Soviet Russia's return to a position of dominant influence in Manchuria by way of its interests in the railway.

Later, on September 20, 1924, the Mukden agreement[23] was signed by Karakhan and Marshal Chang Tso-lin, Miliary Governor of Manchuria since 1911. The negotiations and signing of the Mukden agreement were initially opposed by Koo, who repeatedly assured Karakhan that the Chinese Government had sent its commissioners to Mukden to reconcile any differences with the Government of the Three Autonomous Eastern Provinces. But the Soviets thought that "Chang did not go along wholeheartedly with the Central Peking Government, which was then hostile to him."[24] Karakhan personally complained that "for four months the [Peking] agreement concerning the Chinese Eastern Railway could not be carried out because of the refusal of Chang Tso-lin to recognize [it]." He therefore concluded the Mukden agreement with Chang. Subsequently he explained that this step was "practically nothing else but the execution of the obligation which the Chinese Government had assumed, but which it was unable to carry out."[25]

In spite of the embarrassment caused the Chinese Government by this statement of the Soviet envoy, the Mukden agreement per se had an undeniable value. While reiterating the substance of the Peking agreements, it added a few important and precise arrangements which had been absent from the latter, reducing the period of recovery without payment from eighty to sixty years, providing a commission to dispose of the railway profit, and pledging both Governments not to engage in propaganda "directed against the political and social system of either contracting party." The Mukden agreement was later ratified by the Chinese (Peking) Government on March 15, 1925, as a supplementary document to the Peking agreements.[26]

[23] Russian text in Savvin, *op. cit.*, pp. 135-139; Chinese text in *C.T.S.L.C.P.*, Vol. XVII, chap. vii, pp. 133-138; English text in Shapiro, *op. cit.*, I, 279- 281.

[24] B. Semenov, "Konflikty na KVZhD" ("The Conflicts on the C.E.R."), *Novyi Vostok (The New East)*, nos. 8-9, 1925, p. 1.

[25] Press statement of Karakhan, Oct. 5, 1924, in *Russian Review*, Russian Information Bureau, Washington, Nov. 1, 1924, p. 175.

Vol. XVII, chap. vii, pp. 133-138; English text in Shapiro, *op. cit.*, I, 279-281.

[26] Liubimov, *Ekonomicheskie Problemy Dal'nego Vostoka (Economic Problems of the Far East)*, p. 10.

The Peking and the Mukden agreements of 1924 provided that a conference should be held within one month after the signing of the respective agreement and that detailed arrangements should be completed not later than six months from the date of the opening of the conference, according to the former agreement, and four months, according to the latter.[27] But the plan for calling the conference proved an abortive scheme. Arrangements in accordance with the principles specified in the agreements were not made. Therefore, the seven sections of the Peking agreement on General Principles, the eleven articles of Agreement for the Provisional Management of the Chinese Eastern Railway, and the fifteen sections of Article I of the Mukden agreement remained a skeleton outline of the basic principles for the joint management of the Chinese Eastern Railway during the period of 1924-29.

In accordance with the 1924 agreements, the Sino-Soviet joint management of the Chinese Eastern Railway was inaugurated on October 3, 1924.[28] Members of the board of directors and auditors were duly appointed. General Pao Kuei-ching became the president of the board, and A. N. Ivanov the general manager.[29]

After he had secured China's diplomatic recognition and joint control over the C.E.R., Karakhan's triumphant tone seemed markedly different from his first friendly speeches and remarks made on his arrival in China.[30] Now he said:

The restoration of the Soviet Union's title to the Chinese Eastern Railway opens up broad vistas for economic and political collaboration with China. At present the Soviet Union is gaining a firm foothold in the Far East by *occupying one of the most important positions* of which its enemies were trying to deprive it.

In addition to the *political, economic and other advantages,* the Soviet Union has recuperated, on October 3, a property which according to the most conservative estimate is worth over half a billion gold rubles. The Soviet Union can consider the restitution of its title to the Chinese Eastern

[27] See Article II of the "Agreement on General Principles," Article X of the "Agreement for the Provisional Management of the Chinese Eastern Railway," and Article I (5) of the Mukden Agreement (for texts thereof, see sources cited in n. 22, n. 23 of this chapter).

[28] Semenov, *op. cit.,* p. 1; the C.E.R. Company, *North Manchuria and the Chinese Eastern Railway,* Introduction, p. vii.

[29] *Ibid.,* pp. vii-x.

[30] Karakhan's statements on arrival in Peking, Sept. 2, 4, 1923, *Izvestiia,* Sept. 7, 1923, p. 2; *ibid.,* Sept. 8, 1923, p. 2 (summaries).

railroad as one of the most remarkable instances of return of Soviet property that was seized by its enemies who hoped to use it against the workers and peasants of the U.S.S.R.[31]

As expected, the Japanese Government was not silent after the conclusion of the 1924 Agreements. On October 4, 1924, the Japanese Foreign Minister addressed a note to Karakhan, making reservations in connection with "the rights and interests of Japan and of its citizens in regard to the Chinese Eastern Railway." Karakhan replied that the Soviet Government declined to take note of any Japanese reservations, since "outside of China, no foreign Government or its citizen can claim any rights or interests to the Chinese Eastern Railway."[32] Thus, the Soviet advantages in Manchuria, like the Tsar's, were established through the C.E.R.

Confirming this judgment, both the Commissar and the Assistant Commissar of Communications, IA. E. Rudzutak and G. Pravdin, declared that the "transfer of the C.E.R. to the hands of the U.S.S.R." had great significance in the task of working for closer relations with China. The C.E.R. had increased enormously "the Soviet political and economic weight in the Far East." "With the C.E.R.," they concluded, "our position in the Far East is considerably strengthened, while our rivals, in the persons of Japan and the United States, are correspondingly weakened."[33]

In the light of the national power and international position of the U.S.S.R. at the time, the signing of the 1924 agreements was undoubtedly the most remarkable event of the early period of Soviet diplomatic history. It marked the first significant step in the expansion into a region beyond its own borders of Soviet interests acquired through treaty provisions. Unlike the Soviet expansionist policy in Outer Mongolia and Tannu Tuva,[34] the Soviet Manchuria policy was based on conventional railway diplomacy. It may be asked, then, how the Soviet Government managed to gain Chinese consent to this line of policy. The answer lies in the fact that the Soviets took the initiative in making liberal treaty pledges to the

[31] Karakhan's Statement on Agreement, Oct. 5, 1924, *Russian Review*, Nov. 1, 1924, p. 175; Jane Degras (ed.), *Soviet Documents on Foreign Policy*, Vol. I, 1917-24 (London, New York & Toronto, 1951), pp. 559-560.
[32] Karakhan to the Japanese Foreign Minister, note, Oct., 1924 (exact date unknown), Degras, *op. cit.*, I, 460; *Russian Review*, Dec. 15, 1924, p. 232.
[33] Statements of Rudzutak and Pravdin, *Pravda*, Oct. 8, 1924, p. 3.
[34] Cf. chaps. ix, xi, xiii.

Chinese for the joint exploitation of the Chinese Eastern Railway. China was able to satisfy herself that her care-taking role would come to an end and would be replaced, for the first time, by active participation on a contractual basis in the joint operation of the railway.

DECLARED BASES OF JOINT MANAGEMENT

CHINESE SOVEREIGNTY UNRESERVEDLY RESPECTED

Knowing that China had suffered the tragic lessons of the Tsarist policy of establishing a "state within a state" in Manchuria through the Chinese Eastern Railway,[35] the Soviet Government made solemn and unequivocal pledges at the outset concerning the avowed bases for the railway partnership in order to allay the misgivings of its Chinese counterpart. First of all, it declared that in connection with the joint management, Chinese sovereignty on the railway should be unreservedly respected.

In this regard, both the second paragraph of Section 1 of Article IX of the Peking Agreement on General Principles and the second paragraph of Section 1 of Article I of the Mukden agreement read as follows:

The Governments of the two Contracting Parties declare that with the exception of matters pertaining to the business operations which are under the direct control of the Chinese Eastern Railway, all the matters affecting the rights of the national and local Governments of the Republic of China—such as judicial matters, matters relating to civil administration, military administration, police, municipal government, taxation, and landed property (with the exception of lands required by the said Railway)—shall be administered by the Chinese Authorities.[36]

Moreover, in all the 1924 agreements the Soviet Government gave definite assurance to China that the Chinese Eastern Railway Company hereafter could exercise only its rights as a carrier. It was no longer to have the extensive *de facto* advantages that Tsarist Russia had held at one time, such as the judicial and civil adminis-

---

[35] Skalov, *Sobytiia na Kitaiskoi Vostochnoi Zheleznoi Doroge* (*Events on the C.E.R.*), pp. 22, 23.

[36] Savvin, *op. cit.*, pp. 134, 136; *C.T.S.L.C.P.*, Vol. XVII, chap. vii, pp. 127, 134; Shapiro, *op. cit.*, I, 242, 280.

tration of the railway zone, the stationing of Russian troops therein, and the operation of lands, timber, and coal-mining concessions.[37] As noted in Chapter II, these enumerated advantages previously enjoyed by the Tsarist Government through the Chinese Eastern Railway had resulted in the use of all kinds of questionable practices, including the distortion of the 1896 contract to the extent of violating China's sovereignty and territorial integrity. Thus, under the 1924 agreements, the Soviet Government pledged itself, in theory at least, not to do as the Tsarist regime, according to Skalov, had done in using the Chinese Eastern Railway and the warm-water outlet of Port Arthur as pawns in a game looking to the seizure of all of Manchuria.[38]

Furthermore, according to Article I, Section 5, of the Mukden agreement, Article IX of the Peking Agreement for the Provisional Management of the C.E.R., and Article IX, Section 7, of the Peking Agreement on General Principles, the Soviet Government agreed that the original contract for the construction and operation of the Chinese Eastern Railway of September 8, 1896, was to be completely revised as soon as possible. These stipulations imply that not only those *de facto* advantages acquired by the Tsarist Government through the practice of contractual confusion in regard to the 1896 contract, prejudicing China's rights and sovereignty, but even the contract itself, should be revised completely so as to insure the new character of the Chinese Eastern Railway.

If the Soviet assurances of respect for Chinese sovereignty in the railway zone under the letter and spirit of the 1924 agreements were to be taken seriously, they would in all fairness have carried certain implications as to changes in the position and the operation of the Chinese Eastern Railway. These may be summarized as follows:

The Chinese Eastern Railway Company would no longer have the previously self-assumed *de facto* rights of political administration of its zone.

The company would no longer have the right to construct and to operate the telegraph system necessary for the needs of the line.

The income of the company, as well as goods and materials for

[37] Cf. chap. ii, *supra.*; C.E.R. Company, *North Manchuria and the Chinese Eastern Railway*, p. 398.
[38] Skalov, *op. cit.*, p. 23.

the construction, operation, and repair of the line, would no longer be exempted from any tax or customs duty.

Merchandise imported from Russia into China by the railway and likewise merchandise exported from China into Russia by the same route would no longer pay the reduced rate of less than one-third of the import and export duties of the Chinese Maritime Customs.[39]

The company would no longer be responsible for the transportation of Soviet troops and war materials over the line even directly from one Russian station to another.

The Chinese Government would no longer leave to the company "the absolute and exclusive right of administration of its lands," as had been required under Tsarist Russia's arbitrary and unilateral interpretation of the 1896 contract.[40] The administration of the railway other than for business operations of local scale would be put under the sovereignty and general supervision of China and would be subject to taxes in the same way as other Chinese state and commercial railways. (It is important to note that the rights of the Chinese Government in this respect were reaffirmed clearly after World War II in Article XIII of the Sino-Soviet Agreement on the Changchun Railway, August 14, 1945.)[41] In addition, the Agreement of 1924 implied that the rules in regard to the conveyance of passengers and goods would be framed in accordance with those existing on the Chinese railways, and so not necessarily with those prevailing on the Soviet railway systems.

Moreover, in view of the different political and social structures of the two countries, the Soviet Union was willing to meet the Chinese wishes by agreeing to record in Article II of the Mukden agreement and Article VI of the Peking Agreement on General Principles the pledge of both governments "not to engage in propaganda directed against the political and social systems of either Contracting Party."[42] Thus, the Soviet Government definitely renounced any idea of using the Chinese Eastern Railway as a political tool to interfere with the internal affairs of China.

[39] *Ibid.*, p. 25.
[40] Cf. chap. ii, pp. 55-56, *supra.*
[41] For the English text of the Agreement, see Harriet L. Moore, *Soviet Far Eastern Policy 1931-1945* (Princeton, 1945), p. 270.
[42] See Savvin, *op. cit.*, pp. 134, 138; *C.T.S.L.C.P.*, Vol. XVII, chap. vii, pp. 127, 136; Shapiro, *op. cit.*, I, 242, 280.

"A PURELY COMMERCIAL ENTERPRISE"

The conception of "a purely commercial enterprise" with respect to the construction and exploitation of the Chinese Eastern Railway had been first mentioned in the preliminary negotiations between Li Hung-chang and Count Witte. The problems of profits, bonuses, reserved funds, and losses were mentioned in the Sino-Russian Agreement of August 28, 1896, regarding the Russo-Chinese Bank Association. The same matters were more briefly discussed in the railway contract of September 8/August 27, 1896.[43] But it was not until the Peking Supplementary Agreement of October 2, 1920, that mention was specifically made for the first time of the principle of commercial enterprise as a criterion for the management of the Chinese Eastern Railway. Article VI of that agreement provided:

The rights and obligations of the [C.E.R.] Company will henceforward be in every respect of a commercial character: every political activity and every political attribute will be absolutely forbidden to it. To this end, the Chinese Government reserves the right to prescribe restrictive measures of any character and at any time.[44]

The Soviet Government now reaffirmed this purely commercial criterion for joint management of the railway in Article IX, Section 1, of the Peking Agreement on General Principles, May 31, 1924, and in Article I, Section 1, of the Mukden agreement, September 20, 1924. The text of these relevant passages reads: "The Governments of the two Contracting Parties declare that the Chinese Eastern Railway is a purely commercial enterprise."[45] This statement once more stressed the intention to avoid any recurrence of the railway's former arbitrary role under tsarism in judicial matters, in civil and military administration, in police and municipal government, and in respect to taxation and landed property.

[43] For the Chinese and French texts, see *C.T.S.L.C.P.*, Vol. XVII, chap. vii, pp. 6, 12-13; for the Russian text, see Kliuchnikov and Sabanin, *Mezhdunarodnaia Politika Noveishego Vremeni v Dogovorakh, Notakh, i Deklaratsiikh (International Politics of Most Recent Times in Treaties, Notes and Declarations)*, Part I, p. 280; for the English text, see MacMurray, *Treaties and Agreements with and concerning China 1894-1919*, I, 78.

[44] For the Chinese and French texts, see *C.T.S.L.C.P.*, Vol. XVII, chap. vii, pp. 96, 100-101; for the English text, see *Manchuria Treaties and Agreements*, p. 212.

[45] For the Russian text, see Savvin, *op. cit.*, pp. 134, 136; for the Chinese text, see *C.T.S.L.C.P.*, Vol. XVII, chap. vii, pp. 127, 133.

Also, the preamble to the Agreement for the Provisional Management of the Chinese Eastern Railway stressed that "inasmuch as the Chinese Eastern Railway was built with capital furnished by the Russian Government and constructed entirely within the Chinese territory, the said railway is 'a purely commercial enterprise.' "[46]

So far as Soviet opinion was concerned, the comment made by G. Skalov should be noted:

According to the Treaty of 1924, the Chinese Eastern Railway was recognized as a commercial enterprise to be jointly exploited by China and Soviet Russia. Certainly, there can be no ground for saying that the Soviet Government attempted to maintain for herself any special rights on the road. Both countries had complete equality of rights. Soviet workers on the road were subject to all Chinese laws. Chinese authorities in the area of the road were restored with all their own rights.[47]

It has been stated frequently in Soviet political literature that "Tsarist Russia appeared in China as one of the most wicked imperialists."[48] From 1903 to 1914 the history of the railway showed that the expenses of its upkeep far exceeded the revenues, and only in 1915-17 did the road stop demanding additional funds from the Russian Government.[49] This brief analysis suffices to show that the construction and exploitation of the railway under Tsarist Russia was dictated by motives which were political and strategic rather than commercial.

However, the Russians were convinced, as Skalov said, that "the October Revolution broke the old imperialistic Russia and left no remains; the relation of the U.S.S.R. with China, as with all other countries, is based on the principles of equality and complete independence."[50] Therefore, the apparent inconsistency between this position and Liubimov's assertion that "the return of the Chinese Eastern Railway to the U.S.S.R. acquired the significance of a paramount political factor throughout the Far East" was perhaps the result of an unintentional oversight.[51] His statement was reasonable to the extent that "the Chinese Eastern Railway is an unbreakable

[46] For the Chinese text, see *ibid.*, p. 129; for the English text, see League of Nations, *Treaty Series*, XXXVIII, 194.

[47] Skalov, *op. cit.*, p. 30.   [48] *Ibid.*, p. 26.
[49] Liubimov, *op. cit.*, p. 10.   [50] Skalov, *op. cit.*, p. 26.
[51] Liubimov, *op. cit.*, pp. 3-4.

economic link of the Great Siberian Railway," in the sense of trans-portation.[52]　But fundamentally there can be no doubt that the Chinese Eastern Railway lay within the territory of the Chinese Republic.

As is the case of the Soviet promise to respect the sovereignty of China in the railway zone, the principle of the "purely commercial enterprise," unquestionably agreed upon by the two governments, carried with it a number of implications for the management of the railway as an ordinary business agency.　When these implications are spelled out and set alongside the subsequent actions of the two governments in railway affairs, it becomes evident that although some of the Chinese higher officials were by no means guiltless, the Soviet Government particularly failed to respect the commercial character of the enterprise. Had both sides fully respected the agreed principle, the railway could have been expected to operate within the framework of general Chinese commercial laws and regulations and without any special rights and privileges whatsoever, guided by the following conditions:

The activities of the Chinese Eastern Railway should bear no political character and favor no political group, whether within or outside Chinese territory.

The accounts of the railway should be examined by the competent authorities of the Chinese Government and taxes and duties on business transactions and profits should be duly discharged on an equal footing with other Chinese enterprises, either state or private.

The business policy of the railway should be decided under the general direction of the Ministry of Communications or Ministry of Railways of China.　Although the railway should make a direct contribution to the welfare of the local community and of the railway personnel, its activities should be carried on in the light of the profit principle so as not to increase but rather to diminish the financial burden of both countries concerned.　Accordingly, the efficiency of the railway administration should be further advanced, the railway personnel should be reduced to the minimum number, and the tariff for passenger and freight traffic should be equal on all lines of the

[52] *Ibid.*, p. 10.

railway and maintain a parity relation with the rates of all other railways in China.

EQUAL REPRESENTATION AND MUTUAL CONSENT

Soviet recognition of the principle of equal representation and mutual consent in joint management was in complete contrast to the old order of Tsarist arbitrary management of the railway prior to 1917. Prior to 1917 the Chinese Government could only appoint the president of the board of directors, a figurehead. In Article V of the denounced railway contract of 1896, it is stated that "the [C.E.R.] Company will have the right to employ at will as many foreigners or natives as it may find necessary for the purpose of administration, etc."[53]

The principle of equal representation had first taken root in the Supplementary Agreement of 1920 between China and the Russo-Asiatic Bank. That agreement provided that China should have the right to appoint five of the ten members of the board of directors, one of them to serve as the president of the board. Again in Article V of the agreement: "in order to assure the satisfactory progress of operation of the said railways, the posts of the railway will be shared in an equitable manner between Chinese and Russians."[54]

The principle of equal representation and mutual consent was also clearly stated in Articles I through V of the Agreement on the Provisional Management of the Chinese Eastern Railway of May 31, 1924, which provides that all appointments of personnel of the railway, from the authoritative organ of the board of directors down to the various departments, should be based on the spirit and on the principle of equality. Article I, for example, provided that the board of directors should be composed of ten members, of whom five, including the president of the board, were to be appointed by the Chinese Government, while the other five, including the vicepresident of the board, were to be named by the Soviet Government. Article II stated that the board of auditors of the railway should be composed of five members with two Chinese auditors appointed by the Chinese Government, three Russian auditors ap-

[53] For the Russian text, see Kliuchnikov and Sabanin, *op. cit.*, Part I, p. 278; for the Chinese text, see *C.T.S.L.C.P.*, Vol. XVII, chap. vii, p. 5.

[54] For the Chinese and French texts, see *ibid.*, pp. 96, 100; for the English text, see *Manchuria Treaties and Agreements*, p. 212.

pointed by the Soviet Government, and the chairman of the board elected from among the Chinese auditors. According to Article II, the general manager of the railway was to be a national of the U.S.S.R., and, of the two assistant managers, one was to be a national of China and the other of the U.S.S.R. Under Article IV all chiefs and assistant chiefs of the departments were to be appointed by the board of directors, with this provision: When the chief of a department was a national of one country, the assistant chief was to be a national of the other. Article V provided that "the persons employed in the various departments of the railway shall represent in equal number the nationals of both the Republic of China and the Union of Soviet Socialistic Republic."[55]

All the aforesaid principles and detailed regulations were repeated almost word for word in Article I of the Mukden agreement of September 20, 1924, from section six to section ten.[56]

These stipulations, which laid down the principle of equal representation and mutual consent as a basis for satisfactory joint management of the railway, were not carried out in practice between 1924 to 1931. If they had been applied by the Soviet Government and by the Soviet-appointed general manager of the C.E.R., the development of the railway situation would have been entirely different. For example, since the board of directors was the highest organ of administration, its prerogative should not have been injured either by its members or by any subordinate officer. The directors of the board should neither have abused their powers nor abandoned their responsibilities for any fabricated reasons. In case of disputes, the president of the board should have had the decisive vote, as was later provided in the Sino-Soviet Agreement on the Changchun Railway of August 14, 1945, according to which "the Chairman's [President's] vote counts as two."[57] In addition, since the Chinese Eastern Railway was to be "a purely commercial transport undertaking" under Chinese sovereignty,[58] the appropriate authority of the Chinese Government, such as the Ministry of Com-

[55] For the Chinese text, see *C.T.S.L.C.P.*, Vol. XVII, chap. vii, pp. 129-130.
[56] For the Chinese text, see *ibid.*, pp. 134-135; for the Russian text, see Savvin, *op. cit.*, p. 137.
[57] See Article IV of the Agreement; for the English text, see Moore, *op. cit.*, Supplement, p. 269.
[58] Quoted terminology from Sino-Soviet Agreement on the Changchun Railway, 1945; for text, see *ibid.*, p. 268.

munications or of Railways, should have had the right to adjust and, if necessary, to regulate its business procedure before referring a dispute to both governments for diplomatic settlement. Moreover, the board of directors should have met as often as possible in order to reach mutual agreement on every significant issue regarding the joint management of the railway. Hence, the directors should have worked constantly on the board and should have resided at the seat of the board.

Since all documents of the board of directors had to bear the joint signatures of the president (Chinese) and the vice-president (Soviet), it would have been much better for the general manager (Soviet) and the assistant manager (Chinese) to sign likewise all the documents of the railway administration, in accordance with the spirit of fair play. Furthermore, the Chinese Government should have had the right to appoint one additional assistant manager, on a basis similar to the provision for the appointments to the board of directors, for the purpose of balancing the substantive power of administration.[59]

Since the Soviet Government had admitted by the 1924 agreements that the business interests of the railway should be the guiding principle of the joint management, it would have been logical to assume Soviet approval of the following corollaries: the general manager should abide strictly by this "business first" principle and should never act beyond his authorization. He should not relieve competent railway officials of responsibility for faithfully carrying out the duties entrusted to them. He should not discharge railway employees without adequate reasons, and should not appoint persons who did not possess the experience or qualifications required for important positions.[60]

Since the agreement of 1924 for the joint management of the railway represented a concrete gesture of friendly co-operation between China and the Soviet Union, the organization of the railway on the basis of that agreement should not have been utilized to promote sabotage of its work or separatism or to prevent the railway personnel of either nationality from carrying out their duties.[61]

Similarly, the discipline and efficiency of railway employees

[59] Cf. pp. 178-182, 182-185, 185-192 below.
[60] Cf. pp. 183-184, 185-186, 188-190 below.
[61] Cf. pp. 195-198 below.

should have been constantly improved rather than undermined by any political influence upon the whole administrative structure of the railway. In view of the joint management of the railway by two countries in which the political systems were different, it was just and fair in observing treaty stipulations not to allow any railway organization bearing any political character to play at "intrigue" or to spread a particular political doctrine to the disadvantage of the countries concerned.[62]

With regard to the equal representation of the railway personnel as a whole, it is safe to infer from the letter and spirit of the 1924 agreements that the U.S.S.R. should have welcomed an equal number of railway employees from China on the payroll of the Chinese Eastern Railway. At least, the principle of parity should have been carried out as soon as possible without wilful delay.[63]

As the later conflicts and deadlocks over the Chinese Eastern Railway showed, the basic principles for joint management, as analyzed above, were not observed in practice.[64] The Soviet pledges for genuine joint management thus turned out to be a bait to secure a momentary diplomatic settlement rather than a real guarantee for an enduring partnership pledged to respect the requirements of a going business enterprise.

SYSTEM OF JOINT MANAGEMENT

STRUCTURE OF MANAGEMENT

The structure of the Sino-Soviet joint management of the Chinese Eastern Railway was entirely different from that of the other railways in China proper,[65] and consisted of three main organizations: (*a*) the board of directors, (*b*) the board of auditors, (*c*) the railway administration.[66]

The Board of Directors. The board of directors of the Chinese Eastern Railway was an organization for making resolutions and

[62] Cf. pp. 194-198 below.
[63] Cf. pp. 190-192 below.
[64] Cf. pp. 178-192 below.
[65] Chang Lin, *The Chinese Railways* (Shanghai, 1935), p. 104.
[66] Lie Tsun, *Tung-San-Sheng Ching-chi Shih-kuan Lan-yao* (*An Outline Survey of the Real Economic Conditions in the Three Eastern Provinces*) (Shanghai, 1931), p. 43.

vital decisions. It was the highest organ for formulating the policies of the railway and for managing railway affairs.[67]

According to the 1924 agreements, the railway should establish, for discussion and decision on all matters relative to itself, a board of ten directors, five, including the president of the board, to be appointed by the Chinese Government, and the other five, including the vice-president of the board, to be appointed by the Soviet Government. The president of the board would also be the director-general of the railway, and the vice-president, assistant director-general.[68] The working procedure of the board was defined by the aforesaid agreements as follows:

Seven persons shall constitute a quorum, and all decisions of the Board of Directors shall have the consent of not less than six persons before they can be carried out. The Director-General and the Assistant Director-General shall jointly manage the affairs of the Board of Directors and they shall both sign all the documents of the Board. In the absence of either the Director-General or the Assistant Director-General, the respective Governments may appoint another Director to officiate as the Director-General or the Assistant Director-General (in the case of the Director-General, by one of the Chinese Directors, and in that of the Assistant Director-General, by one of the Russian Directors).

In the board of directors there were four sections with designated functions, for each of which one Chinese and one Russian director were responsible:

(*a*) First section: finance, education, land, medicine, and road protection.

(*b*) Second section: regulations, railway police, material, telephone, and telegraph.

(*c*) Third section: budget, revenue, maintenance, factories, general affairs.

(d) Fourth section: sanitation, purchasing, engineering, jurisprudence, savings, pensions, and awards.[69]

Under the board of directors, besides the whole railway administration headed by the general manager of the railway, there were five

[67] *C.T.S.L.C.P.*, Vol. XVII, chap. vii, p. 174.

[68] For the Chinese text, see *ibid.*, p. 129; for the Russian text, see Savvin, *op. cit.*, p. 136.

[69] Lie, *op. cit.*, p. 44.

more departments, namely: technical, commercial, finance, legal, and general affairs.[70]

As a matter of fact, the chiefs of all the aforesaid four sections and five departments were Russian, and only the assistants were Chinese. Moreover, most of the advisers and secretaries were Russians.[71]

Besides handling the various functions of the board itself, the function of the board of directors, as provided in Articles III, IV, VII, VIII, and IX of the Agreement for Provisional Management and also in Article I of the Mukden agreement, may be stated as follows:

(1) Personnel control: The board of directors had the right to appoint and dismiss the general manager and the two assistant managers, the chiefs and vice-chiefs of the various departments, and the heads of their subdivisions. The board was to decide the scope of the respective competence and duties of the general manager and assistant managers, and supervise them in the discharge of their duties. The board was to direct the work and examine the achievements of the general manager, the assistant managers, and the chiefs of various departments.[72]

(2) Financial control: The board was to examine and pass annually on the estimates and budgets of the railway at a joint meeting of the board of directors and the board of auditors. The board of directors was also to consult the board of auditors in deciding on the annual placing of important construction and other large-scale purchases.[73] The board of directors was to hold all the net profits of the railway pending a final settlement, in a joint commission, of the question of its distribution between China and the U.S.S.R.

(3) Jurisdictional control: The board was to issue all kinds of directives and instructions for the operation of the railway.[74] The most urgent task of the board after its establishment was, in accordance with the Peking and the Mukden agreements of 1924, to revise the statutes of the Chinese Eastern Railway Company as soon as possible. These had been approved on December 4, 1896, by the Tsarist Government alone. This revision, in any case, was to reach

---

[70] *Ibid.*   [71] *Ibid.*

[72] *Ibid.*, p. 43.   Kung-Shang-Fong-Wen-Chu, *Chung-Tung-T'ieh-Lu Wen-t'i* (*The Question of the Chinese Eastern Railway*) (Shanghai, 1929), pp. 16-17.

[73] *Ibid.*   [74] *Ibid.*

completion no later than six months, by the Peking agreement, or four months, by the Mukden agreement, from the date of the constitution of the board of directors.[75]

During the period of joint management the presidents of the board were successively Liu Shan-chin, Yui Chun-han, and Lu Junghuan; the vice-presidents were successively V. P. Pozdeev, L. A. Savrasov, M. M. Lashevich, and V. G. Chirkin.[76]

The Board of Auditors. The board of auditors was the highest organ of supervision and control of the railway.[77] According to Article II of the Agreement for the Provisional Management of the C.E.R. and Article I, Section 7, of the Mukden agreement, the railway was to establish a board of auditors composed of five persons, namely, two Chinese auditors, to be appointed by the Chinese Government, and three Russian auditors, to be appointed by the Soviet Government. The president of the board of auditors was to be elected from the Chinese auditors.[78]

Under the board of auditors there was a control bureau with a chief controller and an assistant controller at its head. In turn, under the control bureau there were three departments: (1) the Secretariat Office, (2) the Revenue Department, with two subdivisions, and (3) the Expenses Department, with three subdivisions.[79]

The chief controller was a Chinese. The assistant controller was

[75] From Oct. 3, 1924, the very beginning of the Sino-Soviet joint management, the first president of the board of directors of the Chinese Eastern Railway was General Pao Kuei-ching, the first vice-president, L. P. Serebriakov; the deputy-to-the-president, Yuan Chi-Kai, the deputy to the vice-president, I. M. Rakitin; the Chinese members were Pan Sing-yuan, Liu Chun-huan, and Liu Chang; the Soviet members were N. K. Klishko and S. I. Danilevsky. For the Chinese text, see *C.T.S.L.C.P.*, Vol. XVII, chap. vii, pp. 130, 135; for the Russian text, see Savvin, *op. cit.*, p. 128.

[76] In the latter part of joint management, the president of the board was Lu Jung-huan; the vice-president, V. G. Chirkin; deputy to the president, Ho Fu-mien; deputy to the vice-president, A. E. Gekker; Chinese members of the board—Pan Tsi-kuang, Li Shao-keng, and Wang Hung-shang; Soviet members—S. I. Danilevsky, S. M. Izmailov, and I. O. Chumanenko. As to other higher executive staffs of the board, the acting manager of the General Affairs Department was Hsia Chung-ji; the Legal Department, V. A. Fiakznovskii; and the Technical Department, V. K. Kalembanovskii. The manager of the Financial Department was A. M. Chizhevskii; and that of the Commercial Department, M. P. Kurenkov.

[77] Cf. *C.T.S.L.C.P.*, Vol. XVII, chap. vii, p. 135.

[78] For the Chinese text, see *ibid.*, pp. 129, 135; for the Russian text, see Savvin, *op. cit.*, p. 137.

[79] See graph in Lie, *op. cit.*, p. 42; and that in *Chung-Tung-T'ieh-Lu Wen-t'i*, p. 10.

a Russian. They examined the accounts according to the resolutions of the board of auditors regarding budget and provisional disbursement. There were more than ten Russian and four or five Chinese inspectors under them.[80]

As to the authority of the board of auditors, in addition to the examination of the annual budgets and estimates for the railway, the board was to appoint the chief controller and the assistant controller of the control bureau, the chiefs of its subordinate departments, their subdivisions, as well as the inspectors.[81]

The Chinese Government, for its part, established the Tupan Office (Office of Director-General) as the highest control organ of the railway; under this there were counselors, secretary-general, advisers, and other personnel, along with the divisions of general affairs, administration, accounting, etc. The Russians at first did not recognize the Tupan Office, but then tacitly consented to its existence after the removal of A. N. Ivanov as general manager.[82]

The Railway Administration. The railway administration was the executive organization of the railway. Its functions were to act on the policies of the board of directors and to be responsible to it for the daily, routine affairs of the railway.[83] A general manager and two assistant managers were at the head of the administration.[84]

According to Article III of the Agreement for the Provisional Management of the C.E.R. and Article I, Section Eight, of the Mukden agreement, the railway was to have a general manager, who should be a Soviet citizen, and two assistant managers, one to be a Soviet citizen, the other to be a Chinese citizen. These officers were to be appointed by the board of directors, and their appointments confirmed by their respective governments. The rights and duties

[80] Lie, *op. cit.*, p. 44.

[81] *Ibid.* During the period of joint management, the presidents of the board of auditors were successively Chen Han, Lieutenant General Chang Shu (acting president), and Liu Tse-jung; the members of the board were C. S. Znamensky, Chang Shu, I. I. Stavetsky, and S. L. Kosiura. The chief controllers of the Control Bureau were successively Liu Tse-jung and Liu Wen. The assistant controller was P. V. Erikin (The C.E.R. Company, *Statisticheskii Ezhegodnik* [*Statistical Yearbook*], p. 7).

[82] Lie, *op. cit.*, p. 45.

[83] *Ibid.*, p. 43; *C.T.S.L.C.P.*, Vol. XVII, chap. vii, pp. 74-75; *Chung-Tung-T'ieh-Lu Went-t'i*, pp. 17-18.

[84] *Chung-Tung-T'ieh-Lu Went-t'i*, p. 17.

of the general manager and assistant managers were to be defined by the board of directors.[85]

The general manager was primarily responsible to the board of directors for all affairs of the administration. He could appoint, dismiss, or transfer those officers of the various departments and subdivisions of the railway administration whose salary was less than 4,200 rubles a year. He might sanction construction work which cost less than 50,000 rubles, or with a contract for less than one year's period. He could also approve the agreements, orders and purchases, but the amount of disbursement was not to exceed ten thousand Chinese dollars. Besides the above-mentioned, all the general management of the railway administration was within the competence of the general manager. All important correspondence of the railway administration forwarded to the board of directors was to be signed by the general manager or by the Chinese and Soviet assistant managers acting as his deputy.[86]

Under the railway administration, there were eighteen departments (including one bureau), as well as commercial schools and a meteorological bureau. All these departments and affiliated institutes were divided so as to be under direct control of the Soviet general manager, the Chinese assistant manager, and the Soviet assistant managers respectively.

Under the Soviet general manager were the following four departments: commercial, general affairs, legal, and accounting, plus a bureau of commercial investigation.

Under the Chinese assistant manager were the following five departments: audit and revenue, telegraph, printing, pension, and Russo-Chinese secretariat.

Under the Soviet assistant manager were the following eight departments: maintenance of the way, traffic, motive power, material, medical, land, veterinary surgeon, and housing, plus commercial schools and a meteorological bureau.[87]

Within each department there were several subdivisions, the number of which was to be determined in accordance with the actual needs of the department concerned.[88]

---

[85] For the Russian text, see Savvin, *op. cit.*, p. 136; for the Chinese text, see *C.T.S.L.C.P.*, Vol. XVII, chap. vii, pp. 129, 135.

[86] *C.T.S.L.C.P.*, Vol. XVII, chap. vii, pp. 174-175; *Chung-Tung-T'ieh-Lu Wen-t'i*, pp. 17-18.

[87] Lie, *op. cit.*, pp. 43-44. *Chung-Tung-T'ieh-Lu Wen-t'i*, p. 16.

[88] *Ibid.*

According to treaty stipulations, the chiefs and the assistant chiefs of the various departments were to be appointed by the board of directors. If the chief of a department was a Soviet citizen, the assistant chief should be a Chinese citizen, and vice versa.[89] Because of the vague wording of this clause in the Peking and the Mukden agreements, most of the chiefs of the various departments were actually Russian.[90] Moreover, in an overwhelming number of cases, when the chief of a department was a Russian, his assistants were one Chinese and one Russian. However, when the chief of a department was a Chinese, both his assistants were Russian. This point was indicated by Mr. Lie as an unfair situation which allowed the Russians to monopolize the authority of the railway administration.[91]

As a matter of fact, during the first years of Sino-Soviet joint management, there were five departments with a Russian chief over one Chinese and one Russian assistant: general affairs, material, commercial, traffic, and motive powers. There were seven departments with a Russian chief and a Chinese assistant: legal, accounting, land, Russo-Chinese secretariat, telegraph, pension, and the bureau of economic investigation. Only two departments had a Chinese chief and a Russian assistant: medical and maintenance of the way.[92]

[89] For the Chinese text, see *C.T.S.L.C.P.*, Vol. XVII, chap. vii, pp. 130, 135; for the Russian text, see Savvin, *op. cit.*, p. 137.

[90] Kan Chin, "Chung-tun-t'ieh-lu chih kuo-ch'u hsien-tsai chi chiang-lai" ("The Past, Present, and Future of the Chinese Eastern Railway"), *Eastern Miscellany*, Vol. XXII, no. 7 (April, 1925), p. 62.

[91] *Ibid.;* Lie, *op. cit.*, p. 44.

[92] Kan, *op. cit.*, p. 62. In the later years of the joint management, the higher executive officers of the railway administration were as follows: general manager, A. I. Emshanov, replacing the previous general manager A. N. Ivanov; Soviet assistant manager, A. A. Eismont; Chinese assistant manager Kuo Tsun-sin; secretary, N. G. Horkov; manager of the General Affairs Department, V. P. Kniazev; managers of traffic, motive power, telegraph, commercial, printing, and housing were respectively E. N. Voitov, A. H. Kalina, A. A. Zateplinsky, A. A. Neopihanov, Chang Yuen-nei, and C. G. Krinsky. The acting managers of the maintenance of the way, material, audit and revenue, land, pension, and Russo-Chinese secretariat departments were respectively Tu Wei-tsin, V. E. Popiel, M. U. Ilinsky, M. K. Gordeev, and concurrently Ho Hsiao-juan, A. A. Sokolov, and Tsai Jung-chang. The acting managers of the Economic Bureau were G. N. Diky and I. Li-chun. The manager of the Rationalization Bureau was M. V. Prianichnikov, and that of the Meteorological Bureau, P. A. Pavlov. The chief accountant was N. A. Pekarsky; the chief medical officer, Wei, Li-kun; the chief veterinary surgeon, A. S. Meshchersky; the acting chief jurisconsult, Tsao Sin. The acting director of Harbin Commercial Schools was N. G. Kozhevnikov; the director of the Central Library of the Railway, N. V. Ustrialov (*Statisticheskii Ezhegodnik*, p. 8).

There was a Conference of Railway Administration, consisting of the following members: general manager, assistant managers, chiefs of various departments and their subdivisions, and the chief controller or their assistants. The function of the conference was to discuss and decide certain business questions of the railway which were beyond the competence of the general manager regarding certain estimates, budgets, contracts, etc. Its position was considered to be in between the board of directors and the railway administration.[93]

The questions to be discussed in the Conference of the Railway Administration were as follows: (1) the projected budget of the revenue and disbursement of the railway and its affiliated enterprises, as well as that of special disbursement. (2) Any individual cases with a budget over $25,000. Cases with a budget over $200,000 were to be passed on by a resolution of the board of directors. (3) Annual estimates of railway transactions. If the estimates were made in accordance with special disbursement, they were to be first presented to the board of directors. (4) All disbursements not designated in the budget, outlay in excess of the business budget and not in conformity with the previous resolutions, and necessary subsequent increases in the budget of a single work or purchase of materials. (5) The examination of any contract regarding a project to be completed within a three years' limit. There was no limit to the number of the contracts, save any made in the resolutions of the board of directors.[94]

There were many affiliated organizations under the control of the railway administration and its various departments:

(1) Under the commercial department: (*a*) 30 commercial agencies (including 12 branches), (*b*) a grand hotel, (*c*) soybeans preservation agency, (*d*) resorts (all directed by the subdivision of auxiliary enterprises of the department).[95]

(2) Under the medical department: (*a*) six hospitals, (*b*) three medical stations, (*c*) warehouses for medical materials, (*d*) the hospital for mental diseases, (*e*) quarantine stations, etc.

(3) Under the land department: (*a*) three vegetable gardens,

[93] *Chung-Tung-T'ieh-Lu Wen-t'i*, p. 18; Lie, *op. cit.*, p. 174.

[94] *C.T.S.L.C.P.*, Vol. XVII, chap. vii, p. 174; *Chung-Tung-T'ieh-Lu Wen-t'i*, p. 19.

[95] Lie, *op. cit.*, p. 45.

(*b*) the agricultural laboratories, (*c*) lending services of agricultural machines.

(4) Under the veterinary department: (*a*) the Hailar wool-washing factory, (*b*) eight veterinary quarantine services, (*c*) kumys dairies.

(5) Under the material department: the Chalainor coal mines.[96]

(6) Under the motive power department: (*a*) the central factory, (*b*) ten railroad repair shops.

(7) Under the telegraph department: (*a*) the Harbin central telegraph office, (*b*) the autonomous telephone exchange, (*c*) the telegraph and telephone factory. (The telegraph and telephone were later, in 1927-28, restored to Chinese management by action of the Chinese Government.)

Other affiliated organizations under the railway administration included several commercial schools, meteorological observatories, etc.[97]

There were many other types of affiliated organizations embracing all railway officers and workers, including (1) co-operatives, (2) libraries, and (3) clubs. The consumers' co-operatives of the railway were established in 1919. By April 1, 1926, membership totaled 6,655. The capital of the co-operatives consisted of Ch$ 61,700 received from sale of shares, Ch$ 63,100 basic capital, Ch$ 43,000 by common accumulation, and Ch$ 130,000 from the Chinese Eastern Railway loan. The head office of the co-operatives was in Harbin, and thus were branch offices at various stations along the railway line. The co-operatives maintained as well four store cars. The central library of the railway was founded in Harbin in 1925 by reorganizing the former railway club library. It was the largest library in Manchuria, with 120,000 books in Russian and other European languages and 20,000 volumes in the Chinese language.[98] There were also libraries in the commercial and other schools affiliated with the Chinese Eastern Railway. Besides, there were three car libraries going back and forth along the lines. The railway clubs

---

[96] *Ibid.*, pp. 45-46; *North Manchuria and the Chinese Eastern Railway*, pp. 448-449.

[97] Lie, *op. cit.*, p. 46.

[98] "Manchzhuriia i K.V.Zh.D." ("Manchuria and the C.E.R."), *Vestnik Man'chzhurii* (*Manchuria Monitor*) (*Harbin*), no. 6, 1928, p. 3.

were established wherever major stations were located: four clubs in Harbin, eight clubs along the western line (from Harbin to Manchuli), seven along the eastern line (from Harbin to Suifenho), and three along the southern line (from Harbin to Changchun).[99]

FINANCIAL SYSTEM

Earnings and Disbursements.   In the Agreements regarding Sino-Soviet joint management of the C.E.R., the stipulations concerning earnings and disbursements of the railway were provisional and ambiguous.   They provided that the net profits of the railway should be held by the board of directors pending a final settlement of its distribution.[100]   But the principle was certain, as Skalov suggested, that "the pure profits shall be divided into two parts on a 50-50 basis."[101]

The earnings of the railway were deposited in the Soviet-owned Dal'bank (the Far Eastern Bank), and were thus removed from Chinese surveillance.[102]   Finally, in August, 1927, after repeated futile efforts on the part of China, the Commissioner of the Special District of the C.E.R., in the name of the Government of Three Eastern Provinces, issued an order to two railway inspectors for drastic action.   Leading a group of police officers and men to the Dal'bank, the inspectors withdrew five million rubles of the total deposit of twenty-five million rubles, US$ 1,600,000 and Ch$ 220,000 and deposited it in the Harbin branch of the official bank of Three Eastern Provinces.[103]

In 1927 Lu Jung-huan, then president of the board of directors, began to negotiate with the Russians on an arrangement for settling the accounts of railway income every five days and for depositing the earnings in the banks respectively designated by China and the U.S.S.R.   Thereafter, it became the practice to entrust the earnings nominally to the board of directors.   As a matter of fact, the cashier was Russian; the Chinese had nothing to do with the daily account

[99] Lie, *op. cit.*, p. 45; *Chung-Tung-T'ieh-Lu Wen-t'i*, pp. 20-21.
[100] For the Chinese text, see *C.T.S.L.C.P.*, Vol. XVII, chap. vii, pp. 130, 135; for the Russian text, see Savvin, *op. cit.*, pp. 137-138.
[101] Skalov, *op. cit.*, p. 30.
[102] It was estimated by Skalov that the total income of the railway in 1924 constituted only 37 million rubles, and in 1928, the amount was raised to 65 million rubles, i.e., almost double (*op. cit.*, p. 46).
[103] Lie, *op. cit.*, p. 46.

of railway earnings and disbursement in spite of the superficial symbol of having a Chinese at the head of the control bureau.[104]

The procedure of railway disbursement required, theoretically, (1) conformity with the rules of budgetary control, (2) sanction of the board of directors, and (3) supervision of the control bureau. The Soviet general manager of the railway was often charged with exceeding his authority, overdrawing money, ignoring the disapproval of the control bureau, and misappropriation. The Soviet general manager in turn often sought justification for his "unbusinesslike action" in the outdated statutes of Tsarist times which were unsuitable for Sino-Soviet joint management.[105]

Currency System. For the many money transactions necessary in the operation of the C.E.R., a currency system using both the Chinese dollar and the gold ruble was established. At first Chinese dollars were accepted by the C.E.R. only in accordance with Order no. 170 issued by the Board of Directors in May, 1920. Permitting half of the payment to be made in Russian banknotes, the order demanded the other half of the payment "in Russian gold or silver coins or full-valued Chinese dollars."[106] No scale of exchange rate between tariff rubles and Chinese full-valued dollars was fixed at that time. The rate of exchange was later announced as one full-valued dollar and ten cents to one tariff gold ruble. By order of the C.E.R. on December 30, 1920, the whole payment was permitted to be made in gold rubles or Chinese full-valued dollars, and the rate of exchange was set at ninety Chinese cents for one tariff gold ruble.[107]

Beginning April 15, 1924, Chinese dollars were also accepted for local traffic, baggage, and freight at the rate of 100 gold rubles to 107 dollars. This rate was for a long time close to the actual exchange ratio between the gold ruble and the dollar, but, beginning with 1926, the dollar exchange dropped, and the railway was said to suffer losses by this inflexible rate.[108] It was estimated that the earnings

[104] *Ibid.*

[105] Hollington K. Tong, *Facts about the Chinese Eastern Railway Situation* (Harbin, 1929), pp. 10, 11, 12.

[106] A. I. Pogrebetsky, "Osnovy Tarifov na KVZhD—'Zoloto ili Serebro'?" ("Basic Tariff Rates on the C.E.R.—'Gold or Silver'?"), *Vestnik Man'chzhurii (Manchuria Monitor)*, no. 5, 1926, p. 7.

[107] *Ibid.*

[108] "Kommercheskaia politika KVZhD za 25 let" ("Commercial Policy of the C.E.R. during 25 years"), *Vestnik Man'chzhurii (Manchuria Monitor)*, no. 6, 1928, p. 7.

of the railway were thus reduced by 10 per cent and the net operating profit by almost 25 per cent.[109]

During the period of Sino-Soviet joint management of the railway, the bookkeeping and accounting unit in all direct traffic remained the gold ruble. In all traffic except local traffic the dollar was accepted at the buying rate advertised by the railway.[110]

One of the most controversial disputes between the Chinese president and the directors of the railway on one hand and the Russians on the other was the question of the tariff calculation or basic rate on the railway.

In the mind of the Chinese, all tariff calculations should have been tabulated in Chinese dollars. There were several basic reasons for giving serious consideration to this point of view: (1) The refusal to use Chinese dollars on the C.E.R.—which, after all, did traverse Chinese territory—was a violation of the sovereignty of the Chinese Republic. (2) Eighty-five per cent of the railway's expenditures were made in Chinese dollars. (3) No losses had been incurred by fixing the tariff on local traffic in dollars. (4) There was no agreed basis for equating all the local currency receipts of the railway with world gold-standard rates. If necessary, up to 15 per cent of the railway's expenditures could be made in a hard currency based on gold. (5) Soviet persistence in calculating income and expenditure in gold rubles contradicted the fundamental principle of free operation of the local national currency, that is, the Chinese dollar.[111]

The Russian standpoint in this respect was stated by Pogrebetsky in the following points: (1) Calculation on the basis of gold ruble was in no way designed to violate the principle of sovereignty, or to infringe on the currency system of China; "the railway authorities must take measures to guarantee maximum advantage of Chinese currency as well as faithfully respect it."[112] (2) To change from a gold basis of calculation to a silver one could mean complete destruction of the commercial interest of the railway. (3) Calculation in

[109] A. E. Groshenin, "Kommercheskaia rabota KVZhD za 1928 g." ("Commercial Task of the C.E.R. in 1928"), *Vestnik Man'chzhurii* (*Manchuria Monitor*) nos. 7-8, 1929, p. 15.

[110] "Kommercheskaia politika KVZhD za 25 let" ("Commercial Policy of the C.E.R. during 25 Years"), *Vestnik Man'chzhurii* (*Manchuria Monitor*), no. 6 1928, p. 7.

[111] Pogrebetsky, *op. cit.*, pp. 10-11.   [112] *Ibid.*, pp. 12, 17.

gold rubles would guarantee the interests of the railway employees in a stable budget. (4) The railway authorities should not commit the enterprise to a commercially disadvantageous basis of calculation.[113]

As a result of this abstract-gold-ruble currency system on the C.E.R., however, Chinese merchants suffered and the Chinese currency system became confused. The Chinese Government resented this situation deeply.[114] In February, 1928, Marshal Chang Tso-lin issued an order to Chang Huan-hsiang, then Commissioner of the Special District of the C.E.R., that thereafter all income of the railway should be calculated in Chinese dollars, in accordance with the exchange rate fixed by the railway. Because of repeated Russian objections, these Chinese measures were not entirely accepted up to the end of the period of joint management now under review.[115]

Tariff System. A new tariff system for goods transported by the C.E.R. was ratified by the board of directors on April 15, 1926, and it was ordered by the board that it be put in force not later than January 1, 1927. At that time the old tariff, which had been in effect since 1913 and had undergone numerous amendments, was to be annulled.[116]

The fundamental principles which were included in the new tariff system were as follows: (1) The revision of the tariff was to be carried out in accordance with the rules for passenger traffic and for shipping goods and luggage along the C.E.R. (2) The Chinese Eastern Railway being a purely commercial enterprise dependent for its maintenance exclusively on its own resources, the sole objective of the new tariff was to increase the revenue of the enterprise. (3) The tariff should be conducive to the development of distant and transit shipments to which the differential tariff system would be applied. (4) The question of special tariffs should be taken up, and the number of these should be reduced as much as possible. All the principles enumerated above were approved by the tariff committee of the board of directors.[117]

[113] *Ibid.*, pp. 11-17.
[114] Lie, *op. cit.*, p. 46.   [115] *Ibid.*
[116] V. N. Kasatkin, "Novyi Tarif Mestnogo Soobshcheniia KVZhD" ("New Tariff of Local Traffic on the C.E.R."), *Vestnik Man'chzhurii* (*Manchuria Monitor*), no. 10, 1926, p. 20.
[117] *Ibid.*

In contrast to the old tariff, which consisted of about ninety different classes and more than forty special tariffs, the new tariff was composed of nineteen fundamental classes and about seventeen special tariffs. Two of the special tariffs for shipments of horses and cattle could not properly be called special, as they could not be inserted in the general tariff tables. The remaining fifteen were created with a view to assisting local industry in shipping certain commodities such as sugar, sugar beets, rice flour, grain products, beans, blocks, veneer, paints, fire clay, iron ore, steel, tin, cast iron, petroleum products, mineral waters, etc.[118]

The entire new tariff system greatly facilitated the work of the railway by reducing the number of classes and special tariffs and by abolishing the coefficient system and obligatory additional fees.[119]

DEADLOCKS IN JOINT MANAGEMENT

As Semenov said, "almost at the very time of the transfer of the Chinese Eastern Railway to the joint management of the U.S.S.R. and China, conflicts began." He pointed out that "on the Chinese Eastern Railway, conflicts occurred one after another."[120] The deadlocks in joint management resulting from these conflicts focused on several principal issues: namely, the revision of the unilateral and obsolete railway statute, the functional defects of the board of directors, the delimitation of the authority of the Soviet general manager, and the equal distribution of the railway personnel among Chinese and Russians.

FAILURE OF REVISION OF RAILWAY STATUTE

The revision of the railway statutes was the immediate and paramount task of Sino-Soviet joint management of the railway, according to the provisions of the 1924 agreements. As early as October, 1924, the Chinese members of the board of directors approached the Soviet members with a request that the regulations concerning the management of the C.E.R., which had been enacted by unilateral Russian action over repeated Chinese protests during the Tsarist period when the railway was entirely under Russian management, be revised in conformity with new agreements and with a view to safe-

---

[118] *Ibid.*, pp. 15-16, 23.   [119] *Ibid.*, p. 25.
[120] Semenov, *op. cit.*, pp. 1, 2.

guarding Chinese sovereignty and interests. The Soviet members agreed to the formation of a committee for the revision of regulations which were, in truth, obsolete. However, they brought to the first committee meeting several proposals which provided for a still further increase in the power of the Soviet general manager. This was contrary to treaty stipulations and was regarded by the Chinese as evidence of an intention to secure complete Soviet control over the railway. The committee met several times, as did the board of directors, but each time the Soviet members were reported as absolutely refusing to consider the Chinese proposal for the limitation of the power of the Soviet general manager and the revision of railway statutes, because they wished to maintain the spirit of the old statutes which symbolized Russian predominance in the making of decisions.[121]

In the spring of 1925 the Chinese members of the board of directors, convinced of the urgency of restraining the one-sided activities of the Soviet general manager in order to protect Chinese interests, again proposed to the Soviet members that the question of statutes be settled without further delay. They finally secured an agreement for the calling of a conference to consider the question. All the preparations for the conference were made, but a month later Mr. Karakhan, then Soviet ambassador to China, demanded that certain conditions, which were considered by the Chinese as "entirely unacceptable" "and not related in any way to the C.E.R.," be fulfilled prior to the beginning of the suggested conference.[122]

As a result, the conference did not take place until August 26, 1925. When the conference convened at Peking, there was merely a formal exchange of greetings by the delegates. Karakhan departed for Moscow on the following day.[123] During his interview with the press in Harbin and in Moscow, Karakhan denied any Soviet responsibility for the postponement of the Soviet-Chinese conference: "The conference was put off because the local Chinese authorities had not fulfilled certain points of the Soviet-Chinese Agreement, such as the [abstention from] continued employment of the White Russians in the [Chinese] military-police force." C. T. Wang, the Chinese negotiator, had assured him that all misunderstandings would be

---

[121] Ho, *Chung-O Wai-chiao Shih* (*Sino-Russian Diplomatic History*), p. 390; Tong, *op. cit.*, p. 5.
[122] *Ibid.*, p. 6.
[123] *North China Herald*, Aug. 29, 1925, p. 242.

righted.   Following this, the conference began its work.[124]

After Karakhan's return from Moscow in December, 1925, the conference was resumed but did not accomplish much. The "final settlement" of the revision of the 1896 contract and the so-called railway statute had thus far still not been achieved.[125]

Following the incident in relation to Soviet General Manager Ivanov in January, 1926, the Soviet Government declared anew its desire to have all the outstanding questions regarding the C.E.R. amicably settled, and immediately sent L. P. Serebriakov, then Soviet Vice Commissar for Communications, and formerly Vice President of the board of directors of the C.E.R., to China to negotiate.[126] There were new statements of friendship and new preparations for the conference, but there was no serious discussion of the questions to be settled.   It was, in fact, reported that the Soviet members did not have any real intention of carrying out the principle of re-vision of the 1896 contract and the "statute" as laid down in the Sino-Soviet agreements.[127]

In this respect, Soviet policy on the Chinese Eastern Railway might be visualized from Chicherin's own statement. He had earlier declared that "those parts of the statute of the C.E.R. which were not altered by the Treaty of May 31, 1924, remained in force."[128]

Afterwards, by means of negotiation, the Chinese made a number of attempts to prevent the further development of abnormal condi-tions on the railway.   But every attempt failed because of the "lack of consent on the part of Soviet vice-president and the impediment to progress on the part of Soviet members; the Soviets, on their side, being quite content with the situation as it was, made no counter-proposals.[129]

Later, at the beginning of 1929, Lu Jung-huan, then director general of the railway and president of the board of directors, in the course of a conversation with Mr. V. G. Chirkin, newly appointed Soviet vice-president of the board, insisted on the early revision of railway statutes so as to settle the outstanding questions.   Mr. Chir-kin agreed to discuss on broad lines all the questions which were

[124] Interviews by Karakhan, Sept. 5 and 10, 1925, *Izvestiia*, Sept. 8, 1925, p. 2, and Sept. 10, 1925, p. 2.

[125] *C.Y.B. 1926* (Peking and Tientsin), pp. 1098-1099.

[126] *Vestnik Man'chzhurii* (*Manchuria Monitor*), nos. 3-4 1926, p. 21.

[127] *North China Herald*, Shanghai, July 10, 1926.

[128] Interview with Chicherin, *Izvestiia*, Feb. 5, 1926, p. 1.

[129] Ho, *op. cit.*, p. 390.

awaiting settlement. The Chinese side at once prepared several proposals based upon the Peking and Mukden agreements of 1924, and sent them to Soviet members on March 1, 1929.

The essence of the proposals was as follows: (1) documents were to be signed jointly by the Soviet general manager and the Chinese assistant manager; (2) all disbursements were to be agreed upon by the control department; (3) unsettled questions were to be submitted to the board of directors; (4) all positions were to be equally distributed, (5) the Chinese language was to be used on a par with the Russian language.

On March 20 the Soviet members submitted a list of counter-proposals, which made no concessions in respect to the important questions raised by the Chinese. On March 27 the Chinese members submitted a series of new proposals of minimum requirements, constituting a far-reaching compromise. Nevertheless, the Soviet members were reported as resorting to a policy of procrastination and insisting upon their original stand against any revision of the railway statutes. Under the circumstances, the Chinese members were compelled to report the matter to their government. The negotiations regarding revision of statutes were thus entering an impasse[130] which was a contributing factor in the Soviet-Chinese frontal clash of 1929.

At this moment of tension in the railway negotiation occurred the Chinese forcible entry and search of the Soviet consulate at Harbin.[131] Immediately thereafter the Chinese Government determined upon a course of decisive action in the railway dispute. Orders were issued through the Manchurian authorities authorizing the president of the board of directors, who was the administrator-in-chief (or *tupan*) of the C.E.R., to deal as he saw fit with any situation that might arise. As late as July 10, 1929, Mr. Lu, then president of the board of directors, made a last appeal to the Soviet vice-president for the early revision of the statutes so as to settle the outstanding questions. According to various Chinese sources, the Soviet vice-president showed no indication that he and his colleague would respond.[132]

[130] *Ibid.*, pp. 390-391; Tong, *op. cit.*, pp. 20-22; *Chung-Tung-T'ieh-Lu Wen-t'i*, pp. 61-62.
[131] Cf. pp. 195-196 below.
[132] *Chung-Tung-T'ieh-Lu Wen-t'i*, pp. 60-61; Ho, *op. cit.*, pp. 392-393; Tong, *op. cit.*, pp. 22-23.

This led Mr. Lu, as president of the board and the *tupan* of the railway, on receiving instructions from the Chinese Government, to take the drastic step of issuing an order independent of the Soviet members of the board for the purpose of carrying out the provisions of the 1924 agreements. His order contained only two of the five Chinese proposals previously mentioned: (1) documents were to be signed jointly by the Soviet general manager and the Chinese assistant manager; (2) the traffic, motive power, commercial, financial, and telegraph departments should be headed by Chinese managers. When the Soviet general manager resisted the order, he was suspended from office by order of the *tupan* on July 11, 1929, pending the adoption of a resolution by the board of directors confirming this action.[133] Although the *tupan* thus exercised his authority to meet an emergency situation, he could not thereby bring about a revision of the railway statutes; over this question the joint management remained in a prolonged deadlock.

OBSTRUCTION OF BOARD OF DIRECTORS

As stipulated in the 1924 agreements, any decision of the board of directors had to have the approval of not less than six of the ten members (five Chinese and five Soviet). Any Chinese measure to which the Soviet members objected could not be passed, and vice versa. With the mutual support of the Soviet members of the board and the Soviet general manager, the hands of the Chinese members of the governing body had thus been tied. Therefore, the Russian members of the board could actually delegate the authority to the Soviet general manager and place the board in a subordinate, auxiliary position, subject to the rule of the Soviet general manager, by the simple device of absenting themselves from meetings or refraining from voting.[134] As Mikhailov stated, "the first conflict" over joint management, occurring in December, 1924, "ended with a defeat of the Chinese section of the board."[135]

Dr. C. C. Wang, former president of the railway, also said in 1925, "It must have required much skill to frame the terms in such

[133] *Ibid.*, p. 23; Ho, *op. cit.*, pp. 392-393.

[134] Harry L. Kingman, *Effects of Chinese Nationalism upon Manchuria Railway Developments, 1925-1931* (Berkeley, California, 1932), p. 62; *North China Herald*, Feb. 13, 1926, p. 279.

[135] Mikhailov, *Chto Proiskhodit na Kitaiskoi Vostochnoi Zheleznoi Doroge?* (*Events Pertaining to the Chinese Eastern Railway*), p. 15.

a pleasant way and yet make them so elastic, if not ambiguous." This elasticity made it possible for the Soviet members of the board to withhold from the Chinese members the parity which they had been promised.[136]

Since the board of directors was paralyzed, it did not function effectively, as it often did not meet for long periods. This was due perhaps less to the Chinese members' not being always on the spot to watch the railway work than to the Russian members' policy of procrastination, either through frequent change of personnel or by sudden resignation when the meetings of the board were called. The Chinese directors should have been severely reprimanded for the grave mistake they had made in allowing General Pao Kwei-ching, the first president of the railway under the new status, to be continually absent from the meetings of the directors, and Mr. Chien, the successor to Mr. Yüan as Chinese vice-president, to avoid going to Harbin in 1925 on the excuse that he was taken up by several other missions.[137]

At the very outset, the obstruction of the board was shown by the fact that in the four months elapsing between board meetings, some five hundred questions had accumulated, awaiting the decision of the board. Even the 1925 budget, which was ready at the beginning of the year, had not been passed by May 1, 1925.[138]

The inability of the board to operate effectively might also have been fully demonstrated in the case of the controversial Order no. 94 issued by Soviet General Manager Ivanov on April 9, 1925. By this order he directed the dismissal of all workmen and employees without either Chinese or Soviet citizenship, effective June 1, 1925, for the purpose of a wholesale supplanting of "White" Russians. Among the writers who have treated this episode, Semenov, in accordance with official Soviet attitude, upheld Ivanov's order as necessary to carry out the 1924 Agreements;[139] but Mikhailov regarded it as a second, more serious and prolonged instance of conflict between the two countries in the management of the railway.[140]

Ivanov's unauthorized action led General Pao Kuei-ching, the

---

[136] C. C. Wang, "The Chinese Eastern Railway," *Annals of American Academy of Political and Social Science,* Vol. CXXII, no. 211, Nov., 1925, p. 68.

[137] *North China Herald,* Oct. 3, 1925, p. 10; Dec. 11, 1926, p. 491; *North China Daily News,* May 2, 1926.

[138] *Ibid.*

[139] Semenov, *op. cit.,* p. 9.   [140] Mikhailov, *op. cit.,* p. 16.

president of the railway, who apparently regarded the situation as an emergency, to declare in turn that the general manager, in issuing such an order without the approval of the board, had "exceeded the rights accorded to him, and therefore the order is fundamentally irregular and cannot possess legal force."[141]   The independent actions of both Ivanov and Pao, taken without consulting the board and giving rise to a serious conflict, certainly left much room for regret.

Karakhan immediately intervened.   He challenged Pao's role and described it as "a criminal and irresponsible act."[142]   In addition to his protests to the Peking Government and the Mukden authorities in this regard, Karakhan instructed the Soviet consul general at Harbin, Grandt, to ignore the Pao order and "see that Ivanov's Order no. 94 be carried out, because it was based on the Sino-Soviet Agreement."[143]

On May 24, 1925, Karakhan sent a note to the Waichiaopu.   In protest, he demanded "the abolition of Pao's order and the dismissal of all non-Chinese and non-Soviet employees of the railway," as well as "the recall of General Pao and the appointment of a new president of the board."[144]   Pao, who had accepted the presidency reluctantly, resigned on June 15, 1925; the resignation was interpreted by Mikhailov as a Soviet triumph.[145]

Earlier, the question of the C.E.R. employees had been settled by an agreement between Soviet Consul General Grandt and Tsai Yun-sheng, the commissioner of the Waichiaopu in Harbin, on June 4, 1925.   Manager Ivanov promptly issued orders on June 4 and 5 to the effect that 424 out of the total of 13,347 employees, or about 3 per cent, were to be discharged.   Thereupon, Grandt triumphantly declared that "we have now fully settled the question with the Chinese representatives in the spirit of justice and mutual friendship."[146]

[141] Pao's order quoted in a TASS dispatch from Peking, May 21, 1925, *Izvestiia*, May 22, 1925, p. 4.

[142] Grandt, Soviet consul general at Harbin and vice president of the board of the C.E.R., to Karakhan, tel., May 19, 1925, *Izvestiia*, May 22, 1925, p. 4.

[143] Karakhan to Grandt, tel., May 21, 1925, *Izvestiia*, May 22, 1925, p. 4.

[144] Karakhan to the Waichiaopu, note, summarized in a TASS dispatch from Peking, May 25, 1925, *Izvestiia*, May 26, 1925, p. 1.

[145] Mikhailov, *op. cit.*, p. 17.

[146] TASS dispatches from Peking and Harbin, June 2 and 6, 1925, *Izvestiia*, June 4, 1925, and June 10, 1925, p. 1.

As a further step, Karakhan simultaneously protested the hostile actions of the Manchurian authorities and pointed out that similar treaty violations had been committed under the protection of the commanding staff of the railway protective forces. He therefore declared that "the U.S.S.R. categorically demands the immediate investigation as well as dismissal and bringing to trial of the said guilty persons of the high commanding staff."[147]

But the Chinese Government took a firm stand. As late as July, 1929, the statement of the Central Executive Committee of Kuomintang referred to the obstruction of the board as mentioned in the above case in the following language: "The Soviet General Manager of the railway had always exceeded his authority, and the Chinese rights were deliberately ignored despite repeated protests launched by the Chinese President of the railway."[148]

Furthermore, the obstruction of the board even affected the composition of the board of directors itself. This might be specially noted in the following paragraph of the statement made by C. T. Wang, then Foreign Minister, after the rupture of Sino-Soviet relations in 1929:

According to the stipulation of the Treaty, the railway shall have a Board of Directors to be composed of ten persons, five Chinese and five Russian, but for the present, Soviet Russia has arbitrarily increased the numbers of Directors from ten to eighteen, of whom fifteen are Russians, the remaining three being Chinese.[149]

Wang referred to this deadlock of the board as "another violation" of the Sino-Soviet agreements of 1924 "on the part of the U.S.S.R."[150]

ACTIVITIES OF THE SOVIET GENERAL MANAGER

As a matter of fact, the board of directors was a figurehead in the administration of the C.E.R., whereas the Soviet general manager was its "supreme ruler." After less than a year of joint management,

---

[147] Karakhan to the Waichiaopu, note, referred to in a Peking dispatch, May 23, 1925, *Izvestiia*, May 26, 1925, p. 1.
[148] *The Sino-Russian Crisis* (published by the International Relations Committee of the Kuomintang) (Nanking, 1929), p. 26.
[149] *Ibid.*, p. 30.
[150] *Ibid.*

the Soviet general manager was described as having become "the practical dictator of the railway."[151]

The Soviet members of the board could easily have their wishes carried out through the Soviet general manager, who could do many "arbitrary things," including encroaching on the rights and privileges of the Chinese authority, abusing his powers to appoint and discharge railway personnel, mobilizing support from political organizations, and disbursing railway revenue without reference to the board.[152]

This situation gave rise to a near crisis in 1926. It appeared that on November 10, 1925, Ivanov, then Soviet general manager, "acting on his own responsibility" issued an order, effective on December 1, forbidding the transportation of Chinese military forces and railway guards on credit. This order probably was occasioned by the Kuo Sung-lin revolt against Marshal Chang Tso-lin. At a meeting of the board of directors held in Harbin on November 30, the Chinese president and members protested this action, and won a reluctant consent from the Russian directors that the Chinese railway guards might continue to ride without prepayment.[153]

A critical situation developed when, on January 16, 1926, Manager Ivanov refused to carry three thousand railway guards because no prepayment had been tendered. He suspended all regular traffic on the Harbin-Changchun line, and a conference held at Harbin proved futile. Thereupon, General Chang Huan-hsiang, military governor of this special area, acting in compliance with Marshal Chang Tso-lin's order, albeit untactfully and irresponsibly, arrested Ivanov and three Russian directors and, for a short time, ran the trains.[154]

Even before the "unlawful" arrest of Ivanov on January 22, 1926, Karakhan, in his note of January 19 to the Waichiaopu, protested "in the most energetic manner" against actions of Manchurian military authorities and requested that agency "to put an end to the outrages and restore order." He also held China responsible "for the damages done to the railway and the coercion committed by the

---

[151] *North China Herald*, Oct. 3, 1925, p. 10; Tao-shing Chang, *International Controversies over the Chinese Eastern Railway*, pp. 129-130; Tong, *op. cit.*, p. 5.

[152] Tong, *op. cit.*, p. 5.

[153] Peking *Leader*, Dec. 5, 1925; Young, *The International Relations of Manchuria*, p. 229.

[154] Peking *Leader*, Jan. 24, 1926; Kingman, *op. cit.*, p. 64; Young, *op. cit.*, p. 231.

Chinese forces."[155]   On January 20 he similarly addressed a telegram to Chang Tso-lin denouncing Chang Huan-hsiang, and concluding: "In sending this I think we have warned you in good time.   We cannot therefore bear the responsibility of any consequences.[156]   He had earlier approved Ivanov's action.[157]   There was thus a prevailing general impression that Ivanov had acted on Karakhan's order.[158]

At this juncture *Izvestiia* furiously commented that "the present conflict bears a completely special form," and that "the unprecedented insolence of the Changtsolinist militarists transcends all the permissible bounds."   It pointed out that "in the last few years, Chang owed the Chinese Eastern Railway over \$14,000,000 for military transportation."[159]

On January 22, hearing of the arrest of Ivanov, Karakhan made a further strong protest against "the unheard-of violation of the agreement of 1924," demanding the immediate release of Ivanov and pointing out all the serious consequences.[160]   On the following day Chicherin sent a three-day ultimatum to the Chinese Government again demanding Ivanov's release and the restoration of order.[161]   *Izvestiia* again emphatically warned Chang: "Really, he does not understand that we cannot permit the playing of such a joke on our prestige. . . ."   It then declared that "if the Chinese Central Government were not in a position to maintain order in the railway area, we would be forced to carry out our treaty obligations for the safeguard of the interests of China and the U.S.S.R."[162]

On January 24, 1926, an agreement was signed by the Soviet consul general at Mukden, Kravkovetskii, and the Commissioner for Foreign Affairs of the Three Eastern Provinces, Kao.   Accordingly, Ivanov was set free on January 25, normal rail traffic was

[155] Karakhan to the Waichiaopu, note, Jan. 19, 1926, *Izvestiia*, Jan. 22, 1926, p. 1.

[156] Karakhan to Chang Tso-lin, tel., Jan. 20, 1926, *Izvestiia*, Jan. 22, 1926, p. 1.

[157] Karakhan to Grandt, tel., Jan. 19, 1926, *Izvestiia*, Jan. 22, 1926, p. 1.

[158] T. V. Butov, a C.E.R. official under Ivanov, recently advised the present writer to this effect in interviews.

[159] "Chzhantszolinovskaia Provokatsiia" ("The Changtsolinist Provocation"), *Izvestiia*, Jan. 22, 1926, p. 1.

[160] Karakhan to the Chinese Foreign Minister, note, Jan. 22, 1926, *Izvestiia*, Jan. 24, 1926, p. 1.

[161] Chicherin to the Chinese Foreign Minister, sent through tel. to Karakhan, Jan. 23, 1926, *Izvestiia*, Jan. 24, 1926, p. 1.

[162] "Naglets Chzhantszolina Nado Polozhit' Konets" ("Chang Tso-lin's Impudence Should Be Put to an End"), *Izvestiia*, Jan. 24, 1926, p. 1.

restored following his release, and the payment for military transportation on the existing credit basis charged against that part of the railway profit belonging to the Chinese Government was authorized.[163]

Shortly thereafter Chicherin expressed his "hope" to C. T. Wang, now Chinese Foreign Minister, that "the deplorable incidents" should be ended once and for all without any possibility of recurrence.[164] Karakhan continued to protest the arrest of the Soviet employees and demanded the dismissal of General Chang Huan-hsiang,[165] who was soon replaced.[166] Chicherin seemed to be pleased with the Manchurian settlement when he said:

The Chinese Government promptly met the Soviet Government half-way and took the step that depended upon it, addressing to Chang Tso-lin, the actual wielder of power in Manchuria, a demand for the restoration of the conditions established by the treaty.[167]

While the deadlock over the powers of the Soviet general manager continued, the incumbent of that office—Emshanov had now replaced Ivanov—persisted, it was said, in doing all he could to advance Soviet interests on the railway at the expense of Chinese interests. Meanwhile, the attempts of the Chinese directors to pass upon the action of the general manager continued to be nullified by the action of the Russian directors in absenting themselves from the meetings.[168] Thus the Soviet general manager was charged not only with having dismissed arbitrarily and without good reason those railway officers whose appointment and discharge were within his power, but also with having removed even higher officers whose appointment and discharge were the prerogative of the board of directors.[169]

Moreover, the Soviet general manager had rendered open and active assistance to the trade unions of officers and workmen of the C.E.R. These had previously existed for the protection of their

[163] TASS communiqué, Jan. 27, 1926, *Izvestiia*, Jan. 26, 1926, p. 1.

[164] Chicherin to C. T. Wang, in Chicherin's tel. to Karakhan, Jan. 29, 1926, *Izvestiia*, Jan. 30, 1926, p. 1.

[165] Karakhan to C. T. Wang, note, referred to in *Izvestiia*, Jan. 30, 1926, p. 1.

[166] Ho, *op. cit.*, pp. 350-351.

[167] Interview by Chicherin on the conflict on the C.E.R., *Izvestiia*, Feb. 5, 1926, p. 1.

[168] Peking *Leader*, Feb. 3, 1926; Young, *op. cit.*, p. 231.

[169] Tong, *op. cit.*, p. 8.

own legitimate interests, but later became powerful political organizations which were deemed by the Chinese to have as their sole object "the Sovietizing of the employees and the spreading of Bolshevism far and wide with the C.E.R. as their basis."[170]   According to the by-laws of the All-Russian Trade Union Central Board, "the All-Russian Professional Union of the Workmen and Employees of the Chinese Eastern Railway" was "affiliated with the [Profintern, or the trade-union arm of the] Third Communistic International."[171] In carrying out the wishes of the trade unions, the Soviet general manager was said to have sacrificed the business interests of the railway and to have relieved various departmental chiefs and other senior officers of their responsibility for the faithful execution of the duties entrusted to them.[172]

The Soviet general manager was likewise accused of having systematically allowed himself "to go beyond the budget and having exceeded his authority to an unlimited extent."   He overdrew money and carried out measures without the board's sanction, to the great detriment of the technical operation of the railway itself.   The board of directors between 1927 and 1928 appropriated 121,460 gold rubles for outfitting the Harbin Central Repair Shop's Club, but the Soviet general manager, on his own authority, disbursed 332,132.56 gold rubles, 210,672.56 in excess of the appropriation.   Because of this and similar cases, the budget committee formed by the board of directors lost its function and became a laughing-stock to the whole railway staff.[173]

The control department, headed by a Chinese, was supposed to control the expenses incurred by the management, but it likewise lost its power.   In 1928 the Soviet general manager spent, "without authorization from any quarter, and "against the disapproval of the control department, more than 600,000 gold rubles in a manner "best known to himself."   Many of the items listed in his accounts—such as loans to the Soviet Government and to various organizations, expenses for parties of investigation sent to Russia, or payment of Soviet staff members of the former navigation department, which had been abolished and the pay of its staff stopped by order of the board of directors—were considered by the Chinese

[170] *Ibid.*, pp. 8-9.   Tao-shing Chang, *op. cit.*, p. 133.
[171] For text of the by-laws, see Tong, *op. cit.*, Appendix F, p. 148.
[172] *Ibid.*, p. 9.   [173] *Ibid.*, pp. 10-11.

as only "a camouflage to secure funds for the conducting of Bolshevik propaganda in Chinese territory."[174]

Regarding the deadlock over the activities of the Soviet general manager, C. T. Wang, then Chinese Foreign Minister, declared in a statement made during the Sino-Soviet crisis in 1929 that the Soviet general manager and other Soviet high officials on the C.E.R. were accustomed to act "beyond their authority and to the prejudice of Chinese interests." "However," he continued, "in the person of the present Director General [General Manager], M. Emshanov, there came a culmination of abuse of authority.[175]

IGNORING THE PRINCIPLE OF "FAIR PLAY"

There were altogether twenty departments for the management of the C.E.R. In conformity with the letter and the spirit of the 1924 agreements, the Chinese should have headed ten out of these twenty departments. However, the principle of equal employment of the nationals of both countries "had never been carried out into full effect, not because of Chinese lack of railway experts, but because of Russia's policy of procrastination."[176] Thus, out of the twenty departments, only six departments had Chinese as their chiefs. Even this result was said to have been "accomplished only after lengthy pourparlers" throughout the whole five-year period of the joint management of the railway. Moreover, the six departments with Chinese at their heads were not important, while all the important departments had been headed by Soviet citizens.[177]

The Soviet general manager was accused of having done everything within his power to defeat the principle of equal representation on the railway staffs by Chinese and Soviet nationals. In consequence, more Soviet citizens had occupied positions of importance, whereas the number of Chinese citizens holding comparatively important positions was very small. During the first four years of joint management, a considerable number of old employees left the service of the C.E.R., and at the same time the staff increased by 40 per cent. These two circumstances should have constituted a sufficient reason to carry out the principle of parity, albeit with a sympa-

[174] *Ibid.*, pp. 11-12.   [175] *The Sino-Russian Crisis*, p. 30.
[176] *North China Herald*, May 7, 1927, p. 237; Tao-shing Chang, *op. cit.*, p. 132; Tong, *op. cit.*, pp. 5-6.
[177] Tong, *op. cit.*, p. 6.

thetic view of the rights of Russian nationals currently employed by the railway, and on condition that they not be dismissed "for the sole purpose of enforcing the said principle."[178] The Soviet general manager was criticized for failing to carry out the principle. Often he was brought to agree to the filling of vacancies by Chinese citizens only after much negotiation. Even for unimportant railway positions, agreement for such appointments could be obtained only with great difficulty.[179]

During the Grandt-Tsai negotiations on the question of the Chinese Eastern Railway employees in June, 1925, *Izvestiia* reported that the Soviet representative went "half way to meet China's interests in the sense of gradual approximation of the number of Chinese employees to the 50 per cent standard" provided in the 1924 agreements.[180] Thus the Soviets themselves admitted that the principle of parity or equal representation had thus far not been carried out as stipulated.

As a matter of fact, the outstanding trend in the personnel administration of the railway under joint management was the marked decrease of Chinese staff in contrast with the unprecedented increase of the total number of railway personnel. For example, the total number of staff members, consisting of staff, temporary, and daily employees, increased extraordinarily from 16,657 in 1924 to 30,185 on July 31, 1928.[181] In the period from October, 1924, to January, 1925, alone, the Chinese employed on the railway decreased from 5,912 to 5,555 while the number of Russian employees increased from 10,833 to 11,251 during the same period.[182] On January 1, 1929, of the 12,000 officers on the regular payroll of the C.E.R. the Chinese numbered less than 3,000, or less than 25 per cent of the total. The rest were Soviet citizens.[183]

The constant decrease of Chinese employees on the C.E.R. reflected the deadlock over the problems of fair play, and the Soviet attitude toward the railway as well as to the agreements concerned.

[178] *Ibid.*, p. 8; Tao-shing Chang, *op. cit.*, pp. 127, 132; Kingman, *op. cit.*, p. 62.

[179] *Ibid.*, p. 63; Tong, *op. cit.*, p. 8.

[180] Harbin dispatch, June 4, 1925, *Izvestiia*, June 6, 1925, p. 1.

[181] Tong, *op. cit.*, p. 16.

[182] *North China Daily News*, May 2, 1925, cited in G. E. Sokolsky, *The Story of the Chinese Eastern Railway*, Shanghai, 1930, p. 48; Kingman, *op. cit.*, p. 63; Tao-shing Chang, *op. cit.*, p. 132.

[183] *Ibid.*, Tong, op. cit., p. 8; the percentage is hereby recalculated and corrected according to the given number.

In this connection, an account of the railway situation by K. K. Kawakami, deserves quotation:

The personnel of the Chinese Eastern Railway is composed of about 30,000 employees, and 75 per cent are Russians. Come what may, the Russians are determined to retain control of the line. The declaration that they made during the revolution to relinquish the railway was just a diplomatic gesture to influence the Chinese Government to recognize the Soviet Government. Today all their efforts are directed toward the taking possession of the rights which they abandoned. On the Board of Directors of that line, China is represented on a basis of equality with Russia. But the actual administration and control of necessary work to ensure the operation and maintenance of the line is in the hands of the Russians. Not one Chinese is employed as a mechanic or as a conductor. Practically all the station masters are Russians. The purchase of material for the line is made by the Russians. Only a few technical experts are Chinese. The operating department and the accounting department are controlled by Russians. This proves that the Chinese are represented only by about 25 per cent of the entire personnel of the line.[184]

In short, the conflicts giving rise to deadlocks in the joint management were various in kind and numerous in number. Karakhan protested the hostile action of the Manchurian authorities on the C.E.R.[185] Likewise, Semenov accused the Chinese authorities in Manchuria of mistaking "our [Soviet] very great complaisance towards China as signs of our weakness," and following through "an extraordinarily aggressive policy on the Chinese Eastern Railway." He made it clear that "this short-sighted policy of the Manchurian generals [had] encountered the deserving repulse of our [Soviet] representatives," thus constituting an unbroken series of conflicts. According to this Soviet commentator, "the real background of these conflicts. According to this Soviet commentator, "the real background of these conflicts," which gradually became insurmountable deadlocks, was "the obstinate 'Sinification'" pursued by the local Chinese authorities and, especially, the Chinese section of the board of the C.E.R.[186] However, judging from the facts of each of the specific issues, this line of Soviet polemics merely provided an excuse for disavowing Soviet responsibility for failure to redeem treaty pledges.

[184] Quoted in *The Sino-Russian Crisis*, p. 14.
[185] *Izvestiia*, May 26, 1925, p. 1, and *ibid.*, May 27, 1925, p. 1.
[186] Semenov, *op. cit.*, p. 2.

V: CONSEQUENCES OF SOVIET RAILWAY POLICY

Encroachment on Chinese Sovereignty and Interests

During the years 1924-29 the Soviet railway policy in Northern Manchuria, in the name of joint management, had in fact pursued essentially the traditional Russian ambition of getting control in the area through the Chinese Eastern Railway. In addition, Communist propaganda and activities, with the alleged aid of the personnel, funds, and facilities of the C.E.R. and the Soviet consulates in Manchuria, presented a potent threat to the tranquillity of China's social and national life. As a result, there were prolonged deadlocks over various aspects of joint management from the very outset, which led in turn to encroachments on Chinese sovereignty and Chinese interests, to China's retaliation through taking the railway into her temporary custody, and finally to the complete cessation of Sino-Soviet relations and the ensuing undeclared war.

It may be recalled that the Russian policy of encroaching upon Chinese sovereignty in Manchuria during the period of Tsarist control of the Chinese Eastern Railway had been denounced repeatedly by Soviet leaders and authors. In accusing the Tsarist "criminal policy" in China of being aimed at turning Manchuria gradually into an "indivisible part" of Russia, V. Avarin, as well as V. I. Lenin, pointed out that the Russians were "actually the masters of Northern Manchuria," in spite of "semi-formal preservation of Chinese sovereignty.[1] Later, however, in the period of Sino-Soviet joint management, the Soviet encroachment on Chinese sovereignty and interests was no less severe, so that the Chinese authorities were driven to

[1] V. Avarin, *"Nezavisimaia" Manchzhuriia ("Independent" Manchuria)* (Moscow, 1934), pp. 39-41; V. I. Lenin, *Polnoe Sochinenie (Complete Works)*, rev. ed., IV, 61, 63.

bitter denunciations of "Russia's plot . . . against the Chinese Government."[2]

The first case affecting Chinese sovereignty was Manager Ivanov's denial of the Chinese prerogative, through "long established custom," to transport her troops and railway guards on credit over the commercial line "in her own territory during time of emergency."[3] This developed into the "Ivanov Incident" of January, 1926, described above.[4] While arguments and accusations were made on both sides, Ivanov's order was interpreted by the foreign press in China as an attempt at playing politics, for he had suspended traffic during a military mutiny in Manchuria, while "he had no right to do this in Chinese territory when managing a purely commercial enterprise."[5]

The second dispute involving Chinese sovereignty grew out of the persistent Soviet claim to the right of navigation in the Sungari, which led to the Chinese seizure of the C.E.R. flotilla in August, 1926, by the edict of Chang Tso-lin. Two reasons for seizure were stated: first, the use by the C.E.R. of the Sungari navigation water was contrary to the 1924 agreements; and second, the seizure of the C.E.R. vessels was also a means of hastening the settlement of the question of the steamers confiscated early by the Soviet Government at Egresheld (a part of the port of Vladivostok serving the C.E.R.) in 1922.[6] The Soviet Government estimated the shipping seized at eleven steamers and thirty barges with a total capacity of twenty thousand tons, and emphatically protested as one-sided the action of the Chinese Government in "violating essential treaty rights of Soviet Russia in Northern Manchuria."[7] As no treaty rights of inland water navigation had ever been granted to the U.S.S.R. by China since the abolition of the unequal treaties between them, the Soviet claim was without ground. Moreover, according to the statement issued by Admiral Sheng Hung-Lieh on receiving the Russian note, the original value of the flotilla was only about two or three million dollars, while that of the Egresheld property was more than

[2] C. T. Wang's speech in *The Sino-Russian Crisis* (pub. by the International Relations Committee of the Kuomintang), pp. 33-34.
[3] Tong, *Facts About the Chinese Eastern Railway Situation*, p. 7.
[4] Cf. pp. 186-188, *supra*.
[5] *North China Herald*, Feb. 13, 1926, p. 279.
[6] *North China Herald*, Aug. 27, 1926, p. 380.
[7] *Ibid.*; London *Times*, Sept. 10, 1926, p. 11.

ten million.[8]   *Izvestiia,* in the name of the Soviet people, again protested Chang Tso-lin's violent action.[9]

The third and most vital encroachment on Chinese sovereignty
was the question of political propaganda avowedly prohibited in
Articles VI and II, respectively, of the Peking and Mukden agreements.   The Chinese authorities stated that for some time Moscow
had been utilizing its position in the Chinese Eastern Railway to
spread Communist propaganda and to damage the existing Chinese
government.[10]   The Chinese thought that the political issue of Communist propaganda had been the basic cause of trouble between China
and the U.S.S.R. ever since 1924, particularly in relation to the
C.E.R.[11]   Indeed, it was Soviet violation of these treaty provisions
and Chinese concern over the problem of Communist propaganda
which led to the subsequent search of the Soviet Consulate General
in Harbin by Chinese police on May 27, 1929.   China held that the
raid was "found necessary as a means of preserving the present regime from being overthrown by violence."[12]   According to the official
report of the raid, "the Russians were conferring on an urgent problem for the Third International having special reference to the
future of Russia in North China, that is, the creating of great disturbances in North China in cooperation with General Feng Yu-
hsiang."[13]   During the raid, literature, documents, pistols, cartridges,
and opium were seized; it was reported that a number of important
documents written in private codes had been thrown into a stove and
burned.[14]   The Chinese authorities also arrested forty-two persons,
including Consul Kuznetsov of Mukden and Consul-General Mel'-
nikov of Harbin.   Mr. Mel'nikov was informed that the raid was
directed not at the consulate but at the Third International.[15]

Four days later, on May 31, 1929, L. M. Karakhan, Acting Commissar for Foreign Affairs in Moscow, sent a protest to the Chinese
Government against the "lawless attack of the police" on the Soviet

[8] *North China Herald,* Sept. 18, 1926, p. 543.
[9] "My Preduprezhdaem" ("We Warn"), *Izvestiia,* Sept. 8, 1926, p. 1.
[10] Kingman, *Effects of Chinese Nationalism upon Manchurian Developments,*
1925-1931, p. 71.
[11] Tao-shing Chang, *International Controversies over the Chinese Eastern Rail-*
way, pp. 135, 137.
[12] *The Sino-Russian Crisis,* p. 12; cf. Kingman, *op. cit.,* p. 71.
[13] Quoted in Tsao, *The Chinese Eastern Railway: An Analytical Study,* p. 101.
[14] Tsao, *op. cit.,* pp. 100, 102.
[15] Kingman, *op. cit.,* p. 71; Tao-shing Chang, *op. cit.,* pp. 138-139.

consulate "after a prolonged campaign raised against the Soviet Union." The Soviet Government demanded the release of the Soviet prisoners in Harbin and the return of the correspondence and other things taken, and it vehemently warned the Nanking Government against further "provocative actions and the violations of treaties and agreements."[16]

Soviet writers of that time thought this raid a link in the series of Chinese "anti-Soviet adventures," exploited by world imperialism after the victory of "counterrevolution" in China, and as a "real prospect for the formation of the existing anti-Soviet front of the imperialists."[17] A Japanese consular report from Harbin surmised that the raid was connected with a "Chinese campaign to gain full control of the Chinese Eastern Railway."[18] However, on June 10 an official spokesman for the Nanking Government was quoted as stating that China had no intention of utilizing the opportunity of the moment to take over the C.E.R. On June 11 C. T. Wang, the Chinese Foreign Minister, disavowed any responsibility for the Harbin affair and offered to make a thorough investigation.[19]

The most important factor affecting Chinese interests in joint management was the activity of the Soviet trade unions. Politically, the unions controlled the various branches of the railway administration. They were charged with exercising an effective supervision over the Soviet staff of the railway, depriving the officers of their responsibility, and "undermining the discipline of the employees." The Chinese feared they were enabling "the Soviet Government to maintain a powerful political influence upon the whole administrative structure of the Railway," and considered them, therefore, "undoubtedly a menace to China."[20] Financially, the unions caused the railway to incur many unproductive expenses, such as the "uncalled-for" increase of salaries and wages, unnecessary appropriations of the fund for extra compensations to the officers acting for absent colleagues, superfluous appropriations for the increase of numerous allowances, pay for railway staff members working in the unions'

[16] *Soviet Union Review* (referred to hereinafter as *S.U.R.*), published by the Soviet Union Information Bureau, Washington, D. C., VII (July-Aug., 1929), 112; Kingman, *op. cit.*, p. 72.

[17] Anatolii Kantorovich, *Amerika v Bor'be za Kitai* (*America in the Struggle for China*) (Moscow, 1935), pp. 422-423.

[18] New York *Times*, May 29, 1929, p. 8; cf. Kingman, *op. cit.*, p. 71.

[19] *Ibid.*, p. 73.   [20] Tong, *op. cit.*, p. 9.

offices, and the inflation of the payroll by incompetent employees, recommended by the unions.[21]

The second factor affecting Chinese interests was the partiality shown by the Soviet general manager for all sorts of Soviet organizations and businessmen. Any Soviet organization could get a reduced rate for shipping goods on the railway. For the development of the port of Vladivostok, an artificial rate was established for the main commodities in order to encourage export through the eastern line. In cases where the railway purchased goods for its own use, the Soviet organizations had often received payment before the materials were actually delivered. And even in purchases of materials considered of the most essential nature, "preference was given to the Soviet contractors, even to the extent of waiving the technical requirements." For instance, the railway placed huge orders for rails with the Soviet syndicate "Yugostal," but the rails supplied by the syndicate proved to be unsatisfactory. Orders for cement had been placed with the Spassky factory in spite of the fact that this factory could not supply cement which would meet the technical specifications. Likewise, the railway always gave preference to the oil of the Soviet Oil Syndicate as against oil of foreign firms, although Soviet oil was more costly. Therefore it is not surprising that the Soviet general manager was accused of "extreme bias" in favor of Soviet institutions, "either commercial or political, against Chinese interests as well as interests of foreign firms desirous of dealing with the railway."[22]

The third factor affecting Chinese interests was the extraordinary increase of railway staffs, which may be shown in official records at the end of each year as given below:

TABLE A

Staff Members of the C.E.R.

	1923	1924	1925	1926	1927
Staff Employees...........	8,971	8,743	9,382	9,781	10,353
Temporary Employees......	980	1,135	1,845	2,670	3,875
Daily Employees..........	6,633	6,779	8,613	9,966	11,000
Total..............	16,584	16,657	19,840	22,417	25,410

[21] *Ibid.*, pp. 9-10.   [22] *Ibid.*, pp. 13-14.

By July 31, 1928, the number of staff members had further increased to 30,185. It is to be noted, then, that during the period of joint management the railway staff was nearly doubled:[23] Thus, in the spring of 1928 the railway was actually unable to meet the payroll for its staff.[24] This abnormal phenomenon was condemned by the Chinese as the result of "the desire of the Soviet management" to give work to many Soviet citizens formally employed or "indirectly working for the Soviet cause."[25]

Another factor affecting Chinese interests was the tremendous increase of expenditure not dependent upon traffic. According to the estimate of railway experts, railway expenses depending upon traffic, such as fuel, lubrication, partial repairs of the rolling stock, etc., increased from 21,849,000 rubles in 1924 to 40,285,000 rubles in 1927, while expenses not depending upon traffic, such as the expenses for the maintenance of the boards and the management of the railway, the upkeep of the minimum staff members, etc., increased from 12,285,000 rubles in 1924 to 25,619,000 rubles in 1927. In the light of expert information, if the expenses not dependent on traffic for the year 1927 had remained the same as those for 1924, as should have been the case, the net profit of the railway in 1927 ought to have amounted to 22,000,000 gold rubles instead of 9,700,000 gold rubles. Moreover, had it been possible to avoid such losses as were suffered from the increase of transport at a lower rate for eastbound freight [1,500,000 to 2,000,000 gold rubles] and from the supplementary enterprises, including the maintenance of the Grand Hotel [up to 2,000,000 rubles], the net profit in 1927 would have been 28,000,000 gold rubles. According to the statistics for the year 1928, the net profit for that year was recorded as 4,700,000 gold rubles, while in reality the railway received a net profit of only 330,000 gold rubles in cash. These facts were used by Chinese critics to throw light on "the intensive political activities of the Soviet management, which were principally responsible for this poor state of finance.[26]

[23] *Ibid.*, p. 16.
[24] Chih, *Tung-T'ieh Wen-ti* (*The Question of the C.E.R.*), p. 64.
[25] Tong, *op. cit.*, p. 16.
[26] *Ibid.*, pp. 17-18.

COMPLETE CESSATION OF SINO-SOVIET RELATIONS

During the period 1927-29 three successive events contributed to the complete rupture of Sino-Soviet relations. The first of these was Chang Tso-lin's search of the Soviet Embassy at Peking on April 6, 1927, for the purpose of arresting a number of Communist leaders including Li Tao-chao, Lu Yiu-yu, and some sixty others, in order to "clean the home front." Whatever the provocation for this action in terms of the role of the Communist movement on the domestic scene, it was clearly in violation of one of the oldest and firmest principles of international law: that of the diplomatic immunity of foreign embassy personnel and the extraterritoriality of the embassy grounds.

The Soviet Government in protest withdrew its ambassador and embassy staff. However, Soviet consuls and commercial representatives remained in various parts of China, and the Chinese chargé d'affaires and consular officers did not leave the U.S.S.R.

The second event involved the expulsion of Soviet consular representatives in leading Chinese cities. On December 14, 1927, the National Government in Nanking, following the Communist uprising at Canton on December 11, withdrew recognition of Soviet consuls in the territory it controlled. Accordingly, the Soviet consular staffs in Canton, Shanghai, Nanking, Chinkiang, and Hankow returned home shortly. At this time, however, there were still Soviet consuls and commercial representatives in Northern China, and the Chinese chargé d'affaires appointed by the Peking Government still maintained perfunctory contact in Moscow.

Finally, on July 17, 1929, as a result of the serious conflict over the Chinese Eastern Railway, the Soviet Government recalled its diplomatic, consular, and commercial representatives, as well as persons appointed by the Soviet Government on the C.E.R., from the territory of China and demanded the departure of Chinese representative and consular officers from the U.S.S.R. By this action and the declaration that railway communications between China and the U.S.S.R. would be blocked, the relations between the two countries were entirely severed.[27] The dispute over the C.E.R. was thus the

[27] Ho, *Chung-O Wai-chiao Shih* (*Sino-Russian Diplomatic History*), pp. 388-389.

chief event responsible for the cessation of relations between the two nations.

On July 10, 1929, the Chinese authorities, acting on information obtained in the Harbin raid, charged the various Soviet officials of the C.E.R. with complicity in the spread of Communist propaganda and instigation of the recent rebellion of Feng Yu-hsiang in Northwest China. Simultaneously they ordered the closing of four Soviet commercial organs, the dissolution of all Soviet trade unions, and the deportation of fifty-nine communists to the frontier.[28]

The next day the Chinese director-general of the railway (the *tupan*) took the fateful action of suspending from office the Soviet general manager, Emshanov, and appointing the Chinese assistant manager in his place. Again, there may have been great provocation for this action—the evidence will be reviewed below—but it was nevertheless an arbitrary act of doubtful legality, and it led to serious consequences for China.

The reason given for the dismissal was Emshanov's refusal to comply with an order from the *tupan* to let the Chinese assistant manager be a cosignatory of railway documents, and to place the traffic, commercial, financial, motive-power, and telegraphic departments under Chinese departmental chiefs. Emshanov's replacement by a Chinese national was regarded as temporary, the Chinese authorities apparently expecting the Soviet Government to appoint a successor without great delay. Nevertheless, opinion on both sides viewed the incident and the events leading up to it as extremely serious. On the one hand, "China believed that the Chinese Eastern Railway had been used by the Soviets as a base of operations dangerous to her peace and safety."[29] On the other hand, Soviet publications pictured the events of July 10 as a raid on the railway management at Harbin and along all lines from Station Manchuli to Station Pogranichnaia, in which Russian personnel had been arrested, deported by force, or asked to leave under various threats, while trade unions, clubs, co-operatives, and newspapers had been dissolved or closed down.[30]

[28] *Chung-Tung-T'ieh-Lu Wen-t'i* (*The Question of the Chinese Eastern Railway*), pp. 62-63; *The Sino-Russian Crisis*, pp. 2-11; Tao-shing Chang, *op. cit.*, pp. 140-141.

[29] Tao-shing Chang, *op. cit.*, pp. 140-141.

[30] G. Voitinskii, "Zakhvat KVZhD i Politika SSSR" ("The Seizure of the Chi-

The Soviet Government immediately issued an ultimatum dated July 13, which was sent by Guedes, Soviet Vice-Commissar of Foreign Affairs, to the Chinese chargé d'affaires, Hsia Weisung. After a long analysis of the troubled situation the Soviet ultimatum denounced the "one-sided and unlawful actions" of the director general of the C.E.R. as constituting "a gross violation of the existing agreements between the U.S.S.R. and China." The Soviet Government, therefore, felt justified in setting forth three demands:

1. The immediate calling of a conference to adjust the questions connected with the Chinese Eastern Railway.
2. The immediate cancellation by the Chinese authorities of all arbitrary orders regarding the Chinese Eastern Railway.
3. The immediate release of all arrested Soviet citizens and the cessation of all persecution of Soviet citizens and Soviet institutions by the Chinese authorities.

The time limit set for the answer of the Chinese Government was three days. In case of "not receiving a satisfactory reply," the Soviet Government would "resort to other means for the protection of the lawful rights of the U.S.S.R."[31]

Izvestiia applauded the Soviet ultimatum of July 13, saying that it would "convince the Manchurian usurpers that they are mistaken in their calculation that their action would provoke no unforeseen consequences." It pointed out that "the responsibility for the consequences rests on the Chinese authorities who have transcended all limits in testing our long-suffering patience."[32]

The Chinese Government wired its reply from Nanking on July 16 and clarified its position in the following words:

According to repeated reports received by the Chinese Government, the Soviet General Manager and other important Soviet officers of the railway have from the very beginning failed to fulfil the terms of the Sino-Soviet agreement of 1924 concerning the provisional management of the railway. During the last few years Soviet railway officers have so

---

nese Eastern Railway and the Policy of the US.S.R."), *Krasnaia Nov'*, no. 9 (1929), p. 142.

[31] For Russian text of the Soviet ultimatum of July 13, 1929, see G. N. Voitinskii, *K.V.Zh.D. i Politika Imperialistov v Kitae* (*The C.E.R. and the Policy of the Imperialists in China*), pp. 58-62; for Chinese text, see Chih, *op. cit.*, Appendix VII; for English translation see *The Sino-Russian Crisis*, pp. 35-39.

[32] "Novaia Provokatsiia na KVZhD" ("The New Provocation on the C.E.R."), *Izvestiia*, July 14, 1929, p. 1.

often violated the agreement that it would not be possible to count the number of violations, and in consequence Chinese officers were unable to carry out their duties under the agreement. What is worse is the fact that Soviet citizens have time and again made use of the railway in conducting their Communist propaganda, an act which was forbidden by the agreement of 1924. For these reasons the authorities of the North-eastern Provinces were obliged to take this necessary action against the Chinese Eastern Railway. That we are not responsible for the violation of the Sino-Soviet agreement and the agreement concerning the provisional management of the C.E.R. is very obvious.[33]

About a thousand Chinese merchants in Russia were then arrested and detained. China did not then suggest a counterproposal. Instead she asked that Russia release her nationals and accord them and their mercantile organizations all necessary protection and facilities. She would then "be ready at the appropriate time to take similar measures toward the arrested Soviet agents and the closed offices." The Chinese note expressed a special hope that "in the present case, the Soviet Government will respect the laws and sovreignty of China and refrain from making any proposals contradictory to the actual facts of the case."[34] Minister Chu Shao-yang was instructed to negotiate with Moscow with a view to settling the dispute on his way to his post as chargé in Moscow and minister to Finland. This suggestion was ridiculed by *Izvestiia* as complete mockery.[35]

On July 17 the Soviet Government in a strongly worded second note stated that the Chinese reply was "unsatisfactory in content and hypocritical in tone." While reserving all rights resulting from the Peking and Mukden agreements of 1924, the Soviet Government decided to take the following measures:

1. To recall all Soviet diplomatic, consular, and commercial representatives from the territory;

[33] Hsia Weisung to Karakhan, note transmitting instruction from the Waichiaopu, July 17, 1929, *Izvestiia*, July 18, 1929, p. 1. Russian text also in Voitinskii, *K.V.Zh.D. i Politika Imperialistov v Kitae* (*The C.E.R. and the Policy of the Imperialists in China*), pp. 62-63; for Chinese text, see Chih, *op. cit.*, Appendix VIII and *Wai-Chiao-Pu Kung-pao* (*Bulletin of the Waichiaopu*), Aug., 1929, pp. 52-53; English translation in *The Sino-Russian Crisis*, pp. 28-29 and *C.Y.B.*, *1929-30* (Peking & Tientsin), pp. 1221-1222.

[34] *Izvestiia*, July 18, 1929, p. 1; *C.Y.B.*, *1929-30*, pp. 1221-1222.

[35] "Razryv Snoshenii s Kitaem" ("Rupture of Relations with China"), *Izvestiia*, July 18, 1929, p. 1.

2. To recall persons appointed by the Government of the U.S.S.R. on the Chinese Eastern Railway from the territory of China;

3. To suspend all railway communications between China and the U.S.S.R.;

4. To order the diplomatic and consular representatives of the Chinese Republic in the U.S.S.R. to leave immediately the territory of the U.S.S.R.[36]

Consequently, Soviet-Chinese diplomatic relations were completely severed. *Izvestiia* hailed the Soviet decision. After referring to the abnormal relationship between the two countries during the past years, it declared that "the breaking of the existing relations at the initiative of the Soviet Government is an act of immense political significance and the strongest blow to the prestige of the Nanking Government."[37]

Izvestiia also reported a statement made by Chiang Kai-shek, head of the Nanking Government, concerning the Sino-Soviet crisis in the Central Committee of the Kuomintang. Touching upon the Chinese Eastern Railway, Chiang reportedly stated that "the Soviet Government repeatedly declared its intention to transfer the railway to China, but it merely tries to strengthen its possession of the road." Chiang was cited as concluding: "Red imperialism is, therefore, more dangerous than the White." This statement, as might be expected, was denounced as "hypocritical."[38]

According to a TASS dispatch, C. T. Wang, the Foreign Minister of the Nanking Government, also made a statement to the effect that "the Chinese Government does not intend to solve the C.E.R. problem by force and hopes to maintain friendly relations with the U.S.S.R." Wang indicated that "at the present moment, China was merely compelled to take up the administration of the C.E.R. temporarily . . . because the Soviet officials had abandoned their duties." Wang gave assurance that China did not contemplate taking over the

---

[36] Karakhan to Hsia Weisung, note, July 17, 1929, *Izvestiia*, July 18, 1929, p. 1; Russian, Chinese, and English texts also in Voitinskii, *K.V.Zh.D. i Politika Imperialistov v Kitae* (*The C.E.R. and the Policy of the Imperialists in China*), pp. 63-65; Chih, *op. cit.*, Appendix IX, pp. 77-79 and *The Sino-Russian Crisis*, pp. 40-41 respectively.

[37] "Razryv Snoshenii c Kitaem" "Rupture of Relations with China"), *Izvestiia*, July 18, 1929, p. 1.

[38] Quoted in a TASS dispatch from Shanghai, July 17, 1929, *Izvestiia*, July 18, 1929, p. 1.

C.E.R. definitively; rather, "the Chinese Government is prepared to restore the previous conditions on the C.E.R. by way of negotiations." He also declared the readiness of the National Government to enter into negotiations. The Wang statement was, however, appraised by *Izvestiia* as nonsensical.[39]

Justifying the measure taken by the Soviet Government in rupturing relations with China, a Soviet commentator, Voitinskii, accused "the Manchurian militarists" and the Nanking Government of replying only with words about their readiness for negotiations while actually continuing to chalk up one accomplished fact after another. According to Voitinskii, the Chinese Government now "demanded from the Soviet Government the legalization of the raid and the nullification of the agreements concluded with China in 1924." He insisted that the Soviet Government was, as a matter of course, "unable to compromise with the Chinese."[40]

On July 19, 1929, the Nanking Government issued a manifesto to various powers following the Soviet note breaking off diplomatic relations. All Chinese legations abroad were instructed, and Dr. Wang Chung-hwei in The Hague was advised to publish the manifesto declaring that the Soviet Government had repeatedly violated the Sino-Soviet Agreements of 1924 both with respect to management of the railway and the pledge not to disseminate propaganda. The communication further charged that the U.S.S.R.

not only made use of the staff members of the railway and its revenue for communist propaganda and to assist various counterrevolutionary elements in China, but also plotted for the overthrow of the Chinese Government.

It based these charges upon the documents which had been captured at the Soviet Consulate General in Harbin and which were now published. After deploring both the Soviet ultimatum and the note cutting off official intercourse between the two countries, thus precluding the possibility of an early amicable settlement of the dispute, the manifesto declared that the Chinese Government, "although imbued with the spirit of the Kellogg Peace Pact, would take legitimate measures for self-defense."[41]

The Soviet spokesman challenged this by saying that "the Chi-

[39] TASS dispatch from Tokyo, July 17, 1929, *Izvestiia*, July 19, 1929, p. 1.

[40] G. Voitinskii, in *Krasnaia Nov'*, no. 9, 1929, pp. 142-143.

[41] Text of the manifesto in *Bulletin of Waichiaopu*, Aug., 1929, pp. 55-58; *The Sino-Russian Crisis*, pp. 25-28.

nese militarists headed by the Nanking bosses threatened to appeal to foreign powers for intervention in the conflict."[42] Foreign powers did in fact show concern over the situation created by the rupture of Soviet-Chinese relations. Following an appeal by American Secretary of State Stimson, the French Government on July 19, 1929, approached the Government of the U.S.S.R. with a "proposal of mediation for the peaceful settlement of the Sino-Soviet conflict." The events and outcome of this "first invocation of the Kellogg Pact" will be set forth below;[43] what is important to note here is the Soviet reaction to the Chinese effort to invoke the interest and support of third powers, particularly of the United States and Great Britain.[44]

According to the judgments of Voitinskii, Mikhailov, and Skalov, the action taken by China on the C.E.R. on July 10, 1929, served no interests but those hostile to China, benefiting those who intended to turn that country from a semicolony into a colony. They thought of the Kuomintang Government as a weapon wielded by imperialist forces led by the U.S.A. against the Soviet Union.[45] Demonstrating how imperialism pushed the Chinese generals to seize the C.E.R., Skalov explained that in the considerations of "the most wild imperialists, especially of the English militarists," the seizure of the C.E.R. might lead to armed collision between China and the U.S.S.R. Any advance of the Red Army into Manchuria would cause a clash between the U.S.S.R. and Japan. Under cover of invoking the interference of the League of Nations, the "imperialists" would create a powerful anti-Soviet bloc. If war were to break out in the East they would blame the U.S.S.R. as a "culprit" and put themselves forward as "protector" of China and decide the war with a blow from the West. If the U.S.S.R. yielded and gave up its rights in the C.E.R., then the decisive force on the C.E.R. would be imperialistic, and the C.E.R. would become a vanguard for the capitalists.[46] Voitinskii emphasized the role of imperialists on the preparation of the conflict on the C.E.R. He charged that the "American

[42] Voitinskii, in *Krasnaia Nov'*, no. 9, 1929, p. 143.

[43] Cf. pp. 210-218, *infra*.

[44] "Predlozhenie Posrednichestva" ("The Offer of Mediation"), *Izvestiia*, July 23, 1929, p. 1.

[45] Voitinskii, in *Krasnaia Nov'*, no. 9, 1929, pp. 148, 149; Mikhailov, *Chto Proiskhodit na Kitaiskoi Vostochnoi Zheleznoi Doroge?* (*Events Pertaining to the Chinese Eastern Railway*), p. 26; Skalov, *Sobytiia na Kitaiskoi Vostochnoi Zheleznoi Doroge* (*Events on the C.E.R.*), p. 14.

[46] Skalov, *op. cit.*, p. 11.

intervention," by proposing the internationalization of the C.E.R., "would accomplish the first step toward the invasion of the U.S.S.R."[47]

DAMAGE TO THE RAILWAY ENTERPRISE

Following the complete rupture of relations between China and the U.S.S.R., the Chinese Eastern Railway was temporarily under Chinese management. In the joint declaration on the C.E.R. question issued by the Political Council of the Northeastern Provinces on July 22, 1929, the Liaoning, the Kirin, and the Heilungkiang Provincial Governments gave support to the stand taken by the Chinese Central Government: "as to the management of the C.E.R. the Chinese Government reports its willingness to respect the 1924 agreement."[48] The statement of the Committee of Communications of the Northeastern Provinces also made it clear that "all action taken by the Chinese authorities was based on the Peking and the Mukden Agreements," and that "the action taken by Tupan Lu Yung-huan was rendered imperative solely to preserve the safety of the North-Eastern Provinces and to maintain order and efficiency on the Chinese Eastern Railway which constitutes the first duty of the Tupan of the Railway."[49]

Once in control of the railway administration, the Chinese attempted to carry out some of the reforms the Russians had blocked. Thus Assistant Manager Fan Tsi-kwang applied the 50-50 principle of employment to correct the discrimination against Chinese nationals in the higher offices. As a result of his efforts, Chinese personnel now headed the departments of traffic, motive power, commercial finance and revenue, housing, Russian and Chinese secretariat, and telegraph, while Soviet citizens continued in charge of the general affairs, maintenance, accounting, pension, veterinary, land, and material departments.[50]

The Soviets on their part reacted not only with strong verbal protests, but also with deeds of violence. There were at the outset

[47] Voitinskii, in *Krasnaia Nov'*, no. 9, 1929, p. 150.

[48] For Chinese text of the joint declaration, see Chih, *op. cit.*, Appendix XI; for English text, see Tong, *op. cit.*, pp. 37-39.

[49] For text of the statement, see Tong, *op. cit.*, pp. 39-42.

[50] *Ibid.*, pp. 24-25.

numerous and widespread resolutions of angry protest against the action of the so-called "Chinese usurpers."[51]   In vain did Chinese spokesmen, such as Foreign Minister Wang, in a speech on July 22, 1929, emphasize that China had not "seized" the railway but had merely "taken an appropriate measure of self-defense."[52]   Soviet commentators accused the "Chinese reactionaries" of hoping to ease their own internal situation and to please the imperialists by seizing the C.E.R. and acting against the U.S.S.R.[53]

The Soviet protest also took the form of direct action on the C.E.R. itself.   It was reported that a number of Soviet workers of the trade unions tried to bring about general strikes and thereby stop traffic on the C.E.R.   Furthermore, "Soviet employees of the railway were compelled by their Government to resign," and the "remaining young members of the Soviet trade unions would see to it that the instruction from Moscow was carried out implicitly."

There were also reports of outright destruction of property. General Me Chung-lin, chief of the police forces of the special administrative areas, stated that on and after July 22, he had heard a good deal about "Communist destructive activities at Manchuli and Suifenho after the Soviet authorities had found that sabotage had no effect upon the Railway."[54]   Tsao Lien-en, a resident investigator in Manchuria (for the Chinese Ministry of Industry, Commerce, and Labor) gave a detailed account of the damage done to the railway by numerous train derailments and bombing outrages, as well as destruction of railway assets by Soviet Russians at all points of the railway, in addition to losses China sustained in the customs revenues and in the decreases of the freight receipts.   The exact losses resulting from such "unscrupulous acts" were said to be difficult to estimate numerically.[55]   According to the data which he and Hollington K. Tong tabulated in the form of a diary, the notable incidents may be listed as follows:

On August 6 a railway bridge across the Hsienling River was bombed.   On August 7 a factory in Machiho was set on fire; in Pristan, Harbin telephone wires at certain sections were cut; and a considerable length of rail at the 946-kilometer point was removed. On August 8 "Soviet agents" damaged a portion of the railway track

[51] M. Mikhailov, *op. cit.*, p. 3.   [52] *The Sino-Russian Crisis*, p. 33.
[53] Mikhailov, *op. cit.*, pp. 14, 18.   [54] Tong, *op. cit.*, pp. 43-46.
[55] Tsao, *op. cit.*, p. 90.

near the Old City of Harbin, and also removed the rails on the other side of the Sungari River. On August 9 the track near the Station Ashibo, about twenty-seven miles from Harbin on the eastern section of the C.E.R., was torn up, causing the complete wreck of a freight train. Owing to this wreck, eastbound traffic was temporarily suspended.[56]

As the daily occurrences continued, train No. 3 on August 17 was bombed while passing the 430-kilometer point; two cars and a portion of the rail were destroyed and several railway employees were wounded. On the same day, bombs were thrown at locomotive No. 67 at the six-kilometer point; two engineers were killed, another injured. On August 29 many shots were fired at the train passing near Suifenho at the 1441-kilometer point, where a considerable quantity of explosives was left behind. On September 3 the fish-plates of rails on the Miling Railway at the 18-kilometer point were loosened, causing the derailment of a train with eight cars, which killed two passengers and injured a large number of others as it turned over.[57]

In addition, two attempts were made to flood the coal mines at Chalainor on July 29 and again on August 8.[58] Most serious of all, many Chinese steamers, including S.S. *Haichen, Ishing, Aigun, Shengyang, Haichong, Weitung, Hungtai, Tungfeng,* and a tow-boat, *Hwakan,* were seized by "Soviet Communists" on the Sungari River and on the Chinese side of the Amur and the Ussuri rivers, and some of them were detained at Khabarovsk. With the exception of women and children, the passengers and crew members, totaling 1,182, were afterwards removed to "a concentration camp" and suffered "most brutal treatment."[59] Likewise cargoes in enormous quantities were confiscated. The total loss resulting from the wrongful seizure of the steamers was estimated at $4,445,000.[60]

Undeclared War as a Test for the Kellogg Pact

Immediately following the complete cessation of its relations with China, the Soviet Government was said to have prepared to force

---

[56] *Ibid.,* pp. 91-93; Tong, *op. cit.,* pp. 46-47.

[57] Tong, *op. cit.,* pp. 47-48; Tsao, *op. cit.,* pp. 93-95.

[58] Tong, *op. cit.,* p. 48.   [59] Tsao, *op. cit.,* pp. 95-97, 99.

[60] *Ibid.,* p. 95.

China to accept its terms through an armed threat. Certainly the Soviet press of this period not only stressed the preparedness of the government for warlike measures, but also suggested a determination to resort to the use of force. No sooner had the break between the two countries taken place than *Izvestiia* raised "the problem of the security of a considerable part of the Soviet eastern frontiers." It declared that the situation compelled the Soviet Union "to take appropriate measures for the defense of its own territory against possible encroachment on the part of the Chinese and White Russian bandits."[61] Nor was passive defense of Soviet territory against the incursion of "bandits" the only measure contemplated. "The workers of the Soviet Union," *Izvestiia* further declared, "in reply to the incident of the C.E.R., demand that a decisive repulse be given to the violators in Manchuria."[62] An even broader basis for Russian intervention in Manchuria was provided by Mikhailov in suggesting action on China's behalf as well as in defense of Soviet interests. "We cannot," he wrote, "permit further mockery on the part of the Chinese counterrevolutionaries. We are strong enough to protect the interests of China and the U.S.S.R. on the Chinese Eastern Railway."[63]

On the Chinese side no similar moves for military readiness or hostile action in the Manchurian border regions were evident. China at this time was caught in inner turmoil, occasioned by the Feng Yu-hsiang rebellion. This rebellion had caused widespread suffering in Northwest China and had resulted in a precarious situation in the Yangtze Valley as well. Under the circumstances, the Chinese felt that the Soviet moves in Manchuria were designed to take advantage of China's internal troubles. There was even some suggestion that the Soviets were promoting or intensifying these internal troubles. Thus the Feng Yu-hsiang movement, according to the Chinese Government, was shown to be effectively connected with the so-called "Soviet plot" revealed in the documents seized in the raid on the Soviet consulate at Harbin.[64] Whether or not this connection existed,

[61] "Razryv Snoshenii s Kitaem" ("Rupture of Relations with China"), *Izvestiia*, July 18, 1929, p. 1.
[62] "Otpor Mass" ("Repulse of the Masses"), *Izvestiia*, July 16, 1929, p. 1.
[63] Mikhailov, *op. cit.*, p. 26.
[64] *Bulletin of the Waichiaopu*, Jan., 1930, p. 87. Photostats of the documents appear in *The Sino-Russian Crisis*, published by the International Relations Committee of the Kuomintang, Nanking, 1929. The Soviet Union charged that the

the Chinese Government was exclusively engaged in suppressing Feng, whom it regarded as operating under Soviet inspiration,[65] and perhaps for this reason could not be too attentive to the Soviet build-up opposite Manchuria.

Thus, in the initial stage after the rupture of Soviet-Chinese relations, the Chinese seem to have made no active war preparations along the Manchurian frontier. The Nanking Government was in no position to do so, and neither the Nanking nor the Mukden Government seems to have had until later any real conception of the seriousness of the situation. There was some reinforcement of local frontier forces, supplemented by a few "student volunteers" from schools and colleges in Manchuria; but no added supplies of arms and ammunition were sent to the frontier corps. Perhaps because no war had been fought in this area since the dawn of the Chinese Republic, no frontier guards were provided by the Mukden or the Nanking Governments.

Hence, in the light of the Russian statements of hostile intentions and the Chinese lack of readiness, *Izvestiia's* assurances to "the toiling masses of the U.S.S.R." that the Soviet Government had taken "all necessary steps for the guarantee of the interests and security of the Soviet state"[66] took on an ominous tone which boded ill for China.

THE FIRST INVOCATION OF THE PEACE PACT

In this state of tension, the United States Government learned from its envoy in Peking, Minister MacMurray, that "the Soviet Government was determined to force the issue with China."[67] Furthermore, there were Chinese and Soviet troop movements toward the Manchurian border with Irkutsk and Chita serving as the Soviet mobilization centers.[68] On July 18, 1929, in view of the Russo-Chinese crisis and "the possibility of an armed clash," Secretary

documents were forged by the White Russians who used the old-style letter Russian typewriter. A close examination of the photostats did verify the point of old-style Russian lettering. Yet, the contention of both sides remained to be judged.

[65] *C.Y.B., 1931* (Peking & Tientsin), p. 496.

[66] Cf. "Razryv Snoshenii s Kitaem" ("Rupture of Relations with China"), *Izvestiia*, July 18, 1929, p. 1.

[67] Minister MacMurray in China to Secretary Stimson, tel., July 17, 1929, *F.R.U.S., 1929*, II, 207.

[68] Same to the same, tel., July 18, 1929, *ibid.*, p. 208.

Stimson, "on the point of celebrating on July 24 the coming into effect of the Kellogg-Briand Peace Pact,"[69] promptly held conversations with the British, Japanese and French ambassadors and particularly with the Chinese minister, C. C. Wu.[70] Later on the same day, the Secretary had a similar conversation with the Italian ambassador in Washington.[71]

During these conversations, Secretary Stimson pointed out to the foreign envoys "the grave responsibility imposed by the present situation upon all the powers signatory or adherent to the multilateral peace pact."[72] He deemed that the Sino-Soviet dispute, according to the claims from both sides, was "of an eminently justiciable nature and one which was particularly fitted for arbitration."[73] He sought international co-operation "in an effort to avert hostilities between China and Russia by calling their attention to the principle of the Pact of Paris signed by them,"[74] and encouraged a pacific settlement by Russia and China of their existing dispute. The foreign diplomatic representatives agreed with Secretary Stimson and telegraphed their respective Governments accordingly.[75] This historical action thus initiated by the United States was the first invocation of the Kellogg Pact.

In a wire to Minister MacMurray in Peking, Secretary Stimson expressed his interest in an amicable solution of the controversy between China and the Soviet Union.

I told Dr. Wu that one of the great difficulties was that China had acted so hurriedly; that the seizure of the railway whether rightly or wrongly was not interpreted by public opinions as an attempt to protect China against attacks of individual propagandists but as an attempt to seize property belonging to Russia and in which she had a joint right of management under the agreement of 1924. I stated that if neutral opinion took this view, probably Russia took the same view and believed that China's action was an attack on her as a nation . . . . He asked me what steps I thought should be taken. I told him . . . the first thing to be done was to make

[69] Stimson to MacMurray, tel., July 19, 1929, *ibid.*, p. 215.
[70] Same to the same, tel., July 18, 1929, *ibid.*, p. 210.
[71] Same to the same, tel., July 19, 1929, *ibid.*, p. 217.
[72] Same to the same, tel., July 18, 1929, *ibid.*, p. 210.
[73] Same to the same, tel., July 19, 1929, *ibid.*, p. 215.
[74] *Survey of American Foreign Relations, 1930* (Publication of the Council on Foreign Relations), New Haven, 1930, p. 414.
[75] Secretary Stimson to Minister MacMurray in China, tel., July 18, 1929, *F.R.U.S., 1929*, II, 210; same to the same, tel., July 19, 1929, *ibid.*, p. 217.

clear the pacific character of China's intentions . . . . I said that I believe China should make it clear from the beginning not only that she was only protecting herself against the acts of progandists but that she had no intention of seizing Russian property . . . . I said that as a friend I thought China should make clear its pacific intentions and readiness to do justice and that China's haste has been one of the causes of the original misunderstanding and must now be offset or remedied in some such way.[76]

In Paris, French Foreign Minister Briand, seemed to appreciate the steps taken by Secretary Stimson in the Russo-Chinese conflict and undertook to discuss the matter with the Soviet and Chinese envoys in Paris on July 19 along the same lines as Secretary Stimson's talk to the Chinese minister in Washington on July 18.[77]

The Italian and Japanese Governments were in full accord with Secretary Stimson in regard to China and Russia.[78] On July 19 the Japanese Foreign Minister, Baron Shidehara, carried a message similar to Secretary Stimson's to the Soviet ambassador and the Chinese minister in Tokyo and called attention to their promises in the Pact for the Renunciation of War. Both envoys replied that their countries did not wish to make war except in self-defense. Baron Shidehara urged that the dispute "be settled by friendly means."[79]

It was perhaps coincidental that almost simultaneously with Secretary Stimson's first invocation of the Kellogg Pact, the Chinese Government, on July 19, was issuing its own manifesto touching upon the Pact:

China however will devote itself to the maintenance of peace, as it is the cherished wish of the Government and the people that world peace be preserved. She will, to the utmost of her ability and consonant with the right of self-protection, abide by the spirit of the Treaty for the Renunciation of War.[80]

In reply to the American-led peace campaign, the Soviet Commissariat for Foreign Affairs issued the following statement on July 22:

[76] *Ibid.*, p. 216.

[77] Memorandum by the assistant to Secretary Stimson (Beck), July 19, 1929, *ibid.*, p. 218.

[78] Memorandum by Secretary Stimson, July 24, 1929, *ibid.*, p. 237.

[79] Secretary Stimson to Minister MacMurray in China, tel., July 24, 1929, *ibid.*, p. 235.

[80] "Manifesto of the Chinese Government," July 19, 1929, Minister C. C. Wu to Secretary Stimson, note, undated, received on July 23, 1929, *ibid.*, p. 231. The same document is printed in *The Sino-Russian Crisis*, Appendix II, pp. 25-27.

In connection with the position brought about as a result of the rupture of Chinese-Soviet relations, the French Government has addressed to the Government of the U.S.S.R. an offer to take upon itself the mediation for the peaceful settlement of the Chinese-Soviet conflict.

This proposal was made in Paris on July 19 by M. Briand directly to the political representative of the U.S.S.R. in France, Comrade Dovgalevskii, and in Moscow was communicated by the French ambassador, M. Herbette, at the instruction of M. Briand, to the People's Vice-Commissar of Foreign Affairs, Comrade L. M. Karakhan, on Sunday, July 21.

Yesterday, July 22, the People's Vice-Commissar of Foreign Affairs, Comrade Karakhan, in the name of the Government of the U.S.S.R. gave the answer to this proposal of France, declaring to the French ambassador in Moscow, M. Herbette, that "the proposal of the Minister of Foreign Affairs of France cannot but be duly appreciated. The Government of the U.S.S.R. must, however, observe that this proposal becomes pointless in view of the refusal of the Chinese authorities to restore the legal basis, violated by them, which is the necessary prerequisite for an agreement, pursuant to the note of the Soviet Government of July 13. As regards the question of possible further complications, the Government of the U.S.S.R. must declare that no one takes so much pains for the preservation of the peace, so far as this depends upon its actions, as the Union Government. There is no ground for doubting that the U.S.S.R. has been and remains the mainstay of the peace of the world.[81]

By July 23 Secretary Stimson "had received assurances from China and Russia that neither would fight except in self-defense, nor would they attack each other."[82] Nevertheless, Stimson thought "the situation remained dangerous so long as it was possible for irresponsible people to provoke a clash." He was "anxious for all moral support." Therefore, on July 23 Secretary Stimson also had a conversation with the secretary of the German Embassy (the German ambassador being away) in which he expressed hope for "Germany's moral support and approval" of the action he had taken on July 18 to invoke for the first time the Kellogg Pact so that "any fighting be stopped."[83]

On the next day, Secretary Stimson was informed through the

[81] "Statement by the Soviet Commissariat for Foreign Affairs," *Izvestiia*, July 23, 1929, p. 1.
[82] Secretary Stimson to Minister MacMurray in China, tel., July 24, 1929, *F.R.U.S., 1929*, II, 236.
[83] *Ibid.*

French Foreign Office that both the Chinese and the Soviet representatives in France had seen M. Briand, with the following results:

> The Chinese Minister had expressed his country's willingness to arbitrate and to abide by its obligations under the peace pact, but . . . the Soviet Ambassador . . . had expressed the opinion that the Soviet Government could not consider arbitration until the Chinese had restored matters to the *status quo ante*.[84]

Simultaneously the Soviet ambassador in Japan presented to Baron Shidehara the substance of this Soviet explanation for declining Briand's mediation proposal.[85]

On July 25 Secretary Stimson, regretting the continuing difficulty between Russia and China but anticipating an ultimate peaceful solution of their controversy, again summoned the British, French, Italian and Japanese ambassadors and the German chargé, and handed and read to them an *aide mémoire* which stated in part:

> Under these circumstances, if a road with honor out of their difficulties can be suggested to these sister nations, who have joined with us in this solemn compact of Peace and who have just signified their desire to maintain it, even in the perplexities which confront them at the present time, it seems that it should be done.
>
> I do not suggest mediation by any nation or a group of nations. Such a course would have its difficulties and might excite unfounded suspicion. I suggest a way by which Russian and China themselves in the exercise of their own sovereign action may create their machinery for conciliation and thus bring about an ultimate settlement of their present dispute, based upon the only foundation upon which such a lasting settlement can be constructed, namely, a full and impartial investigation of the facts.[86]

The Stimson *aide mémoire* enclosed suggestions for a commission of conciliation. They read:

> Pending the investigation mentioned below both countries agree to commit no act of hostility against the other country or its nationals and to prevent their armed forces from crossing the boundaries of their respective countries.

[84] Chargé Armour in France to Secretary Stimson, tel., July 24, 1929, *ibid.*, p. 239.

[85] Memorandum by the Assistant Secretary of State (Johnson), July 25, 1929, *ibid.*, p. 241.

[86] Secretary Stimson to French Ambassador Claudel and certain other envoys, *aide mémoire*, July 25, 1929, ibid., pp. 242-243.

Pending such investigation the regular operation of the Chinese East-ern Railway will be restored and carried on, the interests of both Russia and China in said Railway being guarded by the appointment as President and General Manager with full powers, of a prominent national of some neutral country approved by both China and Russia, and by the recognition and continuance in their respective positions as directors under the agree-ment of May 31, 1924, of the five Russian and the five Chinese ap-pointees.

Pending such investigation the obligations upon both China and Russia of the treaty of 1924, including particularly the obligation of the mutual covenants contained in said treaty—"not to permit within their respective territories the existence and/or activities of any organizations or groups whose aim is to struggle by acts of violence against the governments of either contracting party" and "not to engage in propaganda directed against the political and social systems of either contracting party" will continue in full force and effect.

The grievances and claims of both countries shall be investigated by an impartial commission of conciliation the membership of which shall be agreed upon by Russia and China and which shall have full power to investigate all the facts concerning such grievances and claims and to render to both countries and make public its conclusions both as to the facts and as to any suggested remedies for the future.[87]

These suggestions were subsequently communicated by the envoys to their governments. It was agreed that the matter should be kept strictly secret for the time being "since premature publicity would imperil the proposals being carried out successfully."[88]

M. Briand gave this plan of conciliation his full support: "In his opinion Mr. Stimson's suggestion is in every respect in accordance with the Kellogg Pact," and "its legal basis is strong."[89] M. Briand noted:

In case Russia and China could not reach a settlement by direct commu-nication between themselves the Secretary's note could be forwarded, in accordance with the Kellogg Pact, it being understood that such trans-mission should be made with the approval of the principal Powers interested in the maintenance of the Peace in the Far East.[90]

[87] *Ibid.*, pp. 243-244.
[88] Secretary Stimson to Minister MacMurray in China, tel., July 26, 1929, *ibid.*, p. 247.
[89] The First Secretary of the French Embassy (Henry) to the Assistant Secretary of State (Castle), letter, Aug. 1, 1929, *ibid.*, p. 264.
[90] *Ibid.*

The Japanese Government, while "deeply appreciating" the Secretary's suggestion and being "sincerely willing" to co-operate, was skeptical about the practicability of the suggested plan. The Japanese *note verbale* reads in part:

All official reports which have been reaching Tokyo from various sources tend to strengthen the impression that both China and the Soviet Union are anxious to compose their differences relating to the Chinese Eastern Railway by direct negotiations between themselves.

If the Japanese Government are correctly informed, neither side is likely to welcome any initiative of a third Power or a group of third Powers,—still less any participation by the Governments or nationals,— in the settlement of present difficulty. It is particularly apprehended that the plan under which a national of a third Power is to be appointed, however temporarily, as President and General Manager of the Chinese Eastern Railway, or to take part in the machinery for conciliation, will be resented both in China and in the Soviet Union.

Should the plan in question be rejected by either or both of the two contracting parties, the Powers will find themselves in a peculiarly embarassing position.[91]

Secretary Stimson then made it clear to the Japanese ambassador in Washington:

This suggestion [for a commission of a conciliation] was not in the nature of a mediation by any power or group of powers, but was intended as a suggestion of what was to be voluntary action by China and Russia. . . . The neutral national whose appointment was suggested in the *aide mémoire*, [was] to be chosen not by the neutral countries but by Russia and China themselves . . . . My Government had decided to make this suggestion only in case China and Russia seemed to be unable to get together through negotiation by their own efforts . . . . If Russia and China should be able to get together we would be most happy . . . . If the negotiations between Russia and China continued to go on I should take no further step, but should reserve such action for any emergency which might occur on their failure to go on . . . . So long as Russia and China seemed to be making progress towards direct negotiation I did not intend to make any suggestion.[92]

The German Foreign Office gave a cool reception to Stimson's proposal of conciliation: "It is German policy to keep out of the

[91] Memorandum by Secretary Stimson, July 30, 1929, *ibid.*, p. 260.
[92] *Ibid.*, pp. 260-261.

conflict over the Chinese Eastern Railway and to encourage a direct settlement," considering that "interference by other powers is not desired and would not be accepted by either Russia or China."[93]

The British Government preferred "to await the result of the negotiations, direct or indirect, between the two parties thereto,"[94] because "the conferences between China and Russia immediately commenced," and also because "they feared that the two nations, particularly Russia, would resent any suggestion of a neutral manager of the railroad."[95] The British ambassador in Washington, Sir Esme Howard, told Secretary Stimson that "Russia felt so alone and separated from every one else that his Government felt she would resent any outside mediation."[96]

In the meantime, beginning July 22, Mr. Tsai Yung-sheng, Commissioner for Foreign Affairs in Harbin, had been in touch with Mr. Mel'nikov, the Soviet consul general there, and shortly thereafter the Mukden Government established communication with Moscow.[97] On July 30, in an interview with the Japanese ambassador in Moscow, Karakhan stated that "the Chinese Minister in Berlin had approached the Soviet representative with an offer to negotiate. This has been rejected." Karakhan remarked that "if the Chinese were sincere they could telegraph Moscow direct setting forth their views," and that "there was no need for intervention or mediation by a third power."[98] The Chinese Foreign and Railways Ministers, C. T. Wang and Sun Fo, had also expressed their opinions in favor of direct negotiations.[99]

Thus the first invocation of the Kellogg Pact passed rather quickly from a stage of active efforts to promote conciliation to one of quies-

[93] Ambassador Schurman in Germany to Secretary Stimson, tel., Aug. 5, 1949, *ibid.*, p. 271.
[94] British Ambassador Howard to Secretary Stimson, letter, Aug. 30, 1929, *ibid.*, p. 308.
[95] Memorandum by Secretary Stimson, Aug. 26, 1929, *ibid.*, p. 303.
[96] *Ibid.*
[97] Cf. Karakhan to Chang Hsüeh-liang, letter, Aug. 1, 1929, *Izvestiia*, Aug. 2, 1929, p. 1.
[98] Minister MacMurray in China to Secretary Stimson, tel., Aug. 5, 1929, *F.R.U.S., 1929*, II, 272.
[99] Kuo Wen News Agency (Nanking), dispatch, Aug. 22, 1929, cited in Minister MacMurray in China to Secretary Stimson, tel., Aug. 4, 1929, *ibid.*, pp. 270-271; *North China Standard* (Peking), Aug. 1, cited in the same to the same, tel., Aug. 1, 1929, *ibid.*, p. 263; Reuter, Dispatch from Shanghai, July 25, 1929, cited in the same to the same, tel., July 26, 1929, *ibid.*, p. 250.

cent but interested observation of developments. This passive mood lasted until November, 1929, when the cumulative impact of repeated incidents of violence in the Russo-Chinese crisis prompted a second invocation of the Kellogg Pact, again under the veteran leadership of Secretary Stimson.

THE MOUNTING INTENSITY OF THE UNDECLARED WAR

Meanwhile the two parties to the dispute had taken matters into their own hands, and each was pursuing its own course of action. On July 19, 1929, immediately after China had received the Soviet note rupturing diplomatic relations, Soviet troops were reported to have bombarded the Chinese garrison at Suifeng and five Soviet airplanes were observed over the same Chinese city.[100] The Chinese manifesto of the same date had called the situation to the attention of the various powers.[101] But Soviet sources treated this manifesto as "an appeal of the Chinese counterrevolutionary government to imperialism for help against the U.S.S.R."[102] On July 22 the Chinese Government announced its intention to submit the matter for investigation and settlement in accordance with Articles XII, XVI, and XVII of the Covenant of the League of Nations, "should the Moscow Government deliberately violate the Kellogg Pact."[103] Again after President Hoover had on July 24 proclaimed the famous Kellogg Anti-War Pact to be in force, China, in an identical note to various signatory powers on August 21, called their attention to "the warlike measures of the Soviet Government."[104]

In the Soviet Union, *Izvestiia* again raised the outcry that "we are able to beat off any attack on the Soviet state." It then enumerated the tasks of the Soviet people and state in an effort at mobilizing morale as though the country were in a national emergency on the eve of war.[105]

According to the Japanese military intelligence, reported in an

[100] "A List of Soviet Armed Invasions of the Chinese Northeastern Border" (Monograph of the Waichiaopu, 1929), cited in Tao-shing Chang, *op. cit.*, p. 145.
[101] *Ibid.*, p. 155.
[102] G. N. Voitinskii, *KVZhD i Politika Imperialistov v Kitae*, p. 37.
[103] Quoting from a "Bulletin of the Nanking Government of July 22," in New York *Times*, July 23, 1929, p. 1; T. S. Chang, *op. cit.*, pp. 155-156.
[104] *Ibid.*; New York *Times*, July 25, 1929, p. 1.
[105] "Manchzhurskaia Provokatsiia i Nashi Zadachi" ("The Manchurian Provocation and Our Tasks"), *Izvestiia*, July 20, 1929, p. 1.

American diplomatic cable, "best estimates all sources of information agree as to Russian army Irkutsk [and] east 50,000, composed four infantry divisions, two brigades of cavalry, miscellaneous units, including active aviation [at] Spassk."[106] Before the events on the C.E.R., "the Soviet troops in this region numbered about 34,000."[107] The increase of strength had been "brought about by the recruitment of the various units to war strength and by the transfer of [troops] . . . from Western Siberia."[108] While Russian mobilization was going on in Siberia, a "division of infantry [was]rumored leaving Vladivostok toward Pogranichnaia, with a brigade of mounted troops plus battery on the Suifenho border."[109] Moreover, the Soviet forces had large, three-inch field guns at the front, with additional heavy artillery on reserve at Vladivostok. The Chinese army, on the other hand, was "poorly equipped with ammunition averaging fifty rounds per man."[110]

On August 6 the Revolutionary Military Council of the U.S.S.R. issued a decree for the formation of the Special Far Eastern Army. It read in brief as follows:

1. To unite all the armed forces now stationed on Far Eastern territory into one army, and to call it the "Special Far Eastern Army."

2. To appoint Comrade Blücher as the Commander of the Special Far Eastern Army.

3. Comrade Blücher to take up his duties immediately.[111]

General Vasilii Konstantinovich Blücher (Bliukher), known as "Galen" while a military adviser to the Chinese Nationalists in 1926-27, was selected by Soviet War Commissar Voroshilov for this position[112] and was considered an outstanding choice because he had an

[106] Minister MacMurray in China to Secretary Stimson, tel., July 26, 1929, *F.R.U.S.*, *1929*, II, 249.
[107] Memorandum by the Chief of the Division of Eastern European Affairs (Kelley), Nov. 26, 1929, *ibid.*, p. 352.
[108] *Ibid.*
[109] Minister MacMurray in China to Secretary Stimson, tel., July 26, 1929, *ibid.*, p. 249.
[110] *Ibid.*
[111] The Soviet Union, Commissariat for Foreign Affairs, *Sovetsko-Kitaiskii Konflikt 1929, Sbornik Dokumentov* (*The Soviet-Chinese Conflict 1929: Collected Documents*) (Moscow, 1930), p. 37. For English translation of the decree, see Jane Degras (ed.), *Soviet Documents on Foreign Policy*, II (London, 1952), 391.
[112] *F.R.U.S.*, *1929*, II, 274 n. 49.

"excellent knowledge of the organization of the Chinese military forces and internal political conditions in China.[113]   Besides, his impressive career indicated that he was an old hand at Russian Far East problems.   In 1921-22, in his capacity as Commander-in-Chief, War Minister, and Chairman of the Military Council of the Far Eastern Republic, General Blücher had been credited with the leadership "in the operations of liquidating the White-guardists and Interventionists in the Far East."[114]

General Blücher was later praised for having successfully led into action the Special Far Eastern Army to which the honorary title of "Red Flag" was added.   The Special Red Flag Far Eastern Army (OKDVA)[115] consisted of "two army corps (three rifle divisions, one cavalry brigade, thirty to thirty-five airplanes each) with a total strength of about 113,000 men."[116] During the period between April, 1927 and July 15, 1932, General Blücher was rewarded for his "distinguished battle merits" with the additional honors of an Order of Red Flag and the Orders of Lenin and of the Red Star.   Most of these additional honors would logically be derived from his notable service in command of Soviet military activities in Manchuria.[117]

In reference to these activities Skalov made this observation: "Our forces on the Far Eastern frontiers have been strengthened. The [Special] Far Eastern Army has been organized and has already rebuffed all kinds of attempts to cross our frontiers.[118]

According to Captain Halsey Powell, then American naval attaché in China, who visited the Manchuli front between July 31 and August 2, 1929, on the morning of July 31, "twenty Soviet planes had flown over the border; and a few days before, the Russian artillery had fired over a hundred shells across the frontier.[119]   He reported his interview with General Liang Chung-chia, the com-

---

[113] Memorandum by the Chief of the Division of Eastern European Affairs (Kelley), Nov. 26, 1929, *ibid.*, II, 352-353.

[114] *B.S.E.* (1st ed.), Vol. VI (1927), col. 527; *M.S.E.* (2nd ed.), Vol. I, col. 952.

[115] OKDVA is the abbreviation for Osobaia Krasnoznamennaia Dal'nevostochnaia Armiia; *ibid.*, col. 95.

[116] Memorandum by the Chief of the Division of Eastern European Affairs (Kelley), Nov. 26, 1929, *F.R.U.S.*, *1929*, II, 352.

[117] Cf. *B.S.E.* (1st ed.), Vol. VI, col. 537, and *M.S.E.* (2nd ed.), Vol. I, col. 952.

[118] Skalov, *op. cit.*, p. 35.

[119] The naval attaché in China (Powell) to the minister in China (MacMurray), report, Aug. 2, 1929, *F.R.U.S.*, *1929*, II, 268.

mander of the Manchuli garrison, at the latter's headquarters as follows:

The General stressed the idea of pacific opposition to the Russian demonstration—wherein the Soviets had shelled Chinese territory and had brought tanks to the border firing machine guns, as well as sending airplanes over the Chinese lines daily. Although the forces of the two countries were at some points separated by only a few meters he was confident that his soldiers would not reply to these acts as they had very severe orders from the government that not a shot was to be fired.[120]

Since early August border incidents had begun to increase. The American consul at Harbin, G. C. Hanson, cabled the following:

Letters [dated] August 8-9 from Suifenho indicate Soviet forces have recommenced airplane and firing demonstrations which are causing panic among inhabitants. Chinese military there have advised Chinese Customs staff to withdraw but have ordered railway and telegraph employees stay. Large quantities [of] explosives [were] placed on Chinese Eastern Railway rails near that place which have caused Chinese military fear that their retreat might [at] any time be cut off.[121]

The imminent Soviet attack followed these military demonstrations rather shortly. General Chang Hsüeh-liang, head of the Mukden Government, reported to the National Government that on the afternoon of August 16 the Soviets had attacked Chalainor (Dalainor) "in order to cut the Chinese [Eastern] Railway between Manchuli and Hailar" at its western section. The Nanking Government had instructed Chang "to go no further than self-defense actually required." Chang later stated that "there were repeated incursions of Russians across the line, but that he was keeping his troops in control pursuant to instructions from Nanking."[122]

The situation, however, grew worse. On August 17, at 3 o'clock in the morning, Soviet troops started bombarding Manchuli, and directed further artillery attacks against Chalainor.[123] "Reliable reports" received by the American consul at Harbin showed that

[120] *Ibid.*, II, 269.
[121] Minister MacMurray in China to Secretary Stimson, tel., Aug. 13, 1929, *ibid.*, II, 275.
[122] Memorandum by Secretary Stimson following an interview with Chinese Minister C. C. Wu, Aug. 20, 1929, *ibid.*, II, 293.
[123] Minister MacMurray in China to Secretary Stimson, tel., Aug. 18, 2 p.m., *ibid.*, II, 285.

"clashes have occurred . . . between small detachments [of] Chinese-Soviet troops near Manchuria [Manchuli] Station and Suifenho. [Soviet] heavy aircraft [have been active]; Soviet artillery shooting [has been] taking place near both places evidently to intimidate [the] Chinese."[124] Later on the same day, after investigating the matter, the American consul at Mukden reported further particulars as follows:

Official telegram from Tsitsihar received by [the Mukden] Government this afternoon states that 10,000 Soviet troops with 30 field pieces and machine guns crossed border and attacked between Manchuli and Chalainor. Fifty Chinese soldiers [were] killed.[125]

Following a visit to the Manchuli and Chalainor battlefields, Mr. J. B. Powell, editor and publisher of the *China Weekly Review*, formerly *Millard's Review*, summarized the situation in the following words:

The writer has just visited a battlefield where organized bodies of Chinese and Russian troops had fought for several hours on three separate days, August 16, 18, and 20, the Russians having taken the offensive using armored cars on the tracks of the Trans-Baikal Railway, armor-covered motor-tanks, airplanes, artillery, infantry and cavalry. The Russian forces numbered approximately 5,000 men. They were opposed by about ten thousand Chinese troops stationed behind hastily constructed earthworks the Chinese being equipped with rifles, a few machine guns, several "Stokes" trench-mortars and probably not more than a half dozen pieces of field artillery.

The Russian forces were repulsed with heavy losses . . . . This battle took place on Chinese soil along a line stretching from about ten miles westward of Manchuli to a point about ten miles northward of Chalainor. The total distance of this line is about thirty miles, but actual fighting only occurred at the two ends, Manchuli and Chalainor . . . . The Chinese claim that this fighting took place on Chinese soil, [and] that the Chinese did not fire a single shot until they were attacked by the Soviet troops.[126]

Describing the outbreak of the fighting, General Liang Chung-chia, interviewed by Mr. Powell, told this story:

[124] Same to the same, tel., Aug. 18, 4 p.m., *ibid.*, II, 285.
[125] Same to the same, tel., Aug. 18, 2 p.m., *ibid.*, II, 285.
[126] J. B. Powell, "A Visit to the Manchuli and Chalainor 'Battlefields'" (written for the Chicago *Tribune*), *China Weekly Review* (Shanghai), L (Oct. 5, 1929), 200.

Early on the morning of August 16, a force of Soviet troops rode up to our sentries and ordered them to retire from their posts within fifteen minutes in order to avoid trouble. Since our orders from Mukden and Nanking were to retire rather than offer resistance to the Soviet troops, we followed the instructions and retired, but the Russian forces then advanced within twenty or thirty yards of our infantry posts and fired on our troops with rifles, machineguns and also threw hand-grenades into our trenches. However, at 3:30 o'clock in the afternoon of August 16, a Soviet Russian force of 2,000 infantry and 1,000 cavalry and some 30 pieces of field artillery (the Soviet troops wore the insignia of the 35th and 36th Soviet Regiments; their artillery was of the 4½ centimeter variety) advanced toward our trenches and heavy fighting developed for about four hours. The Russians apparently expected our troops to again fall back or even to flee, but instead they stood their ground and when the Russians neared our trenches we turned loose with machine guns and rifles and inflicted heavy losses on the Soviet troops.[127]

On August 14 a TASS statement charged: "From the very beginning of the conflict on the C.E.R., the White Guardists, under the direct co-operation of the Chinese forces, shelled our border outposts and peaceful inhabitants. For the last few days, there were dead and wounded registered at several places on our side." The TASS item further asserted that the White Russian Guards "even attempted to cross into our territory in the areas of Blagoveshchensk, the mouth of the Sungari River, and Lake Khanka. The attackers were dispersed by the decisive action of our forces."[128]

At the same time, according to official information, fighting occurred on the night of August 17, at Tungning,[129] south of Suifenho. Tungning was then occupied by Soviet troops possibly "consisting of Koreans, Buriats and Magyars" as front-line formations.[130] Two days later customs reports from Taheiho, northwest of Aigun and opposite Blagoveshchensk across the Amur, stated that the "Chinese military are about to evacuate from that place and that raiding parties, presumably Soviet, are crossing the Amur and pillaging on [the] Chinese side."[131] Thus a state of undeclared war actually existed

[127] Cited in *ibid.*, p. 202.
[128] "Provokatsionnye Nalety na Sovetskuiu Territoriiu" ("Provocative Raids on the Soviet Territory"), TASS announcement, *Izvestiia*, Aug. 14, 1929, p. 1.
[129] Minister MacMurray in China to Secretary Stimson, tel., Aug. 20, 1929, *F.R.U.S., 1929*, II, 295.
[130] Same to the same, tel., Aug. 21, 1929, *ibid.*, p. 298.
[131] Same to the same, tel., Aug. 20, 10 A.M., *ibid.*, p. 294.

along the border region of Manchuria. This Skalov indicated by saying that "frontier skirmishes have not only been continued but have been become intensified."[132]

At this juncture the Soviet TASS Agency issued a further statement on raids conducted from China into Soviet territory. This August 18 statement specified that a raid by White Guardists and Chinese bands of an "especially insolent character" had occurred in the areas of Station Manchuli, of Lake Khanka, and of the district of North Poltavskii (twenty-five miles to the southeast of Station Pogranichnaia). It categorically stated that "on all occasions without exception, our frontier forces were restricted to mere firm and decisive repulse of the attacks, the shelling, and the crossing of the frontiers by the White bandits and the Chinese bands."[133]

In connection with the conflicting versions of these alleged border incidents as reported by Russian and Chinese sources, on August 19 the Narkomindel handed the following warning to the German Embassy for transmission to the Nanking and Mukden Governments:

> The various crossings of the Chinese border by the Red Army were the results of raids on the Soviet territory made by Russian White Guards and Chinese detachments. The approval by Chinese authorities of White Guard organizations having ulterior motives creates a menace at the border and indicates the dangerous situation caused by the deeds of the Chinese authorities.
>
> Doing the utmost to prevent the crossing of the border by Soviet troops the Soviet Government holds that the Chinese authorities must disarm the White Guard detachments and prevent all possible raids on Soviet territory by Chinese forces.
>
> Otherwise the guilt of further complications caused by new raids will rest entirely with the Nanking and Mukden Governments.[134]

While no report whatsoever from the non-Soviet sources was available to substantiate the Soviet allegation concerning any Chinese

---

[132] Skalov, *op. cit.*, p. 43.

[133] "Kitaiskie Zakhvatchiki v Gryzne mezhdu Soboiu Prodolzhaiut Politiku Uporstva Voennoi Provokatsii i Pritesnenii Sovetskikh Grazhdan v Man'chzhurii" ("The Chinese Usurpers in Quarrel among Themselves Continue Their Policy of Obstinacy in Military Provocation and Persecution of Soviet Citizens in Manchuria"), *Izvestiia,* Aug. 18, 1929, p. 2.

[134] Narkomindel to the German embassy, statement for the Nanking and Mukden Governments, Aug. 19, 1929, in "Ot Narodnogo Komissariat po Inostrannym Delam" ("From the People's Commissariat for Foreign Affairs,") *Izvestiia,* Aug. 20, 1929; *Sovetsko-Kitaiskii Konflikt, 1929, Sbornik Dokumentov,* p. 39.

or White Russian raids on Soviet territory, *Izvestiia* repeated editorial charges of concentrations of Chinese regular troops and White Russian Guards on the border and their crossing into Soviet territory.[135]

The Chinese flatly denied these Soviet charges of border raids as "unthinkable," "absurd," and "white-washing."[136] They suggested that these "can easily be proved by an international commission of investigation to be untrue."[137] Supporting their denials was the testimony of General Semenov, former commander of the White Russian detachment under the war lord Chang Tsung-ch'ang of Shantung, whose troops had been completely disbanded upon order of Marshal Chang Hsüeh-liang after the defeat of Chang Tsung-ch'ang at Shanhaikwan in 1928, during the Chinese civil war. General Semenov stated in an interview: "Not a single one of the White Russians who are living on Chinese soil would dream of organizing themselves to make raids on Soviet territory."[138]

According to Mr. J. B. Powell, General Liang Chung-chia, in reply to Soviet charges, "branded it as Soviet propaganda and offered to escort a number of American newspaper correspondents throughout his line and encampments to prove that not a single Russian trooper, partisan or irregular was employed." Powell reported his observation as follows:

During a two day inspection of the Chinese lines in this Manchuli-Chalainor sector, the writer probably observed from 8,000 to 10,000 Chinese troops and saw not a single Russian wearing military uniform. He did observe several hundred Russians, residents of this area, but most of them were coal-miners at Chalainor or employees of the Chinese Eastern Railway, a few wearing the uniforms of the railway police which did not participate in the fighting.[139]

After completing his tour at both western and eastern fronts, Mr. Powell again wrote in this respect:

There is very little evidence on the Chinese side of the line, at least from sources available to the foreign newspaper correspondents, to bear

[135] "Provokatsionnaia Rabota Kitaiskikh Militaristov Usilivaetsia," ("The Provocative Work of the Chinese Militarists Is Intensified"), *Izvestiia*, Aug. 21, 1929, p. 1.
[136] Tong, *op. cit.*, p. 59.   [137] *Ibid.*
[138] Cited in *ibid.*, p. 60; Tong interviewed Semenov in Harbin in 1929.
[139] Powell, *op. cit.*, p. 200.

out the Soviet Russian Government's repeated charges of White-Guard attacks across the Sino-Siberian frontier. The writer of these paragraphs visited the Chinese front line trenches at both Manchuli-Chalainor and at Pogranichnaia and probably saw ten or fifteen thousand Chinese soldiers and did not observe a single Russian in Chinese military uniform. Aside from one or two Russian aviation instructors who have been seen at Harbin, wearing the Chinese military uniform, no other Russians have been observed with the Chinese military forces.[140]

Early in September, when American correspondents Powell, Wright, and Goette were at the Manchuli front, they had reported to their respective newspapers of continued Soviet invasion inside Chinese territory.[141] Small-scale raids, involving hundreds of Soviet troops at a time, were frequently reported.[142] Soviet aircraft also bombarded Suifenho, Manchuli, Chalainor, and other target localities.[143] In addition, the Soviets had made "almost daily flights . . . over the Chinese lines" from an airdrome "constructed in the mountains back of Abagaitue," which lies just within the Soviet border in a short distance from Manchuli to the west and from Chalainor to the south. Thus they had "inspected the entire front almost daily."[144]

Since October 1 events had taken a new turn for worse. At that time, the shocking news concerning the massacre of White Russian emigrés by "gangs of well-armed and organized Soviet cavalry"[145] came from the Three-River district located in the Barga region of Heilungkiang Province.[146] The so-called Three-River district fronts on the Argun River north of the Chinese Eastern Railway and east of the Great Hingan mountain range. The area is immensely fertile and prosperous as a source of supply of dairy products for Harbin and other Manchurian cities. Here about five thousand White Russians had settled, many of whom had served under Koltchak and Semenov in Siberia during the Russian Civil

[140] J. B. Powell, "The Soviet Atrocities in Barga" (written for the Chicago *Tribune*), *China Weekly Review*, L (Nov. 2, 1929), 339.
[141] Minister MacMurray in China to Secretary Stimson, tel., Sept. 3, 1929, *F.R.U.S.*, *1929*, II, 313.
[142] Reports of newspapermen and officials who were then inspecting the front, cited in Tong, *op. cit.*, pp. 50-51.
[143] Minister MacMurray in China to Secretary Stimson, tels., Sept. 9, 1929, 5 P.M. and 9 P.M., Oct. 3, 1929, *F.R.U.S.*, *1929*, II, 315, 316, 325.
[144] Powell, "A Visit to the Manchuli and Chalainor 'Battlefields,' " *China Weekly Review*, L (Oct. 5, 1929), 202.
[145] Powell, "The Soviet Atrocities in Barga," *ibid.*, L (Nov. 2, 1929), 337.
[146] MacMurray to Stimson, tel., Oct. 9, 1929, *F.R.U.S.*, *1929*, II, 325.

War.[147] It was reported that there were "four groups of Russian troops, each of about 200 cavalry men, operating now in the Three-River district."[148] One of these Soviet detachments first raided Tanikay village on October 1; other villages and towns of the area were devastated shortly thereafter.[149]

According to a report of T. Leonard Lilliestrom, American vice-consul at Harbin, who had talked to many of the victims in the near-by city of Hailar to which they had fled, a total of ten villages and towns were devastated. The total number of persons killed was first "placed at approximately 1,000, most of them being Russian emigrees."[150] This figure was later reported "to have swollen to a total of nearly 2,000."[151] The killed, for instance, in the town of Usturofok on October 13, also "included a number of Chinese, men, women and children, as well as a few Mongols."[152]

Describing these chilling episodes, Mr. Powell reported:

This massacre of the male inhabitants of Tanikay occurred on Tuesday, October 1. Two days later the same gang of Red Cavalry returned and took away with them practically all the live stock, horses and cattle in the village and also a number of the women and girls, driving them all toward the Siberian border. Immediate after the Tanikay atrocity there followed in rapid succession similar atrocities in other villages, the last incident reported being on October 13 when the town of Usturofok in the extreme northern part of the Barga District was completed destroyed and all persons still remaining in the place, women and children as well as men, were massacred. In the case of Usturofok, which is located on the Argun River, an attempt was made by a small force of Chinese soldiers stationed in the town to put up a defense, but after three attempts to cross the river the Red force finally succeeded under cover of an armored launch and after gaining a foothold on the bank the town was captured and the remaining inhabitants killed.[153]

---

[147] Powell, "The Soviet Atrocities in Barga," *China Weekly Review*, L (Nov. 2, 1929), 339.

[148] I. A. Cooklin, "Soviets Loot White Russian Villages in Manchuria," *China Weekly Review*, L (Oct. 26, 1929), 319. Mr. Cooklin was special correspondent of *China Weekly Review*, writing from Hailar on Oct. 8, 1929.

[149] Powell, "The Soviet Atrocities in Barga," *China Weekly Review*, L (Nov. 2, 1929), 337.

[150] Cited in *ibid*.

[151] "The Red Revenge in Barga," *China Weekly Review*, L (Nov. 9, 1929), 368.

[152] Powell, "The Soviet Atrocities in Barga," *China Weekly Review*, L, 337.

[153] *Ibid.*

Based upon "the best available information" from the refugees and from the Chinese residents of this area, Mr. Powell reported that "Soviet General Blücher sent [these] four gangs of cavalry into the northern Barga district," and that "the small force of Chinese soldiers in the border towns along the Argun" were forced by the "superior forces of Red troops . . . to flee to the interior."[154]   He also testified that "Mr. Lilliestrom was authority for the statement that there were practically no arms, outside of a few old-type hunting guns, in the entire area," because two years before "the Chinese authorities . . . had taken up all guns that could be found in the villages . . . [in order] to break up a gang of Russian and Chinese bandits."[155]   This situation evidently "enabled the Red forces to operate practically at will in the [Three-River] district,"[156] which had presumably been regarded by the Soviets as "a constant source of irritation" and "one of the worst centers of the White Russian menace."[157]

Against this background, the senior (Netherland) minister of the diplomatic corps in Peiping received the following telegram dated October 18:

Red bands raid Russian emigrant settlements [in the] Three Rivers district, torment [to] death, murder all peaceful men, women; number [of] victims grows incessantly. For humaneness beg you as representative [of the] whole civilized world concur putting [an] end [to the] barbarous massacre [of] peaceful unarmed population. Signed [by] representative [of] Russian emigrants in Hailar, Barga, Narbut.[158]

According to American Minister MacMurray, "[The] Senior Minister suggested telegraphing contents of this message to the Secretary of the League of Nations, but it was decided not to do so and interested Ministers are repeating description of it to their Governments. [Besides], it has been given to Reuter's by the Senior Minister."[159]   Meanwhile, in Shanghai the local organization of White Russians had sent telegrams to President Hoover, to M. Briand, to Mr. MacDonald, to the Pope, and to influential statesmen

---

[154] *Ibid.*, p. 338.   [155] *Ibid.*
[156] *Ibid.*
[157] "The Red Revenge in Barga," *China Weekly Review*, L (Nov. 9, 1929), 369.
[158] Quoted in Minister MacMurray in China to Secretary Stimson, tel., Oct. 19, 1929, *F.R.U.S., 1929*, II, 330-331.
[159] *Ibid.*, II, 331.

and philanthropists the world over, "appealing for aid in the allevia-
tion of the plight of the unfortunate refugees in Barga."[160]

As Mr. Powell observed, the Soviets did "not disclaim responsibility" for the massacre.[161] According to him, "the Soviet broad-
casting station at Harbarovsk which broadcasts almost nightly pro-
grams of speeches breathing hatred for Chinese officials, took full
credit for the raids into the Three-River district and alleged that the
Soviet military forces had decided upon this action as retaliation for
alleged 'White-Guard' attacks across the boundary into Soviet territory."[162] He cited a Soviet broadcast announcing that "we have
taught the White emigrees a lesson they never will forget. . . .
These are samples of what we will do as soon as the weather becomes
colder and the rivers are frozen over so our troops can operate on
Chinese territory."[163]

In a message from Hailar dated October 18, Chinese troops
were reported to have been dispatched to the Three-River district
"as soon as the presence of Soviet detachments in the district
became known."[164] Subsequently "several clashes" between them
and Soviet cavalry bands took place in that area. As the Chinese
reinforcements were sent to the region, the Soviet detachments were
"reported to have retreated toward the border."[165]

The events unfolding in the Three-River district may have given
a signal for the further intensification of the Soviet raids and incursions. Following this episode, the most tragic scenes of the Soviet-
Chinese undeclared war occurred at T'ungkiang (Lahasusu or La-
hususu) on the eastern border in October and at Manchuli and
Chalainor on the western border in November.

T'ungkiang is located at the confluence of the Sungari and Amur
rivers. Since the Sungari enters the Amur through a delta dividing
the river into three channels, the area is locally called San-Kiang-Kou,
meaning the mouth of three rivers. T'ungkiang commanded a highly
strategic importance, because with the Chinese navy in control, all
navigation on the Amur between Blagoveshchensk and Habarovsk
could be cut. If, on the other hand, the Russian navy were in con-

---

[160] "The Red Revenge in Barga," *China Weekly Review*, L (Nov. 9, 1929), 368.
[161] Powell, "The Soviet Atrocities in Barga," *China Weekly Review*, L, 338.
[162] *Ibid.*   [163] *Ibid.*
[164] I. A. Cooklin, "Red Terrorism in Barga," *China Weekly Review*, L (Nov. 9, 1929), 377.
[165] *Ibid.*

trol of this point, a Russian army would have access to the rich regions of Kirin Province and Russian gunboats could be sent up to the city of Harbin, the metropolis of North Manchuria. However, following the Chinese Eastern Railway incident of July 10 and the Russian retaliatory seizure of Chinese shipping on the Amur and Ussuri rivers and the detention at Habarovsk of the Chinese passengers and crews of these ships, numbering 1,190 individuals, between July 19 and 29,[166] all three arms of the Sungari River were mined with electric-spark and contact mines which not only prevented the Russian fleet from entering the Sungari but also prevented the Chinese fleet from entering the Amur."[167] According to Mr. Powell, Admiral Shen Hung-lieh, Commander of the Chinese Northeastern Fleet, "called particular attention to this point as definitely indicating China's lack of aggressive designs and her sole intention of protecting her own territory."[168]

On October 12 the Soviet Far Eastern fleet, consisting of nine warships under the command of Admiral Pstozhekov, accompanied by a squadron of more than twenty-five airplanes and more than three thousand cavalrymen and infantry, attacked T'ungkiang. So far as equipment and fighting strength were concerned, the Soviet fleet was more than ten times stronger than the Chinese. After seven hours of severe fighting, the whole Chinese Sungari fleet met total destruction. The Soviets were said to practice "Tsarist barbarity by throwing all captives into the river and drowning them."[169]

As to the actual battle leading to the destruction of the Chinese Sungari fleet and to the Soviet capture of T'ungkiang,[170] a sea captain, who "was in the midst of the Soviet shelling," gave the American vice consul at Harbin, Mr. Lilliestrom, the following story:

On October 12th, at 5:30 in the morning, heavy artillery fire was started from the Soviet flotilla against the Chinese fleet and land positions at Lahasusu. The signal for firing was given by the Soviet gunboat *Liebknecht.* At 6:10 in the morning the Chinese gunboats *Chantai*

[166] J. B. Powell, "The Battle of San Kiang Kou" (written for the Chicago *Tribune*), *China Weekly Review*, L (Nov. 16, 1929), 413.

[167] *Ibid.*, pp. 413-414.

[168] *Ibid.*, p. 414.

[169] Tsao, *op. cit.*, p. 118; Ho, *op. cit.*, pp. 408-409.

[170] Memorandum by the vice consul at Harbin (Lilliestrom), Oct. 28, 1929, transmitted to Assistant Secretary of State Johnson by the consul at Harbin in his covering letter of Oct. 29, 1929, *F.R.U.S.*, *1929*, II, 337.

[*Kiangtai*] and Chanan [*Kiangan*] were sunk. At 6:20 a fire broke out on the Chinese gunboat *Chianping*, which sank at 6:40. At 7:05 the big former German, now Chinese, gunboat *Lichi* [*Lichieh*] was abandoned by its crew and taken in tow by the Russians. It was subsequently brought to Habarovsk. Seven barges, formerly belonging to the Chinese Eastern Railway, were also captured by the Soviet forces, as well as army transport steamer No. 18. These were also taken to Habarovsk. The Soviet gunboats participating in the attack were: *Liebknecht, Kalmuk, Batrak, Arachanin* and *Lenin*. On the *Kalmuk* was killed the chief of the Amur River Fleet, as well as 16 men. The Soviet side lost no gunboats, steamers or barges, nor any planes.

On October 13th at 8:45 in the morning the Chinese troops stationed at and near Lahasusu retreated in complete disorder to Fuchin, 45 versts distant. Soviet infantry and cavalry detachments pursued the retreating Chinese troops and killed great numbers with shrapnel fired from light artillery pieces. . . .

The Soviet casualties were 275 men killed or wounded, while the Chinese casualties were 964 killed or wounded, including 148 sailors from the gunboats and 225 marines killed.

On October 19th several Soviet airplanes appeared over Fuchin, and sunk with bombs the Chinese gunboat *Lisui*. By orders of Admiral Shen there were sunk at a place called Shalbatai, 5 versts below Fuchin, army transport steamer *Lochin* and three barges, in order to prevent the Soviet fleet from sailing up the Sungari river.[171]

T'ungkiang was thus lost, and protests by both China and Russia against each other followed. On October 25, the Chinese Government, unable to persuade the Soviet Government to come to an amicable settlement, issued another manifesto to all the signatories of the Kellogg Pact, charging that the Soviets had assumed the offensive with hostilities always occurring in Chinese territory, and that the Soviet Government must be "responsible for all losses and damage caused to Chinese life and property."[172]

While the Soviet offensive was reported to be intensified day by day, on November 17 the Soviet troops furiously assaulted Chalainor, where three previous unsuccessful attacks had been made on August 16, 18, and 20. It had been learned that in the neighborhood of Chalainor and Manchuli (ten miles apart), there were 30,000 Soviet

[171] *Ibid.*, II, 337-338.
[172] For Chinese text of the manifesto, see Ho, *op. cit.*, pp. 410-412; for English text, see *C.Y.B., 1929-30*, pp. 1227-1229.

troops with thirty tanks, 100 motorcycles, and six armored cars, and also a Russian aerodrome.[173]   The Chinese 17th Brigade offered brave resistance for twenty-four hours.   Finally it was surrounded and totally defeated at the cost of the lives of the Brigade Commander Han Kuang-ti, his three regimental commanders, and 6,000 of the total of 7,000 men.   Following the fall of Chalainor, Manchuli was also enveloped and taken, and its defender, Brigade Commander Liang Chung-chia, made prisoner, the latter dying shortly after his release from Soviet custody.[174]

According to official Chinese figures, as of the end of December, 1929, Chinese casualties, both military and civilian, had exceeded 10,000 and property losses amounted to Ch. $1,000,000,000 (U.S. $500,000,000).[175]

During this period of the undeclared war, the Soviets frequently made the following charges against the Chinese: (1) that cases of the cannonading of Soviet forces and peaceful residents had been much more frequent, and (2) that "the united bands of the Russian White guards and the Chinese *hunhutze* (bandits) have become more and more impudent," and "have more and more often crossed" the Soviet border.[176]   On its side, however, the Chinese Foreign Office, in its October 23 dispatch to all Chinese legations and consulates for transmission to foreign Governments as well as to the press, explained that the Soviet accusation and agitation was designed "to make room for disavowing its responsibility."[177]   And on December 3 the Chinese Government again addressed a note to the Kellogg Pact signatories "for the purpose of drawing their attention to the acts and attitude of the Soviet Government which are contrary to the provisions of the Treaty and requesting that such measures be adopted as may be necessary and appropriate in view of Article II of the Treaty."   After reviewing the incidents of Soviet attacks which showed that "from the beginning it has been apparently the policy of the Soviet Government to use force as a solution of the

---

[173] Tong, *op. cit.*, pp. 53-55; Ho, *op. cit.*, p. 412.

[174] "Biography of Han Kuang-ti," *Hei-Lung-Chiang Chih-kao* (*Draft Gazetteer of Heilungkiang*), Vol. 49, sh. 41-42; "Biography of Liang Chung-chia," *ibid.*, sh. 44-45.

[175] China, *Bulletin of the Waichaiopu*, May, 1931, p. 171; New York *Times*, Dec. 28, 1929, p. 4.

[176] Skalov, *op. cit.*, p. 44.

[177] Telegraphical circular of the Waichiayan, Oct. 23, 1929, quoted in Ho, *op. cit.*, pp. 409-410.

dispute," the note went on to state the Chinese position and to propose concrete measures for a peaceful settlement of the dispute:

The Chinese Government, on the other hand, mindful of its obligations as a Signatory of the Treaty for the Renunciation of War, has in spite of extreme provocation confined itself strictly to measures of self-defense. Chinese troops even after repulsing the invaders have in no instance set foot across the border.   And repeated but unfortunately unsuccessful attempts have been made to reach with the Soviet Government a settlement by pacific means.

Recently in view of Soviet allegations of Chinese responsibility for the warlike conditions along the border, the Chinese Government, aware of the falsity of these allegations, proposed to the Soviet Government the appointment of a mixed commission of inquiry, presided over by a national of a third country, to investigate and report on the responsibility for the frontier situation.   Pending the investigation, both sides were to withdraw their forces from the frontier to a distance of thirty miles.   In case of acceptance by the Soviet Government of these conciliatory suggestions, the Chinese Government stated that it was further prepared to submit the whole case for adjustment to a neutral agency according to the established usage for the peaceful settlement of international disputes.

The Chinese Government has thus continually and consistently demonstrated its faithful and scrupulous adherence to the Treaty for the Renunciation of War.   Nevertheless the Soviet Government seems to persist in its policy of waging undeclared but actual war on China.[178]

The Chinese version of the incidents of the undeclared war was generally accepted in foreign capitals at the time.   In this connection, the following statement made by Arthur Henderson, the British Foreign Secretary, in the House of Commons on December 11, 1929, might serve as a pertinent comment:

I have received no official report of raids by Chinese troops or aircraft over territory of the Soviet Union.   According to my information Soviet troops advanced as far as Chalainor some fifty miles within the western frontier of Manchuria, and Soviet gunboats raided Fuchin, fifty miles within the northern frontier.   Pok'ot'u, about two hundred miles from the frontier, was bombed by Soviet aircraft.[179]

Thus in view of these developments, contemporary Chinese

[178] Minister Wu to Secretary Stimson, letter, Dec. 3, 1929, *F.R.U.S., 1929*, II, 383-384.
[179] Great Britain, *Parliamentary Debates*, CCXXXIII, 438.

writers were firm in concluding that "the Soviet Government did violate the Kellogg Pact" in 1929 in its relations with China.[180]

THE SECOND INVOCATION OF THE PEACE PACT

As early as September and October, 1929, the American consul at Harbin had reported that according to American correspondents in Manchuria, a "state of war exists 500 miles along the border,"[181] and that "regular Soviet troops have invaded and have taken up positions inside Chinese territory and have shelled Chinese outposts."[182]

Beginning November 1, the consul had made frequent reports to the Department of State through the American legation in Peiping that the Soviet forces had launched serious attacks within the Manchurian boundary and conducted heavy bombing up to Mutanchiang, 191 miles from the border town of Pogranichnaia.[183] One of the reports indicates that "[the] Chinese lost 2,000 men killed up to [November 19] . . . on the western front." On November 21 he reported that according to an official source, "Manchuli and Chalainor have both been captured by the Soviets."[184] On subsequent days he reported that "Mishan has fallen into Red hands,"[185] with "Reds advancing from Mishan to Muling,"[186] and that Hailar was being evacuated.[187] Unofficial accounts stated that "the Russians had penetrated two hundred miles into Manchurian territory."[188]

Under these circumstances and with a timely reminder from his predecessor, the co-author of the Peace Pact, Frank B. Kellogg,[189]

[180] Tao-shing Chang, *op. cit.*, p. 160.

[181] Minister MacMurray in China to Secretary Stimson, tel., Sept. 1, 1929, *F.R.U.S., 1929*, II, 311.

[182] Same to the same, tel., Sept. 3, 1929, *ibid.*, II, 313.

[183] Same to the same, tel., Nov. 19, 1929, *ibid.*, II, 344.

[184] Same to the same, tel., Nov. 21, 1929, *ibid.*, II, 344.

[185] Chargé Perkins in China to Secretary Stimson, tel., Nov. 23, 1929, *ibid.*, II, 346.

[186] Same to the same, tel., Nov. 24, 1929, *ibid.*, II, 347.

[187] Chargé Perkins in China to Secretary Stimson, tel., Nov. 26, 1929, *ibid.*, II, 150. The demoralized, disorganized, and retreating Chinese troops on the Manchurian front were reported by the American consul at Harbin to have committed some looting, adding to the misery of the panic-stricken local inhabitants; cf. *ibid.*, II, 350, 353, 358, 365, 380.

[188] *Survey of American Foreign Relations, 1930*, p. 417.

[189] Ambassador Dawes in Great Britain to Secretary Stimson, tel., Nov. 22, 1929, *F.R.U.S., 1929*, II, 346.

Secretary Stimson thought "it is evidently clear that serious hostilities, which approximate a condition of actual warfare, are proceeding between the armed forces of China and Russia in Manchuria and are accompanied by the occupation of territory and by numerous casualties."[190] On November 26 he instructed the American envoys in France, Great Britain, Italy, Japan and Germany to convey to the Foreign Ministers of their respective countries the following:

The United States Government, being alarmed because of the serious extent to which both China and Russia have recently carried hostile acts, is decidedly of the opinion that a further development of the situation along lines which are so fraught with danger to everyone concerned should not be permitted without protest by those powers who sponsored the pact against its violation.[191]

To the respective Ministers for Foreign Affairs the American envoys were later ordered to read and leave in their possession the following American statement in connection with this second invocation of the Kellogg Pact:

The Government and people of the United States have observed with apprehensive concern the course of events in relations between China and Russia in the phase which has developed in reference to the situation in North Manchuria since July 10.

On July 18 this Government took steps, through conversations between the Secretary of State and the diplomatic representatives at Washington of five Powers, to see that the attention of the Chinese and the Russian Governments be called to the provisions of the Treaty for the Renunciation of War, to which both China and Russia were signatories. Both the Russian and Chinese Governments then made formal and public assurances that neither would resort to war unless attacked. Since that time that Treaty has been ratified by no less than fifty-five Powers, including China and Russia.

The American Government desires again to call attention to the provisions of the Treaty for the Renunciation of War, particularly to Article II, which reads, "The High Contracting Parties agree that the settlement or solution of all disputes or conflicts of whatever nature or of whatever origin they may be, which may arise among them, shall never

---

[190] Secretary Stimson to Chargé Neville in Japan, tel. (the same, *mutatis mutandis*, to the diplomatic representatives in France, Great Britain, Italy and Germany), Nov. 26, 1929, *ibid.*, II, 350.
[191] *Ibid.*, II, 351.

be sought except by pacific means;" and the American Government takes occasion to express its earnest hope that China and Russia will refrain from measures of hostility and will arrange in the near future to discuss between themselves the issues over which they are at present in controversy. The American Government feels that the respect with which China and Russia will hereafter be held in the good opinion of the world will necessarily in great measure depend upon the way in which they carry out these most sacred promises.[192]

The American diplomatic representatives were instructed to learn from the foreign ministers whether their respective governments would be ready to make public a statement along lines similar to those of the American one.[193]

French Foreign Minister Briand immediately stated his entire agreement with Secretary Stimson that "France and the United States, as the two original sponsors of the Paris Pact, cannot, in the face of events transpiring now in North Manchuria, stand with folded arms."[194] He agreed to make public a similar statement on a date which was to be fixed to coincide with the issuance of the statement by Secretary Stimson.[195] The British Foreign Secretary and the Italian Minister for Foreign Affairs were in entire sympathy with the action Secretary Stimson had suggested and promised to cooperate in carrying it out.[196] The Japanese and German Foreign Ministers, though expressing their desire for the restoration of peaceful conditions in the Far East, found it "inconvenient" to make a public statement.[197]

On November 30, having received replies from all the governments addressed and finding the replies generally favorable to the

---

[192] *Ibid.;* Secretary Stimson to Chargé Armour in France, tel., Nov. 30, 1929, *ibid.*, II, 367-368; and Secretary Stimson to certain diplomatic representatives, tel., Dec. 1, 1929, *ibid.*, II, 372-373.

[193] Secretary Stimson to Chargé Neville in Japan, tel. (the same, *mutatis mutandis,* to the diplomatic representatives in France, Great Britain, Italy and Germany), Nov. 26, 1929, *ibid.*, II, 351.

[194] Chargé Armour in France to Secretary Stimson, tel., Nov. 28, 1929, *ibid.*, II, 357.

[195] *Ibid.*

[196] Ambassador Dawes in Great Britain to Secretary Stimson, tel., Nov. 27, 1929, *ibid.*, II, 356; Ambassador Garrett in Italy to Secretary Stimson, tel., Nov. 28, 1929, *ibid.*, II, 359.

[197] Chargé Neville in Japan to Secretary Stimson, tel., Nov. 27, 1929, *ibid.*, II, 355-356; Ambassador Schurman to Secretary Stimson, tel., Nov. 28, 1929, *ibid.*, II, 359-360.

principle of his proposal,[198] Secretary Stimson directed the American legation in Peiping to transmit immediately to the national government,[199] and requested the French Foreign Office to convey on behalf of the American Government to the Soviet Government,[200] the American statement as originally proposed on November 26, which may be regarded as the second invocation of the Kellogg Pact.[201]

At the same time, Secretary Stimson sent a circular telegram to more than forty American diplomatic representatives residing in the countries party to the Kellogg Pact, instructing them to present the American statement concerning the Manchurian situation to the governments to which they were accredited. The envoys were directed to express the earnest hope of the United States Government that the governments of the signatories of the Kellogg Pact would find it possible to participate in the action by issuing on their part statements along lines similar to those of the American statement and by communicating simultaneously their respective views to the governments of China and Russia.[202]

Consequently, as of December 12, 1929, thirty-eight signatories in addition to France,[203] Great Britain,[204] and Italy,[205], lent their support to the *démarche* by individual representations.[206] Germany and Japan were two notable exceptions. German Foreign Minister Curtius, however, explained that "the German Government in the special position it occupies in relation to the Chinese-Russian difficulty is already carrying out, along its own established lines, the object" Secretary Stimson suggested.[207] While not in agreement with the

[198] Secretary Stimson to Chargé Armour in France, tel., Nov. 30, 1929, 7 P.M., *ibid.*, II, 366.

[199] Secretary Stimson to Chargé Perkins in China, tel., Nov. 30, 1929, *ibid.*, II, 368.

[200] Secretary Stimson to Chargé Armour in France, tel., Nov. 30, 1929, 8 P.M., *ibid.*, II, 367.

[201] Cf. pp. 235-236, *supra.*

[202] Secretary Stimson to certain diplomatic representatives, circular tel., Dec 1, 1929, *F.R.U.S., 1929*, II, 371-373.

[203] The French text is identical with the translated American text; Chargé Armour in France to Secretary Stimson, tel., Dec. 2, 1929, *ibid.*, II, 375.

[204] The British statement is practically identical with the American version; Ambassador Dawes in Great Britain to Secretary Stimson, tel., Dec. 2, 1929, *ibid.*, II, 375-376; same to the same, tel., Dec. 3, 1929, *ibid.*, II, 379.

[205] Ambassador Garrett to Secretary Stimson, tel., Dec. 2, 1929, *ibid.*, II, 374; same to the same, tel., Dec. 4, 1929, *ibid.*, II, 385.

[206] *Survey of American Foreign Relations*, 1929 (New Haven, 1929), p. 418; cf. *F.R.U.S., 1929*, II, 382, 386, 388 ff.

[207] Ambassador Schurman in Germany to Secretary Stimson, tel., Dec. 2, 1929,

Stimson proposition, Baron Shidehara, the Japanese Foreign Minister, had found it possible to speak to the Chinese and to the Russians privately along the lines of the American statement.[208]

In reply to the American note invoking the Kellogg Pact for the second time, the Chinese Government stated as follows:

. . . Being a signatory of the Treaty for the Renunciation of War, the National Government circularized the other signatories of the aforesaid treaty on August 20, 1929, declaring that China would, apart from adopting measures for self-protection in defense of her territorial sovereignty against external invasion, faithfully abide by Article II of the aforenamed treaty providing for the solution of international disputes by pacific means and that she was ready any time within reasonable limits to negotiate with the Soviet Government for the settlement of the present dispute.   Such declaration was in complete harmony with the intent of the note under reply.   The National Government has always imposed implicit confidence in aforesaid treaty and desisted from acting in any way contrary to its spirit.   It will continue to adhere to its reiterated policy.[209]

The Soviet Government, on its part, sent a reply to the American representations by way of the French Government.   The gist of the Soviet note was as follows:

The U.S.S.R. has practiced since the first day of its existence a policy of peace . . . .   It has constantly followed this policy of peace, and it has the intention to follow it, independently of the Treaty of Paris for the Renunciation of War.

The Government of Nanking, in the course of the last few years, turning aside from the methods which habitually serve [to] resolve, by diplomacy, the disputes which have arisen, has practiced towards the U.S.S.R. a policy of provocation which consists of violating the usual international regulations and treaties . . . .   The Nanking Government has not limited itself to the illegal seizure of the Chinese Eastern Railway, but has mobilized along the Soviet-Manchurian frontier an army, detachments of which, together with the counter-revolutionary Russian bands they contain, made systematic attacks on the U.S.S.R., entering Soviet territory, shooting at units of the Red Army and frontier settlements,

---

ibid., II, 376; memorandum by the Assistant Secretary of State (Castle), Dec. 5, 1929, *ibid.*, II, 395.

[208] Chargé Neville in Japan to Secretary Stimson, tel., Nov. 27, 1929, *ibid.*, II, 355; memorandum by Assistant Secretary Johnson, Dec. 2, 1929, *ibid.*, II, 377.

[209] Chargé Perkins in China to Secretary Stimson, tel., Dec. 4, 1949, *ibid.*, II, 387.

plundering and violating the peaceful population, and causing considerable losses in life and property by these actions. Despite repeated warnings addressed to the Nanking Government through the German Government, these attacks did not cease but rather became more frequent and increased in intensity. These attacks compelled the Soviet Far Eastern Army to take counter-measures in the interests of defense and the protection of the peaceful inhabitants of the frontier region.

Thus, the activities of the Red Army were provoked by considerations of absolutely essential self-defence, and do not in any degree constitute an infringement of any obligations arising out of the Treaty of Paris, which cannot be said about the presence on Chinese territory and in Chinese ports of the armed forces of the Powers which have today addressed identical notes to the Soviet Government.

The Soviet Government notes that the Government of the United States has addressed its note to the Soviet Government at the moment when the Soviet and Mukden Governments have already agreed upon a number of conditions and are conducting direct negotiations which may make possible the speedy settlement of the Soviet-Chinese conflict. In view of this circumstance, the aforementioned note cannot but be regarded as totally *unjustifiable pressure on the negotiations,* and consequently *cannot in any way be considered as a friendly act.*

The Soviet Government further observes that the Treaty of Paris on the Renunciation of War does not make provision for the delegation of the function of guardian of the Pact to any State or group of States. In any case the Soviet Government has never announced its agreement that any Governments should, of their own accord or in consultation with one another, assume such a right for themselves.

The Soviet Government states that the Soviet-Manchurian conflict can only be settled by means of direct negotiations between the U.S.S.R. and China on the basis of conditions known to China and already accepted by the Mukden Government, and that it cannot allow any interference in these negotiations or in the conflict.

In conclusion the Soviet Government cannot help expressing its astonishment that the Government of the United States, which at its own desire has no official relations with the Government of the Soviet Union, finds it possible to approach the Soviet Government with advice and 'instructions.'[210]

[210] Maxim Litvinov to Jean Herbette, French Ambassador in Moscow, note, Dec. 3, 1929, for transmission to the United States Government through the French Government, text in *Sovetsko-Amerikanskie Otnosheniia, 1919-1933* (*The Soviet-American Relations, 1919-1933*) (Moscow, 1934), p. 65; also Chargé Armour in France to Secretary Stimson, tel., Dec. 7, 1929, *F.R.U.S., 1929*, II, 404-406.

To this procedural question as raised by Litvinov in the Soviet note quoted above, Secretary Stimson had a ready answer. On December 4, 1929, before the Soviet communication of the preceding day had been transmitted to Washington, the Secretary of State, having seen the text of the Soviet memorandum as reported in the press, issued a statement which read in part:

Between co-signatories of the Pact of Paris it can never be rightly thought unfriendly that one nation calls to the attention of another its obligations or the danger to peace which from time to time arise . . . . The message of the American Government was sent not from unfriendly motives but because this Government regards the Pact of Paris as a covenant which has profoundly modified the attitude of the world towards peace and because this Government intends to shape its own policy accordingly. . . . The present declaration of the authorities of Russia that they are now proceeding with direct negotiations which will make possible the settlement of the conflict is not the least significant evidence to show that the public opinion of the world is a live factor which can be promptly mobilized and which has become a factor of prime importance in the solution of the problems and controversies which may arise between nations.[211]

Commenting on Secretary Stimson's remarks, *Izvestiia*, in turn, had this to say:

If the United States were aware of the direct negotiations with Mukden, then the American interference in and pressure on the negotiations could not be viewed otherwise than as an unfriendly act. If the American Government were unaware of the direct negotiations with Mukden, especially if its Chinese informants concealed the existing facts which would promote peace, the attitude of the United States, devoid, under the existing mutual relations, of the possibility of receiving direct information from the Government of the U.S.S.R., cannot be recognized as correct, nor as friendly, towards the Soviet Union. It should be further noted that the significance of the Kellogg Pact and the authority of this international act are by no means strengthened, if some signatories reproach some other parties to the Pact of insufficient observance of the treaty, without familiarizing themselves preliminarily and thoroughly with all circumstances of the conflict.[212]

[211] Statement by Secretary Stimson to the press, Dec. 4, 1929, *F.R.U.S., 1929*, II, 388-389.

[212] "Stimson Daet 'Raz'iasneniia' " ("Stimson Gives 'Explanations' "), *Izvestiia*, Dec. 5, 1929, p. 1.

Although the Soviet reply dispelled the rumor concerning the possible mediation of the Sino-Soviet dispute by the United States, Great Britain, and France as a result of their having twice invoked the Kellogg Pact,[213] Soviet writers of the day persisted in their denunciations of the would-be designs of "imperialists" in Manchuria. As Voitinskii writes: "The military and naval attachés of the imperialistic countries have poked their noses into the C.E.R. and have made themselves familiar with strategical and war-material potentialities for marching against the U.S.S.R. under the Chinese flag."[214] Skalov also writes: "It is clear to all walks of the toiling masses in the U.S.S.R. that from behind the back of the Chinese militarists peep the bayonets of world imperialism; hence, obviously our armed collision with China was inevitably the beginning of a general imperialistic war against the U.S.S.R."[215] Such arguments could only serve to enhance the psychological preparedness for war while reducing the hope of peace.

[213] Ho, *op. cit.*, p. 413.
[214] G. N. Voitinskii, *K.V.Zh.D. i Politika Imperializma v Kitae*, p. 37.
[215] Skalov, *op. cit.*, pp. 11-12.

VI: SOVIET ATTITUDE TOWARD THE SETTLEMENT OF THE CHINESE EASTERN RAILWAY DISPUTE

THE KHABAROVSK PROTOCOL OF 1929

Following the Soviet note on July 17, 1929, which marked the complete rupture of Chinese-Soviet relations, several attempts were made to find an amicable settlement of the crisis. The American-inspired mediation proposal of the French Government of July 19 and 25 has already been noted.[1] In addition, there were negotiations on the spot between Tsai Yun-sheng, the Commissioner of Foreign Affairs in Harbin, and Soviet Consul-General Mel'nikov from July 22 to August 4.[2] Further, the German Government tendered its good offices for a "joint declaration" in August and for a mutual exchange of prisoners in October.[3] Throughout these efforts, the Soviet authorities insisted that the Chinese Eastern Railway be returned to its former management—which had lent itself so readily to the securing of Soviet interests in Manchuria—as a prior condition to negotiations on the issues in dispute. The Chinese, for their part, felt that such a condition could not be granted until bilateral talks on the railway situation had been convened. In each case, therefore, the efforts at amicable settlement were futile and were followed by more intensified charges and countercharges from both

---

[1] Cf. pp. 210-216, *supra;* statement of the Narkomindel, July 23, 1929, *Izvestiia,* July 23, 1929, p. 1.

[2] Karakhan to Chang Hsüeh-liang, chairman of the Mukden Government, note, Aug. 1, 1929, *Izvestiia,* Aug. 2, 1929, p. 1; Ho Han-wen, *Chung-O Wai-chiao Shih (Sino-Russian Diplomatic History)*, pp. 404-405.

[3] Statement of the Narkomindel, Aug. 29, 1929, *Izvestiia,* Aug. 31, 1929, p. 1; Ambassador Schurman in Germany to Secretary Stimson, tel., Oct. 14, 1929, *F.R.U.S., 1929,* II, 325-326; N.K.I.D. (the Narkomindel) to German Embassy in Moscow, note, Oct. 18, 1929, *Izvestiia,* Oct. 19, 1929, p. 1.

sides regarding frontier violations and ill-treatment of each other's nationals.[4]

This stalemate was broken only with the Soviet occupation of T'ungkiang on October 12 and then of Chalainor and Manchuli on November 17.[5] Shortly thereafter a preliminary arrangement hastily concluded at Nikol'sk-Ussurisk on December 3[6] paved the way for the Khabarovsk Protocol of December 22 by which the Chinese agreed to restore the *status quo ante* on the Chinese Eastern Railway.[7]

In effect, the Khabarovsk Protocol marked an armistice in the half-year of diplomatic conflict, during which the Russians had managed to re-establish their position in the face of firm Chinese efforts to dislodge them. The episodes of that half-year are worth chronicling in detail, because they present a pattern of Soviet diplomatic and military maneuvers which has since become familiar in other parts of the world.

The Chinese took the initiative in opening direct negotiations on the spot. On July 22, 1929, Tsai was "received at his own request" by Mel'nikov, in Harbin. Tsai stated that he had just arrived from Mukden with instructions from the Mukden Government to propose the following terms for the settlement of the railway controversy:

(1) The liberation of the arrested Soviet workers and civil servants. (2) The appointment by the Government of the U.S.S.R. of the manager of the Chinese Eastern Railway and his assistant. (3) The calling of a conference by the representatives of both Governments to regulate the conflict of the railway in the shortest possible time. (4) The Soviet Government may declare that it does not recognize any postconflict status of the railway and that it is not bound by the postconflict status in any way in the forthcoming negotiations. (5) If the Soviet Government agrees with these proposals, Chang Hsüeh-liang will apply for the consent of the Nanking Government to these proposals.[8]

Mel'nikov "refused to consider these proposals," pointing out to

---

[4] *C.Y.B.*, *1929-30*, p. 1229.

[5] Ho, *op. cit.*, pp. 409-412.

[6] Statement of the Narkomindel, Dec. 4, 1929, *Izvestiia*, Dec. 4, p. 1.

[7] Text of the protocol in statement of the Narkomindel, Dec. 23, 1929, *Izvestiia*, Dec. 23, 1929, p. 1.

[8] Tsai to Mel'nikov, proposals, July 22, 1929, cited in Karakhan to Chang Hsüeh-liang, letter, Aug. 1, 1929, *Izvestiia*, Aug. 2, 1929, p. 1.

Tsai that he had no authority to do so and that the point of view of the Soviet Government had been laid down in its note of July 13. However, in view of Tsai's request that these proposals be communicated to the Soviet Government, Mel'nikov transmitted them to the Narkomindel.[9] Thereupon, Karakhan instructed Mel'nikov to give answer to Tsai for transmission to Chang Hsüeh-liang, to the effect that the Soviet Government "can have no confidence in the proposals emanating from the Mukden Government" through Tsai, but that if the Nanking or the Mukden Government should officially make these proposals with a slight change in the form of point 4, the Soviet Government would adopt a favorable attitude to them. The answer was delivered on July 25.[10]

On July 30 Tsai arrived at the Manchuli Station, and two days later delivered to Mel'nikov, already on Soviet territory, Chang Hsüeh-liang's latter to Karakhan, the contents of which were transmitted to Moscow by telegraph.[11] Karakhan found the letter unacceptable. It had omitted Tsai's proposal for the appointment by the Soviet Government of the manager of the C.E.R. and his assistant and had not complied with the Soviet "formula" for the change of the post-conflict status of the C.E.R. In conclusion, Karakhan warned Chang Hsüeh-liang:

I am thus compelled to declare that, contrary to its own proposal of July 22, the Mukden Government by its new proposal frustrates the possibility of settling the conflict by an agreement which would be possible only by accepting the proposal of the Union Government of July 25. This creates a situation pregnant with new and serious complications, the entire responsibility for which will rest upon the Mukden and Nanking Governments alone.[12]

On August 3, the day after his meeting with Tsai at Manchuli, Mel'nikov deposited with Tsai for transmission to the Mukden Government a note containing three Soviet proposals, namely, to reinstate the discharged personnel of the C.E.R. and restore the old order of things on the C.E.R.; to grant the Soviet armed forces the right of

[9] *Ibid.*

[10] Mel'nikov to Tsai, Soviet counterproposals, July 25, 1929, *ibid.*

[11] Chang Hsüeh-liang to Karakhan, letter, July 29, 1929, *C.Y.B., 1929-30,* p. 1125.

[12] Karakhan to Chang Hsüeh-liang, letter, Aug. 1, 1929, *Izvestiia,* Aug. 2, 1929, p, 1.

protecting the railway; and to terminate Chinese supervision over the Dal'bank.[13]   Tsai told Mel'nikov that the matter had gone beyond his province and telegraphed Chang Hsüeh-liang for instructions.   Chang replied that he could not agree with the Soviet proposal because it would prejudice Chinese sovereignty.   On August 4 Tsai communicated this answer to Mel'nikov, and their talks came to an end.[14]

On August 6, Minister Chu Shao-yang arrived in Manchuli as Chinese plenipotentiary commissioned by the Waichiaopu to conduct negotiations with Russian representatives as the circumstances required.   Tsai Yung-sheng tried in vain to contact Mel'nikov, who refused to meet Chu.   Thus, Chu's mission was fruitless.[15]

In the face of widespread Soviet acts of sabotage and destruction along the railway, Karakhan insisted on holding "the Nanking and Mukden Governments solely and entirely responsible, with all the implied consequences, for the entire material loss resulting from the seizure of the road and the arbitrary taking over of the management thereof."[16]   Yet concurrently with his statement, Soviet forces were engaged in military action in Manchuria.   There were reports of Soviet invasions at Tungning on August 14, 16, and 17, and at Chalainor on August 18.[17]   And when the Chinese protests against Soviet "military pressure [were] aired on August 16 and 24"[18] through the German Government (which had undertaken the protection of Chinese interests in Russia and Soviet interests in China), the U.S.S.R., in turn, protested on August 19 through the same channel against "the frequent attacks on Soviet territory by Russian White Guard detachments organized on Chinese soil."[19] *Izvestiia* also charged a "raid on Soviet territory by regular Chinese troops and the White Guards."[20]

[13] Ho, *op. cit.*, p. 405.

[14] *Ibid.*

[15] *Ibid.*, pp. 405-406; Sun, *Chung-O Chiao-she Lun* (*Sino-Russian Negotiations*), p. 188.

[16] Press statement of Karakhan, Aug. 15, 1929, *Izvestiia*, Aug. 16, 1929, p. 1.

[17] *C.Y.B.*, *1931*, p. 496.

[18] Sun, *op. cit.*, p. 190.

[19] Statement of the Narkomindel, Aug. 19, 1929, in *S.U.R.*, VII (Oct., 1929), 146-147.

[20] "Provokatsionnaia Rabota Kitaiskikh Militaristov Usilivaetsia" ("The Provocative Activity of the Chinese Militarists Is Intensified"), *Izvestiia*, Aug. 21, 1929, p. 1.

On August 27, 1929, the Chinese Mission in Berlin requested the good offices of the German Government to bring the Chinese proposals for joint preliminary declaration to the knowledge of the Soviet Government.[21]   On the following day, the German ambassador in Moscow, von Dirksen, officially handed the proposed declaration to M. M. Litvinov, the Acting Commissar for Foreign Affairs, and stated that the Chinese Government was ready to appoint a representative to sign the following joint statement:

(1) Both parties agree that they will settle all pending questions between them in conformity with the agreement of 1924, and in particular agree upon conditions for the redemption of the Chinese Eastern Railway in accordance with Article 9 of the Peking agreement.   Both parties will appoint immediately properly accredited representatives to a conference to settle all pending questions mentioned in the previous clause.

(2) Both parties believe the position of the Chinese Eastern Railway that developed after the dispute must be altered in accordance with the Peking and Mukden agreements of 1924, on the understanding that all such alterations shall be settled by the conference provided for by the previous article.

(3) The Soviet Government will recommend a new manager and a new assistant manager of the Chinese Eastern Railway, who will be appointed by the Board of Directors of the said railway.   The Soviet Government will instruct employees of the Chinese Eastern Railway who are Soviet citizens to observe strictly the conditions contained in Article 6 of the 1924 agreement.

(4) Both parties will release immediately all persons arrested in connection with the present incident, or subsequent to May 1, 1929.[22]

On August 29 Litvinov delivered to von Dirksen the Soviet draft of the joint declaration and stated that the Soviet Government "saw no basis for the appointment of a *new* manager and assistant manager in place of the manager and assistant manager who had been in their time legally appointed and had fulfilled their functions in strict accordance with the agreements."   However, in the event that the Chinese government should appoint a new president of the railway to replace Lu Jung-huan, the Narkomindel might "put before the Soviet Government the question of appointing a new manager and

[21] Chinese Mission in Berlin to the German Foreign Office, *note verbale*, Aug. 27, 1929, Izvestiia, Aug. 31, 1929, p. 1.
[22] Text in *ibid.* and in Ho, *op. cit.*, p. 406.

assistant manager." Furthermore, he insisted that "the appointment of the manager and his assistant should take place simultaneously with the signing of the joint declaration." While deleting the word "new" regarding the manager and his assistant from the Chinese draft, the Soviet draft also amended the second paragraph of point 3 of the Chinese proposal containing the propaganda prohibition clause as follows:

The Soviet Government will instruct employees of the Chinese Eastern Railway who are citizens of the U.S.S.R., and the Chinese Government will instruct its local authorities and their organs to observe strictly the conditions contained in Article 6 of the 1924 agreement.[23]

On September 6, 1929, with no indication from the Nanking Government of its readiness to accept the Soviet counterproposal, Litvinov declared to the press that "either the Nanking Government itself does not wish to regulate the conflict by mutual agreement," or "some outside power hostile to the U.S.S.R. is hindering such an agreement." "The Soviet Government cannot fail to take note of the completely groundless" and "unjustified" Nanking demands regarding the appointment of a new manager and assistant manager of the C.E.R. Accusations of "Communist propaganda" raised against Emshanov and Eismont were "from beginning to end a deliberate and scurrilous fabrication based on documents forged by illiterates and ordered from White guard organizations to justify the seizure" of the C.E.R. He labeled the statement made in Mukden by John J. Mantell, American adviser of the Nanking Government on railroad affairs, "false and baseless accusations against the Soviet side of the administration" of the C.E.R. "The captious insinuations of Mr. Mantell are a manifestation of the obvious desire of interested imperialist circles to destroy the possibility of a peaceful regulation of the Sino-Soviet conflict, and to bring about an aggravation of our relations with China."[24]

With similar tone and tenor, *Izvestiia* had previously accused the Chinese Government of a policy of adventurous activities and of using "propaganda" as an excuse for the seizure of the C.E.R.[25] Now

---

[23] Text of the Soviet counterproposal in the statement of the Narkomindel, Aug. 29, 1929, *Izvestiia*, Aug. 31, 1929, p. 1.

[24] "SSSR i Kitai: Beseda s Litvinovom" ("The U.S.S.R. and China: Conversation with Litvinov"), *Izvestiia*, Sept. 6, 1929, p. 1.

[25] "Pervyi Shag" ("The First Step"), *Izvestiia*, Aug. 31, 1929, p. 1.

it accused Nanking of a double-dealing and provocative policy. It denounced the Chinese "anti-Soviet demonstration in the Assembly of the League of Nations at Geneva and continued terrorism toward Soviet citizens in Manchuria, while at the same time proposing a peaceful settlement of conflicts with the Soviet Government."[26]

On September 9, 1929, China wired its reply. While yielding to the Soviet amendment to the effect that the word "immediately" be inserted before the word "recommend," she could not see her way clear "to concur in the proposal concerning the appointment of a *new* manager and assistant manager as a preliminary condition for the signing of the joint declaration or the commencement of formal negotiations between the two plenipotentiary delegates." She contended that this latter proposition would be inconsistent with Article 2 of the Chinese draft already accepted by the Soviet Government.[27] This reply reached the Narkomindel on September 11. On September 13 Ambassador von Dirksen transmitted to the Narkomindel a new proposal from the Chinese Government supplementing the preceding reply.[28]

On September 17 the Narkomindel, greatly dissatisfied with the Chinese rejoinders, declared in a verbal note for transmission to the Nanking Government:

The Union Government inserted in the draft declaration proposed by the Nanking Government only the absolutely necessary minimum amendments and changes . . . . The Union Government considered from the very beginning of the conflict, and still considers, that the carrying out of the conditions laid down in these amendments is the elementary prerequisite of the work of the conference.

In its note of September 9, the Nanking Government rejected the minimum amendments designated, thereby annulling its own statement of its agreement to the appointment of a Soviet manager. . . .

A repudiation of its own proposals is likewise contained in the additional proposal of the Nanking Government transmitted to the Union Government on September 13th through the German Ambassador, wherein the Nanking Government substitutes for the question of the appoint-

---

[26] "Politika Dvurushnichestva i Provokatsii" ("Policy of Duplicity and Provocation"), *Izvestiia*, Sept. 6, 1929, p. 1.

[27] Text of the Chinese reply in the German Embassy in Moscow to the Narkomindel, note, Sept. 11, 1929, *Izvestiia*, Sept. 14, 1929, p. 1.

[28] Statement of the Narkomindel, Sept. 14, 1929, *ibid.*

ment of a Soviet manager and assistant manager of the railway, the appointment merely of an assistant manager (prior to negotiations), in clear contradiction both of the Peking and Mukden agreements, and of paragraph 3 of its own draft joint declaration.[29]

In conclusion, the Narkomindel decided that Nanking had rejected "the basic conditions" for signing the joint declaration and conducting negotiations. It placed "the responsibility for the further development of the conflict" squarely on the Chinese Government.[30]

Izvestiia added its voice to the denunciation of Nanking. It charged that the Nanking Government did not respect "elementary mutuality" in regard to the nonpropaganda obligations under Article VI of the Peking agreement. That is, the Chinese were accused of supporting the White Guard organizations,[31] despite the fact that Chang Hsüeh-liang had already issued an order on August 29 to treat armed White Russians everywhere on Chinese territory as bandits.[32] *Izvestiia* also pointed out that by ignoring "the categorical demand of the Soviet Union for the immediate appointment of the manager and his assistant" on the C.E.R., the Nanking Government had tried to legalize the current situation on the railway, which had resulted from its "seizure" by the Chinese authorities.[33] This charge disregarded the repeated assurances of C. T. Wang, Chinese Foreign Minister, that China had no intention of taking the C.E.R. definitively and was ready to settle the dispute by negotiation.[34] As was to be expected, *Izvestiia* hailed the Soviet note of September 17 as a "praiseworthy reply" to the "repetition of the unsuccessful, dishonest maneuvers performed by Mukden under the pressure of Nanking after the July attempts to tie up negotiations."[35]

Voicing his disapproval of the Nanking position regarding the joint declaration, the then Soviet Premier, Alexei Ivanovich Rykov, also declared that the nonacceptance of the Soviet minimum condi-

[29] The Narkomindel to von Dirksen, note, Sept. 17, 1929, *Izvestiia*, Sept. 18, 1929, p. 1.
[30] *Ibid.*
[31] "Nedobrosovestnaia Igra" ("A Dishonest Play"), *Izvestiia*, Sept. 14, 1929, p. 1.
[32] Sun, *op. cit.*, p. 191.
[33] Cf. n. 31.
[34] TASS dispatch from Tokyo, July 17, 1929, *Izvestiia*, July 19, 1929, p. 1; Sun, *op. cit.*, pp. 179, 180.
[35] "Dostoinyi Otvet" ("A Praiseworthy Reply"), *Izvestiia*, Sept. 18, 1929, p. 1.

tions by the Nanking Government meant that the latter "looked at the very negotiations as a means to prolong the conflict."[36]

Following the failure of German good offices to effect a joint declaration, the Soviet military pressure on the Chinese frontier was reportedly intensified, though it had not actually ceased during the preceding period when views were being exchanged through the German Government.[37] At the same time, Soviet protests against "firing and attacks on Soviet territory by Chinese troops and White Guard bands organized by the Chinese authorities" were more vehement and frequent.[38] Ironically enough, each Soviet invasion was followed by a Soviet protest in conventional style. For example, the Soviet protest of August 19[39] followed the Soviet occupation of the T'ungning District on August 17;[40] that of September 6[41] followed the Soviet occupation of the Mishan and Wanching districts on August 23 and 29 respectively, as well as the Soviet assault at Chalainor on September 4.[42] The protest of September 9[43] followed another attack on Chalainor on September 8,[44] while that of September 25[45] followed Soviet occupation of the Suiyuan District on September 19.[46] And the Soviet protest of October 12[47] coincided with the Soviet occupation of the T'ungkiang District on the same day.[48]

In order to ease the situation and facilitate a peaceful settlement, the German Government again tendered its good offices, suggesting a mutual exchange of prisoners. On October 7 it telegraphed a note

[36] Speech of Rykov at the Moscow Regional Conference of Soviets, Sept. 26, 1929, *Izvestiia*, Sept. 28, 1929, p. 2.

[37] Sun, *op. cit.*, p. 194.

[38] Cited from Soviet note to the German Embassy in Moscow, Sept. 28, 1929, in *S.U.R.*, VII (Nov., 1929), 185.

[39] The Narkomindel to the German Embassy in Moscow, note, Aug. 19, 1929, *S.U.R.*, VII (Oct., 1929), 146-147.

[40] Sun, *op. cit.*, p. 194; *C.Y.B.*, *1931*, p. 496.

[41] The Narkomindel to the German Embassy in Moscow, note, Sept. 6, 1929, *S.U.R.*, VII (Oct., 1929), 149-150.

[42] Sun, *op. cit.*, p. 194; *C.Y.B.*, *1931*, p. 496.

[43] The Narkomindel to the German Embassy in Moscow, note, Sept. 9, 1929, *S.U.R.*, VII (Oct., 1929), 150-151.

[44] *C.Y.B.*, *1931*, p. 496.

[45] The Narkomindel to the German Embassy in Moscow, note, Sept. 25, 1929, *S.U.R.* VII (Nov., 1929), 182-184.

[46] Sun, *op. cit.*, p. 194; *C.Y.B.*, *1931*, p. 496.

[47] The Narkomindel to the German Embassy in Moscow, note, Oct. 12, 1929, *S.U.R.*, VII (Nov., 1929), 185.

[48] Sun, *op. cit.*, p. 195; *C.Y.B.*, *1931*, p. 496.

to the Soviet and Chinese Governments proposing that both should stop reprisals and release each other's nationals that had been imprisoned or interned.[49] The Soviet Government, however, refused to accept the German proposal, alleging that China had no intention of respecting her contractual obligations and promises.[50] The Soviet position, as reported to von Dirksen and summarized later in the Chinese manifesto of October 25, was that "no Soviet national would be permitted to negotiate with the [Chinese] National Government, nor would mediation by any third party be accepted" unless the demands put forward in the initial Soviet ultimatum were first granted.[51]

The Chinese Government, in a last effort to get the support of outside powers in the negotiations, transmitted the manifesto of October 25 to all the signatories of the Kellogg Pact, inviting world attention to "the numerous acts of aggression perpetrated by the Soviet Government within Chinese territory." *Izvestiia*, in reply, called the Chinese manifesto "an unprecedented lie," and blamed the failure of the negotiations on Chinese intransigence. "In spite of Nanking's declaration," the article asserted, "the Chinese attempts [to negotiate] remained fruitless." And it reaffirmed the Soviet position that "no matter what negotiations, direct or through mediators," China attempted "with the Soviet Government, [they] remained unsuccessful."[52]

Soviet military pressure by now had placed China in a desperate situation, and her only way out seemed to be unconditional acceptance of the Soviet terms. By November 17 both Manchuli and Chalainor were reported captured by Soviet troops.[53] In the meantime, the Mongols in Hulunbuir (Barga) were aroused to revolt against the Chinese.[54] The loss of strategic points in Hulunbuir, such as Man-

---

[49] Ambassador Schurman in Germany to Secretary Stimson, tel., Oct. 14, 1929, *F.R.U.S.*, *1929*, II, 325-326.

[50] The Narkomindel to the German Embassy in Moscow, note, Oct. 16, 1929, *Izvestiia*, Oct. 18, 1929, p. 1.

[51] Text of the manifesto in *C.Y.B.*, *1929-30*, pp. 1227-1229.

[52] "Besprimernaia Lozh'" ("An Unprecedented Lie"), *Izvestiia*, Oct. 30, 1929, p. 1.

[53] Chinese Minister Chao-chu Wu to Secretary Stimson, letter, Dec. 3, 1929, *F.R.U.S.*, 1929, II, 394.

[54] "The Sino-Russo-Mongolian Struggle in Barga," *China Weekly Review*, Shanghai, L (Nov. 30, 1929), 487-488; "The Soviet Attempt to Steal 76,000 Square Miles of Chinese Territory," *ibid.*, LI (Dec. 28, 1929), 130. Cf. also Powell, "The Soviet Atrocities in Barga" (written for the Chicago *Tribune*), *China*

chuli and Chalainor, alarmed the Chinese.[55]   *Izvestiia* hailed the Soviet military victory of November 17, and claimed that "the decisive action" of a "part of the Far Eastern Red Army" immediately "demoralized the Chinese troops."   According to its account, "over 8,000 Chinese soldiers and officers were disarmed," and "panic swept the Chinese Army, and the Chinese and White Guard detachments retreated in disorder . . . deep into Chinese territory."[56]

The combination of diplomatic impasse and military catastrophe compelled Chang Hsüeh-liang to sue for peace.   Nanking was ready to let the center of gravity for the settlement of the Soviet-Chinese controversy go temporarily to the local authorities.[57]

On November 19, 1929, Tsai Yun-sheng, the Harbin diplomatic commissioner, got in touch with A. Simanovskii, the agent of the Narkomindel in Khabarovsk, by telegraph.[58]   On November 21 Mr. Kokorin, formerly a member of the staff of the Soviet consulate in Harbin and, after the rupture of relations with China, attached to the German consulate at Harbin to render assistance to Soviet citizens, arrived on Soviet territory and transmitted to Simanovskii the official statement of Tsai.   Tsai notified Simanovskii that he had been given full powers by both the Mukden and Nanking Governments for the immediate opening of negotiations to regulate the Soviet-Chinese conflict, and requested that the Soviet Government immediately appoint its representative to meet with him.[59]

On November 22 Kokorin brought back to Harbin Simanovskii's reply, which stated in part:

> The Soviet Government stands for a peaceful regulation of the conflict, but does not consider it possible to enter upon negotiations before the fulfilment by the Chinese of the *preliminary conditions* of which China was informed through the German Government on August 29.   The conditions are in substance as follows:

Weekly Review, L, 337-340; L. A. Cooklin, "Red Terrorism in Barga," *ibid.*, L (Nov. 9, 1929), 377-379.

[55] Ho, *op. cit.*, p. 412.

[56] "Plody Provokatsii" ("The Fruits of Provocation"), *Izvestiia*, Nov. 27, 1929, p. 1.

[57] Sun, *op. cit.*, pp. 196-197.

[58] Tsai to Simanovskii, tel., Nov. 19, 1929, in the statement of the Narkomindel, Nov. 28, 1929, *Izvestiia*, Nov. 28, 1929, p. 1.

[59] Tsai to Simanovskii, letter, Nov. 20, 1929, referred to in statement of the Narkomindel, Nov. 28, 1929, *Izvestiia*, Nov. 28, 1929, p. 1.

1. Official agreement by the Chinese to the restoration of the pre-conflict status of the Chinese Eastern Railway, on the basis of the Peking and Mukden agreements of 1924.

2. The immediate restoration of the rights of the manager and assistant manager of the railway recommended by the Soviet side, in accordance with the Peking and Mukden agreements of 1924.

3. The immediate liberation of all Soviet citizens arrested in connection with the conflict.[60]

On November 26 Chang Hsüeh-liang telegraphed the Narkomindel, expressing his "agreement in principle to the three points in the preliminary conditions." He requested the Soviet Government "to appoint a manager and assistant manager immediately." He also considered it necessary that "accredited persons be appointed by both sides" to work out a procedure for the carrying out of points 1 and 3 of the Soviet preliminary conditions.[61]

In reply, Litvinov recommended "the reinstatement of Emshanov as manager of the railway, and of Eismont as assistant manager." In fulfilment of this condition (point 2), the Soviet Government was to propose that the Chinese representative "be sent immediately to Khabarovsk to meet Simanovskii in considering the technical methods for carrying out points 1 and 3 and in settling questions regarding the time and place of the Sino-Soviet conference."[62]

Izvestiia called the Mukden peace offer a contrast to "the provocative and selfish policy of Nanking," which was an obvious effort to divide the two. It recognized the Mukden proposition as "a prospect for the immediate peaceful adjustment of conflicts," which demanded "deeds" not "words." Above all, it accredited the Far Eastern Red Army with bringing about this triumph.[63]

Incidentally, a note of the Nanking Government of November 14, dated before the fall of Manchuli and Chalainor, but after the Soviet occupation of Tungning, Mishan, Wanching, Suiyuan, and T'ungkiang, was delivered to Litvinov by von Dirksen on November

[60] Simanovskii to Tsai, note, Nov. 22, 1929, in statement of the Narkomindel, Nov. 28, 1929, *Izvestiia*, Nov. 28, 1929, p. 1.

[61] Chang Hsüeh-liang to the Narkomindel, tel., Nov. 26, 1929, in statement of the Narkomindel, Nov. 28, 1929, *Izvestiia*, Nov. 28, 1929, p. 1.

[62] Litvinov to Chang Hsüeh-liang, tel., Nov. 27, 1929, in statement of the Narkomindel, Nov. 28, 1929, *Izvestiia*, Nov. 28, 1929, p. 1.

[63] "Novoe Predlozhenie Mukdena" ("The New Offer of Mukden"), *Izvestiia*, Nov. 28, 1929, p. 1.

29.[64]   The note called attention to the Soviet invasion of Chinese territory, refuted Soviet charges of frontier violation by Chinese troops and White Guard detachments, and proposed the formation of a mixed commission headed by a neutral national and the "withdrawal of armed forces of both countries from the frontier to a depth of 30 miles."[65]   Litvinov flatly rejected the Nanking note, on the grounds that the Soviet Government had already received "official notification from Marshal Chang Hsüeh-liang regarding his acceptance of the preliminary conditions necessary for the quickest possible settlement of the conflict by means of direct negotiations."   Litvinov considered the Nanking note "superfluous"; it "could only prolong the conflict."[66]

Meanwhile, the Nikol'sk-Ussurisk Conference was taking place. On December 1, Tsai Yun-sheng, representative of the Mukden Government, arrived at Nikol'sk-Ussurisk in company with Lee Shao-gen, member of the Board of the C.E.R., to confer with Simanovskii.   On December 3 a preliminary protocol was signed. Tsai declared that the president of the board of directors, Lu Jung-huan, "has been dismissed from that position."   Simanovskii then declared on behalf of the Soviet Goverment that after Lu had been removed from his position, the Soviet Government would be ready to replace Emshanov and Eismont as general manager and assistant general manager.   But the Soviet Government reserved the right to appoint Emshanov and Eismont to other positions on the C.E.R., to which Tsai consented in personal conversation with Simanovskii. Finally, Tsai declared that the Mukden Government would observe strictly the 1924 agreements.   Simanovskii "accepted Tsai's statement with satisfaction," and declared that the U.S.S.R. would "observe them without question."[67]

While the Tsai-Simanovskii talks were in progress, the "second invocation of the Kellogg Pact" was being prepared in the capitals of the world under the moral leadership of Secretary Stimson of the United States and in response to the recently intensified Soviet mili-

[64] *S.U.R.*, VIII (Jan., 1930), 5.
[65] Note of the Waichiaopu to the Narkomindel through the German Government, Nov. 14, 1929, paraphrased in Ambassador Schurman in Germany to Secretary Stimson, tel., Nov. 29, 1929, *F.R.U.S., 1929*, II, 360-361.
[66] Litvinov to von Dirksen, note, Nov. 29, 1929, *S.U.R.*, VIII (Jan., 1930), 5.
[67] The text of the Nikol'sk-Ussurisk Protocol in statement of the Narkomindel, Dec. 4, 1929, *Izvestiia*, Dec. 4, 1929, p. 1.

tary pressure on China. On the same day that the Nikol'sk-Ussurisk preliminary protocol was signed, December 3, the declarations of the other signatory powers began arriving in Moscow.[68] The terms of this intervention and the general substance and tone of the Soviet response have already been noted.[69] Regarding the instant negotiations, however, the Soviet Government charged that the *démarche* of the United States "cannot fail to be considered as a pressure" on the Soviet-Mukden direct *pourparlers* then under way, and consequently "can in no way be considered as a friendly act."[70] *Izvestiia* raised its voice to allege that "the American, French, and British notes represented an attempt of open intervention to disrupt the probable resolution of the Soviet-Chinese conflict."[71] Litvinov himself blamed the governments of these three powers for thus demonstrating their "readiness to render Nanking the requested 'assistance.' "[72]

The Soviet Government showed an awareness of its reliance on military coercive measures to secure favorable terms in a negotiated settlement not only in its rebuff of any third-party reminders of its obligations to use only peaceful measures under the Kellogg Pact, but also in its accounts for home consumption. In both cases, of course, the Soviets insisted they were merely resorting to counter-measures of "legitimate defense"[73] on the Siberian-Manchurian bor-

---

[68] The United States Declaration to China and the U.S.S.R., Nov. 30, 1929, in statement of the Narkomindel, Dec. 4, 1929, *ibid.;* the French and British notes referred to in *ibid.* Cf. also Ambassador Dawes to Secretary Stimson, tel., Dec 3, 1929, *F.R.U.S., 1929*, II, 379. Text of the British statement published in London *Times*, Dec. 3, 1929. For the declarations of other countries, see the following, among others:

Italy: *Izvestiia*, Dec. 5, 1929, p. 1.

Portugal: Minister Dearing in Portugal to Secretary Stimson, tels., Dec. 4 and 6, 1929, *F.R.U.S., 1929*, II, 388, 399.

Egypt: *ibid.*, p. 397.

Little Entente countries: "Vmeshatel'stvo Prodolzhaetsia" ("Intervention Continues"), *Izvestiia*, Dec. 12, 1929, p. 1.

Latin-American countries: *F.R.U.S., 1929*, II: Mexico, 382, 393; the Dominican Republic, 386, 392; Cuba, 389; Peru, 391; Nicaragua, 400.

[69] Cf. pp. 235-241, *supra*.

[70] The Narkomindel to Herbette, for the French and the U.S. Governments, to Urbye for the British Government, reply statements, Dec. 3, 1929, *Izvestiia*, Dec. 4, 1929, p. 1.

[71] "Popytka Otkrytogo Vmeshatel'stva" ("An Attempt at Open Intervention"), *Izvestiia*, Dec. 4, 1929, p. 1.

[72] Litvinov's speech at the second session of the Central Executive Committee, Fifth Convocation, Dec. 4, 1929, *Izvestiia*, Dec. 5, 1929, p. 3.

[73] Term used in Soviet note of Dec. 3, 1929. Cf. n. 70.

der; but in his political report to the Central Executive Committee, Litvinov went further to single out for separate mention the mobilization, power, and bravery of the special Far Eastern Red Army.[74]

The next stage in the direct negotiations opened on December 5, when Chang Hsüeh-liang telegraphed to the Narkomindel his "complete agreement with the results of the Nikol'sk-Ussurisk Conference," and announced the immediate dispatch of Tsai Yun-sheng for the purpose of seeking further agreement.[75] Litivinov replied that Agent Simanovskii was instructed to meet Tsai.[76] The setting for the Khabarovsk *pourparlers* was ready. *Izvestiia* considered it safe to say that the attempt at intervention by the American-French-British "imperialist forces" to grasp the solution of the Soviet-Chinese conflict in their own hands had suffered a crushing blow. It particularly pointed out that so far as "American direct interference" was concerned, the results were "more than a failure."[77] It also reported that Nanking was compelled to approve the Nikol'sk-Ussurisk preliminary protocol, and was clever enough to appoint Tsai as representative of the Chinese Republic for the Khabarovsk negotiations.[78]

On December 13 Tsai arrived in Khabarovsk to confer with Simanovskii. The following day Tsai handed Simanovskii a written statement to the effect that President Lu Jung-huan of the Chinese Eastern Railway had been dismissed from his post on December 7 and that Ho Fu-mian "has been temporarily appointed" to fulfil the duties of the chairman of the board until a new president should be appointed. Simanovskii accepted this as the fulfilment by Mukden of the conditions set forth in the Nikol'sk-Ussurisk protocol regarding Lu's removal, and remarked that "the Soviet Government agreed to recommend" Rudyi and Denisov as new manager and assistant manager of the railway.[79]

On December 22, 1929, the Khabarovsk Protocol was signed by Simanovskii and Tsai. While all outstanding questions were left to

[74] Cf. n. 72.

[75] Chang Hsüeh-liang to the Narkomindel, tel., Dec. 5, 1929, in statement of the Narkomindel, Dec. 7, 1929, *Izvestiia*, Dec. 7, 1929, p. 1.

[76] Litvinov to Chang Hsüeh-liang, tel., Dec. 6, 1929, *Izvestiia*, Dec. 7, 1929, p. 1.

[77] "Krushenie Politiki Vmeshatel'stva" ("Collapse of the Policy of Interference"), *Izvestiia*, Dec. 7, 1929, p. 1.

[78] TASS dispatch from Shanghai, Dec. 10, 1929, *Izvestiia*, Dec. 12, 1929, p. 1. Cf. different tone in Sun, *op. cit.*, p. 201.

[79] Statement of the Narkomindel, Dec. 15, 1929, *Izvestiia*, Dec. 15, 1929, p. 1.

a forthcoming conference, the following three measures were to be carried out immediately:

a) The restoration of the activity of the board of directors of the Chinese Eastern Railway on the basis of the former agreements, and the resumption of duties by the Soviet members of the board. In the future, the Chinese chairman of the board and the Soviet assistant chairman of the board are to act only jointly, in accordance with Article I (6) of the Mukden agreement.

b) The restoration of the former co-relation of the departments headed by Soviet and Chinese citizens and the restoration of the rights of the Soviet chiefs and assistant chiefs of departments.

c) All orders and instructions regarding the railway issued in the name of the board and the administration of the Chinese Eastern Railway since July 10, 1929, are to be considered void unless approved respectively by the lawful board and administration of the railway.

Other provisions included the release by both countries of each other's citizens arrested in connection with the conflict, the immediate restoration of peace on the Sino-Soviet frontiers and the "subsequent recall of the troops by both sides." China also undertook to "disarm the White Russian guard detachments and expel their organizers and instigators" from Manchuria. Both parties further agreed to re-establish consulates in Siberia and Manchuria. All other questions such as the complete resumption of diplomatic, consular, and trade relations were reserved for the Sino-Soviet Conference which was to meet in Moscow on January 25, 1930.[80]

Izvestiia hailed the Khabarovsk Protocol as a "complete victory of the U.S.S.R., inasmuch as the Soviet Union from the very outset did not want anything other than this." It attributed great significance to this act on the alleged ground that "in the so-called Soviet-Chinese conflict," the U.S.S.R. "had to deal with not only the Manchurian generals or even all the Chinese reactionaries, but also the imperialist forces," which "always endeavored to sharpen and utilize" the conflict to advance "their own grasping aims." The paper referred to the American "intervention" through "reminders" as "a concealed attempt at internationalizing the C.E.R." It therefore concluded that "under these circumstances, the victory of the

[80] Text of the protocol in statement of the Narkomindel, Dec. 23, 1929, *Izvestiia*, Dec. 23, 1929, p. 1; also in *C.Y.B., 1931*, p. 497.

Soviet peace policy was, first of all, the victory over the policy of imperialism."[81]

The letter and spirit of the Khabarovsk Protocol, the background and mood of its signing, as well as the tone of the Soviet organ, more or less justified the Chinese opinion that "China had capitulated to the Soviet terms."[82]   The complete restoration of the *status quo ante* with regard to the so-called joint management of the Chinese Eastern Railway was very likely to mean the continued obstruction of the board of directors by its Soviet members,[83] the continuance of limitations on the effectiveness of its Chinese chairman, or *tupan*, and the unlimited *de facto* power of the Soviet manager,[84] as well as the persistent ignoring of the principle of fair play in employment.[85]

Most important of all, the protocol was conspicuously silent on the subject of Soviet propaganda.   No guarantee of noninterference in Chinese internal affairs through the C.E.R. was provided.[86] Thus, the railway would remain "a purely commercial enterprise"[87] in name only, while the protocol would leave Chinese sovereignty and interests continuously at Soviet mercy.[88]

Last but not least, China was now under obligation to the Soviet Union to take measures against White Russians in Manchuria who, in most cases, being long-time residents there or having adopted Chinese citizenship, had been given employment "on the basis of general humanitarian ethics."[89]

Looking back, it now seems that China overstepped the terms of the Railway Agreement when on July 10, 1929, she took the drastic action of arbitrarily dismissing the Soviet manager and assistant manager without first entering into negotiations with the Soviets. Once relations between the two countries had been broken, the Chinese Government would have done better, it would seem, to come to

[81] "Pobeda Mirnoi Politiki Soiuza SSR" ("Victory of the Peaceful Policy of the U.S.S.R."), *Izvestiia*, Dec. 23, 1929, p. 1.

[82] Sun, *op. cit.*, pp. 201, 207-208; Tao-shing Chang, *International Controversy over the Chinese Eastern Railway*, p. 158.

[83] Cf. pp. 182-185, *supra*.

[84] Cf. pp. 185-190, *supra*.

[85] Cf. pp. 190-192, *supra*.

[86] Cf. previous Chinese charges of interference in China's manifestoes, July 20 and Oct. 25, 1929, *C.Y.B.*, *1929-30*, pp. 1223-1224, 1225, 1227.

[87] Cf. pp. 159-162, *supra*.

[88] Cf. pp. 193-198, *supra*.

[89] Tsai to Soviet Consul General Znamenskii, note, Oct. 9, 1930, in *S.U.R.*, VII (Dec., 1930), 195.

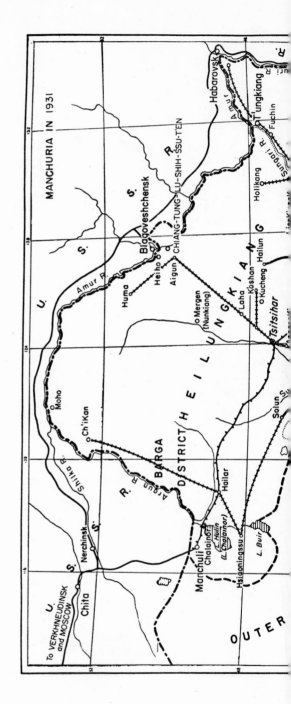

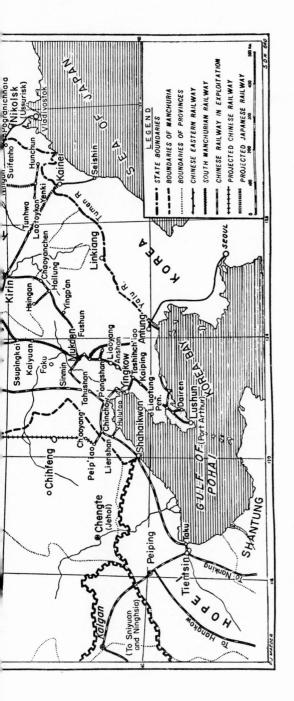

LEGEND

STATE BOUNDARIES
BOUNDARIES OF MANCHURIA
BOUNDARIES OF PROVINCES
CHINESE EASTERN RAILWAY
SOUTH MANCHURIAN RAILWAY
CHINESE RAILWAY IN EXPLOITATION
PROJECTED CHINESE RAILWAY
PROJECTED JAPANESE RAILWAY

terms with Russia on the basis of the joint declaration, even if it meant accepting the entire Litvinov amendment of August 29,[90] in order to avert further bloodshed and to win an additional, explicit promise from the Soviet Government to refrain from propaganda activities. The ill-fated Khabarovsk Protocol, by contrast, very quickly proved an obstacle to the success of the Sino-Soviet Conference in Moscow.

The Moscow Conference of 1930-31

The Sino-Soviet Conference for the final settlement of the Chinese Eastern Railway controversy, as provided in the Khabarovsk Protocol of December 22, 1929, was pregnant with difficulties long before its convocation. It was nevertheless opened in Moscow on October 11, 1930, eight and one-half months behind schedule. During its intermittent sessions, the conference was marked by interminable procrastination on the agenda and procedure. Finally, following the Japanese provoked Manchurian incident of September 18, 1931, the futile conference lapsed from a state of stalemate into abeyance without public notice.

The long delay in the opening of the Moscow Conference beyond the appointed date of January 25, 1930[91] was a source of contention between the U.S.S.R. and China. L. M. Karakhan, Assistant Foreign Commissar, who was named the Soviet representative at the conference on May 7, categorically denied any responsibility on the part of the Soviet Government for this delay.[92] *Izvestiia* attributed the delay to the belated arrival in Moscow of the Chinese delegation headed by Mo Teh-hui, the new president of the Chinese Eastern Railway.[93] In fact, Mo was appointed delegate by the Chinese Government shortly after he had been recommended by Chang Hsüeh-liang on January 11, 1930,[94] long before Karakhan's

[90] Cf. pp. 246-247, *supra*; statement of the Narkomindel, Aug. 29, 1929, *Izvestiia*, Aug. 31, 1929, p. 1.

[91] The date had first been postponed to April 15, then to June 1 before it was finally fixed through Mo Teh-hui's efforts during his conversation with Karakhan on September 19, 1930. Cf. Ho, *op. cit.*, pp. 416-418.

[92] Karakhan's speech at the opening of the Moscow Conference, Oct. 11, 1930, *Izvestiia*, Oct. 12, 1930, p. 1.

[93] "Otkrytie Sovestsko-Kitaiskoi Konferentsii" ("The Opening of the Soviet-Chinese Conference"), *Izvestiia*, Oct. 13, 1930, p. 1.

[94] Ho, *op. cit.*, p. 416.

nomination.   After Mo's arrival on May 9,[95] five months elapsed before the formal conference was opened.

Most prominent among the other reasons for delay advanced by the Soviet side was the demand for the complete ratification of the Khabarovsk Protocol by the Nanking Government and its 100 per cent fulfilment as a prerequisite for the conference.[96]   The Soviets also charged that the Nanking Government was pursuing an anti-Soviet policy in order to win the favor of the "Imperialists" and thus make the latter more willing to yield their privileges in China.[97]

On the other hand, the Chinese side explained that the delay was due to the Soviet's marking time during the concerted insurrection of Feng Yu-hsiang and Yen Hsi-shan in North China.   The Soviet Government seemed to prefer waiting until the Northern rebellion was suppressed in order to see whether Chang Hsüeh-liang would restore his close co-operation with the Central Government or whether he would strive for greater autonomy for the Three Eastern Provinces.[98]   In addition, the dispute over the validity of the whole of the Khabarovsk Protocol and over the scope of negotiations at the conference were thought to be deterrent factors for the earlier opening of the formal conference.[99]

Among outside sources, the *Havas* News Agency and the French press in general repeatedly gave as the cause of the delay the "unacceptable demands" raised by the Soviet Government "for the guarding of the Soviet consulates in China by Red Army men."[100] *Izvestiia* emphatically denounced this report as fabricated by the "company of lie and slander" hostile to the U.S.S.R. and labeled it an "unscrupulous maneuver aiming at further protraction, and if successful, disruption of the Sino-Soviet Conference."[101]   Chinese sources seemed to have refrained from substantiating or mentioning this news dispatch.

Above all, the fundamental stumbling block both for the opening

[95] *Ibid.; S.U.R.*, VIII (June, 1930), 103.

[96] Cf. n. 99; "Dadim Otpor Novoi Provokatsii" ("We Rebuff the New Provocation"), *Pravda*, Jan. 31, 1930, p. 1.

[97] "Nankin i Imperialisty" ("Nanking and the Imperialists"), *Pravda*, Jan. 13, 1930, p. 1.

[98] Ho, *op. cit.*, pp. 416, 417; *C.Y.B., 1931*, p. 498.

[99] Ho, *op. cit.*, pp. 417-418; *C.Y.B., 1931*, p. 498.

[100] TASS dispatch from Paris, June 18, 1930, *Izvestiia*, June 22, 1930, p. 1.

[101] "Gavas Povtoriaet Razoblachennuiu Klevetu" ("Havas Repeats Unmasked Slander"), *Izvestiia*, June 22, 1930, p. 1.

and for the work of the conference was the irreconcilable dispute over the validity of the Khabarovsk Protocol in its entirety. Karakhan reiterated again and again at the opening of the Moscow conference his theme that "along with the 1924 agreements, the Soviet Government considers the Khabarovsk Protocol the most important act, regulating the existing relations between the U.S.S.R. and China and serving as the basis for the conference."[102]   His continued insistence that the Chinese delegation should recognize the Khabarovsk Protocol as the guiding principle of the conference, and his demand that China should strictly fulfil the obligations thereunder embarrassed Mo Teh-hui,[103] whose Government had approved only a part of the protocol which it had authorized Tsai Yun-sheng to discuss at Khabarovsk.[104]

According to *Izvestiia*, the "stubborn refusal" of the Nanking Government to recognize the Khabarovsk Protocol in its entirety as the "contractual basis" for the parley constituted the reason for the delay of the Moscow Conference and the obstacle to the progress of its work.   It pointed out that the recognition by Nanking of the protocol as a whole was not merely a problem of formal procedure, but a matter of "first-class importance" for the Soviet side.   The paper, therefore, concluded that the Soviet Government had the "right to insist on its unconditional recognition and observance by China."[105]

As to the Chinese position, since the Khabarovsk Protocol restored the previous conditions of *de facto* "Soviet monopoly" on the Chinese Eastern Railway and touched upon questions which lay beyond the scope of the railway problem, it aroused great dissatisfaction in the Chinese National Government and the widespread disfavor of Chinese public opinion, which demanded that the National Government disapprove the protocol.[106]   The Waichiaopu, in its statement of February 8, 1930, denied recognition to that part of the protocol which dealt with "questions of general character" and those not

---

[102] Karakhan's speech at the opening of the Moscow Conference, Oct. 11, 1930, *Izvestiia*, Oct. 12, 1930, p. 1.

[103] *Ibid.*; cf. "Otkrytie Sovetsko-Kitaiskoi Konferentsii" ("The Opening of the Soviet-Chinese Conference") (Editorial), *Izvestiia*, Oct. 13, 1930, p. 1.

[104] Chinese Declaration, Feb. 8, 1930, *C.Y.B.*, *1931*, pp. 497-498.

[105] "Otkrytie Sovetsko-Kitaiskoi Konferentsii" ("The Opening of the Soviet-Chinese Conference"), *Izvestiia*, Oct. 13, 1930, p. 1.

[106] Ho, *op. cit.*, p. 415.

arising out of the railway dispute, on which Delegate Tsai Yun-sheng was not empowered to negotiate, contending that he was acting *ultra vires* in so doing. It cited the law of treaties that "any arrangement concluded between the representatives of two countries is subject to the approval or ratification of their respective Governments." While leaving the door open for the Soviet Government to appoint a delegate to China to discuss general problems, the Nanking statement announced that the measures for resolving railway disputes, as stipulated in the Khabarovsk Protocol, had been put into effect.[107]

Izvestiia attributed to the Waichiaopu the statement that the Nanking Government had attempted to declare the Khabarovsk Protocol invalid "under the ridiculous pretext that its plenipotentiary acted beyond his power." "Regarding the protocol," the paper declared, "the Soviet Government, no matter under what circumstances, can never ignore the attempt of the Nanking Government to repudiate its voluntarily undertaken obligations."[108]

In his speech at the opening session of the Moscow Conference, Mo Teh-hui, head of the Chinese delegation, solemnly declared that "China has not for one moment digressed from the observance of the legal agreements concluded between China and the U.S.S.R." While avoiding specific mention of the Khabarovsk Protocol, in accordance with the stand of his Government, Mo further stated that "there can be no doubt that every treaty *legally concluded* between China and the U.S.S.R. will meet with the strict observance on the part of China, as a binding international obligation."[109]

During the following discussion, the Soviet delegation brought forward the question of "the necessity for clear and unequivocal recognition by the Chinese delegation of the Khabarovsk Protocol."[110] *Izvestiia* regretted that the speech of the Chinese delegate was limited to "vague assurances." It pointed out that so far as the validity of the protocol was concerned, "no slightest obscurity" about its "strict observance" could be permitted.[111]

[107] Chinese Declaration (Waichiaopu statement), Feb. 8, 1930, *C.Y.B.*, *1931*, pp. 497-498.
[108] "Otkrytie Sovetsko-Kitaiskoi Konferentsii" ("The Opening of the Soviet-Chinese Conference"), *Izvestiia*, Oct. 13, 1930, p. 1.
[109] Mo Teh-hui's speech, Oct. 11, 1930, *Izvestiia*, Oct. 12, 1930, p. 1.
[110] Statement of the Narkomindel, Oct. 12, 1930, *ibid.*
[111] "Otkrytie Sovetsko-Kitaiskoi Konferentsii" ("The Opening of the Soviet-Chinese Conference"), *Izvestiia*, Oct. 13, 1930, p. 1.

In fact, Karakhan soon admitted in writing that in regard to the Chinese Eastern Railway, "China is generally fulfilling her obligations under the Khabarovsk Protocol." He enumerated point by point the provisions relating to "workers and employees on the railway," "the restoration of the Soviet consulates," and that "the security and normal work of Soviet economic organizations were also fulfilled."[112] He even added that China was carrying out the stipulations of the protocol regarding the White Guards[113] and the scope and work of the Moscow Conference. Therefore, he concluded that "the main points of the Khabarovsk Protocol may be considered as already fulfilled."[114]

The Moscow Conference suffered rough sailing during its prolonged voyage. It struck one rock after another: the disputes over its agenda, over the maintenance of the existing administration of the railway, over the question of the redemption of the railway, and even over the arrangements for its regular meetings.

The mission of the Chinese delegation to the Moscow Conference was "for the exclusive purpose of effecting a readjustment of the Chinese Eastern Railway,"[115] which meant to China the redemption by her of the C.E.R. as provided in the 1924 agreements and the Khabarovsk Protocol.[116] This is why the Moscow parley was often referred to by Chinese authors as the Sino-Soviet conference on railway redemption.[117] However, when the question of agenda came up for a decision, Karakhan sought to widen the scope of the conference. Not only the Chinese Eastern Railway problem should be discussed, but also questions relating to trade, diplomatic relations, right of navigation on the Amur and the Sungari rivers, the independence of Outer Mongolia, the delimitation of the Sinkiang boundary, and the indemnity to the U.S.S.R. for her military expenses during the conflict as well.[118] When China rejected these new

[112] Karakhan to Mo Teh-hui, letter, Nov. 10, 1930, *Izvestiia*, Nov. 11, 1931, p. 1.

[113] Cf. "Prekrashchenie Deistvii Belykh" ("Discontinuance of the Activities of the Whites"), *Izvestiia*, Oct. 19, 1930, p. 1.

[114] Karakhan to Mo Teh-hui, letter, cited in "Otkrytie Sovetsko-Kitaiskoi Konferentsii" ("The Opening of the Soviet-Chinese Conference"), *Izvestiia*, Oct. 13, 1930, p. 1.

[115] Chinese declaration, Feb. 8, 1930, *C.Y.B., 1931*, p. 498.

[116] Mo Teh-hui to Karakhan, letter, Nov. 17, 1930, *ibid.*, p. 499; Chinese text in Ho, *op. cit.*, p. 420.

[117] Ho, *op. cit.*, p. 424; Sun, *op. cit.*, p. 210.

[118] Ho, *op. cit.*, pp. 417-418.

proposals, Soviet troops were reported massing on the Manchurian border. Some interpreted these military demonstrations as being calculated to induce China to show a more conciliatory attitude in the Moscow Conference.[119]   The final agenda included three items: the Chinese Eastern Railway, trade, and diplomatic relations.[120]

After the opening session on October 11, the second meeting of the conference was not held until December 4. In the meantime, Karakhan and Mo debated on the question of the preservation of the existing regime of the C.E.R. in the form to which it had reverted under the Khabarovsk Agreement. The Soviet Government was anxious to have China recognize the existing status; Karakhan insisted that "so long as the present state of affairs regarding the railway is not changed by a change of its administration, or by mutual agreement, or by China purchasing the railway, the present status of the railway as based on the Peking and Mukden treaties shall not be altered by one-sided action."[121]   Mo contended that the present status of the C.E.R. "was not entirely in correspondence with the stipulations of the Peking and Mukden agreements."[122]   Again Karakhan retorted that the present administration of the C.E.R., "in whole and in part must not be subjected to a change by unilateral and arbitrary actions of one party or the other," and that any change of the administration of the C.E.R. "in any of its parts can be effected only through a mutually agreed decision."[123]   Soviet policy in this respect was apparently bent toward perpetuating the predominant position of Soviet Russia on the railway which had prevailed prior to the conflict, and thus toward preventing in effect the complete and faithful carrying out of the 1924 agreements.

Only after his return from a three-month home trip to report to his Government between December, 1930, and March, 1931, did Mo bring up the problem of railway redemption.[124]   During the discussion of redemption at the third to eighth sessions of the conference from April 11 to June 4, Karakhan threw in the challenge

[119] New York *Times*, Oct. 29, 1930, p. 8.

[120] Karakhan to Mo Teh-hui, notes, Nov. 10 and 23, 1930, *Izvestiia*, Nov. 11, 1930, p. 1; *S.U.R.*, VIII (Dec., 1930), 198; Ho, *op. cit.*, pp. 418, 419.

[121] Karakhan to Mo, Nov. 10, 1930, *Izvestiia*, Nov. 11, 1930, p. 1.

[122] Mo to Karakhan, note, Nov. 17, 1930, *C.Y.B.*, *1931*, p. 499; also in Ho, *op. cit.*, p. 420.

[123] Karakhan to Mo, note, Nov. 23, 1930, *S.U.R.*, VIII (Dec., 1930), 198; *C.Y.B.*, *1931*, p. 499.

[124] Ho, *op. cit.*, pp. 423-425.

that "there were preliminary conditions for the Chinese purchase, with which the Chinese Government must comply before any practical results could accrue from the conversations." He added that "as soon as the evaluation of the railway property was obtainable, it would be up to the Chinese Government to decide on the methods to be used for effecting such redemption."[125] But even the question of evaluation was very complex and was hotly debated.[126]

Finally, there was the Soviet "policy of procrastination" in regard to the sessions of the conference. For instance, Mo had to remind Karakhan on November 17, 1930, that he earnestly hoped for the resumption of the conference sessions "at an early date" in order to "proceed promptly with its work and come to a speedy conclusion."[127] Again on November 28, Mo wrote to Karakhan that "the important point at the present time is the continuation of our conference."[128] Karakhan repeatedly used the excuse of illness for postponing sessions of the conference. And as a pretext for postponing the ninth session from June 16 to June 21, 1931—over Mo's protest—he cited the giving of a reception to the diplomatic corps.[129] This Soviet policy was said to have for its purpose the natural death of the conference.[130] The purpose, whether intended or not, was achieved. With the opening of the Japanese adventure in Manchuria on September 18, 1931, the Moscow Conference expired.

Russia's subsequent illegal sale, on March 23, 1935, of the Soviet-Chinese joint interests in the Chinese Eastern Railway to Japan in the name of her puppet Manchukuo showed a sharp change in Soviet policy in Manchuria as expressed through the Chinese Eastern Railway, compared to the policy of the preceding period. The Soviet Government effected the sale of the railway through prolonged and deliberate efforts, at a meager sum of 140,000,000 yen, and in violation, moreover, of Articles IX and I respectively of the Peking and Mukden agreements of 1924. This unilateral action on the part of the Soviets aroused profound suspicion as to their real interest in the railway as compared with previous claims. It seemed to be clearer than ever that the Chinese Eastern Railway was to the U.S.S.R. what

---

[125] *C.Y.B., 1931-32* (Peking & Tientsin), p. 267.
[126] Ho, *op. cit.*, pp. 424, 425.
[127] Mo to Karakhan, note, Nov. 17, 1930, *C.Y.B., 1931*, p. 499.
[128] Mo to Karakhan, note, Nov. 28, 1930, *ibid.*, pp. 499-500.
[129] *Bulletin of the Waichiaopu*, June, 1931, p. 192; Ho, *op. cit.*, p. 425.
[130] *C.Y.B., 1932* (Peking & Tientsin), p. 267.

it had been to her Tsarist predecessor: merely a weapon for encroaching upon Manchuria when it was under a weaker state like China.

The Far Eastern policy of both Tsarist and Soviet Russia centered on Manchuria. To gain access to Manchuria, the Tsarist Government had, under various pretexts constructed the Chinese Eastern Railway, which then became Russia's all-encompassing excuse for her illegal control of and interference with the affairs of Manchuria, and thus with the internal affairs of China.

During the fourteen years that the Tsarist government dealt with the C.E.R., from 1903 when the construction of the railroad was completed until the time of the Russian Revolution in 1917, a state within a state was actually maintained in the northeast corner of China. Under Lieutenant-General Horvath's dictatorship in the so-called railway zone, all legislative, judicial, administrative, and military power, including control over customs tariffs and over education, was actually in the hands of Russia.

When the Soviet government came into power, it gave only lip-service to the sovereign rights of China, though enough to induce China to sign the Peking and Mukden agreements of 1924. Thereafter, freshly armed with a show of legality, the Soviet Union once more assumed control of the C.E.R., through which it again proceeded to interfere in Manchuria and in China.

But Russia was not satisfied with the political influence she wielded over Manchuria. Her eyes were on the wealth of agricultural, sylvan, and mineral resources of the territory. Through the Chinese Eastern Railway, she acquired extensive lumber and coal concessions by the agreements of 1907 and 1908. To these were added the telegraph lines and other tangible advantages. During the period of Sino-Soviet joint management, actual Soviet control over a network of auxiliary enterprises enabled Soviet Russia, in a somewhat different manner, to control the economic life of North Manchuria.

Nor did Russia neglect the military basis for her influence in Manchuria. Resorting to tactics of confusion, Russia sent and maintained along the railroad the so-called Railway Guards as a part of the later Russian Trans-Amur Army. In 1898 Russian troops had interfered in Manchuria and emerged with the compulsory lease of Port Arthur and Dairen. During the construction of the C.E.R., the railway guards aroused the resentment of the Manchurian people, who then started the Boxer movement. Tsarist War Minister Kuropatkin saw his opportunity and moved in Russian troops to occupy the whole of Manchuria. Next, the Russo-Japanese War of 1904-5, which was being fought on Chinese soil, brought still more Russian troops to the area. Thereafter, until the Russian Revolution, Russia made no effort to remove her troops from Manchuria. The Soviet Union, in turn, launched a military expedition invading Manchuria from October through December, 1929, following the complete cessation of the Sino-Soviet diplomatic relations growing out of the dispute over the joint management of the C.E.R.

Thus, throughout its history the Chinese Eastern Railway has served both Tsarist and Soviet Russia as a most effective agent in the promotion of their Far Eastern policy and the furthering of their designs on Manchuria. In this respect, both Tsarist and Soviet Russia may be said to have fostered a consistent expansionist policy by means of the Chinese Eastern Railway, at the expense of a weak neighbor.

PART TWO. OUTER MONGOLIA:
CENTER OF RUSSIAN AND SOVIET
STRATEGY IN THE FAR EAST

VII: MONGOLIA'S RELATIONS WITH CHINA AND RUSSIA IN HISTORICAL PERSPECTIVE

In the thirteenth century the Mongol tribes of Central Asia had risen to the height of their power. A warlike people, respected and feared by Europe and Asia alike, they had swept across the breadth of Asia in a series of daring, brilliant campaigns that included Russia and China among their conquests. Under a succession of powerful and gifted rulers they were able to administer their vast empire and maintain their rule over China for ninety-eight years, and over Russia for more than two centuries. But as quickly as their star had risen, it fell; a few centuries later, the descendants of Genghis Khan, "ruler of all men," were to be found at one time or other under the control of Russia or China, though neither country had ever conquered them in open warfare.

The early history of the Mongols is very obscure. It is a story of nomadic tribes suddenly rising to power and as quickly losing their hold. Until the seemingly miraculous rise of Targontai and then his son Temuchin, who became the Genghis Khan, the strategic and military prowess of the various Mongol tribes was limited to local skirmishes and conquests of brief duration.

In antiquity, the people inhabiting the tableland of Mongolia were known as the Hsiung-Nu or the Huns (from the third century B.C. to the first century A.D.). They roamed over an area bound by Siberia in the north, the Chinese provinces of Chihli, Shansi, Shensi, and Kansu in the south (roughly the edge of the Great Wall), Sinkiang or Chinese Turkestan in the west, and Hulunbuir or Barga of Manchuria in the east. They were strong and prosperous in the Tsin and the Han dynasties (206 B.C.–25 B.C.). Later they were divided into northern and southern units. When the northern

Hsiung-Nu suffered defeat at the hand of the Han general, Tou Hsien, they migrated to the west, and the southern Hsiung-Nu came under the control of the Han dynasty.

During the later Han period (25 B.C.–219 A.D.), the descendants of the Tung-hu nomads known as the Wu-Huang and the Hsien-Pei launched repeated raids on the northern frontier of China whenever they had mustered sufficient strength. The Wu-Huang were defeated by Ts'ao Ts'ao, the Chinese general, and moved as a group into the interior of China. During the Wei dynasty (220-64) Mongolia existed as a part of the extensive domain of the Wu-Wu or Rou-an.

During the Tsin dynasty (265-416), the southern Hsiung-Nu (317-439) in the northern part of Shansi grew populous and powerful, and for over a century their five tribes led invasions from the north. In the Yellow River basin they maintained their domain until the beginning of the fifth century, when a branch of the Hsien-Pei nomads under their chieftains, the Tobas, descended upon these war-worn barbarians and destroyed the kingdoms. The new rulers then established the first of several dynasties known in history as the Northern dynasties (439-580).

When China was again unified under the Chinese Sui (581-617) and Tang (611-907) dynasties, Mongolia was ruled by the T'u-Chüeh or Turks, a branch of the Hsiung-Nu (from the sixth to the middle of the eighth century). Then the empire of the T'u-Chüeh was destroyed by the Hui-Heh of the Wigurs in the middle of the eighth century, and the tribes scattered in all directions, particularly westward. Descendants of the Hsien-Pei nomads living on the Inner Mongolian prairie and known as the Ch'itans established the Liao dynasty (907-1125). Thereupon the Manchurian tribe of Nüchen revolted against the Ch'itans and replaced the Liao dynasty with the Chin dynasty (1115-1234). First the Liao and then the Chin dynasties claimed the fealty of Mongolia, but in the end the Chin empire fell to the Mongols as they swept eastward under the leadership of Genghis Khan.

In the Chinese chronicles the name of the Mongols is recorded as early as the Tang dynasty (618-907), possibly in the ninth century.[1] In racial stock the Mongols are said to be the hybrids of the

[1] VI. Kotvich, *Kratkii Obzor Istorii i Sovremennogo Polozheniia Mongolii* (*A Brief Survey of the History and Contemporary Situation of Mongolia*) (St. Peters-

Tung-Hu and the Turks and cousins of the Ch'itans.[2] The original homeland of the Mongols was the area between the Onon and Kerulen rivers southeast of Lake Baikal, or the northeastern corner of present-day Mongolia.

In their early history, the Mongols, while under the control first of the Liao and then the Chin dynasties, were divided into a number of tribes, each under the rule of its own prince. These tribes or clans waged petty wars with one another, uniting occasionally in greater undertakings, such as a war against China.

At the beginning of the thirteenth century, the history of the Mongols took on world-wide significance. In 1206 Temuchin (1162-1227), son of a petty chieftain who had won recognition from the Court of Chin, seized control of his father's tribes after the latter's death and in a series of daring and courageous battles united all the Mongol tribes under his authority. He formed them into one nation and proclaimed himself supreme ruler: Genghis Khan (Very Mighty King). Under his leadership the Mongol armies swept over northern China, then west and south over Azerbaijan, Georgia, and northern Persia. Relentlessly the Mongol armies moved westward until Transoxania was invaded and Bokhara taken (1219); Samarkand captured (1220), and Khorasan and Merv devastated. In 1223 the battle of the Kalka River in southern Russia saw the defeat of a strong force of Russians and Cumans. Thus before he died in 1227, Genghis Khan had become the first ruler of the vast realm of the Mongol empire which stretched from the China Sea to the banks of the Dnieper.

In a career as dramatic and colorful as that of Genghis Khan, Ogotai pushed forward the frontiers won by his father until Eastern Europe lay before his armies. After he had been elected Kjakan or chief Khan by plenary kuritai on the Kerulen, he marched southward to complete the downfall of the Chin dynasty, which until then had controlled the territory north of the Yellow River (1234). Following this victory his armies also invaded Korea (1231) and the lands of the southern Sung dynasty (1233-34), and laid waste Meso-

burg, 1914), p. 5. Cf. *Chou-T'ang-Shu* (*An Old Version of the History of the Tang Dynasty*), Vol. 199; *Hsin-T'ang-Shu* (*A New Version of the History of the Tang Dynasty*), Vol. 219; Ho Chien-min, *Hsiung-Nu Min-T'su Kao* (*A Study on the Hsiung-Nu Race*) (Shanghai, 1939), pp. 2-3.

[2] Ho Chien-min, *op. cit.*, pp. 4-7.

potamia and Azerbaijan (1235), and Georgia and Armenia (1233-34). Eastern Europe knew the might of the Mongol hordes from 1237 until 1241 when Batu, the son of Ogotai's deceased eldest brother Juchi, and General Sabotai led 600,000 troops into and devastated an enormous area including Moscow and Kiev northward to Novgorod. In 1241 they invaded Hungary, then Poland, crossed the Danube, and advanced as far as the Adriatic, pillaging and murdering the length and the breadth of the continent.[3]

In 1241,when Ogotai died, Batu, whose forces had finally met with stubborn resistance in Bohemia, was recalled. He withdrew from the lower Volga whence he had summoned the Russian princes to do him homage as the victorious khan.

It may be recalled that Genghis Khan, before his death, had partitioned his empire among a grandson and three sons: to Batu, son of Juchi, Kipchok in Russia; to Chagatai, the former Kara-khitai empire; to Ogotai, Outer Mongolia; and to Tului (regent 1727-29), Eastern Mongolia and North China. Consequently, in 1242, Batu, now supreme on the lower Volga as the ruler of the Khanate of the Golden Horde, built a populous and beautiful city for his capital, Sarai.

For two centuries thereafter this khanate was suzerain (sometimes referred to as sovereign) of all Russia. Aside from levying tributes and taking military contingents, however, the new rulers left the Russian princes in control and the Russian church undisturbed. The khans of the Golden Horde demanded only that the princes gave their allegiance and the people their tribute. The existing Russian political, economic, and social organization and structure were left largely unchanged.

As for the eastern part of the empire, there was a series of short reigns from 1246 until 1259,[4] when Kublai, one of the younger sons of Tului and grandson of Genghis Khan, declared himself supreme khan. Instead of residing at Kara-Korum, which had been built with the assistance of Chinese artisans during Ogotai's reign, he established his capital at Peking and proclaimed himself Emperor of China in 1264. By the reckoning of Chinese historians, Kublai actually sat

[3] Kotvich, *op. cit.*, pp. 5-6.
[4] Guyuk, son of Ogotai (1246-48); Turakina, widow of Ogotai (regent, 1242-46); Guyuk's widow (regent, 1249-51); Mongka, son of Tubui (1251-59).

on the throne of China from 1280 A.D., as Emperor Shih-Tsu of the Yüan dynasty (1280-1368).

The Mongol Empire was reunited when Kublai defeated and captured his brother, Arikboga, who had been proclaimed Khan of Kara-Korum in 1260, and later, in 1277 and again in 1287-88, overcame the dissension of Khaidu, head of the house of Ogotai. Kublai also won the support of his brother Hulagu and the successor Ilkhans of Persia, and, in theory, of the Golden Horde on the Volga. Thus the Mongol Empire under Kublai Khan at the south reached the Ganges River of India and the Persian Gulf; at the west, Egypt, the Black Sea, and the banks of the Dniester; at the north, Central Russia and Lake Baikal; at the east, the Chinese and Korean shores along the Pacific Ocean.

This empire, the size of which the world had never seen before, was not of long duration. In spite of their prowess and their talents, the Mongols were unable to hold for long all the conquered territories with their conglomerate of nationalities. After the death of Kublai Khan (1294), the empire as such existed only in name. By the end of the thirteenth century, authority had been delegated to so many khans that the empire was actually a number of quite separate principalities. In Persia the reign of the Ilkhans ended in 1439, when the dynasty was succeeded by a number of lesser families.

The Mongol reign in China lasted scarcely a century. In 1368 the last Yüan emperor, Shun-Ti or Togon-Temur, fled China, pursued by Chinese revolutionary forces. Chu Yuen-chang, an ex-Buddhist priest, who had led the victorious assault, ascended the throne as Emperor Hung-Wu (1368-99), founder of the Ming dynasty (1368-1644). Togon-Temur's remaining forces were pursued into Mongolia and crushed by an army of 400,000. Meanwhile a quick succession of brief reigns followed in the eastern Mongol royal houses. In the 1380's Emperor Hung-Wu's army again invaded Mongolia and this time overwhelmed the Mongolian forces near Lake Buyur. This marked the collapse of the eastern branch of the Mongols, for thereafter the Mongol tribes began to break away from all governing centers. Instead they established scattered communities, each with its own chief, over the whole of eastern Mongolia.[5]

[5] D. Pokotilov, *History of the Eastern Mongols during the Ming Dynasty from 1368 to 1634* (Chengtu, 1947), pp. 5-15.

Meanwhile, in Russia the Mongol yoke had not yet been thrown off. In 1380 the Tartar armies had been defeated at the battle of Kulikovo by the Russians under Grand Duke Dimitri, surnamed Donskoi in memory of this successful battle, but the victory was in no sense decisive. On several occasions thereafter the Tartars advanced to the very gates of Moscow. Still Kulikovo had broken the prestige of the Tartar arms and turned the Mongol tide. Had it not been for Tamerlane, another great Mongol conqueror, Russia too might have shaken off the Tartar yoke in the fourteenth century. As it happened, not until 1480 did Ivan III (1462-1505), later called "the Great," and actually the first national sovereign of Russia, succeed in undermining the Tartar power, and finally annexing most of the rival principalities.

The opposing armies had confronted each other on the River Oka, but there had been no battle. Earlier Ivan had seen the wisdom of winning over the unruly elements within the ranks of the Golden Horde and negotiating with the dissatisfied neighbors of the Tartar state. Then winter came to the aid of the Russians and forced the Tartars into retreat, many of them deserting to the Russian side. Tribute ceased to be paid; within less than twenty years the Golden Horde disappeared.

During the Chinese Ming dynasty (1368-1644), the Mongols in their homeland in Mongolia were divided into a number of independent feudal principalities which waged constant internecine wars in competition for the throne of the khan or for preference in trade with China. Toward the fifteenth century the Mongols were divided into two groups: eastern (Khalkhas, Buryats, Charhars, Tumets), and western or Oirats group (Derbets, Oirats, Olets). Later the eastern Mongols were in turn divided into the southern Mongols (Chahars, Tumets, etc.), roaming south of the Gobi desert, and the northern Mongols (Khalkhas, Buryats), occupying the area north of the desert.

All eastern Mongols were at first subject to Togon-Temur Khan, last of the Yüan emperors, who had fled from Peking, and then to his son Bilikt (1370-78), who again made Kara-Korum the Mongolian capital. Later descendants of Togon-Temur were called by the Chinese "Hsiao-wang-tzu," "small" or "petty" khans. In 1402 Gun-Temur revived the former name of the Mongol dynasty—

"Tatan"—and engaged in a contest with the western Mongols for power. China was said to have seized the opportunity presented by the enmity between the western and eastern Mongols and dispatched troops against both warring factions at separate times. In this way the military strength of the Mongols was completely divided and overcome.[6]

In a subsequent battle, in 1425, the western Mongols under the command of Makham Khan defeated the eastern Mongols and seized control of all Mongolia. To maintain this power over the eastern Mongols, the Oirat princes concluded a military alliance under the name of Durbun-Oirat, and laid plans to seize the northern frontier provinces of China. But the Ming emperor then entered into the fray and lent his support to the eastern Mongols, who then crushed the Oirat army.

However, by the year 1434, the Oirats had again risen to power. It was during the rule of the Oirat Khan Esen (Yehsien) (1449-53) that attempts were made to unite the Mongol tribes and to re-establish Mongol rule over China. Esen actually took prisoner the Ming Emperor Ying-Tsung (1436-49 and 1457-64) at T'umu in 1449, and thereafter proclaimed himself Khan of all Mongolia (1453). But in the same year he was killed while struggling with the other princes for the khan's throne. With his death Oirat power and rule came to an end.[7]

From 1453 to 1644 ruling power rested in the tents of the eastern Mongols, but they were able to produce only a rapid succession of khans who possessed neither economic nor political power. Hence this was known as "the period of minor khans." Then under the rule of the eastern khan, Dayan (1470-1543), who was considered a fifteenth-generation descendant of Genghis Khan, the Mongols were once more united. It proved to be the last time Mongolia knew any kind of unity, for after the death of Dayan in 1544, in accordance with the instructions he left, the Mongolian territory was divided among his eleven sons into eleven completely independent units. Among the later minor khans, only Tumet Khan Altan (sixteenth century) and Charhar Khan Lingdan (seventeenth century) are worth mentioning.[8]

[6] "Mongoly" ("The Mongols"), *B.S.E.* (1st ed.), Vol. XL (1938), col. 62.
[7] Pokotilov, *op. cit.*, pp. 56-60.
[8] *Ibid.*, pp. 79-81.

Northern Mongolia became known as "Khalkha" in the sixteenth century, when one of Dayan Khan's sons, Geresentsze-Dzhalapr (1479-1543), inherited this region north of the Gobi desert from his father and called it the "shield" (barrier). Khalkha was not brought into direct contact with China until the time of Geresentsze's grandson, Batai-Tushetu Khan.[9] By this time, however, Khalkha had long been under attack from the western Oirats.

After the death of Esen, little is known of the activities of the Oirat (Western) Mongols until the sixteenth century, when, crowded out by the Khalkhas, part of them went northward to Western Siberia and the other part southward to Tibet. In 1630, those who were said to have gone over to the Siberian steppe, to the Urals and to the Volga, organized the Kalmyk Khanate. The others under the Oirat Gushi Khan occupied Tibet in 1637, where, while holding temporal power for themselves, they delegated the spiritual power.

One of the Oirat princes, Batur Khan, in an attempt to unite the Oirat tribes called a conference of the Oirat princes in 1640. His hopes of ending the conflicts between the princes and uniting forces in a common struggle against the growing power of the Manchus were not realized, however, and no real unity was achieved. When he died in 1663, neither his son Senge (died 1671), nor Senge's brother Galdan (Boshoktur Khan), who succeeded Senge, attempted anything in that direction. Instead Galdan seized Eastern Turkestan in 1679, and from 1688 on waged war with the Khalkhas for control of the trade route through Khalkha, which led from Central Asia to Russia and China and from China to Russia (the Kiakhta route). After lengthy wars, Galdan defeated the Khalkhas, who then fled to the border region of southern Mongolia.[10]

As for the southern Mongols, there was first a brief alliance with the Manchus and then a period of protection from these enterprising neighbors to the East, which in turn became allegiance to the new leaders. The Manchus had achieved unity under the leadership of Nurharch in 1618 and gained the support of the Charhar Mongols, which previously had been given to the forces of the rapidly declining Chinese Ming dynasty. Since at this time the northern Mongols had not yet accepted the destiny of the Manchus, that part

---

[9] "Mongoly," ("The Mongols"), *B.S.E.* (1st ed.), Vol. XL, cols. 62-63.

[10] A group of these Khalkhas fled to Russia, and were thereafter called Selegin Buriat.

of Mongolia south of the Gobi desert became known as Inner Mongolia; that north of the Gobi, Outer Mongolia.

Thus it came to pass that in 1644, when China was embroiled in civil war, the Manchus availed themselves of the request of the Chinese Ming General Wu San-kuei to drive off the bandit Li Tzu-ch'eng and surprised Peking. By this stroke the resistance of the last Ming princes (1644-60's) was broken and the Ch'ing dynasty firmly established.[11]

It was in 1688, shortly after the Manchu conquest of China, that the Khalkha princes of northern or Outer Mongolia were defeated by Galdan, the Oirat ruler of Dzungaria. They retreated to the border of southern Mongolia, where they applied to the Manchu Government of China for help. Emperor K'ang-Hsi went to the defense of the Kalkhas and in 1691 called an assembly of the Mongol princes at Dolon Nor in Inner Mongolia. There he lost no time in establishing and strengthening the ties of these princes with China. The T'uhsieht'u Khan and the Hutukhtu or Living Buddha of Urga were solemnly invested as new vassals and given "the official documents and the great seal. Thus, Khalkha officially became a dependency of China."[12]

With the beginning of the seventeenth century Russia could boast of a record of conquest and expansion. It was now over a century since the Golden Horde in Russia had been put down. In Siberia, the peoples of the northern regions had offered no resistance, so that the Russian flag was carried south on the Ob, Illtysh, and Yenisei rivers, up to the very door of the Mongols.

It has been said that almost the entire seventeenth century was a period of rivalry between Russia and the Chinese Empire over Mongolia. Toward the end of the Ming dynasty China retreated behind the Great Wall and the Russians entered Khalkha unhampered. In 1616 Russia sent its first mission to Altyn (Golden) Khan, prince of the western part of Khalkha, who had his capital near the upper Yenisei, to obtain his help against the Kirgiz and to persuade him to acknowledge allegiance to the Tsar. This he did vaguely

[11] Since the ruling house of the Ching dynasty was Manchu, the term "Manchu" has been used interchangeably with "Chinese," particularly in reference to the government, during the period 1644-1911.

[12] Michel N. Pavlovsky, *Chinese-Russian Relations* (New York, 1949), p. 19.

without actually committing himself, so that the Russian mission was not able to obtain any definite results.[13]

In 1632 Altyn Khan, possibly concerned about the growing power of the Manchus, reportedly sent an emissary to Tomsk to express his desire to place himself under Russian protection. In 1634 a second Russian mission arrived in Mongolia but departed without having obtained any satisfaction. Yet soon after, the Altyn Khan sent gifts to Moscow and asked presents in return. Moscow satisfied a part of the Khan's demand and sent a new mission headed by Grechanin. This mission was said to have succeeded in bringing back in 1634 "a written document in which Altyn Khan formally acknowledged himself a subject of the Tsar.[14]

However, these good terms with Moscow were to last for only a few years. In 1646 old Altyn Khan sent one of his sons to the court of Emperor Shun-Chih in Peking to present his tribute, while his other son, Lobzdan, suddenly advanced with a large army against the Russian Kirgiz. Just as the Russian towns of Tomsk, Krasnoyarsk, and Kuznetsk were about to fall, Altyn Khan's death forced Lobzdan to return in order to assure his succession. Grechanin, therefore, succeeded only in obtaining from the new Khan Lobzdan consent to an alliance with Russia for help against the Oirats (Dzunghars), but not allegiance to the Tsar as his subject.[15] Thus with the Southern Mongols throwing their lot in with the Manchus of China since 1636, and with Dzungharia's Galdan in the west on excellent terms with the Russians, Sino-Russian rivalry over Mongolia was considerable by the latter half of the seventeenth century. The Cossack advance on the Amur was already a point of serious contention. Therefore, in 1682, Emperor K'ang-Hsi, while starting his great campaign on the Amur, also sent a Chinese mission bearing rich gifts to Khalkha. His next move was to ask the Khalkhas to stop trade with the Russians at Nerchinsk so that the Russians on the Amur might be blockaded.

In 1686 the Khalkha Mongols, at a general conference at Khurien-Beltchir, heard of the Russian advance in Trans-Baikalia. Aware of

[13] *Ibid.*, pp. 6-9; "Mongols" *Encyclopaedia Britannica* (11th ed.; Boston, 1911), XVIII, 715.

[14] This document was said to have been presented by Russian plenipotentiary Savva Vladislavich for display when the Treaty of Kiakhta was signed in 1727 (Pavlovsky, *op. cit.*, p. 10).

[15] *Ibid.*, p. 12.

their own weak position, they decided to seek Chinese protection. Shortly thereafter, in 1688, on the eve of the conference with the Russians at Nerchinsk and just before the Khalkhas were driven south by Galdan, Emperor K'ang Hsi, apparently to facilitate the Mongol petition for protection, sent to Urga his emissary Arani, head of the Li-fan-Yüan (Board of the Administration of Dependencies), and later one of the delegates at Nerchinsk. It is not unlikely that his presence influenced the Hutukhtu and, through him, the Council of the Khalkha princes in that year to decide "to place themselves under the protection of China,"[16] thus paving the way for the official ceremony at Dolon Nor in 1691 when Khalkha "officially became a dependency of China."[17] From that time until 1911, the Khalkha Khans and the Hutukhtu of Outer Mongolia paid to the Manchu Court an annual tribute of "nine whites" ("chiu-pai," or eight white horses and one white camel).[18]

During the Khalkhas' negotiations with China for protection, the Russians were not inactive. Golovin, Russian plenipotentiary at Nerchinsk, spent more than two years in Selenginsk and Udinsk, near the frontiers of Outer Mongolia, before proceeding to Nerchinsk. He was instructed to approach the Hutukhtu and the T'uhsieht'u Khan before negotiating with China. There was a courier, Vasilii Perfiliev, carrying presents and a letter from Golovin, in Urga in 1687. Later, Stepan Korovin, the emissary of Golovin, appeared and remained from the end of 1687 until the beginning of 1688. A second emissary, Kachanov, was there in 1688, probably at the same time as the Chinese envoy Arani.

Later events indicated that these Russian diplomats were not very successful. There were reports of a strong force sent by Tushetu (Ochiroi) Khan to intercept Golovin's army. Selenginsk and Udinsk were besieged and Golovin's safety imperiled. When the siege was lifted and the troops had returned to Mongolia,[19] Galdan began his assault on Khalkha. Thus Galdan seemed to have

[16] *Ibid.*, p. 15; Kotivich, *op. cit.*, p. 10.

[17] Pavlovsky, *op. cit.*, p. 19.

[18] *Li-Fan-Yüan Tse-li (Code of the Board of the Administration of Dependencies,* referred to hereinafter as *L.F.Y.T.L.*) (1908), Vol. XIV, sh. 3; Vol. XV, sh. 10-11; Vol. XVII, sh. 1; Vol. XVIII, sh. 1-2. This code was first proclaimed by Emperor K'ang-Hsi in 1698, and later revised by Emperor Ch'ien-Lung in 1789, and by Emperor Chia-Ch'ing in 1815.

[19] Pavlovsky, *op. cit.*, p. 16.

come to the rescue of Golovin, and accomplished his own end of defeating the Khalkhas. The Hutukhtu and T'uhsieht'u Khan and their whole entourage of tens of thousands, with women and children, were forced to seek refuge on the frontiers of China. Emperor K'ang-Hsi viewed this new development with alarm, and went to the defense of the Khalkhas against their enemy. Personally commanding one of the two forces, the emperor marched triumphantly into Mongolia. In 1696, Galdan was crushed by Chinese forces near Urga and took poison the next year while he was still in the field against the Chinese. Galdan's successors, however, were not willing to let the Chinese relax. For almost the whole of the next century, through the reign of three successive emperors—K'ang-Hsi (1662-1722), Yung-Cheng (1723-35), and Ch'ien-Lung (1736-95)—China was at war.[20] This phase of Mongol-Sino-Russian relations was summed up by Pavlovsky as follows:

The diplomatic success which China had gained in Urga in 1688 was counteracted by the fact that it involved her in a war against the Dzunghars [Oirats]. The struggle was to be a terrible one. It was to last, with short interruptions, for more than sixty-five years; diminishing considerably the resources of China; and account to a great extent for her political decline in the nineteenth century. The entire foreign policy of China was for a long time to be influenced by this war. The Russians were only too pleased by this. Already in Nerchinsk the Chinese had shown themselves more conciliatory than they had been a year earlier, and in order to insure Russian neutrality they offered to grant ever greater trading facilities.[21]

On the other hand, as a result of this prolonged warfare, the Khalkha Mongols were enabled to return to their homeland in about ten years. Also Urianghai, which had been under the Mongols, passed over into Chinese hands; and Chinese control was firmly established in Kukunor (1720's), Tibet (1721-51), and Sinkiang (1755).[22]

As for the governing of Inner and Outer Mongolia, the Mongols were organized into "banners," each under a hereditary chieftain. These banners formed leagues, each with a captain-general and a

[20] Kao Po-yen, Meng-Ku yü Chung-Kuo (Mongolia and China) (Peiping, 1936), pp. 65, 68-72.
[21] Pavlovsky, op. cit., p. 18.
[22] Kao, op. cit., p. 72.

deputy captain-general, whose selection had to be approved by the Imperial Government.[23] Inner Mongolia leagues were directly under the Li-Fan-Yüan in Peking, while those of Outer Mongolia were responsible to the chiang-chun or military governor of Uliassutai, whose jurisdiction extended also to Urianghai. An imperial representative was stationed at Urga and one at Kobdo to serve as associates of the military governor at Uliassutai.[24]

While Emperor K'ang-Hsi permitted the internal administration of Khalkha to remain in the hands of the Mongols, he created seventy-two new princes, their number to increase later, in order to weaken the power of the khan and the Hutukhtu. At the same time he encouraged the revival of Lamaism, which had made the Mongol ruling class in China a special elite during the Yüan dynasty. It was through the manipulation of the "incarnation" of the Chebutsum-Damba Hutukhtu or Living Buddha of Urga as spiritual leader that the Manchu dynasty consolidated its control in Mongolia.[25]

Outer Mongolia's acceptance of the suzerainty of the Chinese Empire of the Manchus did not, however, in the least diminish Russia's interest in that region. On the contrary, during the later years of Peter the Great's reign, commissioners, as they passed through Urga on their way to Peking, tried Christianity as a means of winning over the Mongols. It is on record that Peter the Great instructed the Metropolitan Bishop of Tobolsk to convert the Hutukhtu at Urga to Christianity. Missionaries were sent to the Third Hutukhtu in the hope that "once they had caught the Hutukhtu, his followers would without trouble embrace the new faith [of the Orthodox Church of Russia]."[26] This and another attempt in 1719 both proved unsuccessful. Nevertheless Russia remained friendly with the Mongol princes and sent students to Mongolia, ostensibly to learn the Mongol tongue. Even at this early period, it must be noted, her future policy of penetrating into Outer Mongolia was not far from view. All this time Russia was not unaware of the events in Outer Mongolia, but she chose to believe that she had certain claims derived from the brief submission of the Altyn Khan in 1634. Therefore, the fact that the Treaty of Nerchinsk of 1689 had fixed

[23] *Ibid.*, pp. 74-80; Vol. I, sh. 1-9, *L.F.Y.T.L.*, Vol. III, sh. 1-2; Vol. VI, sh. 6-8; Vol. XIII, sh. 1-2, 8-9, 10.
[24] *Ibid.*, Vol. V, sh. 19; Vol. VI, sh. 13-14.
[25] *Ibid.*, Vol. LVI, sh. 21-22; Vol. LVII, sh. 3, 3-13.
[26] Pavlovsky, *op. cit.*, p. 16.

the border between Russian and Manchuria only to the east of the Argun River gave her little concern. On the other hand, China was quite anxious to establish a definite boundary with Outer Mongolia along the enormous frontier more than twelve hundred miles long west of the river.

China's objections to Russia's claims were for a long time unavailing. However, China's interest in fixing the boundaries of Outer Mongolia became the more urgent as the "desertion" of Mongol nomadic tribesmen across the frontier increased, especially following the campaigns against the Dzunghars in 1718 and thereafter. In 1720, when, at an audience given to Russian envoy Ismailov, Emperor K'ang-Hsi insisted on the fixing of the Mongolian frontier, Sino-Russian relations were strained and then broken off for five years. Not until the accession of Yung-Cheng did reconciliation become possible.[27] Therefore, the question of the frontier was not settled until August 27, 1727, when Count Sava Vladislavich Razousinskii, envoy to Peking from Empress Catherine I signed the Treaty of Kiakhta after two years of negotiations. This agreement marked the frontier eastward from Kiakhta to the Argun River, and westward from the same point to Shabina Dabeg, a pass in the Sanyan Mountains. Since Razousinskii felt that his country was faced with war if he did not sign the treaty, he decided in favor of the more prudent act. As may be seen from the following quotation, his conclusions were not the result of hasty reasoning.

We may easily conceive of a war with China, but we must take into consideration the fact that this would not be an easy undertaking. We would have to concentrate at the border at least ten regiments of the line and an equal number of irregulars, which would have to face all the Chinese forces and perhaps the Mongolian as well. The cost of such an undertaking, even assuming that it should be successful, will never be recovered even in hundred years. We would have to build fortresses, maintain strong garrisons there, supply them continuously with food and ammunition. Peace would be menaced for a long time, trade with China would be interrupted, and the Siberian population would become impoverished. Moreover, the Chinese would never acknowledge defeat; they would begin to arm themselves to an even greater extent, and learn our military arts.[28]

[27] *Ibid.*, pp. 20-22; Weigh, *Russo-Chinese Diplomacy*, pp. 21-25.
[28] Cited in Pavlovsky, *op. cit.*, pp. 29-30.

It is quite likely that as a consequence of Razousinskii's attitude, Russia recognized Chinese sovereignty in Mongolia in the Treaty of Kiakhta and assumed a position of "armed neutrality" when China warred on the Dzunghars. The status established by the Treaty of Kiakhta was actually maintained for nearly two centuries.[29]

However, the surface tranquillity of Mongol-Sino-Russian relations imposed by the Treaty of Kiakhta did not remain unbroken. In 1733, when China was in serious battle with the Dzunghars, Lorenz Lange, who had been advocating an "active" Russian policy, suggested making demands on Peking in regard to Outer Mongolia and the Amur. In the same year the Mongols were said to have sought Russian protection against the harsh treatment of the Chinese. The Hutukhtu himself showed so much friendship toward Russia that the Manchu emperor had him move to Dolo Nor, in Inner Mongolia, away from the Russian border and Russian influence.[30]

In 1756, Ch'ing-Kung-Tsa-Pu, one of the most influential of the Mongol princes then at the head of an army guarding communications for the Chinese forces in battle with the Dzunghars, revolted. Within a few months the revolt had spread over almost all of Outer Mongolia. It was an uprising of the princes against the severity with which the emperor punished those responsible for the lack of success in the military operations against the Dzunghars. The descendants of Genghis Khan, furthermore, resented being treated like mere subjects and punished as such.[31]

Ch'ien-Lung's answer was a decree asserting his right to compensate and punish "according to law" all servants of the state, including the Mongol princes.[32] It was not surprising, therefore, that the five most influential Mongol chiefs—among them the T'uhsieht'u Khan and the Hutukhtu himself—should choose this time, a most critical one for China, to approach the Russians. They went to Jacobi, commandant of Selenginsk, and asked him to announce to St. Petersburg their willingness to accept the status of a protectorate and to become Russian subjects. When the proposal reached Gover-

[29] *Ibid.*, pp. 22, 25, 30-31.
[30] *Ibid.*, pp. 31-32.
[31] *Ch'ien-Lung Shih-lu* (*The Factual Records under the Reign of Emperor Ch'ien Lung*, referred to hereinafter as C.L.S.L.) (n.d.), Vol. DXXIII, sh. 15; Pavlovsky, *op. cit.*, pp. 32-34.
[32] Decree of Emperor Ch'ien-Lung, Aug. 18/July 23 (Chinese lunar calendar), 1756, *C.L.S.L.*, Vol. DXVII, sh. 8.

nor Miatlev, he urged immediate acceptance of the Mongol offer. For thus, he argued, "the Chinese army will be cut off from its bases, and Russia will be able to dictate terms to Peking."[33]   However, "complete instructions" from St. Petersburg came too late; Chinese forces had put down the revolt and "the Emperor of China had become reconciled with the princes."[34]

During the reign of Catherine II (1762-96), when trade difficulties occurred at the frontier, Gerhard Friedrich Muller, an influential historian, submitted to the court a secret memorandum entitled "Reflection on the War with China." Therein he proposed war as the only solution which, in the situation, would achieve the principal demands of Russia: first, the return of the Amur, "the Russian river," and then of Mongolia, "the country of Altyn Khan, a Russian subject."[35]

Catherine II herself proceeded more cautiously.   Under her reign, Sino-Russian relations reached a stability hitherto unknown. Much of this was due to the long and patient negotiations of Kropotov, who was twice sent to China.   The question of Mongol deserters was settled in two stages: in 1768 an addendum to the Treaty of Kiakhta was signed by Kropotov, and in 1792 a supplementary protocol was signed by Nagil.   Thereafter the number of frontier incidents diminished and trade in Kiakhta proceeded without interruption. Clearly this policy of maintaining the status quo was beneficial to both Russia and China, as no event of any great moment occurred during the years of the next half century to disrupt their relations. Nevertheless, Russia was not without strong advocates for expansion in Outer Mongolia.   Some Russian commentators claimed that the Buryats of Russian Transbaikalia belonged to the same stock as the Mongols of Outer Mongolia and that the Urianghai region had always belonged to Russia "juridically."[36]   As early as 1852 Governor General Muraviev of Eastern Siberia was taking steps to stir the Mongols to rebellion against the Chinese authorities.   Zenovick, his agent, went among some of the Mongol princes and predicted the

---

[33] Pavlovsky, op. cit., pp. 34-35.

[34] Ibid., p. 35.

[35] Nicholas Bantysh-Kamensky, Collection of Diplomatic Matters between the Russian and the Chinese Governments from 1619 to 1792 (Kazan, 1882), Part I, sec. 1, pp. 378-393.   Cited in Pavlovsky, op. cit., p. 37.

[36] "K Voprosu ob Avtonomii Mongolii" ("The Problem of Mongolian Autonomy"), Vestnik Azii (Asiatic Herald) (Harbin), nos. 35-36, 1915, p. 113.

downfall of the Manchu dynasty, and the advisability of joining ranks with Russia. Furthermore, Zenovick asserted, the Russian Government could not even conceive of continued Chinese rule over Manchuria and Mongolia. In 1854, when China was critically embroiled in the dispute with Great Britain, Muraviev thought the time was ripe to push Russian claims. Thereupon he proposed to St. Petersburg that he claim Mongolia as a Russian protectorate. A less hasty approach was recommended by a special committee which reduced Muraviev's ambitions to a project for further consideration. It was considered far more desirable to win the sympathies of the Urga Hutukhtu and perhaps to forge friendly ties with the leading princes. In a similar fashion, the activities of Muraviev in 1860 were neutralized by the cautious St. Petersburg Amur Committee.[37]

Russia's official interest in Outer Mongolia in the nineteenth century may be said to have been limited to economic matters. In 1860 the first Russian trading firm was established in Urga. In the next year a Russian consulate was opened there. Thereafter, a series of trade pacts was concluded to control the commercial traffic then passing between Russia and China. The Peking Trade Agreement of February, 1862, allowed Russian merchants with small capital to trade in Mongolia free of duty. In the St. Petersburg Treaty of 1881, detailed regulations governed the transit of goods passing through Mongolia from Russia to China, and entrance points on the Mongolian frontier for Russian merchants were specified. In addition, Russia secured the right to open consulates in Kobdo and Uliassutai, among other places, provided that the commercial development so warranted. Toward the end of the nineteenth century Russia began to seek special railway rights in Manchuria and Mongolia. In an Anglo-Russian exchange of notes in April, 1899, Russia obtained British agreement to abstain from competing for railway concessions in the region north of the Great Wall, and she in turn promised not to interefere with British interests in the Yangtze basin. In June, 1899, Russia, acting within her special rights in her so-called sphere of influence, secured from China the promise that "if railroads are in future built from Peking to the north or to the northeast towards the Russian frontier," China, if not constructing them herself, would

---

[37] A. Popov, "Tsarskaia Rossiia i Mongoliia v 1913-1914 gg." ("Tsarist Russia and Mongolia, 1913-1914," referred to hereinafter as "Tsarskaia"), Introduction, in *K. A.* (Moscow-Leningrad), XXXVII (1929), 7.

reserve the right of construction for the Russian Government or a Russian syndicate.[38] However, as the activities of the Russian Government were concentrated chiefly on Manchuria rather than Outer Mongolia, the nature of Russian trade in Outer Mongolia did not appear impressive in the second half of the nineteenth century. Only when 1904 ushered in the Russo-Japanese War and heralded the emergence of Japan as a new and victorious power in the Far East did Tsarist Russia feel forced to give up its interests in South Manchuria. Then it turned the greater part of its attention to Mongolia. Politicians in St. Petersburg immediately began an all-out campaign to resolve the "Mongolian question"; "official circles, representatives of commerce and industry, the press, various societies, all set to work"[39] on a new program that would compensate for the Port Arthur-Mukden failures.

In 1905 a Russian consulate was opened at Uliassutai; and, in 1911, one at Kobdo. About 1908, large Russian firms in Moscow and Tomsk began to see possibilities in the economic structure of Mongolia, where previously only small Russian establishments had sought to compete with the numerous Chinese shops (there were twelve Chinese firms for every one that was Russian). In the Ministry of Trade and Industry, a special "Departmental Committee" was created in 1909 to collect information on the Mongolian market,[40] and in 1910 a committee was set up in Irkutsk to reinforce and encourage trade with Mongolia. There was a scheme afoot to connect Mongolia with the Trans-Siberian Railway.[41] Eventually, several trade expeditions made their way to Mongolia. All these activities, while ostensibly commercial, could not conceal Russia's political interest. Members of the expeditions advocated the establishment of a Russian commercial bank in Mongolia, in part to aid the Russian merchants but also to "compete" with the Chinese credit system then in force all over Mongolia.[42]

The revitalized Russian interest in Outer Mongolia evidently had an immediate reaction on China. For almost two centuries China

[38] MacMurray, *Treaties and Agreements with and Concerning China 1894-1919*, I, 204, 207-208.
[39] I. Maiskii, *Sovremennaia Mongoliia* (*Contemporary Mongolia*) (Irkutsk, 1921), p. 253.
[40] Popov, "Tsarskaia," *K.A.*, XXXVII, 11.
[41] Maiskii, *op. cit.*, p. 253.
[42] Popov, "Tsarskaia," *K.A.*, XXXVII, 11.

had followed a buffer-state policy with regard to Outer Mongolia, refraining from colonizing the vast Mongolian region and maintaining it as a strategic "vacuum." But now this policy was reversed; in 1906 a bureau for the colonization of Mongolia was created in Peking to encourage Chinese emigration to Mongolia. Russia, having profited from the Chinese frontier "vacuum" policy in the past, did not at all welcome this alteration of what was in effect a no-man's land in Outer Mongolia.[43] Thus the stage was set for a new struggle between Russia and China in Outer Mongolia.

In Peking, Ivan J. Korostovets, the Imperial Russian Minister, supported an active Russian policy in Outer Mongolia. In a long memorandum of November 3, 1910, he pointed out that if China were successful in her efforts to make a province of Outer Mongolia, Russia's security would be threatened. Therefore he recommended that a "strong protest" be addressed to China, and at least tacit support be solicited from Great Britain and Japan.[44]

However, when the Foreign Minister, Sazonov, heard from the Russian representatives in Great Britain and Japan, he did not find the reports encouraging. The Japanese Foreign Minister felt that if strong measures were taken against China, the Chinese would only seek the help of the United States and Germany; as for Great Britain, her current policy did not permit interference in the internal affairs of Asiatic countries. Furthermore, the British felt that this particular question had little to do with British interests.[45]

Nevertheless, agitation for an aggressive Russian policy continued vehement. A certain Men'shikov wrote in the pages of the *Novoe Vremia* (*New Times*) in February, 1911:

They write to me that the general staff of the Japanese armed forces visited the whole of Northern Mongolia and the Ili district [in Sinkiang] as early as the last year before the Chinese Revolution, as if having it in view. Naturally enough, Mongolia will look for support after having declared its independence; if Russia will not give such a support, then Japan will be asked for it. . . .

. . . Mongolia is bound to place itself under the protection of some

[43] Pavlovsky, *op. cit.*, pp. 40-42.

[44] Dispatch of Korostovets of Nov. 3, 1910, file no. 104, referred to in Popov, "Tsarskaia," *K.A.*, XXXVII, 8.

[45] Letter of Benckendorv, Dec. 10, 1910, referred to in Popov, "Tsarskaia," *K.A.*, XXXVII, 9.

country, and if Russia will not give such protection, then Japan will; in the latter case it will no longer be the problem of how to keep Eastern Siberia, but Central and Western [Siberia] as well.[46]

Rish, for instance, reported that the partisans of *Novoe Vremia*, speculating on the advantages to be secured, "urged the Imperial Government not to procrastinate. Their scheme for Russian annexation of the immense Mongolian empire was emerging in a manner resembling the conquest of the Siberian empire by the adventurous Ermak."[47]

In this respect Kushelev wrote, "[One] group thinks that in the present political situation the absolutely necessary and the only solution is the annexation by Russia of Mongolia and of the Northern part of Chinese Turkistan as far as the Great Desert of Gobi, following a boundary along the mountain range of Tienshan and further eastward to the city of Taonanfu [in Manchuria]. . . . Personally, I subscribe completely to this last opinion."[48]

Another author from the same Suvorin school offered: "if Russia wants and succeeds in occupying Mongolia, then innumerable advantages will be secured."[49] Rish pointed out that "Russian diplomacy, which occupied itself with realizing these projects, was forced out of necessity to cut down its appetites in the settlement of the 'Mongolian question' in view of Japan and other imperialist countries."[50]

Other factions lent strong voices to the cry for expansion into Outer Mongolia. In describing the means and manner in which Mongolia was transferred into the Russian sphere of influence in the period preceding World War I, Shoizhelov recorded "the attempt to transform the area into another Bukhara or Khiva. And the entire public opinion of the contemporary Russia of landowners and of the bourgeoisie demanded it."[51] For instance, the *Journal of Commerce and Industry*, the organ of manufacturers, wrote:

Mongolia and Northern Manchuria naturally gravitate, geographically and economically, toward Russia. These are the regions which should be

[46] Cited in A. Rish, "Mongoliia na Strazhe Svoei Nezavisimosti" ("Mongolia Guarding Her Independence") *Tikhii Okean* (*The Pacific Ocean*), no. 4 (6) (Oct.-Dec., 1935), p. 99.
[47] *Ibid.*   [48] Cited in *ibid.*, pp. 99-100.
[49] Cited in *ibid.*, pp. 100.   [50] *Ibid.*
[51] S. Shoizhelov, "Avtonomnoe Dvizhenie Mongolii i Tsarskaia Rossiia" ("The Autonomous Movement of Mongolia and Tsarist Russia"), *Novyi Vostok* (*The New East*), nos. 13-14, 1926, p. 359.

under exclusive Russian influence. We must do business there and control their markets. Moreover, our frontier with China is unnatural, sinuous, difficult to defend, and completely contrary to physico-geographical conditions. A natural boundary of Russia should consist of the deserts of Mongolia (Gobi). Those lifeless seas of sand can be compared to the oceans which separate peoples and states. Also two different and absolutely incompatible races, like the yellow and the European, ought to be separated by real obstacles to a mass invasion. If we do not think about that at present, and if we allow the Chinese to control Mongolia and Manchuria, then the roads which are to be constructed by them through the desert, close to us along the Russian frontier, would be utilized to strengthen their economic and political position to such an extent that we Russians will be pushed westward back to the Urals. . . .

Here you have a natural frontier for Russia! Mongolia and Northern Manchuria ought to be ceded to us, with the same conditions prevailing as those governing Khiva and Bukhara, and those governing Korea in respect to Japan. Also, Russia should immediately draw that line which may still be drawn with ink. If this political and historical business should be long postponed, then it is possible that such a line will have to be drawn with a "red stroke" [i.e. by blood]. Whatever can be achieved at this time by peaceful means must later on be considered a possible cause for war.[52]

Toward the latter part of 1911, events gave Russia further opportunity and pretext to expand her Mongolian program. As Maiskii put it, "The Chinese Revolution of 1911 created an extraordinarily favorable condition for the prompt realization of the plans for political occupation—the immediate result being the Mongolian coup d'etat of 1911-12."[53] Nevertheless, Sazonov's policy in the Far East remained one of moderation. Because of the "international constellation in Europe," he opposed any "one-sided engagement" of Russian military forces in the Far East.[54]

The policy of moral support for the Mongol princes rather than actual intervention, as laid down by the Tsarist Foreign Ministry in 1905, was, on the surface, still in force in 1911. When a delegation of Mongol princes asked the Russian Government to take

[52] *Dal'nevostochnoe Obozrenie (Far Eastern Review)* (St. Petersburg, 1910), pp. 70-71, cited in Shoizhelov, *op. cit.*, pp. 359-360.
[53] Maiskii, *op. cit.*, p. 253.
[54] German minister in Vienna to Chancellor Bethomann-Hollwog, Feb. 20, 1911, in Germany, *Die Grosse Politik der Europäischen Kabinetter 1871-1914* (Berlin), Vol. XXXII, no. 11792, p. 216.

Khalkha under its protection, Korostovets was told that "the internal situation in Khalkha does not in any way affect our vital interests." Its importance lay in its potential use in achieving "our political tasks in China."[55]

Yet Outer Mongolia's declaration of independence in the latter part of 1911 "must be attributed to the work of Russian agents."[56] A report of a special conference of ministers on the Far East convoked in August, 1911, admitted that *"Some of our agents in Mongolia have collaborated to a considerable extent in the formation of the belief among the Mongols that they can count on Russian support, when they break off with China* [italics added by S. Shoizhelov]; nevertheless, in the prevailing political situation it would be desirable to intervene actively in Mongolian affairs."[57]

[55] Sazonov to Korostovets, tel., July 27, 1911, file no. 1046, as cited by Popov in "Tsarskaia," *K.A.*, XXXVII, 9.

[56] Popov, "Tsarskaia," *K.A.*, XXXVII, 7.

[57] Report of Special Council of Ministers, Aug. 4, 1911, as cited by Shoizhelov, *op. cit.*, p. 355.

VIII: THE RUSSIAN ROLE IN OUTER MONGOLIAN INDEPENDENCE OF 1911

RUSSIAN CHALLENGE TO CHINESE POLICY IN OUTER MONGOLIA

Since 1691, when Northern Mongolia accepted Manchu sovereignty for saving her from the Djungar (Dzhungar) invasion, the Manchu policy toward Mongolia had consisted of a few rather generous principles: namely, division of the Mongols into separate small units, segregation of the Mongols from the Chinese, favoritism toward the Mongol princes, and encouragement of Lamaism. This policy of Emperor K'ang-Hsi and his successors may initially have facilitated the maintenance of Manchu rule in Mongolia. At the same time, from the standpoint of the local population, it may have been, as a Soviet writer later described it, a "skilful and farsighted policy of the highest degree."[1] But when Russia became interested in expanding its influence into this region, the traditional Manchu policy could scarcely provide the needed bulwark against Russian infiltration and expansion.

Thus when Tsarist Russia turned its attention to Mongolia in 1905 as compensation for the disastrous Russo-Japanese War, the Manchu Government naturally had to adopt new measures to maintain its position. Yet any means of self-defense it attempted was opposed and criticized by Russia. Conflict was bound to ensue. As one Russian author flatly challenges, "From the very moment of the conclusion of the Portsmouth Peace Treaty, China blindly entered into political struggle with us, and last year [i.e., in 1911] we were obliged to deliver an ultimatum to her."[2]

[1] I. Maiskii, *Sovremennaia Mongoliia* (*Contemporary Mongolia*), p. 240.
[2] IU. Kushelev, *Mongoliia i Mongol'skii Vopros* (*Mongolia and the Mongolian Problem*) (St. Petersburg, 1912), p. 53.

Of the measures adopted by the Manchu regime, the one most resented by Russia was that of promoting Chinese colonization in Mongolia. Even today Mongolia has an extremely sparse population—about 800,000 people in an enormous area of 580,158 square miles. Throughout the period of Manchu rule, therefore, there had been ample room for an influx of immigrants. The Manchu policy of colonization was actually of fairly recent origin, however: not until 1902 did the Manchu Court formally open Mongolia to Chinese settlers. Moreover, the early settlements were not entirely haphazard, but were organized and directed by an Imperial Commissioner sent out from Peking. Beginning in 1903, many Mongol-inhabited regions were reorganized into *hsiens* or counties. In 1906, the former Li-Fan-Yüan, or the department in charge of Tibetan and Mongolian affairs, was raised to the status of a ministry and given the task of inaugurating large-scale systematic colonization in Mongolia. In 1910 all the decrees, regulations, etc. previously promulgated to prevent Chinese reclamation of Mongol land, to prohibit intermarriage between the Chinese and Mongols, and to require the use of the Chinese language were abrogated. In 1911 a colonization bureau was opened in Urga to expedite the colonizing movement from Inner China.[3]

The problem of Chinese colonization in Mongolia was so serious in the eyes of the Russians that many Russian authors described it as "one of the most burning problems of the political situation in the Far East."[4] They were very much concerned about the energetic measures taken by the Manchu Government for colonizing and fortifying the northwestern part of Mongolia.[5] They thought that the Manchu policy of driving away the friendly Buryats and Kazakhs from the frontier region and replacing them with Chinese settlers was aimed at getting the Mongolian land for the Chinese people and at weakening the Mongols and expelling the Russians in favor of the Manchu Government.[6] They considered Chinese colonization in Outer Mongolia "a barrier preventing the penetration of the inten-

[3] Kushelev, *op. cit.*, p. 54.
[4] B. Guryev, "Territorial'naia Neprikosnovennost' Mongolii po Ulozheniiu Lifan Iuania" ("Territorial Inviolability of Mongolia in the Code of Li Fan Yüan"), *Vestnik Azii (Asiatic Herald)*, no. 6, 1910, p. 6.
[5] *Ibid.*, p. 13.
[6] Kushelev, *op. cit.*, p. 58.

sified Russian influence."[7]   Furthermore, they charged that Chinese colonization in Outer Mongolia was violating the century-old regulations on the territorial inviolability of Mongolia as established by the Li-Fan-Yüan, and staging "the last act of a great drama being performed before our eyes; the annihilation of a once powerful nation—the Mongols."[8]   They feared that through colonization "China with her more than four hundred million population would soon become the immediate neighbor of Russia."[9]

Another phase of Manchu policy challenged by Russia was the political reform conducted in Outer Mongolia.   Soon after the young and energetic Santo, the last Manchu Amban at Urga, assumed office in 1910, a kaleidoscopic cluster of governmental bureaus sprang up like mushrooms—the Bureau of Military Affairs, the Headquarters of the Garrison Troops, the Board of Internal Revenues, the Board of Public Health, the Preparatory Board for Constitutional Government, the Board of External Affairs, the Board of Reclamation, the Board of Commercial Survey, and so forth.   In addition, schools of all grades for both sexes were opened.   To defray the upkeep of these new establishments, such heavy taxes were imposed upon the Mongols that "the Mongols, in dread of these crushing burdens, escaped from their homes, leaving the several *banners* around the capital almost a no-man's land."[10]   Thus, anti-Manchu sentiment among the Mongols was widespread.

In the opinion of the Russians, the purpose of Manchu political reform in Outer Mongolia was twofold: to abolish the autonomy of the Mongol princes in order to reduce Mongolia to the status of a Chinese province, and "to deprive Russia of the special position which she had enjoyed among the Mongols since ancient times because of the proximity and the close unity between the Russian and the Mongolian border territories."[11]   So, in Kushelev's words, "To make a long story short, the underlying motive of the reform

---

[7] Anatolii Kallinikov, *Revoliutsionnaia Mongoliia* (*Revolutionary Mongolia*) (Moscow, 1925), p. 64.

[8] Guryev, *op. cit.*, p. 13.

[9] *Ibid.*

[10] Ch'en Ch'ung-tsu, *Wai-Mong Ching-Shih-Shih* (*A Modern History of Outer Mongolia*) (Shanghai, 1922), p. 5.

[11] Kushelev, *op. cit.*, pp. 53-54.

in Mongolia is a clear expression of mistrust and unfriendliness toward Russia."[12]

Allied with political reform, there were also a number of economic and financial measures taken by the Manchu Government. These included the adoption of a plan for Chinese mining enterprises, the introduction of a project for building the Kalgan-Urga railway, and the establishment of a commercial-industrial bank in Mongolia. The Russian commentators interpreted these measures being carried out by the Manchu amban as a repressive policy directed against Russian influence in Outer Mongolia, including the Kobdo and Altai regions. They blamed the Peking Government for undertaking intensive efforts to force the Russians and Russian trade from Mongolia while simultaneously adopting measures of a strategic character. As Kushelev said, "All the measures have one purpose: to create a strong base in northern Mongolia for possible action against Russia."[13]

Another cause for Russian opposition to the Manchu policy in Outer Mongolia was the plan to establish permanent Manchu garrisons there. The Peking Government was planning to station two thousand additional troops at Urga by the end of 1911; after that date the total number was to be increased to 10,000, which would be detailed to garrison the other key posts in Outer Mongolia. However, it was reported in Russian sources that China had decided to transfer military forces of not less than ten battalions from China proper to northern Mongolia in addition to the organization of the general staff, the establishment of military schools, and the formation of the Mongolian army, and that the amban at Urga had demanded the increase of military guards "not only against spies, but also against foreign enemies [i.e., the Russians]."[14]

As noted above, the Mongols resented the new, aggressive policy conducted in their semiautonomous land. In desperation, the princes and leading lamas of Outer Mongolia met in July, 1911 and decided to dispatch a delegation to Russia.[15] Its avowed purpose was to solicit the good offices of the Tsar against the "oppressive" policy of the Manchu Court.[16]

[12] *Ibid.*, p. 54.   [13] *Ibid.*, p. 57.
[14] *Ibid.*, p. 56.   [15] Treated extensively in the next section.
[16] Shoizhelov, "Avtonomnoe Dvizhenie Mongolii i Tsarskaia Rossiia" ("The Autonomous Movement of Mongolia and Tsarist Russia"), *Novyi Vostok* (*The New East*), nos. 13-14, 1926, p. 354.

Wasting no time, Neratov, temporarily in charge of the Tsarist Ministry of Foreign Affairs, reported to Tsar Nicholas II that the present Mongolian compaign could be profitably utilized in Russian relations with China. Whereupon he recommended that the Mongolian problem be given serious consideration at a special conference of cabinet ministers usually concerned with this matter.[17]

Tsar Nicholas II approved Neratov's suggestion, and on August 4, 1911, the conference took place under the chairmanship of Prime Minister Stolypin. Other participants included Kokovtsev, Finance Minister, Grigorovich, Navy Minister, Timashev, Minister of Commerce and Industry, Neratov, Polivanov, temporarily in charge of the Ministry of War, and Zhilinskii, Chief of the General Staff.[18] Concerning Mongolia, the Conference declared:

The reforms planned by China in Mongolia—Chinese tillers to colonize the strip of land bordering us, the linking of the same by railways, at points which would be close to this frontier, with Chinese administrative centers, and the distribution of the Chinese troops, especially the appearance of considerable Chinese armed forces in the close neighborhood of our possessions, cannot fail to disturb us. Therefore, the Mongolian question is for us of great importance, and our support of the Mongols in their aspiration to counteract the above-mentioned undertaking of the Chinese Government would fully correspond with our interests."[19]

The conference went on to oppose colonization of Mongolia by the Chinese, the establishment of a Chinese administration, and the reinforcement of the Chinese armed forces as undesirable and threatening to the security of the Russian frontier.[20] In other words the proposals and plans of the Chinese Government concerning Khalkha were interpreted as an "hostile act"[21] requiring action on the part of Russia.

Hence, at the conclusion of this conference Neratov sent Korostovets in Peking the following instructions concerning the enlightenment of the Chinese ministers:

[17] Neratov to Tsar Nicholas II, report, July 11, 1911, in Shoizhelov, *op. cit.*, p. 354.
[18] *Ibid.*
[19] Protocol of the Special Conference of Aug. 4, 1911, quoted in Shoizhelov, *op. cit.*, p. 355.
[20] Neratov to Korostovets, secret tel., Aug. 6, 1911, no. 228/229, in Shoizhelov, *op. cit.*, p. 355.
[21] *Ibid.*

The Imperial [Russian] Government cannot be indifferent to the way in which the Chinese Government conducts its Mongolian policy. We are very closely concerned with maintaining tranquillity in Mongolia, which borders our possessions for many thousands of versts, and which represents large commercial interests of ours. Meanwhile, plans for administrative and military reforms in Mongolia advanced by the Chinese Government are causing such excitement among the Mongols that our possessions can easily be affected. The experiment of Inner Mongolia shows that the introduction of reforms produces bands of robbers with whom the Chinese authorities admit themselves to be unable to cope. It follows that administrative and military reforms planned by China for Khalkha may necessitate our taking certain steps to safeguard our borders and avoid further aggravation of the situation in Khalkha.

Finally, and most important of all, we remind the Chinese Government of the fact that its planned reforms, especially the creation of a Chinese army in Mongolia, will lead to a disturbance of the balance of power at the frontier. This cannot but reflect on the totality of the relations between the two countries. If, as the newly arrived Chinese plenipotentiary, Lou Tseng-tsiang, assured us, the Peking Government is interested in the maintenance and development of Russo-Chinese friendship, it should consider our demands. . . .[22]

In reply, the Chinese note acknowledged Russia's neighborly solicitude but went on to state that the reform which was being introduced was for the benefit of the Mongols. In view of the Mongol misgivings, however, instructions had been sent to the amban at Urga to proceed with caution and to consult the feelings of the native people.[23]

The Russian attitude toward China's position in Outer Mongolia was revealed more clearly by the historical fact that by early October, 1911, a number of Russian troops were already pouring into Outer Mongolia under the pretext of protecting the Russian consulate at Urga, with total disregard for the telegram which the Hutukhtu had sent to head them off.[24] Apparently the help the Living Buddha and the Mongol princes sought was Russian diplomatic protection rather than armed intervention, to say nothing about the presence of sizable Russian forces. But since Russia had a design of its own,

---

[22] *Ibid.*, p. 356.

[23] E. T. Williams, "The Relations between China, Russia, and Mongolia," *American Journal of International Law*, Vol. X, no. 4 (Oct., 1916), pp. 802-803.

[24] Ch'en Ch'ung-tsu, *op. cit.*, p. 6.

it preferred to take matters into its own hands and enter into a decisive role in the orientation and development of the Mongolian "independence" movement.

RUSSIA AND OUTER MONGOLIAN "INDEPENDENCE" DURING THE CHINESE REVOLUTION

Side by side with diplomatic intervention, the Russian Government did not overlook any opportunity to take a direct hand in the Mongolian development. The moment for a coup d'état arrived when several major developments precipitated Russian participation in the Mongolian "independence" movement.

Aside from Mongolian resentment against Chinese policy of vigorous reform in their domain, Mongolian indebtedness to Chinese merchants had by then accumulated to a large sum. According to Russian sources, by the end of last century the Mongolian population was in debt to Chinese firms for about 50 or 60 million rubles.[25] As Rish said, the Mongols' much desired separation from China was connected with the hope for a possibly automatic cancellation of debts to Chinese moneylenders, debts which had been carried from year to year without any settlement.[26]

The Chinese Revolution of 1911 had an immediate effect on the "independence" movement in Outer Mongolia. Like others,[27] Shoizhelov was well aware of the opportune time and circumstances provided by the political upheaval in China.[28] This influence was evidently reflected in the Mongolian declaration of independence itself. The Mongolian declaration, distributed in the name of the all-nation conference, states:

At the present time in the South, in the provinces of Manchuria and China, a seditious uprising is under way, menacing the structure of the Manchu dynasty. Our Mongolia in its original founding was an individual state and for the reason of ancient right, Mongolia proclaims itself an independendent state under a new government, endowed with authority

[25] Rish, "Mongoliia na Strazhe Svoei Nezavisimosti" ("Mongolia Guarding Her Independence"), *Tikhii Okean* (*The Pacific Ocean*), no. 4(6) (Oct.-Dec., 1935), p. 99.
[26] *Ibid.*
[27] For instance, B. Perlin, *Mongol'skaia Narodnaia Respublika* (*The Mongolian People's Republic*) (Moscow, 1941), p. 17.
[28] Shoizhelov, *op. cit.*, p. 357.

to manage its affairs independently of others. In view of what has been stated above, let it be known that from now on we Mongols shall obey neither Manchu nor Chinese officials, whose administrative authority is being completely abolished and who, as a consequence, should be sent home.[29]

The most important factor of all, however, was the readiness of Tsarist Russia to avail itself of the above-noted opportunities for decisive action. As Rish points out, the Mongolian "independence" or "revolution" "would not have taken place if the area had not at this time been successful in consolidating itself internally under Russian imperialism, which was supporting and instigating the seditionist tendencies of Mongolian princes."[30]   In the losing of the Russo-Japanese War he saw the background for the current engineering of the Tsarist policy for Mongolia:

Russian autocracy, defeated in the Russo-Japanese war, conceived again, just a few years after that serious setback, expansion plans in the Far East, plans aiming at compensation for concessions in Manchuria wrested from it by Japanese imperialism. The inspirers and ideologists of the new ambitions proved to belong to the same circles as those who had pushed the Tsarist autocracy to its own misfortune, into the war with Japan.[31]

The Russian maneuver, which not long thereafter led to Mongolian "independence" may be characterized as consisting of two aspects, political and military. Politically, Russo-Mongolian cooperation had been developing significantly since 1905. According to a telegram dispatched by Limba, the Russian consul-general in Urga, to the Russian Ministry of Foreign Affairs on July 27, 1905, the Mongol princes feared that the Manchu Government intended to reorganize the Mongolian administration and colonize Mongol land. And this, in addition to the fact that they themselves were aiming to unite the separate principalities into a state independent from China, had induced them to apply to the Russian consul-general at Urga "for advice and protection."[32]   Again in 1910, the Urga

[29] Quoted in *ibid.*
[30] Rish, *op. cit.,* p. 99.
[31] *Ibid.*
[32] Popov, "Tsarskaia Rossiia i Mongoliia v 1913-1914 gg." ("Tsarist Russia and Mongolia, 1913-1914," citing tel. of Liuba, July 27, 1905, and report of Kuzminskii, Sept. 4, 1905, *K.A.,* XXXVII, 4.

Hutukhtu, failing in his year-long struggle with the Manchu authorities, appealed to Russia for help.[33]

A dramatic illustration of Russian support for Mongol resistance and rebellion against China is provided by the story of Bair Toktokho Taiji. After a quarrel with his feudal overlord in 1910, this Mongol nobleman of Barga collected a force of a hundred men and took up arms against the Manchu rule. The Russians, in answer to his request, accepted him and his men as Russian subjects and granted them five thousand acres of land near Nerchinsk. From Trans-Baikal Taiji and his men made frequent raids into the Tsetsen Khan *aimak* or district in eastern Mongolia. Extending his activities to Outer Mongolia with the help of the Russian authorities, this agent of Tsarism urged the Mongol khans and princes to revolt and set up an "Autonomous Mongolia" under the aegis of Russia. His propaganda won a good deal of support, especially with the influential Prince Khandachin Wang, who rapidly emerged as the leader of the "independence" movement.[34]

In the summer of 1911 the Hutukhtu of Urga called a conference of the princes and ecclesiastical leaders, ostensibly to consider the proposal of the Manchu Court to colonize northern Mongolia with Chinese settlers. The covert purpose was to consider the possibility of completely ridding themselves of Chinese rule. Only eighteen of the princes present were actually engaged in the planning of the revolt.[35] These khans of the steppe held secret meetings, sometimes in the houses of Russian colonists in Urga, and sometimes in the forest on the slopes of the holy mountain Bogdo-Ula.[36] They decided "to send a deputation to St. Petersburg in order to ask the 'White Tsar' to accept the Mongols under his protection."[37] Lavdovskii's telegram from Urga on July 15, 1911, thus reported their action:

After a prolonged discussion, all came to the conclusion that the reforms conducted by the Chinese aimed at final subjugation of Mongolia, and that protest against the Chinese action was useless. Determined to appeal to us [i.e., Russia] without further delay with the request for protection . . . after a few days, a deputation of the clergy, the princes, and the

---

[33] Cited in *ibid.,* XXXVII, 6.
[34] G. D. R. Phillips, *Russia, Japan and Mongolia* (London, 1942), p. 21.
[35] *Ibid.;* Kallinikov, *op. cit.,* pp. 64-65.
[36] Phillips, *op. cit.,* p. 21.
[37] Kallinikov, *op. cit.,* p. 65.

people will leave for St. Petersburg, where they will make a formal request for the acceptance of Khalkha as a protectorate under Russia. Fearing that the Chinese Government, on finding out the matter, will take repressive measures against the Mongols, the hutukhtus and the princes request the immediate dispatch of Russian troops to Urga, under any pretext, in order to prevent Chinese coercion.[38]

On August 2, 1911, Khandachin Wang (Prince Handa Dorji), heading a Mongolian delegation, arrived in St. Petersburg for a three-week visit as had been planned. There he and his delegation were given a warm welcome in the Russian capital and were promised support.[39] However, the Tsarist Government, in response to their appeal for promoting outright Mongolian independence, apparently showed some restraint. The special conference of leading members of the Russian Government, referred to above, met on August 4 and gave the reason for this restraint, though equivocably, in the conference protocol:

At present the Imperial Government is compelled to take an active part in the settlement of various acute problems in the Near and the Far East; [on the other hand] to play an active role in the Mongolian question and thereby weaken our influence in the affairs of the West would be extremely undesirable. The approaching crisis in Mongolian affairs is not unexpected; for a long time we have rendered the Mongols our support and our protection.[40]

On August 6, 1911, in accordance with a decision reached at the special conference and approved by Nicholas II, Neratov sent by telegraph the following instructions to minister Korostovets in Peking.

The Mongolian delegation arrived in St. Petersburg and was received by me. Its wishes can be summed up as aiming at our support in their separation from China and at defending thereby their present social order against attempts on the part of the Peking Government to reduce Khalkha to a Chinese province. My conversations with the delegates prompted me to conclude that the Mongols themselves realize their lack of unity and impotence in the struggle against the Chinese.

Discussing the question of our attitude toward that delegation, we found it indispensable to support the Mongols in their attempts to defend

---

[38] Popov, "Tsarskaia," *K.A.*, XXXVII, 6.
[39] Phillips, *op. cit.*, p. 21.
[40] Cited in Shoizhelov, *op. cit.*, pp. 354-355.

their own way of life . . . . In view of the general political situation, [however,] we did not believe it possible to co-operate with the desire of the Mongols to break off from China and we have adopted the following program: we shall promise the delegation our help in preserving the particular status of Khalkha and in guaranteeing the personal safety of the delegates, as well as that of the Hutukhtu and of the princes who sent them; therefore, in accordance with our position, we shall immediately reinforce the guards of the consulate in Urga with two hundred men equipped with machineguns . . . . Somewhere in the course of your explanation, it would be desirable if you could by some means make the Chinese understand that we shall not remain indifferent to the fate of the Mongolian deputies and of the persons who have sent them and that this delegation is considered by us as a somewhat naïve demonstration against Chinese oppression, which, however, on no account deserves punishment.[41]

As the Soviet regime was to show later by way of some secret Tsarist documents, the Tsarist political and diplomatic maneuver on the eve of Mongolian "independence" served to a large degree as a smoke screen for secret military arrangements with the Mongols in engineering a coup d'état.

At about the same time that the Mongols were soliciting Russian support, one Captain Makushek, in a note to the Russian Ministry of Foreign Affairs on "The Coming Coup d'État in Mongolia and the Means for Its Realization," presented a comprehensive plan for assisting the Mongol uprising. It called for the organization of a network of storage depots for arms under the flag of commercial firms, the formation of partisan detachments, and an armed demonstration for the seizure of power. On seeing this note, Kozakov, a leading expert on Far Eastern affairs in the ministry, is reported to have remarked: "What nonsense!" But Sazonov, then Russian Minister for Foreign Affairs, in his secret telegram no. 1125 of August 10, 1911, to Korostovets, found the plan "in principle, entirely possible," and gave instructions that "in case of failure of our representations in Peking and of the inevitable uprising of Khalkha," he should deliver the arms to the Mongols.

Sukhomlinov, the Minister of War, gave an order to transfer 15,000 rifles and 7,500,000 cartridges to the headquarters of the

[41] Neratov to Korostovets, secret tels. nos. 228-229, Aug. 6, 1911, in Shoizhelov, *op. cit.*, pp. 355-356.

Irkutsk Military District.[42]   At the beginning of November, 1911, at the request of a representative hutukhtu authorized by the princes, these firearms, along with 15,000 sabers, were given to the Mongols by the Irkutsk headquarters in the form of a private transaction.[43] Thus there is much evidence to support the view that military "assistance from Russia played a very important part [in the forthcoming coup d'état].   The arms used by the Mongols [in Urga] and the Barguts [in Barga] were supplied chiefly by Russia."[44]

The assistance sent from Russia to aid the Mongol cause took the form not only of arms and training, but also, in one striking instance, of leadership as well.   The siege of Kobdo was under the direction of Ja-Lama, a strange, romantic lama who was a Kalmyk Mongol from Astrakhan on the Volga.   He had first appeared in Khalka in 1890 and had, with the support of Khandachin Wang, begun to agitate for Mongolian independence.   He soon had to flee the Manchu authorities and, although captured at one time, he managed to escape with the help of a Russian official.   In 1910 he came back, proclaiming himself the reincarnation of the Mongol hero Amursana, the eighteenth-century fighter for Mongolian independence.   Under this aura, Ja-Lama rapidly gained the support of the whole Kobdo region, and later mobilized five thousand men to take the city of Kobdo in August, 1912.[45]

After the political, diplomatic and military cornerstones had been laid by the Tsarist and the Mongol collaborators, the next step could only be a coup d'état.   And so Kallinikov, like Perlin[46] and others, points out: "Having secured the support of the Tsarist Government, the plotters began energetically to prepare for the coup d'état."[47]

At this moment, Santo, the Manchu amban in Urga, was proceeding with his drastic policy in Outer Mongolia.   As a result secret Mongolian opposition increased in vigor and Urga became the center of a conspiracy of anti-Manchu princes who gathered around the Urga Hutukhtu as their leader.[48]   The Chinese Revolution, which broke

---

[42] Sukhomlinov to Sazonov, letter, Oct. 17, 1911, file no. 4271, cited in Popov, "Tsarskaia," *K.A.*, XXXVII, 13.

[43] Sukhomlinov to Neratov, letter, Nov. 3, 1911, file no. 340, cited in *ibid.*, XXXVII, 13.

[44] *C.Y.B., 1919* (London & New York, 1920), p. 588.

[45] Phillips, *op. cit.*, pp. 22-23.   [46] Perlin, *op. cit.*, p. 17.

[47] Kallinikov, *op. cit.*, p. 65.   [48] *C.Y.B., 1919*, p. 587.

out on October 10, 1911, "made their task easier for the Mongols."[49] On December 1/November 18 the Mongols seized the opportunity to carry out a coup d'état. It was reported in the Russian sources that the coup was accomplished without any bloodshed and that the Mongols offered terms to the Manchu garrison while the Manchu amban was said "to have taken refuge in the Russian consulate." The report went on to say that the city of Urga was in the hands of the rebels and that "the Chinese (Manchu) amban, escorted by the guards of the Russian Cossacks, left after a few days for Kiakhta in order to return home through Russia, and the troops of the Manchu garrison were sent out immediately after him."[50]

According to Shoizhelov, at the "last conference" of the plotters on December 1/November 18, 1911, the date of the Urga coup, the Aimak and Khoshun princes, as well as the clergy, "decided not to recognize henceforth the authority of the Chinese Government and to proclaim Mongolia an independent state headed by Chebutsum Damba Hutukhtu."[51] As for the details, the resolutions passed urged nonrecognition of the Chinese Republic, utmost resistance to the Republic's claim of sovereignty in Mongolia, refusal to pay taxes to the Manchus and the Chinese, and expulsion of all Chinese colonists from Mongolia.[52]

Late in December the "independence" of Outer Mongolia was formally proclaimed with the birth of the new state, named "the Empire of Mongolia." On December 28/16 during a majestic ceremony, at a large, solemn assembly the Urga Hutukhtu was crowned the khan of all Khalkha, otherwise known as Great Khan of the "Empire."[53] Subsequently a Mongol ministry of five portfolios— interior, foreign affairs, finance, war and justice—was formed. But almost from the very beginning the influential princes in Urga split into two factions. One was styled the Military or pro-Russian party, the other the Nationalist or Da Lama's party, which advocated a conciliatory policy toward China. At first the Da Lama, a most influential and popular personality, assisted by the Kharchin Prince Hai San Kung who was universally recognized as the cleverest or-

[49] Perlin, *op. cit.*, p. 17.
[50] Kallinikov, *op. cit.*, p. 65.
[51] Shoizhelov, *op. cit.*, p. 356.
[52] Chu, *Chin-shih-lien lai chi Chung-O Kuan-hsi (Russo-Chinese Relations of the Last Ten Years)*, p. 134.
[53] Shoizhelov, *op. cit.*, p. 356; *C.Y.B.*, *1919*, p. 587.

ganizer of the coup d'état, seemed to have the upper hand.   But later, in the autumn of 1912, a new post, that of premier, was created and given to Sain Noyan Khan of the pro-Russian party for the express purpose of counteracting the Da Lama, who was Minister of the Interior.   Thereafter the Da Lama's party became nearly power-less; but "a general reaction of feeling against Russia appeared to have set in."[54]   In the aftermath of the Urga coup there were de-velopments which soon had far-reaching consequences.

In January, 1912, Hulunbuir, or Barga, which had been re-garded as part of China's Heilungkiang province, followed the example of Khalkha, as the state of affairs in China proper gave the Barguts their opportunity to revolt.   Their demands upon local representatives of the Peking Government having been rejected, the Barguts, after two small engagements, expelled all the Chinese officials and troops from their territory.   Thereupon the Barguts, "either with or without the knowledge or advice of Russia, proposed to the Urga Hutukhtu that Barga should form part of his new dominions."   This offer was accepted, and in May, 1912, a leading Bargut, Shen Fu, was installed at Hailar as the Urga Hutukhtu's viceroy with the title of amban.[55]

During the early part of 1912, the newly formed Urga Govern-ment extended its authority first to Uliassutai and then gradually to the district of Kobdo.   The latter town and its environs were the scene of several engagements between the Mongols and Chinese troops based in the Altai district.[56]   It is recorded in Russian sources that on the day of the coronation of the Urga Hutukhtu, the Manchu Chiang-Chun in Uliassutai surrendered that territory to the Mongol forces.   Similarly, in May 1912, five thousand men of the Khalkha and Urianghai troops under Ja-Lama besieged the former Manchu garrison at Kobdo.   Reinforcements were dispatched from Gucheng and Sume to relieve the beleaguered garrison, but, unable to sustain the stubborn siege, it capitulated in August before they could reach it. The reinforcements thereupon went into winter quarters at a place about sixty miles from Kobdo, and returned to their bases the fol-lowing spring.[57]

[54] *C.Y.B.*, *1919*, p. 587.
[55] *C.Y.B.*, *1919*, p. 588.
[56] *Ibid.*, p. 589.
[57] Kallinikov, *op. cit.*, pp. 65-66.

The Altai district, it should be noted, was not involved in the struggles over Outer Mongolian "independence."[58]   To the governorship of this district the Peking Government at the end of 1911 had appointed Prince Palta, perhaps the most remarkable figure in the whole Mongolian question.   In spite of attempts to persuade him to change sides, he remained faithful to China, so that even after the later Russo-Chinese Declaration of 1913 Altai remained outside Autonomous Outer Mongolia.   That it did so was certainly due in part to Prince Palta's action, but the fact that Russia presumably preferred the Mongolian Altai Mountains as the southern boundary of the new buffer state may also have been a factor.[59]   In any case, it was from this background that the Chinese Government in 1919 ordered the incorporation of the Altai district into Sinkiang Province.

Incidentally, following the Mongolian declaration of "independence," Russian military intervention became bolder.   Immediately after the Urga coup d'état, the creation of a Mongol army was undertaken in Urga, under Russian training.   In March, 1912, a Russian officer, Captain Vasiliev, with ten instructors, began to train troops near Urga.   Later the "Mongolian Brigade" was formed at Hunjir Bulun (five miles from Urga), with the help of a training depot under Nadezhnyi, a Russian colonel, and ten officers and a staff. From these and similar bands of Russian-trained Khalkhas came the threat to move southward into Inner Mongolia in the latter part of 1912.   They appeared with many Inner Mongols in Ulanchar, Chahar, Silingol, and northern Chou Uda to attack the Chinese.[60]

At that time Peking was constantly warned that the Khalkhas, pursuing their program of Pan-Mongolianism, intended to move southward.   In August of that year there occurred the first serious outbreak in Inner Mongolia, led by Prince Wuteh.   This rebellion was speedily and severely crushed by Chinese troops rushed from Chihli.[61]   However, during this period the adroit Mongolian cavalry frequently ambushed Chinese units and inflicted considerable casualties.

[58] In the old days this area was under Kobdo and was undoubtedly considered part of Outer Mongolia.
[59] *C.Y.B.*, *1919*, p. 589.
[60] *Ibid.*, pp. 589-590.
[61] *Ibid.*

From China's point of view, Mongol "independence" could not be recognized. In order to counteract the secession, soon after the triumph of the revolution a mandate declaring China's five races as constituent parts of the new republic was issued. In February, 1912, after Dr. Sun Yat-sen had voluntarily resigned from the presidency of the republic in favor of Yüan Shih-k'ai, the new President made strenuous but futile efforts to persuade the Hutukhtu to come back into the orbit of the republic. The Hutukhtu shunned direct negotiations with Peking and suggested discussion by proxy through the Russian minister at Peking. Having failed to dissuade the Urga Government itself, Peking thereupon centered its attention on trying to retain the adherence of the Inner Mongolian princes. The result was that most of the princes outside Khalkha and Kobdo declared their adherence, outwardly at any rate, to the republic.[62]

In the meantime, as a peaceful settlement with Outer Mongolia could not be reached by any means, the patience of the Chinese Government was exhausted, and it decided to resort to arms. But many obstacles stood in the way. On the one hand, the new government was not yet recognized by other powers; domestic affairs were still rather chaotic; and the strength of the infant republic was too feeble to undertake such a campaign.

And on the other hand, Russia, posing as the patron of her new protégé, came forward to notify the Chinese Government that she could not view with indifference the dispatch of any Chinese troops to repress the Mongolian revolution. These factors combined to deter China from action. President Yüan could only instruct the Chinese minister to Russia to negotiate a solution, while sending a number of representatives to Outer Mongolia to carry on the work of persuasion.[63]

Soviet commentators have quite correctly attributed the movement for Outer Mongolian "independence" to the work of Tsarist agents.[64] In Popov's words: "There is no doubt about the role of the Tsarist diplomatic agents in Mongolia. They were not passive

[62] *Ibid.*, p. 589.
[63] Duke Frans O. Larson, *Larson, Duke of Mongolia* (Boston, 1930), pp. 227 ff.; Chang Chung-fu, *Chung-Hwa-Ming-Kuo Wai-chiao-Shih* (*A Diplomatic History of the Republic of China*), I (Peiping, 1936) 80-82; Chu, *op. cit.*, p. 244.
[64] Cf. Gerard M. Friters, "The Prelude to Outer Mongolian Independence," *Pacific Affairs*, X (June, 1937), 168.

observers of the occurring events and automatic transmitters of the 'independent' decisions of the Mongolian princes."[65]

Even as early as the 1890's, "efforts of major proportions to organize and direct the Mongol nobility toward the White Tsar" were not unknown, as is shown by the letters of Badmaev to Alexander III, Nicholas II, and Witte.[66] On one of the first of these letters, in which Badmaev outlined an elaborate plan for the "annexation of Mongolia, Tibet and part of China to Russia," Alexander III made the notation: ". . . it is so new, unusual and fantastic that it is difficult to believe in the possibility of success."[67]

The part played by Tsarist agents in promoting Mongolian "independence" was even more obvious in the later period. Leo Pasvolsky said of it: "To what extent the events in Mongolia since 1911 have been the work of the agents of the Russian Imperial Government is not known, but that such agents had a hand in their unfolding, especially after the Chinese Revolution, appears fairly certain."[68]

The strong support of the Russian military and political intervention were vividly described by Popov:

While Korostovets exchanges caustic remarks with the Chinese ministers in Peking, the movement in Mongolia continues to expand and take an organized form.

The administrative head of the Russian consulate in Urga, participating in the delivery of arms to the Mongols and observing the course of all insurrectionary plans, kept the ministry fully informed regarding the course of events.

In telegram no. 1102, dated November 18, 1911, he [the consul-general] informed [the ministry] of the first results of the application of Russian arms by the Mongols—the overthrow of the Chinese authorities in Khalkha and the declaration of Mongolian independence.[69]

To the Tsarist program of expansion, Russia's role in Outer Mongolian "independence" made a considerable contribution. Shoizhelov summed up its results in his fairly comprehensive comment:

[65] Popov, "Tsarskaia," Introduction, *K.A.*, XXXVII, 7.
[66] *Za Kulisami Tsarizma. Arkhiv Tibetskogo Vracha Badmaeva (Behind the Scenes of Tsarism: Archives of the Tibetan Physician Badmaev)* (Leningrad, 1925), pp. 49-112.
[67] *Ibid.*
[68] Leo Pasvolsky, *Russia in the Far East* (New York, 1922), p. 55.
[69] Popov, "Tsarskaia," Introduction, *K.A.*, XXXVII, 13, 14.

The place liberated from the Manchu rulers was immediately occupied by the representatives of Tsarist Russia, to which the political leaders and the clergy appealed for help. The Tsarist Government utilized the hopes of Mongolia for emancipation to advance its own greedy designs on the country. Thus, the fate of Mongolia fell into the hands of the Tsarist diplomats.[70]

[70] S. Shoizhelov, "Natsional'no-Osvoboditel'noe Dvizhenia v Mongolii" ("National Liberation Movement in Mongolia"), *Novyi Vostok (The New East)*, no. 6, 1924, p. 246.

IX: RUSSO-MONGOLIAN DIRECT NEGOTIATIONS OF 1912-13

Russo-Mongolian Agreement of 1912

With the Mongolian situation firmly under her control, Russia continued to exploit the troubled state of China's Government. On November 3/October 21, 1912, Ivan Korostovets, state councillor and plenipotentiary for negotiations with the Mongolian Government, together with Sain-Noyan Khan, Mongolian President of the Council of Ministers, and his five cabinet members signed an Agreement intended to clarify relations between Russia and autonomous Mongolia, with an attached protocol defining Russian trade rights.[1] The terms of the Agreement were as follows:

1. Russia was to assist Mongolia to "maintain the autonomous regime which she has established, and therein to exercise her right to have her national army, and to admit neither the presence of Chinese troops on her territory nor the colonization of her land by the Chinese";

2. Mongolia was to permit, "as in the past, Russian subjects and Russian trade to enjoy the rights and privileges" enumerated in the seventeen articles of the added protocol. No rights not enjoyed by Russian subjects in Mongolia would be granted to the subjects of any third Power;

3. If the Mongolian Government concluded a separate treaty with China or another foreign Power, there should be no infringement upon the provisions of the present Agreement, and no modifications thereof should be made without Russian consent.

[1] For Russian texts, see *Izvestiia Ministerstva Inostrannykh Del* (*Bulletin of the Ministry of Foreign Affairs*), 1913, II, 16-23; for English translation, see MacMurray, *Treaties and Agreements with and Concerning China, 1894-1919*, II, 992 ff.; for Chinese translation, see *Kuo-Chih Tiao-Yao Ta-Chuan* (*A Complete Collection of International Treaties*), III, 21-22.

Thus the protocol entitled Russian subjects to all the privileges they had enjoyed under former Russo-Chinese treaties, and at the same time converted Outer Mongolia into an economic fief of Russia. The Russians could move or reside anywhere in Outer Mongolia, engage in every kind of business, commercial, industrial, or otherwise; could make contracts of every kind; could export and import goods free of duties, taxes, or other dues; could have allotments on lease, and acquire them as private property or for cultivation; could obtain concessions of any kind; and Russian credit institutions could maintain branches in Mongolia and transact all kinds of business there.

Russia's willingness to carry on negotiations with the Mongolian Government of "the Unanimously Proclaimed" in defiance of traditional Chinese-Mongolian relations indicated the direction and the scope of Russia's ambition. As Vollosovich indicates, "on the foundation of the Russo-Mongolian Treaty there was laid down the so very Russian principle"[2] which was clearly stated in the preamble of the said Agreement:

In accordance with the desire unanimously expressed by the Mongolians to maintain the national and historic constitution of their country, the Chinese troops and authorities were obliged to evacuate Mongolian territory, and Djebzoun Damba-Hutukhtu was proclaimed Ruler of the Mongolian people. The old relations between Mongolia and China thus came to an end.

A *fait accompli* had thus been created. "The previous connection between Mongolia and China came to an end, while the new one, in the sense of Chinese suzerainty unilaterally recognized by Russia, had not yet emerged." Therefore, during the period "from October 21 [i.e., November 3], 1912, to October 23 [i.e., November 5], 1913, Mongolia, in relation to Russia, was an independent state . . . because the intercourse between the two governments was carried out directly, not through China."[3] Russia's attitude and action in concluding this Agreement were commented on by a semiofficial Russian journal at that time. *Vestnik Azii* noted that no country will conclude treaties with vassal states without the knowledge of their suzerains

[2] M. Vollosovich, "Rossiia i Mongoliia" ("Russia and Mongolia"), *Vestnik Azii* (*Asiatic Herald*), nos. 31-32, 1914, p. 42.
[3] *Ibid.*, p. 43.

and "in the given case, the treaty was signed not only without asking the consent of the suzerain but against its protests."[4]

Russian official sources had been less outspoken, but still asserted the factual independence of Mongolia from China. Thus, somewhat earlier, Sazonov, in a telegram to Krupenskii in Peking, had noted: "We [the Russian Government] do not want to recognize the independence of Mongolia from China; nevertheless it cannot be denied that such an independence exists."[5] Thus, the acknowledgment of the Tsarist Government led the general Russian public into thinking that "Mongolia, or at least Outer Mongolia, had been made an independent country—practically since the declaration of her independence on November 18 [December 1], 1911, and legally since October 21 [November 3], 1912"[6]—the date the Russo-Mongolian Agreement was signed.

Russian ambition could also be seen in the fact that in the Agreement of November 3/October 21, 1912, Russia approved the replacement of the name "Outer Mongolia" by "Mongolia" alone; actually, the extent of territory covered by the Agreement had not yet been determined. It was clear to the Russians that, in the eyes of the Chinese, this kind of wording was bound to constitute "a menace that threatened to extend the agreement to include the other Mongol regions adjoining Khalkha."[7] In their own eyes, however, the Russians interpreted the function of the agreement as merely "for the defense of their own interests in Mongolia."[8] But the extent of their interests was left undefined, and thus open to a broad interpretation. In fact, some Russians saw in the Russo-Chinese declaration concerning Mongolia, announced in Peking on November 5/October 23, 1913, evidence that the Agreement of November 3/October 21, 1912, had actually compelled the Chinese Government to submission, "to become more compliant."[9]

[4] N. Shteifel'd, "Vazhnaia Dedomolvka v Urginskom Dogovore" ("Important Omission in the Urga Treaty"), *Vestnik Azii (Asiatic Herald)*, no. 15, 1913, p. 23.
[5] Sazonov to Krupenskii, tel. no. 19, Oct. 16, 1912, in Russia, Ministry of Foreign Affairs, *Sbornik Diplomaticheskikh Dokumentov po Mongol'skomu Voprosu, 23 Avgusta 1912 g.–2 Noiabria 1913 g. (A Collection of Diplomatic Documents Relative to the Mongolian Question, Aug. 23, 1912–Nov. 2, 1913*, referred to hereinafter as *S.D.D. po M.V.*) (St. Petersburg, 1914), p. 19.
[6] Vollosovich, *op. cit.*, p. 43.
[7] *Ibid.*, p. 42.
[8] Kallinikov, *Revoliutsionnaia Mongoliia (Revolutionary Mongolia)*, pp. 66-67.
[9] *Ibid.*, p. 67.

The sequence of events leading to the signing of this Russo-Chinese declaration shows the Chinese efforts to restrict the interpretation of Russian interests in Mongolia and uphold traditional Chinese interests. Three days after the signing of the earlier Russo-Mongolian agreement, the Russian Foreign Minister, Sazonov, instructed Krupenskii to inform the Chinese Government of the conclusion of the pact, with the hope that "the Chinese Government will find no obstacles that will prevent it from concurring in the principles of the present agreement so as to lay a foundation for the mutually profitable solution of the whole Mongolian problem."[10] The Chinese Foreign Minister, Liang Ru-hao, was determined to protest and deny the validity of the agreement, regardless of the Russian threat to strengthen the newly created Mongolian regime in case their "hope did not come true."[11] His reply to the Russian minister in Peking on November 8/October 26, 1912, was that the contents of the Agreement would be discussed by the Chinese Government. At the same time he gave as the immediate reaction of his Government the view that "the Chinese Government cannot recognize as valid, an agreement concluded by a foreign Power with one of the constituent parts of China without the consent of the Central Government."[12]

A day earlier Krupenskii had already been notified by the Chinese Foreign Office that "Mongolia is a constituent part of China and, even though disturbances are going on there, it is absolutely incapable of concluding agreements with foreign countries."[13]

On the same day Liu Ching-jen, then Chinese minister in St. Petersburg, visited the Russian Foreign Minister and made the same statement concerning the Chinese nonrecognition of the Russo-Mongolian agreement. Sazonov explained to the Chinese minister that Russia would not view Mongolia as completely independent from China and would agree to recognize Chinese suzerainty over it, provided China participated in the agreement. The Chinese minister objected and instead asked for further significant concessions from Russia. Sazonov, on the other hand, threatened that Chinese unwillingness to discuss the Mongolian question with Russia would

[10] Sazonov to Krupenskii, tel. no. 26, Oct. 24, 1912, *S.D.D. po M.V.*, p. 31.
[11] *Ibid.;* also Krupenskii to Sazonov, tel. no. 28, Oct. 26, 1912, *S.D.D. po M.V.*, p. 32.
[12] Krupenskii to Sazonov, tel. no. 28, Oct. 26, 1912, *S.D.D. po M.V.*, p. 32.
[13] Krupenskii to Sazonov, tel. no. 27, Oct. 25, 1912, *S.D.D. po M.V.*, p. 32.

compel the latter "to deny the recognition of the vassal relationship of Mongolia towards China."[14]

On November 16/3, 1912, the Chinese Foreign Vice-Minister cited the protest of the Waichiaopu (the Chinese Foreign Office) of November 7, and also the reply given the Russian minister by the Chinese Foreign Minister. Then he declared to Krupenskii that "by no means can China recognize the latter [the agreement], because any agreement concerning Mongolia, which is a part of China, should be concluded with the Central Government, but not with Urga, which represents merely an insignificant part of Outer Mongolia."[15] Besides, "the signing of the agreement was a surprise to the Chinese Government, and such an unfriendly action on the part of Russia could achieve nothing."[16] Therefore, the Chinese Government asked that Russia "renounce her agreement with the Mongols, after which it will be ready to proceed with the negotiations" with the Russian Government for "an amicable settlement of the Mongolian problem."[17]

On November 19/6, 1912, the Chinese minister at St. Petersburg again paid a visit to the Russian Foreign Minister and requested the Russian Government to renounce the agreement with the Urga Government. He assured Minister Sazonov that after such a renunciation China would be ready to negotiate with Russia "for a solution of the Mongolian question." However, both Krupenskii and Sazonov replied that the Chinese suggestion came too late to be taken into consideration.[18]

On November 23/10, 1912, the Chinese Foreign Minister summoned the Russian minister to inform him that "the Chinese Government insisted on the stand that, with the conclusion of an Agreement between Russia and China, the Russo-Mongolian agreement should lose its force." But the Russian minister would not agree.[19]

At this time, Chinese opinion was quite indignant about the Russo-Mongolian negotiations and transactions. Krupenskii reported that "at the conferences of different political parties here [in Peking],

[14] Sazonov to Krupenskii, tel. no. 29, Oct. 27, 1912, *S.D.D. po M.V.*, p. 33.
[15] Krupenskii to Sazonov, tel. no. 30, Nov. 3, 1912, *S.D.D. po M.V.*, pp. 33-34.
[16] *Ibid.*, p. 34.
[17] *Ibid.*
[18] Sazonov to Krupenskii, tel. no. 31, Nov. 6, 1912, *S.D.D. po M.V.*, pp. 34-35; also Krupenskii to Sazonov, tel. no. 30, Nov. 3, 1912, *S.D.D. po M.V.*, pp. 33-34.
[19] Krupenskii to Sazonov, tel. no. 34, Nov. 10, 1912, *S.D.D. po M.V.*, p. 36.

and at the meetings in Shanghai and in Canton, militant resolutions have been carried, and telegrams expressing similar strong feelings were being received from various provinces."[20]

Parallel to these diplomatic conversations were a number of military moves and countermoves. While the Mongols were making "military preparations and sending troops to the border of Outer Mongolia, China also began to assemble troops, on the border of Inner Mongolia at Kalgan; at Mukden, Kwanchengtze, Hailar, and Tsitsihar in Manchuria; and advancing from Urumchi in the province of Sinkiang towards Uliassutai and Kobdo."[21]   The Russian consul at Uliassutai also reported to Minister Sazonov that the Dudu (Governor) of Sinkiang had given orders to take military measures against the Mongols in Kobdo and then in Khalkha, "if they should not resume their former relations with China."[22]

To forestall this possibility, Krupenskii was instructed by Sazonov to call the attention of the Chinese Foreign Minister to "the military preparation of the Governor of Altai District, Prince Palta," warning him that, if Russian interests had to be "safeguarded," it might lead to complications in Russo-Chinese relations.[23]

Regarding the Russo-Mongolian agreement and the supplementary protocol, a Chinese author, Tennyson Tan, concluded that "Russia's action . . . was a violation of the laws of nations; she did not observe the restrictions imposed upon countries neutral towards civil factions of another country."[24]   He also deplored "the immediate recognition of the Mongolian independence at the very hour of China's internal unrest; it was an inexcusable want of friendship on the part of Russia towards China."[25]

Foreigners also observed that "Russia, under whose shadowy wing the new state had been set up, had hastened to bolster its position" by signing the Agreement.   It would not be an exaggeration to say that "Mongolia liberated herself from Chinese colonization to become a colony of Russia."[26]

[20] Same to the same, tel. no. 30, Nov. 3, 1912, *S.D.D. po M.V.*, p. 34.
[21] H. G. C. Perry-Ayscough and R. B. Otter Barry, *With the Russians in Mongolia* (London, 1914), p. 27.
[22] Sazonov to Krupenskii, tel. no. 35, Nov. 11, 1912, *S.D.D. po M.V.*, p. 37.
[23] *Ibid.*
[24] Tennyson Tan, *Political Status of Mongolia* (Shanghai, 1932), p. 47.
[25] *Ibid.*
[26] E.g., Phillips, *Russia, Japan, and Mongolia*, p. 23.

Although the Chinese authorities persistently opposed the Russo-Mongolian agreement of 1912,[27] the additional seventeen-article protocol on Russian trade rights did not share the same fate. As a concession to Russia in exchange for Russian co-operation in settling the Mongolian problem, China finally recognized the protocol.[28] The formal recognition was first clearly stated in the fourth principle of the Russo-Chinese declaration of November 5, 1913, which reads as follows:

China declares itself ready to accept the good offices of Russia for the establishment of its relations with Outer Mongolia, in conformity with the principles set forth above and with the stipulations of the Russo-Mongolian Commercial Protocol of October 21, 1912 [November 3, 1912].

Later, in the Russo-Sino-Mongolian Tripartite Agreement of July 7, 1915, China reaffirmed her intention to abide by the Protocol in question, as Article XXI of the Tripartite agreement provided:

The stipulations of the Sino-Russian Declaration and the Notes exchanged between China and Russia of the 5th day of the 11th month of the 2nd year of the Republic of China [October 23, 1913], as well as those of the Russo-Mongolian Commercial Protocol of the 21st October 1912 remain in full force.

REPORTED RUSSO-MONGOLIAN SECRET MILITARY
AGREEMENT OF 1913

According to a Japanese source, in 1913 (exact date of signature not yet known) a secret military agreement was concluded between Russia and Outer Mongolia with the following provisions:

1. In view of the lack of military knowledge on the part of the Mongolian people, the Russians should be entrusted with the management of all military affairs in the event that Outer Mongolia should be at war with other countries, and the commander-in-chief of the Mongol army must be a Russian officer with full power of command.

---

[27] *Kuo-Chih-Tiao-Yao Ta-Chuan*, III, 22.
[28] China, Delegation to the Sino-Russian Conference, *Hui-I Tsan-k'ao Wen-chi* (*Sino-Russian Conference: Reference Documents*), I (Digest of Sino-Russian Old Treaties), 1.

2. Likewise, in such an event the Russian commander-in-chief should have the right to recruit his army in such a way as he might choose.

3. The Russian Government would contribute, as it saw fit, to the Mongol expenditures incidental to training and equipping the Mongol army.

4. In case the Russian commander-in-chief should resign during his five years' tenure, he should be replaced by another Russian officer recommended by the Russian Ministry of War.[29]

This secret military agreement has been little known in the outside world, and there may be doubt as to whether it was enforced or not. However, after a careful examination of the published Tsarist documents, there is reason to believe that scattered traces of the operation of some agreement of this nature have been found. For example, the Russo-Mongolian Brigade agreement of February 16/3, 1913, often referred to in official Russian communications,[30] quite likely served either as a prelude to, or even as a part of, this reported secret military agreement.

The Brigade agreement, signed shortly after the Russo-Mongolian Urga agreement of November 3/October 21, 1912, was fixed for one year's duration, and subject to renewal. By its terms the Mongolian Government undertook "for the defense of its territory to organize a brigade of two cavalry regiments . . . one machine-gun command and a platoon of artillery with a total of 1,900 men, and to invite the Russian staff of instructors," composed of seventeen officers and forty-two noncommissioned officers, for the training of the brigade. To cover "all expenses in connection with the organization of armed forces in Khalkha [Outer Mongolia] and with the invitation of Russian instructors," the Mongolian Government was to "deposit with the Imperial [Russian] Consulate the sum of 350,000 rubles, the expenditure of this sum entrusted to the [Russian] instructors by the Russian Government."[31]

Later, apparently referring to the Russo-Mongolian secret mili-

[29] Japan, Zen Rin Cho Kai (Good Neighbor Association), *Mo Ko Tai Kang* (*A General View of Mongolia*) (Tokyo, 1938), Appendix II, pp. 532-533.

[30] Referred to in the secret tel. of Miller, no. 12, Jan. 29/16, 1914, in A. Popov, "Tsarskaia Rossiia i Mongoliia v 1913-1914 gg." ("Tsarist Russia and Mongolia in 1913-1914"), *K.A.*, XXXVII, 62.

[31] Popov, "Tsarskaia," *K.A.*, XXXVII, 62 n. 1.

tary agreement and particularly to the Brigade agreement, the Tsarist Ministry of Foreign Affairs told Sain Noyan Khan, the Mongolian special envoy:

For the creation of a trained army, the Imperial Russian Government has dispatched, at the disposal of the Mongolian Government, instructors who, in accordance with the agreement worked out for this purpose, were entrusted to form a brigade of Mongolian forces. All the arms necessary for this brigade, including guns and machine-guns, have been supplied. . . . Undoubtedly, the correctly organized Mongolian Brigade under the command of Russian officers represents immeasurably greater strength than men without military training and without commanders, to whom the Mongolian Government might distribute the large amount of armament requested.[32]

In a confidential letter suggesting that a new loan be given the Urga regime, Russian Foreign Minister Sazonov explained to Minister of Finance B. H. Kokovtsov that:

The two-million-ruble loan given to the Mongols by the Russian Government has been almost entirely used up. Approximately a quarter of the sum has paid for the maintenance of the Brigade, organized in Mongolia under the command of our [Russian] instructors, and serving our [Russian] political purposes to a significant degree.[33]

In January, 1914, Miller, the Russian diplomatic agent in Mongolia, asked the Russian Foreign Minister for instructions as to:

Whether the previous Agreement on the Mongolian Brigade should be prolonged or if a new Agreement were to be signed; what would be the conditions, such as the number of our [Russian] instructors and sergeants, their salaries, allowances of the Mongolian soldiers, and the effective period.[34]

In reply, Sazonov instructed Miller to prepare the Mongols for a renewal of the agreement on the Mongolian Brigade. He pointed out that "the continued existence of the Mongolian Brigade is an essential factor for Russian influence and for the integrity of the

[32] The Ministry of Foreign Affairs to Sain Noyan Khan, the Mongolian special envoy, note no. 969, Jan. 3, 1914/Dec. 21, 1913, in Popov, "Tsarskaia," *K.A.*, XXXVII, 47.

[33] Sazonov to Minister of Finance Kokovtsov, letter, Nov. 23, 1913, in Popov, "Tsarskaia," *K.A.*, XXXVII, 34.

[34] Tel. no. 12 of Miller, Jan. 29/16, 1914, in Popov "Tsarskaia," *K.A.*, XXXVII, 62.

Mongolian state," because "it is the most reliable weapon of the Central Urga Government in its struggle against the possible secessionist movement of the individual princes."

Also, to meet the wishes of the Mongolian Government, a plan for the reorganization of the Brigade was drafted. The Brigade was to be composed of "two cavalry regiments of four hundred men each, one battery of four guns and one four-machine-gun detachment, with a total number of one thousand men." In order to retrench the finances of the Brigade, the number of the Russian instructors was to be reduced to "one commander, seven or nine officers, and twenty-three or twenty-five of lower ranks."[35]

As Tsarist General Averianov was "to inspect the Brigade and to check its monetary account together with a representative of the Mongolian Government," the detailed working plan for the removal of the agreement had to be deferred until the arrival of General Averianov at Urga. Sazonov also stated that "General Averianov would come to Urga in the first days of May," since it was close to "the time of the expiration of the present agreement on the Brigade, the beginning of which we [the Russian Government] date from the middle of May, when the first Mongol soldiers were included in the Brigade."[36]

Such evidence from various Russian sources indicates that it is more likely than not that a Russo-Mongolian military arrangement resembling the Russo-Mongolian secret military agreement reported by the Japanese source must in fact have existed. Certainly the Mongolian Brigade was the only Mongolian regular, trained army. It was headed by a Russian commander and Russian assistants dispatched by the Russian Government, who, in other words, were appointed and recalled by the Tsarist Ministry of War. The military equipment of the Mongolian Brigade, or the Mongolian Army, was supplied by the Tsarist Government. The expenditures of this Mongolian Brigade were wholly financed by a Russian loan.

From November, 1913, to January, 1914, an important Mongolian mission headed by the Mongolian First Minister, Sain Noyan Khan, visited St. Petersburg. According to Sain Noyan Khan's own statement, the purpose of his mission to Russia was "to secure Rus-

---

[35] Sazonov to Miller, tel. no. 477, March 12/Feb. 27, 1914, *M.O. v E.I.*, Ser. III, Vol. I, doc. no. 431, p. 566.

[36] *Ibid.*, p. 567.

sian co-operation for the incorporation of Inner Mongolia into the domain of the Urga Hutukhtu and to obtain a new loan and additional arms."[37]

In his letter to the Russian diplomatic agent in Mongolia, Russian Foreign Minister Sazonov referred to this visit. "It was evident that the arms were required for continued warfare against China, a matter brought out by the Mongolian minister himself."[38] The quantity of arms Sain Noyan Khan asked was first designated as "100,000 rifles, ten guns, and forty machine guns, with an appropriate quantity of shells and cartridges."[39] As a result of Russian advice, though Sain Noyan Khan continued to insist on arms, he reduced his request to 20,000 rifles with 20,000,000 cartridges, six guns with 3,000 shells and four machine-guns with 400,000 bullets. For these he suggested payment in cash or half of the amount of the purchase in advance with the payment of the balance postponed until a year from the date of receiving the arms. To support Sain Noyan Khan's position in Urga and at the same time secure a promise on the part of the Mongolian Government not to buy weapons from the agents of other foreign firms, the Tsarist Government decided to satisfy his request for arms.[40]

In spite of the fact that Sain Noyan Khan had been recommended by Russian Foreign Minister Sazonov as a Russian sympathizer who worked on behalf of Russian influence in Outer Mongolia,[41] and despite the presence in the delegation of Prince Udai, whom Peter Badmaev had singled out to the Tsar,[42] Sain Noyan Khan's mission was not a completely happy one. Indeed the Tsarist Government did not hesitate to remind him that the Mongolian Government had promised "to settle the problem of inviting [additional] Russian advisers when he [Sain Noyan Khan] should arrive in St. Petersburg." "Refusal to fulfil the promise could not fail to reflect on Russo-Mongolian relations."[43]

[37] Foreign Minister to the diplomatic agent in Mongolia, letter, Jan. 30/17, 1914, *K.A.*, XXXVII, 63, 65.
[38] *Ibid.*, p. 66.
[39] *Ibid.*
[40] *Ibid.*, p. 67; p. 47.
[41] Sazonov to Kokovtsov, draft letter, in Popov, "Tsarskaia," *K.A.*, XXXVII, 33.
[42] Dr. P. A. Badmaev to Tsar Nikolai Romanov, letter, dated Jan. 5, 1914 (Dec. 23, 1913), *K.A.*, XXXVII, 48-49.
[43] Foreign Minister to the diplomatic agent in Mongolia, letter, dated Jan. 30/17, 1914, *K.A.*, XXXVII, 66.

However, even if this reference to Russian advisers might not have had too close a connection with the reported secret military agreement, which could have been concluded in the middle of May, 1913, published Russian secret documents give little reason to doubt the understanding between Russia and Mongolia in military matters.

The new status of Outer Mongolia was also reflected clearly in the study by Kushelev, a well-informed Russian commentator of that period, who accepted as a fact Russia's provision of armaments and military instructors. For example:

Now Mongolia does not take a single step without fixing her eyes on her neighbor, recognized by her as her unique friend, brother, and protector. . . . From those telegrams and similarly from private letters of the Mongols to the Russians, it is apparent that at all times they do not cease to supplicate the Russians to give them immediate assistance in the following respects: (1) conducting negotiations with China; (2) supply of money; (3) supply of arms; (4) sending advisers for administering the country; (5) sending instructors for the organization of armed forces, which absolutely did not exist and do not yet exist for the Mongols. "Rule us and teach us"—these voices are sounding in the speeches of the Mongolian dignitaries and ordinary nomads alike.[44]

None of the available Chinese source materials have touched specifically upon the reported secret military agreement. However, they do disclose a number of relevant facts: for instance, the fact that the Russian Government had presented a large number of rifles to the Mongolian Government for the coronation of the Hutukhtu; that there had been forty-five Russian officers serving in the Mongolian army; or that the Russian Government had provided the Mongols with armaments and ammunition.[45]

Though direct evidence of the agreement has not come to light, the Japanese source had no reason to fabricate an unnecessary rumor about such an agreement, since Japan had already reached a full accord with Russia in the understandings of 1907, 1910, and 1912; whereas the agreement in question was obviously directed against China because of her intentions to recover her position in Outer

[44] Kushelev, *Mongoliia i Mongol'skii Vopros* (*Mongolia and the Mongolian Problem*), p. 84.
[45] Ch'en Ch'ung-tsu, *Wai-Mong Ching-Shih-Shih* (*A Modern History of Outer Mongolia*), Part I, pp. 26-28; Chang Chung-fu, *Chung-Hwa-Ming-Kuo Wai-chiao Shih* (*A Diplomatic History of the Republic of China*), I, 122-123.

Mongolia. It must be remembered, too, that Soviet publication of the Tsarist documents has not yet been completed; hence, direct evidence of the reported secret military agreement may some day be forthcoming.

Thus, although the existence of some kind of military assistance arrangement between Russia and Outer Mongolia is clearly shown by the evidence, the existence of the reported secret military agreement remains conjectural. It may be suspected, however, from a number of events and situations—such as the Sino-Russian joint declaration of 1913, the preliminary negotiations for and the convocation of the Russo-Sino-Mongolian Conference at Kiakhta leading to the later tripartite agreement, the lack of enthusiasm on the part of the Russian Government toward Pan-Mongolianism, and the tensions in the Balkans—that Tsarist Russia did not, in any case, pay too much attention to any such secret military agreement nor devote itself too conscientiously to its faithful execution.

X: RUSSIAN "MEDIATION" REGARDING OUTER MONGOLIA 1913-15

Motives and Tactics of Russian "Mediation"

That Russia should attempt to arrange a settlement between China and Outer Mongolia was the logical next step in Russian policy toward Mongolia after the establishment of Mongolian "independence" and the Russo-Mongolian direct negotiations. The goal of the Russian mediation efforts was a treaty or agreement recognizing Russian legal rights in Mongolia. Russia was motivated by both political ambition and fear: ambition to secure a positive guarantee that Outer Mongolia would be Russia's protégé, and fear that this prize would be jeopardized by military conflict between China and Outer Mongolia. It was thus to Russia's advantage to interpose herself between China and Outer Mongolia and to interfere with whatever direct relationship or arrangements there might be between the two governments.

To this end Sazonov instructed Korostovets in September, 1912, to warn the Mongols that Russia would not recognize a Sino-Mongol agreement concluded without Russia's participation, and at the same time to come to an agreement with the Chinese Government on Mongolia's fate. Sazonov advanced this Russian mediation policy on the ground that Russian "interests" in Outer Mongolia "do not permit us to be satisfied with those promises which the Chinese would give to the Mongols, as we do not doubt that they would be broken on the first possible occasion and we must provide a guarantee that such a breach of faith will not take place."[1]

Another motive of Russian "mediation" was the fear in the minds

[1] Sazonov to Korostovets, tel. no. 11, Sept. 29, 1912, *S.D.D. po M.V.*, p. 8.

of high Russian officials, including Sazonov, Neratov, and Kozakov, that the Mongols would definitely break with China. Such a break would compel Russia to defend Mongolia in the event of Chinese oppression with armed forces.[2] In the end, the Russian officials came to the conclusion that some sort of autonomous regime was the desired solution, and that they would try to obtain the consent of the Chinese Government for the establishment of such a regime.[3]

As early as the end of November, 1911, Russian fears of military conflict were revealed in an official communiqué which contained a warning to China and Outer Mongolia. Again, Sazonov explained in his speech in the Duma, on April 13, 1912, that Russia could not help but be interested in the establishment of lasting order in the territory adjoining Siberia in which Russia had commercial interests, and that "an armed struggled between Mongols and Chinese was not desirable, because our interests would inevitably suffer."[4] "We have tried to avoid this dilemma [of military conflict] and we have declared ourselves ready to undertake mediation between the Chinese and the Mongols for the conclusion of such a compromise, as would, as far as possible, respect the wishes of the Mongols to preserve their peculiar customs, and the wish of China to re-establish her suzerainty over Mongolia."[5]

In accordance with the Russian program of "mediation," three conditions were set forth in the above-mentioned communiqué and in Sazonov's speech, both issued with the approval of the Tsar: (1) the administration of Khalkha should be left to a national government; (2) Chinese troops should not be permitted to enter this territory; (3) the colonization of Mongolian land by Chinese should cease.[6] These conditions were designed to meet Mongolian demands and were directed against measures which the Chinese had thought

[2] Popov, Introduction to "Tsarskaia Rossiia i Mongoliia v 1913-1914 gg." ("Tsarist Russia and Mongolia in 1913-1914") *K.A.*, XXXVII, 1929, 13.

[3] Kozakov, Nov. 9, 1911, no. 1853, referred to in Popov, "Tsarskaia," *K.A.*, XXXVII, 13.

[4] "Pravitel'stvennoe Soobshchenie 29 Dekabria 1911 goda o Mongolii" ("Governmental Message of December 29, 1911 on Mongolia"), *Pravitel'stvennyi Vestnik* (*Governmental Herald*), republished in *Izvestiia Ministerstva Inostrannykh Del* (*Bulletin of the Ministry of Foreign Affairs*, referred to hereinafter as *I.M.I.D.*), no. 3, 1912, pp. 85-86.

[5] G. E. Grumm-Grzhimailo, *Zapadnaia Mongoliia i Uriankhaiskii Krai* (*Western Mongolia and the Urianghai Region*), II (Leningrad, 1926), 748-749.

[6] Sazonov to Krupenskii, tel., Oct. 16, 1912, *S.D.D. po M.V.*, no. 19, p. 20; governmental message, Dec. 29, 1911, in *I.M.I.D.*, no. 3, 1912, p. 85 (cf. n. 4).

fit to introduce in Outer Mongolia in recent years, i.e., the establishment of a Chinese administration, the formation of Chinese regular troops, and the colonization of Mongolia by the Chinese. However, the Russians believed that the three conditions could be taken "as a basis for a possible agreement between the Chinese and the Mongols."[7]

Accordingly, the Russian chargé d'affaires in Peking was instructed to propose to the Chinese Government that Russia was ready to act as mediator between the Chinese and the Mongols. He declared that, if the Chinese Government were prepared to negotiate on this basis, Russian diplomacy would be directed toward inducing the Mongols not to sever their connection with China but rather to observe the obligations taken upon themselves.[8]

In order to carry out "mediation," which was actually a policy of self-interest, Russia had resorted to warning and pressure in relation to both China and Outer Mongolia. Russia warned China in the official communiqué of December 29, 1911, that Russia's "large interests in Mongolia do not permit the Imperial Government to ignore the Government which has been practically established in Outer Mongolia." The communiqué emphatically declared that if "Mongolia severs her connection with China, the Imperial Government, with every desire to see the Sino-Mongolian dispute ended, will be compelled by force of circumstances to enter into business relations with the Mongolian Government."[9]

On October 16, 1912, Sazonov instructed the Russian minister in Peking, Krupenskii, to point out to the Chinese Government that "we do not wish to recognize Mongolia as independent from China, but we cannot help but see that such independence has already existed *de facto* for over a year. It will depend on China as to how far we shall go in recognizing this fact."[10] The Chinese Government was also cautioned that if, in spite of warnings, it should "dispatch troops against Western Mongolia [Kobdo], such action would force us [Russia] to re-examine our attitude to [Outer] Mongolia both from the point of view of her proclaimed independence as well as from that of the territorial extent of Autonomous Mongolia."[11]

[7] *Ibid.*   [8] *Ibid.*, p. 86.
[9] *Ibid.*
[10] Sazonov to Krupenskii, tel., Oct. 16, 1912, *S.D.D. po M.V.*, no. 19, p. 19.
[11] *Ibid.*, p. 20.

It was difficult, however, to get the Chinese Government's consent to the Russian conditions, as the feelings of the new parliament of the Republic were running high when the text of the Russo-Mongolian agreement of 1912 became known. The Russian consul in Kalgan reported military preparations and concentration of Chinese troops in districts bordering Outer Mongolia.[12] Thereupon, Krupenskii was instructed to point out to the Waichiaopu that in view of the fact that "our [Russian] forces entered into Mongolia and stayed there in accordance with the wishes of the Mongols, the dispatch of Chinese troops into Mongolia will mean an act of war."[13]

Besides giving this warning, Sazonov also ordered Krupenskii to draw the attention of the Chinese Government to the fact that it was not Russia, "but China, who was interested in recognition by the Mongols of their link with the Chinese Government." Therefore, "China cannot put forward demands [upon Russia] for her own sovereign rights in Outer Mongolia," whereas Russia did have "the right to demand that China" perform "certain obligations."[14]

In order to assume effectively the role of "mediator," Tsarist Russia constantly threatened China with a change of attitude for the worse. As Sazonov pointed out, by the end of April, 1913, China was again strongly warned that if she persisted in delaying the signing of an agreement with Russia on Outer Mongolia and in agitating against Russia among the Mongol princes, Russia would "enter into new relations with the Mongolian Government, and then negotiate on a completely different basis with the Chinese Government."[15] It was under this heavy Russian pressure that the Peking Government finally declared its "readiness" to accept Russian good offices by signing the 1913 Sino-Russian declaration, and appointed Pi Kwei-fang, formerly High Commissioner of the Manchu Court in the Altai region and the royal Special Commissioner in Urga, to negotiate with the Mongols through the "mediation" of the Tsarist consulate in Urga.[16]

Nor did Outer Mongolia fare any better. The Russians told the Mongols, in Sazonov's own words that

[12] Krupenskii to Sazonov, tel. no. 45, Nov. 30, 1912, *S.D.D. po M.V.*, p. 45.
[13] Sazonov to Krupenskii, tel. no. 48, Dec. 10, 1912, *S.D.D. po M.V.*, p. 49.
[14] *Ibid.*
[15] Sazonov to Krupenskii, tel. no. 60, April 24, 1913, *S.D.D. po M.V.*, p. 60.
[16] Pi Kwei-fang, *Wai-Mong Chiao-sheh Shih-mo Chi (A Report on the Negotiations Concerning Outer Mongolia) (Peking*, 1928), Sh. 3, 5.

the Khalkhas [Outer Mongols] are not prepared by their history for an independent state-life. Being nomads, for centuries accustomed to obey the Peking Government, the Mongols of Khalkha possess neither a military nor a financial organization, nor leaders, without whom an independent state is impossible . . . . Peace could only be preserved in Khalkha if she knew that her two powerful neighbors, Russia and China, had come to an agreement about her future.[17]

The Russian envoy, Korostovets, warned the Living Buddha in August, 1913, that Russia "never promised full independence to Mongolia, as we have no reason to undertake such a task."[18] Chebu-tsum Damba Hutukhtu, following this hint to recognize ties with the Chinese Government by accepting its suzerainty, formally requested Russia to act as a mediator in "concluding a treaty of peace between Mongolia and China."[19]

These efforts of Russian diplomacy show how keenly Russia desired to have its role of "mediator" recognized by China especially, and by Outer Mongolia as well. Such recognition would imply acceptance to a certain extent of a special Russian position in Mongolia, and would also prevent any direct settlement between China and Outer Mongolia without Russian interference.

RUSSO-CHINESE DECLARATION OF 1913

The Russian "mediation" between China and Outer Mongolia was precipitated by the conclusion of the Russo-Mongolian agreement of November 3/October 21, 1912, which offered an urgent challenge to the Chinese.[20] On learning of this agreement, the Chinese Government lodged a protest with the Russian Legation on November 7; Foreign Minister Liang Ru-hao also stated to the Russian minister China's determination not to recognize the agreement. However, the attitude of Krupenskii remained unyielding. Finding himself in a very awkward position, Foreign Minister Liang resigned and was succeeded by Lou Tseng-tsiang. Minister Lou thereupon embarked on formal negotiations with Russia, while the French minister at Peking served as a mediator in a private capacity.

[17] Cited in Grumm-Grzhimailo, *op. cit.*, II, 748-749.
[18] Korostovets to Sazonov, tel. no. 68, April 30, 1913, *S.D.D. po M.V.*, p. 61.
[19] Miller to Sazonov, tel. no. 84, Aug. 24, 1913, *S.D.D. po M.V.*, p. 73.
[20] Chen Po-wen, *Chung-O Wai-Chiao-Shih (Sino-Russian Diplomatic History)*, 2nd ed. (Shanghai, 1931), p. 152.

Because of the Russo-Japanese secret treaty of 1907 and the subsequent visit of Sazonov to London to assure the British Government of its rights in Tibet in exchange for Russia's position in Mongolia, Japan and Great Britain refrained from intervening in the Sino-Russian dispute concerning the said agreement. Thus without external assistance, China was compelled to fall back on direct bilateral negotiations with Russia for the purpose of concluding a Russo-Chinese agreement abrogating the Russo-Mongolian agreement in question.[21]

During the period of Sino-Russian dispute about the Russo-Mongolian agreement of 1912, opinion in Russia, much as in China, was divided among three distinct lines of action: prompt military action; settlement from within Mongolia; and diplomatic negotiations between China and Russia.[22] In favor of war, Count Bennigsen said:

War against China is inevitable . . . . And as we shall never become China's friend, the sooner we equip ourselves for the tussle the better . . . . After a successful campaign we could assure our safety by forming two separate states out of Mongolia and Sin Dsian [Sinkiang], and deny the Chinese admission by means of various restrictions.[23]

The liberal elements thought that the best policy in Russian relations with China, and also with England and Japan, was "to maintain the *status quo*": "It is not in our [Russian] interest to annex Mongolia. The best solution for the whole question is to leave Mongolia alone."[24] Official Russia, through Foreign Minister Sazonov, was for a compromise of these two extreme views. Urging a middle course in order to protect Russian interests in the Far East, Sazonov stated plainly in the Duma on April 13, 1912: "We should demand three conditions from China as a basis for negotiations. China should promise, first, not to colonize Mongolia; second, not to send troops to Mongolia; and third, not to interfere with the internal politics of Mongolia."[25] This policy remained in force after Russia had

[21] *Ibid.*, pp. 84-85.
[22] Weigh, *Russo-Chinese Diplomacy*, pp. 173-174.
[23] Count Bennigsen, "Some Data about Contemporary Mongolia," pp. 39, 40, quoted in E. J. Dillon, "The Chinese Pale of Settlement," the *English Review*, XIII (Jan., 1913), 299.
[24] *Literary Digest*, XLIV (March 9, 1912), 475.
[25] C. L. Chu (ed.), *Chin-shih-lien lai chi Chung-O Kuan-hsi (Russo-Chinese Relations of the Last Ten Years)*, p. 145.

signed the agreement with Mongolia in November, under the pretext of Chinese nonco-operation. Because Russia had many problems in the Balkans at that time, while President Yüan Shih-k'ai could not afford to send an expeditionary force to Outer Mongolia, a political settlement appeared to be desirable to both of them.

For the purpose of discussing measures to be taken by the Chinese Government, its State Council met several times and decided on the following principles to guide it in its negotiations with Russia: (1) to demand the abrogation of the Russo-Mongolian Agreement; (2) to revise the Russo-Mongolian agreement into a Sino-Russian agreement on the basis of Chinese proposals; (3) to reduce and moderate the Russian proposals in order to formulate a Sino-Russian convention; (4) to select and recognize those provisions in the Russo-Mongolian Commercial Protocol which were not contradictory to the projected agreement in order to retain Chinese sovereignty.[26]

The Russian attitude, on the other hand, was very firm. Throughout repeated consultations, Krupenskii never gave his concurrence to taking up the first two Chinese guiding principles even as bases for negotiations. He held that Russia could never renounce her newly signed agreement with Urga, and that the Chinese demand on this point would "certainly make an unfavorable impression" on the Tsarist Government.[27]   Sazonov also pointed out to the Chinese minister in St. Petersburg that "the only alternative to the existing situation acceptable to both sides could be found in the conclusion of an agreement between the Imperial [Russian] and the Chinese Governments on the Mongolian question in accordance with the principles of our [Russian] agreement with the Urga Government."[28]

On November 30, 1912, Krupenskii submitted the first Russian counterproposal to the Chinese negotiator. Thereafter, proposals and counterproposals were exchanged on December 7 and 17, 1912, and on January 4 and 11, 1913, respectively.[29]   After a strong Russian threat at the end of April that "Russia would enter into new relations with the Mongolian Government,"[30] a projected agreement of six clauses was reached on May 20, 1913.

[26] Ch'ü Hsi, *Tzu-Chih Wai-Meng-Ku* (*The Autonomous Outer Mongolia*) (Shanghai, 1918), pp. 42-43.
[27] Krupenskii to Sazonov, tel. no. 30, Nov. 3, 1912, *S.D.D. po M.V.*, pp. 33-34.
[28] Sazonov to Krupenskii, tel. no. 31, Nov. 6, 1912, *ibid.*, pp. 34-35.
[29] Ch'ü Hsi, *op. cit.*, pp. 43-52.
[30] Sazonov to Krupenskii, tel. no. 66, April 24, 1913, *S.D.D. po M.V.*, p. 60.

This agreement provided, first, that recognizing Mongolia as an integral part of the territory of China, Russia promised not to seek to dissolve this bond and to respect the historical rights accruing therefrom to China. The second provision was that China agreed not to modify the historical autonomy of Outer Mongolia but to give the Mongols of Outer Mongolia the responsibility for the defense and the maintenance of order in their own territory, and the exclusive right to maintain their military and police organization, as well as the right to prohibit the colonization of their lands by people other than Mongolian subjects. Thirdly, Russia, on her side, was to promise not to send troops into Outer Mongolia with the exception of consular guards, not to undertake the colonization of the territory of Outer Mongolia, and not to be represented in that territory by any other institution than the consulates allowed by the treaties. In the fourth clause, China, desirous of using peaceful methods in the exercise of her authority over Outer Mongolia, declared herself prepared to accept the good offices of Russia to establish on the above basis the principle of her relations with Outer Mongolia so that the central authority of this region should recognize its historical character as a local authority in a part of China. The fifth clause provided that, in consideration of the good offices of the Russian Government, the Chinese Government would consent to confer on Russian subjects in Outer Mongolia the commercial advantages enumerated in the protocol concluded at Urga. In the final clause, all international acts concerning modifications of the system of government in Outer Mongolia which might later be concluded by the Russian Government with the authorities of that region were to be valid in so far as they should have been approved by the Chinese Government as a result of direct negotiations between China and Russia.[31]

On May 26, 1913, the six-clause projected agreement was passed by the Chinese State Council. Two days later, it was transmitted to the Chinese House of Representatives. After a protracted discussion in the House and fruitless additional negotiations with Russia on the basis of the minor revisions made by the House, the agreement as originally projected was passed in the House on July 8. However, the Chinese Senate, which was at this time dominated by the Kuomin-

[31] Neratov to Krupenskii, tel. no. 89, Sept. 11, 1913, *ibid.*, pp. 76-77.

tang, thought that too much was given to Russia and so rejected the preliminary agreement on July 24/11.[32]

Russia was greatly irritated by this rejection and decided to withdraw from the previous agreement. On July 26/13, 1913, following the instructions of Sazonov, Krupenskii dispatched a note to the Chinese Foreign Office. In it he indicated the objection of the Tsarist Government to the Chinese proposals of revision, expressed its regret that "the negotiations did not lead to the desired results," and declared on its behalf that "Russia remains free to act" with respect to the Mongolian question. The note also advanced four new prerequisite conditions, which were much harsher than the previous ones, namely, that China acknowledge the autonomy of Mongolia (with the exception of the district forming Inner Mongolia) and the rights ensuing from such autonomy for the said territory; that Russia acknowledge the suzerainty of China over Mongolia and the rights involved in such suzerainty; that China express her readiness to accept the good offices of Russia for the establishment of her mutual relations with the Mongolian Government on the basis of the principles expressed in the Russo-Mongolian agreement and the protocol of 1912; and that questions touching the interests of Russia and China in Mongolia and arising from the new state of affairs in that country be settled through subsequent discussion by the respective governments.[33]

On receiving the Russian note, President Yüan was angered at the adverse attitude of the Tsarist Government and at the vain efforts of scores of preceding conferences. He therefore accepted the resignation of Foreign Minister Lou Tseng-tsiang. Russian Minister Krupenskii thereupon informed his government that until a new Foreign Minister was appointed, no definite answer from China might be expected.[34]

On July 16, 1913, a Russian newspaper in St. Petersburg commented that the Chinese Government wanted to recognize Mongolian autonomy only in name, while in fact intending to oppose it

[32] Krupenskii to Sazonov, tels. nos. 72, 73, 80, June 17/4, 1913; June 19/6, 1913; and July 24/11, 1913, *ibid.*, pp. 63-64, 64-65, 71.

[33] For text in Russian, see Sazonov to Miller, tel. no. 78, July 1, 1913, *S.D.D. po M.V.*, p. 70; for text in French, see *ibid.*, tel. no. 75, pp. 67-68; for text in Chinese, see Ch'ü Hsi, *op. cit.*, p. 56.

[34] Krupenskii to Sazonov, tel. no. 80, July 11, 1913, *S.D.D. po M.V.*, p. 71; Ch'ü Hsi, *op. cit.*, p. 56.

and to nullify it. The editorial continued, "there was no more room for Russia to make concessions; therefore, the negotiations broke off and Russia notified the Peking Government of her free action."[35] Thus, the negotiations were actually interrupted for two months.

Not until September 18, 1913, did the new Chinese Foreign Minister Sun Pao-ch'i resume conversations with Russian Minister Krupenskii, whose previous proposition of four prerequisite conditions was consented to by the Chinese Government in a formal statement. Since the Russian Minister refused to negotiate on the basis of the former projected agreement of six clauses on the ground that the state of things had changed, new proposals and counterproposals were again exchanged in ten conference meetings lasting until the end of October.[36]

Finally, China and Russia came to an agreement. It was embodied in a declaration of five articles and an exchange of notes in four articles. On November 5/October 23, 1913, the declaration was signed and the notes formally exchanged by Sun Pao-ch'i and Krupenskii, after the texts had been passed by the Chinese State Council and approved by President Yüan. This time the Chinese Parliament was not consulted, because the declaration was not considered a treaty; in fact, the Kuomintang had been dissolved by a Presidential mandate and no session of the Parliament had since been reconvened. The declaration and the attached document were simultaneously made public by the two contracting parties on November 22/9, 1913. The provisions were:

1. Russia would recognize China's suzerainty over Outer Mongolia;

2. China would recognize the autonomy of Outer Mongolia;

3. Both China and Russia pledged themselves to abstain from intervention in the internal administration of Outer Mongolia, from sending troops there, and from colonizing the land;

4. China declared herself ready to accept the good offices of the Russian Government in the settlement of her relations with Outer Mongolia, and China and Russia agreed to settle in subsequent conferences questions pertaining to their respective interests in Outer Mongolia.[37]

---

[35] Ch'ü Hsi, *op. cit.*, p. 57.   [36] *Ibid.*, pp. 57-65.
[37] Krupenskii to Sazonov, report no. 105, Oct. 23, 1913, text of declaration and exchange of notes attached, *S.D.D. po M.V.*, pp. 87-90; for Chinese text, see *Kuo-*

In the notes exchanged, it was provided that "Russia recognizes that the territory of Outer Mongolia forms a part of the territory of China" (Article 1), and that "as regards questions of a political and territorial nature, the Chinese Government shall come to an agreement with the Russian Government through negotiations in which the authorities of Outer Mongolia shall take part" (Article II).[38] Thus, nominally, China was the acknowledged suzerain of Outer Mongolia, but, in reality, Outer Mongolia was put under the joint protection of China and Russia.

It is agreed among many Chinese historians and diplomatic negotiators that in comparison with the previously projected six-clause agreement of May, 1913, the final declaration, together with the exchanged notes, was far more unfavorable to China than the original draft. The latter had stated that Russia would respect various Chinese territorial rights in Outer Mongolia, that Russia would recognize the central authorities of Outer Mongolia as Chinese local officials, and that any agreement of international character between Russia and Outer Mongolia should be approved by the Chinese Government. All these provisions disappeared in the final document. Moreover, the stipulation regarding "the exclusive right of the Mongols of Outer Mongolia to provide themselves for the international administration of Autonomous Mongolia and to settle all questions of a commercial and industrial nature relating to that country" (Article III) was very broad in scope. It accorded exactly with Russia's most strongly held purpose at that time: to exploit Outer Mongolia economically while keeping it a buffer state under Russian domination.[39]

On the part of Outer Mongolia, there was considerable uneasiness over the Russo-Chinese declaration, in spite of the repeated Russian assurance given to the Urga Government first by Korostovets and then by Miller that its purpose was to strengthen Mongolian relations.[40]

Chih-Tiao-Yao Ta-Chuan (*A Collection of International Treaties*), Part I, Vol. III, p. 21; for text in English, see MacMurray, *Treaties and Agreements with and Concerning China 1894-1919*, II, 1066.

[38] MacMurray, *op. cit.*, II, 1066.

[39] Ch'ü Hsi, *op. cit.*, p. 68; Pi *Wai-Mong Chiao-sheh Shih-mo-Chi* (*A Report on the Negotiations Concerning Outer Mongolia*), sh. 6.

[40] Sazonov to Korostovets, tel. no. 55, Feb. 4/Jan. 22, 1913, and Miller to Sazonov, tel. no. 79, July 19/6, 1913, *S.D.D. po M.V.*, pp. 54-55, 71.

On December 16/3, 1913, after receiving the Urga Hutukhtu's instruction of November 25, Special Mongolian Envoy Sain Noyan Khan, then at St. Petersburg, wrote a letter to Sazonov, who had transmitted the texts of the Russo-Chinese declaration and the exchange of notes to him on November 7. A note of largely similar contents was addressed to Liu Chin-jen, then Chinese minister at St. Petersburg, on the next day. Sain Noyan Khan stressed the fact that after a careful study of the contents of the declaration, the Mongolian Government believed that its existing political structure and its independence in all aspects of internal administration and in friendly relations with other powers had been guaranteed and recognized by Russia and China. "However," he declared, "the Mongolian Government had repeatedly warned Russia and China that Mongolia has definitively broken her relations with China and that she will not recognize any dependency settled without her consent." Therefore, he continued, "the Mongolian Government reserves the right to determine its attitude toward the clauses in the declaration and in the notes regarding the mutual relationship between Mongolia and China."[41]

Though the Mongols received the declaration with almost open displeasure, it is interesting to notice that in his letter to Sazonov, Sain Noyan Khan thanked Russia deeply on behalf of his Government "for all she [Russia] has done for the strengthening of the foundation of the independent existence of the Mongolian state." He also assured Sazonov that "the Mongolian Government, highly appreciating the friendly mediation of Russia and willing to establish normal good-neighborly relations with China, declares its complete readiness to participate in the tripartite conference provided in the declaration and in the notes." In return he appealed to Sazonov for Russia's "strong support" in the forthcoming negotiations, with regard to Outer Mongolia's claim for jurisdiction over Inner Mongolia.[42]

Immediately after the signing of the declaration, government spokesmen at St. Petersburg expressed satisfaction at their diplomats' success in evading on the one hand the "unreasonable Chinese attempt" to reject Mongolian autonomy and on the other "the helpless

[41] *K.A.*, XXXVII, 37-38, 39-40.
[42] *Ibid.*, pp. 37, 38.

Mongolian hope" of full independence.[43]   The Russians also rejoiced that they had at last compelled the Chinese to concede to them the commercial privileges stipulated in the 1881 St. Petersburg Treaty, which they had for the last three years tried in vain to renew.[44]

However, some of the Russian commentators viewed the declaration and the exchanged notes of November 5/October 23, 1913, as "naturally contradictory with the Russo-Mongolian agreement of November 3/October 21, 1912."[45]   To them it seemed a retreat from the earlier position, which would have the effect of leading the Mongols, who were not skilled "in the fineness of European diplomacy, to the conclusion that Russia sold Mongolia to China."[46]

One need not follow this extreme interpretation to conclude that with the Russo-Chinese declaration and notes of 1913, not only was Russian *de facto* domination over Outer Mongolia officially, though belatedly, acknowledged, but also Tsarist Russia became more or less a legal comaster of that area.   The role of "mediator" had been used to good advantage.

Russo-Sino-Mongolian Tripartite Agreement of 1915

Having successfully brought China to a recognition of Outer Mongolia's autonomy in the Russo-Chinese declaration of 1913, Russia next directed her efforts toward finding a stable basis for the status of Outer Mongolia as its protégé.   To this end the Russians pressed the Mongols to participate in a tripartite conference as provided by Article IV of the Russo-Chinese declaration.   In Sazonov's words, "Autonomous Outer Mongolia owed her existence exclusively to Russian efforts."[47]   In order fully to secure and consolidate her exclusive domination in Outer Mongolia, Russia endeavored to isolate the Mongols from any diplomatic and trade relations with other powers.[48]   The best way to achieve the isolation and control of Outer Mongolia, it was felt, was to forestall the latter's independence by leaving it under China's weak suzerainty.

[43] Ch'ü Hsi, *op. cit.*, pp. 68-69.   [44] Weigh, *op. cit.*, p. 180.

[45] B. S. Kalinskii "Mongoliia" ("Mongolia"), *Sibirskii Torgovo-Promyshlennyi Ezhegodnik* (*Siberian Commercial-Industrial Yearbook*), 1914-15, no. 8, Part II, p. 212.

[46] Vollosovich, "Rossiia i Mongoliia" ("Russia and Mongolia"), *Vestnik Azii* (*Asiatic Herald*), nos. 31-32, 1914, p. 46.

[47] Sazonov to Miller, letter, Jan. 30/17, 1914, *K.A.*, XXXVII, 64.

[48] *Ibid.*, pp. 67-68.

The diplomatic agent in Urga, Miller, in communicating the text of the Russo-Chinese declaration and notes to the Mongolian Government, had once more to explain to the Mongolian ministers that "full separation from China was impossible" and that Russia was not willing to defend their full independence against China, nor to fight for the inclusion of Inner Mongolia in the territory of Outer Mongolia. But Russia "promised to support the Mongols' demands within the legal and wise limits" which were fixed by the Russo-Chinese declaration.[49] Though the Mongol ministers were at first "bewildered" by this explanation, the aim of Russian policy in Outer Mongolia after the Russo-Chinese declaration was, in Miller's words, to lull them with the hope of reasonable results from tripartite negotiations.[50]

Tsarist Russia, while satisfying the Mongols' demand for money and arms during Sain Noyan Khan's mission, in order to strengthen her influence in Outer Mongolia and to forestall activities of the Chinese and possibly others, refused categorically to recognize Sain Noyan Khan as the representative of an independent entity. The Mongol envoy became acquainted with the Russo-Chinese declaration only after his arrival in St. Petersburg. Disappointed particularly with the provision for Russia's recognition of Chinese suzerainty over Outer Mongolia, he addressed a note to Sazonov and to all diplomatic representatives in St. Petersburg, including the Chinese ministers, denouncing the Russo-Chinese declaration and averring that Mongolia had entirely broken with China.[51] But when Sain Noyan tried to obtain interviews with the foreign diplomats in St. Petersburg, Sazonov pointed out to him that it was impossible for Mongolia to obtain recognition of her independence by the other powers. The majority of them did not desire the disintegration of China nor the creation of an autonomous Mongolia effected exclusively through the efforts of Russia.[52]

To remove the possibility that Outer Mongolia would be independently active in the international arena, Mongolian representation

---

[49] Sazonov to Miller, tel. no. 106, Oct. 25, 1913, and Miller to Sazonov, tel. no. 107, Nov. 2, 1913, *S.D.D. po M.V.*, pp. 90, 91.

[50] Miller to Krupenskii, tel. no. 303, Nov. 15/2, 1913, *K.A.*, XXXVII, 21.

[51] Sain Noyan Khan, Mongolian Prime Minister and Special Envoy to Sazonov, letter, Dec. 16/3, 1913, *K.A.*, XXXVII, 37-38; to Chinese minister in St. Petersburg, note (copy), Dec. 17/4, 1913, *ibid.*, pp. 39-40.

[52] *K.A.*, XXXVII, 63-64; Sazonov to Miller, confidential letter, Jan. 30/17, 1914, *K.A.*, XXXVII, 63-64.

was discouraged even in Russia. When the Mongolian Prime Minister informed the Russian Government before his departure that he would leave behind him a substitute, Tserendorchzhi, who would be "in charge of his seal and in permanent telegraphic connection with the Urga Government," this act was viewed by the Russians as "an attempt to establish a permanent diplomatic representation of the Mongolian Government in St. Petersburg." It was explained that the Russian Government did not wish such a relationship with Mongolia and would refuse to have official relations with his substitute.[53] Thus all possible complications which might arise from personal contact of the Mongols with foreign legations were also prevented.

Russia's policy and practice of isolating Outer Mongolia covered not only diplomatic, but also commercial fields. In the Russo-Chinese declaration Russia had recognized "the exclusive right" of the Outer Mongolian Government "to settle all questions of a commercial and industrial nature." Yet Sazonov remarked in October, 1914, that "the right to conclude trade agreements remains likewise a dead letter if Russia and China agree to regard the conclusion of a trade treaty as a political act outside the limits of the Mongol Government's political jurisdiction as defined in the declaration of November 5, 1913."[54]

Under the sway of this Russian policy of isolating and controlling Outer Mongolia with Chinese suzerainty as a cause for common complaint, it is natural that Sain Noyan Khan, the Mongolian Prime Minister, in his letter to Sazonov, assured the Tsarist Foreign Minister that "the Mongolian Government, highly appreciating the friendly mediation of Russia and willing to establish normal good-neighborly relations with China, declares its complete readiness to participate in the tripartite conference provided in the declaration and in the notes."[55]

Thus, the Russian efforts to assume the role of "mediator were crowned with success when, on September 9, 1914, the representatives of Russia, China, and Outer Mongolia met at Kiakhta. The conference lasted until June 7, 1915, when an agreement was reached.[56]

[53] *Ibid.*, pp. 67-68.

[54] Sazonov to Krupenskii, tel. no. 3499, Oct. 28/15, 1914, *M.O. v E.I.*, Ser. III, Vol. VI, Part I, p. 427; *M.O. v E.I.*, Ser. III, Vol. VI, Part I, pp. 427-428 n. 1.

[55] Sain Noyan Khan to Sazonov, in letter, Dec. 16/3, 1913, in Popov, "Tsarskaia," *K.A.*, XXXVII, 38.

[56] For Russian text, see Kliuchnikov and Sabanin, *Mezhdunarodnaia Politika*

General Pi Kwei-fang and Chen Lu, Chinese Minister to Mexico, signed for China. Russian Councillor of State Alexandre Miller, Diplomatic Agent and Consul General in Mongolia, signed for Russia. Cho-nang Peitzu and T'uhsieht'u Ch'in Wang signed for Outer Mongolia.

The tripartite agreement in regard to Outer Mongolia, provided *inter alia,* for the following:

1. Outer Mongolia recognized the Russo-Chinese declaration and notes exchanged on November 5, 1913, and hence the suzerainty of China.

2. China and Russia agreed that Outer Mongolia formed a part of China, but that it should have autonomy in the administration of its internal affairs, without the interference of the contracting parties.

3. Autonomous Mongolia should have no right to conclude international treaties with foreign powers respecting political and territorial questions, but might conclude treaties and agreements of a commercial and industrial nature. As regards questions of political and territorial nature, the Chinese Government was obliged to come to an agreement with the Russian Government through negotiations in which Outer Mongolia should participate.

4. The ruler of Outer Mongolia should be invested by the President of the Chinese Republic.

5. No Russian or Chinese troops were to be stationed in Outer Mongolia except for a limited number of consular and military guards.

6. The Chinese Amban (Commissioner) at Urga and his assistants in various localities of Outer Mongolia were to exercise general control lest the acts of the Autonomous Government of Outer Mongolia and its subordinate authorities impair the suzerain rights and interests of China and her subjects in Autonomous Mongolia.

7. The Russo-Mongolian protocol of 1912 relating to Russian commercial rights in Outer Mongolia should remain in force; that is, Russia was assured of all commercial prerogatives obtained from the erstwhile Independent Mongolian Government.

Noveishego Vremeni v Dogovorakh, Notakh i Deklaratsiiakh (International Politics of Most Recent Times in Treaties, Notes and Declarations), Part II (Moscow, 1926), pp. 34-35; for Chinese text, see Pi, *Wai-Mong Chiao-sheh Shih-mo Chi (A Report on the Negotiations Concerning Outer Mongolia),* sh. 15-25; for English text, see MacMurray, *op. cit.,* II, 1239-1244.

Other articles dealt with such matters as boundaries, customs, administration of justice, telegraph and postal communications, and honor.

In a word, by this agreement, which formed the basis of Russo-Sino-Mongolian relations until the Russian Revolution, Russia retained all her vested rights—among them the right of free trade in Outer Mongolia—and was assured of an Autonomous Outer Mongolian buffer which she desired. China secured nothing substantial except the right of representation in political and territorial matters pertaining to Outer Mongolia; but even this had to be shared with Russia. China and Russia were legally required to exercise a joint protection over Outer Mongolia; it might be more apt to say, as one American writer expressed it, that by this agreement China recognized the autonomy of Outer Mongolia, under China's suzerainty but as Russia's "Protectorate."[57]

Moreover, as Maiskii pointed out, the tripartite agreement, which provided at its face value, for "the recognition of Chinese sovereignty [in fact, suzerainty] over Outer Mongolia by Russia and the corresponding recognition of Outer Mongolia's autonomy by China, was merely a trick of temporary character."[58] It allowed "the Russian agents accompanied by military forces and openly based in the city of Urga to manipulate the Mongolian cabinet in compliance with Russian plan."[59] It was apparently for precisely this reason that immediately after the signing of the Tripartite agreement, a leading newspaper of St. Petersburg praised the Tsarist diplomats for their success as skilful "mediators" in pursuing the golden mean between "the unreasonable Chinese attempt" not to recognize Mongolian autonomy and "the helpless Mongolian hope" to become an independent state.[60] Outer Mongolia was thus described as "obviously a semi-independent state under Russian protection."[61]

Thus, taking advantage of "China's internal difficulties" during the years of revolution and unrest, Tsarist Russia, as indicated by Maiskii, step by step acquired a firm grip on Outer Mongolia.[62]

[57] Leonard Ludwin, "Mongolia Against Japan," *The New Republic*, XCIV, March 23, 1938, 188.

[58] Maiskii, *Sovremennaia Mongoliia (Contemporary Mongolia)*, p. 263.

[59] *Ibid.*   [60] Ch'ü Hsi, *op. cit.*, p. 90.

[61] Ho Han-wen, *Chung-O Wai-chiao Shih (Sino-Russian Diplomatic History)*, pp. 292-293.

[62] Maiskii, *op. cit.*, p. 263.

XI: RUSSIAN SUPREMACY OVER OUTER MONGOLIA UP TO 1917

RUSSIAN ECONOMIC DOMINATION

The Tsarist Russian Government, by taking advantage of the Kiakhta Tripartite agreement of 1915, secured "enormously extensive and exclusive rights" in Outer Mongolia, thus "turning Outer Mongolia into an actual colony of Tsarist Russia."[1] A series of "one-sided, enslaving agreements for various concessions with Outer Mongolia" was concluded.[2] It provided Outer Mongolia with a number of loans, while taking Mongolian finance under its own administration through the creation of a post of Russian financial adviser in Urga. In addition, there were a Russian bank, Russian-sponsored communications projects, and a Russia-oriented trade policy. Taken together, these measures of Russian economic domination were considered by Miller, the Russian Diplomatic Agent in Urga, as designed to "help the Mongols to oppose Chinese and foreign economic pressure."[3]

As Maiskii has pointed out, in two successive years, 1913 and 1914, Tsarist Russia had given Outer Mongolia three separate loans totaling more than five million rubles for the establishment of Mongolian armed forces and the re-organization of Mongolian administration.[4] Taking advantage of Sain Noyan Khan's sojourn in St. Petersburg in 1913-14, Russia tried to satisfy his "request for a loan." The purpose of making the loan, Sazonov explained, was to

---

[1] *M.S.E.* (2nd ed.), Vol. VII (1938), col. 45.

[2] *Ibid.*, cols. 45-46.

[3] Dispatch of Miller, Nov. 21/8, 1913, in Popov, "Tsarskaia Rossiia i Mongoliia v 1913-1914 gg." ("Tsarist Russia and Mongolia in 1913-1914"), *K.A.*, XXXVII, 321.

[4] Maiskii, *Sovremennaia Mongoliia (Contemporary Mongolia)*, pp. 279, 280.

win Sain Noyan's "support for our [Russian] activities in [Outer] Mongolia.[5]

From the beginning of the loan arrangements the Russians laid stress on the condition that the funds could not be put at the disposal of the Mongolian Government without Russian control.[6] In order to bargain for Sain Noyan's consent to such control in connection with the loan, the Russian Government refused to arrange an audience with the Tsar for Sain Noyan Khan and threatened not to recognize his position as a plenipotentiary equipped with full powers.[7] Shortly before his return home early in 1914, Sain Noyan signed a contract appointing S. A. Kozin, an official of the Russian Ministry of Finance, as adviser on the organization of finance of the Mongolian Government for the administration of state property and for the outlining of reforms.[8] Later he also took charge of the administration of public revenues and of the treasury.[9] The right of administration was considered a sufficient guarantee to effect such prolongation of financial control.[10] Kozin remained in the post of financial adviser until 1917. In order to fulfil his "mission" of Russian control over Mongolian economy and finance, "Kozin created a special *'Administration of the Russian Adviser'* which drew a considerable number of experts from Russia." According to Maiskii, the entire up-keep of the "Administration of Russian Adviser" was charged to the Russian loan account.[11]

In spite of the creation of the "Administration of the Russian Adviser" there were interdepartmental frictions and conflicts among the Russian bureaucracy both at home and in Urga. Kozin played the role of economic tsar in Outer Mongolia.

According to Maiskii, Russian domination may be discerned in the decrees of the Urga Living Buddha concerning compulsory land cultivation and the internal organization of the administrative ma-

---

[5] Sazonov to Kokovtsov, draft of letter, confidential, in Popov, "Tsarskaia," *K.A.*, XXXVII, 34, 35.

[6] Sazonov to Miller, tel. no. 81, Jan. 24/11, 1914, *M.O. v E.I.*, Ser. III, Vol. I, doc. no. 91, pp. 97-98.

[7] Sazonov to Miller, letter, Jan. 30/17, 1914, in Popov, "Tsarskaia," *K.A.*, XXXVII, 66.

[8] *Ibid.*

[9] Contract of Jan. 7, 1914/Dec. 25, 1913, in *D.I.B.Z.D.I.*, Vol. I, Part I, p. 78.

[10] Sazonov to Finance Minister Bark, letter, July 6/June 23, 1914, *M.O. v E.I.*, Ser. III, Vol. IV, doc. no. 101, pp. 139-141.

[11] Maiskii, *op. cit.*, p. 280. Italics added.

chinery.[12] One of the most striking results achieved by the "Administration of the Russian Adviser" was the elimination of the original Mongolian financial system and the establishment of a highly centralized state treasury for the convenience of control by Tsarist Russia. This action was in vivid contrast with Russia's repeated charges that China was destroying Mongolian historical institutions. It was also apparently in violation, both in letter and in spirit, of Articles II, III, V, and VI of the Russo-Sino-Mongolian tripartite agreement, regarding noninterference in the "system of autonomous internal administration existing in Outer Mongolia."[13]

Moreover, in 1915-16, Baron P. A. Witte, assistant to Kozin, led an expedition to investigate Outer Mongolia geographically and statistically in order to find new sources of state income and objects for investment which would promote Russian economic exploitation. In 1916 Witte created and assumed the chairmanship of a special administration of state properties which introduced new taxes, issued regulations for the renting of land for haymaking, pasture, and cultivation, established statistical research institutes, and opened factories in Urga,[14] thus strengthening Russia's economic hold in Outer Mongolia.

Russian economic control over Outer Mongolia, exercised through its agents headed by the Russian financial adviser, was based on Russian loans, which found their entering wedge in the extreme inadequacy of the budget of the Mongolian Government in carrying out the political, economic, and military assignments of its Russian overlord. Of the ordinary expenditures of the Mongolian Government, only one half went for the maintenance of the central and local institutions and offices; the other half was required for the armed forces and a reform fund. Even so, the ordinary budget could not cover the expenses of the military expeditions made in connection with the events of 1911, nor the payment of the debt already owed to Russia.[15] These had to be covered in an extraordinary budget,

---

[12] *Ibid.*

[13] MacMurray (ed.), *Treaties and Agreements with and Concerning China 1894-1919*, II, 1240.

[14] "Mongol'skaia Navodnaia Respublika" ("The Mongolian People's Republic"), *Sibirskaia Sovetskaia Entsiklopediia* (*Siberian Soviet Encyclopedia*, referred to hereinafter as *S.S.E.*), III (Moscow, 1932), 528-529.

[15] Cf. "Chronicle" on Mongolia, *Vestnik Azii* (*Asiatic Herald*), no. 37, 1916, p. 125.

receipts for which came from further Russian loans. With the loans went Russian advice to the Mongolian Government on budgetary policy. These tactics led the Mongols into a vicious circle which resulted in Russian economic domination in Outer Mongolia.

The loan agreement signed in July, 1914, provided a new loan amounting to three million rubles, given without interest. The loan was to be used for the rehabilitation of finances, internal reforms, the improvement of cattle breeding, and "the maintenance and training of the army with the help of Russian and Mongolian instructors." The loan was to be secured by customs revenues. Should the receipts prove to be insufficient, the Mongolian Government promised to give an additional guarantee. Repeated lack of punctuality in payment was to give the Russian Government the right to establish an effective control of the revenues serving as a guarantee for the loan and to administer them on the Mongolian Government's account.[16]

In the negotiations for a loan the Russian Government was anxious to exclude the possibility of the Mongols' borrowing from foreign sources, especially from the Chinese, for fear of the reestablishment of the latter's influence. Originally the reports that China had offered to repay on the Mongols' behalf the loan given by Russia and had also offered credits to the Mongolian Government were denied by the Chinese Foreign Minister upon strong Russian diplomatic remonstrances to Peking. The Russians intimated that if the Chinese Government continued to disregard Mongolia's autonomy, Russia would have to change her moderating influence on Urga.[17]

In November, 1913, Miller proposed to consolidate Russian financial control in Outer Mongolia by establishing, in addition to the appointment of a Russian financial adviser, a Russian bank in Urga.[18] This proposal attracted the attention of Nicholas II who commented that it should "be dispatched to the Ministry of Finance promptly."[19] Offers were made by the Russo-Asiatic Bank and by

[16] Miller to Sazonov, tel. no. 192, July 21/8, 1914, *M.O. v E.I.*, Ser. III, Vol. IV, doc. no. 315, pp. 369-370.

[17] Sazonov to Krupenskii, tel. no. 289, Feb. 19/6, 1914, *M.O. v E.I.*, Ser. III, Vol. IV, doc. no. 279, pp. 350-351.

[18] Dispatch of Miller, no. 321, Nov. 21/8, 1913, in Popov, "Tsarskaia," *K.A.*, XXXVII, 27.

[19] Miller to Sazonov, tel. no. 13, Jan. 29/16, 1914, comment of Jan. 30/17, 1914, *M.O. v E.I.*, Ser. III, Vol. I, doc. no. 137, pp. 157-158.

the Siberian Commercial Bank. As the political side of the question was of great significance, in July, 1914, the interministerial conference considered all aspects of the organization of such a Russian credit institution. The conference concluded that it would be necessary to create a special form of bank in Mongolia, in order for it to be regarded by the Mongols as the national bank which they themselves had intended to found by offering a concession to a private person. Moreover, a Mongolian national bank, as opposed to a private bank, would be able "to accomplish certain other functions of political character which await the bank in the future."[20]

The plan for the Mongolian national bank worked out by the Credit-Chancellory in collaboration with the Siberian Commercial Bank was based on the Iuferov concession previously granted in October, 1912, but not utilized. The proposed bank would have the sole right to issue bank notes in both Mongolian and Russian monetary units and to organize their circulation. It was also considered essential to facilitate trade relations between Russia and Mongolia. The directorate of the bank was to be established in St. Petersburg, the administration in Urga. Two officials of the Mongolian Government had the right to buy the whole of the bank after five years. If this right was not exercised the whole property of the bank would pass into the possession of the Mongolian Government after eighty years. In return for this concession the Mongolian Government agreed to protect the bank against any losses and in emergencies recover amounts owed to it. The branches of the bank were to be under the protection of the Russian Government. The first share capital was fixed at one million rubles. Additional capital could be raised with the authorization of the Russian Ministry of Finance. The bank was officially opened on May 27/14, 1915.[21]

The monopolistic character of Russian financial control in Mongolia through the Russian Financial Adviser and the Russian-managed Mongolian National Bank was shown in the Mongolian rejection of a Chinese banking plan. In 1915 the Chinese Amban, Cheng Lo, requested the Mongolian government to permit the opening of a Chinese bank. Under Russian influence the Mongolian Government

[20] Journal of the Inter-Ministerial Conference, July 15/2, 1914, *M.O. v E.I.*, Ser. III, Vol. IV, doc. no. 241, pp. 289 ff.

[21] Tel. no. 1318 of Khionin, May 27/14, 1915, *M.O. v E.I.*, Ser. III, Vol. VIII, Part II, p. 272 n. 2.

declined the request on the ground that the opening of a Chinese bank was a violation of the Kiakhta agreement,[22] although in fact there was no such prohibition within the agreement.

Cheng Lo once again made the request with the explanation that the proposed bank was not a purely Chinese commercial bank but an international bank based on the shares of stock held in America, China, and other countries. The Mongolian Government then inquired of the Russian consul whether the Chinese information regarding foreign capital involvement was true and whether the opening of the bank could be authorized. The reply from the Russian consulate was as follows:

So far as is known to the consulate, the bank "Chih-Pian-Yin-Hang" is a purely Chinese mortgage bank, and if it were to open in Mongolia, it would, on the one hand, violate the Kiakhta Treaty, and on the other, bring nothing except harm to the Mongolian people because all Mongolian princes and lamas would be heavily in debt to this bank, thus laying a great burden on the whole population.[23]

This refusal to approve the establishment of a Chinese bank was, in the words of Sazonov, "a great success for us."[24] Thus, no Chinese bank actually could materialize during the period of Tsarist rule in Russia.[25]

Until 1912, the date of the proclamation of Mongolian independence, many large Chinese companies were active in Mongolia, with thousands of branches scattered in the interior of the Mongolian steppes. Supported by some large Chinese banks, the companies engaged in commercial operations either independently, or using foreign capital circulating at the time within the interior of the "China beyond the Wall."[26] In 1912, the Chinese were driven out of Mongolia and the Russians monopolized all the markets, and, moreover, became surfeited with a huge stock of merchandise left

[22] "Chronicle" on Mongolia, *Vestnik Azii* (*Asiatic Herald*), no. 37, 1916, p. 128.

[23] *Ibid.*, p. 129-130.

[24] Sazonov to Miller, tel. no. 4444, Sept. 10/Aug. 28, 1915, *M.O. v E.I.*, Ser. III, Vol. VIII, Part II, p. 272.

[25] Telegram of diplomatic agent no. 109, April 5, 1916, cited in A. Gladstern, "Mongolska Politika Timchasovoho Rossigskoho Uviadu" ("The Mongolian Policy of the Russian Provisional Government"), in *Skhidnii Svit* (*The World of the Orient*, referred to hereinafter as S.S.) no. 5, Kharkov, 1928, p. 167.

[26] N. K. Penskii, "Ekonomicheskoe Vzaimootnoshenie SSSR s Mongoliei" ("Economic Interrelations of the U.S.S.R. with Mongolia") *Novyi Vostok* (*The New East*), nos. 10-11, 1925, pp. 163-164.

at bargain prices by the hastily liquidated Chinese companies. It seemed as if the propitious moment had arrived for Russian commerce to develop fully its potentialities so that it would be able to control the Mongolian market permanently.[27]

However, the ultimate result was that the Chinese merchants were replaced by Russian merchants for only a short time. In the three years following (1913-15) despite their monopoly advantages, Russian merchants were far from dominant in the Mongolian markets. The Russo-Mongolian commercial turnover constituted scarcely one-third of the total turnover of Outer Mongolia's foreign commerce, and Russian capital did not succeed in consolidating the positions of the merchants.[28]

On the other hand, it is interesting to note that Russian sources admit that "in terms of commercial profits and cheating the population, the Russian merchant succeeded and even surpassed his Chinese counterpart."[29] According to the testimony of Boloban, the agent of the Russian Ministry of Commerce and Industry in Outer Mongolia, "the wholesale surcharges on merchandise sold by Russian commercial companies to retailers of the Khoshuns were 100 per cent higher than prices in Moscow, not including transportation expenses.[30] And yet, the disproportionately high prices of merchandise illustrated only one side of the story. "Having preserved a semi-barter system under the name of 'zadachi,' Russian merchants, like their Chinese predecessors, cornered the Mongolian raw material market, mercilessly cheating and looting the peasant masses."[31]

Concerning the practices of the Russian merchants Boloban wrote:

Based on the extreme poverty of the Mongols, those peculiar "zadachi" drew the whole of Mongolia into a bondage of indebtedness. No matter where you may have been in Mongolia, complaints about Russian merchants could be heard with the implication that under the Chinese, everyone was better off. The Chinese used to make profits at 36 per cent and never brought about the complete ruin of the masses, because they saw that the Mongol was their client, indispensable to the selling of their mer-

[27] *Ibid.*, p. 168.
[28] *Ibid.*, p. 169.
[29] Rish, "Mongoliia na Strazhe Svoei Nezavisimosti" ("Mongolia Guarding Her Independence"), *Tikhii Okean* (*The Pacific Ocean*), no. 4(6), Oct.-Dec., 1935, p. 100.
[30] Cited in *Ibid.*
[31] *Ibid.*

chandise; but Russians do not bother about that and look with indifference at the ruin of their clients.[32]

As a result "the Russian *obivalory* [swindlers] were," as Rish pointed out, "less adjusted to the conditions of the Mongolian market than the Chinese companies with their wide commercial ramifications, and soon had to give back to their Chinese competitors the positions they occupied."[33]   The import of Russian merchandise into Mongolia fell from 4.5 million rubles in 1907 to 2.4 million rubles in 1915.   By 1916 the export of merchandise from Russia to Mongolia had fallen to its lowest point.[34]   Because of World War I Russian commerce experienced still further setbacks.   Nevertheless Russian capital maintained its monopoly.   In the buying and exporting of Mongolian raw materials, the value reached 11.5 million rubles in 1915.[35]

The Chinese disputed vigorously, but in vain, the right of the Mongolian Government to conclude agreements concerning telegraphs or railways with the Russian Government, contending that they were not treaties of an industrial and commercial character, such as Mongolia was allowed to conclude, but rather treaties of a political and territorial character.[36]   In the field of communications, the Mongols conceded to Russia telegraph and railway agreements in exchange for supplies of money and arms.   As in banking and other fields, the chief Russian aim regarding Mongolian communications was to exclude any possible concessions to foreign powers or their nationals.

In May of 1913 Russia secured a telegraph concession in Western Mongolia.   The Mongolian Government bound itself to offer to the Russian Chief Administration of Posts and Telegraphs not only "the right of exploitation and complete control" (Article I), but also any concessions for telegraph lines made "in any other direction whatsoever" (Article V).[37]   By the end of 1913 the construction of other telegraph lines was under negotiation.   In the case of the concession for the Mondy-Uliassutai telegraph, in order to make the Mongolian

---

[32] Cited in *ibid.*, pp. 100-101.   [33] *Ibid.*, p. 101.
[34] Penskii, *op. cit.*, p. 169.
[35] Kallinikov, *Revoliutsionnaia Mongoliia* (*Revolutionary Mongolia*), p. 34, cited in Rish, *op. cit.*, p. 101.
[36] Miller to Sazonov, tel. no. 272, Dec. 29/16, 1914, *M.O. v E.I.*, Ser. III, Vol. VI, Part II, doc. no. 709, p. 293.
[37] Text in MacMurray, *op. cit.*, II, 1038-1039.

Government more willing to sign the agreement, Miller originally proposed an advance payment of ten thousand rubles; in the end he succeeded without any advance.[38]

Russian economic control in Outer Mongolia even led to Russian interference with the establishment by China of postal and telegraphic communications in that territory, even though it had been openly recognized by Russia, in Article II of the 1915 agreement, that Mongolia was under the suzerainty of China. In denouncing to the Mongolian Government the planned opening of the Chinese postal and telegraphic offices in Kobdo and Uliassutai, the Russian consul at Kobdo emphatically stated:

Such activities of the Chinese officials [the opening of postal and telegraphic offices] are [again] a violation of the Kiakhta Treaty, and for this reason [I] ask the government of Autonomous Mongolia to prohibit the opening of the above mentioned offices; in case of rejection on the part of the Chinese officials, notify me, the consul.[39]

In the field of railway construction, Russia's desire to exclude other powers and to achieve dominance for itself was likewise apparent. Frequent proposals for a Russian railway through Mongolia, among them those of Badmaev, had been made in the years before 1913,[40] but these bore no significant connection with the agreement on railway concessions finally reached in September of 1914. In fact, in 1913 the Russians objected to the project of building the Kiakhta-Urga railway chiefly on the grounds that it would not pay. In view of the very limited foreign trade of Outer Mongolia, Sazonov considered that "the time for such an undertaking has evidently not yet come.[41]

Under these circumstances, Russian policy aimed to prevent the building by private enterprise of a railway from Kiakhta to Urga, as well as from Kalgan to Urga, the latter project having been contemplated by the Chinese for a long time. Russia therefore proposed that the Mongols conclude an agreement to the effect that any railways constructed in Mongolia should link up with the Russian

[38] Miller to Sazonov, tel., April 3/March 21, 1914, *M.O. v E.I.*, Ser. III, Vol. II, doc. no. 148, p. 196.
[39] "Chronicle" on Mongolia, *Vestnik Azii (Asiatic Herald)*, no. 37, 1916, p. 130.
[40] Cf. chap. i, *supra*.
[41] Sazonov to Kokovtsov, letter, Jan. 2, 1914/Dec. 20, 1913, *M.O. v E.I.*, Ser. II, Vol. XX, Part II, doc. no. 989, p. 423.

railway system. According to Sazonov, this proposed agreement would prevent the construction of railways by Chinese or others and leave it to Russia to decide when to take advantage of the concession, meanwhile being able easily to postpone the date "on different pretexts."[42]

With the purpose of obtaining a stipulation amounting to a Russian monopoly of railway construction in Outer Mongolia, Miller warned Sain Noyan Khan that if Mongolia, after all the benefits which Russia had bestowed on her, were to give a concession for a railway from Kalgan to Urga—or in any other direction—to any outsider, Russia would regard such a step as an obviously unfriendly act "against which she would know how to take adequate measures to safeguard her special interests in adjacent Mongolia."[43]

In order to obtain the railway concessions in Outer Mongolia, Russia did not hesitate to grant more favorable terms to the Mongols in their demands for more credit and arms.[44] Indeed, Sazonov urged Sukhomlinov, the War Minister, "not to delay the signing of the arms agreement with Outer Mongolia" nor the dispatch of the arms to the Mongols, in view of the railway negotiation in Urga which was of "very grave importance to us."[45] Russia signed the loan and arms convention in June, 1914,[46] and the railway agreement followed in September.[47]

The railway convention of 1914 reaffirmed that, before the granting of railroad concessions to any one, the Mongolian Government should "by virtue of the relations of close friendship with the neighboring great Russian Nation," consult the Russian Government as to whether the projected railroad was injurious to Russia's "strategic" and "economic" interests (Article V). In addition, by the same provision, the Russians considered the stipulation in Article I that the

[42] Miller to Sazonov, tel. no. 107, April 13/March 31, 1914, *M.O. v E.I.*, Ser. III, Vol. II, doc. no. 216, p. 300.

[43] Miller to Sazonov, dispatch no. 73, March 20/7, 1914, *M.O. v E.I.*, Ser. III, Vol. II, doc. no. 57, p. 55 ff.

[44] *Ibid.*

[45] Sazonov to Sukhomlinov, letter, June 21/8, 1914, *M.O. v E.I.*, Ser. III, Vol. III, p. 381 n. 3.

[46] Sazonov to Miller, tel. no. 1549, July 29/16, 1914, *M.O. v E.I.*, Ser. III, Vol. V, doc. no. 220, p. 209.

[47] Sazonov to Miller, tel. no. 1448, July 19/6, 1914, *M.O. v E.I.*, Ser. III, Vol. IV, doc. no. 282, p. 337; Miller to Sazonov, tel. no. 192, July 21/8, *M.O. v E.I.*, Ser. III, Vol. IV, doc. no. 315, pp. 369-370. Text of the Russo-Mongolian Railway Agreement of Sept. 30, 1914, in MacMurray, *op. cit.*, II, 1178-1179.

Mongolian Government has a "perpetual right" to construct a *useful* railroad with its own means as giving them "a right to intervene in case of the construction of a railway detrimental to Russia's interests, by some other agency than the Mongolian Government." Moreover, the direction of the railway should be deliberated and decided upon jointly by the Russian and the Mongolian governments (Article II). The railroads were to connect with the Russian railroads (Article IV). In short, all future Mongolian railroads were to be placed within the Russian railway system, under Russian control.

In foreign trade as in other fields of economic activity, Russia desired eventually to establish a monopolistic position in Outer Mongolia, and thus to counteract the severe competition of Chinese goods and the somewhat lesser competition of foreign goods assembled in China. In order to impose some restrictions on Chinese and foreign trade in Outer Mongolia, Russia sought the introduction of *likin* (internal customs) charges similar to the internal duties levied in China.[48] During the Kiakhta negotiations of 1915 Russia tried hard to win the Chinese assent to the establishment of the *likin* system in Outer Mongolia, contending that it was an administrative measure which an Autonomous Mongolia was fully entitled to employ as long as equality of rights between Chinese and Mongols was maintained.[49] But while it is true that the Tripartite Agreement established Outer Mongolia's right "to conclude with foreign powers international treaties and agreements respecting all questions of a commercial and industrial character," it should be noted that this stipulation was inserted only in order to satisfy the Mongols and to give Russia a "legal right" to conclude such treaties with the Mongolian Government.

Any move to extend to other governments this 'legal right" to conclude treaties with the Mongolian Government was frowned upon by Russia. For example, when Boloban, an official of the Russian Ministry of Trade and Industry, made the mistake of taking this clause of the tripartite agreement at its face value (much as a colleague of his in the Ministry of Finance had done in a similar case in 1914), he was soon corrected by Sazonov. Boloban was held

[48] Special Journal of Russian Council of Ministers, May 7/April 24, 1914, *M.O. v E.I.*, Ser. III, Vol. II, doc. no. 368, pp. 480-481.

[49] Sazonov to Miller, tel. no. 564, Feb. 12/Jan. 30, 1915, *M.O. v E.I.*, Ser. III, Vol. VII, Part I, doc. no. 183, pp. 244-245.

to be entirely mistaken in viewing the Mongolian Government as in any way capable of concluding trade treaties with other powers; such treaties, on the contrary, would lead not only to the penetration into Mongolia of foreign influences, but also to claims of foreign powers for most-favored-nation treatment—for the same right of trade free of duty there as Russian nationals enjoyed.[50]

As a result of Russian commercial exploitation in Outer Mongolia and of Russian involvement in World War I, Russian export and import trade with Outer Mongolia went into a state of decline. However, Tsarist Russia never gave up her monopolistic designs. On February 3, 1916, a conference of the Far Eastern Section of the Export Chamber was opened in Petrograd under the chairmanship of State Counsellor E. L. Zuboshev, to deal with the restoration of Russian economic influence in Mongolia. It stressed the "necessity of a more active policy on the part of the agents of our [Russian] government in Mongolia, who so far have not demonstrated sufficient energy in fighting for Russian economic interests there."[51]

RUSSIAN POLITICAL INTERFERENCE

In the years between the Mongolian declaration of independence in 1911 and the Russian Revolution in 1917 the Tsarist Government sought by every means to meddle in the affairs of the Mongolian people and to impose on them Russian methods of regulation and control. Both the internal and the external affairs of Autonomous Mongolia were subject to the close scrutiny of the Russian foreign minister and his agents. Any activities or situations which did not conform with the Russian conception of friendly Russian-Mongolian relations were immediately altered.

One example of the Russian intervention was shown in the efforts of the Mongol leaders to integrate the various Mongol peoples of Inner Mongolia, Barga, Urianghai, and Outer Mongolia into a single political unit, that is, to achieve a Mongol State that would permit external independence as well as "internal autonomy." Since a plan for a Greater Mongolia would have presented several compli-

[50] Sazonov to Miller, letter no. 4319, Sept. 27/14, 1915, *M.O. v E.I.*, Ser. III, Vol. VIII, Part II, doc. no. 796, pp. 379-381.

[51] "Chronicle" on Mongolia, *Vestnik Azii (Asiatic Herald)*, no. 37, 1916, pp. 124-125.

cations for Russian foreign policy, the Tsarist Government immediately took steps to prevent such a concert of potential power. Korostovets was instructed to oppose vigorously all such schemes[52] at the same time that he was required to gain the good will of the Mongol princes and obtain a number of trading rights and privileges for Russian subjects.

Russia's objection to an independent Greater Mongolia was derived chiefly from her desire at this time to preserve the status quo in the international scene. A complete separation of such a vast area from the territory of China would have been interpreted as nothing less than a Russian violation of the territorial integrity of China; as a result, international pressure would have been brought to bear on Russia. As it was, her policy for the gradual control of Central Asia was already suspect, and her various activities in the direction of Mongolia were not without observers.

Certainly Sazonov, in his speech of April, 1913, left no doubts about Russia's refusal to sanction a union among the Mongol tribes.[53] He gave as reasons for this categorical refusal only the disparity of the tribes and the immense obstacles to political unity. But it is more likely that he was thinking of the reaction of Japan, to whom such a union would have meant a breach of the Russo-Japanese secret agreement of 1912, in which their respective spheres of influence had been outlined.

Since Russia's interest in an autonomous Mongolian state was limited to the expansion of Russian political control and Russian trade privileges, it was to her advantage and profit to limit the range of activity of the new Mongolian state. For in the final analysis, a large independent unit might begin to withhold co-operation and perhaps even to take matters into its own hands by appealing to the other powers.

In achieving an autonomous status for Outer Mongolia the Mongol leaders had had hopes of establishing diplomatic relations with her neighbors, but in this area also the Russian Government saw fit to raise vigorous objections. When Sain Noyan Khan, the Mongolian Prime Minister, learned of the Russo-Chinese protocol on his

---

[52] Sazonov's Duma speech in April, 1913, cited in Grumm-Grzhimailo, *Zapadnaia Mongoliia i Uriangkhaiskii Krai* (*Western Mongolia and the Urianghai Region*), II, 746-747.
[53] *Ibid.*

arrival in St. Petersburg, he sent notes of protest to all the diplomatic representatives in the capital, including the Chinese minister, and sought interviews with them. Sazonov thereupon spared no time in pointing out to him the impossibility of Mongolia's obtaining recognition of her independence by the other powers.

Then again when Sain Noyan Khan, on the eve of his departure, thought to leave behind in St. Petersburg a substitute (Tserendorchzhi), who would be "in charge of his seal and in permanent telegraphic connection with the Urga Government," he was told that this attempt to establish a permanent diplomatic representation of the Mongolian Government in St. Petersburg was not desirable in Russia's view.[54]   Thus, by refusing to have official relations with his substitute, the Russian Foreign Office at one stroke destroyed all possibility of personal contact between the Mongols and the foreign legations.

In the matter of Mongolia's internal affairs and governmental organization, also, Russia did not hesitate to impose her will.   Russian agents, the staff of the Russian consulate general in Urga, and the Russian financial adviser urged reform and reorganization in various spheres.   The decrees of the Hutukhtu concerning compulsory land cultivation betray considerable Russian influence.   Similarly, internal reforms grew out of the Russian geographical and statistical surveys of Outer Mongolia begun by Baron P. A. Witte in 1915-16 in an effort to find new sources of state income.   Witte was able to make good use of these studies when, in 1916, he became head of the newly created Special Administration of State Properties, through which a veritable era of reform was instituted.

These internal reforms were by no means accepted without opposition within the country.   In particular, the tax reforms introduced by Witte evoked the anger and opposition of the Lamaist church dignitaries.[55]   Prior to these reforms, the 125,000 *shabinar*, or serfs belonging to monasteries, had been considered the direct personal subjects of the Living Buddha and the church had claimed for them exemption from taxation.   From the Russian point of view, the Church's opposition was considered an act of insubordination to be crushed.   A. Miller, the Russian Consul General at Urga, thought

[54] Sazonov to Miller, confidential letter, Jan. 30/17, 1914, in Popov, "Tsarskaia," *K.A.*, XXXVII, 63-64.

[55] "Mongol'skaia," in *S.S.E.*, III, 529.

the moment opportune for separating the Church from the State and planned a coup d'état with the help of armed force.[56] But the energetic and much feared Miller left Urga that very year, 1916, and the efforts of his successor, Orlov, were frustrated by dissensions among the Russian population in Mongolia which were the direct outcome of the Russian February Revolution.[57]

Before Miller left Urga, he did send the Mongolian Government a note expressing the wish of the Imperial Russian Government that the ecclesiastical personnel in governmental posts be removed from office and replaced with secular employees.

Misunderstandings often occur between the temporal and the ecclesiastical authorities. These frictions not only hinder the decision of important and urgent problems, but also spoil the relationship between the two peoples. Therefore, the Russian Government asked the Mongolian Government to dismiss the clergymen occupying high offices and to replace them with secular persons. Notifying you on behalf of my government, I asked the Mongolian Government to report this matter to the Ruler of Autonomous Mongolia, Bogdo Cheptsum Damba Hutukhtu Khan, and report the subsequent action to me.[58]

This intervention was but the insult added to the earlier injury sustained in 1913, when *Shine-Tole,* a Mongolian language magazine published by the Russian consulate general, printed an incendiary article criticizing the self-seeking policies and the greed of the Mongolian ministers and dignitaries.[59] All these activities did not serve to decrease or alleviate the growing sensitivity of the Mongolians to Russian interference in their affairs.

A third area in which Russia maintained a check on the Mongolians was in their relations with China. In 1914 Hulunbuir (Barga), a part of the Chinese province of Heilungkiang, expressed a desire for an autonomous internal administration under the suzerainty of China.[60] When Russia saw in the situation a means of

---

[56] Report of Russian diplomatic agent in Mongolia to Russian Mission in Peking of April 12, 1919, as cited in Gerard M. Friters, *Outer Mongolia and Its International Position* (Baltimore, 1949), pp. 111-112 n. 222.

[57] *Ibid.,* p. 112.

[58] "Chronicle on Mongolia," *Vestnik Azii (Asiatic Herald),* nos. 38-39, 1916, p. 202.

[59] "Pis'ma iz Mongolii" ("Letters from Mongolia"), *Vestnik Azii (Asiatic Herald),* no. 37, 1916, p. 127.

[60] Cf. p. 85, *supra.*

exerting pressure on the Chinese Government in connection with the tripartite negotiations, Krupenskii, Russian minister in Peking, was instructed to declare to the Chinese that Russia would not permit any decision on the destiny of Barga without her knowledge and collaboration and would recognize no agreement made directly between the Chinese Government and the Barga authorities.[61]

With the signing of the tripartite agreement in June, 1915, Tsarist Russia had actually won consent to the regulation of Mongolia's relations with China.   In political and territorial questions between these two, Russia was to act as mediator.   The *likin* tax established between China and Mongolia was not applicable to Russia, whose goods entered Mongolia free of tax, and the Mongolian National Bank was Russian-controlled.   The fact that Russia would not tolerate agreements detrimental to her interests limited the right of the Mongolian Government to conclude commercial agreements.   Politically, Mongolia was required to address herself first to Russia.   Thus did Russia step between the Chinese and the Mongols to prevent their coming to an understanding, whether political, economic, or military.

Finally, in the ceremonial exchange between Mongolia and China, Russia saw fit to intervene and assert her influence.   Shortly after the signing of the tripartite agreement, Amban Cheng Lo informed the Mongolian Government that the President of China was prepared to invest the Living Buddha with his official golden seal and the diploma of merit.   This right to confer the title of Bogdo Chebutsum Damba Hutukhtu Khan of Outer Mongolia on the Urga Living Buddha belonged by agreement to the President of China, yet when China proceeded to her duty, Russia objected.

In June, 1915, Sazonov instructed Krupenskii that the investiture should not "take the character" of the normal ceremonies for the foreign rulers dependent on China.   Russia could not tolerate the "return of the times when Mongolia was joined to China," or the neglect of the "position which Russia had tried to obtain for herself."[62]

Whether or not he was influenced by the Russian protest, the

[61] Krupenskii to Sazonov, tel. no. 32, Feb. 6/Jan. 24, 1914, *M.O. v E.I.*, Ser. III, Vol. I, doc. no. 191, pp. 232-233.

[62] Tel. of the Foreign Minister, no. 6038, Dec. 30, 1915, as cited in Gladstern, *op. cit.*, p. 167.

Urga Hutukhtu did in any case refuse to accept the seal. He avowed he would not kowtow or kneel and knock his forehead on the ground in homage to the seal, or to the Chinese officials who were to conduct the ceremony. As the head of the dominant religion of Mongolia, he did not wish to degrade himself by kneeling before secular and mortal Chinese. Such an act would violate the doctrine of Buddha. Therefore he said, "In the future I shall categorically refuse to accept all rewards, since I have no need of them at all."[63]

Even the right of the Chinese amban to a private audience with the Hutukhtu was curtailed by the Russians. On October 10, 1916, when Amban Ch'en Lo went to the Urga palace on appointment, he was told, falsely, that the Living Buddha had gone to the "Maidari" temple. On the twenty-sixth day of that same month when he requested an audience, he was reluctantly granted a brief one, which proved in fact, to be merely a social call.[64]

Russian imperialistic aspirations in Outer Mongolia[65] are clearly traceable in a vivid description written as early as 1913. The author of *Mongolia and Its Contemporary Importance to Russia*, Tomilin, who was closely connected with the War Department, phrased it in the following manner:

In its own interests, commercial and military, Russia must deprive China of any opportunity to move close to our boundaries and to establish itself thereat. This can be done by consolidating the independence of Mongolia from China. Along with a move so uniquely advantageous to us the question inevitably arises: Is Mongolia able to maintain its own independence? . . . The only answer is: No . . . China is too big and Mongolia too small and helpless. Both by open force and economic tactics China can destroy the recently constituted state of nomads. There is no other solution to the Mongolian problem, but the fulfilment of their fervent hopes for the incorporation of Mongolia with Russia forever. Therewith we shall achieve every possible thing: we shall rescue the Mongolian people from a sure destruction under the pressure of China; we shall find faithful subjects in the acquired population, fit for military service, and loving us, who will become our combat vanguards; we shall

[63] "Chronicle" on Mongolia, in *Vestnik Azii* (*Asiatic Herald*), no. 37, 1916, p. 127.

[64] *Ibid.*, pp. 127-128.

[65] Shoizhelov, "Avtonomnoe Dvizhenie Mongolii i Tsarskaia Rossiia" ("Autonomous Movement of Mongolia and Tsarist Russia"), *Novyi Vostok* (*The New East*), nos. 13-14, 1926, p. 361.

fulfil our historical task of uniting the Mongolian peoples whose millions are already distributed among us; we shall have a rich region with fertile land, which is also suitable for our settlers; we shall obtain an extensive market for selling our goods and produce; we shall open a source abundant with raw materials not only for Siberia, but for European Russia as well; we shall draw nearer to China and facilitate the sale of our own products there; we shall seize a wide, impassible belt in the desert in central Mongolia which will firmly guarantee us from Asiatic invasion. All these are immeasurable advantages.[66]

To indicate the extent to which Mongolian affairs were being taken over and controlled by Russia is to outline the steps Russia took in the gradual annexation of Outer Mongolia. Had it not been for the intervention of the Russian Revolution, one can imagine how far Russia might have gone. At it was, Kushelev was able to claim, "Now, Mongolia does not move a single step without turning her eyes to her great neighbor, recognized by her as her unique friend, brother, and protector."[67]

[66] V. Tomilin, *Mongoliia i Ee Sovremennoe Znachenie dlia Rossii* (*Mongolia and Her Contemporary Importance for Russia*) (Moscow, 1913), pp. 17-18.

[67] "Chronicle" on Mongolia, in *Vestnik Azii* (*Asiatic Herald*), nos. 38-39, 1916, p. 202.

XII: THE RUSSIAN REVOLUTION AND OUTER MONGOLIAN ORIENTATION

CANCELLATION OF OUTER MONGOLIAN AUTONOMY

As soon as the Russian Revolution broke out in 1917, the Tsarist Government's hold on Outer Mongolia was naturally weakened. During the Kerensky regime, Russia was powerless to direct her attention to matters in Mongolia. But two new factors loomed large in the Outer Mongolian picture: the White Russian movements and the intercession of Japan.

A White Russian, Semenov, who owed his allegiance to the Tsar and also claimed to have Mongolian blood in his veins, determined to take up the unfinished business upon his own responsibility. He planned to establish a Pan-Mongolian state, consisting of Inner and Outer Mongolias, Hulunbuir, Tibet, and other districts where the Mongolian dialects were spoken, with Hailar designated as the seat of the projected government. Accordingly, two conferences were called by him in 1919, at which some self-appointed representatives of the above-mentioned districts were present.

Japan, meanwhile, was not slow to see her opportunity. In 1918 she began invading Siberia under the pretext of supporting the Allied intervention there. In line with this move, Japanese agents suddenly appeared at Urga, bent upon cajoling the Hutukhtu to join Semenov's party.[1] Their arguments, however, proved futile.

These surrounding dangers were already enough to arouse Mongol fears. Yet, simultaneously, internal unrest was growing in proportion. Prior to their declaration of autonomy, the Mongols had to contribute only a limited amount of money to the revenue

---

[1] Cf. *Conference on the Limitation of Armaments* (official bulletins published in the Washington Conference), 24th meeting, p. 1394 and especially a "concise statement" read by Baron Shidehara, the Japanese delegate, p. 1398.

of the Hutukhtu.   But under the autonomous government, levies had become quite burdensome.   The Russian Revolution made it necessary for the government to prepare for any possible exigencies, which meant additional hardships for the Mongol tribes.   And now that Russian protection, however onerous, was no longer to be counted on, the Mongols felt the danger of isolation and of being exposed to foreign aggression—from Japan on the east, the Red Russians on the north, and the Chinese irredentists on the south.   To add to the internal unrest, the Russian currency which for many years had been widely used as the medium of exchange, was now "not worth a Continental."

Seeing that the situation was ripe for outside intervention, the Chinese swung into action.   According to the tripartite agreement of 1915, Chinese troops, as well as Russian troops, could not be stationed in Outer Mongolia.   Now, however, Outer Mongolia was compelled to seek Chinese aid.   In June, 1918, China was asked to send a battalion of troops, or more if necessary, into Outer Mongolia to strengthen its defense; these troops were to be withdrawn as soon as the situation could be stabilized.   By March, 1919, a battalion (actually two battalions) of Chinese cavalry was already drilling at Urga.   Its presence led the Russian minister at Peking to lodge a protest on April 3, to which the Chinese Government merely replied:

The internal chaos of Russia has not yet been wiped out.   Troops of many countries are still in Russian territory.   Why did the Russian Government not lodge protests to all those countries?   Moreover, inasmuch as Outer Mongolia is an integral part of Chinese territory, China cannot remain indifferent to the maintenance of order in that region.   The Chinese Government, when required by the conditions in Outer Mongolia to send troops there for the purpose of maintaining order, is taking a justifiable measure . . . . Therefore, the Russian protest sounds only too out of place.[2]

Early in February, 1919, the Chinese Government instructed the High Commissioner at Urga to initiate negotiations with the Outer Mongolian Government with a view to concluding a new treaty in place of the tripartite agreement.   If such a new treaty could be signed in time, it might be advantageously used as a legal excuse to keep the Russians out and as a bargaining tool in the later negotia-

---

[2] Chang Chung-fu, *Chung-Hua-Min-Kuo Wai-chiai Shih* (*A Diplomatic History of the Chinese Republic*), I, 360 n. 48.

tions over the recognition of a new Russian Government. The gist of the instructions was as follows:

The new treaty should be negotiated on a basis of the transfer to us [China] of all of the rights and interests which Russia has acquired under the Russo-Mongolian Protocol of 1912. Besides . . . there should be no restriction upon the stationing of Chinese troops in Outer Mongolia. . . . The purpose is to eliminate Russian influence on the one hand, and to strengthen the solidarity between us and the Mongols on the other.[3]

The efforts of the Chinese commissioner met with favorable response from the Mongols. In a conference of the princes and the lamas, it was decided that Semenov's suggestion of resuming independence should be rejected, and that China's aid should be solicited. The princes favored outright cancellation of autonomy, while the lamas wanted to preserve it. In August, 1919, the princes expressed their desire *sub rosa* to the High Commissioner and asked for substantial aid from the Chinese Government to ward off possible Russian intervention and to iron out the internal difficulties among the Mongols themselves. Up to this point the Russians were unaware of the intrigue being carried out against them.

The Peking Government saw no objection to meeting these requests, and official endorsement was granted accordingly. At the same time the Hutukhtu, persuaded by his princes, also accepted the proposed cancellation. Thus, a protocol consisting of sixty-three articles was initiated and sent to Peking for sanction.[4] In this agreement fair treatment and considerable latitude in the management of their own affairs were promised to the Mongols by the High Commissioner.

Thus far, Mongolian-Chinese relations were going smoothly; under the friendly and tactful negotiations of the Chinese Resident Minister, Chen I, the leading Mongol princes and lamas, as noted above, were giving favorable consideration to a termination of their autonomy. But unpleasant things were in store, for at this juncture, unfortunately, there arrived on the scene an ambitious but unruly protégé of the then Premier Tuan Ch'i-jui, one General Hsü Shu-tseng, better known as "Little Hsu." During Tuan's premiership, just prior to his election as President of the Republic, Hsü Shih Ch'ang served as Vice Minister of the War Office, also headed by Tuan as Minister. Sometime during this period—the details are not readily available—Hsü submitted to the government, at Tuan's suggestion, a program for frontier pacification. Hsü was thereupon appointed Defense Commissioner for the Northwestern frontier on June 13, 1919; on June 24 he was made concurrently Commander-in-Chief of the Northwestern Defense Force.[5] In this new capacity he lost no time in sending reinforcements to Urga, so that by autumn the Chinese forces stationed there had grown to approximately four thousand men.[6] He also petitioned the government for a free hand in dealing with the situation in Mongolia; this granted, he soon made himself virtually the "uncrowned king" of Mongolia,[7] to the sorrow of the Mongolian people and the lasting detriment of the Chinese influence there.

Toward the end of October, 1919, General Hsü arrived in Urga, ostensibly to inspect the Chinese garrisons there as part of his official duties, but secretly determined to take Chinese-Mongol relations into his own hands. At this time Resident Chen I had just received instructions from Premier Chin Yün-p'eng of the Peking Government, informing him that General Hsü had been sent to Outer Mongolia in a military capacity to inspect troops only. Negotiations with the Mongols on the cancellation of autonomy were to remain the charge of the Resident. Chen therefore decided not to disclose to Hsü the secret conditions agreed upon with the Mongols. Hsü, however, before his departure from Peking, had secured a copy of the document concerned and had announced his own view that the conditions should be simple and to the point. Though Peking had instructed him to consult Chen on whatever modifications he deemed necessary, Hsü chose not to discuss his views with the Resident.

[5] Tuan Ch'i-jui, "Lu-Chün Shang-chiang Yüan-Wei-Chiang-Chün Hsü-chün Shen-tao-pei" ("Monument at the Grave Avenue of General Hsü Shu-tseng"), *Shih-Hsi-Hsien I-kao (Papers Left by General Hsü Shu-tseng at the Retrospect Study)* (1931), Appendix B, sh. 2; Wang Shu-nan, "Yüan-Wei-Chiang-Chun Hsü Fu-chün Chia-chuan" ("Biography of General Hsü Shu-tseng"), *ibid.*, Appendix A, sh. 2; K'o Shao-wen, "Yüan-Wei-Chiang-Chün Lu-chün Shang-chiang Hsiao-Hsien Hsu-kung Mou-chih-ming," ("The Epitaph of General Hsü Shu-tseng"), *ibid.*, Appendix C, sh. 1.

[6] *C.Y.B. 1921-22*, p. 576.

[7] Weigh, *Russo-Chinese Diplomacy*, p. 190.

Thus the relations between the two became extremely strained, and co-operation between them was completely out of the question.[8]

As the arrogant Hsü felt that his colleague Chen I was proceeding too slowly in the negotiations, he directly telegraphed Peking his opposition to the conditions underlying the cancellation of autonomy. Upon meeting Patama, Premier of Outer Mongolia, he suggested to him also that no conditions should be fixed in advance, and that the correct procedure was for the Mongols, led by the Hutukhtu, to file a petition to cancel autonomy. Shortly after his arrival at Urga, he had demanded a private audience with the Hutukhtu, who, possibly on the advice of Chen, took his time in granting the request. While awaiting the Hutukhtu's reply, Hsü visited the leading princes of Outer Mongolia, gave them costly presents, and persuaded them to send in "voluntarily" a petition for the cancellation of their autonomy. This petition required the ratification of the Hutukhtu, but since he was playing for time, he referred the matter to the two Houses of the Mongolian Parliament. Aside from the members of the two Houses who had received gifts from General Hsü, the majority voiced vehement disapproval. After this demonstration, the Hutukhtu received both General Hsü and Resident Chen and relayed the negative decision. During the course of the interview, General Hsü had had his troops lined up in front of the Hutukhtu's palace in a display of armed force. But the Living Buddha was not to be frightened into submission. He refused persistently to give in to Hsü's demand.

Infuriated by the Hutukhtu's determined opposition, General Hsü struck out those clauses in the sixty-three article protocol proposed by Chen I which promised good treatment to the Mongols, retaining only eight articles which were far more severe than those originally presented. In addition, he sent an ultimatum to the Mongolian Premier demanding acceptance of the new terms within thirty-six hours, failing which both the Living Buddha and the Premier would be placed under arrest and escorted to Kalgan.[9] Unwilling to sign the so-called petition, the Hutukhtu referred the question to the Parliament. Great indignation arose from all sides when General Hsü's new terms were made known in the two Houses, and hot debates ensued. A large faction in favor of armed resistance

[8] Chang Chung-fu, *op. cit.*, I, 352.
[9] Chang Chung-fu, *op. cit.*, I, 352.

modified their stand only when they understood the impossibility of opposing Hsü's better-equipped army. After increased pressure and threats from General Hsü, the members of the Parliament were finally forced to have the petition signed by the various ministers and vice-ministers of the government departments. This General Hsü accepted; the lack of the Hutukhtu's signature he explained to his government at Peking with the contention that the Living Buddha never personally signed a document. The Mongol "petition" thus signed on November 16, 1919, reads in part:

It is our hope that the Central Government will organize the system of Government of Outer Mongolia in accordance with the circumstances of various banners and leagues . . . . It is our only desire that the Republic of five races should thrive and its people enjoy peace and prosperity. Since we are willing to renounce autonomy, all these instruments are null and void automatically. As to the commercial enterprises started by the Russians in Outer Mongolia, the Central Government must undertake the responsibility of making the arrangements with the Russians when their new government is established, so as to promote friendship between China and Russia and to protect our interests.[10]

Accordingly, the President of China proclaimed the cancellation of Outer Mongolian autonomy on November 22, 1919. The proclamation said, in part:

Their petition is hereby granted and the desires of the people of Outer Mongolia are hereby complied with. The dignity of the Hutukhtu shall, hereafter, be preserved and the rights and privileges of the chiefs of the Four Leagues respected. The old system prevailing under the late Manchu dynasty is hereby restored, and specially favorable treatment shall be given Outer Mongolia. I, the President, hope that peace and good relations will forever be maintained between the Central Government and Outer Mongolia.[11]

Concurrently with this Presidential proclamation, another order was issued conferring upon the Living Buddha the dignified title of the "Lishan Fuhua Bogdo Chebutsum Damba Hutukhtu Khan of

[10] *Millard's Review*, XI (Dec. 6, 1919), 12-13; Wang Chin-yu, *Hsien-Tai Wai-Mong Chi Kai-Kwan* (*An Outline of Contemporary Outer Mongolia*) (Shanghai, 1935), pp. 64-65.
[11] *Millard's Review*, XI, 13; Chang Chung-fu, *op. cit.*, I, 353-354; Kao Po-yen, *Meng-Ku yü Chung-Kuo* (*Mongolia and China*) (Tientsin, 1927), pp. 130-132; Ch'en Ch'ung-tsu, *Wai-Meng-Ku Ching-shih-shih* (*A Modern History of Outer Mongolia*) (Shanghai, 1922), Part III, pp. 5-7.

Outer Mongolia." The ceremony for conferring the title was scheduled for New Year's Day of 1920, in Urga.[12] In January, 1920, the region of Hulunbuir (Barga) sent in a similar petition requesting cancellation of the autonomy granted it by the Sino-Russian protocol on Hulunbuir in 1915.[13]

The Chinese proclamation of the cancellation of Outer Mongolian autonomy aroused immediate Russian reaction and protests. Minister Kudachev, then still recognized by the Chinese, sent a complaint to the Chinese Government. But since the Tsarist regime was already overthrown and all of Russia was in turmoil, the Russian protests, however strongly worded, received scant attention from China.[14]

In this manner, the autonomous regime of Outer Mongolia was canceled "voluntarily." This vast area, once an outlying tributary of the Chinese Empire, henceforth was again to be at the disposal of the Peking Government.

Judging from the immediate gains, General Hsü's move was for China a most successful stroke of opportunism. But the aftereffects of his coercion proved that it was indeed a most regrettable mistake for China. First of all, the cancellation of autonomy had already been desired and proposed by the Mongols and a settlement by means of diplomacy, with satisfaction to both parties, was already at the point of accomplishment. If the Chinese authorities had properly exploited the situation, as had the Russians before them, the result would have been a master stroke indeed. To substitute force for diplomacy at this time only made bitter foes of potential friends and suggested that the Chinese, too, were resorting to the measures of imperialism from which, both before and after this date, they suffered and therefore condemned on the part of others.

Secondly, this unwise action reawakened in the Mongols a strong distrust of China which could not thereafter be dispelled. As a result, the Mongols felt they had no other course but to turn for help to Semenov, from whom they had previously been so anxious to keep aloof. If the Chinese Government had had more

---

[12] Ch'en Ch'ung-tsu, *op. cit.*, Part III, pp. 7-8, 11-12; Chang Chung-fu, *op. cit.*, I, 354-355; *C.Y.B.*, *1921-22*, p. 578.

[13] Tsou & Chu (eds.), *Hu-Lun-Pei-Erh Kai-yao* (*An Outline of Hulunbuir*), pp. 64-67; Ch'en Ch'ung-tsu, *op. cit.*, Part III, pp. 8-9; Kao, *Meng-Ku-yü Chung-Kuo* (*Mongolia and China*), p. 133.

[14] *C.Y.B.*, *1921-22*, p. 759; Ch'en Ch'ung-tsu, *op. cit.*, Part III, pp. 7-8.

respect for the dignity of the Mongols and had tried to secure their whole-hearted co-operation, it would have been well-nigh impossible for Semenov to succeed in his invasion of Outer Mongolia. Thus the actions of General Hsü, in the eyes of the Chinese, could only be regarded in retrospect as a major crime against his own country as well as against Mongolian-Chinese friendship.

The day after he had compelled the Outer Mongolian leaders to sign the petition, General Hsü set out with it for Peking,[15] stopping at his headquarters at Kalgan en route. Before returning to Peking he issued orders placing Resident Chen I and his staff under house arrest, lest they intrigue against him in his absence. Upon his arrival in Peking, Hsü urged the government to cancel the position of the Resident and withdraw Chen I altogether from Urga. He suggested also that an official be given full charge of rehabilitation affairs in Outer Mongolia. To this the Government consented. On December 1, 1919, General Hsü, instead of being censured, was appointed High Commissioner for Northwestern Frontier Defense concurrently in charge of the rehabilitation and pacification of Outer Mongolia. Chen I was then ordered back to Peking. Thereafter, all important posts in Outer Mongolia were filled by General Hsü's men. On December 2, 1919, General Hsü became Special Envoy with the privilege of conferring titles on the Living Buddha.[16]

Though General Hsü's rule in Urga was not of long duration, he did not lose time "strengthening" Chinese "influence" at the expense of Mongolian friendship and at the risk of Mongolian hostility. His high-handed methods ran completely counter to the program he outlined in a treatise two years later.[17] He disarmed the unresisting Mongol forces and his troops occupied the former Mongolian ministries. The offices of the former autonomous government were then merged with the office of the high commissioner. The latter became a ponderous structure of eight departments: general administration, finance, commerce, post, agriculture and husbandry, forest and mines, education and religion, and defense.[18] Then, in an

---

[15] The Mongol petition was signed in duplicate, one presented to Resident Chen I and the other to General Hsü. Cf. Chang Chung-fu, *op. cit.*, I, 352-353.

[16] Ch'en Ch'ung tsu, *op. cit.*, Part III, pp. 10-12; Chang Chung-fu, *op. cit.*, I, 355.

[17] Hsü Shu-tseng, *Chien-kuo Ch'üan-cheng* (*Notes on National Reconstruction*) (1921), sh. 107-111.

[18] Ch'en Ch'ung-tsu, *op. cit.*, Part III, pp. 12-14.

imposing proclamation in the Mongolian language, General Hsü admonished the Mongol people to propagate their Yellow Religion faithfully, to increase their population, to develop their industries and commerce, and to educate themselves and their children, as the only means to strengthen their country.[19]

During his brief incumbency, General Hsü instituted a number of bold measures. In regard to military measures, he sent three battalions of Chinese troops to garrison the border posts against the possibility of an invasion by White Russian forces. The burden of provisioning the greater part of the Chinese forces, however, was placed upon the Mongols. In the field of economic development, a Frontier Development Bank, with a capital of $10,000,000 was established, with its head office at Peking and a branch office at Urga. Use of Russian currency was outlawed. But, finding the meager income extracted from the Mongols insufficient for his grandiose plans, General Hsü, in direct contradiction to his announced program of pacification and industrial development, in effect mortgaged the mining and agricultural resources of Mongolia to secure a loan of fifteen million dollars from the Sino-Japanese Exchange Bank. Later he was said to have secured another loan of twenty million dollars from the Japanese, allegedly to construct a railway connecting Kalgan and Urga.

Shortly after taking over the Mongolian offices and instituting these measures, General Hsü returned to Peking, leaving the task of pacification and rehabilitation of Outer Mongolia to his deputy at Urga, Li Yüan. But his conduct in Mongolia was a principal factor contributing to a general revulsion of public opinion in China against the Anfu Club, of which General Hsü was a prominent member.[20] Before long, the Anfu Club was overthrown and Wu P'ei-fu took over the reins of government. The liquidation of Hsü's sorry policy in Outer Mongolia began forthwith. On July 4, 1920, General Hsü was removed from office, being replaced as acting commander by his deputy, Li. Three weeks later the offices of Commissioner of Frontier Defense and of Commander of Defense Forces, both controlled originally by General Hsü, were officially abolished. Finally, on August 15, 1920, the Peking Government designated the former Resident, Chen I, as High Commissioner for Urga, Uliassutai,

[19] *Millard's Review*, XI (Jan. 31, 1920), 412-413.
[20] Ch'en Ch'ung-tsu, *op. cit.*, Part III, p. 26; Weigh, *op. cit.*, pp. 197-198.

Kobdo, and Tannu Urianghai (Tannu Tuva) with jurisdiction over civil and military affairs, and with residence in Urga.

But it was too late. Although Chen I had maintained friendly relations with the Mongols, the hearts of the Mongols were now lost to the Chinese people as a result of the disgraceful and inhuman practices of General Hsü, who, in order to make up for funds owed his troops, had allowed them to kill and plunder the local population. The end of Chinese rule and influence in Outer Mongolia was quick in coming, hastened by local disaffection and outside intervention in the form of two White Russian drives on Urga led by Baron Ungern-Sternberg, an aide of Semenov.

The first attack on the Mongolian capital came in October, 1920, before Chen I had arrived at his post. The assault was repulsed, but the Chinese forces made the mistake of holding the Hutukhtu in captivity on the suspicion that he might communicate with Ugern. They thus committed an unprecedented sacrilege in Mongol eyes. Ungern's second attack caught Chen I before his defense preparations could be completed; Urga fell to the White Russians on February 1, 1921, and the Chinese forces were reported to have been completely annihilated.[21] The short-lived Chinese rule in Outer Mongolia had brought only ill for the Mongolian people.

THE WHITE RUSSIANS AND THE INDEPENDENT GOVERNMENT OF OUTER MONGOLIA

For about a year, then, Baron Ungern-Sternberg, a White Russian and a lieutenant of Semenov, became the central figure on the Mongolian scene. This man, half Magyar, half Russian, was married to a Manchurian princess, and was deeply versed in Buddhist mysticism. He sought to establish a Buddhist empire embracing Mongolia and Tibet, with the Hutukhtu as the titular head and himself as the actual ruler of the state. He and his band, pressed by the Reds, filtered into Outer Mongolia in August, 1920, and launched an attack on Urga in October.[22]

[21] Ch'en Ch'ung-tsu, *op. cit.*, Part III, pp. 33, 45-46, 47-56; Weigh, *op. cit.*, pp. 198-199. Disagreement was reported between Brigadier Commander Ch'u Ch'i-Ch'iang and Regimental Commander Kao Tsai-t'ien, the only high field commanders then in Outer Mongolia; Kao, *op. cit.*, pp. 135-139.

[22] A. E. Khodorov, "Mongolia and its Claimants," *The Living Age*, CCCXIV (Aug. 5, 1922), 337.

The vigilant Chinese garrisons succeeded in repulsing the invaders, but they did not stop there. The Hutukhtu and several princes were put under custody on the charge of disloyalty toward the Republic. The confinement of the Hutukhtu was regarded as an unprecedented sacrilege in the eyes of the Mongols; hostile sentiments ran high and a revolt seemed imminent. Mongol discontent was raised to an even higher pitch when the Chinese troops availed themselves of this opportunity to plunder the foreign population of Urga, including about two thousand Russians, many of whom were imprisoned, ill-treated, and even shot.

In spite of such internal instability, the Chinese grip on the Mongolian situation would not have been lost so easily, as it turned out later, if the Peking Government had applied itself to the task of strengthening the frontier defense. But several things went wrong. An appropriation of $500,000 was made to Marshal Chang Tso-lin, who pocketed the sum and did not send out any reinforcements. As had been anticipated, the mad Baron came back in February, 1921, with five thousand Russian, Mongolian, Buriat, and Japanese soldiers, and routed the handful of Chinese soldiers. Before the Chinese reinforcements could arrive, Urga had fallen into Ungern's hands.

Immediately after the fall of Urga, an "Independent Government of Outer Mongolia" was set up on March 21, with the Hutukhtu as the puppet ruler, and Ungern, who had declared himself a Mongolian subject, as his supreme military adviser and, needless to say, as the real dictator. His authority was shortly extended to other parts of Outer Mongolia, when the towns of Kobdo, Uliassutai, and Wang-Kuren were captured by local Russian White Guards.[23] A reign of blackest terror existed. A cruel purge was conducted among the Mongols, the Chinese, the Jews and even his own followers.[24] In May, 1921, on the occasion of the triumphant coronation of the Hutukhtu, he launched a fantastic appeal, full of quotations from the Apocalypse and the Lamaist scriptures, for a punitive expedition against the Red Russians. Soon he was marching northward toward Kiakhta.[25]

---

[23] *C.Y.B.*, *1923*, p. 675.
[24] F. Ossendowski, "With Baron Ungern at Urga," *Asia*, XXII (Aug., 1922), 614-618.
[25] *C.Y.B.*, *1923*, p. 676.

Meanwhile, under the auspices of the Red Russians, a People's Revolutionary Party of Mongolia had been organized in 1918 in Trans-Baikalia, Siberia,[26] and on March 13, 1921, a Provisional People's Revolutionary Government of Mongolia was proclaimed by the party at Kiakhta. This provisional government immediately solicited the intervention of the Russian communists. The request was readily honored. A joint military expedition organized by Soviet Russia and the Far Eastern Republic then swept into Mongolia and in May defeated Ungern's men in an encounter in the vicinity of Kiakhta. Ungern was captured alive. Later, according to the sentence passed by the Extraordinary Siberian Revolutionary Tribunal, the baron was executed.[27] The Red forces marched into Urga in July, 1921. On July 12, the Independent Government of Mongolia was officially dissolved, and its functions taken over by the Provisional People's Revolutionary Government.

At the end of July, 1921, the new government sent a request to Russia that the Red army remain in Mongolia so as to preserve the "security of the territory of Mongolia and of the frontier of the R.S.E.S.R.," until "the complete removal of the menace from the common enemy." Such a request was naturally granted.[28] So, during the short period of one year and a half, the Chinese had come and gone; the White Russians had come and gone; the Japanese were abiding by their hands-off policy; and the Soviet Russians had come to stay in Outer Mongolia.

[26] Alfred L. P. Dennis, *The Foreign Policy of Soviet Russia* (New York, 1924), p. 322; Tennyson Tan, *The Political Status of Mongolia*, p. 66; *C.Y.B.*, *1923*, p. 675.

[27] P. Ogin, *Mongol'skaia Narodnaia Respublika* (*Mongolian People's Republic*) (Moscow, 1939), pp. 22.

[28] Pasvolsky, *Russia in the Far East*, p. 176; Paul S. Reinsch, "Manchuria, Mongolia, and Siberia," *The Nation*, CXIV, May 3, 1922, 525.

XIII: OUTER MONGOLIA UNDER
SOVIET CONTROL AFTER 1921

SOVIET MILITARY OCCUPATION AND THE MONGOLIAN
PEOPLE'S GOVERNMENT

Commenting upon Soviet policy in Outer Mongolia, Pasvolsky wrote: "Though the details differ, the basic lines of Imperial [Russian] and of Soviet diplomacy in this particular instance coincide most remarkably."[1] Each created a Mongolian "government" based on force of arms, and thus controlled all phases of life in Outer Mongolia. Friters went further and pointed out that "the 'imperialistic genius' of Soviet Russia, a phrase against which I. Maiskii, Soviet Ambassador in London, protested in a speech in the summer of 1936, has certainly shown a greater ability in the treatment of the Mongols than Tsarist Russia."[2] More than a decade before, Friters had been able to observe that "Soviet Imperialism has achieved a disguised annexation of Mongolia."[3]

The entry of Soviet armed forces into Outer Mongolia and the subsequent occupation of the region were clearly in tune with the Soviet-sponsored Mongolian People's Revolutionary Party and government. To illustrate how the Mongolian incident of 1921 was the direct consequence of a well-planned Soviet strategy, a "policy of coordination of activities," Pasvolsky wrote:

There was a special reason, too, for the formation of such a [Mongolian People's Revolutionary] party. The Soviet technique of promoting revolutions in territories bordering on Russia consists of bringing into life in

[1] Leo Pasvolsky, "The Ways of Soviet Diplomacy," *The Independent*, Vol. CVIII, no. 3807, March 4, 1922, p. 213.
[2] Gerard M. Friters, *The International Position of Outer Mongolia* (Dijon, 1939), p. 111.
[3] Carlo Sforza, "Imperialistic Russia in China," *Foreign Affairs*, Vol. VI, no. 1, Oct. 1927, p. 69.

such a territory a Communist group, however small and insignificant; of inducing such a group to proclaim itself the provisional revolutionary government of the territory in question and to appeal to Moscow for military assistance, which would be immediately furnished. This was the program gone through in the Caucasus and elsewhere. And this was precisely the plan worked out for Mongolia.[4]

The Soviet plan of penetration into Outer Mongolia took definite form as early as August, 1919, at the beginning of a decisive offensive in the Civil War against the White forces in Siberia.[5] The Soviet Government had then sent a special appeal to the Mongolian people which read:

As soon as Russian workers and peasants took over the government from Tsarist generals, gendarmes, and capitalists on October 25, 1917, they immediately addressed the workers of the world, proposing to establish an order in which no one big and powerful state would be allowed to incorporate by force, or to hold within its boundaries, small and powerless nations. At the same time, the government of workers and peasants canceled all secret pacts with Japan and China, by means of which the former Tsarist Government wrested Mongolia from China under a pretext of Mongolian autonomy, supposedly in the interests of the Mongolian people, in order to establish its own representative in Urga, exhaust the Mongolian people's wealth, and betray those people to Russian merchants and exploiters of the masses . . . . The Russian people do not endorse the pacts negotiated with the Japanese and Chinese governments which concerned Mongolia, as she is a free country. Russian advisers, Tsarist consuls, bankers, and the rich, who keep the Mongolian people in bondage by force and by bribery and totally exploit them, must be driven from Mongolia. All authority and all courts of Justice ought to be controlled by the Mongolian people. No foreigner may interfere with the internal affairs of Mongolia. Contrary to the stipulations of 1913, Mongolia, as a free country, is entitled to direct relations with all other nations without any tutelage on the part of Peking or Petrograd. The Soviet Government, publicly making this known to the Mongolian people, invites them to open diplomatic relations with the Russian people at once and to send the envoys of the free Mongolian people to welcome the Red armed forces.[6]

[4] Pasvolsky, *Russia in the Far East,* pp. 114-115.

[5] Perlin, *Mongol'skaia Narodnaia Respublika* (*The Mongolian People's Republic*), p. 19; Shoizhelov, "Avtonomnoe Dvizhenie Mongolii i Tsarskaia Rossiia" ("The Autonomous Movement of Mongolia and Tsarist Russia"), *Novyi Vostok* (*The New East*), nos. 13-14, 1926, p. 362.

[6] Text in V. D. Vilenskii (Sibiriakov), *Sovremennaia Mongoliia* (*Contemporary Mongolia*) (Moscow, 1925), pp. 52-53; Shoizhelov, "Avtonomnoe Dvizhenie Mon-

In November, 1920, the Soviet regime defeated the various White armies and consolidated its rule over most of the territories of the former Tsarist Empire. On November 11, 1920, Chicherin sent a note to China with the reassurance that Russian military units would appear in Chinese territory as "friendly troops who would consider their task fulfilled after the final destruction of White Guardist bands in Mongolia and the restoration of Chinese sovereignty, and would then immediately leave Chinese territory."[7] On December 31, 1920, the Peking government, in a note delivered to the Soviet representative, Krassin, through the Chinese ambassador in London, told the story of the first Soviet attempt to send troops into Outer Mongolia:

> In his telegram of November 10, the Russian Commissar of Foreign Affairs stated that the Soviet Government, upon the request of the Chinese authorities in Urga, ordered the Siberian Command to dispatch troops to Mongolia in order to assist in the liquidation of the Semenov bands, whereupon those troops were to return to Russian Soviet territory. On November 27 another telegram stated that, since the Chinese troops had already driven out the Semenov bands, the Soviet Government did not intend any longer to send troops there; however, should the followers of Semenov be found again within the boundaries of Mongolia, and should the Chinese authorities apply to Russia for assistance, such assistance would be given.
>
> We consider it necessary to state that the crossing of the frontiers of one country by the troops of another violates the sovereignty of that country, and that the statement in the first telegram to the effect that we asked for assistance is not true. Though the dispatching of troops did not actually take place, there still remains the offer of military assistance, which we should not accept.[8]

Subsequently, the Red Army actually crossed the frontier into Outer Mongolia. Again, the reason given for the crossing was a "request" for assistance on the part of Chinese authorities, which, in Pasvolsky's opinion, "would seem rather doubtful" in view of China's attitude, explicitly stated in the note quoted above. The ostensible objective of the Soviet expedition was to attack some detachments of anti-Soviet forces in Eastern Siberia which had fled to China and had been interned by the Chinese in the district of Chuguchak. These

golii i Tsarskaia Rossiia" ("The Autonomous Movement of Mongolia and Tsarist Russia"), *Novyi Vostok* (*The New East*), nos. 13-14, 1926, pp. 362-363.

[7] *C.Y.B.*, *1924-25* (Peking & Tientsin), p. 860.

[8] Russian version of the note in *Izvestiia*, Jan. 5, 1921.

forces were commanded by General Bakich and were joined in May by remnants of detachments under the command of Gnoev, who had until then operated in the Semipalatinsk district of Sibera.

On May 24 the Red army attacked the Bakich forces and surrounded Chuguchak. Bakich retreated in the direction of Mongolia with the Red Army in pursuit, and was reported in June as attempting to effect a junction with the forces of Baron Ungern, operating on Mongolian territory.[9]

Thus commenced the Soviet expedition to Outer Mongolia. Previously, in March, 1921, the Soviet-sponsored Mongolian "People's Revolutionary Party" had proclaimed itself the government in Kiakhta and had attempted without success to capture Urga, the Mongolian capital. It had at its disposal an army organized and equipped on Russian territory.[10] It was with the help of these forces that the Red Army, which had concentrated in the Baikal region, defeated Ungern's troops and took Urga on July 12.[11]

The subsequent Soviet military occupation of Outer Mongolia was also a response to a Mongolian "request." Immediately following the liquidation of the White Russian forces at the end of July, 1921, the Mongolian People's Revolutionary Government addressed an official appeal to the Moscow Government, in which it requested the latter "not to withdraw Soviet troops from the territory of Mongolia" until the "menace of the common enemy" no longer existed. The appeal explained that the Mongolian People's Revolutionary Government had not succeeded as yet in organizing and perfecting its apparatus of governmental authority and needed the aid of the Red Army for reasons of security.[12]

The Soviet Government immediately acceded to this request. Through the representative of the Narkomindel at Irkutsk, Chicherin transmitted to the revolutionary government of Mongolia a note, which began as follows:

The Russian Soviet Government, in alliance with the Government of the Far Eastern Republic, ordered its troops, operating side by side with the revolutionary army of the Provisional Government of Mongolia, to deal a crushing blow to the common enemy, the Tsarist General Ungern,

[9] *Izvestiia,* June 11, 1921.   [10] *Izvestiia,* Nov. 6, 1921.
[11] A. E. Khodorov, "Mongolia and Its Claimants," *The Living Age,* CCCXIV (Aug. 5, 1922), 337.
[12] Russian text of the appeal in *Izvestiia,* Aug. 10, 1921.

who has subjected the Mongolian people to unprecedented enslavement and oppression; violated the rights of autonomous Mongolia; at the same time threatening the security of Soviet Russia and the inviolability of the territory of the fraternal Far Eastern Republic.[13]

Such was Chicherin's explanation for the appearance of Soviet troops on Mongolian territory. In giving the Mongolian "request" a "complete satisfaction," the Soviet Government expressed its appreciation of the appeal addressed to it by the Mongolian Provisional Revolutionary Government "that the Soviet troops should not be removed from the territory of Mongolia." The Soviet Government thus considered the appeal a manifestation of "close and friendly bonds" uniting the people of Russia with the people of Mongolia. It announced its firm decision to withdraw the Red Army just as soon "as the menace to the free development of the Mongolian people and to the security of the Russian Republic and of the Far Eastern Republic shall have been removed." But the Soviet Government was "in complete accord with the Revolutionary Government of Mongolia" that the moment for such a withdrawal of its troops had not yet arrived. Therefore, the Soviet Government decided to comply with the Mongolian request and ordered its troops to remain in the territory of Mongolia.[14]

The military occupation of Outer Mongolia by Soviet armed forces was for many years the source of a major dispute between China and Soviet Russia. The Chinese Government found it difficult to tolerate the Soviet action. Wellington Koo, for one, asserted that Russia actually ruled in Outer Mongolia. Joffe denied this assertion but explained that Russian forces remained temporarily on Mongolian soil solely to prevent Mongolia from becoming once again the assembly area for White Guardist forces in the Russian Far East and in Chinese territory.[15] Nevertheless, the very fact of military intervention has been taken by many to prove that Soviet Russia's activities were from the outset a direct continuation of Tsarist policy.

It has been reported frequently that Soviet Russia withdrew her troops from Outer Mongolia at the beginning of 1925. The report stems from a long exchange of notes between the Soviet and Mon-

---

[13] Full text in *Izvestiia*, Aug. 12, 1921.

[14] *Ibid.*

[15] U.S.S.R., Narkomindel, *Mezhdunarodnaia Politika RSFSR* (*International Politics of the R.S.F.S.R.*) (Moscow, 1922), p. 71.

golian governments on the occasion of the fulfilment of the 1921 promise to do so.[16] Possibly, with the White Russian bands destroyed or disbanded, and no military action to fear from China, Soviet Russia was content to send materials and instructors on a larger scale than under the Tsarist regime. Yet, since information from Outer Mongolia was restricted to Soviet channels, the Russian report of evacuation can hardly be regarded as genuine proof. Even if the Red Army did evacuate Outer Mongolia, this does not preclude the possibility that Soviet Russia tendered other aid to Mongolia during the years of 1925-31. In the words of Doksom, the President of the Little Hural, Soviet Russia provided "manifold assistance in regard to technical equipment and military training of our army" throughout the period.[17]

After Japan's occupation of Manchuria in 1931, however, Soviet Russia did not resort any longer to camouflage but engaged more or less openly in strengthening her military position along the frontier of Manchuria, in Outer Mongolia.

The "People's Revolutionary Government" of Outer Mongolia was created on March 13, 1921, by the Mongolian People's Revolutionary Party which has been termed by a critic in the West as "an agency of the Soviet Government."[18] Writing of Outer Mongolia from the Soviet point of view, Murzaev described the connection between the Mongolian national revolution and the U.S.S.R. in the first years as a "firm and disinterested friendship."[19] In reality, the Mongolian People's Revolutionary Party and Government both served as Soviet protégés, greatly facilitating the entry of the Red Army and the subsequent occupation of the country.

Before the Red Army entered Mongolia a conference had taken place at Kiakhta in March, 1921, under the auspices of the People's Revolutionary Party. The party was a small one; even its official membership did not number more than 160. It was first organized in 1918 from partisan groups of Mongols in Transbaikalia, which

[16] Doksom, "Istoricheskie Uroki 15 Let Revoliutsii" ("Historical Lessons of Fifteen Years of Revolution"), *Tikhii Okean* (*The Pacific Ocean*), no. 3 (9) (July-Sept., 1936), pp. 73-74.

[17] *Ibid.*, p. 75.

[18] David J. Dallin, *The Rise of Russia in Asia* (New Haven, 1949), p. 190.

[19] E. M. Murzaev, *Mongol'skaia Narodnaia Respublika, Fisiko-Geograficheskoe Opisanie* (*The Mongolian People's Republic: A Physical Geographical Description*) (Moscow, 1948), p. 3.

lies north of Urga and borders upon Russia. Under Soviet sponsorship the Mongolian People's Revolutionary Party followed the example of the Russian Communist Party, whose guiding hand and spirit was evident at every stage of its activity.[20]

The party was immediately accepted into the Communist International, and placed under its control.[21] Two delegates participated in the Third Congress of the International in July-August, 1921. While the party did not call itself Communist, it was in fact a segment of the Russian Communist Party working in a backward area, very much like those in Kirgizia, Uzbekistan, and Turkmenia. In its program the party did not advocate "socialization of all the means of production," but called for "political democracy" in the manner of the usual Soviet interpretation, i.e., one-party rule, with no opposition tolerated. It claimed to be "a bourgeois-democratic system of a new type," which aimed at eliminating the capitalist stage of development.[22]

At the Kiakhta conference, a "Provisional Revolutionary Government of Mongolia" was set up, and on April 10, 1921, the government officially asked the Soviet Government for assistance. Inasmuch as all the details had been prearranged, the request was, of course, granted. In order to avoid further international complications, the Soviet position in world affairs at that time being already precarious, the U.S.S.R. tried to present the Mongolian incident as a purely national movement. The fact of the Soviet Army's presence was kept in the background. Similarly, because of the Soviet-Chinese diplomatic dispute over Outer Mongolia, the Soviet Government even considered it necessary to retain the Hutukhtu as titular head of the state, and the Mongolian People's Revolutionary Party found it convenient to proclaim Mongolia a constitutional monarchy.

But as Kallinikov points out, "Bogdo-Gegen (the Urga Hutukhtu) reigns but does not rule."[23] The real power rested entirely with the People's Revolutionary Government, later called the People's Government. This government was the political tool of the dominant and monopolistic People's Revolutionary Party of Mongolia. Members of the government and the leadership of the

[20] Dallin, *op. cit.*, pp. 189-190.
[21] *New International Yearbook, 1944* (New York & London, 1945), p. 396.
[22] *Pravda*, April 8, 1936.
[23] Kallinikov, *Revoliutsionnaia Mongoliia (Revolutionary Mongolia)*, p. 76.

armed forces were recruited from its ranks. A congress of the party deliberated every problem relating to economics, administrative tasks, mutual relations between the center and the periphery, and cultural activities, in addition to problems concerning the party itself.[24]

After China's practically futile claim of sovereignty over Outer Mongolia in the Peking agreement of 1924 and the death of the Urga Hutukhtu in the same year, the Soviet-sponsored Mongolian People's Revolutionary Party took steps to abolish the nominal monarchy and establish a full-fledged "People's Republic."

Thus, Soviet penetration and control of Outer Mongolia in 1921, through military occupation and "friendly government," succeeded in setting up the first example of a so-called "People's Republic." It was also the first instance of extension of Soviet control over a neighboring, non-Russian area.

SOVIET-MONGOLIAN TREATY RELATIONS

In 1919 the Karakhan Declaration was addressed to the Chinese Government.[25] The Soviet Government issued in the same year a special message to the Mongolian people calling Mongolia a "free country" and suggesting immediate entry into diplomatic relations with Russia.[26] This declaration itself had no immediate effect; Outer Mongolia was again in the firm grip of China, and Soviet Russia was not in a position to intervene at that time.

In 1921 the presence of the Red Army in Outer Mongolia and the establishment of the Soviet-sponsored Mongolian Provisional Revolutionary Government brought Soviet Russia back into the political scene. In order to legalize her hold on Outer Mongolia, Soviet Russia signed a secret agreement in Moscow on November 5, 1921, "for establishing friendly relations" with the People's Revolutionary Government.[27] The preamble stated that, in contrast to treaties made "by the cunning and predatory Tsarist Government,"

[24] I. I. Genkin, "Dva S'ezda Mongol'skoi Narodnoi Revoliutsionnoi Partii" ("Two Sessions of the Mongolian People's Revolutionary Party"), *Novyi Vostok* (*The New East*), no. 12, 1926, p. 186.

[25] Cf. chap. iii, pp. 137-139, *supra*.

[26] See Doksom, *op. cit.*, p. 72.

[27] Text in Shapiro, *Soviet Treaty Series*, Vol. I, 1917-28, pp. 137-138; also in *C.Y.B., 1923*, p. 677.

the agreement was one of "free friendship and collaboration between the two neighboring states."

The Soviet-Mongolian treaty was thus concluded. It provided for mutual recognition between the two governments without mentioning China (Article I). The reciprocal establishment of consulates in necessary places at the governments' discretion was provided for, and Russia undertook to construct postal and telephone communication lines in Mongolia; the latter obligated herself to cede to Russia such territory as would be needed for the construction of railroads (Article 3). The Tannu Tuva or Urianghai area adjoining Mongolia in the west, and claimed by Mongolia as part of its state, was not acknowledged as such by the Soviet Government. Instead, Tannu Tuva was set up as a separate state and secretly marked for annexation, which eventually took place in 1944.[28]

After the conclusion of the treaty, ties between official Mongolia and Russia became closer, as might be expected. Two Russian Communists, Okhtin and Berezin, arrived in Urga and became the real masters there. A third representative, Butin, acted as financial "adviser" to the Mongol Government, the role formerly played by Kozin in the period prior to 1917.[29]

In order not to complicate the negotiations with China then being undertaken by the Paikes Mission, the text of the treaty with Mongolia was not published. When rumors of the treaty reached Peking, the Chinese Foreign Minister asked Paikes, the Soviet envoy, for an explanation. Paikes denied the existence of the treaty. Finally, however, it had to be made public. Irritation at Russian tactics mounted high in Peking. On May 1, 1922, the Chinese Foreign Minister addressed a note to Paikes, in which he said:

Now the Soviet Government has suddenly gone back on its own word and, secretly and without any right, concluded a treaty with Mongolia. Such action on the part of the Soviet Government is similar to the policy the former Imperial Russian Government assumed toward China.

It must be observed that Mongolia is a part of Chinese territory and as such has long been recognized by all countries. In secretly concluding a treaty with Mongolia, the Soviet Government has not only broken faith with its previous declarations but also violates all principles of justice.

The Chinese Government finds it difficult to tolerate such an action,

[28] Cf. chap. xiv.
[29] Cf. chap. xi, pp. 342-343, *supra.*

and therefore we solemnly lodge a protest with you to the effect that any treaty secretly concluded between the Soviet Government and Mongolia will not be recognized by the Chinese Government.[30]

Thus by 1922 the issue of Mongolia had become the most important matter in dispute between the Soviet and Chinese governments. In all negotiations carried on at that time by China with the Soviet envoys, "the Russian offers were turned down by the Chinese Government which demanded the prior evacuation of Mongolia," in an effort to prevent the detachment of Mongolia from China.[31]

Moscow seemed to be determined not to return Mongolia to China until China herself should turn pro-Soviet and firmly ally herself with Russia. In this connection Grigorii Zinoviev, President of the Third International, said at the First Session of the Revolutionary Organizations of the Far East in 1922:

. . . a definitive solution of the Mongolian question will not become possible until the Chinese shall liberate themselves from the yoke of their oppressors, until they drive from their borders the soldiers of foreign imperialist nations, until the revolution shall be victorious in their country.[32]

In all its negotiations with Paikes and Joffe, the Chinese Government returned again and again to the question of Mongolia. In an official report the Narkomindel stated that, because of dissension over Mongolia, the long-awaited Sino-Soviet agreement was incapable of achievement. Though ideally Russia would have liked to obtain official recognition from Peking, the actual extension of Russian hegemony over Outer Mongolia was considered more important.[33]

---

[30] Waichiaopu to Paikes, note, May 1, 1922, *C.Y.B., 1923*, p. 680.

[31] *Ibid.*

[32] Speech of Zinoviev, cited in T. Ryskulov, "Velikii Khuruldan Mongolii" ("The Great Huruldan of Mongolia") *Novyi Vostok* (*The New East*), nos. 8-9, 1925, pp. 218-219.

[33] A secret Soviet-Mongolian agreement was reportedly concluded in Moscow on February 22, 1923. This alleged agreement appears to have included far-reaching economic, political, and military provisions. Mining resources were to be put under the management of Soviet trade union organizations. A revolutionary and a military committee were to be set up to exercise governmental functions, among them the convocation of a people's assembly and preparation of a constitution. The secret agreement in question reportedly provided that "Soviet troops might be stationed in Outer Mongolia in order to help the Mongolian people resist Chinese encroachment." According to Ho Han-wen, the existence of this agreement was first reported by *Hua-Pei-Min-Hsin-Pao* (*North China Star*), Tientsin, shortly after its supposed signing. For a summary of the text of the alleged secret agreement, see Ho Han-wen, *Chung-O Wai-Chiao-Shih* (*Sino-Russian Diplomatic History*), pp. 300-

After three years of negotiations in which the Mongolian problem was the focal point, the Chinese Government came to the conclusion that it had no means at its disposal with which to restore its previous position in Mongolia, and that it had to acknowledge the *fait accompli* in Outer Mongolia. It then reverted to the same construction that had been used by both Russia and China before the Revolution: a compromise wherein Russia recognized Chinese sovereignty over Mongolia on paper, while China acknowledged Russia's actual dominance there. On this basis a treaty was finally concluded between China and the U.S.S.R. on May 31, 1924. As for Outer Mongolia, Article V of this Peking Agreement on General Principles read as follows:

The Government of the U.S.S.R. recognizes that Outer Mongolia is an integral part of the Republic of China and respects China's sovereignty therein.

The Government of the U.S.S.R. declares that, as soon as questions of the withdrawal of all troops of the U.S.S.R. from Outer Mongolia, namely the time limit of the withdrawal of such troops and the measures to be adopted in the interests of the safety of the frontiers, are agreed upon at the conference as provided in Article II of the present Agreement, it will effect the complete withdrawal of all troops of U.S.S.R. from Outer Mongolia.[34]

Thus, in strict accordance with the treaty provision, Soviet Russia reaffirmed that Mongolia was a Chinese possession—using exactly that term, "sovereignty," which Tsarist Russia had obstinately refused to use in 1912-15 when conceding only Chinese "suzerainty." As a matter of fact this was merely an "agreement on general principles." The conference scheduled within a month after the signing of the Peking agreement to make detailed arrangement for carrying out the provisions was not convened. Apart from the promise for the withdrawal of troops, the Peking agreement contained no concrete proposal for re-establishment of direct contact between the Chinese Government and the Mongolian authorities. Moreover, Chicherin, Commissar for Foreign Affairs, made it clear at the end

---

301. The agreement does not appear in Shapiro, *Soviet Treaty Series*, Vol. I, 1917-28; nor was it recorded in Degras (ed.), *Soviet Documents on Foreign Policy*, Vol. I, 1917-24.

[34] Text in Shapiro, *op. cit.*, I, 242.

of the same year that Russia did not intend to tolerate any interference by China in Outer Mongolian affairs:

> We recognize the Mongolian People's Republic as part of the Chinese Republic, but we recognize also its autonomy in so far-reaching a sense that we regard it not only as independent of China in its internal affairs, but also as capable of pursuing its foreign policy independently.[35]

In the same year, 1924, neither the proclamation of the Mongolian People's Republic following the death of the Urga Living Buddha in July, nor the constitution adopted in November declaring Mongolia to be "an independent People's Republic" referred to Chinese "sovereignty" as the term had been used in the Sino-Soviet agreement.[36]

Drafted on the Soviet pattern, the Outer Mongolian constitution of November 26, 1924, empowered the government of the "Mongolian People's Republic to represent the 'Republic' in international relations; to conduct diplomatic negotiations; and to conclude political, commercial, and other treaties with the Powers."[37] This implied that Outer Mongolia was itself a sovereign state.

According to the definition given by prominent scholars in international law such as Hall, Lawrence, Oppenheim, Moore, Hyde, Hackworth, Jessup, Eagleton, *et al.*, sovereignty means an absolute, uncontrolled state will, or the right of property and exclusive control within, and supremacy over, territory. As to agreement-making power, Hall states, that "the power of a state to enter into a valid engagement with another may be impaired by reason of the dependence of the former upon an independent state."[38] The control exercised by the independent state over foreign relations of the dependency may serve to preclude it from making agreements in its own behalf. Therefore, as Pavlovsky observed, the Soviet-initiated Russo-Mongolian agreement of 1921 and the Peking agreement of 1924 which constituted the basis of the international status of Outer

[35] Cited in Kallinikov, *op. cit.*, p. 95.

[36] *C.Y.B.*, *1928* (Peking & Tientsin), p. 383.

[37] For text of the Constitution of the Mongolian People's Republic, see *C.Y.B.* *1926*, pp. 795-796.

[38] W. E. Hall, *A Treatise on International Law*, 8th ed., edited by A. P. Higgin (Oxford, 1924), p. 105; cf. also pp. 55-57. The passage is also cited in C. C. Hyde *International Law Chiefly as Interpreted and Applied in the United States* (Boston 1947), I, 1377.

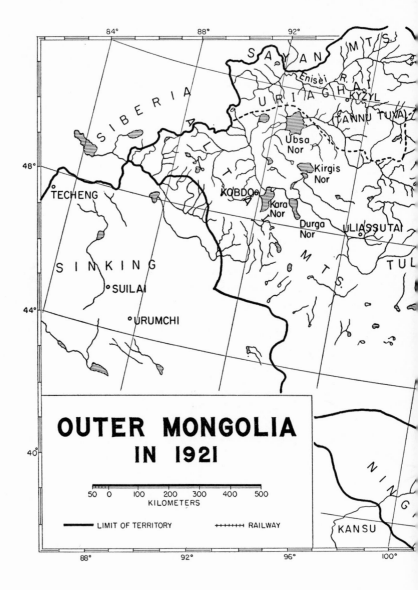

OUTER MONGOLIA
IN 1921

KILOMETERS

50 0   100   200   300   400   500

——— LIMIT OF TERRITORY   ++++++ RAILWAY

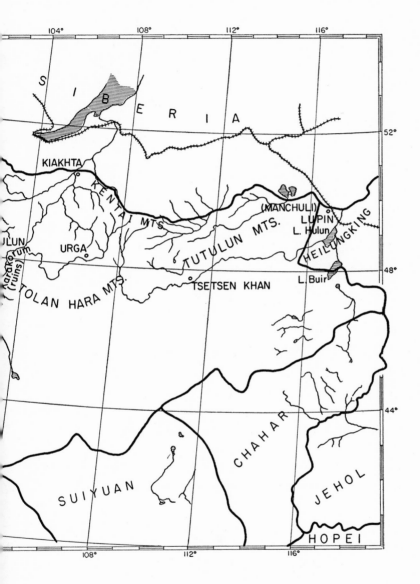

Mongolia were, in reality, mutually contradictory.[39] The Soviet expedient of paying lip service to Chinese sovereignty over Outer Mongolia facilitated the Soviet Union's designs. It also must have encouraged Japanese militarist circles in their ambition to establish a puppet regime through which they were, after 1931, to attempt to rule and exploit Manchuria.

Furthermore, the Sino-Soviet Agreement of 1924, which formed the basis for Soviet-Chinese treaty relations up to 1945, stood in contradiction to the various agreements between Russia and Mongolia (the Soviet-Mongolian treaty of 1921, the Gentlemen's Agreement of 1934, and the mutual assistance pact of 1936) in recognizing Chinese sovereignty over Mongolia. It contained no mention of Outer Mongolia's autonomy, as had the Sino-Russian Agreement of 1913 and the Tripartite Agreement of 1915. No Sino-Soviet convention was concluded in which Outer Mongolia participated. Thus, if China did not officially recognize Outer Mongolia's autonomy, neither did Outer Mongolia accept Chinese sovereignty. As Pavlovsky pointed out,

The absence of a tripartite treaty similar to that of 1915, or a direct Sino-Mongol convention, was particularly disadvantageous to China, since it permitted Mongolia to interpret her autonomy as widely as she wished and permitted Russia, while admitting Chinese sovereignty, to turn this wider interpretation to account.[40]

During the period under review in this study, there were several other important agreements between the U.S.S.R. and Outer Mongolia, notably the telegraphic Agreement of October 3, 1924,[41] and the railroad agreement of 1926,[42] the agreement regarding navigation on Mongolian rivers by Soviet vessels of July, 1926,[43] and the protocol regarding the prolongation of the telegraphic agreement of February 22, 1927.[44]

In the light of these various attempts of the U.S.S.R. to consolidate Soviet control in Outer Mongolia through the rather obvious

---

[39] Pavlovsky, *Chinese Russian Relations*, p. 89. Some scholars, however, consider that in the light of agreements concluded with the Turkish dependencies in the nineteenth century, the Mongolian case was not a unique one.

[40] Pavlovsky, *op. cit.*, p. 90.

[41] Text in Shapiro, *op. cit.*, I, 281.

[42] Referred to in *ibid.*, p. 313; text not available.

[43] Text not available; referred to in Shapiro, *op. cit.*, I, 320.

[44] Text in Shapiro, *op. cit.*, I, 326.

device of Soviet-Mongolian treaty relations, it is not surprising that Stalin should regard Outer Mongolia as a protectorate even before the signing of the mutual assistance pact on March 12, 1936. On March 1, 1936, in an interview with Roy Howard of the Scripps-Howard newspapers, Stalin said; "If Japan is determined to attack the Mongolian People's Republic, we will have to assist them . . . . We will help the Mongolian People's Republic as we helped her in 1921."[45]

PHASES OF SOVIET CONTROL

POLITICAL ASPECTS

Soviet control of Outer Mongolia may be considered under three major headings: political, economic, and military.

Politically, a one-party dictatorship, closely affiliated with the Russian Communist Party, dominated the domestic scene and directed foreign affairs exclusively through Russian Channels. Economical control took the form of the Mongol bank, jointly owned by the Mongolian administration and the Soviet State Bank in Moscow but controlled by a Soviet staff, and the Russian state monopoly which handled the Mongolian export-import trade. As for military control, Russia depended on Soviet officers who staffed and supervised the Mongolian Army and Air Force, as well as a police system organized by Soviet experts and patterned on the G.P.U (later the N.K.V.D.). These two latter aspects will be treated in detail subsequently.

To return to the sovietization of the political activity of Mongolia, both Mongolian and Soviet sources indicate that it was the victory of the October Revolution that made the revolutionary movement possible in Outer Mongolia.[46] Thus in March, 1925, the regular plenary session of the Central Committee of The People's Revolutionary Party of Mongolia (PRPM) adopted a new program, of which paragraphs 12 and 13 read:

Mongolian working masses realize that they have liberated themselves and have consolidated their independence in the wake of the Great October

[45] Cited in Ogin, *Mongol'skaia Narodnaia Respublika* (*Mongolian People's Republic*), p. 53.

[46] *M.S.E.* (2nd ed.), Vol. VII, cols. 56-57; Murzaev, *op. cit.*, p. 18.

Revolution and in the course of the successful campaign launched by the Soviet Government against imperialist intervention in the Far East. The future of their own relationship with the contemporary world situation necessitates that the working masses of Mongolia definitely view the Comintern and the U.S.S.R. as the only revolutionary centers willing to aid the oppressed peoples of the Orient. So speak the working masses of Mongolia and its vanguard, the People's Revolutionary Party of Mongolia.[47]

And again, Tsiren-Dorzhi, then Chairman of the Council of Ministers of the Mongolian People's Republic, following this approved party line, credited Russia with the very existence of his government. He was completely endorsed by Shoizhelov, who quoted him:

> Comrade Tsiren-Dorzhi is absolutely right, (November, 1925) in an article entitled "The October Revolution and Mongolian People" in which he says: ". . . the toiling people of Mongolia got their independence and their chance for a free and happy life only as a result of the great October Revolution. For, if the October Revolution had not succeeded, then the Soviet Government would not have been established in Russia; if the Soviet Government had not been established, then the Third Communist International would not have had that solid basis which is given to it today by the Soviet Union; if the U.S.S.R. and the Comintern had not existed, under no circumstances would the Mongolian people have been able to achieve a free and happy life.[48]

The People's Revolutionary Party of Mongolia,[49] the only political party of the country, was first formed in the Russian territory of Kiakhta under the leadership of Russian-educated Sukhe Bator.[50] After Sukhe Bator died in 1923, a collaborator with the Soviet cause, Choibalsan, was selected as his successor.[51] Aided by its Revolutionary League of Youth, the party, with its Soviet-created elite,

---

[47] *Izvestiia Ulan-Bator-Khoto* (*Izvestiia of Ulan-Bator*), cited in S. Shoizhelov, "Perelomnyi Moment v Istorii Natsional'no-Osvoboditel'nogo Dvizheniia Mongolii" ("The Turning Point in the History of National Liberation Movement in Mongolia," referred to hereinafter as Shoizhelov, "Perelomnyi"), *Novyi Vostok* (*The New East*), nos. 10-11, 1925, p. 206.

[48] *Izvestiia Ulan-Bator-Khoto* (*Izvestiia of Ulan-Bator*), Nov. 7, 1925, cited in S. Shoizhelov, "Avtonomnoe Dvizhenie Mongoliia i Tsarskaia Rossiia" ("The Autonomous Movement of Mongolia and Tsarist Russia"), *Novyi Vostok* (*The New East*), 1926, nos. 13-14, p. 363.

[49] Cf. pp. 370, 371, 374, *supra*.

[50] *M.S.E.* (2nd ed.), Vol. VII, col. 56.

[51] *M.S.E.* (2nd ed.), Vol. VII, col. 58. Marshal Choibalsan died in Moscow on Jan. 26, 1952.

carried out Soviet policy in Outer Mongolia from the initial step to the final consolidation of control.

In order to sovietize Outer Mongolia politically, the People's Revolutionary Party of Mongolia had to pass through two principal stages: The first stage was a period of a "national united front against foreign oppressors," the slogan of which was "to struggle for national independence." During this period, the activities of the party did not deviate toward a struggle against feudal and theocratic groups. On the contrary, the party was forced to make concessions in the sphere of internal politics and to organize a national anti-imperialist united front (which included feudal and theocratic groups).[52]   In the development of its all-embracing activities, the party gave much attention to the expansion and intensification of activities among the masses of "Khudons" or provinces. The delegate of the Comintern, Amagaev, persisted in trying to make the party congress aware of the necessity for close co-operation among the party, the middle classes, and the proletarian elements of the country.[53]   These efforts were directed toward forming a coalition government headed by a constitutional monarch, Bogdo Chebutsum Damba Hutukhtu,[54] whom a Soviet expert referred to as one of the most prudent among theocrats and feudals.[55]

The second stage was marked in the beginning by the appearance of class stratification among the directing circles of the party. This development paved the way for the replacement, in the name of national liberation, of the coalition government by a much more stringent party dictatorship. Many measures were carried out to "purge the party ranks of all undesirable elements."[56] The Soviet-controlled party now tried to get rid of the so-called anti-party group of Lama Bodo (the first Premier) and others. They were accused of having

. . . followed a policy of subordinating the party's Central Committee to

[52] Shoizhelov, "Perelomnyi," *Novyi Vostok* (*The New East*), nos. 10-11, 1925, p. 204.
[53] Genkin, *op. cit.*, p. 186.
[54] Shoizhelov, "Perelomnyi," *Novyi Vostok* (*The New East*), nos. 10-11, 1925, p. 204.
[55] Shoizhelov, "Avtonomnoe Dvizhenie Mongolii i Tsarskaia Rossiia" ("The Autonomous Movement of Mongolia and Tsarist Russia"), *Novyi Vostok* (*The New East*), nos. 13-14, 1926, p. 352.
[56] Shoizhelov, "Perelomnyi," *Novyi Vostok* (*The New East*), nos. 10-11, 1925, p. 206.

the coalition government, opposing the execution of social and economic reforms, trying to introduce elements of hostility into the relations between Mongolia and the U.S.S.R. and co-operating with Chinese militarists and the Japanese, as well as other imperialists . . . in their struggle to thwart friendly relations between the working classes of the U.S.S.R. and Mongolia.[57]

The influence of the right wing of the People's Revolutionary Party of Mongolia was finally removed at the Third Congress of the party in August, 1924, which "condemned both rightists, headed by Commander-in-Chief Danzan, and ultra-leftists such as Buyan and others."[58] As a result, the coalition period was brought practically to an end. As Genkin puts it:

The fellow travelers of the Mongolian revolution escaped either freely or under force, and some were even shot, for example, Bodo, the first Premier of the new government, and Danzan, the first chairman of the Central Committee of the party and Commander-in-Chief. Those who remained at their posts tried not to deviate from the main lines set by the leftist elements of the party; they endeavored to become more leftist themselves and were in harmony with the radical elements.[59]

According to Murzaev's study, it was an act of Soviet expediency to set up, in the first stage in the Mongolian political transformation, a constitutional monarchy headed by Chebutsum Damba Hutukhtu, in order to utilize his popular support and minimize opposition. Immediately after the death of the Living Buddha in July, 1924, the Central Committee of the PRPM passed a resolution to establish the "People's Republic" on July 11.[60] This move accomplished a clever and a successful transition to a more open Soviet form of administration.

The constitution of the "Mongolian People's Republic" of November 26, 1924, was nearly identical with that of the R.S.F.S.R. of July 10, 1918. The Mongolian Constitution of 1924 as well as the subsequent constitution of June 30, 1940, defined the Mongolian People's Republic as "an independent state of the working people [*arats*—herdsmen and peasants, workers and intelligentsia] who abolished the imperialist feudal yoke in order to assure the non-capitalistic development of the country for a transition to socialism

[57] *Ibid.*, p. 204.
[58] *Ibid.*, p. 206.
[59] Genkin, *op. cit.*, p. 186.
[60] Murzaev, *op. cit.*, p. 18.

in the future.[61] According to the Mongolian constitutions the supreme political organ is a legislative body called the Great People's Khural, convened not less often than once in three years. Subordinate to this body and responsible to it is the Small Khural, which, for the execution of its ordinary duties, elects a presidium from among its members and also appoints the "Council of Ministers."[62] Except for the use of tribal terminology in the naming of political offices, the structure of the hierarchy exactly follows the Soviet pattern.[63]

Owen Lattimore once indicated that the Mongolian regime "required a preliminary reign of terror" to establish itself.[64] Bloody purges have been carried out frequently in compliance with Soviet orders and policies. The fact that the Mongols, from the Soviet point of view, were not entirely trustworthy was reflected by the execution of Prime Minister Bodo on April 10, 1922, only a few months after Soviet recognition. Fifteen other officials were arrested and shot. They were chiefly accused of connections with and conspiracy with the Chinese. Further revolts took place at the end of 1922.[65]

In 1924, between the death of the Living Buddha and the proclamation of the Mongolian People's Republic, the commander-in-chief of the Mongolian Army, Danzan, was also excuted after having been charged with making an anti-Russian speech.[66] According to Captain Bimba, a former Soviet-trained Mongolian officer, Premier Choibalsan, who was concurrently chief of the Mongol G.P.U., assassinated War Minister Demid, Premier Gendun, General Damba, and General Malji.[67] As Genkin reported, 5,550 out of 6,200 members were dismissed from the party after the purge of 1924-26.[68] Thus Bimba concluded: "the perfection of the terrorist organization

[61] *Ibid.*

[62] *M.S.E.* (2nd ed.), Vol. VII, col. 56.

[63] V. Durdenevskii, "Narodni Respubliki Tsentralnoi Azii, Mongolska ta Tuvinska" ("The People's Republics of Central Asia—Mongolia and Tuva"), *Skidnii Svit* (*The World of the Orient*), Kharkov, no. 3 (9), 1929, p. 108.

[64] Cf. O. Lattimore, "Mongolia," in *C.Y.B.*, *1933*, pp. 191-201.

[65] Maslennikov, "K Mongol'skomu Voprosu" ("About the Mongolian Problem"), *Mirovoe Khozaistvo i Mirovaia Politika* (*World Economics and World Politics*), Moscow, May 5, 1936, p. 81.

[66] Durdenevskii, *op. cit.*, p. 108.

[67] Captain Bimba, *Red Hand Over Outer Mongolia*, a pamphlet published in 1938, p. 29.

[68] Genkin, *op. cit.*, p. 185.

[G.P.U.] paved the way for the complete Sovietization of Outer Mongolia."[69]

Apparently Soviet political control over Outer Mongolia extended beyond the organization of the party and the government. Communist ideology as interpreted by the Soviet leaders was a basic part of their program during the early years of the Mongolian "liberation." As Rinchino pointed out: "There are translations of the 'Communist Manifesto,' of single articles and pamphlets written by V. I. Lenin and other authors, there is a translation of the 'Theory of Historical Materialism' by C. Bukharin, and there are translations of many other authors who wrote on economics and the co-operative movement."[70]

In foreign relations, Outer Mongolia was firmly under Soviet control. As Genkin pointed out, "Outer Mongolia does not look with hope either to Versailles or to Locarno but to the U.S.S.R."[71] David Dallin also indicated that "Mongolia was regarded as the most obedient of all Soviet satellites; this small nation was not expected to conduct an independent foreign policy."[72] In the first years of Outer Mongolia's "independence" a few attempts were made by the Mongols themselves to establish international ties with other governments besides Russia. Bogdo Khan (Holy Lord), the religious leader and semimonarch, tried to enter into direct negotiations with the United States and Japan until his death in 1924. Danzan, the Vice-Premier, wanted an agreement with China. These and similar attempts were frustrated by Moscow, and among the accusations which eventually led to Danzan's execution his connection with China was uppermost. Evidently Soviet policy was directed toward avoiding diplomatic recognition of Outer Mongolia which would entail the establishment of foreign legations and the arrival of observers in Ulan Bator.

ECONOMIC ASPECTS

Economic Sovietization of Outer Mongolia found expression in the Mongolian constitution of 1924. This consitution stipulated that

[69] Bimba, *op. cit.*, p. 29.
[70] Rinchino, "K Voprosu o Natsional'nom Samoopredelenii Mongolii v Sviazi c Zadachami Kitaiskoi Revoliutsii" ("The Problem of National Self-determination of Mongolia in Relation to the Tasks of the Chinese Revolution"), *Revoliutsionnyi Vostok* (*The Revolutionary East*), no. 2, 1927, p. 69.
[71] Genkin, *op. cit.*, pp. 58-59.
[72] D. Dallin, *Soviet Russia and the Far East* (New Haven, 1948), p. 356.

"all the lands and mineral wealth, forests and waters and their resources . . . [are] the property of all the people. The unified economic policy of the country . . . [is] to be concentrated in the hands of the government, and a state monopoly of foreign trade . . . introduced." The new constitution, ratified on June 30, 1940, adds industrial enterprises, transport and communication systems, banks, etc., to state property. In fact the Russo-Mongolian bank project was approved by Moscow early in 1924.[73]

In June, 1924, the Mongolian Industrial and Commercial Bank was established in Urga with a monopoly status. Branches were opened later in Uliassutai, Kobdo, Altan-Bulak (opposite Kiakhta), and several other places. The ownership of the bank was divided equally between the Mongolian Government on the one hand, and the Soviet State Bank and the People's Commissariat of Finance. The members of the directorate and practically all the staff, however, were Russian. There was only one Mongolian official on the directorate. The notes issued by the bank were called *tughrik*. The *tughrik* was minted as a silver coin in Moscow, where the Mongol bank notes were also printed.[74] Earlier in 1923, under Soviet guidance, "the Mongolian Central People's Co-operative" had been created. Through these two agencies—the co-operative and the Mongol Industrial and Commercial Bank—the Mongolian Government attempted to carry out monetary reforms which aimed at replacing the Chinese currency then in circulation with a Mongolian national monetary unit.[75]

In the transitional period which immediately followed the death of the Urgan Hutukhtu in 1924, the question of liquidating the wealth left by the Living Buddha became the key to the subsequent policy of handling private property in Outer Mongolia. According to Genkin, the Central Committee of the People's Revolutionary Party itself was not in unanimity regarding this problem at the time of the congress." On the contrary, the issue aroused considerable debate, Genkin reported:

    [73] *C.Y.B., 1924*, p. 582.
    [74] L. Zolotarev, "Denezhnaia Reforma v Mongolii" ("The Bank Reform in Mongolia"), in *Novyi Vostok (The New East)*, nos. 13-14, 1926, pp. 234-236.
    [75] N. N. Tugarinov, "Biudzhet Mongol'skoi Narodnoi Respubliki" ("The Budget of the Mongolian People's Republic"), *Novyi Vostok (The New East)*, no. 15, 1926, p. 170.

The right wing (Tseren-Dorchzhi, Amor, Maksarzhap, and others) wanted to channel the whole of the property of Bogdo to religious causes, reasoning that the will of the donors must not be violated: money and cattle had been donated at the time for specific religious purposes. This opinion found few partisans among members of the Congress. In fact, some energetic voices demanded a confiscation of the entire legacy of Bogdo Khan into the people's treasury. However, the overwhelming majority of the delegates adopted the proposal of the Commander-in-Chief, Choibalsan (a representative of the left wing of the Central Committee), to divide the patrimony of Bogdo-Gegen into three equal parts and apportion one part each to religious causes, education of the people, and health services, respectively.[76]

During the period when the NEP (New Economic Policy) was in force in Russia—until 1929—the traditional economic system of Outer Mongolia was subjected to certain modifications. Russian and Chinese tradesmen disappeared from the scene, while large "cooperative" enterprises were encouraged; foreign trade was already veering toward Russia. But the turning point came with the Seventh Congress of the Soviet-sponsored Mongolian People's Revolutionary Party. It coincided with the inauguration of the Soviet drive toward collective farming, industrialization, and the five-year plans. The congress in Ulan Bator resolved that in Mongolia, too, the immediate goal was "the creation of a socialist economy." During the following three years the wealth of Mongolian princes, well-to-do lamas, and, in particular, of the monasteries, was expropriated. A five-year plan for the development of the Mongolian economy was adopted and integrated with the Soviet plan.[77]

The period 1929-32 was one of violent socialization. According to Soviet information, livestock-raising was the primary source of livelihood for 90 per cent of the Mongolian population, and wealth in the form of cattle was virtually the only "capital" in Outer Mongolia. The most sweeping of all economic transformations was the abortive *kolkhoz* (collective farm) experiment. After six hundred "feudals" (princes and monasteries) had been deprived of their herds, their entire wealth was given to the newly founded collectives.[78]

[76] Genkin, *op. cit.*, p. 188.
[77] *M.S.E.* (2nd ed.), Vol. VII, col. 52.
[78] *Ibid.*

By the summer of 1931, 740 *kolkhozy*, with a total of 174,988 members and dependents, had been created. This upheaval involved a considerable percentage of the inhabitants of a nation whose total population was below the million mark. The resentment of the thousands of shepherds was intense. Unable to resist brute force, they retaliated by killing their livestock or driving it across the border into Inner Mongolia or into Manchuria, in typical nomad fashion. A great catastrophe was in the offing. A purge within the government was initiated in which overzealous "leftists" were made responsible for a policy originally dictated by Moscow. The Mongolian People's Revolutionary Party held a plenum of its Central Committee in June, 1932, to condemn its own policy as a "left-wing deviation." Now it was admitted—with Moscow's consent—that Outer Mongolia was not ripe for socialism. She was proclaimed to have entered the road of "noncapitalist, anti-imperialist" development, which would "in time" make possible the transition to a socialist economy. The *kolkhoz* experiment was then abandoned, and the right of *arats* (herdsmen and peasants) to hold private property was again recognized; but trade—in particular, the important cattle trade—was concentrated in the hands of "co-operative" enterprise, which was in fact an agency of the state.[79]

Soviet circles boasted of measures adopted by the Soviet-dominated Mongolian Government in developing veterinary care, haymaking, and well-drilling so as to increase the number of cattle from 12.2 million head in 1918 to 22.4 million head in 1935.[80] This improvement in the livestock did not necessarily add materially to the wealth of the natives: as Mongolian officers Captain Aligatza and Lt. Chamsu later reported, "the Mongolians are required to deliver to Soviet agents half of the meat for every cow slaughtered. The Mongolians are not allowed to kill their cattle unless they obtain a permit from the control organs concerned, which are usually dominated by the Russians."[81]

After a period of respite and relaxation, the program of collectivization was soon resumed and intensified. Since the Outer Mongolian economy would eventually be integrated into the Soviet system, Genkin's comments made before the initial drive of collectivization were still valid:

[79] *S.S.E.*, II, 88.   [80] *M.S.E.* (2nd ed.), Vol. VII, col. 55.
[81] New York *Times*, March 22, 1948.

We must say that in case of greater consolidation of the socialistic structure of the U.S.S.R. and quicker revolutionizing of the laboring masses in Europe and America, cattle-breeding Mongolia will be forced to adjust its economic life in order to be able to accelerate and join the sphere of socialist economy, leaving behind the intermediary stages of bourgeois and capitalistic development.[82]

Industrially, Outer Mongolia was still very backward; the U.S.S.R., occupied by industrial projects at home, was apparently able to offer little help. Up to 1945, in fact, Outer Mongolia had only 24 mining, extractive, and manufacturing enterprises, 330 enterprises connected with the food industry, and 160 handicraft enterprises.[83] In the light of later revelations that Outer Mongolia had made an enormous "material contribution" to the Soviet war efforts during the years 1941-45,[84] it is most likely that these industrial enterprises existed in the main for the extension of Soviet economic development.

Commercially, Soviet Russia exploited Outer Mongolia as a closed market. According to Soviet information, about 70 per cent of commodity circulation in Outer Mongolia was in the hands of co-operatives[85] which acted as agencies of the Soviet-dominated Mongolian government. Mongolian export trade was controlled by a state monopoly. The dominant commercial position of the Soviet was not achieved without years of political pressure to alter the traditional commercial orientation of Outer Mongolia. Penskii provided the reasoning and appeal in 1925:

As for the problem of Soviet participation in the commercial turnovers of Mongolia at the present time, one must necessarily admit that so far the volume of trade relations is of little importance. These turnovers are considerably below the prewar level . . . . The figures for imports for the year 1924-25 do not exceed 50 per cent of the prewar figure. . . . There is no doubt that Autonomous or Outer Mongolia, since achieving its independence, is rapidly becoming economically strengthened by eliminating all influences exerted by Chinese and other foreign capital, and the economic situation is also becoming more and more favorable to the

---

[82] Genkin, *op. cit.*, p. 189.

[83] Murzaev, *op. cit.*, p. 36.

[84] Cf. Mongolian reply to the United Nations Committee on the Admission of New Members, Aug. 28, 1946, New York *Times*, Aug. 29, 1946.

[85] *M.S.E.* (2nd ed.), Vol. VII, col. 55.

U.S.S.R. Thus, our economic agencies must take some necessary steps to establish close economic relations between the U.S.S.R. and Mongolia.[86]

Of a similar opinion, Rinchino wrote in 1927:

On the whole, ethnographic Mongolia gravitates economically to the markets of China and the Pacific Ocean: from 80 to 90 per cent of total Mongolian production is directed to these markets. Even Outer Mongolia, regardless of its proximity to the U.S.S.R. . . . from Altai to Manchuria, gravitates to these cited markets, and roughly 70 per cent of all imports and exports of Outer Mongolia flows between these markets.[87]

Before 1928 China occupied first place in Mongolian foreign trade because of her traditional influence, but thereafter Soviet Russia assumed a monopoly. Mongolian commercial relations with Germany were also terminated in 1929 at Moscow's behest, after having been maintained for four years during a high point of Soviet-German friendship. It was reported that "all direct and lasting connections between Outer Mongolia and the non-Soviet world were severed in 1929."[88] Since 1929 there have been virtually no foreigners other than Russians at work in Outer Mongolia.[89]

Thus Mongolian commerce became channeled to Russia exclusively. Faced with a shortage of foreign exchange ever since the Revolution, Russia could hardly obtain raw materials other than by such tactics of semirequisition as were practiced in Outer Mongolia. In this way Soviet Russia placed herself in a commercially most advantageous position, acquiring Mongolian raw materials with very little foreign exchange and imposing Soviet manufactured goods of inferior quality on the Mongols for sale. Henry R. Lieberman, after interviewing two Mongolian officers, Captain Aligatza and Lieutenant Chamsu, reported: "in order to meet Russian demands, the Mongolians are forced to barter their cattle for Russian manufactured goods at a very unfavorable price . . . . Since they [the Mongols] are prohibited to trade with any country other than Russia, they are inevitably subject to Russian exploitation."[90]

[86] Penskii, "Ekonomicheskoe Vzaimootnoshenie SSSR s Mongoliei" ("Economic Interrelations of the U.S.S.R. with Mongolia"), *Novyi Vostok* (*The New East*), nos. 10-11, 1925, pp. 169-174.
[87] Rinchino, *op. cit.*, p. 68.
[88] Serge M. Wolf, "Mongol Delegations in Western Europe, 1925-1929," *Journal of the Royal Central Asian Society*, London, XXXII (July-Oct., 1945), 289.
[89] Friters, *The International Position of Outer Mongolia*, p. 39.
[90] New York *Times*, March 22, 1948.

Soviet economic control of Outer Mongolia also covered the field of communication. All important settlements in Outer Mongolia became linked with the U.S.S.R. by motor highway as well as by telegraph. Regular air-communication services were established between Ulan-Bator and Altan-Bulak in Mongolia, and Ulan-Ude in the U.S.S.R.[91] All these processes of economic development of Outer Mongolia under Soviet guidance resulted in the integration of the Mongolian economy into the Soviet economic blood stream, thus fortifying the power of the Soviet Union.

MILITARY ASPECTS

Outer Mongolia was first occupied by the Soviet Red Army in 1921 in the name of "liberation." Thereafter, Outer Mongolia was controlled not only by the Russian-trained and equipped Mongolian Army but also by garrisons of the Soviet Army, openly or under guise. The Mongolian Army was for the most part staffed and advised by Soviet officers under Marshal Choibalsan, concurrently head of the Mongolian government and armed forces. Thus, Soviet control in Outer Mongolia was active in all Mongolian military affairs: organization, training, occupation, commitments, mobilization, and militarization.

According to Japanese reports, a Mongolian Army was created in the twenties and expanded considerably during the late thirties, apparently coinciding with the general growth of Soviet military power. The Japanese described the Mongolian Army as similar to the Soviet Army in every respect, with Soviet officers playing a prominent role in its training. They observed that it was staffed by Soviet officers, as was the Mongolian Air Force; just as in Soviet Russia, a "Bureau of Political Education" existed in the army; and military supplies came from the Soviet Union. In 1930 the former Mongolian People's Revolutionary Army was renamed the Red Army, its publication bearing the same name as that of its Moscow counterpart—*The Red Star*.[92] In 1937 Japan estimated the Mongolian armed forces at 25,000 men. The Eighth Congress of the Mongolian People's Revolutionary Party declared that the Mongolian Red Army "must strengthen its close bonds with the Red

[91] *M.S.E.* (2nd ed.), Vol. VII, col. 55.
[92] Y. Misshima and T. Goto, *A Japanese View of Outer Mongolia* (Tokyo, 1937), p. 56.

Army of the Soviet Union, which is the defender of the world's proletariat."[93]   Thus, the Mongolian Army had become a tool of the Soviet Red Army, perhaps even a component thereof.

As indicated by Captain Bimba, Soviet Russia required the Mongolian regime to establish a National Red Military Academy at Ulan Bator (Urga) as successor to the former Officer Training Corps under Tsarist control.   The instructors were for the most part Soviet Russians, with a few Soviet-trained Mongols of the rank of regimental commander.   In addition to preliminary courses, the instruction included military strategy, topography, communication, the science of fortification, and Russian language.   Political education was emphasized.   According to Bimba, the cadets were indoctrinated "over and over again that in order to attain complete independence, there was no other way for Outer Mongolia than to rely upon Soviet civilization and military force."[94]

It is generally believed that ever since the Red Army marched into Outer Mongolia in 1921, Soviet military occupation there has been in operation under one pretext or another.   Ostensibly the Red Army was "requested" by the Soviet-sponsored Mongolian Government to remain in Mongolia to preserve the security of Mongolia and the U.S.S.R.   The alleged Soviet-Mongolian secret treaty of 1923 provided that "Soviet troops might be stationed in Outer Mongolia in order to help the Mongolian people resist Chinese encroachment."[95]   Phillips, however, has presented the Soviet contention that Soviet occupation forces were withdrawn from Outer Mongolia contrary to the desire of the Mongolian "People's Government" following the conclusion of the Sino-Soviet Agreement of 1924.[96]   The U.S.S.R. itself officially declared that the withdrawal took place in 1925.[97]   But the reported withdrawal seemed to be doubtful in the light of continuing reports of Mongolian hatred for Soviet military occupation.   Furthermore, according to the eye-witness report of Captain Bimba, an uprising was planned for the spring of 1937 by many Soviet-trained yet nationalist-minded Mongolian officers, "to

[93] Cited in Dallin, *Soviet Russia and the Far East,* p. 81.

[94] Bimba, *op. cit.,* p. 7.

[95] For the text of the alleged secret treaty of Feb., 1923, see Zen Rin Cho Kai (Good Neighbor Association), *Mo Ko Tai Kang (A General View of Mongolia)* (Tokyo, 1938), Appendix II (6), pp. 550-551.

[96] Phillips, *Russia, Japan, and Mongolia,* p. 47.

[97] Cited in Doksom, *op. cit.,* p. 76.

force all of the Soviet troops stationed in Outer Mongolia to with-draw."[98] Because of this plot against Soviet occupation forces, a host of Mongolian political and military leaders, including Premier Gendun, Foreign Minister Sanbowa, War Minister Demid, Vice-War Minister Dalijap, and General Shionbul, President of the Military Academy, were victims of the subsequent purge and military coup organized by Soviet occupation troops and reinforcements with the help of the pro-Soviet faction headed by Choibalsan.[99] In the absence of reliable information from within the Soviet orbit, it is impossible to say to what extent, during the period since 1924, Russian troops have actually occupied Outer Mongolian territory. But it is clear that the Soviet-Mongolian "gentleman's agreement" of 1934, the mutual assistance protocol of 1936, and the military alliance of 1946 have all provided convenient legal bases for the continued presence of Soviet military forces in Outer Mongolia.

The extent of Soviet military control in Outer Mongolia was also indirectly reflected by events. Stalin, in a declaration to the world on March 1, 1936, committed the U.S.S.R. to defend Outer Mongolia.[100] In 1939, during the border incident at Nomonhan with Japanese forces from Manchuria, thousands of Russian planes and hundreds of tanks were believed to have entered the conflict under the mutual assistance protocol. The close collaboration and extensive contribution to the Soviet war cause in mobilization and fighting on the part of Outer Mongolia against Germany and Japan during World War II gave further evidence of military affiliation with Russia.

According to recent revelations by two Soviet-trained Mongolian officers, Captain Aligatza and Lieutenant Chamsu, Outer Mongolia's military strength consisted of twelve divisions and forty "border units" totaling 113,650 men. Soviet tanks and airplanes were attached to each division.[101] This picture showed that with a population around 900,000 and a Soviet-supervised armed force of 113,650,

---

[98] Bimba, *op. cit.*, p. 16.

[99] *Ibid.*

[100] Cf. *The Soviet Union and the Path to Peace*, A Collection of Statements and Documents, 1918-36 (London, 1936), p. 15.

[101] Each division contains fourteen battalions and every battalion four companies, totaling about 7,000 officers and men. Each of the border units has one company of less than 500 men. Besides, there were more than 9,600 cadets of the military academy and some special service troops. New York *Times*, March 22, 1948.

or one-eighth of the total population, Outer Mongolia had been transformed into a militant state under Soviet control.

The extent of Soviet control through political, economic, and military channels was indicated in 1936, when the Mongolian Government, whose claim to speak for the Mongolian people it owed to Soviet intervention, stated in a note to Moscow:

The Mongol working people and their government consider that henceforth the people of the Soviet Union and of our republic are bound by an unseverable community of fate, interests and great ideas . . . and, particularly, the people and government of our republic firmly trust in the aid of the U.S.S.R. and the Red Army if, contrary to expectations, conditions develop similar to those of 1921. . . .[102]

Commenting on Soviet control of Outer Mongolia, Maiskii likewise came to this conclusion: "It is our opinion that if Autonomous Mongolia has every reason to tie its fate with the fate of Russia, then Russia has every sufficient reason to manifest its special interest toward Autonomous Mongolia."[103] He pointed out that Autonomous Mongolia had undoubted importance to Russia in two respects: economic and political. He boasted that Russian policy "will not only serve its own interests but also accomplish its natural mission . . . for the victory of the advanced European civilization over the backward civilization of the Asiatic Continent."[104] Long known elsewhere as the White Man's Burden, this idea, when embraced by Russia, could only mean Soviet imperialism.

[102] Doksom, *op. cit.*, p. 74.
[103] Maiskii, *Sovremennaia Mongoliia (Contemporary Mongolia)*, p. 331.
[104] *Ibid.*, pp. 331-332.

XIV: TSARIST AND SOVIET POLICY IN TANNU TUVA

TANNU TUVA, which until 1921 was known internationally as Urianghai and in China as Tannu Urianghai, has long been a land of great promise. It is important in terms of "geopolitics" because it is an elevated Asiatic hinterland. It is a focal point of military strategy in Central Asia. Moreover, it is rich in natural resources, both agricultural and mineral.

Until 1911 Tannu Tuva, then Urianghai, administratively constituted a part of Western Outer Mongolia under the jurisdiction of the Chinese *Chiang-Chun,* or Military Governor, at Uliassutai. At the time of the Mongolian independence movement in that year, Russia took it over from Outer Mongolia and proclaimed a protectorate over it in 1914.[1] During the internal strife in Russia following World War I, it came again under Chinese jurisdiction but in 1921 the Soviets proclaimed it an independent "republic" under the tribal name of Tannu Tuva. In 1926, under Soviet auspices,[2] it was definitely separated from the rest of Outer Mongolia by treaty with Russia, against the will of both Mongolia and Tannu Tuva.

On October 13, 1944, Tannu Tuva was annexed by the U.S.S.R. as an autonomous region of the R.S.F.S.R. (Russian Soviet Federated Socialist Republic).[3] China was then still its nominal sovereign under both the Sun-Joffe declaration of 1923 and the Koo-Karakhan agreement of 1924, but Russia made neither any arrangement with China, nor any public announcement. As a matter of fact, Soviet determination to keep Tannu Tuva isolated prevented even the

[1] *B.S.E.* (1st ed.), Vol. LV (1947), col. 109.
[2] *The Encyclopaedia Americana,* 1943 ed., XXVI, 249.
[3] *B.S.E.* (1st ed.), Vol. LV, col. 110; Professor Schuman gives the date of the establishment of the Tuvinian Autonomous Region as October, 1945, which is not compatible with the cited Soviet source; cf. Frederick L. Schuman, *Soviet Politics at Home and Abroad* (New York, 1946), p. 313 n.

informed quarters in China and the outside world, including the United States, from learning of the action until a very much later time, and even then only through indirect channels. This unilateral, outright annexation is not even in accord with the later Sino-Soviet Agreement of 1945, by which both the U.S.S.R. and China undertook to guarantee the independence of Outer Mongolia as a whole.

STRATEGIC SIGNIFICANCE OF TANNU TUVA

Tannu Tuva is located in the Asiatic hinterland. At the northern tip of Outer Mongolia, it is bounded by Russian Siberia on almost three sides. It borders the Buriat Mongolian A.S.S.R. on the East, Irkutsk Province on the Northeast, Krasnoiarsk Territory on the North, and Altai Territory on the West.

The geographic importance of Tannu Tuva lies in its strategic location between China and Russia and next to Outer Mongolia, of which it has traditionally been considered a part. A Tannu Tuva in Russian hands would mean a shorter and a strategically more favorable border line with China or with an independent Outer Mongolia than would a Tannu Tuva in the hands of either of the latter. As a Tsarist War Minister once observed, a "considerable shortening of the frontier or our Empire with Mongolia would assure ourselves of the feasibility of making expeditions from Irkutsk and Tungka at the shortest distance from Uliassutai."[4] This was also important, he added, from a purely military point of view, as the Chinese troops in the district of Altai in Sinkiang were 300 to 600 versts away.[5] With Tannu Tuva lost to Russia, China or an independent Outer Mongolia would be left in a very strategically disadvantageous position: what was formerly a spearhead of northern defense would become a foreign-controlled natural stronghold which would point toward the heart of Western Mongolia and its center, Uliassutai, endangering the security of Sinkiang Province.

Tannu Tuva lies across Russia's direct approach to the western parts of Outer Mongolia: Kobdo and Uliassutai. Historically, this direct overland approach has followed one of two routes: the Ussinsk and the Tchuisk tracks. The first runs from Minusinsk via Ussin-

---

[4] Letter of Sukhomlinov, of March 14/1, 1914, no. 4253; quoted in Friters, *The International Position of Outer Mongolia*, p. 76.
[5] *Ibid.*

koje and Buluk to Dohahol. It would add greatly to the importance of this route if the potentialities of navigation on the Upper Yenisei should be developed between Minusinsk and Krasnyi or Kyzyl. The second road, the Tchuisk road, was one of the oldest routes from Siberia via Urianghai to Mongolia, beginning in Biisk and proceeding by way of Koshgatsh to Kobdo. It is a most hazardous route and during the Russian Civil War was the scene of many encounters. One Soviet writer points out that the route is politically important as "geographically the nearest road to the east."[6]

Before the political upheaval in Tannu Tuva, the major outlet was by water transport. There was also a passable road connecting Tannu Tuva with Minusinsk, a river port on the Yenisei. Now, Tannu Tuva has automobile, water, and air transport, but land transport still possesses great significance. Military actions during the period of Russian revolution and civil war produced more than nine hundred kilometers of automobile road. Along certain branches of the Yenisei flowing out of Tannu Tuva there is steamship transportation. In 1942 the freight turnover in Tannu Tuva was estimated at 2,193 thousand tons-kilometers. Fourteen districts of Tannu Tuva are now connected by graded roads with the capital city of Kyzyl, a name of which means "red." The Red City, in its turn, is connected by an automobile highway with Abakan, a station on the Trans-Siberian Railway and the center of the Khakas Autonomous District. All districts have telephone and radio communications with Kyzyl. There is a telegraph line connecting Kyzyl with Minusinsk.[7] These Soviet efforts to promote communication facilities have apparently been motivated by, and have further increased, the strategic importance of Tannu Tuva.[8]

Since Soviet industralization brought the Kuznets coalfield, which lies northwest of Tannu Tuva into prominence, the U.S.S.R. has given more emphasis to the strategic significance of Tannu Tuva. Whatever others may think of their conduct toward a weaker neighbor, the Soviets have undoubtedly thought it essential to move forward Russia's frontier as far as possible from her vital center. The mountain chains of Sayan and Tannu-Ola which surround Tannu

[6] Kashintsev, "Tchuiskyi Trakt v Mongolii" ("The Tchuisk Road in Mongolia"), *Novyi Vostok* (*The New East*), 1925, nos. 8-9, pp. 142-143.

[7] *B.S.E.* (1st ed.), Vol. LV, col. 115.

[8] Friters, *The International Position of Outer Mongolia,* p. 97.

Tuva from north and south have almost no passes. Russian control of Tannu Tuva would make the southern borders of Siberia practically impregnable to attack by enemy land forces.[9] Its strategic importance seemed to have been recognized by the government of Peter the Great when the latter vaguely claimed the whole river basins of Ob, Yenisei, and Lena, though this claim was not stressed by the government of Nicholas II. The seizure of Tannu Tuva by Russia meant that the latter's frontier with China or with an independent Outer Mongolia was no longer formed by the Sayan mountains but by the Tannu-Ola mountain chains, which slope more steeply to the south and could be more easily defended. Communications could be improved to hasten the sending of reinforcements there.[10]

ECONOMIC ATTRACTION OF TANNU TUVA

Tannu Tuva, though little explored as yet, is known to be rich in minerals.[11] As early as the middle of the nineteenth century, Russian gold prospectors began to mine along the tributaries of Bii-Khem and Ulu-Khem. Beneath the earth of Tannu Tuva are also copper ores of different types, as well as traces of iron ores and asbestos in the basin of the Khemchik. The largest asbestos deposit in Ak-Touvuran contains a reserve estimated at 1,600,000 tons. There are large coal reserves estimated at many tens of millions of tons along the Bii-Khem and the tributaries of the Ulu-Khem.[12]

At present, mining is the leading industry in Tannu Tuva. There are five gold fields, several coal mines, salt piles, and asbestos works.[13] Thus Tannu Tuva, with an area of 64,000 square miles and a population of about 65,000, is in an extremely favorable position to assure its inhabitants of the necessities of life in exchange for its great mineral wealth.[14]

Another special feature of Tannu Tuva's unlimited natural re-

[9] Fedor S. Mansvetov, "Russia and China in Outer Mongolia," *Foreign Affairs,* Vol. XXIV, no. 1, Oct., 1945, p. 148.

[10] *Bol'shoi Sovetskii Atlas Mira* (*Great Soviet Atlas of the World*), 1937, I, 131-132.

[11] *M.S.E.* (1st ed.), Vol. VIII (1930), col. 986.

[12] *B.S.E.* (1st ed.), Vol. LV, col. 113.

[13] *Ibid.*, p. 114.

[14] *The Encyclopaedia Americana,* 1943, XXVI, 249. Also see "Geographical Summaries of World Spheres of Influence" in *Encyclopaedia Britannica World Atlas* (1946), p. 124 (the figure therein is the 1938 estimate).

sources is its abundant water power. A network of rivers constitutes the water system of the Upper Yenisei.[15]

Tannu Tuva abounds in valuable fur-bearing animals, among which are black and silver foxes, sables, ermines, otters, and so forth, and other valuable game animals such as elk and deer. Over 70 per cent of the adult agricultural inhabitants engage in hunting as a subsidiary profession.[16] Lakes Ulu-Kul, Tolzhi-Kul, and Dzhauai-Kul are rich in fish, which are almost entirely ignored by a native people so well blessed by nature.[17]

The basis of the economy of Tannu Tuva is livestock raising.[18] The chief mass of cattle is concentrated in the western part of Tannu Tuva. In the central part, the proportion of large cattle rises, while in the eastern part, reindeer breeding is also developed.[19]

Agriculture in Tannu Tuva, as in the regions of Western Mongolia, was originally taught by the Chinese.[20] In 1931 the sown area in Tannu Tuva was 19.7 thousand hectares (one hectare equal to 2.47 acres).[21] The Soviet efforts in increasing its agricultural cultivation in latter years fully indicated how the Soviets have appreciated the virgin soil of Tannu Tuva.

The first Russian merchants came to Urianghai in 1867 and established three trading stations there. Their business was so prosperous that Siberian merchants, one after another, began to penetrate into the interior of the country. Up to the nineties of the last century, almost the whole territory of Urianghai was covered with

[15] *B.S.E.* (1st ed.), Vol. LV, col. 112.

[16] *Ibid.*, p. 114.

[17] Douglas Carruthers, *Unknown Mongolia* (London, 1913), I, 217, 221.

[18] According to the figures of the Russian Emigration Office, the Urianghais—the Tuvinian people—possessed in 1916 up to 108,000 head of horned cattle, more than 500,000 head of sheep and goats, and about 112,000 horses. In 1923 the commercial deputation of the Soviet Commisariat of Foreign Trade estimated that the Tuvinian people had 136,870 head of horned cattle, 108,580 horses, and 564,390 sheep and goats. In 1926, according to the report made by the Ministry of the Interior to the Fourth Great Khurudan, or general assembly of the Tuvinian "Republic," horned cattle were counted at 149,985 head. In 1930, there were altogether 1,030,000 head of cattle; in 1941, 1,462,000 head (small cattle, i.e., sheep and goats predominated). M. Safianov, "Kolonial'naia Politika Torgovogo Kapitala v Tannu-Tuve," ("The Colonial Policy of Commercial Capital in Tannu Tuva,"), *Novyi Vostok* (*The New East*), nos. 23-24, 1928, p. 169.

[19] *B.S.E.* (1st ed.), Vol. LV, col. 113.

[20] Grumm-Grzhimailo, *Zapadnaia Mongoliia i Uriankhaiskii Krai* (*Western Mongolia and the Urianghai Region*), III, 474.

[21] *B.S.E.* (1st ed.), Vol. LV, col. 114.

Russian trading stations.[22]   Most trade was conducted on credit, a practice so profitable to the Russian merchants that sales on credit guaranteed by the local society, or sometimes by an administrative unit as a whole, brought them one hundred per cent profit or more a year.   In 1896, according to the figures of Usinsk border administration, imports into Urianghai were 118,550 rubles, while exports were 125,000 rubles.   The accuracy of these figures is open to doubt, since in that year up to five thousand sables alone were exported at a reported price not less than 250,000 rubles.   The profit surpassed imagination.   The number of Russian commercial enterprises in Urianghai increased each year and their capital grew rapidly, accumulating at an impressively high rate.[23]

According to a Soviet author, the Tuvinian people (the Urianghais), were cruelly exploited by the Russian merchants who took sheep from them in return for having given them, years earlier, a little box of matches, or who seized the best Tuvinian pastures and hay harvests.[24]

Russian merchants in Tannu Tuva were assured of a privileged position.   As Safianov pointed out, they obtained from the Usinsk border administration preferential certificates guaranteeing them extraordinary privileges and protection while engaging in business operations across the border.   "Their rights were indeed various," he says, and "they were protected by the force and authority of a great power."[25]   In supplementing and developing the Peking treaty of 1860, the Russo-Chinese treaty of 1881 gave additional rights for Russian commerce in Outer Mongolia, including Tannu Tuva, as well as in Western China.   Russian commercial exploitation in Tannu Tuva was marked by tremendous capital accumulation for the Russians on the one hand and the aroused indignation of the Tuvinians against Russian merchants on the other.   As Safianov relates, "after the incident at Beselkov's trading station, attacks on Russian trading stations occurred repeatedly.   These were sometimes accompanied not only by burning but also by killing.   For this, the Tuvinian people were severely punished by the Chinese authorities."[26]

[22] Safianov, *op. cit.*, pp. 156-157.   [23] *Ibid.*, pp. 158-159.

[24] V. IUdin, "Sovremennoe Sotsial'no-Economicheskoe Polozhenie Tuvinskoi Respubliki" ("Contemporary Social-Economical Situation of the Tuvinian Republic"), *Revoliutsionnyi Vostok (The Revolutionary East)*, no. 3, 1928, p. 292.

[25] Safianov, *op. cit.*, p. 159.   [26] *Ibid.*

From the very outset, the Chinese merchants were not on an equal footing with the Russian merchants in Urianghai trade. As late as 1903 there was still in effect a decree issued by the Manchu Government prohibiting Chinese merchants from going into Tannu Tuva, though Chinese commercial capital is said to have appeared there as early as 1895. In 1910 there were more than thirty Chinese shops. To obtain trading rights, the firm had to pay a yearly tax of about one thousand *lan* or kuping *taels* in Uliassutai. It was a surprise to the Russian traders that the Tuvinian buyers always went to the Chinese merchants. The reason was that the Chinese merchants offered to the Tuvinians on credit their most preferred goods: green tea, tobacco, and bean oil for cooking. Besides, the Chinese, in accordance with old customs, entertained their Tuvinian customers with yellow-colored Chinese grain wine.[27]

However, as Safianov puts it, "the negative character of Chinese trade did not prevent it from marching victoriously along the road of conquest of the Tuvinian market."[28] In ten years of trade, Chinese merchants dominated the Urianghai market. They opened new firms, dictated prices, and even forced Russian merchants to act as their commissioners.[29] This inferiority of Russian trade in Tannu Tuva commercial competition created a resentment against the Chinese merchants, so that when the upheaval did come to Urianghai in 1911, Russian-inspired political pressure was applied to eliminate the influence of these Chinese merchants.

As early as the spring of 1920, a Soviet mission headed by Kashnikov came to Urianghai to discuss, among other things, the opening of Soviet trade in Urianghai. In 1922-24, as a consequence of these negotiations, Soviet co-operatives claimed the right to establish branches in Tannu Tuva against the opposition of the Tuvinians.[30]

While Soviet control of Tannu Tuva was still weak both politically and economically, some Chinese firms reappeared in this commercial vacuum in 1922 and quickly reoccupied their former dominant position. A new competition immediately began. Close collaboration in the development of commercial ties between the U.S.S.R. and the Tuvinian "Republic" was created. Tuvinian co-operatives and Soviet commercial organizations, such as agencies of Sibgostorg (Siberian

[27] *Ibid.*, pp. 159-160.
[29] *Ibid.*
[28] *Ibid.*, p. 161.
[30] *Ibid.*, p. 169.

State Trading Organization) and the Commercial-Industrial Bank, were established. Furthermore, a conference on the promotion of close commercial relations was held at the end of 1923.[31]

It seems quite warranted to conclude, therefore, that commercial considerations strongly motivated both Tsarist and Soviet Russia to take decisive action in Tannu Tuva.

TSARIST POLICY IN URIANGHAI

ENCOURAGEMENT OF COLONIZATION

Russian colonial policy in Urianghai or Tannu Tuva appeared to pursue a course similar to its traditional adventures in Siberia. A quasi-geopolitical rationale for its actions was provided, among others, by G. E. Grumm-Grzhimailo, a leading Russian geographer and anthropologist, who made a field study in Urianghai. "All Russian history," he observed, "presents a picture of the gradual movement of the Slav races to the east and the assimilation by them of the peoples of lesser culture." The Urianghai region "represents only the last step of this movement, which is as natural and lawful as progression of national masses, beginning from the immigration of the Phoenicians and the ancient Greeks, who made possible the spreading of culture within the limits of the then known world."[32] "To think otherwise," he added, "means to deny one of the laws that rule the world: the weaker yields his place to the stronger, physically or mentally."[33] These words certainly reveal the very roots of Russia's colonial ambition for Urianghai, a land of unexploited treasure. It is even more astonishing to learn from observations made by Russian writers that the Urianghais or Tuvinian people are "in the process of dying out."[34]

The first Russian settlers were farmers, the Martynov and Funtikov brothers, who came to Urianghai in 1885. When news of the Russian agricultural colony in Urianghai reached Uliassutai in 1888, the Manchu Chiang-Chun seemed not to take it too seriously and only prohibited the settlement of new colonists. The policy of Russian border authorities was also slightly modified as a result of

---

[31] *Ibid.*, p. 170.
[32] Grumm-Grzhimailo, *op. cit.*, III, 541.
[33] *Ibid.*   [34] E.g., Grumm-Grzhimailo in *ibid.*

vigorous protests from the Urianghais that their pastures had been seized by the Russians. However, these measures did not stop the settlers. Russian trading stations in Turan and Uiuk grew into large villages.[35]

As a Soviet author commented, State-Secretary Kulomzin showed interest in the problem of colonization in Urianghai in 1903, and "from that time on, the Tsarist Government made this region an objective of its aggressive policy, and began a systematic settlement of Urianghai by Russian colonists."[36] In 1907, in the bordering province of Usinsk, a border chief was appointed to observe and perhaps to approve all the co-operative measures in the colonization in Urianghai. As a result, in a short interval of time, the central region of Urianghai had been covered by a network of Russian villages. In this way, the writer pointed out, "Tsarist Russia, principally through its merchant-settlers, opened a way for herself to the Urianghai territory."[37]

In 1913 the border administration of the Usinsk territory was reorganized into a commission. To assist the chief for border affairs of the Usinsk Province, the officials of colonial administration were commanded to extend managerial and economic-cultural assistance to the Russian settlers in the Urianghai land. Thus, "persistently carrying out the plan of strengthening the Urianghai territory for Russian people," Grumm-Grzhimailo says, "the Russian Government from this time on carried on organizational work in the region on a large scale, and only the World War and the revolution following it put an end to this work."[38]

SEPARATION AND ISOLATION

In the period from 1911 to 1917, the Urianghais, the Mongols, and the Chinese all endeavored to maintain the territorial integrity of Outer Mongolia as a geographical and political unit, and attempted to forestall Tsarist efforts to carve off Urianghai from the rest of Outer Mongolia. But by political pressure, diplomatic intrigue, and actual and military maneuver Tsarist Russia successfully frustrated their efforts.

In accord with the terms of a number of treaties between China

[85] *Ibid.*, pp. 536-537. [86] IUdin, *op. cit.*, p. 292.
[87] *Ibid.*
[88] Grumm-Grzhimailo, *op. cit.*, III, 547.

and Russia, Urianghai was traditionally considered to be under Chinese sovereignty.[39] The Sino-Russian Kiakhta treaty of 1727 designated the Sayan Mountains as the dividing line between the respective domains of China and Russia. Thus Urianghai was legally established as Chinese territory and administratively constituted a part of Outer Mongolia.[40] Subsequently, the Treaty of Tarbahatai (or Chuguchak) of 1864 and the Treaty of Uliassutai of 1870 further demarcated the boundaries along the Sayan Mountains; following them, many stone signs with carved inscriptions were erected to indicate the demarcation line.[41] Nevertheless, the Russians continued to look upon Urianghai as a possible and desirable prey within easy reach.

No sooner had the Chinese Revolution broken out than Russian troops occupied the territory of Urianghai, synchronizing their maneuvers with those in eastern Outer Mongolia.[42] When the new regime was established in Urga in 1911 under Russian sponsorship, the leading men in Urianghai addressed themselves to the Hutukhtu in Urga in order to unite the five *khoshuns*, or districts, of Urianghai in a special *aimak*, or province, under his leadership.[43] In 1912 Noyan Gombodji, the then Mongol amban, and previously subordinate to the Manchu chiang-chun or military governor at Uliassutai under the Manchu Empire, brought Urianghai into line with the Outer Mongolian independence movement. But in 1913 he came under the influence of Russian "forward policy" in that region. In 1924 the Governor-General of Irkutsk recommended the further strengthening of Russian influence in Urianghai in order to prevent the affiliation of the latter with its "spiritual sovereign," the Urga Living Buddha.[44]

During the Russo-Mongolian negotiations in 1912, Korostovets, the Russian negotiator and former minister to Peking, balked at the idea that the frontier between Mongolia and Siberia should continue

---

[39] Mansvetov, *op. cit.*, p. 148.

[40] Wang, Chin-yu and Shih, Shou-chang, *Chung-O Yueh Chu* (*Sino-Russian Treaties and Annotations*), Vol. I, Treaty of Kiakhta.

[41] Tsou Tai-chün, *Chung-O Chieh Chi* (*Sino-Russian Boundary Demarcations*) (Wuchang, 1911), Vol. II, chaps. ii-iii.

[42] Liu Ching-chang, *Mongolia, An Object of International Rivalries in the Far East* (Unpublished Master's thesis in Boston University), chap. ix.

[43] Friters, *The International Position of Outer Mongolia*, p. 74.

[44] Gerard M. Friters, "The Development of Outer Mongolian Independence," *Pacific Affairs*, X (Sept., 1937), p. 326.

to include Urianghai within Mongolia.[45]   The Mongols, who asserted that independence would be a fiction, without a recognized frontier for their nation, were rebuffed. In July, 1914, Miller, the Russian diplomatic agent at Urga, again warned the Mongols that the question of Urianghai must under no circumstances be raised during the forthcoming tripartite conference at Kiakhta, inasmuch as it had already been settled by the Russians.[46]   In 1916 the Mongols again requested the admission of Mongol officials into Urianghai as successors to the former Manchu officials.   The Russian reply was that the Chinese claim to Urianghai was so doubtful that it was out of the question for China to cede the territory to Mongolia while Mongolia itself had no claim in its own right.[47]

According to Article IV of the Russo-Chinese Declaration of 1913, "Autonomous Outer Mongolia shall comprise the regions which have been under the jurisdiction of the Chinese Amban at Urga, of the Chinese Protector-General [or Military Governor] at Uliassutai, and of the Chinese Amban at Kobdo." Therefore, the realm of Autonomous Outer Mongolia would logically be interpreted as including Urianghai.   However, Russia harbored no intention of loosening her hold on the seized territory.   In contravention of Article V of the 1913 declaration, which provided that the exact boundaries of Outer Mongolia should be the subject of the subsequent conference, Miller foiled the Chinese efforts to put Urianghai on the agenda of the Kiakhta conference in 1915 by merely saying that the frontier should remain as before.[48]

Again, under the Treaty of Kiakhta, China claimed that the Mongols had agreed to admit Chinese officials to regulate mixed Mongol-Chinese questions. Both China and Outer Mongolia argued that Urianghai was an integral part of Outer Mongolia. Therefore, the Mongols must either prevent Russia from treating Urianghai as Russian territory or admit Chinese officials to Urianghai, since they themselves recognized the territory as under Chinese suzerainty. As Mr. Friters points out, "to the latter alternative the Mongols agreed;

[45] Cf. Korostovets to Sazonov, tel. no. 6, Sept. 27, 1912, *S.D.D. po M.V.*, p. 5.
[46] Miller to Sazonov, letter no. 212, Aug. 1/July 19, 1914, *M.O. v E.I.*, Ser. III, Vol. V, doc. no. 447, pp. 353, 354.
[47] Ivan J. Korostovets, *Von Cinggis Khan bis zur Sowjet-republik*, Berlin, 1926, p. 197; Friters, "The Development of Outer Mongolian Independence," *Pacific Affairs*, X, 327.
[48] Cf. n. 47 *supra*.

but Mongols and Chinese were frustrated when Russia ordered a detachment of Cossacks, posted at Kobdo in Outer Mongolia, to move into Urianghai."[49] The Chinese officials then gave up the attempt to enter.

At the end of 1916 China adopted another course. The Chinese minister at St. Petersburg asked Russia to recognize the jurisdiction of the Chinese commissioner at Uliassutai over Urianghai as part of Outer Mongolia. This forced Russia to reaffirm her previous position to the effect that "Urianghai was under Russian protection and that it did not belong to Autonomous Mongolia and therefore formed no part of the district of Uliassutai and could not come under the jurisdiction of a Chinese official."[50]

Russian policy succeeded not only in separating Urianghai from Outer Mongolia but also in isolating it from the outside world. Tsarist Foreign Minister Sazanov declared that in exchange for receiving Russian protection "the Urianghais must first of all give up the right of external relations and must pledge themselves to form connections with their neighbors only through the official stationed in the territory by the Governor-General of Irkutsk."[51] Thus, in July, 1914, an instruction was communicated by the Chief of Frontier Affairs, Zereni, to Amban Gombodji and other Urianghai officials:

Your duty is to maintain no relations of any kind with foreign states, including Mongolia. In case such relations should be necessary, they can only be conducted through me as the representative of the Russian Government in the territory of Urianghai or by a person deputized by me.[52]

PROTECTION AIMING AT EVENTUAL ANNEXATION

In discussing Russian policy toward Urianghai in 1911, the Tsarist Council of Ministers agreed that none of the historical docu-

---

[49] Friters, "The Development of Outer Mongolian Independence," *Pacific Affairs*, X, 328. Also see Liu Kwei-nan, "Wai-Meng Chih Kao-chu yu Chiang-lai" ("The Past and the Future of Outer Mongolia"), *Eastern Miscellany*, Shanghai, Vol. XXXII, no. 4, 1935, p. 66.

[50] Goremykin's initial reply, dated April 22, to Sazonov's letter of April 12, 1914, cited in Friters, "The Development of Outer Mongolian Independence," *Pacific Affairs*, X, 328; Liu Kwei-nan, *op. cit.*, p. 67.

[51] Sazonov to Nicholas II, report, April 11/March 29, 1914, signed by the Tsar, April 17/4, 1914: "Agreed," *M.O. v E.I.*, Ser. III, Vol. II, doc. no. 203, p. 281.

[52] Text of Russian Declaration to Amban Gombodji, July 17/4, 1914, *M.O. v E.I.*, Ser. III, Vol. IV, doc. no. 267, p. 326.

ments, which went back to the eighteenth century and showed that some of the Urianghai tribes had paid tributes in furs to both Russian and Manchu officials, could serve as proof of the allegiance of that territory to Russia. As for more recent agreements, the Protocol of Chuguchak of 1864 again denied any possible Russian claim to the territory beyond the Sayan Mountains. The journal of the Council of Ministers concluded, with the approval of the Tsar, that the only possible policy for Russia was one of peaceful penetration beyond the Sayan Mountains. Thus, the policy of St. Petersburg toward Urianghai was "to strengthen it gradually for Russia."[53] Sazonov himself was convinced that it was necessary to tackle the question of the territory of Urianghai "carefully and gradually."[54]

However, the Governor-General of Irkutsk believed in the necessity of an active policy. In forwarding a demand of the inhabitants of Urianghai to be received as Russian subjects, the Governor-General pointed out to the Tsar that, though it was perhaps not advisable to receive them formally as Russian subjects, it was most desirable to furnish them with a definite answer to the effect that Russia would be prepared to take them under her protection. Sazonov agreed with this proposal. In his opinion, there was no necessity to take radical measures immediately to annex the Urianghai territory. The Assistant Minister for Land Organization and Agriculture, on the other hand, favored a strong policy of immediate and complete annexation. The War Minister agreed with Sazonov's policy, provided that it was regarded as "the first step on the way towards the complete affiliation of the whole territory with our Empire."[55] While acknowledging Sazonov's prudence in not annexing Urianghai, and criticizing his policy concerning the territory, Russian Prime Minister Goremykin considered the establishment of a protectorate to be "a further step on the road which, it is my deep conviction, leads ultimately to complete and definite affiliation of the territory of Urianghai with a great and powerful Russia."[56]

[53] Grumm-Grzhimailo, *op. cit.*, III, 546.

[54] Sazonov to Minister of War Sukhomlinov, Minister of the Interior Maklakov, and Assistant to the Head of the Chief Administration of Land Organization Ignatiev, letter no. 181, March 10/Feb. 25, 1914, *M.O. v E.I.*, Ser. III, Vol. I, doc. no. 409, pp. 535-536.

[55] Letter of Sukhomlinov, March 14/1, 1914, no. 4253, quoted in Friters, *The International Position of Outer Mongolia*, p. 76.

[56] Letter of Goremykin, April 22/9, 1914, cited in Friters, "The Development of Outer Mongolian Independence," *Pacific Affairs*, Vol. X, no. 3, p. 328.

Thus, according to a Soviet author, V. IUdin, "The representatives of the Tsarist Government, having become unlimited masters in Urianghai, ceased to trouble themselves with masking from the native people the cynical seizure and exploitation of that territory."[57] Hence the conquerors, "using open threats as the most reliable measures," spoke to the Urianghai inhabitants in "tough and clear language" in order to "hold the conquered people in obedience." Immediately after the occupation of Urianghai, the Commissar for Urianghai Affairs, Grigor'ev, in a circular sent to Urianghai princes and officials, wrote:

The Great Russian Empire, proclaiming the event of taking the Urianghai land under its protection, accepted this land and the Urianghai people living thereon in its individual charge. Therefore, from the day of proclamation of the said protection, no other states whatsoever, except the above mentioned Great Russian, can, without the consent of the latter through their ordinary subjects [citizens], missionaries, or officials, develop any kind of activities in Urianghai, and moreover infringe upon its administration, i.e., tax the people, try the Urianghais, punish them, demand explanation from Urianghai officials or from the princes themselves; on the contrary, each foreign state is responsible to the Russian Government.[58]

The tactful explanation of Russian policy given by Grumm-Grzhimailo was that "the establishment of a republican regime in China, the proclamation of Mongolian independence and the banishment of Chinese authorities from Kobdo and Uliassutai, to which administration the Urianghai territory belonged," broke off the dependence of Urianghai on China; and since Outer Mongolia could not claim any right on it, "Urianghai, in this manner, was practically a no man's land."[59] In spite of this explanation, the Soviet critics of Russian aggression have been frank and impressive enough. IUdin has the following straightforward comment:

The aggressive policy of the Tsarist Government with regard to this territory was successfully accomplished in 1913 by the recognition on the part of the princes, the rulers of Urianghai, of the 'protection' of Russia; the territory has been incorporated into Yenisei Province, and subsequently in 1914, there followed a 'highest order' concerning the appointment of a commissar for the affairs of the Urianghai territory. *Thus, with forced tempo, the Tsarist Government took in hand the potentially rich Urianghai*

[57] IUdin, *op. cit.*, p. 203.   [58] *Ibid.*
[59] Grumm-Grzhimailo, *op. cit.*, II, 794.

territory, which had important strategic significance for Russian imperialism as a foremost outpost for its further aggressive plans in Central Asia.[60]

As if with deep sympathy for the subjugated Urianghai people, the Soviet author rejoiced that the October Revolution soon "put an end to the predatory policy of the Tsarist Government, and the Tuvinian people threw off the yoke of alien mastery."[61]   However, the effect of subsequent Soviet policy on the fate of Tannu Tuva remains to be examined.

Soviet Policy in Tannu Tuva

New Stream of Colonization

Generally speaking, it is not so easy to discuss a particular phase of Soviet policy as it is of Tsarist policy.   The secrets of the latter have been revealed to some extent, and its harsh aspects criticized and denounced by Soviet authors.   Soviet policy we can observe only obliquely.   Yet, in most cases, it is possible to apply Soviet criticisms of Tsarist policy to Soviet policy itself.   The two are essentially similar, with the Soviets perhaps more tactful, more secretive, and more positive.

So far there is no special literature dealing with Soviet colonization in Tannu Tuva, but Mansvetov and others estimate that the Russian population now surpasses that of the native people there.[62] This alone indicates the necessity for full investigation and pioneer exploration of the subject.

Judging from population figures of different years in different sources, the population of Tannu Tuva has increased rapidly and certainly out of proportion to its past record.   For example, according to Soviet figures the population increased 38.4 per cent in the fourteen years from 1925 to 1939.[63]   In 1927, according to Soviet figures, the population was 70,200, including 12,000 Russians; in 1941, it had become 95,000 with 86 per cent said to be Tuvinians.[64]   This meant an increase of 35.4 per cent in another sampling of fourteen

---

[60] IUdin, *op. cit.*, pp. 292-293.   Italics added.

[61] *Ibid.*, p. 294.

[62] Mansvetov, *op. cit.*, p. 152.

[63] *B.S.E.* (1st ed.), Vol. LV, col. 113.

[64] For 1941 figure, see *ibid.*; for 1927 figure, see *M.S.E.* (1st ed.), Vol. VIII, col. 986.

years. If the population estimate of 1938, according to Anglo-American sources, is 65,000, including 12,000 Russians,[65] and the Soviet figure for Tuvinian population in 1946 is 95,000, the population increase in the period of eight years is 46.2 per cent. Since Russian writers have spoken of the "dying off" of the whole Tuvinian race, its birth rate cannot be high. Thus, this extraordinary increase must be explained by immigration, which is possible only from the U.S.S.R.

Another notable sign of Soviet colonization in Tannu Tuva is reflected in the boom of all types of Soviet Socialist institutions there, such as the collective use of agricultural machinery, and the establishment of factories or combines, schools, newspapers, and scientific and cultural institutions of a Soviet type.

As noted above, since the years of Soviet *de facto* rule, the acreage of cultivated land in Tannu Tuva has been greatly increased and many *artely*, associations, and *sovkhozy* have been organized. According to Soviet claims, the present cultivation of land there is conducted with modern, complex agricultural machinery.[66] If this is true, then the increasing needs of agricultural machinery must to a certain extent parallel the increase of Russian agricultural immigrants, because the Soviets would not entrust their precious machinery to the less educated natives. The same is true of the immigration of industrial workers, as Soviet information indicated that there are now in Tannu electrical stations, a state printing establishment, a factory for mechanical repairs, a sewing combine, leather works, etc.[67] It is fairly clear, as Professor Cressey points out, that in the Soviet "export of automobiles and trucks, cotton cloth, and textile and agricultural machinery to peripheral states such as Outer Mongolia, Tannu Tuva, Chinese Sinkiang . . . political ends have been in-

---

[65] For Anglo-American figures, see *The Encyclopaedia Americana*, 1943 ed., XXVI, 249; "Geographical Summaries," *Encyclopaedia Britannica World Atlas*, p. 124.

[66] In 1941 there were in Tannu Tuva 37 tractors, two combine machines, 6,700 iron ploughs, 1,200 mowing machines. In 1945 there were four MTS (Machine-Tractor Stations) with the number of tractors increased to 115 and combine machines to 12. Since Soviet industrialization of agriculture has not yet been developed to a high degree, modern agricultural machinery is not yet in wide use, even in the European portion of the U.S.S.R., especially during wartime (it is only infrequently that one sees any along the railway line to the east). Therefore such an increase in the use of agricultural machinery in the primitive agricultural economy of Tannu Tuva must be unusual. *B.S.E.* (1st ed.), Vol. LV, cols. 114-115.

[67] *Ibid.*, col. 115.

volved."[68]   In the present case, colonization of a political nature is evidently among the "political ends" of the U.S.S.R. in Tannu Tuva.

According to Soviet figures, in Tannu Tuva there were only four schools with sixty students in 1924-25. The number of students and the variety in types of educational institutions were greatly increased in later years.[69] This increase might prove not only the accomplishments but also the needs, in part at least, of the Soviet colonists in Tannu Tuva.

As to other cultural organizations, it may also be said that they are needed more by Russian immigrants than by native Tuvinians who by nature prefer to dwell peacefully in seclusion.[70] Thus, the prosperity of the cultural establishment in Tannu Tuva may reflect more the rapid increase of Russian population and intelligentsia than the success of the highly publicized civilizing mission.

It is generally known that the U.S.S.R. suffers from a shortage of manpower at home. It is also believed by demographic scientists that the U.S.S.R. has ample room to absorb a great population growth.[71] However, it is not difficult to explain why there was a new stream of Soviet colonization to Tannu Tuva. Even though anxious to increase her own population, the U.S.S.R. did not hesitate to pour more colonists into Tannu Tuva for the reason that she had no doubts but that Tannu Tuva would eventually belong to her. Secondly, Soviet colonists there were a means of consolidating possession of the Tuvinian land for the U.S.S.R. in a great task of empire building.

RENEWED SEPARATION AND ISOLATION

After the Russian Revolution in 1917, Urianghai became a battleground of the Russian Civil War. Utilizing this opportunity, the

[68] George B. Cressey, *The Basis of Soviet Strength* (London, 1946), p. 143.

[69] In 1939 there were 42 summer schools with 1,640 children. In 1945-46, in Tannu Tuva there were altogether 10,517 students studying in the teachers' college, the medical college, the veterinary technical school, the party school, and the institute of language, literature, and history. Other cultural organizations include 51 village reading rooms, 17 district clubs, 67 libraries, and other political-educational institutions. Soviet sources also indicated that since the creation of the Tuvinian written language in 1930, 18 per cent literacy had been attained by 1931 and greater achievements were made in later years. *B.S.E.* (1st ed.), Vol. LV, col. 115.

[70] Carruthers, *op. cit.*, I, 213-214.

[71] Frank W. Notestein and others, *The Future Population of Europe and the Soviet Union* (New York, 1944), pp. 70-71.

Chinese Government began taking steps in January, 1919, to restore the old Manchu position there. From then on, it conducted a campaign against the White Russians in Urianghai and wiped them out in June of the same year.[72] A Special Assistant Commissioner was thereafter appointed to reside in Urianghai for recruitment and rehabilitation. Thus, Urianghai had returned to China's fold even before the rest of Outer Mongolia had surrendered its autonomy in November, 1919. However, the Urianghai fear of alienating the White Russians, together with the inefficiency of the Chinese garrisons, made it easy for the Soviets in 1921 to come in and to drive out the Chinese officials and garrisons in the name of world revolution and liberation of the oppressed peoples of the East. Actually, according to one interpretation, the Soviets desired to compensate for the great setbacks in the West since the signing of the humiliating Brest-Litovsk Treaty of March 3, 1918, in spite of the fact that the treaty itself was annulled by the Soviets on November 13 of the same year. They also wished to obtain a base for supporting the then Far Eastern Republic, near Lake Baikal, as a buffer state between the R.S.F.S.R. and the Interventionists, since it was being threatened at the time by Japanese imperialism.

After the Soviet occupation, an assembly of the khoshuns of Urianghai was called on August 13, 1921, under Soviet tutelage to declare the independence of Urianghai, which Soviet Russia immediately recognized on September 9, 1921.[73] To mark the new status, the name of Urianghai was changed in 1921 to the tribal name of Tannu Tuva (Tangno Toba).

In 1924 the inhabitants of Urianghai declared their affiliation with Outer Mongolia.[74] Soviet Russia was as intolerant of such a move as Tsarist Russia would have been. As Dr. Friters points out, "troops were sent which successfully suppressed the revolt."[75]

So far as Outer Mongolia was concerned, it became clear during the third session of the Mongolian People's Party Congress in August, 1924, that the Mongols desired to include the territory of

[72] Liu Ching-chang, *op. cit.*, chap. ix.
[73] *Ibid.*
[74] V. Durdenevsky, "Narodni Respubliiki Tsentralnoi Azii, Mongolska ta Tuvinska" ("The People's Republics of Central Asia—Mongolia and Tuva"), in *S. S.*, no. 3 (9), 1929, p. 108; Friters, *The International Position of Outer Mongolia*, p. 96.
[75] *Ibid.*

Urianghai in the Mongolian People's "Republic."[76] However, they were told by the representative of the Soviet Union, Vasiliev, that the Russians would not countenance the Mongol desire to regain Tannu Tuva. He also stressed the importance of the Comintern role in the development of Outer Mongolia.[77] Since Russian troops had suppressed the Urianghai revolt, the Mongolian People's Party Congress was, therefore, faced with a *fait accompli;* nonetheless, it adopted a resolution asking for a Russian-Mongolian Commission to regulate the question of Urianghai.[78] Moscow cleverly met the desires of Mongols only in a minor point. A small, sparsely inhabited strip of territory (about 16,000 square kilometers), called Darkhat, west of Koso Kol (Lake) was given to Outer Mongolia.[79] Immediately thereafter, in 1925, a mission in Moscow drew up, without further territorial changes, a treaty of friendship between the "People's Republic" of Tannu Tuva and the Mongolian "People's Republic," modeled on the Soviet-Mongolian Agreement of 1921.[80] In this new agreement, finally signed in August, 1926, the two governments reluctantly recognized each other's independence and agreed to send representatives to the respective capitals.[81]

"To divide and rule" has long proved to be a most effective doctrine, and the fundamental core of any aggressive policy. Very little of the Soviet policy in Tannu Tuva has been made public. However, the opinions of Soviet writers may suffice to provide good evidence on the Soviet attitude under the given circumstances. As Professor V. Durdenevsky states bluntly: "Mongolia and Tannu Tuva cannot join. The idea is *clearly* and absolutely impossible." He cites the different language (Turkic) of Tannu Tuva, and the fact that that country's economic development demands conditions for farming similar to those in the Siberian districts. Moreover, the inhabitants "do not consider themselves at all as Mongols . . . the misuse of power by feudal lords who had all come from Outer Mongolia made them not very friendly towards Mongols." Tuva's people and the

[76] *Ibid.*
[77] Max Beloff, *The Foreign Policy of Soviet Russia,* London, 1947, I, 243.
[78] Korostovets, *op. cit.,* p. 340; cited in Friters, *The International Position of Outer Mongolia,* p. 96.
[79] *Ibid.,* pp. 96-97; W. Leimbach, *Landeskunde von Tuwa* (Gotha, 1936), p. 101.
[80] Friters, *The International Position of Outer Mongolia,* p. 97.
[81] *Ibid.;* Durdenevsky, *op. cit.,* p. 114.

Mongols, he concludes, will not become one nation.[82]   In fact, as Dr. Friters points out, "Soviet Russia's policy in Tuva has ever since been directed towards ensuring that a different national feeling is developed there." Soviet agricultural policy has aimed at settling the inhabitants and thereby drawing them away from a nomadic life like that of the Mongols. Intensive colonization by Russians, and the introduction of a national Tuvinic written language (which until 1931 had been Mongolian) have been, according to him, other important "means of separating Tuva from Outer Mongolia, and at the same time increasing Soviet Russia's hold on the country."[83]

Under Soviet *de facto* control, as under the Tsarist "usurpers," Tannu Tuva has been separated from Outer Mongolia and isolated from the outside world as well. All borders of Tannu Tuva, like those of the rest of Outer Mongolia, have remained closed except those contiguous to Soviet Russia.[84] The Chinese Republic has been unable to enter into direct relations with Outer Mongolia as a whole and with Tannu Tuva in particular. As Larson points out, "every attempt is made to keep news from coming out concerning conditions, so that at this time, Outer Mongolia [including Tannu Tuva] has no communication with the rest of the world except through Soviet channels."[85]

Soviet diplomacy is often credited with the ability to manipulate all possible measures to meet its own ends. This is true of her policy of isolating Outer Mongolia in general and Tannu Tuva in particular. In spite of a series of treaties between the U.S.S.R. and Outer Mongolia, and between the U.S.S.R. and Tannu Tuva—treaties bitterly opposed by China, who claimed that her sovereignty was thus violated—Mr. Litvinov repeatedly assured the Chinese Government, in reply to its protests, that the Soviet Government continued to recognize Chinese sovereignty over Outer Mongolia under the Sino-Soviet agreement of 1924.[86] From the Chinese point of view, this recognition should have covered Tannu Tuva as well, since it had traditionally been considered part of Outer Mongolia. In giving continuous lip service to Chinese sovereignty in Outer Mongolia,

[82] *Ibid.*, p. 101.
[83] Friters, *The International Position of Outer Mongolia,* p. 97.
[84] Mansvetov, *op. cit.,* p. 150.
[85] Larson, *op. cit.,* p. 240.
[86] *Pravda,* April 8, 1936; Moscow *Daily News,* weekly edition, April 15, 1936; full text of Litvinov's statement in New York *Times,* April 8, 1936.

therefore, the Soviets were engaged, intentionally or not, in a diplomatic maneuver to advance their own interests. By not clarifying and bringing into the open their own views on the status of Tannu Tuva, the Soviets risked complicating the international situation, but they could at the same time quiet Chinese doubts and avoid offending Chinese pride. Most important of all, they could use the gesture of recognizing Chinese sovereignty to maintain "a convenient legal fiction which prevents direct relations between Outer Mongolia and foreign states."[87]

The Soviet policy of isolating Tannu Tuva is all-embracing. Like the rest of Outer Mongolia, Tannu Tuva had had no trade relations with the other states. While Article XIX of the Consular Regulations of the U.S.S.R., adopted in January, 1926, provides that a Soviet consul may represent another state as well as the Soviet Union, the implication in relation to Outer Mongolia as a whole and Tannu Tuva in particular may be easily seen.[88] Moreover, since 1921 there has been less and less actual communication between Tannu Tuva, together with the rest of Outer Mongolia, and China. Since 1925, Chinese merchants have been virtually excluded. Their properties were overtaxed until nothing was left, and their lives were endangered.[89] From that time on, even postal communication with Tannu Tuva and the rest of Outer Mongolia has been possible only by way of Siberia.[90] An appeal by the Chinese Government to Outer Mongolia (including Tannu Tuva) to attend a conference on Mongolian and Tuvinian affairs in 1930 received no response.[91]

All in all, the separation and isolation of Tannu Tuva aimed at by Soviet policy have been successfully completed. It is clear that the Soviets played a triple game: (1) They used China to keep foreign countries out of Outer Mongolia as a whole. (2) They used Outer Mongolian "independence" to oust China. (3) They used Tuvinian "independence" to counteract Mongolian efforts. Through these procedures the Soviet Union reduced Tannu Tuva to an area *verboten* to outside political influences.

[87] Friters, "The Development of Outer Mongolian Independence," *Pacific Affairs*, X, 334.

[88] *Ibid.*, p. 325.

[89] "Wai-Meng chih Shan-yu" ("The Commerce in Outer Mongolia"), *Eastern Miscellany*, Vol. XXVIII, no. 6 (March, 1931), p. 38.

[90] *Ta Kung Pao*, Tientsin, Feb. 27, 1931; also cited in Friters, "The Development of Outer Mongolian Independence," X, 335.

[91] *Ibid.*; *Chinese Affairs* (Nanking), May 31, 1930, pp. 1-2.

NEW TACTICS OF PROTECTION AND ANNEXATION

After the February Revolution in Russia in 1917, the Provisional Government took measures to strengthen Urianghai for Russia. On June 13, 1917, the Russian-Tuvinian Territorial Congress confirmed "the preservation of supreme civil power for her."[92] After the October Revolution, Soviet authority was established in the Russian settlement in Urianghai on March 8, 1918. When the Chinese authorities came back to Urianghai in January, 1919, to "restore sovereignty" and to protect Chinese merchants, the territorial congress of Russian colonists had replaced the commissar of the Russian Provisional Government and had elected a territorial Soviet of Deputies.[93] After the establishment of a White regime in Siberia, the Chinese authorities in Urianghai were in a position to fight against the White encroachment until they were finally driven out in 1921 by the Soviet troops.

On August 13, 1921, under Soviet auspices, the first congress of the representatives of the Khoshun in Urianghai, with the participation of the delegates from the Siberian Revolutionary Committee and the Mongolian People's "Revolutionary Government," proclaimed Urianghai an independent state. It also elected a government, adopted a provisional constitution, and established "friendly relations" with the Russian settlement in Urianghai.[94]

On September 9, 1921, when the new tactics of Soviet domination in Urianghai had already been in effect, Soviet Russia (or the R.S.F.S.R.) renounced the Tsarist protection of Urianghai established in 1914[95] in the face of Chinese protest.[96]

On December 12, 1921, the Great Khuruldan or General Assembly again proclaimed Urianghai a "people's state" and adopted a constitution annulling all the debts of the people incurred before 1921. Under an agreement with the Tuvinian authorities, the Soviet citizen-colonists organized a self-governing labor colony. The path of Soviet control in Urianghai was, however, none too smooth, for a rebellion of the feudal lords and lamas broke out in the spring of 1924. The insurrection was put down by the Soviet occupation authorities only in the summer of that year.[97]

[92] *M.S.E.* (1st ed.), Vol. VIII, col. 987.   [93] *Ibid.*
[94] *Ibid.*, cols. 987-988.   [95] *Ibid.*, col. 988.
[96] Zen Rin Cho Kai, *Mo Ko Tai Kang*, p. 220.
[97] *M.S.E.* (1st ed.), Vol. VIII, col. 988.

On July 22, 1925, a treaty of friendship was signed between the U.S.S.R. and Tannu Tuva, in which the U.S.S.R. once again confirmed its renunciation of the protection established by Tsarist Russia over Urianghai.[98] Since this move closely followed the suppression of the Tuvinian rebellion and the consolidation of Soviet control, it provides evidence that the U.S.S.R. prefers *de facto* and effective control to nominal protection, the title of which may do harm rather than good for Soviet prestige in the minds of oppressed, innocent peoples. Professor Schuman said, "Tannu Tuva had already become an 'independent' Soviet protectorate in 1923."[99] In the *Encyclopaedia Britannica World Atlas* Tannu Tuva was referred to as a Soviet protectorate.[100] From a legal point of view, the basis of these assertions should be re-evaluated.

On November 24, 1926, the Great Khuruldan, in its fourth session, declared for the third time the new status of Tannu Tuva. This time, a "People's Republic" of Tannu Tuva was proclaimed, and again, as a matter of course, a constitution was adopted. Under this constitution the country was declared an independent republic; all the land, its natural deposits, waters, forests, and their resources were to be the property of all the people; foreign trade was to be a monopoly of the state; a People's Revolutionary Army was to be organized; the church was to be separated from the state, etc.[101]

A Soviet writer, Professor V. Durdenevsky, made a comparison between the Constitution of the R.S.F.S.R. of July 10, 1918, and the Constitution of the Mongolian "People's Republic" of November 26, 1924, as well as with the Constitution of Tannu Tuva of November 24, 1926. He observed that while the names of the different national institutions are naturally different, the preamble and the construction are nearly identical.[102] Therefore, it may be safely assumed that Soviet Russia's constitution has provided the basis for that of Tannu Tuva. Since then Tannu Tuva has undergone a process of sovietization. The old conception of protection over Tannu Tuva has certainly been supplanted by the newer tactics of undeclared protection or solid control. The effect of the new tactics of protection has been

[98] *Ibid.* The text of the Soviet-Tuvinian Treaty, however, does not appear in *Izvestiia*, nor in Shapiro's *Soviet Treaty Series*, Vol. I, 1917-28.

[99] Schuman, *op. cit.*, p. 251.

[100] *Encyclopaedia Britannica World Atlas*, p. 124.

[101] *M.S.E.* (1st ed.), Vol. VIII, col. 988.

[102] Durdenevsky, *op. cit.*, p. 108.

indicated by professor Cressey: under Soviet tutelage, Tannu Tuva, as in the case of Outer Mongolia, is "recognized as being under Chinese suzerainty, but there has been no effective Chinese influence for decades."[103]

The primary channel of Soviet control in Tannu Tuva has been through its People's Revolutionary Party, which the Soviet supervisors have taught to struggle against "the Chinese-Mongol bandits."[104] This phase of indoctrination seems to have ended only after the complete annexation of Tannu Tuva to the R.S.F.S.R.[105] Organizational work for the Tuvinian Revolutionary Party started at the end of 1921. Under Soviet sponsorship, a conference of Tuvinian revolutionaries convened on October 29, 1921, and an organization bureau was formed. The first Congress met on February 28, 1922, when the Tuvinian "People's Government" was established.[106] However, as soon as the Second Congress convened on July 6, 1923, the former party was dissolved because of Soviet dissatisfaction, and a new one was organized. The Fourth Congress met in October, 1925; the Seventh Congress, in 1928. The Central Committee was authorized to establish party cells and branches of the league of revolutionary youth throughout the country.[107]

Sovietization had many harsh aspects. During the Second Plenary Session of the Central Committee of the party in 1929 the right-wing leadership, which had intended to retain Lamaism as a state religion in the old sense, in contradiction to the proclaimed constitution, was completely destroyed. Under the watchword of "antifeudal revolution," the Eighth Congress paved the way for socialist reconstruction and collectivization. When, in April-May, 1930, the so-called "counterrevolution of the Tuvinian nobles and the Russian kulak-colonists" broke out with the intent "to overthrow the 'Revolutionary Government,'" it was also put down by force.[108] Resolutions were adopted in the Central Committee of the People's Revolutionary Party to confiscate the property of the exploiter class, to conduct agricultural collectivization "on an unconditionally voluntary basis," "to struggle for complete independence from the imperialist countries and to co-operate closely with the oppressed peoples

---

[103] Cressey, *op. cit.*, p. 16.   [104] *M.S.E.* (1st ed.), VIII, 989.

[105] The passages concerning the Tuvinian struggle for national liberation in *M.S.E.*, completely disappear in *B.S.E.* (1st ed.), Vol. LV, published in 1947.

[106] *M.S.E.* (1st ed.), Vol. VIII, col. 989.

[107] *Ibid.*   [108] *Ibid.*

and the working class of the whole world."[109]   It is no wonder that Owen Lattimore speaks of the Russian "ability to rule Tannu Tuva and Outer Mongolia by 'conversion,' enlistment and amalgamation superior to that of either China or Japan."[110]

But this was not all. A long-prepared secret annexation of Tannu Tuva took place on October 13, 1944. There was no official Soviet statement, no announcement by the Soviet TASS agency, no news dispatch in this respect in any Soviet, Chinese, American, or other newspapers. It was first mentioned in the United States in 1946 by Professors Schuman and Lattimore, neither of whom at that time cited the exact date of the annexation.[111]   A new political-administrative map of the U.S.S.R. which includes Tannu Tuva in its domain first appeared in 1946.[112]   The exact date of annexation was not known until the publication of the fifty-fifth volume of the *Bol'shaia Sovetskaia Entsiklopediia* in 1947.

In the analysis of the motives of Soviet outright annexation of Tannu Tuva, two major factors, strategic importance and economic attractiveness, have been discussed in detail in the previous pages. It may be recalled that, when the unilateral Soviet action took place, armistices with Rumania and with Finland had been concluded in the previous month (September 13 and 19, 1944), Bulgaria had accepted preliminary armistice terms (October 11, 1944), and the Red Army had entered Czechoslovakia and Poland. Extension of the Soviet sphere of influence in the west tempted the victorious Soviets to incorporate outright their valuable old satellite to the East. Moreover, the then secret annexation occurred at a time when the allies were most friendly toward one another and, more important still, when the United States and Great Britain were most anxious to have Russia enter the fray and declare war on Japan, even if it meant taking decisions without a full consultation with their Chinese ally beforehand. Thus no serious opposition to the annexation was to be expected. Even the censored information of the *fait accompli* was allowed to leak out prematurely. Actually, the West knew nothing of the annexation until later. However, the effect was

[109] *Ibid.*

[110] Lattimore, *Manchuria: Cradle of Conflict*, p. 253.

[111] Schuman, *op. cit.*, p. 313 n.; Owen Lattimore, "The Outer Mongolian Horizon," *Foreign Affairs*, XXIV, no. 1, 4 (July, 1946), 649.

[112] Consult N. S. Kuznetsov and F. N. Protas (eds.), *Politiko-Administrativnaia Karta Soiuza SSR (Political-Administrative Map of the U.S.S.R.)* (Moscow, 1946).

dangerous; aside from the aftermath in power politics, a far-reaching moral issue in international relations was involved: whether it was to be true, as an old Chinese saying observes, that "to steal a fruit means theft, while to steal a country does not."

THE FUTURE OF TANNU TUVA

Tannu Tuva (or Urianghai) was treated as a colony within a neighboring country in the Tsarist period. As Tsarist Prime Minister Goremykin once sagely confessed, "in intercourse with Asiatic states, the principles of international law are not completely applicable."[113]   Therefore, only by ignoring the actual state of affairs and even displaying a kind of naiveté could one evaluate Tsarist policy in Urianghai in any terms other than exploitation and conquest.

In the aftermath of the favorable international position brought about by the Anglo-Russian entente of 1907, Russia showed a renewed interest in Urianghai, as in the other border regions of the Far East. Taking advantage of China's internal weakness, the Tsarist Government reanimated its plans for empire building in the Urianghai region in conflict with Chinese interests there, in spite of the historic claims of Outer Mongolia to this territory, and at the expense of the Tuvinians themselves.

Like "old wine in a new bottle," the former Tsarist policy has reappeared in Tannu Tuva in a new Soviet guise. In spite of the fact that at the very outset of the Soviet era, on September 9, 1921, Soviet Russia published a statement to the Urianghai people wherein she disavowed "the predatory policy of the Tsarist Government and solemnly declared that she does not look at the Urianghai territory as her own property,"[114] the Soviet words have not been proved by deeds. Actually, Tannu Tuva has long been behind the iron curtain. Now, even the mask of Tuvinian "artificial independence" as a "People's Republic" created by the Soviet school of methodology has been cast aside. Tannu Tuva has been annexed to the U.S.S.R. not as a Union Republic, nor an Autonomous Republic, but as an autonomous region. It is in the same category as any other non-autonomous region, district, or locality, according to Article 94 of the

[113] Grumm-Grzhimailo, *op. cit.*, II, 791.   [114] IUdin, *op. cit.*, p. 295.

Stalin constitution. There is certainly no room for self-determination of peoples in an administrative unit which serves only to enforce laws and regulations of the various hierarchies of Soviet Russia. Hence, the position of Tannu Tuva has certainly not been elevated but depressed; the treatment she underwent is clearly not one of liberation but of subjugation.

By nature, the Tuvinians are one of the most peace-loving peoples in the world. They want very little, and are easily contented.[115] They were probably an independent people until the coming of Genghis Khan in the thirteenth century, when they became subjects of that great conqueror. Later, the allegiance which they at first owed to the Mongols passed to the Manchu rulers at Peking, and until 1911 remained under the administration of a Manchu official of military rank resident at Uliassutaii.[116] In spite of Tsarist and Soviet ambition, Chinese sovereignty over Urianghai was recognized by the whole world.[117]

Traditionally, Tannu Tuva has been regarded as a part of Outer Mongolia.[118] In the Soviet-Chinese exchange of notes of August 14, 1945, wherein the independence of Outer Mongolia was recognized and guaranteed by the interested parties, no separate provision was made for Tannu Tuva. Hence, one can advance the interpretation that under these documents, Tannu Tuva should occupy the same position as the remainder of Outer Mongolia; in other words, it should be a component of an independent Outer Mongolia. If such be the case, would not the right of Russia to annex the region in 1944 be subject to question?

It is felt that the situation of Outer Mongolia and Tannu Tuva today is due to a certain extent to the inability of the Chinese Government to handle the matter and to present a firm stand. To discharge its obligation to Outer Mongolia in general and to Tannu Tuva in particular as guarantor of Mongolian independence was, however, not easy for China, especially when pitted against the stronger will and might of Soviet Russia. Logically speaking, the present status as well as the future of Tannu Tuva are rightfully problems to be resolved and settled in the Security Council of the United Nations.

[115] Carruthers, *op. cit.*, I, 212.
[116] *Ibid.*, p. 204.
[117] Cressey, *op. cit.*, p. 16.
[118] This represents a prevailing Chinese point of view. Lattimore, "The Outer Mongolian Horizon," *Foreign Affairs*, XXIV, no. 4 (July, 1946), 649-650.

XV: CONCLUSION

THE HISTORY of modern Russia presents a chronology of expansion: the growth of Muscovy from one small principality among many to a vast Eurasian land empire. "For five centuries," as Kennedy has expressed it, "the Russians have been seeking a final frontier which they never find."[1]

Russia's policies in the Far East have long revealed territorial ambitions. By the Treaty of Aigun of 1858, she acquired the entire left bank of the Amur River. Again, in 1860, by the Treaty of Peking, she had secured that back window looking out on the Pacific Ocean, Vladivostok. When Japan defeated China in the war of 1895, Russia sought control of China. And again in the years between 1923 and 1927 the Soviet government attempted to impose its influence on China. Now, in a third attempt, Soviet Russia has made its voice heard and its strength felt in the China which has emerged since World War II.

With the construction of the Chinese Eastern Railway, Russia found reason to send troops into Manchuria as "railway guards" to protect her investment and her nationals. From 1900 until 1905, under the pretext of quelling the Boxer uprising, the Russian Army took over Manchuria. Not until the Japanese intervened with arms did Tsarist Russia remove herself from South Manchuria and Korea.

Among the territories acquired by Russia in the century following the Napoleonic Wars, Manchuria loomed largest in political and economic importance. To carry out her Manchuria policy, Russia utilized to the fullest extent the advantages and privileges made possible by the Chinese Eastern Railway.

In the Tsarist period, the main offices of the Russian railroad in Harbin developed into a Russian government for Northern Man-

[1] A. L. Kennedy, "The Expansion of Russia," *Quarterly Review*, CCLXXXV (Jan., 1947), 1.

churia. New areas of control were brought under the office of the railway manager with the unjustified creation of several departments not specifically provided for in the railway agreements: a department of schools, a department of churches, a health department, etc. Russian courts were set up, and without the consent of China, in total disregard of Chinese laws, the Russian system of local administration was introduced. When in January, 1908, the Chinese government formally protested, a diplomatic dispute ensued. Difficulties and protests notwithstanding, the Russian city administration had also begun to collect taxes.

During the Soviet period the agreement of 1924 was concluded, under which the two partner nations were to enjoy strict equality in the matter of the Chinese Eastern Railway. In practice, however, the Soviet government was concerned only with her own interests and was desirous of monopolizing the control of the railroad. March, 1926, saw the appointment by the Politburo of a commission to formulate Soviet policy with regard to this issue. Its members included Voroshilov, Chicherin, and Dzerzhinskii. Trotsky was the chairman. The commission decided on "strict maintenance of actual control of the line in the hands of Soviet authorities."[2] In addition, after 1945 the Soviet Union was to resume control of Port Arthur and Dairen, a move which would be at the expense of Chinese political independence and territorial integrity. As a Washington *Post* editorial phrased it, "Russia has taken the place of Japan as the arch-imperialist, at the expense of China."[3]

After her defeat by Japan in 1905, Russia began to reach out again along another route—this time through Mongolia. By fostering the Urga coup d'état, the seizure of Kobdo and the Mongolian independence movement, Tsarist Russia turned Outer Mongolia into a protectorate. From 1912 until the present day (with the exception of a short interval around 1919 when Chinese administration was restored) both Tsarist and Soviet Russian policies have succeeded in quietly detaching Outer Mongolia, including Tannu Tuva, from China and attaching it to Russia in fact, if not in name. Tsarist expansionism has carried over into the Soviet era.

Even in the early years of the Soviet regime in Russia, Com-

[2] L. Trotsky's statement in *Biulleten' Oppozitsii* (*Bulletin of the Opposition*), 1929, No. 3.
[3] Washington *Post*, June 10, 1949.

munist doctrine and tactics fused with the traditional Russian imperialism. In those years, as has been pointed out by Professor Mosely,
"the device of promoting a 'People's Republic' as an intermediate
status between full independence and a Soviet regime found useful
application."[4] Tannu Tuva was first declared by the Soviet Union to
be a "People's Republic" after it was made an "independent republic"
in 1921. Again, a "People's Republic" was proclaimed in Outer
Mongolia in 1924, after the death of Chebutsum Damba Hutukhtu,
the nominal head of a regime friendly to the Soviet Union.

Tannu Tuva, a country almost the size of Great Britain and
possessed of almost unlimited natural resources, was a part of Outer
Mongolia under the jurisdiction of the Manchu Military Governor
at Uliassutai until 1911. At the time of the Chinese Revolution and
the Mongolian "independence" movement, Tsarist Russia claimed it
and then proclaimed a protectorate over it in 1914. When the
Soviets marched into the area in 1921, it was proclaimed an independent people's republic. On October 13, 1944, without any agreement whatsoever with China, then still its nominal sovereign under
the Sun-Joffe declaration of 1923 and the Koo-Karakhan agreement
of 1924, Tannu Tuva was annexed outright by the Soviet Union as
an autonomous district of the R.S.F.S.R.

Along the Sino-Russian border from Sinkiang to Manchuria the
Soviets had a hand in the affairs of all the outlying territories of
China. In addition to the Tsarist methods of political infiltration
and intrigue, economic exploitation and domination, and military
occupation and acquisition, the Soviets resorted to Communist propaganda and Communist agents. With the aid of Sukhe Bator and,
later, Choibalsan, Outer Mongolia was integrated with the Soviet
Union politically, economically, and militarily. Today, Outer Mongolia exists only in name.

The Soviet Union emerged from World War II as the strongest
power in Europe and in Asia. According to Professor Kerner, the
party line for the postwar era—amounting to world revolution—
has ended all doubts as to the Soviet Union's serious intentions.[5]
This policy is a combination and most effective application of Com-

    [4] Philip E. Mosely, "Aspects of Russian Expansion," *The American Slavic and
East European Review*, VII (Oct., 1948), 208.
    [5] Robert J. Kerner, "The Setting of Far Eastern Policy," *Far Eastern Review*,
Vol. XVIII, no. 3 (Feb. 9, 1949), p. 27.

munist imperialism and Russian expansionism. Thus, Professor Mosely says: "Soviet power and influence abroad are more extensive than the Imperial Government dreamed of."[6]

It has been stated that "the Communism which Lenin's dynamism gave to the world is the first and last formula for power."[7] Communism is the current instrument of Russian policy. James Byrnes, reviewing his term as the United States Secretary of State, has spoken out against "aggression by subterfuge or political infiltration" and against conducting a war of nerves to gain strategic ends.[8] Spokesmen of other peace-loving nations likewise regard these methods as contrary to the spirit of the United Nations Charter. The Soviet Union, in its actions, has plainly violated the first article of the Charter which described the purpose of the United Nations. History has recorded the disruption of the League of Nations by Germany, Italy, and Japan. To permit the continued expansion of the Soviet Union endangers the validity of the United Nations and may lead to its destruction.

[6] Mosely, *op. cit.*, p. 209.
[7] "Communism and Russian Foreign Policy," *Quarterly Review*, CCLXXXIV, April, 1946, 134.
[8] James F. Byrnes, *Speaking Frankly* (New York and London, 1947), pp. 312, 313.

APPENDIX

APPENDIX: CONSTRUCTION AND ECONOMIC OPERATIONS OF THE CHINESE EASTERN RAILWAY

Railway Lines and Equipment

A brief description of the physical aspects or actual conditions of the Chinese Eastern Railway may prove helpful in factual analysis of the important roles, economic, political, and strategic, played by the railroad during the period under review.

In the years 1911-31, the total length of the main line of the C.E.R. at the disposal of Russian and Soviet policy was 1,078.93 miles, or approximately 1,722.24 kilometers or 1,618 versts. The main line was divided into three sections: (1) the Western Line, from Harbin to Manchuli (Station Manchuria), 584.13 miles, or about 943.72 kilometers, or 876 versts; (2) the Eastern Line, from Harbin to Suifenho (Pogranichnaia), 343.12 miles, or about 552.38 kilometers, or 515 versts; (3) the Southern Line from Harbin to Kwanchengtze near Changchun, 149.02 miles, or about 238.46 kilometers, or 224 versts.[1] There was also a branch line of 2.66 miles from Harbin-Central to Harbin-Pristan. The total trackage including sidings was 1,854 miles.[2]

The capital of the Chinese Eastern Railway consisted largely of the expenditure for its construction. But due to lapses of time be-

---

[1] C.E.R. Company, *Spravochnik po Severnoi Man'chzhurii i K.V.Zh.D.* (*A Reference Book on North Manchuria and the C.E.R.*, hereinafter referred to as C.E.R. Company, *Spravochnik*) (Harbin, 1927), p. 290; P. Ivangorodskii, "K Voprosu o K.V.Zh.D." ("The Problem of the C.E.R."), *Sibirskie Ogni* (*Siberian Light*), no. 3 (June-July, 1925), p. 168; E. A. Khodorov, "Kitaiskaia Vostochnaia Zheleznaia Doroga" ("The Chinese Eastern Railway"), *Mezhdunarodnaia Zhizn'* (*International Life*), no. 1, 1924, p. 31; The Chinese Eastern Railway Company, *North Manchuria and the Chinese Eastern Railway* (Harbin, 1924), p. 434.

[2] C.E.R. Company, *Spravochnik*, pp. 290-291.

tween calculations and the divergent attitudes and nationalities of the agents who made them, discrepancies are often found in the figures. The most astonishing and exaggerated figure, referred to by Mikhailov in 1926, is that of 1,200 million rubles as the total sum of money invested by the Russian people in the Chinese Eastern Railway.[3] The comparatively modest figure given by Skalov is 378 million rubles, with the loss of 178 million rubles during the first two years excluded.[4] Another account made by Khodorov fixes the total sum borne by the Russian state for the construction and deficit of the railway to 1924 as 461,980,457 gold rubles.[5]

The official Chinese documentation, published by the communications and the railways ministries recorded the capital of the Chinese Eastern Railway, managed by the Russo-Chinese Bank, as 350,000,000 rubles in 1896. According to the Railway Statutes ratified by unilateral Russian action on December 4, 1896, the stock of the railway company totaled 5,000,000 rubles divided into 1,000 shares of 5,000 rubles each, to be bought only by Chinese and Russian citizens. If the sale of stocks were not adequate, the Railway Company would borrow from the Russian Government at an interest rate of six per cent. It estimated the total expense by 1902, for the construction of the Railway, including surveying service, land purchase, and the building of Port Arthur, to be more than 300 million rubles.[6]

The general expenditure for the construction of the Chinese Eastern Railway on January 1, 1928, as stated in the statistical yearbook of the railway, may be listed as follows:

	(Rubles)
1. Cost of works and expenditure other than cost of rails, fastenings, and rolling stock	189,274,289.36
2. Cost of rails, fastenings, and rolling stock	50,904,076.72
3. Cost of works and expenditure incurred owing to the peculiar conditions of the construction of the railway	49,245,614.66
4. Cost of works and expenses incurred owing to disturbances in 1900	72,040,097.63
5. Expenses connected with the creation of the turn-over funds	7,844,100.00
6. Interest and redemption paid on the capital during the construction of the Railway	35,753,756.80

[3] M. Mikhailov, *Chto Proiskhodit na Kitaiskoi Vostochnoi Zheleznoi Doroge?* (*Events Pertaining to the Chinese Eastern Railway*), p. 13.

[4] Skalov, *Sobytiia na Kitaiskoi Vostochnoi Zheleznoi Doroge* (*Events on the C.E.R.*), p. 8.

[5] E. A. Khodorov, *op. cit.*, p. 31.

[6] *C.T.S.L.C.P.*, Vol. XVII, chap. vii, pp. 18, 20, 370.

7. Losses from the sale of construction materials.................. 19,089,190.75
8. Cost of property transferred by the former Marine Navigation Department in consequence of its liquidation:
    (a) real estate...................................... 362,500.00
    (b) chattels.. 53,479.84
9. Expenditure connected with the preliminary survey of Kirin branch. 32,263.24
10. Additional expenditure for increasing:
    (a) the density of traffic............................ 15,548,335.52
    (b) the carrying capacity............................ 6,595,198.16

        GRAND TOTAL COST............................ 446,742,882.68
Written off:
    (a) In accordance with the advice of the Control Bureau... 77,878.30
    (b) Cost of the line ceded to Japan in accordance with the
        Portsmouth Peace Treaty....................... 81,015,463.21

Cost of the construction of the Railway on January 1, 1928.......... *365,649,541.17

*See the C. E. R. Company, *Statisticheskii Ezhegodnik (Statistical Yearbook)* (Harbin, 1929), p. 45.

The Chinese Eastern Railway during the period 1911-31 was perhaps the richest railway in China. According to the estimate of its rolling stock, there was a maximum of 536 locomotives, 11,509 freight cars with a total capacity of 224,607 tons, and 810 passenger coaches with a total seating capacity of 23,789 persons. (The average haul per ton was 339 kilometers, and the average per train was 257 tons.) The gauge of the railway was five feet, according to the Russian standard, and each rail was 35 feet long, weighing 65 pounds to the foot; or 2,275 pounds in all.[7]

For the course of the years of 1913-28, the railway equipment and servicing may be described as follows:

1. *Rolling stock: Engines.* The C.E.R. always had plenty of locomotive stock on reserve. The number of locomotives available, the average number in service, and the proportion of locomotives by types in use as against number available in the years under review may be seen in the tables below.

Certain measures to redistribute the supply of locomotives were taken in the period of joint management, 1924-29. This redistribution allowed the operation of trains of increased and more uniform weight, since each section had its special type of locomotive; a procedure which lightened repair work, making it possible to operate with smaller quantity of spare parts in stock. In the years 1924-29, out of seven types of locomotives available only three types were kept in operation, all the other types being placed in reserve because of their weak traction capacity. At the same time, all atten-

[7] Tsao, *The Chinese Eastern Railway: An Analytical Study*, p. 10.

Appendix

TABLE 1
Work of Locomotive Stock of the C.E.R. (A)*

Year	Existing number of all locomotives	Average number of locomotives in service	In reserve and in good order
1913...............	491	205	192
1914...............	491	224	176
1915...............	491	274	113
1920...............	505	266	22
1921...............	536	229	95
1922...............	536	186	209
1923...............	536	139	308
1924...............	532	137	308
1925...............	528	131	304

*See C. E. R. Company, *Spravochnik*, p. 321.

TABLE 2
Work of Locomotive Stock of the C.E.R. (B)*
(*Average in Service/Existing number*)

	1924	1925	1926	1927	1928
Tank Locomotives.............	2/ 34	2/ 30	0/ 23	0/ 19	0/ 18
Passenger Train Locomotives.....	20/ 83	16/ 83	18/ 83	25/ 83	33/ 83
Freight Train 10-Wheeled Locomotives...............	58/278	54/278	41/277	43/276	43/271
Freight Train 8-Wheeled Locomotives...............	4/ 13	3/ 13	1/ 13	0/ 13	0/ 13
Freight Train Decapod Locomotives...............	54/124	56/124	57/124	66/124	71/124
Grand Totals........	137/532	131/528	117/520	134/515	147/509

*See *Statisticheskii Ezhegodnik*, p. 19-20.

tion was concentrated on the repair of the types of locomotives in operation so as to double the weight limit of trains. As increasing shipments demanded a greater number of engine runs, long runs for engines were introduced in 1925. The operation of locomotives became more efficient because the average annual run of a working locomotive increased.[8]

2. *Rolling Stock: Coaches.* The number and percentage of the

[8] "Sluzhba tiagi K.V.Zh.D. za 25 let" ("Traction Department of the C.E.R.— during 25 years"), *Vestnik Man'chzhurii* (*Manchuria Monitor*), no. 6, 1928, pp. 20-21.

TABLE 3

PASSENGER CAR STOCK OF THE C.E.R. (A)*

Year	Existing number of passenger coaches	Number of passenger coaches in service	Percentage of passenger coaches in service
1913............	734	358	48.8
1914............	716	378	52.8
1920............	648	255	39.4
1921............	793**	228	28.7
1922............	807	292	36.2
1923............	744	279	37.5
1924............	733	311	42.4
1925............	728	311	42.7

*See C. E. R. Company, *Spravochnik*, p. 322.
**The sudden increase of coaches was due to large number coming from other railways during the period of the Russian Civil War.

TABLE 4

PASSENGER CAR STOCK OF THE C.E.R. (B)*

Existing number of cars (including cars or other railways)	1924	1925	1926	1927	1928
In service.........................	311	311	314	388	452
In reserve.........................	221	235	241	208	163
In bad order.......................	201	182	168	122	99
TOTALS......................	737	723	723	718	714
Existing number of cars (excluding cars of other railways)	1924	1925	1926	1927	1928
In service.........................	292	304	305	349	408
In reserve.........................	172	181	195	178	136
In bad order.......................	144	124	110	64	43
TOTALS......................	608	609	610	591	587

*See *Statisticheskii Ezhegodnik (Statistical Yearbook)*, p. 21

passenger coaches in service in relation to the number available during the years 1913-25 and the average disposition of passenger coaches during the years 1924-28 may be seen in tables three and four.

3. *Rolling Stock: freight cars.* The number and percentage of freight cars in service in relation to their existing number during the years 1913-25 as well as the average disposition of freight cars during the years 1924-28 may be seen in tables five and six.

4. *Repair of Rolling Stock.* At the end of each operational year, a plan for repairing the rolling stock for the ensuing year was

Appendix

TABLE 5

FREIGHT CAR STOCK OF THE C.E.R. (A)*

Year	Existing number of cars	Number of cars in service	Percentage of cars in service
1913.............	8,428	5,938	70.4
1914.............	7,473	5,082	68.0
1920.............	12,171**	9,109	74.8
1921.............	12,417	7,159	57.7
1922.............	12,411	5,711	46.0
1923.............	12,239	5,225	42.7
1924.............	12,259	4,609	37.6
1925.............	12,069	5,514	45.7

*See Spravochnik, p. 322.
**The sudden increase of freight cars was due to large number coming from other railways during the period of the Russian Civil War; most of these incoming cars were in bad order.

TABLE 6

FREIGHT CARS STOCK OF THE C.E.R. (B)*

Average annual number of cars	1924	1925	1926	1927	1928
In service................	4,376	4,019	4,048	4,322	6,187
In reserve................	6,924	7,578	7,374	6,895	4,929
In bad order.............	935	659	820	647	507
TOTALS.............	12,235	12,256	12,242	11,864	11,623

*See *Statisticheskii Ezhegodnik*, p. 21.

worked out; each class being specified for repair at the particular time of the year when it was least needed in service. Most shops in Harbin and along the lines were equipped for electric welding and for the use of compressed air.[9]

5. Water Supply. A regrouping of all boilers and pumps was effected in all water towers in accordance with their capacity and the water supply requirements of the particular stations. With a view to reducing fueling expenses, and in order to keep strict control thereof, water meters were installed in all water towers, premiums were issued for fuel saving, and at the more important points, water heaters for boilers were installed. With the construction of electric power plants, water towers underwent electrification; there were, in 1928, seven such water towers, and two more were under construction.[10]

[9] *Ibid.*, p. 23.   [10] *Ibid.*

6. *Railway Electrification.* In 1925 the Traction Service Department (motive power) submitted a plan for the construction of thirteen electric power stations, and this plan was gradually put through. By the end of 1928 the railway possessed ten electric power stations, located in Harbin, Tsitsihar, Fularki, Chalantun, Barim, Mientuhe, Hengtachetze, Sanchaho, Kwanchengtze, and Chalainor, and one more was under construction. The annual electric energy produced increased from 2,985 thousands of kilowatts in 1924 to 6,332 thousands of kilowatts in 1928.[11]

PASSENGER TRAFFIC

During the period under review, the Chinese Eastern Railway, being the only convenient railroad in North Manchuria, and representing a chief link of a great international overland route from the shores of the Pacific to those of the Atlantic, performed two fundamental functions in regard to passengers. On the one hand, it served a local population of fourteen million by connecting the vital centers of the land and opening a route to South Manchuria and China proper. On the other hand, it played an important part in the Europe-Asia through traffic.[12]

Passenger traffic on the C.E.R. in the years of Sino-Soviet joint management may be analyzed under the following four heads: (1) Passenger traffic in general, (2) Immigration, (3) Local traffic, (4) Europe-Asia through traffic.

PASSENGER TRAFFIC IN GENERAL

The intensive colonization of North Manchuria and the considerable growth of its economic activity could not help but have a bearing on the volume of C.E.R. passenger traffic. Reciprocally, the growth of passenger traffic was also facilitated by a number of measures undertaken by the C.E.R., such as the sale of passenger tickets and the receiving of freight originating in a number of populated centers, sometimes situated at a considerable distance from the

[11] *Ibid.; Statisticheskii Ezhegodnik,* p. 27, Fig. 23.
[12] C.E.R. Company, *Spravochnik,* p. 356; A. I. Groshenin, "Kommercheskaia Rabota K.V.Zh.D. za 1928 Goda" ("Commercial Work of the C.E.R. in 1928"), *Vestnik Man'chzhurii (Manchuria Monitor),* nos. 7-8, 1929, p. 22.

railway.[13] The growth of passenger traffic in general during the period under review is illustrated by tables seven and eight below.

TABLE 7
PASSENGER TRAFFIC ON THE C.E.R. (A)*

Year	I Class	II Class	III Class	IV Class	Total
1913............	10,983	66,291	882,439	217,682	1,177,302
1914............	8,843	60,757	868,950	140,595	1,079,150
1920............	11,884	88,117	1,271,351	824,747	2,196,099
1921............	11,804	63,183	949,370	1,021,478	2,045,835
1922............	5,084	32,582	908,348	1,209,248	2,155,362
1923............	4,429	24,376	776,011	1,562,136	2,366,952
1924............	4,408	23,877	1,141,178	1,013,963	2,183,426
1925............	5,001	22,263	1,316,970	1,110,088	2,454,322

*See C. E. R. Company, *Spravochnik*, p. 356.

TABLE 8
PASSENGER TRAFFIC OF THE C.E.R. (B)*
(*In thousands individuals*)

	1924	1925	1926	1927	1928
In class cars on a general traffic rate...	2,098	2,407	3,212	4,289	4,885
Children and passengers transported in class cars on reduced tariff......	81	46	61	83	91
Immigrants........................	1	—	—	81	53
Military..........................	134	104	107	74	111
Persons under arrest and their escort..	2	1	0.3	0.2	0.3
Railway guides....................	2	2	3	4	6
TOTAL OF PASSENGERS........	2,318	2,560	3,383.3	4,531.2	5,146.3

*See *Statisticheskii Ezhegodnik (Statistical Yearbook)*, p. 49, Fig. 5.

The special features of local life explained the unequal distribution of passenger traffic of the railway during different seasons of the year. The following table gives the mean monthly number of passengers carried, showing the minimum and maximum numbers during the years 1926-28:

[13] Groshenin, *op. cit.*, p. 22. V. C., "Rabota K.V.Zh.D. za Tri Goda—3 oktiabria 1924 g.–3 oktiabria 1927 g." ("The Work of the C.E.R. in Three Years—Oct. 3, 1924–Oct. 3, 1927"), *Vestnik Man'chzhurii (Manchuria Monitor)*, no. 10 (1927), p. 3.

TABLE 9
TRANSPORTATION OF PASSENGERS BY MONTHS ON THE C.E.R.*
(*in thousands individuals*)

	Minimum	Maximum	Average Per Year
1926...................	160.1	363.8	273.0
1927...................	259.6	483.2	371.5
1928...................	300.3	607.8	419.6

*See Groshenin *op. cit.*, p. 22.

IMMIGRATION MOVEMENT

In North Manchuria, as in any other country still in the process of colonization, the incoming passengers exceeded outgoing, as the following figures will show; numbers are in thousands.

TABLE 10
IMMIGRATION MOVEMENT ON THE C.E.R.

	1926	1927	1928
To the C. E. R. from other railways through traffic connections.....................................	13.4	18.0	12.3
Dispatched on the C. E. R. from all terminal stations..	551.6	836.0	810.4
From Changchun-Kwanchengtze (included in figures above)...........................	(492.5)	(703.8)	(678.3)
TOTAL.............................	565.0	854.0	822.7
From the C. E. R. to other railways through traffic connections.....................................	39.7	59.0	31.7
Arrived from C. E. R. at all terminal stations.........	429.8	509.0	594.9
At Changchun-Kwanchengtze (included in figures above).....................................	(348.0)	(414.1)	(488.8)
TOTAL.............................	469.5	568.0	626.0
Excess of arrivals over departures....................	95.5	286.0	196.1

The above figures show that through traffic on the C.E.R. was prevalent on the southern route and that it was subject to considerable fluctuations. This is explained by influx of passengers from the south, which, in addition to general economic reasons, was often due to the occurrence of such common calamities as droughts, inundations, wars, etc.[14]

[14] Groshenin, *op. cit.*, p. 23.

LOCAL TRAFFIC

Local traffic on the C.E.R. depended entirely upon local living conditions and proceeded along lines parallel with the general growth of North Manchuria, as the following table will show:

TABLE 11

LOCAL TRAFFIC ON THE C.E.R.*

Year	I Class	II Class	III Class	IV Class	Total
1913	6.6	45.2	794.1	194.8	1,040.7
1914	6.2	45.2	765.0	122.4	938.8
1920	11.6	87.2	1,255.6	824.5	2,178.9
1921	10.9	61.9	947.7	1,021.0	2,041.5
1922	3.8	30.5	901.8	1,208.7	2,144.8
1923	1.8	22.0	760.0	1,561.9	2,346.7
1924	2.6	21.5	1,106.4	1,013.8	2,144.3
1925	3.2	19.2	1,247.7	1,090.8	2,379.9
1926	4.0	26.0	1,814.0	1,376.0	3,223.0
1927	2.0	30.0	1,995.0	2,267.0	4,380.0
1928	5.0	40.0	2,789.0	2,098.0	4,991.0

*Table was based on data in *Spravochnik*, p. 358 and *Statisticheskii Ezhegodnik* (*Statistical Yearbook*), p. 50, Fig. 8 Passengers carried under the general and reduced tariffs, including passengers of the border stations, except troops and prisoners in the local traffic of the C. E. R.

This table shows that the local traffic of the C.E.R. was third and fourth class, usually represented by members of the local farming and working population. Another very considerable group of local passengers was composed of local merchants traveling for business, mainly over short distances, for the most part at the height of the cereal season, with activity gradually declining toward the summer and stopping altogether during the Chinese holidays. A third, and larger, group of local passengers was made up of laborers and colonists arriving from China proper and South Manchuria. The largest numbers of such passengers usually traveled in spring (March, April, and May), and toward the end of autumn when the laborers returned home after the harvesting of crops.[15]

EUROPE-ASIA THROUGH TRAFFIC

In 1902, prior to the opening of the C.E.R. to traffic, there was held in Paris the first conference dealing with the questions of

[15] *Ibid.*, p. 24.

establishing direct communication with Asia through Siberia. Later, at a conference in Brussels in 1907, there was worked out and ratified an "agreement relative to the establishment of direct international communication with China and Japan through Siberia," between the railroads of England, Austria, Belgium, Germany, the Netherlands, Russia, and France, and the C.E.R.. The opening of this traffic took place on July 14, 1908. The Japanese Government Railway and the South Manchuria Railway in 1909 entered into an agreement with the C.E.R., and in 1910 opened up direct traffic routes— the Chinese Eastern-South Manchurian-Manchurian-Japanese routes, while in 1912 agreements were concluded relative to international communication by way of Siberia. Finally, in 1914, just before the war, the Northern Chinese and Korean railroads also entered into the agreements. The war of 1914-19 interrupted this international traffic at the very beginning of its development, but, beginning with 1920, normal trade connection between the Far East and Europe began gradually to be resumed.[16]

In 1925, the People's Commissariat of Communications of the U.S.S.R. took the initiative in calling a number of conferences with both western European and Chinese government railways, Japanese transportation enterprises, and the C.E.R. In May, 1926, there began to be operated direct trains from Manchuli Station to the western frontiers of the U.S.S.R., connecting there with direct trains to Berlin and Paris, and the number of passengers began to increase to such an extent that it was found necessary to pay particular attention to the resumption of through traffic. The Berlin conference of 1926 worked out a tariff and an agreement covering "direct Europe-Asia service via Siberia" and the date for its opening was placed at May 15, 1927. Finally, after the Riga conference in 1927, direct Europe-Asia service went into effect on May 15, 1928.

It took fifteen days to travel from Shanghai, through Dairen, Moscow, Riga, and Ostend, to London instead of the thirty- to forty-five-day journey by sea.[17] After 1926 detailed statistics are available as the following table shows:

[16] A. P. Kobzarev, "God Priamogo Evropeisko-Aziatskogo Soobshcheniia" ("A Year of European-Asiatic Through Traffic"), *Vestnik Man'chzhurii* (*Manchuria Monitor*), no. 5, 1929, p. 21.
[17] C.E.R. Company, *Spravochnik*, p. 358.

Appendix

TABLE 12

TRANSIT PASSENGERS CARRIED VIA STATION MANCHULI*

Year	West	East	Total
1926...................	1,001	932	1,934
1927...................	2,082	1,692	3,774
1928...................	3,347	3,514	6,861

*See Kobzarev's article in *Vestnik Man' chzhurii* (*Manchuria Monitor*), no. 5, 1929, p. 23.

During the above mentioned three years, the total number of through passengers increased three and one-half times. Through traffic during the first months of 1929 indicated an increase of passengers in the year of 1929 to 9,000.[18]

As to the nationality of transit passengers, data for 1928 indicated that the first place among passengers proceeding from the Far East to Europe was occupied by Japanese, who comprised approximately 25 per cent of all passengers. They were followed by Germans (19 per cent), citizens of the U.S.S.R. (10 per cent), British and French in almost equal numbers (7-8 percent) and finally, Americans and Chinese (5 per cent each). Data on passengers in the opposite direction showed practically the same percentages.[19]

As to the transit service in 1927, the C.E.R., in accordance with agreements made between it and the railways of the U.S.S.R. and the Administration of the Through Traffic Sleeping Cars (formerly the International Sleeping Car Company) at Leningrad, opened facilities for accepting advance reservations on the Siberian Express at Shanghai, Tientsin, Dairen, Yinkow, Mukden, Changchun, and Harbin.[20] By 1929 the through passenger communication via Siberia had broadened its scope even beyond that of prewar times to include all the countries of Europe and Asia bound by commercial interests.[21]

FREIGHT TRAFFIC

In spite of the fact that a number of new railroads had been built within the borders of North Manchuria in later years, the Chinese

[18] Kobzarev, *op. cit.*, p. 23.
[19] *Ibid.*, p. 24.
[20] *Ibid.*, p. 23.
[21] *Ibid.*, p. 25.

Eastern Railway remained the principal transportation artery of the country. The import and export freight carried on the C.E.R. represented practically 100 per cent of the entire export and import traffic of North Manchuria.[22] The general situation of freight traffic of the C.E.R. during most of the period under review is shown in the following table:

TABLE 13
FREIGHT TRAFFIC ON THE C.E.R.*
(In thousands of tons)

Year	Export	Import	Transit	Local	Total
1911	719.1	190.9	75.4	242.4	1,226.9
1912	550.4	234.2	90.1	242.8	1,117.1
1913	553.7	270.3	96.1	244.1	1,164.7
1914	506.1	270.3	83.5	226.1	1,086.0
1915	778.1	312.9	406.2	316.1	1,813.3
1916	633.9	314.5	730.8	407.9	2,086.8
1917	981.3	332.5	303.0	404.6	2,021.3
1918	725.7	216.2	9.8	322.7	1,274.4
1919	633.9	263.7	77.0	308.0	1,282.6
1920	886.2	214.6	1.6	424.3	1,526.7
1921	1,294.1	301.4	—	440.6	2,036.1
1922	1,376.0	348.9	—	737.1	2,462.0
1923	1,646.2	407.9	—	727.3	2,781.4
1924	1,882.2	427.5	—	702.7	3,012.4
1925	2,240.9	430.8	—	704.3	3,376.0
1926	2,526.0	515.0	—	1,179.0	4,220.0
1927	2,766.0	538.0	—	1,578.0	4,882.0
1928	2,686.0	617.0	—	2,123.0	5,426.0

*Table based on data in C. E. R. Company, *Spravochnik*, pp. 327-335, and *Statisticheskii Ezhegodnik*, p. 58, Fig. 15

It is interesting to note from the above table that the transit freight of the C.E.R., except in the years 1915 and 1916 when Tsarist Russia was engaged in World War I, was but a surprisingly small quantity and percentage. These data certainly offer small justification for Russia to exploit this railway with the alleged purpose of connecting the two parts of her territory.

For a more detailed analysis of the later period of joint management, when more statistics of specific classification were available, the freight traffic on the C.E.R. may be analyzed under the following four heads: general, export, import, and local.

[22] V. G. Shishkanov, "Importnye Gruzy na K.V.Zh.D." ("Import Freight Movement on the C.E.R."), *Vestnik Man'chzhurii* (*Manchuria Monitor*), no. 9, 1929, p. 20.

FREIGHT TRAFFIC IN GENERAL

The commercial activity of the C.E.R. showed rather favorable results for the period of joint management with reference to the increase in the volume of freight carried, as the following figures prove:

TABLE 14
COMMERCIAL GOODS CARRIED ON THE C.E.R.
(By slow freight, excepting goods carried by the piece)

Year	Thousands of Tons*	Percentage
1924...............................	3,011	100
1925...............................	3,377	115
1926...............................	4,220	140
1927...............................	4,882	162
1928...............................	5,426	180

*The figures are derived by simplifying Fig. 14 in *Statisticheskii Ezhegodnik*, pp. 56-58.

The total increase in the commercial work of the railway was not evenly reflected in the activity of its individual sections, as the following table will prove:

TABLE 15
FREIGHT TURNOVER OF THE LINES OF THE C.E.R.
(By slow freight, excepting goods carried by the piece, in thousands of tons)

Shipments	Western Line	Harbin Terminals	Eastern Line	Southern Line
1926...............	1,184	1,006	789	727
1927...............	1,499	1,244	955	646
1928...............	1,513	1,345	1,177	775
Arrivals				
1926...............	359	927	114	294
1927...............	418	1,154	162	382
1928...............	489	1,394	277	580

The above quoted figures show the somewhat slower development of shipments on the western line in 1928, the result of the attraction of considerable quantities of grain to the Hu-Hai Railway. In this respect the Taonan-Tsitsihar Railway diverted freight only to a slight degree from the nearby stations of the C.E.R.[23]

The quantities of goods carried by the C.E.R. were very un-

[23] Groshenin, *op. cit.*, p. 17.

evenly distributed by months. Their volume depended exclusively upon local conditions such as periods of harvesting, the condition of roads, weather, market, and so forth. Hence, a characteristic feature of the commercial freight traffic of the C.E.R. was to be found in the fact that cereals held the foremost position as regards the quantities of goods carried.[24]

A more comprehensive picture of the commercial work of the C.E.R. during the period of joint Sino-Soviet management is given in the following table, showing the quantities of goods carried in the different kinds of traffic:

TABLE 16

KINDS OF TRANSPORTATION ON THE C.E.R.*

(By slow freight, excepting goods carried by the piece, in thousands of tons)

	1924	1925	1926	1927	1928
Local Traffic.........	702	704	1,179	1,578	2,123
Exports.............	1,882	2,241	2,526	2,766	2,686
Imports.............	428	432	515	538	617
TOTAL.........	3,012	3,337	4,220	4,882	5,426

*See *Statisticheskii Ezhegodnik (Statistical Yearbook)*, p. 58, Fig. 15.

The dynamics of freight traffic become more striking if the statistics in the above table are regrouped, excluding the turnover of goods at the terminal stations of Kwanchengtze and Suifenho (Pogranichnaia) from the items of local traffic and adding arrivals and shipments of goods, as the case may be, to the respective items for imports and exports. Thus, in average, the export freight occupied 61 per cent, import 13 per cent, and local 26 per cent respectively of commercial goods carried on the railway in the years 1926-28.[25]

EXPORT FREIGHT

Up to and including 1917, exports from North Manchuria were largely handled by the Ussuri Railway for the reason that it had an exit through the port of Vladivostok. Beginning in 1918, the predominant importance in connection with exports was assumed by the

[24] *Ibid.*, p. 16.
[25] Shishkanov, *op. cit.*, p. 21.

South Manchuria Railway. In 1926 the weight scale fluctuated strongly, and in 1927 the Ussuri Railway again took the upper hand in the matter of exports from North Manchuria, with the result that the competing enterprises reached an agreement relative to the equal distribution of Manchurian exports.[26]

About 80 per cent of the exports consisted of cereals. It should be noted that in respect of quantity, export consignments still held the first place in the commercial activity of the railway, to which they supplied about 65 per cent of all business. Because of the growth of local traffic, exports rather declined during the period of joint management.[27]

The distribution of exports by routes is shown in the following table:

TABLE 17
DISTRIBUTION OF EXPORTS ON THE C.E.R.*
(*By slow freight, excepting goods carried by the piece, in thousands of tons*)

	1924	1925	1926	1927	1928
Beyond Suifenho	761	808	1,207	1,489	1,503
Arrival at Suifenho from the C. E. R.	9	7	7	10	17
TOTAL	770	815	1,214	1,497	1,520
Beyond Kwanchengtze	1,121	1,143	1,319	1,279	1,183
Arrival at Kwanchengtze from the C. E. R.	57	78	179	268	404
TOTAL	1,178	1,221	1,498	1,547	1,587
GRAND TOTAL	1,948	1,836	2,712	3,044	3,107

*See *Statisticheskii Ezhegodnik (Statistical Yearbook)*, Figs. 15, 16, 17.

In correlating exports and imports, it can be seen that the C.E.R. aided the systematic growth of exports from 1903 up to 1927, there having been an increase of almost 4300 per cent during the twenty-five years and one of 15 per cent from 1924 to 1928; and aiding as well the steady growth of imports, in which there was a 1300 per cent increase for the whole period and a 16 per cent increase during the years 1924-28.[28]

[26] *Ibid.*, p. 15.
[27] Groshenin, *op. cit.*, p. 15.
[28] Shishkanov, *op. cit.*, p. 10.

IMPORT FREIGHT

The large development of import operations on the railway during the later period of joint management resulting from the growth of the population, the increase in agricultural output, and the work of industrial establishments in North Manchuria may be seen in the following table:

TABLE 18

DISTRIBUTION OF IMPORTS ON THE C.E.R.*

(By slow freight, excepting goods carried by the piece, in thousands of tons)

	1924	1925	1926	1927	1928
Via Suifenho	66	49	78	82	94
Shipped to C. E. R. from Suifenho	2	2	3	5	7
TOTAL	68	51	81	87	101
Via Kwanchengtze	361	383	437	457	523
Shipped to C. E. R. from Kwanchengtze	39	44	70	81	119
TOTAL	400	417	507	538	632
GRAND TOTAL	468	468	588	625	733

*See *Statisticheskii Ezhegodnik (Statistical Yearbook)*, p. 59, Figs. 18, 19.

The average distribution of goods imported into North Manchuria in the years of 1924-28 was about 15 per cent via the Ussuri Railway and about 85 per cent via the South Manchuria Railway.[29]

Fuel, or coal, for the requirements of the Chinese Eastern Railway, for industrial purposes, and for private consumption in the country had, up to 1929, been the principal item of importation. Another item carried in bulk was salt, which came exclusively via the South Manchuria Railway, there being a specially fixed tariff for the Chinese Government salt monopoly. Under the category of importation of goods for mass consumption, the principal items were kerosene, alabaster, chalk lime, sugar, cereals, fresh fruits and berries, piece goods, bags, iron, steel, and pig iron. Other items were mineral oils, benzine, construction materials, paint, stone, fish, crabs and sea cabbage, leather, groceries, tea, tobacco and tobacco products, vegetables, mushrooms, soap, drugs, perfumeries, cosmetics, yarns, thread, rope, readymade clothing, cotton, copper, brass, lead, ma-

[29] *Ibid.*, p. 22.

chinery, agricultural machinery, tools, glass and glassware, pottery, porcelain, paper, etc.[30]

In addition to goods for mass consumption by the native population, which were largely supplied by China through Yinkow and by Japan through Dairen, North Manchuria received through the corresponding representatives from the various countries the following goods: (1) petroleum products from America, England, and Soviet Russia; (2) sea and fish products from the Soviet Far East and Japan (3) all kinds of technical equipment from America, England, and particularly Germany; (4) agricultural machinery and equipment from America and Soviet Russia; (5) piece goods from Soviet Russia, England, and other countries.[31]

LOCAL FREIGHT

The discontinuance of transit shipments and the absence of financial support from the outside during the years of joint management made the C.E.R. base its prosperity principally upon the local economy. According to Soviet interpretation, the commercial policy of the railway, in favoring local economy in general and industrial activity in particular, had a considerable influence upon the development of local traffic. Moreover, the decline of the local dollar shifted a number of export and import goods over to the broken tariff and thereby also increased the volume of goods carried in the local traffic.[32] The commercial goods transported by slow freight, carried on the railway in local traffic, may be seen in the following table:

TABLE 19

LOCAL TRAFFIC ON THE C.E.R.*

(*In thousands of tons*)

	1924	1925	1926	1927	1928
Local traffic (except goods carried by piece)..	702	704	1,179	1,577	2,123
Shipments by the piece..................	13	8	11	15	20
GRAND TOTAL..................	715	712	1,190	1,592	2,143

*See *Statisticheskii Ezhegodnik (Statistical Yearbook)*, pp. 59-61, Fig. 21.

[30] *Ibid.*, pp. 22-23. [31] *Ibid.*, p. 23.
[32] Groshenin,*op. cit.*, p. 15.

AUXILIARY ENTERPRISES

According to Russian source accounts, the Chinese Eastern Railway was engaged in several auxiliary enterprises for the sake of giving consigner and consignee the maximum of cargo turnover and profits, of promoting industry and commerce, and of developing culture in general.[33] In the commercial activities of the railway, the auxiliary enterprises of the commercial department played a very substantial and significant role. Thus, by ever-expanding auxiliary enterprises, the C.E.R., under the predominance of Tsarist and Soviet Russia, became a giant in North Manchuria and dominated economic life in that area. Revenue of the auxiliary enterprises increased year after year during the period of joint management as the following table may show:

TABLE 20

REVENUE OF THE AUXILIARY ENTERPRISES OF THE C.E.R.*
(*In thousands of gold rubles*)

	1924	1925	1926	1927	1928
Loan operations	1	8	35	38	74
Insurance Operations	—	1	57	45	50
Storage Operations	24	41	68	88	86
Commission operation	—	0.2	2	7	10
Transport operations	256	458	1,398	2,043	2,948
Customs operations	448	488	750	905	952
Sale of tickets	1	10	24	52	76
Assignment of warehouses	—	—	94	97	**
TOTAL	730	1,006.2	2,428	3,275	4,196

*See *Statisticheskii Ezhegodnik (Statistical Yearbook)*, p. 31, Fig. 30; some figures are different from those in the article by V. G. Shishkanov in *Vestnik Man'chzhurii (Manchuria Monitor)*, no. 7, 1927, p. 17. Statistics of this kind for the earlier period are not available.
**The revenue from the assignment of the warehouses enters into the total operation revenue of the railway.

The main categories of the auxiliary enterprises sponsored and controlled by the C.E.R. may be described as follows: (1) the network of supplementary enterprises of the commercial department of the railway, including fifty commercial agencies and branch agencies in China and the U.S.S.R. (Moscow and Vladivostok), for six kinds of operations, namely, transport, customs, loan, insurance, commission, and storage; (2) the Grand Hotel in Harbin; (3) the Hailar

[33] C.E.R. Company, *Spravochnik*, p. 416.

wool-washing factory; (4) six health resorts; (5) three agricultural experimental farms with laboratories and three agricultural machine stations; (6) the Harbin veterinary hospital and quarantine, and disinfection services in Manchuli and Hailar, etc.[34]

Special attention in the work of auxiliary enterprises was directed to transport operation. In 1927 almost two-fifths of the total freight turnover of the railway passed first of all through the division of auxiliary enterprises of the commercial department. Assuming that the volume of goods handled in this manner in 1924 was 100 per cent, the records showed the following percentage of goods passing through the division as: 1925—179 per cent, 1926—538 per cent, 1927—833 per cent.[35]

The second significant element of the work of auxiliary enterprises was customs operation. The customs agencies were opened for the purpose of handling all customs, tax, veterinary, and forwarding formalities in connection with shipments passing in transit from the U.S.S.R. to stations of the C.E.R. and vice versa, as well as in connection with shipments in transit through Manchuria from one section of the U.S.S.R. to another. According to official statistics, the customs agencies were already handling over two-thirds of the freight passing through the frontier point.[36]

In 1924 the loan operations were partially in the form of transportation payments as loans secured by freight, and beginning with 1926 they began to receive intensive development. As in 1925 there were issued loans in the aggregate of 325,000 rubles; in 1926, 1,326,148 rubles; in 1927, 1,618,802 rubles. According to railway regulations, loans were divided into two groups: short term and special account, secured by goods, and warehouse or transportation documents, covering both through and local communications, or by way-bills. The railway also opened credits by paying transportation charges on freight addressed to its clients. This was the

[34] *Chung-Tung-T'ieh-Lu Wen t'i* (*The Chinese Eastern Railway Question*), pp. 23-27; C.E.R. Company, *Spravochnik*, pp. 417-422.
[35] V. G. Shishkanov, "Dopolnitel'nye Predpriiatiia Kommercheskoi Chasti K.V. Zh.D." ("Supplementary Enterprises of Commercial Department of the C.E.R."), *Vestnik Man'chzhurii* (*Manchuria Monitor*), no. 10, 1927, pp. 4-5.
[36] *Ibid.*; I.A.S. and A.V.M., "Kratkii Obzor Operatsii Dopolnitelnykh Predpriiatii Kommercheskoi Chasti KVZhD so Dnia Ikh Uchrezhdeniia" ("Brief Outline of Operations of Additional Enterprises of Commercial Department of the C.E.R. from the Date of Their Establishment till the Year 1928"), *Vestnik Man'chzhurii* (*Manchuria Monitor*), no. 8, 1928, p. 18.

most popular form of credit. The principal class of freight against which loans were granted were those of beans and of cereal freight in general, followed by coal, while the last place was taken by sundry goods.[37]

The insurance operations were complementary to warehousing, loans, and transport operations, and their development was directly dependent upon the development of the latter operation. The operations themselves were divided into two basic categories: insurance against fire damage to property and freight in the warehouses of the railway, and insurance of freight in transit. The insurance operations during the period of 1926-27 increased by one-half over the preceding period of 1925-26.[38]

The commission operations were entirely new enterprises established in the second half of the year 1925. These agencies received from the clients of the railway commissions to buy and sell goods.[39]

The storage operations were established to maintain proper and practically constructed warehouses at points of destination and transfer in order to attract freight. According to the data covering the receipt and delivery of goods in 1927, the greatest quantity of goods in the warehouses was beans, which constituted the principal freight carried by the C.E.R. The second place was taken by coal and timber, i.e., the storage operations handled principally those goods which were the basis for railway transportation. The warehouses were scattered in Manchuli, Fuliaerhti, Anda, Tuichinshan, Ashiho, Pogranichnaia, Sanchiaho, Yaomon, Hailar, Tsitsihar, Mankou, Harbin, Hailin, Sungari, Kwanchengtze, and other places.[40]

FINANCIAL ACCOUNTS

The C.E.R. was well known for its heavy losses from the time of its construction to the year 1922. During the years 1911-15, the net income of the railway increased considerably in comparison with that of the year 1910. Even the year of the commencement of World War I saw an increase of income against that of 1913 of 720,000 rubles. However, the increase of income was constantly

[37] *Ibid.*, p. 21.
[38] *Ibid.*
[39] C.E.R. Company, *Spravochnik*, p. 422.
[40] I.A.S. and A.V.M., *op. cit.*, p. 20.

outrun by even greater increase of expenditure.[41] This meant that the C.E.R. was being used as a means of furthering Russia's colonial ambitions and was not a commercial undertaking.[42] During the period of joint management, according to Russian reports, the financial result of the operation of the railway was surprisingly favorable. The years between 1925 and 1927 were especially the golden age of the railway, with a net profit of 37,954 thousand rubles, revenue increasing by 135 per cent and expense by 161 per cent.[43]

The following table shows the annual principal account of the financial results of the railway for the years 1924-28:

TABLE 21

ANNUAL ACCOUNT OF THE C.E.R.

(*In thousands of gold rubles*)

	1924	1925	1926	1927	1928
Total Revenues	37,632	48,691	55,717	60,553	64,875
Total Expenses	24,842	29,826	30,800	45,029	53,210
Total Profits	12,790	18,865	24,917	15,524	11,665

The total profits in the above table do not represent the net gains of the C.E.R. during the years under review. From those sums are to be subtracted sinking funds and other appropriations for the maintenance of the Tupan Office [Office of the Director General or the President of the railway], schools, railway police, and guards as the following table may show:

TABLE 22

NET PROFITS OF THE C.E.R.

(*In thousands of gold rubles*)

	1924	1925	1926	1927	1928
Total Profits	12,790	21,865	24,987	15,525	11,775
Sinking Funds	1,520	2,903	3,976	5,736	6,966
Appropriations	3,833	3,289	3,617	3,456	4,246
Net Profits	7,417	15,673	19,094	6,333	563

[41] "Deiatel'nost' K.V.Zh.D. v 1915 g." ("Work of the C.S.R. in 1915"), *Vestnik Azii* (*Asiatic Herald*), no. 37, 1916, p. 114.
[42] Tsao, *op. cit.*, p. 60.
[43] Shishkanov, "Dopolnitel'nye Predpriiatiia Kommercheskoi Chasti K.V.Zh.D." ("Supplementary Enterprises of the Commercial Department of the C.E.R."), *Vestnik Man'chzhurii* (*Manchuria Monitor*), no. 10, 1927, p. 5.

The following two classified tables show the detailed accounts of revenues and expenses of the C.E.R. for the years 1924 to 1928:

TABLE 23

ANNUAL REVENUES OF THE C.E.R.*

(*In thousands of gold rubles*)

Classified items	1924	1925	1926	1927	1928
Revenues from passenger and freight receipts.........	34,825	42,178	49,740	57,410	60,678
Other revenues not relating to railway transport.....	976	1,431	1,745	1,309	2,023
Sinking funds and revenues from savings and banking operations.............	70	4,480	2,172	Figure unavailable	Figure unavailable
Revenues from railway materials..............	159	Figure unavailable	932	932	1,423
Revenues from other railway commercial enterprises...	32	20	494	121	Figure unavailable
Revenues from the transport of freight of auxiliary enterprises.............	106	422	502	515	644
Auxiliary enterprises.......	157	162	202	176	87
TOTAL..............	37,959	48,693	55,787	60,463	64,857

*See *Statisticheskii Ezhegodnik*, p. 47.

TABLE 24

ANNUAL EXPENSES OF THE C.E.R.*

(*In thousands of gold rubles*)

Classified items	1924	1925	1926	1927	1928
Board of directors..........	1,550	982	1,397	7,248	10,901
General administration.....	4,392	4,328	6,184	8,524	7,952
Workers' department.......	4,019	4,694	5,942	7,625	9,096
Locomotive and rolling stock department............	2,475	2,517	2,899	3,406	3,928
Electricity department......	430	460	522	578	603
Engineering department....	7,033	7,281	8,779	10,547	11,808
Payment for use of other railways..............	No	66	No	No	No
Damages to railway assets...	No	2,213	No	No	110
Miscellaneous expenses.....	1,576	1,129	1,078	1,889	3,433
Repairs for the railway.....	374	468	448	467	670
Losses of auxiliary enterprises	2,839	2,526	2,378	5	5
Sinking funds.............	1,520	2,903	2,276	5,736	6,966
Maintenance for tupan office, schools, cultural institutions, police and railway guards................	3,853	3,689	3,617	3,456	4,246
TOTAL..............	30,061	33,256	35,520	49,481	49,718

*See *Statisticheskii Ezhegodnik*, p. 47.

BIBLIOGRAPHY

Note: This bibliography does not claim to cover the whole field of publications concerning Russian and Soviet policy in Manchuria and Outer Mongolia. It is, however, as far as we are able to ascertain, a rather complete and up-to-date one concerning the period dealt with. No mention has been made of articles of news value only, though reference to them will be found in the footnotes. It also omits books which have been mentioned in footnotes only to substantiate minor points. For a full bibliography of Russian books and articles on all aspects of Mongolian affairs, see E. N. Yakovleva, *Bibliografiia Mongol'skoi Narodnoi Respubliki* (Moscow, 1935). A useful, though not extensive bibliography can also be found in Dr. Hugo Knoepfmacher's *Outer Mongolia, A Selection of References* (New York, 1944).

I. PRIMARY SOURCES

A. GOVERNMENT PUBLICATIONS

i. *China*

Delegation to the Sino-Russian Conference. *Chung-O Hui-i Tsan-k'ao Wen-chien (Sino-Russian Conference: Reference Documents)*. 6 vols. in 1 case. Peking, 1923.

The Manchu Government. *Kwang-Hsu Tiao-yo (Treaties under the Reign of Kwang-Hsu)*. 4 cases.

Ministries of Communications and Railways. *Chiao-t'ung-shih Lu-cheng Pien (History of Communications: Part of Road Administration)*. Vol. XVII. Nanking, 1931.

Ministry of Foreign Affairs. *Documents with Reference to the Sino-Russian Dispute 1929*. Nanking, 1929.

————. "Su-O Ch'in-jao Wo-kuo Tung-Pei Pien-chiang An" ("The Case of the Soviet-Russian Invasion of Our Northeastern Frontiers"). *Foreign Affairs Gazette*, Vol. II, sec. 5, Sept., 1929.

Peking Metropolitan Police Headquarters, Inspection Bureau, Commission for Translation and Compilation. *Su-Lien Yin-mou Wen-cheng Hui-pien* (*Collection of Documentary Evidence of the Soviet Conspiracy*). Peking, 1928.

ii. *Russia*

Ministry of Foreign Affairs. *Izvestiia Ministerstva Inostrannykh Del* (*Bulletin of the Ministry of Foreign Affairs*). 5 vols. Petrograd, 1912-1917.

―――. *Sbornik Diplomaticheskikh Dokumentov po Mongol'skomu Voprosu.* 23 Avgusta 1912 g.―2 Noiabria 1913 g. (*Collection of Diplomatic Documents Concerning the Mongolian Question.* August 23, 1912―November 2, 1913). St. Petersburg, 1914.

R.S.F.S.R. *Soglasheniia mezhdu Rossiei i Kitaem po Voprosam Zhelezno-dorozhnym, Pochtovo-telegrafnym i Tamozhennym* (*Agreements between Russia and China in Regard to Railways, Posts and Telegraphs, and Customs*). Petrograd, 1918.

iii. *U.S.S.R.*

Akademiia Nauk SSSR (The Academy of Sciences of the U.S.S.R.). *Istoriia Mongol'skoi Narodnoi Respubliki* (*A History of the Mongolian People's Republic*). Moscow, 1954.

―――. *Materialy Komissii po ussledovaniiu Mongol'skoi i Tannu-tuvinskoi NP* (*Materials from the Commission for Research on the Mongolian and Tuvinian People's Republics*). Moscow, 1929.

―――. Mongol'skaia Komissiia (The Mongolian Commission). *Trudy* (*Works*), No. 1. Moscow, 1952.

―――. *Mongol'skaia Narodnaia Respublika: Sbornik Statei* (*The Mongolian People's Republic: A Collection of Articles*). Moscow, 1952.

The Chief Archival Administration of the People's Commissariat of the Interior. *Krasnyi Arkhiv* (*The Red Archives*) (a historical journal). 105 vols. Moscow, 1922-41 (Especially Vols. 2, 37, and 52).

Commission for the Publication of Documents during the Period of Imperialism attached to the C.E.C. *Mezhdunarodnye Otnosheniia v Epokhu Imperializma: Dokumenty iz Arkhivov Tsarskogo i Vremennogo Pravitel'stva.* (*International Relations during the Period of Imperialism: Documents from the Archives of the Tsarist and the Provisional Governments*). Series II: Vols. XVIII, XIX, and XX, each in two parts, cover the period 1900-13. Series III: Vols. I-X (Vols. VI-VIII in two parts each), cover years 1914-17. Moscow, 1931-39.

Narkomindel (People's Commissariat for Foreign Affairs). *Ezhegodnik*

Narodnogo Komissariata po Inostrannym Delam na 1925 (*Yearbook of the People's Commissariat for Foreign Affairs for 1925*). Moscow, 1925.

————. *Mezhdunarodnaia Politika: Dogovory, Deklaratsii i Diplomaticheskaia Perepiska* (*International Politics: Agreements, Declarations and Diplomatic Correspondence*), A. V. Sabanin (ed.). Moscow, 1931.

————. *Mezhdunarodnaia Politika v 1929 godu: Dogovory, Deklaratsii i Diplomaticheskaia Perepiska* (*International Politics for 1929: Agreements, Declarations and Diplomatic Correspondence*). Moscow, 1930.

————. *Sbornik Deistvuiushchikh Dogovorov, Soglashenii i Konventsii Zakliuchennykh s Inostrannymi Gosudarstvami* (*Collection of Active Treaties, Agreements and Conventions Concluded with Foreign States*). Moscow, 1927.

iv. *United States*

Department of State. *Foreign Relations of the United States.* Washington, D. C. Diplomatic papers since 1861, especially volumes relating to Russia and China, such as those of 1910; 1918, Russia, II; and 1929, II.

Eighty-fifth Congress, House of Representatives, Committee on Un-American Activities. *Communism in China: Consultation with Dr. Peter S. H. Tang, September 29, 1958.* Washington, D. C., 1959. This transcript illustrates the new role which Manchuria and Outer Mongolia have been assigned by the Moscow-Peking Axis.

B. COLLECTIONS OF SELECTED DOCUMENTS

"Akty i Dokumenty: Sovetsko-Kitaiskii Konflikt 1929 goda" ("Acts and Documents: The Soviet-Chinese Conflict of 1929"), *Mezhdunarodnaia Zhizn'* (*International Life*), Vol. II, 1931, pp. 125-129.

Bukhartzev, D. *Desiat' Let Sovetskoi Diplomatii: Akty i Dokumenty* (*Ten Years of Soviet Diplomacy: Acts and Documents*). Moscow, 1927.

Far Eastern Republic. *Letters Captured from Baron Ungern in Mongolia.* Washington, 1922.

Grimm, E. D. (ed.). *Sbornik Dogovorov i Drugikh Dokumentov po Istorii Mezhdunarodnykh Otnoshenii na Dal'nem Vostoke* (*Collection of Treaties and Other Documents on International Relations in the Far East*). Moscow, 1927.

Huang, Yueh-po, and others (comp.). *Chung-wai T'iao-yo Hui-pien*

(*An Annotated Collection of Treaties Concluded between China and Foreign States*). Shanghai, 1935.

Kliuchnikov, IU. V., and Sabanin, Andrei (ed.). *Mezhdunarodnaia Politika Noveishego Vremeni v Dogovorakh, Notakh i Deklaratsüakh* (*International Politics of Most Recent Times in Treaties, Notes and Declarations*). 3 vols. Moscow, 1925-29.

Korovin, E. A. *Mezhdunarodnye Dogovory i Akty Novogo Vremeni* (*International Treaties and Acts of the New Period*). Moscow, 1924.

K.V.Zh.D. *Sbornik Dokumentov Otnosiashchikhsia k Kitaiskoi Vostochnoi Zheleznoi Doroge* (*A Collection of Documents Relating to the Chinese Eastern Railway*). Harbin, 1922.

MacMurray, J. V. A. (ed.). *Treaties and Agreements with and Concerning China, 1894-1919.* 2 vols. New York, 1921.

Manchuria Treaties and Agreements (Pamphlet Series of the Carnegie Endowment for International Peace, No. 44). Washington, D. C., 1921.

Shapiro, Leonard (ed.). *Soviet Treaty Series: A Collection of Bilateral Treaties, Agreements and Conventions, etc., Concluded between the Soviet Union and Foreign Powers.* Washington, Vol. I (1917-28), 1950; Vol. II (1929-39), 1955.

Siebert, B. De, and Schreiner, G. A. *Entente Diplomacy and the World.* New York and London, 1921.

Sovetskii Soiuz v Bor'be za Mir: Sobranie Dokumentov i Vstupitel'naia Statia (*The Soviet Union in the Struggle for Peace: Collection of Documents and an Introductory Article*). Moscow, 1929.

Tsiang, T'ing-fu (ed.). *Chin-tai Chung-Kuo Wai-chiao-shih Tzu-liao Chi-yao* (*A Collection of Basic Material on Modern Chinese Diplomatic History*). Vols. I & II, Shanghai, 1931, 1934.

Tung-Pei Wen-ti Yo-chu Tsung-shu: Chung-O Hsieh-ting, Fung-O Hsieh-ting, Pei-Li Yi-ting-shu (*A Collection of the Texts of the Sino-Russian Agreements, the Mukden Agreement, and the Khabarovsk Protokol*). Peking, 1930.

Wang, Yien-wei, and Wang, Liang (eds.). *Ching Chi Wai Chiao Shih Liao* (*Chinese Diplomatic Documents: the Later Period of the Ching Dynasty*). 12 cases. Peking, 1932.

Wilbur, C. Martin and How, Julie Lien-ying (eds.). *Documents on Communism, Nationalism, and Soviet Advisers in China 1918-1927.* New York, 1956.

C. SEMIOFFICIAL REPORTS

Chicherin, G. V. *Vneshniaia Politika Sovetskoi Rossii za Dva Goda* (*Foreign Policy of Soviet Russia in Two Years*). Moscow, 1919.

Doksom. "Istoricheski Uroki 15 Let Revoliutsii" ("Historical Lessons of Fifteen Years of Revolution"), Report by Doksom, Chairman of the Little Hural at the 21st Jubilee Session of the Little Hural at Ulan Bator, in *Tikhii Okean* (*The Pacific Ocean*), No. 3(9), Moscow, July-Sept., 1936, pp. 63-94.

Gendun. "Iz Doklada Premierministra MNR Genduna VII Velikomu Khuralu" ("Extract from the Report of the Prime Minister of the Mongolian People's Republic, Gendun, to the Seventh Great Hural"), in *Tikhii Okean* (*The Pacific Ocean*), No. 1(3), Jan.-Mar., 1935, pp. 250-267.

Hsu, Shih-ch'ang. *Tung-San-Sheng Cheng-lueh* (*The Record of the Administration of the Three Eastern Provinces*). 40 vols. in 7 cases. Mukden, 1911.

Joffe, A. A. "Russia's Policy in China," in *The Living Age*, Jan., 1923, pp. 73-76.

Karakhan, L. M. "Soviet Notes on the Chinese Eastern Railway Seizure," in *Soviet Union Review*, Vol. VII, No. 9 (Sept., 1929), pp. 130-134.

K.V.Zh.D. *Kitaiskaia Vostochnaia Zheleznaia Doroga, Istoricheskii Ocherk* (*The Chinese Eastern Railway: A Historical Sketch*). Vol. I (1896-1905). St. Petersburg, 1914.

Lenin, V. I., Stalin, J., and Molotov, V. *The Soviet Union and the Cause of Peace*. New York, 1936.

Litvinov, M. M. *Vneshniaia Politika SSSR: Rechi i Zaiavleniia, 1927-35 gg.* (*Foreign Policy of the U.S.S.R.: Speeches and Statements, 1927-35*). Moscow, 1935.

Maiskii, I. "Russia's Foreign Policy" and "The U.S.S.R. and Outer Mongolia," in *The Challenge to Democracy* (Speeches delivered to the Liberal Summer School). London, 1936.

Pi, Kwei-fang. *Wai-Mong Chiao-sheh Shih-mo Chi* (*A Report on the Negotiations Concerning Outer Mongolia*). Peking, 1928.

Popov, A. "Tsarskaia Rossiia i Mongoliia v 1913-1914 gg." ("Tsarist Russia and Mongolia in 1913-1914"), Foreword to the Collection of Documents in *Krasnyi Arkhiv*, Vol. XXXVII, 1929, pp. 3-14.

D. INTERVIEWS

Ludwig Besharov, May, 1949.   P'o Tao-ming, Feb., 1956
Chin Shao-fen, Feb., 1952.   Sun Su-ch'in, Feb., 1952
Fu Ju-lin, Mar., 1956.   Tsin Ti-tsing, Feb., 1952
Nicholas N. Poppe, Jan., 1956.   T. V. Butov, Feb., 1952.
Tinuwa Hutukhtu, June, 1949.   Chu Hsin-min, Feb., 1956.
John B. Tsu, Feb., 1956.

E. CONTEMPORARY NEWSPAPERS AND PERIODICALS

The China Weekly Review (formerly *Millard's Review*), Shanghai.
The Far Eastern Review.
Foreign Affairs.
Krasnaia Nov' (*The Red Virgin Soil*).
Izvestiia, Moscow.
Mezhdunarodnaia Zhizn' (*International Life*).
The London Times.
The New York Times.
North China Herald.
Novyi Vostok (*The New East*).
Pravda, Moscow.
Revoliutsionnyi Vostok (*The Revolutionary East*).
The Soviet Union Review (formerly *Russian Review*) and *Soviet Russia,*
    Washington, D. C.
Ta Kung Pao, Tientsin.
Tung-Fang Tse-chih (*Eastern Miscellany*), Shanghai.
Vestnik Azii (*Asiatic Herald*), Harbin; especially years 1910-16.
Vestnik Man'chzhurii (*Manchuria Monitor*), Harbin.

II. GENERAL REFERENCES

Bol'shaia Sovetskaia Entsiklopediia (*Great Soviet Encyclopedia*). Moscow,
    first ed., 1926-47, 65 vols.; second ed., 1949-58, 51 vols. and annual
    supplement.
The China Year Book. H. G. W. Woodhead (ed.). London and New
    York (1912-19), Peking and Tientsin (1921-) in particular for the
    years 1914-32.
The Chinese Eastern Railway Co. *North China and the Chinese East-
    ern Railway.* Harbin, 1924.
Hsü, Hsi. *Tung-San-Sheng Chih-lueh* (*The Annals of the Three East-
    ern Provinces*). Shanghai, 1915.

K.V.Zh.D.   *Kratkii Obzor Raboty K.V.Zh.D. i Kraia* (*A Brief Survey of the Function of the Chinese Eastern Railway and the Region*). Harbin, 1928.

————. *Severnaia Man'chzhuriia i Kitaiskaia Vostochnaia Zheleznaia Doroga* (*North China and the Chinese Eastern Railway*). Harbin, 1922.

————. *Spravochnik po Severnoi Man'chzhurii i K.V.Zh.D.* (*A Reference Book on Northern Manchuria and the C.E.R.*). Harbin, 1927.

————. *Statisticheskii Ezhegodnik* (*Statistical Yearbook*). Harbin, 1929.

Malaia Sovetskaia Entsiklopediia (*Small Soviet Encyclopedia*). Moscow, first ed., 1928-31, 10 vols.; second ed., 1933-47, 11 vols.

Sibirskaia Sovetskaia Entsiklopediia (*Siberian Soviet Encyclopedia*). 3 vols. Moscow, 1932. Especially "The Mongolian People's Republic," in Vol. III, pp. 508-542.

III. SECONDARY TREATMENT

A. MEMOIRS AND BIOGRAPHIES

Iswolsky (Izvolskii), Alexander. *Recollections of a Foreign Minister.* New York and Toronto, 1921.

Li, Hung-chang. *Li-Wen-Chung-Kung Chuan-chi* (*The Collected Works of Viceroy Li Hung-chang*).

Witte, Sergei Iulevich. *Vospominaniia* (*Memoirs*). 2 vols. Berlin, 1922.

Yamolinsky, A. (trans. and ed.). *The Memoirs of Count Witte.* New York, 1921.

B. GENERAL WORKS

Baddeley, John F. *Russia, Mongolia, China.* 2 vols. London, 1919.

Bau, M. J. *Foreign Relations of China.* New York, 1921.

Beloff, Max. *The Foreign Policy of Soviet Russia, 1929-1941.* 2 vols. London, 1947, 1949.

————. *Soviet Policy in the Far East, 1944-1951.* New York, 1953.

Chang, Chung-fu. *Chung-Hua-Ming-Kuo Wai-chiao Shih* (*A Diplomatic History of the Republic of China*). Peiping, 1936.

Ch'en, Po-wen. *Chung-O Wai-chiao-shih* (*Sino-Russian Diplomatic History*). Shanghai, 1st ed., 1928; 2nd ed., 1931.

Cheng, Tien-fong. *A History of Sino-Russian Relations.* Washington, 1957.

Chiang, Kai-shek. *Soviet Russia in China.* New York, 1st ed., 1957; rev. ed., 1958.

Chu, C. L. (ed.). *Chin-shih-lien lai chi Chung-O Kuan-hsi* (*Russso-Chinese Relations of the Last Ten Years*). Harbin, 1926.

Clyde, Paul H., *International Rivalries in Manchuria, 1689-1922*. Columbus, 1926.

Conolly, Violet. *Soviet Economic Policy in the East*. London, 1933.

Dallin, David J. *The Rise of Russia in Asia*. New Haven, 1949.

──────. *Soviet Russia and the Far East*. New Haven, 1948.

Dennis, Alfred L. P. *The Foreign Policy of Soviet Russia*. New York, 1924.

Fischer, Louis. *Soviets in World Affairs*. 2 vols. New York, 1930.

Golder, Frank. *Russian Expansion in the Pacific*. Cleveland, 1914.

Ho, Han-wen. *Chung-O Wai-chiao Shih* (*Sino-Russian Diplomatic History*). Shanghai, 1935.

Hu, Chiu-yuan. *O Ti Ching Hua Shih Kang* (*A Short History of Russian Aggression in China*). Taipei, 1952.

Kerner, Robert J. *Northeastern Asia, a Selected Bibliography*. Berkeley, 1939.

Khodorov, A. E. *Mirovoi imperializm v Kitae* (*World Imperialism in China*). Shanghai, 1922.

Lobanov-Rostovsky, Andrei. *Russia and Asia*. Ann Arbor, 1951 (originally published by Macmillan, New York, 1933).

Maiskii, I. *Vneshniaia Politika RSFSR, 1917-1922 gg.* (*The Foreign Policy of the R.S.F.S.R., 1917-1922*). Moscow, 1923.

Michael, Franz H. and Taylor, George E. *The Far East in the Modern World*. New York, 1956.

Pasvolsky, Leo. *Russia in the Far East*. New York, 1922.

Pavlovsky, Michel N. *Chinese-Russian Relations*. New York, 1949.

Potemkin, V. P. (ed.). *Istoriia Diplomatii* (*History of Diplomacy*). 3 vols. Moscow, 1941-45.

Savvin, V. P. *Vzaimootnosheniia Tsarskoi Rossii i SSSR s Kitaem* (*Relations of Tsarist Russia and the U.S.S.R. with China*). Moscow, 1930.

Sun, Chi-i. *Chung-O Chiao-she Lun* (*A Study of Sino-Russian Negotiations*). Shanghai, 1931.

Tang, Peter S. H. *Communist China Today*. 2 vols. New York, 1957, 1958.

Tanin, M. *Mezhdunarodnaia Politika SSSR 1917-1924 gg.* (*International Politics of the U.S.S.R. 1917-1924*). Moscow, 1925.

Vernadsky, George V. *Political and Diplomatic History of Russia*. Boston, 1936.

Vilenskii, V. (Sibiriakov). *Kitai* (*China*). Moscow, 1923.

──────. *Kitai i Sovetskaia Rossiia* (*China and Soviet Russia*). Moscow, 1919.

Walker, Richard L. *China Under Communism*. New Haven, 1955.
Wei, Henry. *China and Soviet Russia*, Princeton, N. J., 1956.
Weigh, Ken Shen. *Russo-Chinese Diplomacy*. Shanghai, 1938.
Wen, Kung-chih. *O-Lo-Ssu Chin-lueh Chung-Kuo Tung-shih* (*The Tragic History of the Russian Aggression in China*). Shanghai, 1932.
Whiting, Allen S. *Soviet Policies in China, 1917-1924*. New York, 1954.
Wu, Aitchen K. *China and the Soviet Union*. New York, 1949.
Yakhontoff, Victor A. *Russia and the Soviet Union in the Far East*. New York, 1931.
Zhukov, E. M. (ed.). *Mezhdunarodnoe Otnoshenie na Dal'nem Vostoke, 1870-1945 gg.* (*International Relations in the Far East, 1870-1945*). Moscow, 1951.

C. SPECIAL STUDIES

Alekseev, I. *Chto Proiskhodit na KVZhD?* (*What Is Happening on the Chinese Eastern Railway?*). Khabarovsk, 1929.
"Aratskoe Revoliutsionnoe Dvizhenie v Doavtonomnoi Mongolii" ("Arat Revolutionary Movements in Pre-Autonomous Mongolia"), in *Revoliutsionnyi Vostok* (*The Revolutionary East*), No. 5, 1934, pp. 137-156 and No. 6, 1934, pp. 43-64.
Avarin, V. *Imperializm v Man'chzhurii* (*Imperialism in Manchuria*). 2 vols. Moscow, 1934.
Badmaev, P. *Rossiia i Kitai* (*Russia and China*). St Petersburg, 1905.
Banzaragachi, B. *Mongol'skaia Narodnaia Respublika, Geograficheskii i Politiko-Ekonomicheskii Ocherk*. (*The Mongolian People's Republic, A Geographical and Politico-Economic Sketch*). Ulan-Bator, 1951.
Blagoveshchenskii, M. N. *Die Mongolische Volksrepublik*. Berlin, 1951.
Bogolepov, M., and Sobolev, M. *Ocherki Russko-Mongol'skoi Torgovli* (*Sketches of Russian-Mongolian Trade*). Tomsk, 1911.
Carruthers, Douglas. *Unknown Mongolia*. 2 vols. London, 1913.
Chang, Chia-fan. *Hu-Lun-Pei-Erh Chih-lieh* (*Annals of Hulunbuir*). Shanghai, 1923.
Chang, Tao-shing. *International Controversies over the Chinese Eastern Railway*. Shanghai, 1936.
Ch'en, Ch'ung-tsu. *Wai-Meng-Ku Ching-shih-shih* (*A Modern History of Outer Mongolia*). Shanghai, 1926.
Chen, Yen-hsing. "O-Kuo chih Tung-fang Cheng-t'se yu Chung-Tung-T'ieh-Lu" ("Russia's Far Eastern Policy and the Chinese Eastern Railway"), *Social Science Magazine*, Nov., 1929, pp. 21-32.

Chiang, Hsin-teh. "Chung-O Hui-I ti Chien-yeh" ("The Eve of the Sino-Russian Conference"), *Eastern Miscellany*, Vol. XXVII, No. 8 (April 25, 1930), pp. 11-23.

Chiang (Tsiang), Ting-fu. "Tung-Pei Wai-Chiao-Shih chung ti Jih-O Mei-yueh" ("The Secret Russo-Japanese Treaties in the Diplomatic History of the Northeast"), *Tu-li P'ing-lun (Independent Review)*, No. 8 (July 10, 1932), pp. 17-20.

Chih, An. "Chung-Tung-T'ieh-Lu yu Ti-Kuo-Chu-I" ("The Chinese Eastern Railway and Imperialism"), *Tsing-Hua Weekly*. Vol. XXX (Jan., 1930), pp. 13-14.

Chih, Jen-hsi. *Tung-T'ieh Wen-ti (The Question of the Chinese Eastern Railway)*. Shanghai, 1929.

"Chinese Eastern Railway and Its Zones," *Far Eastern Review*, Vol. XX (1924).

Chung, Yun. "Chung-Tung-T'ieh-Lu Wai-chiao Mi-wen" ("Secret Diplomacy Concerning the Chinese Eastern Railway"), *Eastern Miscellany*, March, 1931.

"Comintern's Plottings in Manchuria," *Contemporary Manchuria*, May, 1938, pp. 146-158.

Davidov, D. A. *Kolonizatsiia Man'chzhurii i S.-V. Mongolii (Colonization of Manchuria and Northeastern Mongolia)*. Vladivostok, 1911.

Deane, Frederick. "The Chinese Eastern Railway," *Foreign Affairs*, Oct., 1924, pp. 147-153.

Demidov, S. S. *Mongol'skaia Narodnaia Respublika (The Mongolian People's Republic)*. Moscow, 1952.

"Development of Outer Mongolian Independence," *Pacific Affairs*, Vol. X, No. 3 (Sept., 1937), pp. 315-336.

Doronin, M. *Zakhvat Kitaiskoi Vostochnoi Zheleznoi Dorogi (The Seizure of the Chinese Eastern Railway)*. Novosibirsk, 1929.

Durdenevsky, V. "Narodni Respubliki Tsentralnoi Azii, Mongolska ta Tuvinska" ("The People's Republics of Central Asia—Mongolia and Tuva"), *Skhidnii Svit (The World of the Orient)*, Kharkov, No. 3 (9), 1929.

Friters, Gerard M. *The International Position of Outer Mongolia*. Dijon, 1939.

———. *Outer Mongolia and Its International Position*. Baltimore, 1949.

———. "The Prelude to Outer Mongolian Independence," *Pacific Affairs*, Vol. X, No. 2 (June, 1957), pp. 168-189.

Fu, Jeng-en. "Po-Li-Hui-I chih Chien-chien Hou-hou" ("The Beginning and the End of the Conference of Khabarovsk"), *Current Events*, March, 1930, pp. 112-119.

Gastov, G. "K Zakhvatu KVZhD" ("The Seizure of the Chinese Eastern Railway"), *Novyi Vostok*, Vol. XXVI-XXVII (1929), pp. 3-10.

Geleta, Jossef. *The New Mongolia*. London, 1936.

Genkin, I. I. "Dva S'ezda Mongol'skoi Narodnoi Revoliutsionnoi Partii" ("Two Sessions of the Mongolian People's Revolutionary Party"), *Novyi Vostok* (*The New East*), No. 12, 1926, 184-195.

Gordenko, M. K. *Obzor Lesnykh Kontsesii Kitaiskoi Vostochnoi Zheleznoi Dorogi* (*A Survey of Forest Concessions of the Chinese Eastern Railway*). Harbin, 1923.

Groshenin, A. I. "Kommercheskaia Rabota KVZhD za 1928 goda" ("Commercial Work of the C.E.R. in 1928"), *Vestnik Man'chzhurii*, Nos. 7-8, 1929.

Grumm-Grzhimailo, G. E. *Zapadnaia Mongoliia i Uriankhaiskii Krai* (*Western Mongolia and the Urianghai Region*). Vol. I, St. Petersburg, 1914; Vol. II, Leningrad, 1926; Vol. III, Part I, Leningrad, 1926; Vol. III, Parts II-IV, Leningrad, 1930.

Han, Chih-hsin, and Yang, Chien-hai. "Man-Chou Chung-O Shih-chien chih Hsieh-chen" ("The Truth about the Sino-Soviet Dispute in Manchuria"), *Eastern Miscellany*, Oct., 1929, pp. 53-66.

Hazard, John N. "The Constitution of the Mongol People's Republic and Soviet Influences," *Pacific Affairs*, Vol. XXI, No. 2 (June, 1948), pp. 162-167.

"The Historical Setting of Inner Mongolian Nationalism," *Pacific Affairs*, Vol. IX, No. 3 (Sept., 1936), pp. 388-405.

Hornbeck, Stanley K. *American Policy and the Chinese-Russian Dispute*. Washington, D. C., 1929.

Hu, Hsiang-ling. "Chung-O tsai Man-Chou chih Chung-tu" ("The Sino-Russian Conflict in Manchuria"), *Central University Fortnightly*, Dec., 1929.

IAkimova, Tamara A. *Mongol'skaia Narodnaia Respublika* (*The Mongolian People's Republic*). Moscow, 1956.

Inrevskii. "Iz Istorii Kitaiskoi Vostochnoi Zheleznoi Dorogi" ("The History of the Chinese Eastern Railway"), *Mezhdunarodnaia Zhizn'*, Vol. XI (1926), pp. 80-84.

IUdin, V. "Sovremennoe Sotsial'no-Ekonomicheskoe Polozhenie Tuvinskoi Respubliki" ("Contemporary Social-Economic Situation of the Tuvinian Republic"), *Revoliutsionnyi Vostok* (*The Revolutionary East*), No. 3, 1928.

Ivangorodskii, P. "K Voprosu o KVZhD" ("The Problem of the Chinese Eastern Railway"), *Sibirskie Ogni* (*Siberian Light*), Vol. III (1925), pp. 163-177.

Kallinikov, A. *Revoliutsionnaia Mongoliia* (*Revolutionary Mongolia*). Moscow, 1925.

Kao, Po-yen. *Meng-Ku yü Chung-Kuo* (*Mongolia and China*). Tientsin, 1927.

Kawakami, K. "Russo-Chinese Conflict," *Foreign Affairs*, Vol. VIII, No. 1 (Jan., 1930), pp. 52-68.

Khalkin, N. "The Stages of the Development of the Mongolian People's Republic," *Pravda* (Moscow), April 8, 1936, p. 2.

Kharbinskii, S. *Chto Takoe Kitaiskaia Vostochnaia Zheleznaia Doroga i Kuda Idet Ee Milliony?* (*What Is the Chinese Eastern Railway and Where Do Its Millions Go?*). St. Petersburg, 1908.

Khodorov, A. E. "KVZhD" ("The C. E. R."), *Mezhdunarodnaia Zhizn'* (*International Life*), No. 1, 1924.

———. "Sovetskoe Predstavitel'stvo v Kitae" ("Soviet Representation in China"), *Izvestiia.* October 7, 1922.

Korostovets, Ivan IA. *Von Ginggis Khan zur Sowjetrepublik.* Berlin, 1926.

Kudriavtsev, P. *Upravlenie i Sud na Kitaiskoi Vostochnoi Zheleznoi Doroge 1917-1918 gg.* (*Administration and Legal Procedure on the Chinese Eastern Railway*). Irkutsk, 1930.

Kung-Shan-Fong-Wen-Chu. *Chung-Tung-T'ieh-Lu Wen-ti* (*The Question of the Chinese Eastern Railway*). Shanghai, 1929. This book was written under the auspices of the Department of Industry and Commerce of the Chinese government.

Kuo, Ti-cheng. "O-kuo Tung-kung-t'se-lueh ti Yen-chiu" ("A Study of the Russian Policy of Eastward Expansion"), *Eastern Miscellany*, Sept., 1930, pp. 19-32.

Kushelev, IU. *Mongoliia i Mongol'skii Vopros* (*Mongolia and the Mongolian Question*). St. Petersburg, 1912.

Lattimore, Owen. *Manchuria: Cradle of Conflict.* 2nd ed. New York, 1935.

———. *The Mongols of Manchuria.* New York, 1934.

———. "The Unknown Frontier of Manchuria," *Foreign Affairs*, Vol. XI (Jan., 1933), pp. 315-330.

Lei, Yin. "Chung-Tung-Lu wei Su-O Tung-fang Ching-chi Cheng-t'se chih Wu-ch'i chi Wu-Kuo chih Ken-pen Chieh-chueh-t'se" ("The Chinese Eastern Railway as the Weapon of Soviet Russian Far Eastern Economic Policy and China's Counter Policy toward a Solution"), *Three Eastern Provinces Economic Monthly,* Vol. I, No. 7 (Nov., 1929), p. 1, and Vol. I, No. 8 (Dec., 1929), p. 1.

Liang, C. P. "History of the Chinese Eastern Railway," *Pacific Affairs,* Vol. III, No. 2 (Feb., 1930), pp. 188-211.

Liubimov, N. N. *Ekonomicheskie Problemy Dal'nego Vostoka (Economic Problems of the Far East).* Moscow, 1925.

Ma, Ho-t'ien. *Chinese Agent in Mongolia.* Baltimore, 1949.

Maiskii, I. *Sovremennaia Mongoliia (Contemporary Mongolia)* (Report of the Mongolian Expedition organized by the Irkutsk Office of the All-Russian Central Union of Consumers' Societies, "Tsentrosoiuz"). Irkutsk, 1921.

————. "Mongolia" in *Novyi Vostok,* No. 1, 1922, pp. 152-183.

Makhnenko, V. A. *Gosudarstvennyi Stroi Mongol'skoi Narodnoi Respubliki (The Governmental System of the Mongolian People's Republic).* Moscow, 1955.

————. *Mongol'skaia Narodnaia Respublika (The Mongolian People's Republic).* Moscow, 1955.

————. *Stroitel'stvo Osnov Sotzialisma v Mongol'skoi Narodnoi Respublike (Building the Foundation of Socialism in the Mongolian People's Republic).* Moscow, 1955.

Mansvetov, Fedor S. "Tsarist and Soviet Policy in the Far East," *Foreign Affairs,* Vol. XII (July, 1934), pp. 654-663.

————. "Strategic Mongolia," *Asia and the Americas,* April, 1945, pp. 202-205.

————. "Inside Outer Mongolia," *Asia and the Americas,* May, 1945, pp. 244-247.

————. "Russia and China in Outer Mongolia," *Foreign Affairs,* Vol. XXIV (Oct., 1945), pp. 143-152.

Markov, M. "25th Anniversary of the Mongolian People's Republic," *Pravda* (Moscow), July 11, 1946, p. 3.

Martynov, E. I. *Rabota Nashikh Zheleznodorozhnykh Del'tsov v Man'chzhurii (Work of Our Railway Business Men in Manchuria).* Moscow, 1914.

Maslennikov, V. "K Mongol'skomu Voprosu" ("About the Mongolian Question"), *Mirovoe Khoziaistvo i Mirovaia Politika (World Economics and World Politics),* Moscow, May, 1936, pp. 77-81.

Mikhailov, M. *Chto Proiskhodit na Kitaiskoi Vostochnoi Zheleznoi Doroge? (Events Pertaining to the Chinese Eastern Railway).* Moscow, 1926.

"Mongols of the Chinese Border," *Geographical Magazine,* Vol. VI, No. 5 (March, 1938), pp. 327-344.

Moskovskaia Torgovaia Ekspeditsiia v Mongoliu (*Moscow Commercial Expedition to Mongolia*). Moscow, 1912.

Murzaev, E. M. *Mongol'skaia Narodnaia Respublika, Fisiko-Geograficheskoe Opisanie* (*Mongolian People's Republic: A Physical Geographical Description*) (Published by the Institute of Geography). Moscow, 1948.

———. *Mongol'skaia Narodnaia Respublika* (*The Mongolian People's Republic*). Moscow, 1952.

Nasyrov, V. M. *Kitaiskaia Vostochnaia Zheleznaia Doroga* (*The Chinese Eastern Railway—Concerning the Events of 1929*). 2nd ed., enlarged and corrected. Khabarovsk, 1929.

Nilus, E. Kh. (ed.). *Istoricheskii Obzor Kitaiskoi Vostochnoi Zheleznoi Dorogi* (*An Historical Survey of the Chinese Eastern Railway, 1896-1923*). Harbin, 1923.

Nin, Tien-hsia. "Chung-Tung-T'ieh-Lu yu O Jih Mei chih Kuanhsi" ("The Chinese Eastern Railway in Its Relations to Russia, Japan and the United States"), *Eastern Miscellany*, Dec., 1927, pp. 31-42.

Norton, N. K. "International Aspects of the Chinese Eastern Railway," *Annals of the American Academy of Political and Social Science*, Nov., 1930, pp. 308-317.

Ogin, P. *Mongol'skaia Narodnaia Respublika* (*Mongolian People's Republic*). Moscow, 1939.

"Perelomnyi Moment v Istorii Natsional'no-Osvoboditel'nogo Dvizheniia v Mongolii" ("The Critical Period in the History of the National Emancipation Movement in Mongolia"), *Novyi Vostok*, Nos. 10-11, 1925, pp. 203-211.

Perlin, B. *Mongol'skaia Narodnaia Respublika* (*The Mongolian People's Republic*). Moscow, 1941.

Perry-Ascough, H. G. C., and Otter-Barry, R. B. *With the Russians in Mongolia*, with a Preface by the Right Hon. Sir Claude MacDonald. London, 1914.

Phillips, G. D. R. *Russia, Japan and Mongolia*. London, 1942.

Pi, Kwei-fang. *Hu-Lun-Pei-Erh Wen-t'i* (*The Problem of Hulunbuir*). Peking, 1914.

Powell, J. B. "Has the Chinese Position in Manchuria Been Weakened?" *China Weekly Review*, Jan. 4, 1930.

Price, Ernest B. *The Russo-Japanese Treaties of 1907-16 Concerning Manchuria and Mongolia*. Baltimore, 1933.

Quigley, H. S. "Kellogg Pact Invoked in the Soviet-Chinese Dispute," *Current History*, Vol. XXXI, No. 4 (Jan., 1930), pp. 758-763.

————. "The Struggle to Control the Chinese Eastern Railway," *Current History*, Vol. XXX, No. 6 (Sept., 1929), pp. 1100-1110.

Ravenstein, Ernest G. *The Russians on the Amur*. London, 1861.

Rish, A. "Mongoliia na Strazhe Svoei Nezavisimosti" ("Mongolia Guarding Her Independence"), *Tikhii Okean (The Pacific Ocean)*, No. 4(6), Oct.-Dec., 1935.

Rockhill, W. W. "The Question of Outer Mongolia," *Journal of the American Asiatic Association*, Vol. XIV, No. 4 (May, 1914), pp. 102-109.

Romanov, B. A. *Rossiia v Man'chzhurii (Russia in Manchuria)*, Leningrad, 1928.

Ryshik, I. "Khoziaistvennoe i Kulturnoe Stroitel'stvo Mongol'skoi Narodnoi Respubliki" ("Economic and Cultural Reconstruction of the Mongolian People's Republic"), *Planovoe Khoziaistvo (Planned Economy)*, No. 6, 1936, pp. 169-190.

Ryskulov, T. "Velikii Khuruldan Mongolii" ("The Great Khuruldan of Mongolia"), *Novyi Vostok*, Nos. 8-9, 1925, pp. 215-229.

Safianov, M. "Kolonial'naia Politika Torgovogo Kapitala v Tannu-Tuva" ("The Colonial Policy of Commercial Capital in Tannu Tuva"), *Novyi Vostok (The New East)*, Nos. 23-24, 1928.

Savvin, V. P. *Vzaimootnosheniia Tsarskoi Rossii i SSSR s Kitaem (Relations of the Tsarist Russia and the U.S.S.R. with China)*. Moscow, 1930.

Semenov, B. "Konflikty na Kitaiskoi Vostochnoi Zheleznoi Doroge" ("Conflicts on the Chinese Eastern Railway"), *Novyi Vostok*, Nos. 8-9 (1925), pp.1-2.

Shambolon, D. "Kak Ne Sleduet Stavit' Vopros o Natsional'nom Samoopredelenii Mongolii" ("How One Should Not Put the Question of the National Self-determination of Mongolia"), *Revoliutsionnyi Vostok*, No. 3, 1928, pp. 235-240.

Shivendyb, B. *Narodnaia Revoliutsiia v. Mongolii i Obrazovanie MNR 1921-1924 (The People's Revolution in Mongolia and the Formation of the Mongolian People's Republic 1921-1924)*. Moscow, 1956.

Shlezinger, B. "Chastnyi Kapital v Mongolii" ("Private Capital in Mongolia"), *Novyi Vostok*, Nos. 16-17, 1926-27, pp. 91-104.

Shoizhelov, S. "Avtonomnoe Dvizhenie Mongolii i Tsarskaia Rossiia" ("The Autonomous Movement of Mongolia and Tsarist Russia"), *Novyi Vostok*, Nos. 13-14, 1926, pp. 351-363.

————. "Perelomnyi Moment v Istorii Natsional'no-Osvoboditel'nogo Dvizheniia Mongolii" ("The Turning Point in the History of National Liberation Movement in Mongolia"), *Novyi Vostok* (*The New East*), Nos., 10-11, 1925.

Skalov, G. B. *Sobytüa na Kitaiskoi Vostochnoi Zheleznoi Doroge* (*Events on the Chinese Eastern Railway*). Moscow, 1929.

Skvirskii, F. B. "Tsarskaia Avantiura na Dal'nem Vostoke" ("Tsarist Adventure in the Far East"), *Vestnik Man'chzhurü*, I, (1931), 92-97.

Sokolsky, G. E. *The Story of the Chinese Eastern Railway*. Shanghai, 1930.

Solomenik, V. "Bor'ba za Sovetskuiu Vlast' v Polose Otchuzhdeniia KVZhD 1917-1920 gg." ("The Struggle for the Soviet Regime in the Chinese Eastern Railway Zone 1917-1920"), *Dalistpart*, III (1925), 51-81.

Sung, T'ao. "Chung-O-Hui-I chih I P'ieh" ("A Glimpse at the Sino-Russian Conference"), *Eastern Miscellany*, Vol. XXII, No. 17 (Sept. 10, 1925), pp. 5-6.

Tan, Tennyson. *The Political Status of Mongolia*. Shanghai, 1932.

Tang, Peter S. H. "Foreign Relations," *A Regional Handbook on Northeast China* (compiled by the Far Eastern and Russian Institute, University of Washington, Seattle). New Haven, 1956, pp. 397-424.

Tanin, M. *Desiat' Let Vneshnei Politiki SSSR, 1917-1927* (*Ten Years of Soviet Foreign Policy, 1917-1927*). Moscow, 1927.

Tishchenko, P. S. *Kitaiskaia Vostochnaia Zheleznaia Doroga, 1 Iulia 1903 g.–1 Iulia 1913 g.* (*The Chinese Eastern Railway, July 1, 1903-July 1, 1913*). Harbin, 1913.

Tomilin, V. *Mongoliia i Ee Sovremennoe Znachenie dlia Rossii* (*Mongolia and Its Contemporary Importance for Russia*). Moscow, 1913.

Tong, Hollington K. *Facts about the Chinese Eastern Railway Situation* (With documents). Harbin, 1929.

Tsao, Lien-en. *The Chinese Eastern Railway: An Analytical Study*. Shanghai, 1930.

Tsapkin, N. V. *Mongol'skaia Narodnaia Respublika* (*The Mongolian People's Republic*). Moscow, 1948.

Vargin, N. *Mongol'skaia Narodnaia Respublika* (*The Mongolian People's Republic*). Moscow, 1949.

Vernadsky, G. "Russian Interests in Mongolia and Manchuria," *Proceedings of the Institute of International Relations*, (Sixth Session) Vol. VI, Berkeley, 1930, pp. 168-173.

Viktorov, S., and Khalkin, N. *Mongol'skaia Narodnaia Respublika* (*The Mongolian People's Republic*). Moscow, 1936.

Vilenskii, V. "Kitaiskaia Kommunistcheskaia Partiia" ("The Chinese Communist Party"), *Novyi Vostok* (*The New East*), No. 2, 1922.
————. "Sovetskaia Rossiia i Mongoliia" ("Soviet Russia and Mongolia"), *Izvestiia*, November 2, 1920.
Vladimir (pseudonym). *Russia on the Pacific and the Siberian Railway.* London, 1899.
Voitinskii, G. "Zakhvat KVZhD i Politika SSSR" ("The Seizure of the Chinese Eastern Railway and the Policy of the U.S.S.R."), *Krasnaia Nov'*, No. 9 (1929), 142-150.
————. *KVZhD i Politika Imperialistov v Kitae* (*The C.E.R. and the Policy of the Imperialists in China*). Moscow, 1930.
Vollosovich, M. "Rossiia i Mongoliia" ("Russia and Mongolia"), *Vestnik Azii* (Asiatic Herald), Nos. 31-32, Nov.-Dec., 1914, pp. 42-49.
Wang, C.C. "The Chinese Eastern Railway," *Annals of the American Academy of Political and Social Sciences*, Vol. CXXII (Nov., 1925), pp. 57-69.
————. "A Solution of the Chinese Eastern Railway Conflict," *Foreign Affairs*, VIII (Jan., 1930), 294-296.
Wentsel, A. "Znachenie Kitaiskoi Vostochnoi Zheleznoi Dorogi v Dal'-nevostochnom Voprose" ("The Significance of the Chinese Eastern Railway in the Far Eastern Problem"), *Ekonomist* (*Economist*), IV-V (1922), 177-199.
Williams, E. T. "The Treaty of Kiakhta," *American Journal of International Law*, X (1916), 798-808.
Wolff, S. M. "The People's Republic of Mongolia," *The Contemporary Review*, March, 1929, pp. 362-368.
Yavdynsky, J. *The Chinese Eastern Railway Problem in Contemplation of the Law.* Shanghai, 1934.
Young, C. W. *The International Relations of Manchuria.* Chicago, 1929.
Yu, Kan. "Ha-Fou Sou-ch'a O-Ling-Kuan Shih-chien" ("The Case Concerning the Search of the Russian Consulate in Harbin"), *Eastern Miscellany*, Vol. XXVI, No. 12 (June 25, 1929), pp. 6-8.
————. "Su-O Ta-chu Ch'in-lueh Pien-ching" ("Soviet Russia's Invasion of China's Frontier"), *Eastern Miscellany*, Vol. XXVI, No. 16 (Aug. 25, 1929), pp. 1-3.
Yuan, Wen-chang. *Tung-Pei T'ieh-lu Wen-t'i* (*The Railway Problem of the Northeast*). Shanghai, 1932.
Zotov, K. "Dal'nevostochnyi Teatr Voennykh Deistvii" ("The Far Eastern Theater of Military Operation"), *Morskoi Sbornik* (*Marine Symposium*), X (1929), 93-113.

INDEX

DATE DUE